6TH EDITION

CONSUMER BEHAVIOR

AND MARKETING ACTION

HENRY ASSAEL
New York University

SOUTH-WESTERN College Publishing
An International Thomson Publishing Company

Publishing Team Director: John Szilagyi
Acquisitions Editor: Dreis Van Landuyt
Developmental Editor: Alice Denny
Production Editior: Kelly Keeler
Production House: WordCrafters Editorial Services, Inc.
Ad Permissions: Naples Publication Services
Photo Editing: Cary Benbow
Cover Design: Tin Box Studio
Cover Illustrator: Leslie Cober-Gentry
Internal Designer: Mike Stratton
Marketing Manager: Sarah Woelfel

Library of Congress Cataloging-in-Publication Data
Assael, Henry.
Consumer behavior and marketing action / Henry Assael.—6th ed.
p. cm.
ISBN 0-538-86770-1
1. Consumer behavior. 2. Motivational research (Marketing)
I. Title.
HF5415.3.A83 1998
658.8′342—dc21 97-37073
CIP

Printed in the United States of America
3 4 5 D1 2 1 0 9

International Thomson Publishing
South-Western College Publishing is an ITP Company. The ITP trademark is used under license.

BRIEF CONTENTS

PART V

CONSUMERS AND CULTURAL INFLUENCES 455

PART VI

GROUP INFLUENCES 531

CONTENTS

PART III

PREFACE

Since its first edition was published in 1981, *Consumer Behavior and Marketing Action* has been noted for tying together the conceptual foundations of consumer behavior with an applications orientation. The simple premise is that if consumer needs are to drive marketing strategies, a better understanding of these needs should be the foundation for strategy development.

This integration between concepts and strategy is accomplished in several ways. First, and most important, each chapter has examples of strategic applications integrated with concepts, providing the most recent examples of marketing strategy. Second, an opening vignette dealing with a specific example of marketing strategy illustrates many of the basic concepts in the chapter. For example, the chapter on complex decision making cites Saturn's success in establishing a strong, cult-like following and its appeal to both utilitarian and hedonic needs. The chapter on perceptions considers McDonald's unsuccessful attempt to change consumer perceptions of it to a more adult-oriented fast food establishment with the introduction of the Arch Deluxe sandwich. The third vehicle for integration of strategy and concepts is a set of boxes in each chapter that further deals with strategic applications.

CHANGES IN THE SIXTH EDITION

The new edition of *Consumer Behavior and Marketing Action* includes several important changes:

A More Macro Orientation

This edition takes a more macro orientation in studying consumer behavior by focusing on hedonic and experiential processes in purchasing and consumption. Chapter 1 calls this perspective a holistic approach in that it stresses the broader, culturally derived context of purchasing and consumption.

An important manifestation of this focus is the distinction, maintained throughout the text, between a hedonic and a utilitarian perspective. This distinction is applied to all facets of consumer behavior—needs, motives, information processing, and marketing stimuli.

In addition, the text focuses on the experiential dimensions of consumer behavior by emphasizing the consumption experience as well as the purchasing process. An experiential hierarchy of effects is also discussed, leading to action based on consumer emotional responses to a brand.

Most chapters have a section dealing with ethical issues regarding consumer behavior concepts. For example, the chapter on consumer involvement considers the desirability of increasing involvement with social issues such as AIDS prevention and teenage drinking. The chapter on information processing considers the less efficient processing capabilities of younger and older consumers and raises the question of business's responsibilities to these two groups. The chapter on marketing communications considers the potential for consumers to misperceive advertising claims and the responsibilities of marketers to insure that claims are not deceptive and irresponsible.

In addition, placing the chapter on consumerism in the front of the book provides a further focus on the ethical and policy implications of consumer behavior and marketing strategy. This emphasis on societal implications of consumer behavior serves two purposes. First, it provides a balance between the strategic focus throughout the book and a focus on consumer rights. Second, it conforms to the current emphasis on ethical issues in the business curriculum. Ethical issues that relate to misleading labeling, inadequate environmental protection, irresponsible targeting of children and minorities, and deceptive advertising and sales practices can now be more easily woven into conceptual discussions given their early introduction in the text.

The sixth edition of *Consumer Behavior and Marketing Action* reflects the increasing importance of new technologies in consumer decision processes. Various chapters have boxed items titled *Consumer Behavior and the New Technologies*. For example, Chapter 1 cites Levi Strauss as tapping the global youth market on the World Wide Web, and Chapter 7 on information acquisition cites P&G's Internet sites designed to encourage information acquisition through "cyber-surfing." In addition, Web site addresses are frequently listed when referring to specific companies and agencies.

The new edition reinforces the focus on the global dimensions of consumer behavior because of the increasing realization that global communications have produced similar needs and tastes among consumers worldwide. This emphasis is reflected in Chapter 15 on cross-cultural influences in consumer behavior. It is also emphasized in a boxed item in most chapters titled *Global Applications of Consumer Behavior.*

Additional changes of note in the new sixth edition of *Consumer Behavior and Marketing Action* include:

- A shorter and more concise 18-chapter book, reduced from the 20 chapters in the fifth edition. Material on market segmentation and product positioning has been integrated throughout the book. Further, the chapters on word-of-mouth communications and diffusion processes have been combined into one chapter dealing with group communications.
- A complete update of demographic trends in Chapter 12, particularly the aging of the baby boom generation as they reach 50, and the increasing importance of generation X.
- A change in focus from family decision making to household decision making in Chapter 17 to reflect the diminished role of the traditional household and the increasing importance of single-parent and childless households.
- Citing the most recent lifestyle trends in Chapter 13, namely a more isolate lifestyle, a more frugal lifestyle, greater time pressures, and more emphasis on self-awareness.
- An update of cross-cultural and subcultural trends in Chapter 15.

Professors who adopt the text for their classes may request the ancillaries by calling the ITP Academic Resource Center at 1-800-423-0563.

- *Instructor's Manual* (ISBN: 0-538-86771-X) contains teaching suggestions, lecture notes, and guidelines for the end-of-chapter questions and research assignments.
- *Transparency Masters* (ISBN: 0-538-86774-4) of figures from the text may be used to make overhead acetates or photocopied handouts.
- *Test Bank* (ISBN: 0-538-86772-8) contains short-answer questions and problem sets for each chapter of the text. The test bank is also avail-

able in a computerized format (ISBN: 0-538-86773-6) that allows the instructors to edit and add questions.

ACKNOWLEDGEMENTS

I am indebted to a number of people for their help in completing the sixth edition. The following reviewers provided excellent insight and suggestions for preparation of the manuscript for the new edition: Russell W. Belk, University of Utah; Cynthia Huffman, University of Pennsylvania; David M. Lee, Quinnipiac College; Mike D. Reilly, Montana State University; and Richard F. Yalch, University of Washington.

I would also like to thank a highly effective team of people at South-Western College Publishing for their assistance. Particular thanks go to my editor, Dreis Van Landuyt, for his constant support in every facet of the book. Special thanks go to my developmental editor, Alice Denny, who was a constant participant in developing the new edition from the start. Her input was invaluable in helping to shape the book. I would also like to thank my production editor, Kelly Keeler, for overseeing every detail of the book and insuring a rigorous schedule. Thanks also to Jo-Anne Naples for obtaining permissions and for an excellent job of photo-researching. Thanks also to Laura Cleveland for a very effective job of copy-editing.

As in the first five editions, final thanks are reserved for my special partner, Alyce Assael, for having spent long days searching out references and periodicals. As always, her help and support are invaluable.

Henry Assael
New York University

PART I

CONSUMER BEHAVIOR: A MANAGERIAL AND CONSUMER PERSPECTIVE

This introductory section views consumer behavior from both a manager's and a consumer's perspective. In Chapter 1, we take a managerial view of consumer behavior. Such a view recognizes that marketing strategies must be based on consumer needs and that it is the manager's responsibility to satisfy those needs at a profit to the firm. As a result, marketing managers must understand what underlies consumer needs. Such understanding requires a knowledge of the individual consumer and the consumer's environment—culture, society, families, and social groups.

In Chapter 2, we suggest that in the pursuit of profits, managers must recognize their responsibilities to both the individual consumer and to society. Recognizing a responsibility to consumers goes beyond fulfilling needs for particular products or services. It requires acting to insure product safety, to protect children from undue marketing influences, to provide consumers with accurate product information, and to safeguard the environment. These responsibilities should be regarded as basic consumer rights. The attempt to insure such rights is known as *consumerism* and is the responsibility of business, government, and consumers themselves.

This section attempts to provide a balanced perspective to ensure that we do not lose sight of management's responsibilities to the consumer as we describe consumer behavior applications in a marketing strategy context.

CONSUMER BEHAVIOR: A MANAGERIAL AND CONSUMER PERSPECTIVE

Chapter 1

LEVI STRAUSS & CO. FOCUSES ON THE CONSUMER

Marketers have come to realize that their effectiveness in meeting consumer needs directly influences their profitability. The better they understand the factors underlying consumer behavior, the better able they are to develop effective marketing strategies to meet consumer needs.

This introductory chapter establishes a managerial orientation to the study of consumer behavior. It considers the reasons why the study of consumer behavior is important. In so doing, the chapter:

- Defines the strategic applications of consumer behavior.
- Describes the information required to understand consumer behavior.
- Considers differing approaches to studying consumer behavior.
- Reviews the organization of the text.

The next chapter considers the study of consumer behavior from a consumer's, as opposed to a manager's, perspective. A consumer perspective of the field naturally leads to public policy questions that deal with protecting consumer rights in areas such as environmental protection and product safety.

http://www.levi.com/

In the past, many business firms were not very concerned with understanding consumer behavior. They were more focused on tracking sales results with little concern for why consumers did what they did. Consider Levi Strauss & Co. Until the mid-1980s, the company sold jeans to a mass market. It did not have to understand the dynamics behind the sales of jeans or be concerned with segmenting its markets as long as the sales of jeans kept increasing. But, then jeans sales in the market as a whole took a slide. Why? Basic demographic and social trends started affecting sales. Baby boomers (those born between 1946 and 1964) were getting out of jeans, and teens—the most loyal of jeans purchasers—represented a shrinking proportion of the market.

http://www.dockers.com/

http://www.levi.com/hanger

Levi Strauss & Co. quickly came to recognize that it was facing different demographic and lifestyle segments with different needs regarding casual wear. As a result, the company broadened its line to include casual cotton pants and then targeted different lines to different consumer segments. In 1986, Levi Strauss & Co. introduced Dockers® khakis for the baby boomers' looking for more options, then comfortable Action Slacks for the over-50 group and 501® buttonfly jeans targeted to teens (see Exhibit 1.1).[2] Then, Levi Strauss & Co. further segmented the market by introducing Loose jeans, a line of fashion-forward denims targeted to generation Xers (those born between 1965 and 1976), and in 1994, a new line of jeans positioned for kids ages 8 to 14.[3]

Levi Strauss & Co. has demonstrated savvy in targeting consumers. It foresaw the trend toward casual business wear (see Exhibit 1.1), a trend that saw the percentage of companies allowing casual wear at least once a week to grow from 36 percent in 1992 to 75 percent in 1995.[4] To appeal to this growing segment, Levi Strauss & Co. works with human resource managers of larger companies to develop their casual dress policy. In short, consumer trends of the 1980s and 1990s led the company to move from mass marketing to a strategy of market segmentation.

http://www.levi.com/inner_seam/eu

The company has also followed a global strategy by recognizing the differing needs of consumers around the world. By using James Dean as the centerpiece of its advertising, under the tag line "Heroes Wear Levis," it catered to the desire of European and Asian teenagers in search of American icons[5]. It even took its mission campaign, casualization of the workplace, global in 1996 by staging mock demonstrations in the business centers of cities from Milan to Manila. Men, dressed in suits, cut off their ties, stripped down to their boxer shorts, and donned khakis.[6]

Rapid changes in the marketing environment such as those experienced by Levi Strauss & Co. have led marketing managers to analyze more closely the factors that influence consumer choice. Managers are now concerned with delivering benefits to consumers, learning about and changing consumers' attitudes, and influencing consumer perceptions. They realize that marketing plans must be based on the psychological and social forces that are likely to condition consumer behavior—forces such as the aging of baby boomers, increasing concern with health and nutrition, greater emphasis on value, and greater focus on a clean environment.

EXHIBIT 1.1
Levi Strauss & Co.'s market segmentation strategy

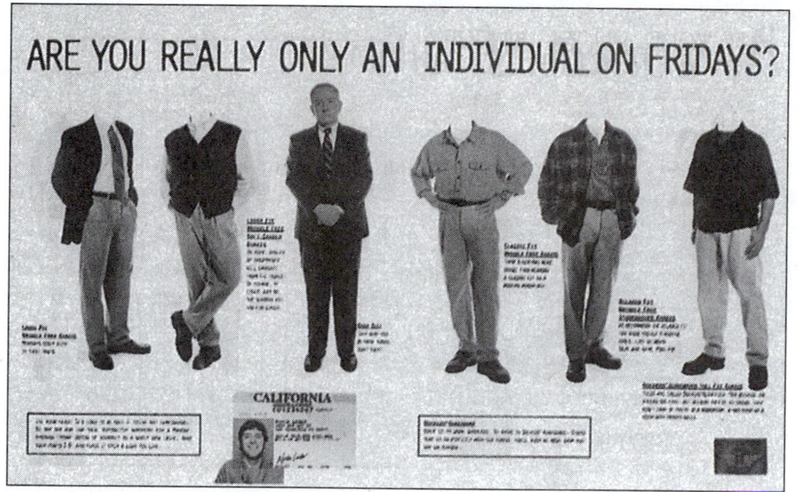

Targeting Casual Wear in the Office

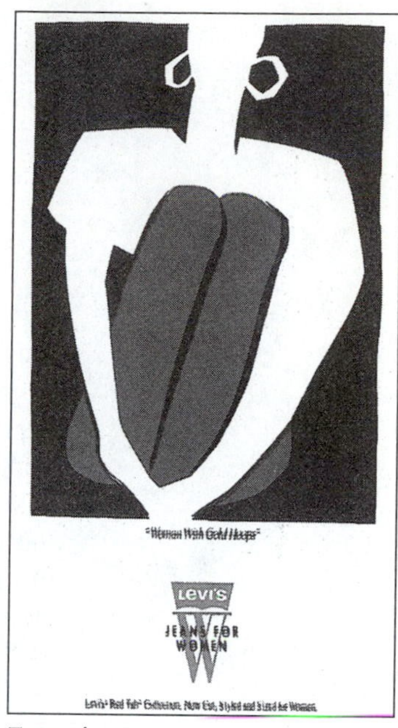

Targeting Women

Targeting Teens

The result of this realization is a new emphasis on consumer information. To paraphrase one marketing executive, the most successful companies will be those that get their hands on information that identifies and explains the needs and behavior of consumers.[7]

Much of this text will be devoted to a better understanding of terms such as *consumer benefits, perceptions,* and *attitudes* and how they influence development of successful marketing strategies. Because it recognized that jeans could no longer provide baby boomers with the benefits they needed, Levi Strauss & Co. was successful in introducing its Dockers® line of casual pants. The company determined that baby boomers' perceptions linked Levi Strauss & Co. to jeans and that it would have to change this perception to market the Dockers® khakis successfully. Levi Strauss & Co. also had to change the perception that their jeans were only for men in order to successfully target the female consumer (see Exhibit 1.2). Levi Strauss & Co. wanted to develop more positive attitudes to-

EXHIBIT 1.2
Levi Strauss expands its consumer base to females

ward its new product lines, thus increasing the chance that the targeted demographic group would buy.

Companies that fail to recognize consumer needs are more likely to make costly mistakes. Consider Sears, the number-one retailer in the United States until 1990, when it fell to third place. Before its slide, Sears had a clear focus on how to satisfy its customers: offer a wide variety of low-priced merchandise to middle America. However, Sears failed to see the implications of more working women and the greater affluence of dual-earning households. These demographic shifts meant that consumers wanted a greater variety of name brands at reasonable prices.

While other mass merchandisers were moving to specialty, name-brand goods, Sears was slow to change. It continued to offer what consumers perceived as low-quality merchandise in aging stores with garish displays. By 1993, the company recognized it needed a drastic repositioning. It put greater focus on fashion by emphasizing name-brand apparel in a boutique-like setting and introducing a line of cosmetics. Part of the focus on fashion was a new advertising campaign, "The Softer Side of Sears," introduced in 1995 (see Exhibit 1.3).

EXHIBIT 1.3
Sears adapts to consumer trends with a new emphasis on fashion

Sears is climbing back to dominance by reinventing itself to better meet the needs of a more affluent customer base.[8]

As the Levi Strauss & Co. and Sears examples show, the basic philosophy required for successful marketing—the importance of satisfying consumers—may be simple, but its implementation is complex. It requires that the company:

- Define consumer needs.
- Identify consumer segments that have these needs.
- Position new products or reposition existing products to meet those needs.
- Develop marketing strategies to communicate and deliver product benefits.
- Evaluate these strategies for their effectiveness.
- Ensure that such strategies do not deceive or mislead consumers and that they are implemented in a socially responsible manner.

Underlying these strategic requirements is the importance of obtaining information on consumer needs, consumer perceptions of new and existing brands, attitudes toward these brands, intentions to buy, and past purchasing behavior.

DEVELOPING A CONSUMER-ORIENTED VIEW OF MARKETING STRATEGY: THE MARKETING CONCEPT

The philosophy that marketing strategies rely on a better knowledge of the consumer is known as the **marketing concept.*** The marketing concept states that marketers must first define the benefits consumers seek in the marketplace and gear marketing strategies accordingly. Acceptance of this concept has provided the impetus for studying consumer behavior in a marketing context.

First formulated in the early 1950s, the marketing concept seems so logical today that we may wonder why marketers did not turn to it sooner. There are two reasons. First, marketing institutions were not sufficiently developed before 1950 to accept the marketing concept. Consumer behavior research was in its infancy. Moreover, advertising and distributive facilities were more suited to the mass-production and mass-marketing strategies of that time. The implementation of the marketing concept requires a diversity of facilities for promoting and distributing products that meet the needs of smaller and more diverse market segments. This diversity in marketing institutions did not exist before 1950. Instead, the emphasis was on economies of scale in production and marketing. Before the 1950s, for example, Coca-Cola was a one-product company; Chevrolet had only one model.

http://www.cocacola.com/

http://www.chevrolet.com/

*All terms in bold type are defined in the Glossary at the back of the text.

The second reason the marketing concept was not accepted until the 1950s is that prior to that time there was no economic necessity to do so. During the Depression, there was little purchasing power to spur an interest in consumer behavior. During World War II and immediately after, scarcities were prevalent. There was no competitive pressure to discover consumers' motives or to adjust product offerings to consumer needs. Manufacturers could sell whatever they made.

The end of the Korean War in 1953 changed this sales-oriented focus. The conversion to peacetime production was rapid and efficient. Different marketers brought out similar lines of refrigerators, ovens, and cars but now they found consumers reluctant to buy. Consumers had become more selective in their purchasing habits after two major wars and a Depression, and they were now reluctant buyers. The economy experienced its first true buyers' market. For the first time, supply exceeded demand, and inventories built up in the face of consumer purchasing power.

Some marketers reacted by intensifying the old strategies: pushing the existing line, heightening selling efforts, repeating selling themes, and pushing excess inventories on unwilling distributors and dealers. Others reacted with more foresight by recognizing that the right combination of product benefits would influence reluctant consumers to purchase. These manufacturers researched the market to identify consumer needs and to develop products to fit those needs. This newer approach resulted in an expanded set of product offerings. It also caused advertising strategy to shift from the repetitive campaigns designed to maintain brand awareness to more creative, diverse campaigns designed to communicate product benefits.

Marketers began talking in behavioral terms. In this new context, a product must be positioned to deliver a set of benefits to a defined segment of consumers. Advertising's goals are to communicate symbols and images that show how the brand delivers these benefits, to create a favorable attitude toward the brand, and to induce trial. Advertising is also intended to reinforce the consumers' choices to influence them to repurchase.

Implications for Consumer Behavior

http://www.avon.com/

The shift from a sales orientation to a behavioral or consumer orientation did not occur overnight. It is still going on today. Avon Products reflects this shift. Before 1980, the company's sales-oriented management failed to see the potential impact of an increasing proportion of working women on its primary means of distribution: door-to-door sales of cosmetics. The simple fact was that fewer women were at home to open the door for the Avon salesperson. In addition, more affluent and aware female consumers were beginning to look down on Avon's low-price, bargain basement image.[9]

The shift to a consumer orientation required a new management team, which promptly commissioned a large-scale study of women's cosmetic needs and attitudes toward Avon products. On the basis of the study, the company repositioned itself to appeal to affluent working women with higher-priced prestige perfumes and began distributing them through department stores. To reinforce a more savvy and up-to-date image, Avon became an official sponsor of the 1996 Olympic team, describing Jackie Joyner-Kersee, an Olympic gold medalist, as "Just another Avon Lady" (see Exhibit 1.4).

Avon is also appealing to its traditional base by sending its Avon sales reps to the office to reach less affluent working women and to offer them traditional Avon products.[10]

The shift to a consumer orientation by companies such as Avon and Levi Strauss & Co. has changed the nature of marketing operations by:

- *Providing a spur to consumer behavior research.* Both Levi Strauss & Co. and Avon conducted studies of consumer needs, attitudes, and purchasing behavior as a basis for their shift in strategy.
- *Creating a more customer-oriented framework for marketing strategies.* Levi Strauss & Co. could no longer rely on a mass-market approach. It recognized it had to broaden its line beyond jeans to satisfy baby

▶EXHIBIT 1.4
Avon becomes more consumer oriented by updating its image

boomers first and then baby busters. It also realized it would have to differentiate its appeals based on the needs of these segments—an appeal to baby boomers based primarily on fit and to baby busters based primarily on design.

http://www.pg.com/

GLOBAL APPLICATIONS OF CONSUMER BEHAVIOR

▶ Procter & Gamble Fails to Export Its Consumer Savvy to Japan

Lack of adequate knowledge of foreign consumers' needs and customs often results in U.S. companies mismarketing abroad. Consider Procter & Gamble (P&G), a company renowned for its ability to meet the needs of American consumers with leading packaged goods such as Tide detergent, Crest toothpaste, Folgers coffee, and Pampers disposable diapers. Until recently, when it came to marketing in Japan, P&G appeared to be a novice. It made the basic mistake of assuming the marketing strategies that worked at home would also work abroad.

Its experience in disposable diapers was instructive. In the words of its current CEO, when P&G introduced Pampers in Japan in 1977, it used "American products, American advertising, and American sales methods and promotional strategies." The product was relatively thick and bulky, designed for American mothers who intended to leave diapers on their babies for longer periods. P&G did not realize that Japanese women are among the most compulsive cleaners in the world and change their babies' diapers twice as often as the average American mother. Japanese companies saw an opening and introduced a thinner, leak-resistant diaper better suited to the needs of Japanese mothers. As a result, Pampers' market share plummeted from 90 percent in 1977 to 7 percent in 1985.

At that point, the new head of international operations, Edward Artzt, recognized the fallacy of ignoring cross-cultural differences and encouraged development of an improved diaper with one-third the thickness of the original model. By 1990, the new diaper captured almost one-third of the Japanese market and became the prototype for Ultra Pampers in the United States.

P&G is now a company attuned to cross-cultural differences, especially since Artzt became CEO. From 1990 to 1993, under Artzt's leadership, the company became a world player in cosmetics. It is also aggressively moving into Eastern Europe. In each case, it is not doing so hesitantly, given its new-found confidence in defining and meeting the needs of foreign consumers.

Sources: "Procter & Gamble: Winning in Japan," *Discount Merchandise* (September 1994), p. 54; "Procter & Gamble Is Following Its Nose," *Business Week* (April 22, 1991), p. 28; "At Procter & Gamble, Change Under Artzt Isn't Just Cosmetic," *The Wall Street Journal* (March 5, 1991), pp. A1 and A8; "Japan Rises to P&G's No. 3 Market," *Advertising Age* (December 10, 1990), p. 42; Edward Artzt, "Winning in Japan: Keys to Global Success," *Business Quarterly* (Winter 1989), pp. 12–16.

▶EXHIBIT 1.5
Levi's World Wide Web site appeals to global youth

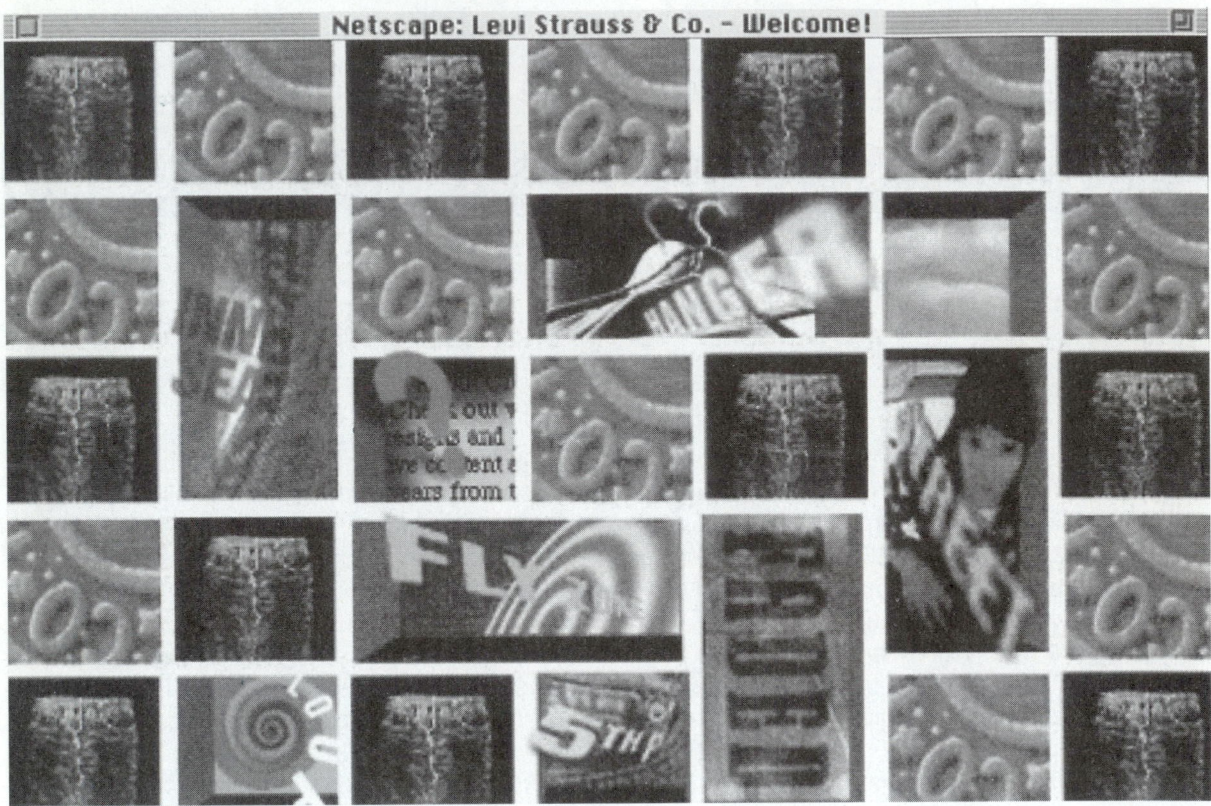

- *Encouraging measurement of the factors that influence consumers to purchase.* Levi Strauss & Co. had to determine what factors influence choice of slacks among its various age segments.
- *Emphasizing market segmentation.* As we saw, Levi Strauss & Co. grouped its customers primarily into age segments. Avon also had to identify segments such as affluent working women (targets for more expensive perfumes), less affluent working women (targets for sales calls at the workplace), and the traditional stay-at-home or work-at-home women (targets for sales calls at home).
- *Emphasizing product positioning to meet consumer needs.* Products are developed and advertised to establish qualities that set them apart from the competition and to relate these qualities to the needs of a defined market segment. Based on the theme, "We're going to make you feel beautiful," Avon developed a campaign for its products aimed at less affluent working women. How did it arrive at this positioning strategy?

Avon's research showed that less affluent working women wanted to improve their feelings about themselves and to better accept themselves.

- *Creating greater selectivity in advertising and personal selling.* Emphasis is now on selective marketing rather than on mass marketing. Avon's separate strategies to target more affluent working women, less affluent working women, and women at home are examples.
- *Creating more selective media and distributive outlets.* There are now more specialized magazines, greater uses of catalogs and phone orders, and more specialized wholesalers and retailers. As we saw, Avon is broadening its base beyond door-to-door selling by relying more on direct customer orders.

In summary, in accepting the marketing concept, marketing management has recognized that the determinants of consumer behavior have a direct bearing on the formulation of marketing strategies.

CURRENT TRENDS IN CONSUMER BEHAVIOR

The preceding historical perspective shows that successful companies adapt to changing consumer needs and environmental trends—the needs of aging baby boomers in the case of Levi and the needs of an increasing proportion of working women in the case of Avon.

The mid-1990s have seen equally important consumer behavior trends that will influence marketing strategies. Three in particular are a greater value orientation on the part of consumers, a desire for and access to more information, and a desire for more customized products to fit consumer needs.

A Greater Value Orientation

Steep recessions in the 1980s and 1990s have made consumers more price-sensitive. Today, with the realization that growth is not unbridled and that there are limits to future purchasing power, consumers are viewing price more in the context of value, that is, getting your money's worth. In the booming 1980s, many consumers held a different view: acquisition for its own sake. The emphasis on value has led to a preponderance of "cross-shoppers," that is, the person who buys his suits at Brooks Brothers but goes to Kmart to buy socks or the consumer who buys premium ice cream and generic paper towels.[11] This dichotomy makes sense in that consumers see value at both high price ends and low price ends in certain product categories.

Greater sensitivity to value has led companies to keep prices down without sacrificing quality—one reason why companies are putting such great emphasis on Total Quality Management (TQM) programs. National marketers market product lines with both premium-priced and lower-priced brands. Similarly, retailers such as Nordstrom and Saks Fifth Avenue, prestige department stores, have opened discount clearinghouses, and Mercedes has developed less expensive models that advertise performance and safety over snob appeal.[12] The emphasis on EDLP (every day low prices) by leading marketers such as Procter & Gamble is also an indication of a greater value orientation. Another is the resurgence of emphasis on building brand equity, that is, communicating the value of a brand in the context of quality and price.

The American consumer is becoming a more aware and self-assured shopper. One reason is the greater accessibility of information and shopping options. The expansion of cable TV channels has made product information more available on the airwaves through home shopping channels, infomercials (commercials that are almost program length), and an expanded advertising base. The greater incidence of home computers and advances in interactive technologies have expanded the availability of product information in cyberspace. With the increasing educational levels of American consumers, these additional information sources are likely to be used.

The strategic consequences of these changes on consumer behavior are yet to be felt. It is likely that marketers will expand the range of product options to consumers and insure that fuller product information is provided than is now typically the case. Marketers will also consider a broader range of media options in communicating to consumers in the future, and a broader range of delivery options as well (home shopping channels, telephone buying, electronic kiosks, buying on the Internet).

One indication of future change is Procter & Gamble's introduction of eight Web sites on the Internet in 1996 to promote its brands.[13] P&G saw the sale of home computers surpass that of TV sets for the first time in 1994 and recognized the potential of the Internet as a source of product information.[14] The Web site for Hugo Boss men's fragrances comes with cutting-edge color graphics and funky poems targeted to generation Xers. The company is predicting that spending on Web advertising will jump from $74 million in 1996 to $2.6 billion in 2000.

Their greater sophistication, access to more information, and emphasis on value has led consumers to desire products more closely fitted to their needs. Consumers today are looking for more options at lower prices. They want sneakers for different activities, snacks for different times of day, clothes that are custom-fitted, and cars with a specific set of options and accessories.

CONSUMER BEHAVIOR AND THE NEW TECHNOLOGIES

▶ Levi Strauss & Co. Taps the Global Youth Market on the World Wide Web

In the eyes of the world's youth, Levi Strauss & Co. stands for American pop culture. That is one reason why scarce Levi jeans can sell for hundreds of dollars on the gray and black markets in Eastern European countries and stories abound of teens taking their jeans off and selling them on the streets for exorbitant sums.

Levi Strauss & Co. extended its global brand equity through the World Wide Web. On September 29, 1995, it went live on the Web by unifying all of its brands in one global campaign on one Web site (http://www.levi.com). Levi Strauss & Co. can use the Web as a global medium to leverage its position as an American icon among youth worldwide. As one executive involved in establishing the site said, "Global youth culture is part of the fabric of the brand and the Levi company."

Through its Web site, Levi Strauss & Co. targets 15- to 24-year-olds with content about street fashions, cultural trends, company history, and product information in separate sections on its site. It hopes to expand its user base on the Web through interactive word-of-mouth communication, that is, one youth telling another about the site through the Internet.

When Levi launched its Web site, it featured seven sections (see Exhibit 1.5). One, titled "Faded," features historical clips from a different decade each month while communicating "how society influenced what Levi Strauss & Co. was doing." The "Street" section features fashions in a different city each month. Another section called "Fly Zone" was devoted to portraying youth culture. The section has featured an interview with a well-known graffiti artist and contains a "Bomb the Wall" area where viewers can post their own computer-generated artwork.

Levi's focus on the World Wide Web goes beyond the global youth culture. It is already developing a more customized marketing strategy by utilizing another interactive technology—in-store kiosks that enable consumers to get product information and place custom-sized orders at retail.

Levi's global strategy and pop culture status appear to be naturals for the World Wide Web.

Source: Adapted from "Unzipped: A Levi's Site for Culture, Not Just Clothes," *IQ* (November 20, 1995), pp. 8–12.

Because of this trend, two marketers have argued that a totally new set of marketing strategies will arise in the future. Instead of product managers selling one product at a time to as many customers as possible, *custom managers* will sell as many products as possible to one consumer at a time.[15] Marketers are not quite at that point, but the trend to customization is accelerating. Marketers are targeting smaller segments and even individuals. Consider the following:

http://www.ford.com/

http://www.mot.com/

http://www.Nikonusa.com/

- Ford builds its Thunderbirds with 69,120 combinations, so consumers can come close to designing their own cars.
- Motorola offers 29 million different combinations of pager features designed to customer orders.[16]
- Nikon's sunglasses division markets five lens types and more than 30 frames for activities ranging from skiing to driving to water sports.[17]
- Levi Strauss allows customers in its stores to place alteration directions in a "sizing computer" which is connected to a Tennessee factory where robotic arms cut the personalized jeans to the consumer's measurements.[18]

THE INFORMATION BASE FOR UNDERSTANDING CONSUMER BEHAVIOR

Most marketing firms have a *marketing information system* designed to provide data on what consumers do and why. Such a system is obviously important in understanding consumer behavior and developing marketing strategies. A marketing information system should have the capability of collecting two types of data: secondary and primary.

Secondary data are existing data from published sources or from company records. **Primary data** are data collected by the company for the specific purpose of answering its research questions.

Secondary Data

Generally, companies will first analyze secondary data before collecting primary data. Three sources of secondary data that are important to understanding consumers are census data from the U.S. government, syndicated services that track consumer trends, and databases that provide information on the characteristics of purchasers of certain products and services.

Census Data

Census data provide a storehouse of demographic information that is constantly used by marketers. We have seen that important demographic trends such as aging baby boomers and the increasing proportion of working women have influenced Levi Strauss and Avon to change their long-term marketing strategies. The census in 2000 will be even more important in tracking demographic trends such as the changing composition of dual-earning households, an increasing birth rate, and the increasing importance of minorities in the U.S. economy.

Syndicated Services

Syndicated services are firms that collect data periodically and sell it to subscribing companies. Syndicated services serve two important functions in the context of consumer behavior. First, they track behavior in the form of sales data. Second, they provide a basis for understanding such behavior by periodically collecting information on consumer attitudes, perceptions, and lifestyles.

http://www.nielsen.com/

Two companies, A.C. Nielsen and Information Resources Inc., provide information on consumer behavior by reporting scanner data from retail stores. Such data breaks out sales by type of product, retail store, price, and region. These firms also maintain panels of consumers that use special coded cards when purchasing which identify their demographic and lifestyle characteristics. This permits marketers to connect what people do to who they are.

Syndicated services also track consumer attitudes, opinions, and lifestyles and divide consumers into segments that might better explain their purchasing behavior. For example, one service, the Value and Lifestyle Survey (VALS), interviews 2,500 respondents yearly and divides them into segments such as achievers (affluent people who get satisfaction from their jobs and families) and experiencers (younger people who strive for wealth and power and spend heavily on new products). Marketers can determine what products these segments are buying and can thereby get a better understanding of their purchasing behavior.

Database Marketing

Database marketing utilizes information about individual consumers and allows companies to customize their offerings accordingly. Database marketing has been made possible by interactive technologies that allow consumers to respond directly to company offers and inquiries and by powerful computers that can merge and analyze this data.

An example is Levi Strauss's "sizing computer" which allows customers to provide alteration data while shopping in the store. In so doing, Levi gained a valuable database on individual consumers. By maintaining files of these consumers in a database, Levi can now reach them with direct-mail promotions. Similarly, when General Motors launched its credit card in 1992, it was not so much to give its customers rebates on GM cars through the cards, but rather to establish a database of 12 million GM cardholders. GM surveys its cardholders to determine what they are driving, when they next plan to buy a car, and what kind of vehicle they would like.

http://www.gm.com/

Such databases raise issues of invasion of privacy. There is a thin line between using consumer data collected in the course of doing business and invading one's privacy regarding personal information. One logical solution is to inform consumers that data is available regarding their characteristics and purchasing patterns and to ask their permission to use it.

Primary Data

In most cases, secondary data is not sufficient to develop marketing strategies to meet consumer needs. Companies collect primary data to meet their informational needs. They conduct surveys to determine consumers' attitudes toward their products and intentions to buy. They determine consumer reactions to advertisements, price promotions, and new product concepts. And, they test new products on select consumer groups.

Consumer researchers collect primary data by utilizing qualitative research, survey research, experimentation, and observation.

Qualitative Research

Qualitative research is designed to provide more information about consumers' underlying motives by asking them questions in an unstructured manner. It allows researchers to form hypotheses regarding consumer actions and to better define research areas to determine the kinds of questions to ask in more structured surveys or experiments. The two most frequently used qualitative approaches are focus-group interviews and projective techniques.

Focus-group interviews are informal, open-ended group discussions that are guided by a trained moderator who keeps the discussion focused on a series of topics of interest to the marketing firm. One airline used focus groups to research fear of flying among businesspeople. Standard surveys did not lend insight into these fears. Group discussions allowed consumers to be more open about their fears. These focus groups showed that it was not so much fear of flying that deterred businesspeople as it was guilt that if they died they would leave behind their loved ones. As a result, the airline developed an ad campaign that focused on the joy of coming back to the family from a business trip rather than the more rational appeals of direct flights and on-time arrivals.

Projective techniques involve presenting ambiguous materials to consumers that are designed to induce them to project subconscious feelings and attitudes. If the desired information is very personal or deep-seated, consumers can be given a cartoon and asked to fill in the bubble, an unfinished sentence and asked to complete it, or a situation and asked to project the people they would associate with it. In each case, consumers are more likely to project their true feelings because the questions are not asked directly.

http://www.panasonic.com/

Panasonic used projective techniques to determine whether its positive image in consumer electronics could carry over to office automation. Researchers asked consumers to select photos of people they associated with IBM, Xerox, Canon, and Panasonic products. Respondents associated photos of older, distinguished, and affluent people with IBM and Xerox. They selected photos of younger, upstart professionals with Panasonic.[19] The company used these findings to develop an ad campaign for its office automation products, "The Panasonic boom, the next generation," showing the independent baby boomers of the 1960s and 1970s now in management positions (see Exhibit 1.6).

EXHIBIT 1.6
Panasonic's ad campaign based on qualitative research

Survey Research

Survey research is designed to collect structured data through a questionnaire given to a sample of respondents that is representative of a population. If General Motors wanted to determine attitudes toward GM cars among foreign car owners, it might develop a questionnaire to elicit attitudes toward domestic and foreign cars and ask these questions among a representative sample of foreign car owners (the population). GM could then determine the reasons for resistance toward its particular divisions among foreign car owners, the characteristics of car owners holding these negative views, and whether it can develop strategies to change these attitudes.

The GM survey is known as a cross-sectional design; that is, it conducts research at a particular point in time. If GM were to track changes in attitudes and behavior among the same sample of foreign car owners over time, this would be a longitudinal design. Companies frequently conduct longitudinal studies by forming panels of consumers to track changes in attitudes and behavior. One of the first such longitudinal panels was formed by General Electric in the late 1960s to track the acquisition of major appliances among new households.

Experimental Research

Experimental research attempts to test for cause-and-effect relationships under controlled conditions. Researchers try to determine the effects of marketing stimuli such as alternative product characteristics, advertising themes, or price levels (the cause) on consumer responses (the effect). In trying to establish such cause-and-effect relationships, the researcher must try to control all factors except the marketing stimulus being tested so that consumer responses can be attributed to that stimulus.

http://www.fritolay.com/

Frito-Lay ran experiments under controlled conditions and found it could reduce the oil in its light chip line (the stimulus or cause) by one-third without a decrease in consumer taste ratings (the response or effect). Beyond that level, taste ratings plummeted. Frito-Lay gave groups formulations with one-sixth less oil, one-third less, one-half less, and so on. When it ran tests on these various formulations, the company matched each group on key consumer characteristics to make sure that the results were due to the oil level in the chip rather than to some extraneous factor such as frequency of snacking or age of the respondent.

Observational Research

Researchers also observe consumers to determine what they do in the process of buying a product, using it, or being exposed to a marketing communication. For example, how long do consumers examine a product in a supermarket before putting it in the shopping cart, or how accurately do consumers follow directions on a label in food preparation?

By observing consumers, Corning Glass found that sales of its Pyrex measuring cup were slumping because they were uncomfortable with the handle on the cup. A change in design followed. Curad Battle Ribbon adhesives were developed as a result of direct observation of children decorating bandages with crayons and felt-tip pens. These studies are obtrusive in that respondents are aware of the presence of researchers, and such awareness can influence results. In an example of unobtrusive observation, researchers determined they could not get reliable estimates of alcohol consumption through direct questioning so they measured the number of empty bottles in the garbage.[20]

Another form of observation is participant observation in which a researcher lives with a group or family in a particular culture and observes their behavior. Such in-depth observation is derived from cultural anthropology and is called **ethnography.** Although rare, ethnographic studies are occasionally used by marketers. A leading advertising agency selected a small Illinois town for in-depth study to try to gain insights into typical consumer concerns and preoccupations. Researchers visit the town to talk to residents, attend town functions, engage in social events, and try to be "part of the scene."[21]

APPROACHES TO STUDYING CONSUMER BEHAVIOR: A MANAGERIAL VERSUS A HOLISTIC APPROACH

There are two broad approaches to the study of consumer behavior. A *managerial approach* views consumer behavior as an applied social science. It is studied as an adjunct to and a basis for developing marketing strategies. A *holistic approach* views consumer behavior as a pure rather than applied social science. In this view, consumer behavior is a legitimate focus of inquiry in and of itself without necessarily being applied to marketing.

Although it may appear that the first view has the most credence for marketers, in reality, a holistic approach also provides a useful perspective to strategy in many cases.

A Managerial Approach

A managerial approach to consumer behavior tends to be more micro and cognitive in nature. It is *micro* in emphasizing the individual consumer: his or her attitudes, perceptions, and lifestyle and demographic characteristics. Environmental effects—reference groups, the family, culture—are studied in the context of how they influence the individual consumer. In being more micro, a managerial orientation is also more *cognitive;* that is, it emphasizes the thought processes of individual consumers and the factors that go into influencing their decisions.

Marketing managers find such a focus on the individual only natural. The goal of all marketing strategy should be to satisfy the needs of individual consumers in a socially responsible manner. Information is collected on the consumer's needs (desired product benefits), thought processes (attitudes and perceptions), and characteristics (lifestyles and demographics). This information is then aggregated to define segments of consumers that can be targeted with the company's offerings. Thus, a more affluent, older baby boom segment might be identified that likes casual wear and emphasizes performance over status. Identification of such a segment would have implications for marketers of everything from clothes to home computers and from yogurt to cars.

But there are risks in taking too rigid a managerial perspective. First, it might overemphasize the rationality of consumers. The cognitive view is that consumers search for and process information in some systematic manner in an attempt to meet their needs. But in many cases, such systematic processing may not occur, as when consumers buy products for their symbolic value, on impulse, or on an addictive basis. Using a strictly cognitive approach may not reveal the underlying nature of the consumer's decision in these cases.

Second, a micro view might overlook the dynamics of environmental factors independent of the individual. For example, a perspective on gift giving in the context of ritual behavior would be culturally derived and might be insightful for many marketers. Yet such a perspective might be overlooked if the focus is primarily on individual consumers.

Third, a managerial perspective tends to focus more on purchase than on consumption. This is only natural since marketing managers emphasize sales results as represented by purchasing behavior. But, recently, the focus has increasingly shifted to what happens after the purchase. Satisfaction is generally defined by the consumption, not the purchase experience. A whole new area in marketing called **relationship marketing** recognizes that marketers must maintain a relationship with their customers after the purchase. And to a large degree, this relationship will depend on the consumption experience.

A Holistic Approach

A holistic approach is more *macro* in its orientation. It tends to focus more on the nature of the consumption experience than on the purchasing process because it stresses the broader, culturally derived context of consumption. Consumption is seen as being symbolic as well as functional, antisocial as well as social, and idiosyncratic as well as normative. Purchase behavior is of little inherent interest outside of its impact on the consumption experience. When it is studied, it is in the context of shopping rather than decision making because shopping is frequently culturally derived.

Whereas a managerial orientation is more interested in predicting what the consumer might do in the future, the holistic approach is more interested in understanding the environmental context of the consumer's actions.

A holistic approach also has its drawbacks. The most important is that findings regarding the culturally derived meaning of consumer actions and consumption experiences may not be actionable from a marketer's perspective. This need not bother those who study consumer behavior for its own sake, but findings from consumer behavior should be actionable for marketing strategies in a business context. Thus, the title of this book: *Consumer Behavior and Marketing Action.*

Second, a holistic approach does not put sufficient emphasis on purchase decisions. Marketers must understand how consumers reach decisions if they are to influence them.

Third, although many consumer decisions are not made through a process of systematic processing, many are. Some understanding of such cognitive processes is necessary if marketers are to attempt to meet consumer needs.

A Balanced View

This book clearly takes a managerial perspective in viewing the study of consumer behavior as a basis for developing marketing strategies to meet consumer needs. But it also recognizes the value of a broader, holistic perspective in moderating a strictly cognitive and micro view. For example, the discussion of consumer decision making considers both information processing and the symbolic role of products. The discussion of the consumer environment considers its effects on both consumer purchases and the consumption experience.

A MODEL OF CONSUMER BEHAVIOR

As noted, the premise of this text is that marketing strategies must be based on the factors that influence consumer behavior. Figure 1.1, a simple model of consumer behavior, emphasizes the interaction between the marketer and the consumer. Consumer decision making—that is, the process of perceiving and evaluating brand information, considering how brand alternatives meet the consumer's needs, and deciding on a brand—is the central component of the model.

Two broad influences determine the consumer's choice. The first is the individual consumer whose needs, perceptions of brand characteristics, and attitudes toward alternatives influence brand choice. In addition, the consumer's demographics, lifestyle, and personality characteristics influence brand choice.

The second influence on consumer decision making is the environment. The consumer's purchasing environment is represented by culture (the norms and values of society), by subcultures (a part of society with distinct norms and val-

FIGURE 1.1 Simple model of consumer behavior

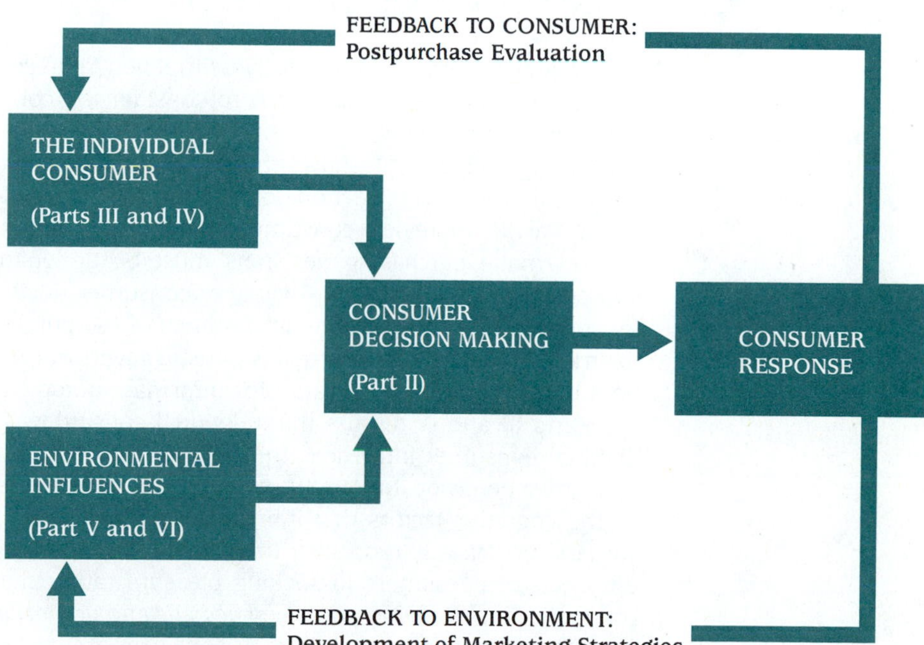

ues in certain respects), and by face-to-face groups (friends, family members, and reference groups). Marketing organizations are also part of the consumer's environment since these organizations provide the offerings that can satisfy consumer needs.

Once the consumer has made a decision, postpurchase evaluation, represented as feedback to the individual consumer, takes place. During evaluation, the consumer will learn from the experience and may change his or her pattern of acquiring information, evaluating brands, and selecting a brand. Consumption experience will directly influence whether the consumer will buy the same brand again.

A feedback loop also leads back to the environment. Consumers communicate their purchase and consumption experiences to friends and family. Marketers also seek information from consumers. They track consumer responses in the form of market share and sales data. However, such information neither tells the marketer why the consumer purchased nor provides information on the strengths and weaknesses of the marketer's brand relative to those of the competition. Therefore, marketing research is also required at this step to determine consumer reactions to the brand and future purchase intent. This information permits management to reformulate marketing strategy to better meet consumer needs.

ORGANIZATION OF THIS TEXT

The model in Figure 1.1 is an oversimplified representation of consumer behavior. The purpose of this text is to consider the components of the model in detail and, in so doing, emphasize consumer behavior applications to marketing strategy. Figure 1.1 shows that we will consider a portion of the model in each of the remaining sections of this text.

In Part II, we review consumer decision making. The process by which consumers make purchasing decisions must be understood in order to develop strategic applications. As we will see, consumer decision making is not a uniform process. It varies by the importance of the purchase to the consumer, the degree to which the consumer is satisfied with the purchase, and the willingness of the consumer to search for information and brand alternatives.

Parts III and IV discuss the individual consumer. The way in which the individual consumer influences the decision process is central to understanding consumer behavior. In Part III, we consider consumers' *thought processes,* that is, the cognitive factors that influence decision making. We also consider consumers' *experiential processes,* that is, decisions that are governed more by the emotions of consumers in seeking pleasure rather than purely by utility from products. This distinction between *hedonic* and *utilitarian* products will be a common theme in this section. Part IV considers the individual consumer's characteristics, namely demographic, lifestyle, and personality characteristics that influence consumers' decisions.

In Parts V and VI, we cover the environmental factors influencing behavior. In Part V, we start with the broadest set of environmental influences, **culture,** that is, the widely shared norms and patterns of behavior of the society in which the consumer lives. In this section we also consider **subcultures,** groups with norms and values that distinguish them from the culture as a whole, and **cross-cultural influences** that identify differences in cultural values between nations. We then consider face-to-face groups in Part VI and how they influence consumer behavior. One chapter describes **reference groups,** so-called because they provide consumers with a means of comparing and evaluating their attitudes and behavior with the group's. Another describes the most important group of all, the family. Part VI also describes communications from the environment to the consumer through word-of-mouth and through a broader process of the diffusion of information across groups.

CONSUMER BEHAVIOR FROM A CONSUMER'S PERSPECTIVE

Until now, we have emphasized the managerial implications of studying consumer behavior. This is a logical perspective for current and future business managers. However, when viewed through consumers' eyes, consumer behavior can take on a very different perspective.

Managerial and consumer perspectives differ on at least three dimensions. First, because of the profit motive, managers have a vested interest in presenting their products in the best light possible. Consumers are interested in evaluating information in light of their own needs. As a result, managers tend to view product information as a vehicle for influence. Consumers view information as a vehicle for making better choices.

Second, most marketing strategies are product-specific. Managers introduce, price, advertise, and distribute individual brands. Consumers must make decisions across a range of brand alternatives. Further, consumers often view an individual product as part of a larger constellation that reflects their lifestyles. Buying health foods, wearing Levi jeans and Reebok sneakers, and owning a cellular telephone may not appear to be related; however, they may reflect the lifestyle and desires of an individual consumer. These products are related in the consumer's mind, not in the marketer's.

Third, managers view competition as a threat. Consumers view competition as an opportunity to gain additional alternatives, frequently at lower prices.

The differences between the managerial and consumer views of consumer behavior could lead to potential abuses by marketers and suboptimal choices by consumers. The manager's product-specific, profit-oriented, anticompetitive perspective could lead to deceptive advertising, limited product choices, inadequate attention to product safety, and an attempt to skirt ecological responsibilities.

Fortunately, these inequities are the exception rather than the rule. In most cases, abuses of consumer rights do not occur because of the inherent protection of a free marketplace. Marketers can best maximize profits by offering consumers quality products and accurate information to ensure a loyal customer base. However, abuses have occurred with enough regularity to promote a *consumer movement* that seeks to protect consumer rights through the activities of consumer groups, government agencies, and at times even business organizations.

The consumer movement is the public policy representation of the consumer perspective and attempts to ensure the consumer's right to product safety, accurate information, sufficient choice, and a clean environment. As such, it is the countervailing force to a managerial perspective of consumer behavior.

In the next chapter, we consider consumer rights and the firm's social responsibility in ensuring these rights.

SUMMARY

This introductory chapter has established the text's orientation by linking consumer behavior to marketing strategy. The need for consumer information to establish marketing strategies is recognized. Such consumer information permits marketing managers to:

- Define consumer needs.
- Identify consumer segments that have these needs.
- Develop marketing strategies targeted to these segments.
- Evaluate marketing strategies.
- Ensure that marketing strategies are implemented in a socially responsible manner.

A historical perspective shows that a consumer orientation developed out of economic necessity in the 1950s. With the advent of a buyer's market, marketing managers began to identify consumer needs in a competitive environment and to gear marketing strategies accordingly. A better understanding of consumer needs, perceptions, attitudes, and intentions became necessary.

Current trends suggest that marketers must continue to be sensitive to changes in consumer needs, demographic characteristics, and lifestyles in order to develop effective marketing strategies. Three changes in particular are likely to have an impact on marketers:

1. A greater value orientation on the part of consumers.
2. Greater interest in and access to information on products and services.
3. The desire for more customized products.

Marketing firms need some systematic basis for collecting information. Most have a marketing information system designed to provide data on what consumers do and why. Such information systems are designed to collect both secondary data (existing data from published sources or company records) and primary data (data collected by the company to answer its research questions).

The common sources of secondary data are the U.S. government, syndicated services, and databases on individual consumer characteristics that allow companies to customize their offerings. The usual means of collecting primary data are qualitative research, surveys, experimentation, and observation.

Although this text takes a managerial approach to the study of consumer behavior, it also recognizes the usefulness of an alternative view—a holistic approach. A managerial approach tends to emphasize individual consumers, their thought processes, and the impact of the environment on their needs and attitudes. A holistic approach tends to stress consumer experiences—primarily consumption—rather than purchase behavior and the general context of the consumer's environment.

One following a holistic approach tends to view consumer behavior as a field of study in and of itself without necessarily deriving managerial and strategic implications.

The text is organized after the model in Figure 1.1, which has four components: consumer decision making and the three elements that influence consumer decision making—the individual consumer, environmental influences, and communications from the environment to the consumer. In addition to the introductory section, these four components make up the four parts of the text.

QUESTIONS

1. In what ways is the study of consumer behavior linked to the development of marketing strategies?
2. Why did Levi Strauss & Co. switch from a mass-market strategy to a strategy of market segmentation? How did it adjust its product line to reflect changes in consumer demographics and lifestyles?
3. A vice president of marketing for a large soft drink company often states that sales are the ultimate criterion of marketing effectiveness and, therefore, one must look primarily at the relationship between marketing stimuli (price, advertising, deals, coupons) and sales. What arguments could you, as director of marketing research, present in support of consumer research to demonstrate that sales figures alone are not sufficient to evaluate marketing strategies?
4. What were the conditions leading to the development of the marketing concept?
5. What caused Avon to shift from a sales to a marketing orientation in the 1980s? What Avon strategies reflected this shift?
6. What is the relationship between a greater value orientation on the part of consumers and the "cross-shopper" effect? What are the strategic implications of a greater value orientation?
7. In what ways does the consumer have more access to information today? Are consumers likely to use these new information sources? How are marketers responding to their availability?
8. Two marketing analysts predict that instead of product managers selling one product to many consumers, we will begin to see *custom managers* selling many products to one consumer. What does this mean and why did these analysts make this prediction?
9. What are the roles of primary and secondary data in conducting consumer research? What are the roles of qualitative and survey research in collecting primary data?
10. What is the distinction between a managerial and a holistic approach to the study of consumer behavior? What are the advantages and disadvantages of both?

RESEARCH ASSIGNMENTS

1. Log onto Levi Strauss's Internet site at http://www.levi.com. Browse the various pages and answer the following questions:
   - In what ways is Levi Strauss trying to treat the market for jeans as a global market?
   - What product information is supplied at this site? In what language is this information conveyed? Does this conflict with your previous answer?
   - What purpose(s) do the various sections of the site serve?
   - How would you improve the site?
2. Do a content analysis of two issues of *Advertising Age*, one from about 1960 and one current issue, by determining the frequency of the appearance of certain basic marketing references.
   - How frequently mentioned in the 1960 and the current issues are (a) marketing research, (b) test marketing, (c) new product development, (d) market segmentation, (e) product positioning, (f) lifestyles, (g) advertising regulation, (h) environmental concerns, and (i) advertising to African Americans and Hispanic Americans?
   - What are the implications of the frequency of the references to these subjects in 1960 and currently?
3. Attempt to trace a large manufacturer's development of a marketing concept and evolution of a behavioral orientation for consumer packaged goods. Do so by tracing references to the company in business periodicals and, when possible, by interview-

ing company executives who have been with the company in marketing for 10 years or more.

- How have marketing research procedures changed, particularly in regard to (a) product testing, (b) advertising evaluation, (c) in-store testing, and (d) utilization of concepts of market segmentation and product positioning?
- What changes have occurred in the organization of the research function?

CONSUMER RIGHTS AND SOCIAL RESPONSIBILITY

Chapter 2

THE BODY SHOP: A FOCUS ON CONSUMER RIGHTS AND CORPORATE RESPONSIBILITY

In Chapter 1, the focus was primarily on the strategic implications of consumer behavior. Equally important are considerations of consumer rights in the marketplace. Consumers have a right to accurate and full information, to safe products, to adequate product choices, and to products that do not harm the environment. In this respect, it is important to view purchasing decisions from the consumer's as well as the manager's perspective. Without a focus on consumer rights, businesses could easily engage in abuses such as deceptive advertising, failing to provide consumers with full information on product contents, developing unsafe products, or charging unreasonably high prices.

In this chapter, we will:

- Consider basic consumer rights.
- Describe the historical development of these rights.
- Focus on four issues that have been a battleground for consumer rights in the 1990s: (1) environmental protection, (2) accurate health and nutritional claims, (3) regulation of advertising to children, and (4) consumer privacy.

- Assess the marketing firm's social responsibilities in insuring consumer rights and addressing social issues.

To some extent, competitive forces and government regulation act to insure consumer rights, but not fully. The socially responsible firm will recognize its responsibility to provide consumers with full and accurate information and safe products. Beyond such recognition, the socially responsible firm will also realize it has a responsibility to address social issues, such as insuring a clean environment, discouraging drug use and teenage drinking, avoiding indirect appeals to youth to smoke (for example, by the use of cartoon characters), and accounting for the inability of young children to evaluate ads and promotional appeals.

http://www.the-body-shop.com/

Some businesses have begun to recognize that social responsibility should be part of their strategic focus. A good example is The Body Shop and its iconoclastic founder, Anita Roddick. Roddick has tapped into a vein of environmentalism and corporate mistrust that runs deep among many of today's consumers. In her native Britain, for instance, one study suggests that 56 percent of shoppers are suspicious of environmental claims.[1] "Consumers crave information, not another bloody marketing hyperbole," says Roddick.[2] Roddick clings to a simple credo: make sure your customers trust you to sell them products that are part of the solution, not the problem.

Roddick has been following her own advice since 1976, when she opened her first London store full of bottles containing her handmade lotions and shampoos. Roddick drew a solid following among a new generation of consumers who were carefully scouring labels for proof that products they bought were all natural.

The Body Shop's popularity really took off in the mid-1980s, when a wave of consumer protests were launched against companies accused of abusing animals for commercial profit. Widely publicized boycotts were organized against fur makers for inhumanely trapping animals and against cosmetics companies for testing their products on animals.[3] Roddick became one of the movement's most fiery supporters, going so far as to sell bath soaps in the shape of endangered animals and to label her products with the explicit promise that she did not engage in animal testing.[4] Her latest cause is a campaign against Shell because of reported human rights abuses in Nigeria.[5]

That, however, would have been of little impact had her products not caught the imagination of shoppers. Blue corn oil made by indigenous Indian tribes from the American Southwest became a best-selling face lotion; mixtures from obscure African villages began appearing in bathrooms from Duluth to Dallas. By 1993, she was ringing up $266 million in sales from 900 stores.[6] That reach has led Roddick to attempt to influence how her shoppers act once they leave her stores. She encourages recycling, for instance, with an offer that gives a discount to those who bring back empty bottles for refilling.

But the very consumer distrust of such corporate actions as self-serving caught up with Roddick. Critics began accusing her of latching onto every cause to build her media celebrity status, thereby getting free advertising. They cited Body Shop

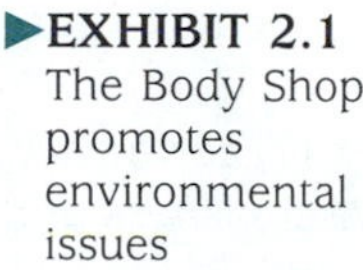
▶EXHIBIT 2.1
The Body Shop promotes environmental issues

claims of using only organic ingredients as false and the fight against animal testing as a straw man because testing had decreased by the time Roddick got on the bandwagon.[7] Others considered the charges unfair, pointing to Roddick's willingness to spend corporate profits on social causes. Roddick waves off such criticism, saying that she is trying to create a new definition of corporate responsibility. "I thought it was very important that my business concern itself not just with hair and skin preparation, but also with the community, the environment, and the big wide world beyond cosmetics," she says[8] (see Exhibit 2.1).

Clearly, Roddick's business ethics are perfectly timed for the desires of a public that has begun to rebel against businesses that purposefully mislead, offer a restricted choice of alternatives, or sell unsafe products. The manifestation of this trend has come to be known as **the consumer movement.** Broadly defined, the consumer movement represents activities by consumer groups, government agencies, and at times business organizations that are designed to protect the consumer.[9] The term *consumer movement* is somewhat misleading since there is no actual organization of consumers but, instead, a conglomeration of groups with separate concerns. As a result, the activities of these groups in the consumer interest have also been referred to as **consumerism.**

✦ THE CONSUMER MOVEMENT

The primary concern of the consumer movement is to ensure the consumer's rights in the process of exchange. These rights include the right to be informed, to be told the truth, to be given adequate alternatives, and to be assured of safety in the process of consumption.[10]

Three types of organizations make up the consumer movement: (1) consumer-oriented groups concerned primarily with increasing consumer consciousness and providing consumers with information to improve their basis for choice, (2) government legislation and regulation, and (3) at times, business through competition and self-regulation. These forces are summarized in Figure 2.1.

The Role of Consumer Activists and Organizations

The most visible forces in the consumer movement have been consumer activists. Upton Sinclair exposed the unsanitary conditions in Chicago's meat packinghouses in his book *The Jungle*. During the Depression in the 1930s, several authors continued to expose unsafe food and drug products. In the 1960s, Rachel Carson wrote about the dangers of pesticides and food additives in her book *Silent Spring,* and Ralph Nader wrote about the failure of the automobile industry to maintain safety standards in *Unsafe at Any Speed.* In the 1980s, Dennis Hayes founded an environmental group called Green Seal to monitor environmental claims and to expose companies that use such claims to sell products without protecting the environment.

Consumer Organizations

Consumers Union, the oldest consumer group which was established in 1936 as a product-testing and consumer education agency, now has a membership of 2

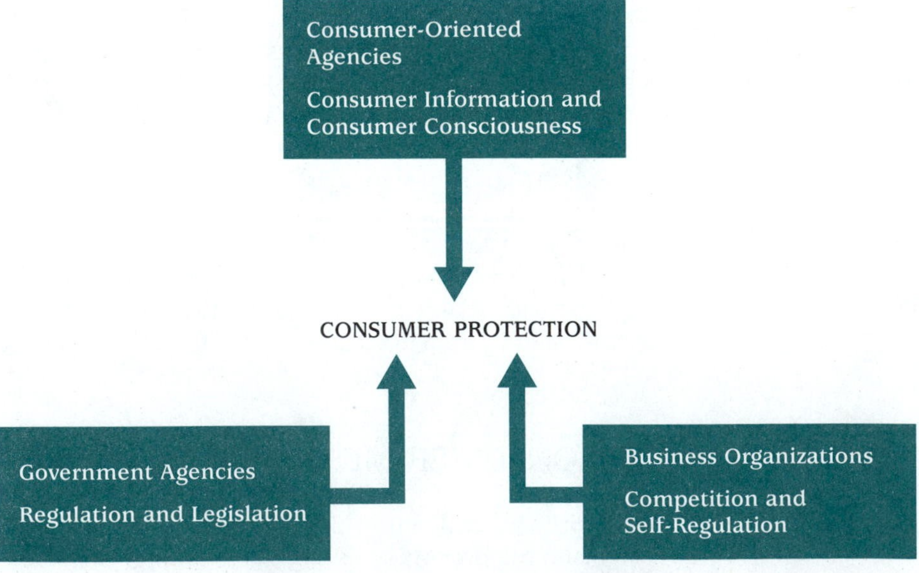

FIGURE 2.1 Agencies involved in consumerism

Source: Adapted from Jagdish N. Sheth and Nicholas Mammana, "Why Consumer Protection Efforts Are Likely to Fail," Faculty Working Paper No. 104, College of Commerce and Business Administration, University of Illinois at Urbana-Champaign, April 11, 1973, p. 3. Reprinted with permission from Jagdish N. Sheth, Emory University.

million and publishes *Consumer Reports* magazine. It has undertaken broad consumer education programs regarding interest rates, life insurance, product safety, doctor selection, and the problems of low-income consumers. Consumers regard Consumers Union as an objective, impartial third party that can assess product quality and consumer complaints through its product-testing facilities.

http://www.greenpeace.org/

Other groups such as the Sierra Club, the National Audubon Society, and Greenpeace have been active on environmental issues. In another area of concern, the Citizen Health Research Group and the Center for Science in the Public Interest monitor health claims. The latter is also active in monitoring cigarette and alcohol advertising to minorities and teens.

Consumer Boycotts

One primary means consumer activists and organizations have used to pressure business organizations is boycotts. Protesting higher prices, supermarket boycotts in 1966 and meat boycotts in 1973 received national attention. One of the most effective boycotts was of California grapes to protest grape growers' treatment of migrant workers.

http://www.starkist.com/

In 1988, thousands of consumers joined Action for Corporate Accountability when it resumed a lapsed six-year boycott of Nestlé S.A. for violating World Health Organization standards on marketing infant formula to developing nations.[11] Then, in 1990, a potential boycott of H. J. Heinz's Star-Kist tuna and Van Camp's Chicken of the Sea caused both companies to promote a plan to protect dolphins when fishermen net tuna.[12]

Overall, consumers' group action has been sporadic and uncoordinated. For instance, in 1991, Jesse Jackson's PUSH organization tried convincing the major sneaker companies to put their money in black-owned banks and to hire African-American executives, but the organization had few tangible results. The feminist organization Media Watch tried to boycott Guess? jeans for sexist advertising and had mixed results. On average, there are more than 100 national boycotts each year and most fail.[13] The reason is that consumers are difficult to organize and to represent because of their diverse interests.

The Role of Government

Government has a responsibility to protect consumer interests and does so through legislation and the actions of regulatory agencies.

Legislation

In the area of legislation, Congress has outlawed deceptive packaging, required warning labels on cigarettes, mandated full disclosure of all finance charges in consumer credit agreements, prohibited the sale of unsafe products to children, and required full disclosure of health claims and ingredients for food products. The most important consumer protection laws passed since 1966 are listed in Table 2.1. States also have a legislative role in protecting consumer rights. State laws have required unit pricing on food products and open dating of perishable

TABLE 2.1
Key consumer rights legislation

Far Packaging and Labeling Act	1966	Requires manufacturers to disclose ingredients and volume on the package
Federal Cigarette Labeling Act	1967	Requires warning label on cigarette packages and advertising
Truth-In-Lending Act	1968	Requires full disclosure of all finance charges in consumer credit agreements
Child Protection Act	1969	Allows the Food & Drug Administration to remove dangerous children's products from the market
Consumer Product Safety Commission Act	1972	Establishes the Consumer Product Safety Commission to recall and ban unsafe products
Magnuson-Moss Warranty Act	1975	Sets disclosure standards for product warranties
Nutritional Labeling and Education Act	1990	Regulates health claims and requires disclosure of nutritional content
Clean Air Act	1990	Establishes strict controls on companies to avoid air pollution and acid rain emissions
Children's Television Act	1990	Reduces the number of commercials during children's TV programs and requires more educational programs for children

foods and drugs. States and local communities have also enforced laws regarding recycling and waste disposal.

Regulation

Federal regulatory agencies play a critical role in ensuring consumer rights. The two most important are the **Federal Trade Commission (FTC)** and **Food and Drug Administration (FDA).** The FTC, established in 1914 to curb the monopoly powers of big business and unfair trade practices, is also a watchdog over deceptive advertising. The FDA, created in 1906 as a result of the outcry over Sinclair's *The Jungle,* sets product standards and requires disclosure of product contents. The **Federal Communications Commission (FCC)** oversees advertising directed to children.

http://www.kraftfoods.com/

Since 1991, the FDA has been particularly active in controlling health claims and ensuring accurate labeling as a result of passage of the Nutritional Labeling Act in 1990. Based on FDA actions in a two-year period, Kraft-General Foods had to stop exaggerating the calcium content of its Kraft Singles cheese; [14] Citrus Hill was made to take the word *fresh* off its orange juice label because it is made from concentrate; and restaurants have been ordered to begin backing up nutrition claims with hard data on their menus.[15]

Two other agencies, established in the 1970s, are important. The **Consumer Product Safety Commission (CPSC)** is empowered to set product safety standards to protect consumers from risk or injury. The **Environmental Protection Agency (EPA)** sets controls on industry emissions, toxic wastes, and automobile pollution.

The Role of Business Organizations

Business has been both reactive and proactive in protecting consumer rights. It has been reactive in responding to government regulation. In reacting to government, businesses must conform to a variety of laws dealing with areas such as pollution controls, product safety, product labeling, truth in advertising, and controls over price fixing and antimonopoly activities. They must also conform to guidelines established by regulatory agencies such as the FTC's restrictions on deceptive advertising and health and the FDA's nutritional labeling requirements. At times, the business community has strongly resisted such regulation. For example, when the Carter Administration put more teeth into the Environmental Protection Agency and sought greater powers for the FTC and the FDA, the response from business was intense. One casualty of this lobbying effort was failure to create a cabinet-level Office of Consumer Representation.

http://www.ge.com/

http://www.pg.com/

A more proactive response from business is self-regulation. Many companies are adopting sophisticated antipollution policies, forthright labeling practices, and new channels for customers to exercise their rights. For example, Lever Brothers commits itself to using recycled plastics in packages for its household products; General Electric spends millions on reducing pollutants that deplete the ozone barrier; Procter & Gamble is advertising refills for its products to reduce waste by 25 to 35 percent; and Wal-Mart is experimenting with an eco-store that features recycling as its wall-to-wall theme.[16] But as we saw in the case of The Body Shop, the public is often skeptical of such efforts, regarding them as self-serving rather than motivated by a true interest in environmental protection or consumer rights.

The Consumer Movement: A Global Perspective

The consumer movement is not just an American phenomenon. In fact, for much of the past 25 years, it has been a global one. The ecological focus of consumerism began in Western Europe, where the Green movement took root as a political force in the early 1980s to protest acid rain's detrimental impact on Europe's forests. By decade's end, Greens had become establishment politicians, accounting for 14.5 percent of the parliamentary vote in the United Kingdom, 14 percent in Belgium, 8.4 percent in West Germany, and 10.5 percent in France.[17]

The Greens pressured federal, state, and local agencies in their countries to mobilize, and these agencies, in turn, made the message clear to industry. Nonpulp diapers were introduced in Britain; Germany's federal Environmental Protection Agency established a Blue Angel label for products declared environmentally sound; an Ecover line of nonpolluting cleaning products was sold in Belgium; and a line of green products was unveiled in Canada.[18] Overall, the public mood seems best summed by a 1990 poll that showed 75 percent of Western European consumers factored in the greenness of a product when making their purchase decision.[19]

One area in which Western Europe lagged behind the United States was in regulating the promotion of cigarettes. But that has changed. The European Union

EXHIBIT 2.2
An antismoking message in Scotland

banned cigarette ads on TV in 1989, 19 years after the U.S. ban.[20] There is also more of a concerted effort to prevent teenage smoking, as illustrated by the striking ad in Exhibit 2.2 by the Health Education Board of Scotland. In addition, consumer activists are emerging in Asia to attack cigarette marketing meth-

GLOBAL APPLICATIONS OF CONSUMER BEHAVIOR

▶ Environmentalism Has a Long Way To Go in Eastern Europe

Through much of this century, the chokehold of centralized planning and massive spending on arms led to one environmental crisis after another in the nations of Eastern Europe and the former Soviet Union. The most famous was the nuclear meltdown at Chernobyl. As William Reilly, former head of the Environmental Protection Agency, wrote in 1992:

> To those who doubt the wisdom of pollution control . . . let them travel to Eastern Europe. Let them see the Vistula River in Poland, over 80 percent of it so corrosive that it is useless for even cooling machinery. Let them experience sulfur dioxide levels in Krakow, so high that 500-year-old monuments have crumbled in just 40 years. Let them confront Eastern Europe's high rate of infant mortality, lung disorders, worker absenteeism, and premature death. Poland, Hungary, Bulgaria, Romania and Czechoslovakia, not to mention Russia itself—these are entire nations living in the dark shadow of an environmental catastrophe.

With the possible exception of the Czech Republic, not much has improved in these countries since Reilly's pessimistic statement. In 1996, the European Union sent a stern message that unless they attempt to tackle these environmental problems, they would not be considered for future membership. "The message here was: environment is not something you can forget about," according to one official. "We're saying you have to take this seriously, and now is the time."

The warning was based on a visit to Eastern Europe by the European Union's new Environment Commissioner. After the visit, a blunt memo from the commissioner's office stated that some Eastern European countries had no strategy to deal with environmental problems. The warning is well taken because, according to one report, Eastern European chemical works and power plants are still infusing the air and water with amounts of waste that far surpass international standards. Toxic dumps still contaminate groundwater, and raw sewage from cities still spews into rivers and coastal waters. Even more discouraging, countries that have instituted new regulations have no efficient means of enforcement.

The one ray of light is growing awareness among these countries that economic growth might be hindered without more awareness of consumer interests, and a fledgling green movement that is starting to exert some pressure on public officials. But Eastern Europe has a long way to go to establish a consumer-friendly environment.

Sources: "Clean Up Your Land, European Union Tells Ex-Eastern Bloc," *The New York Times* (September 25, 1996), p. A11; "Environment Inc.," *Business Horizons* (March-April 1992), p. 9.

ods, bolstered by a World Health Organization report that found U.S.-style tactics "caused immediate jumps in consumption among women and teens, traditionally non-smoking groups in less-developed countries."[21]

Unfortunately, in other parts of the globe such as Japan and Eastern Europe, consumerism has received less emphasis (see the Global Applications box). In Japan, for example, a powerful alignment between government and industry has put more emphasis on forming protective trade barriers than in protecting consumer rights.[22] While cooperation between government and industry may be suited to Japanese preferences for harmony and consensus, it leaves consumers with fewer brand alternatives. However, because of the first victory in 1993 of parties more sympathetic to free-trade principles and consumer rights, the pendulum may soon start swinging toward consumerism. The same trend can be seen in the nations of Eastern Europe and the former Soviet Union.

THE HISTORY OF THE CONSUMER MOVEMENT IN THE UNITED STATES

A history of the consumer movement reveals the nature of attempts to protect consumer rights and the progress of corporate America in accepting a concept of social responsibility for its actions.

Three Periods of Consumerism from 1890 to 1980

The first recorded consumer protest in this country occurred in 1775 in Massachusetts where people who sold tainted food were sentenced to the pillory.[23] The real consumer movement started at the turn of the century and was followed by three distinct periods prior to 1980 when consumer protection became a national issue. Each of these periods was marked by rising consumer prices coupled with muckraking exposés, which resulted in consumer protection legislation.

First Period of Consumerism

The first period came at the turn of the century, a time when huge corporations such as Standard Oil were amassing power. As a result, the Sherman Antitrust Act was passed in 1890 to limit big business from restraining competition. Also, national brands began gaining prominence and consumers were focusing on their performance. In 1906, the FDA was established to regulate these brands. That was also the year that Sinclair's *The Jungle* created such an outcry about unsanitary food processing that Congress passed the Meat Inspection Act. Another development in this period was passage in 1914 of the Federal Trade Commission Act, which established the FTC to curb monopoly and unfair trade practices.

Second Period of Consumerism

The Great Depression and the 1933 book *100,000,000 Guinea Pigs,* which exposed unsafe medicines, cosmetics, and foods, sparked the second period of consumerism. They led to other exposés of advertising through two books, *Our Master's Voice* and *The Popular Practice of Fraud,* and exposés regarding the preparation of foodstuffs through two other books, *Eat, Drink and Be Wary* and *American Chamber of Horrors: The Truth About Food and Drugs.* Thanks to such books, Consumers Union was formed in 1936 and the Wheeler-Lea Amendment to the Federal Trade Commission Act was passed in 1938. The amendment extended the powers of the FTC to prosecute unfair and deceptive trade practices, particularly advertising.

Third Period of Consumerism

The third period of consumerism began in the 1960s, when another series of exposés followed the relative quiet of the post-World War II years. In 1962, Rachel Carson's *Silent Spring* made consumers aware of the dangers of pesticides and other chemicals in foods and other products. In 1965, Ralph Nader's *Unsafe at Any Speed* exposed the automobile industry's disregard for even rudimentary safety precautions. Nader's study was instrumental in the passage of laws to set safety standards for cars.

Former EPA head William Reilly described the 1970s as a period marked by an "astonishing record of legislation to protect the environment, with the passage of laws to restrict air pollution, control toxic substances, promote resource conservation, and protect drinking water."[24] From 1974 to 1978, federal expenditures on consumer safety, job safety, and other industry-specific regulation increased by 85 percent.[25] President Carter created a cabinet post to deal with energy conservation and the environment. Further, new agencies such as the EPA were formed and older regulatory agencies were rejuvenated. The FDA became more activist, requiring additional information on food labels. The FTC established clear rules to define deceptive advertising, made cigarette companies disclose harmful tar content on their packages, and energetically investigated TV advertising's effect on children.[26] By decade's end, the FTC's budget had increased by 500 percent.[27]

The Decline of Consumerism in the 1980s

The Reagan Administration reversed the drive to regulation and deemphasized consumer issues. The basic philosophy was stated in Reagan's 1982 economic report: "While regulation is necessary to protect such vital areas as food, health and safety, too much unnecessary regulation simply adds to the costs to businesses and consumers alike without commensurate benefits."[30]

To the Reagan Administration, self-regulation was preferable to government regulation in protecting consumer interests. Regulatory agencies were required to justify their actions with a cost-benefit analysis demonstrating the value of their proposals.[31] Unlike the 1970s, when the burden of proof was on industry to ensure consumer protection, the burden was now on the regulatory agencies.

Coinciding with this shift were severe cutbacks in most of the agencies' budgets. The greatest effect on marketing came from cutbacks at the FTC that produced a one-third reduction of staff[32] and resulted in a sharp reduction in the regulation of advertising activities.

http://www.epa.gov/

Environmental control was also deemphasized, and the EPA was weakened by a 50 percent staff cut.[33] The administration also deregulated the airline industry, substantially reduced the enforcement powers of the Consumer Product Safety Commission, eliminated the nutritional educational program at the Department of Agriculture,[34] and rolled back automobile emission and pollution control standards.

By 1989, when the Bush Administration came to power, the marketing industry had grown used to relaxed rules on everything from children's advertising to nutritional labeling. Swinging the pendulum back toward consumerism yet again, the Bush Administration slowed the pace of deregulation and put more teeth into some of the agencies that were all but ignored during the Reagan years. By 1990, for instance, the FTC's new chairperson said that the advertising industry would be held accountable for ads or practices regarded as unfair and deceptive.[35] If there was a single reason for this change of course, it was that most surveys showed American consumers thought deregulation hurt them.

http://www.ftc.gov/

THE REBIRTH OF CONSUMERISM IN THE 1990S

A rebirth of consumerism has occurred in the 1990s, primarily as a reaction to the deregulation of the Reagan years. The Bush Administration initiated this rebirth, and the Clinton Administration is carrying it forward.

Four issues have dominated the attention of consumer activists, government, and business in the 1990s: (1) the environment, (2) health claims, (3) advertising to children, and (4) the right to privacy and nondisclosure of personal information.[36]

The New Environmentalism

The 1990s has seen greater enforcement of environmental controls and new initiatives to promote a clean environment. The impetus for these moves does not come from government but from an increased awareness among consumers for protecting the environment. Highly publicized environmental disasters such as the Exxon Valdez oil spill and the record oil spill Iraq caused during the Gulf War in 1991 have reinforced the belief among consumers that the environment is deteriorating.

A 1995 survey found that 63 percent of Americans consider themselves environmentalists and that 62 percent said they would give priority to the environment over economic growth. Some consumers act on these concerns. For example, 14 percent of consumers stopped buying Exxon products because of the Exxon Valdez oil spill.[37]

On the other side of the coin, consumers do not necessarily buy green products. Unless they consider environmentally sound products to be the equal of regular brands based on quality and purpose, most consumers are unlikely to pay the higher prices such products often require. When green goods were a novelty, shoppers were willing to spend more to test them; but as time passed, they began to apply the same value and quality standards to green products as to any other product. Some recycled tissues, for instance, are not as soft; certain recycled paper is not appropriate for all uses. This is even true in an increasingly environmentally conscious European market. As *The Wall Street Journal* reported in 1995, "Most consumers in Europe don't want to pay extra for eco-friendly products, while others simply believe green detergents and cleaners don't work as well."[38]

The new environmentalism of the 1990s has found a voice in each of the three parties to consumerism in Figure 2.1: the consumer, government, and business organizations.

Reaction of Consumer Activists and Agencies

Increased environmental concerns have led consumer groups and politicians to target marketers they believe produce needless pollutants and clog precious landfill space. Such actions often center on consumer organizations that have played a public role in opposing business activities that harm the environment. The most prominent is the Sierra Club, an organization that seeks to protect land areas from development and publicizes negative environmental activities. Another, the Environmental Defense Fund, attempts to increase public awareness regarding issues such as waste disposal and encourages consumers to recycle trash (see Exhibit 2.3). The EDF was instrumental in influencing McDonald's to change its packaging from plastics to paper.

http://www.sierraclub.org/

http://www.edf.org/

One consumer group that highlights the positive is California's Green Cross Certification program, which awards a stamp to products made from the highest possible percentage of recycled material. Clorox was the first to receive an award for the recycled content of its bleach boxes. Willamette Industries also received one for its 40 percent recycled grocery bags.[39]

Government Controls

The new environmentalism also has resulted in renewed activism by government. In 1990, the Clean Air Act was passed and required companies to conform to strict controls to avoid air pollution and acid rain emissions. The bill will cost American companies an estimated $21 billion by the turn of the century.[40] The Clinton Administration has strengthened the commitment to conservation. In 1993, it established a new White House Office of Environmental Policy and signed a biodiversity treaty to protect plant and animal life worldwide. Clinton

EXHIBIT 2.3 An environmentally oriented ad from a consumer organization

also signed a law in 1996 to protect millions of acres of forests and grasslands in the southwest from mining and lumbering. And in the same year, the Clinton Administration directed the EPA to focus all environmental protection standards on the risks that pollution poses to the health of children, leading to tougher rules on pollution emissions.[41]

The federal government has not undertaken this mission alone. From coast to coast, local governments are recognizing that shrinking landfill space and finite resources make environmental policy good policy. In Texas, a law that went into effect in early 1994 requires 40 percent of all solid waste to be recycled. Other states are trying to lessen gasoline consumption by encouraging carpooling, mass transit, and even walking.[42] Some municipalities are even joining with business to educate consumers. The St. Lawrence County Solid Waste Disposal Authority, for instance, has teamed up with P&C Food markets of Syracuse, New York, to give environmental shopping tours to the chain's customers.[43]

Reaction of Business

The reaction of the third leg in the consumer movement, business organizations, has been mixed. On the positive side, some companies have begun to take steps to ensure environmentally responsible actions. In late 1993, the three largest American automobile makers agreed to work with the White House to create jointly the technology that would produce a reliable and well-priced car that is three times more energy efficient than present models.[44] Japanese carmakers http://www.honda.com/

such as Honda have begun using their fuel efficiency to appeal to environmentally minded consumers.

Companies have taken other actions to promote environmental controls; for example:

- Reynolds Wrap promotes recycling (see Exhibit 2.4), while Crane Papers advertises the natural content of its products (see Exhibit 2.5).
- McDonald's switched from plastic to paper wrapping and uses recyclable products to build its restaurants.
- Following McDonald's lead, six major paper users, among them Time Warner and Johnson & Johnson, agreed in 1993 to help the Environmental Defense Fund build a market for recycled paper by using second-hand pulp.[45]
- Sears, Roebuck & Co. has asked its 2,300 suppliers to cut packaging use 25 percent, while Pepsi-Cola has introduced 2-liter bottles made from 25 percent recycled materials.[46]
- Monsanto organized a task force of scientists and engineers to analyze the effects of any new materials and chemicals on the environment and on users. It views the task force as an "early warning system" that is intended to "blow the whistle on any new product concept that may introduce unacceptable hazards to users."[47]

http://www.mcdonalds.com/

http://www.timewarner.com/

http://www.jnj.com/

http://www.sears.com/

http://www.monsanto.com/

EXHIBIT 2.4
Reynolds promotes recycling

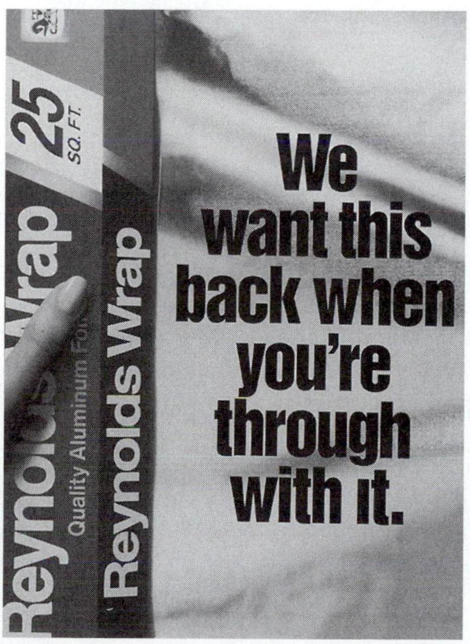

EXHIBIT 2.5 Crane & Co. promote environmentally friendly paper.

Marketers have also unleashed a torrent of new products with environmental claims. In 1991, 13.4 percent of all consumer products introduced were positioned as green, up from 4.3 percent in 1989.[48]

On the negative side, many of these "green" claims are dubious at best. For example, when Hefty, Glad, and Handi-Wrap trash bags added chemicals to promote the decomposition of their products, they advertised them as biodegradable. The problem is that biodegradability requires the action of sunlight, and most of these products wind up in landfills where they do not actually decompose.

Such claims have led to a series of actions on the federal and state levels. The FTC and eight states are investigating whether recycling claims violate truth-in-advertising laws. In addition, the FTC has issued a set of guidelines on environmental labeling. For example, calling a trash bag recyclable is now considered misleading because bags are not generally separated from other trash at landfills.[49]

Advertising Health Claims

A second issue that has generated consumer activism in the 1990s is concern with health claims on foods. Changing lifestyles have led to an increased focus on health and nutrition. Now, consumers are more aware of nutritional information in ads and on packages.

In one recent survey, over half of consumers interviewed said that health claims are an important factor in influencing their purchasing decision, and 44 percent said they read most health and nutritional information on the package.[50] The focus on health claims has been heightened by greater awareness of the potential harm cigarettes, liquor, drugs, and even coffee can cause. This concern was shown in another poll that found three of four consumers support warnings on beer, wine, and liquor advertising and packaging.[51]

Reaction of Consumer Activists and Agencies

Protection of consumer rights in advertising health claims has been the primary responsibility of only one of the three legs of the consumer movement: government agencies (see Figure 2.1). Although they have begun to raise their voices, consumer activists and organizations have played a minor role in this area. In 1993, for example, the Center for Science in the Public Interest and 274 other consumer protection groups wrote to President Clinton, pushing for the resignation of the FTC's chairperson, a Bush appointee named Janet Steiger. The letter urged Clinton to draw from state and local consumer protection officials who are more concerned with health claims for future appointments.[52]

Government Controls

By 1990, studies casting doubt on many health claims caused Congress to pass the Nutrition Labeling and Education Act, which requires fuller disclosure of the nutritional content of foods in packaging. For example, one study found that oat bran was no more effective in lowering a person's cholesterol or risk of heart disease than any other food with fiber such as whole wheat bread.[53]

In conjunction with the Nutritional Labeling Act, the FDA developed new rules requiring that advertisers substantiate their claims for foods such as oat bran and high-fiber cereals with scientific evidence.[54] In 1991, the FDA forced Kellogg to withdraw its claim that Heartwise cereal helped reduce cholesterol. More recently, the FDA softened its stand, allowing companies like Quaker Oats to advertise the health benefits of oatmeal (see Exhibit 2.6).

http://www.kelloggs.com/

The FDA has also forced several food makers to eliminate no-cholesterol claims on vegetable oils. The agency said that such claims were misleading since they implied that no-cholesterol products are fat-free, which is not the case. Procter & Gamble immediately took no-cholesterol claims off its Crisco and Puritan oils.

Individual states have also taken a more activist role in protecting consumer interests. In 1989, officials of several states stopped Campbell ads that promoted its soups as sources of calcium and fiber and prevented Nestlé's Carnation unit from claiming that its Good Start formula is hypoallergenic.[55]

EXHIBIT 2.6 Quaker Oats advertises the health benefits of oatmeal

Reaction of Business

Food and drug companies have attempted to get on the nutritional bandwagon with a proliferation of products that claim to have fewer calories, less salt, lower fat, less cholesterol, more calcium, and higher vitamin content. Some companies have specialized in all-natural products. For instance, Tom's of Maine started with an all-natural toothpaste and is now branching out into other all-natural drug products. In 1995, Frito-Lay sank $225 million into developing low- or no-fat versions of its entire snack food line.[56] However, with about 60 percent of foods sold in U.S. grocery stores having nutritional labels and one-third of all food advertising containing some kind of health message,[57] it is no wonder that consumers are confused. Consider the following:

- Klondike Lite ice cream bars, introduced in 1989, claimed to have half the calories and fat of the originals. Ads never cited the fact that the bars were only half the size of the originals.[58]

- Taco Lite, a product of Taco Bell, actually raises cholesterol more than the regular product, according to a spokesperson for the Center for Science in the Public Interest.[59]
- Best Foods' Mazola Light Corn Oil Spread promises no cholesterol and low sodium, with 50 percent fewer calories than margarine. Still, one tablespoon contains 50 calories and is 100 percent fat.[60]
- Entenmann Bakery's "no-cholesterol, low-calorie" cherry coffee cake must be served in tiny 1.3-ounce servings if it is to fulfill its low-calorie, low-fat claim.[61]

Companies are becoming more conscious of health and nutritional claims as a result of the FDA's more activist stance and new laws requiring fuller disclosure of nutritional contents. Kellogg's change in name from Heartwise to Fiberwise is an example.

Advertising to Children

A third issue that is receiving increasing attention from consumer activists is advertising to children. Perhaps the most visible issue is cigarette companies appealing to adolescents. No campaign has drawn more fire than the Joe Camel campaign, which R. J. Reynolds launched to resuscitate its ailing Camel brand. The campaign rescued Camel from obscurity to make it the sixth most popular brand in the nation. While Reynolds' stated intent is to appeal to smokers over the age of 21, antismoking activists insist that the cigarette maker's real desire is to attract teens with a likeable cartoon character. After Joe Camel came on the scene, Camel's market share among underage smokers increased from less than 1 percent to 32.8 percent.[62] The FDA reports that children were as familiar with Joe Camel as with Ronald McDonald. Equally disturbing, one survey found that when asked to name a familiar cigarette, 90 percent of children 8 to 13 years old named Camel.[63]

The basis for this concern is a study that found that adolescents are more likely to be affected by advertising than by peer pressure. Further, adolescence is a time of identity formation which makes teens particularly subject to advertising symbols connoting that it is "cool" or "with it" to smoke.[64]

Concern also centers on the effect of advertising on younger children. Younger children may not understand that an advertiser's motive is to persuade and influence and may not even be able to tell the difference between a TV program and a commercial. As a result, they may be more disposed to regard anything said in a commercial message as truthful. Aggravating this merger of advertising and content is the practice of making children's ads look like part of the program. This concern is heightened by the fact that children from ages 6 to 13 spend more time in front of the television than they do in school.[65]

Others have argued that exposing children to advertising permits them to become more informed consumers at an early age. They learn to discriminate claims and to process marketing information. Eliminating advertising would deprive them of such consumer socialization, and they would then become more vulnerable consumers later in life.

However, a number of studies support the position that excessive advertising to children is not in their best interest. Rubin found that younger children do not understand the purpose of a commercial as fully as older children.[66] In support of this study, Stephens and Stutts found that children between ages 3 and 5 had difficulty distinguishing between TV programming and commercials.[67] Roedder, Sternthal, and Calder found that preteens are likely to respond to the immediate influence of a commercial in buying decisions. They tend to ignore their own past experiences with products.[68] Similarly, Brucks, Armstrong, and Goldberg found that preteens do not refer to prior knowledge of products and brands when watching commercials.[69] All of these studies support the notion that children may be unduly influenced by advertising because they have not developed their perceptual discrimination and information processing abilities.[70]

Both consumer organizations and government agencies have been active in controlling advertising to children. The response of business has been mixed.

Reaction of Consumer Activists and Organizations

Whereas government agencies have taken the lead in protecting consumer rights regarding nutritional claims, consumer organizations have taken a more active part regarding advertising to children. Advocacy groups such as the Action for Children's Television (ACT) have attacked advertising to children as unfair and deceptive for the reasons just cited.

Consumer agencies have singled out specific products and brands for criticism, particularly those that pose safety and health problems for children. For example, Hormel's Kid's Kitchen is the same product as the company's Top Shelf line of microwaveable entrees—except that it is positioned to children. Advertising touts the product as one that teaches children confidence and self-reliance. This implies that children can just pop it into the microwave. Parents are concerned that very young children might try to prepare the product.[71] Similarly, in 1996, small, local breweries began introducing lemonade flavor drinks that contain the same level of alcohol as beer. Brands with names like Two Dogs Lemon Brew and Hooper's Hooch are targeting younger people more used to orange soda than beer. Anheuser-Busch and Miller are carefully testing their own versions but are still staying on the sidelines for fear of a public backlash.[72]

http://www.cancer.org/

A coalition of groups, including ACT and the American Cancer Society, has lobbied the FTC to ban the use of all cartoon characters to sell cigarettes because of their appeal to minors. A group called the Smoking Control Advocacy Resource Center has publicized the past role of cigarette companies in consciously promoting cigarettes to the youth market. An RJR memo dated 1976 made public by the group states:

> Evidence is now available to indicate that the 14- to 18-year-old group is an increasing segment of the smoking population. RJR-T[obacco] must soon es-

tablish a successful new brand in this market if our position in the industry is to be maintained over the long term.[73]

Government Controls

Concern about advertising and marketing practices to children has resulted in greater government controls in the 1990s. In 1990, Congress passed the Children's Television Act which reduces the amount of commercials on children's television programming from as many as 14 minutes of ads per hour to no more than 10 minutes per hour on weekends and 12 minutes on weekdays. Broadcasters must also offer more educational programs for children.[74] Implementation of the Children's Television Act was so successful that, at the end of 1992, Action for Children's Television decided to disband.[75]

Although guidelines limiting commercial time have been effective, government regulation has had less success in controlling commercial content. The Joe Camel experience demonstrates this difficulty. In 1992, Surgeon General Antonia Novello demanded that Reynolds stop using the Joe Camel promotion, only to be rebuffed by the company. Later, when she asked magazines to stop accepting the ads, Novello did not fare much better.[76] In 1994, the FTC also refused to recommend an outright ban of the campaign, although the Commission was badly divided on the issue.[77]

Reaction of Business

The reaction of business to the issue of children's advertising has been mixed. Most advertisers avoid manipulating advertising claims to influence children unduly, and the Joe Camel experience seems to be the exception rather than the rule. Companies are particularly sensitive to the charge that they may be endangering the welfare of children or are acting in bad taste. While R. J. Reynolds has been stubbornly insistent that its Joe Camel character is not affecting children and seems to fuel the fires by including the character in catalogs featuring sports wear and other products, Kenner Products reacted differently to parents' concerns about a line of its toys. When parent groups railed at Kenner Products in 1993 for introducing a line of wheeled action toys called Savage Mondo Blitzers that had names such as Chunk Blowers, Puke Shooters, and Butt Kickers, the company did an about-face and discontinued the line.[78]

The Right to Privacy

Another issue that has received attention from consumer advocates in the 1990s is the right to privacy.[79] In the last 10 years, with the availability of increasingly powerful computers, companies can merge and analyze vast amounts of consumer data from sources such as credit card bills, telephone records, and coupon redemptions. The problem is that such information can be used without the consumer's consent. For example, a customer renting a car from Hertz might get a letter from Ford saying it is "collecting information" on people who rent their products. One report even accused MCI of using phone records to identify peo-

http://www.hertz.com/

http://www.mci.com/

ple customers frequently call so it could ask them to join MCI's discount calling circle.

Databases are sometimes welcomed by consumers. For example, frequent purchaser programs at department stores such as Bloomingdale's identify heavy purchasers and provide services such as sending reminders to spouses to buy birthday presents or offering free delivery. But the potential for using personal information is of increasing concern to consumers as an invasion of privacy. Surveys show that 76 percent of consumers are "very concerned" about the amount of personal data accumulated by business, and 93 percent feel that companies should be legally required to ask permission before using it.

The New York Attorney General's Office reflected this concern when it took action against American Express for making its 20 million cardholder database available to The Sharper Image to enable it to better target its customers. New York State argued that customers "should not unknowingly have their spending patterns and lifestyles analyzed . . . for the use of merchants fishing for good prospects." As a result, American Express has been giving customers a choice as to whether they want to be contacted.

http://www.americanexpress.com/

As the technology for reaching individual consumers becomes more sophisticated, calls for regulation will grow louder. As of 1996, more than 300 bills are pending in state legislatures to regulate access to such information. At the federal level, there has been a proposal to establish a U.S. Privacy Protection Commission. As one legislator said, consumers should be given the right to be given notice and to say no to the disclosure of private information.

ADDITIONAL CONSUMER RIGHTS

The recent trend toward greater consumer protection reflects certain basic rights that were first formulated in 1962 by President John F. Kennedy in a message to Congress titled *Special Message on Protecting the Consumer Interest.* This was the first message a president ever delivered on this topic. For the federal government to meet its responsibilities to consumers in the exercise of their rights, Kennedy stated that legislative and administrative action was required. He spelled out four rights that have served as a basis for consumer protection:

1. ***The right to safety.*** To be protected against the marketing of goods that are hazardous to health or life.
2. ***The right to be informed.*** To be protected against fraudulent or misleading information, advertising, labeling, or other practices and to be given the facts needed to make an informed choice.
3. ***The right to choose.*** To be assured access to a variety of products and services at competitive prices.
4. ***The right to be heard.*** To be assured that consumer interests will receive full and sympathetic consideration in the formulation of government policy.[80]

A fifth right should also be added to this list:

5. ***The right to be a minority consumer without disadvantage.*** To ensure that minority groups or low-income consumers will not be at a disadvantage in relation to any of the above rights as compared to other groups.

In this section, we will consider each of the five consumer rights that companies should be responsible for fulfilling.

The Right to Safety

Government agencies, businesspeople, and consumerists generally agree that abuses related to product safety must be eliminated. Most companies try to ensure product safety and reliability, but abuses occasionally exist.

http://www.cpsc.gov/

The primary government agency responsible for eliminating these abuses is the Consumer Product Safety Commission. The Commission can ban the sale of products, require manufacturers to perform safety tests, and require repair or recall of unsafe products. It operates a hotline to report hazardous products and also runs the National Electronic Injury Surveillance System, a computer-based system that monitors 119 hospital emergency rooms across the country. On the basis of this system, the Commission computes a product Hazard Index. Among products with the highest hazard index are cleaning agents, swings and slides, liquid fuels, snowmobiles, all-terrain vehicles (ATVs), and, more recently, in-line skates. It reported 105,000 in-line-skate related injuries between 1993 and 1996. The CPSC also has been active in recalling products at an average of 200 per year.

The CPSC's action against manufacturers of ATVs demonstrated how the Commission tries to ensure product safety. All-terrain vehicles had been linked to over 900 deaths from 1982 to 1987. In 1987, the Commission filed suit against ATV manufacturers. In April 1988, all ATV manufacturers signed a consent decree agreeing not to sell any three-wheeled ATVs and to restrict sale of four-wheeled models to certain age groups.[81]

The trend toward strengthening consumers' safety rights is spreading around the globe. In Japan, the nascent consumer movement may finally be increasing awareness of product safety as a consumer issue. Under current law, the consumer is the one who has to prove a product caused damage—the opposite of U.S. law. The Japanese have a term for the futility of trying to collect damages: *nakineiri,* or "crying oneself to sleep." Although a study by the Ministry of International Trade and Industry recently concluded that the time was not ripe for consumerist-style laws, the 1993 parliamentary victory of parties less committed to government protection of business may hasten change.

The Right to Be Informed

The consumer's right to be informed covers two components: the right to be protected against misleading and deceptive information and the right to be given sufficient information to make an informed choice. The explosion of media outlets makes these rights even more important today. Statistics show the typical American spends 9 percent of his or her time watching commercials and gathering information about products.[82]

Deceptive Advertising

Over the years, the Federal Trade Commission has established a set of clearly defined guidelines for determining what is deceptive advertising. Advertising need only have the capacity to deceive to be considered deceptive. That is, the FTC does not need to prove deception actually occurred. Furthermore, the advertiser can be ignorant of any false claim and still be liable. Consumer researchers have tried to grapple with the question, Where does puffery end and deception begin?

Gardner identified three types of deceptive advertising.[83] The first is **fraudulent advertising,** that is, a straightforward lie. The second is **false advertising,** which involves a claim-fact discrepancy. That is, the product's claimed benefits are fulfilled only under certain conditions that may not be clear in the advertising. Or, the product must be used in a certain manner or with certain precautions. For example, Superior Rent A Car advertised a $69-a-week rate in Miami's Yellow Pages, but it never disclosed that the rate applies only to cars with manual transmissions.[84]

A third type of deception is **misleading advertising.** It involves a claim-belief interaction. In this case, an advertisement interacts with certain consumer beliefs and results in a misleading claim. For example, Nutri/System weight-loss centers foster the belief through advertising that prospective customers will likely lose up to 100 pounds with its product. In fact, the results were so uncommon that the Federal Trade Commission sued the company in 1993 for making unsubstantiated claims.[85]

In some cases, the FTC has asked certain companies not only to stop making deceptive claims but also to correct these claims publicly. The rationale for requiring such **corrective advertising** is that deceptive claims have a residual effect and, if uncorrected, could remain in consumer memory for a period of time. Without corrective advertising, companies continue to benefit from such past claims. For example, the FTC required:

- ITT-Continental to correct past advertising that its Profile Bread was effective in weight reduction.
- Warner-Lambert to correct the claim that Listerine helps prevent colds.
- Hawaiian Punch to correct its claim that its drink was composed of natural fruit juices, when actually it contained only 11 to 15 percent fruit juice.[86]

http://www.warner-lambert.com/

Do such corrected claims have an impact on consumer beliefs? One study found that the proportion of consumers who believed that Hawaiian Punch contained little fruit juice went from 20 percent to 70 percent during the period of corrective advertising.[87]

Deceptive advertising is not just an American phenomenon. In China, inadequate regulation of ads has led some businesses to use deceptive advertising to boost profits. In one case, a skin care product promising more delicate skin succeeded in producing rashes. In another case, a soft drink claiming 100 percent natural ingredients was made of preservatives and artificial coloring. China has had laws against misleading advertising since 1987, but in a country more concerned with industrial production than consumer rights, they are rarely enforced.

Control of Other Deceptive Marketing Practices

Deception can occur in other areas of marketing strategy besides advertising. Packaging can be deceptive when a company reduces the contents or size of the package while maintaining price. Such a practice would represent a deceptive price increase since consumers are getting less for the same price. During the 1991–1992 recession, Star-Kist tuna decreased the contents of its cans by about 6 percent. Procter & Gamble and Kimberly Clark decreased the number of disposable diapers in a standard package by about 10 percent, and Lipton cut the weight of a jar of instant tea by about 7 percent. In each case, the company maintained the price of the product.[87]

Deception can also occur in pricing practices. One such practice, **bait-and-switch pricing,** involves a low-price offer intended to lure customers into a store where a salesperson tries to influence them to buy higher-priced items. Such practices are illegal, and the FTC and states' attorneys general police them. An example of this is the case of Craftmatic, which advertised low-priced therapeutic chairs on television. It then sent salespeople into the field to sell more expensive models to the elderly. A Massachusetts judge barred the practice after the state's attorney general's office revealed the scam.[88]

Selling practices can also be deceptive, for example, a realtor who glosses over defects in a home. However, government can do little to legislate fair sales practices. If the sales transaction is fraudulent, the consumer can take the seller to court; but few consumers do. In most cases, companies have become more sensitive to the need to maintain high standards in selling.

The Provision of Adequate Information

Does the right to information include the right to adequate information to ensure a wise purchase? There are two positions on this issue. The view of most businesses is that the buyer should be guided by his or her judgment of the brand's quality. Consumer activists believe that business and impartial sources should provide full information and should reveal performance characteristics.

Regardless of the position one takes, the trend is toward more disclosure of information. An increasing number of states are requiring unit pricing of grocery products and open dating of perishables. Recent rules formulated by the Food and Drug Administration require more information on certain food labels.

http://www.fda.gov/

The question of the efficacy of providing more information to consumers does not resolve a basic question: Will consumers use the additional information provided? One study found that when consumers were given clear and concise performance information on carpeting, they used it because they regarded the information to be helpful and easy to employ.[89]

However, consumers do not always use the information marketers provide to make purchase decisions. If product involvement is low, informational requirements may be minimal. Adequate information is not as important a consumer rights issue for low-involvement products such as toothpaste or paper towels.

The Right to Choose

Consumer satisfaction requires the ability to evaluate alternatives in the marketplace. Consumer advocates argue that large corporations restrict choice by discouraging market entry. The marketer of a leading brand may advertise heavily, preempt shelf space within the store, and offer frequent price deals and coupons. Such actions tend to make competitive entry more difficult and thus restrict choice. Scott Paper's attempt to enter the disposable diaper market failed because of the dominance of P&G's Pampers. Supermarkets generally do not stock more than two brands because of space restrictions, and Scott had difficulty gaining adequate coverage.

The potential for market dominance may create monopoly powers that restrict consumer choice. The federal government has played an active role in preventing the restraint of competition by enforcing the antitrust laws. As we have seen, however, enforcement varies across political administrations. The Reagan Administration's emphasis on self-regulation prompted a proposal "to take the FTC out of the antitrust field entirely."[90] In the early 1980s, the Commission reduced antitrust enforcement activities by 50 percent and cut its antitrust and consumer protection staff by 25 percent.[91] Although the FTC has not been divorced totally from antitrust issues, its reduced powers prompted it to drop a 10-year-old "shared monopoly" case against the ready-to-eat breakfast cereal industry[92] and to accept large mergers such as Philip Morris's acquisition of General Foods and Kraft.

The Clinton Administration is less likely to condone such mergers and acquisitions. Clinton's new antitrust chief, Anne Bingaman, says, "The general philosophy is more active antitrust enforcement."[93] As a result, the Justice Department began investigating Microsoft, the computer software giant, as a possible monopoly. In 1996, it also brought charges against Toys R Us for limiting the consumer's choices in toys by cutting deals with manufacturers to prevent discounters and warehouse clubs from selling the identical items.[94] The philosophy behind these moves is to try to protect consumers by insuring adequate choice and competitive prices.

The Right to Be Heard

The consumer has the right to express dissatisfaction with a product and to have complaints resolved (redressed). Most surveys agree that the overall level of product dissatisfaction among consumers is low. But the level of product dissatisfaction is increasing. The 1991–1992 recession resulted in a greater value orientation on the part of consumers. Consumers are taking a more critical look at products and are demanding product quality at fair prices. Consumers are increasingly dissatisfied with the higher prices of national brands relative to their quality. There has been a general decrease in loyalty to national brands and a significant move to private labels (that is, retailer-controlled brands) because these brands often offer the same quality at lower prices.

If not satisfied, consumers can react in three ways.[95] The first and most common is simply not to buy again. A second reaction is to express dissatisfaction to others. Such negative word-of-mouth is the most harmful effect of dissatisfaction because it goes beyond one consumer's reaction. One study found the average dissatisfied customer "bad-mouths" the product to 9 or 10 other people.[96]

A third reaction is to seek redress. But few dissatisfied customers actively bring their complaints to the marketer's attention. One survey by the RAND Corporation, a nonprofit organization, found that even when they are injured by a product, only 1 in 50 consumers seeks redress.[97] An earlier study by A. C. Nielsen of food products and health and beauty aids found that only 3 percent of all dissatisfied consumers brought their complaints to the attention of the manufacturer.[98] Both studies demonstrate that the manufacturer is almost totally cut off from direct consumer feedback regarding dissatisfaction with the product.

Why do so few consumers bother to take action in expressing their dissatisfaction? The reason is that they are not sufficiently involved with the product to go out of their way to complain. Many consumers in the studies cited earlier simply said it was not worth the time and effort. When financial risk and product involvement are higher, complaint behavior increases. When a wide array of higher-priced products were studied, one-third of all dissatisfied customers voiced complaints to manufacturers or retailers.[99]

Another possible explanation for the lack of consumer follow-up when dissatisfied is that there are no formal channels for redress. Letters of complaint are usually too much trouble to write and a minority of better-educated consumers are more likely to write them. Also, excessive red tape in retail stores frequently discourages product returns.

Manufacturers have begun to provide consumers with direct channels to voice complaints through toll-free telephone numbers. Whirlpool was among the first to do so and was followed by Procter & Gamble, General Electric, Clairol, Pillsbury, General Mills, and many others. General Electric has programmed over 750,000 possible answers to customer inquiries and complaints. Thus, when consumers call, representatives will have a ready response.[100] A company's average cost to answer a complaint is about $3, often more than the cost of the product. However, the cost is generally worth it. One study found that quick and positive resolution of a complaint leads to repeat purchases 80 to 90 percent of the time.[101]

The Right to Be a Minority Consumer Without Disadvantage

The four consumer rights that have been discussed may have little relevance for low-income minority consumers. Minority consumers living in poverty:

- Are more exposed to unsafe products.
- Have less access to information.
- Have fewer choices of alternative brands.
- Have less access to means of redress.

The consistent finding is that, compared to other consumers, low-income consumers do not always have the information necessary for a satisfactory choice. They often lack the freedom to go outside their local community to engage in comparison shopping and lack the means for redress if the product fails.[102]

Consumer activists also complain about marketing campaigns that they believe encourage unhealthy or unsafe product choices for minorities. They have been particularly forceful in their efforts to call attention to cigarette and alcohol advertising in minority neighborhoods, where the incidence of lung cancer and liver damage are high. The Reverend Calvin Butts of Harlem, for one, has taken scores of his followers on marches through the neighborhood where they paint over billboards selling cigarettes and alcohol. Some consumer organizations publish literature that attempts to educate minority consumers about how the major food, alcohol, and cigarette companies target them. The Center for Science in the Public Interest published two such books: *Marketing Disease to Hispanics* and *Marketing Booze to Blacks*.

Perhaps the most publicized protest involved R. J. Reynolds' 1989 launch of Uptown, a cigarette that was targeted specifically to African Americans. The objective was to increase sagging sales by aiming at a segment that had a higher proportion of smokers. This was the first time that a new cigarette was designed especially for a minority group, instead of the usual practice of advertising existing brands across the racial spectrum. As a result, it drew a torrent of criticism, particularly since Uptown was very high in nicotine.[103] African-American leaders and consumer activists charged that the company was taking unfair advantage of inner-city minorities. In 1990, the Secretary of Health and Human Services said, "Uptown's message is more disease, more suffering, and more death for a group already bearing more than its share of smoking-related illness and mortality."[104]

R. J. Reynolds responded to the Uptown uproar by discontinuing the brand. Why the difference in its actions with Joe Camel and Uptown? Because the intended target saw the Uptown campaign as an affront, while the intended target for Joe Camel embraced the ads. By and large, cigarette and alcohol companies have not been overly responsive to complaints about their advertising tactics. The major beer companies, for example, continue to market their potent malt liquor brands almost exclusively to African Americans despite outrage by health officials. As a result, this area will continue to provide fertile ground for consumer advocates for some time to come.

SOCIAL RESPONSIBILITY

Based on the corporate actions just cited, the record of Corporate America is fairly mixed regarding the protection of consumer rights. The social responsibility of marketing organizations can be assessed in two areas: first, their ability to impose restraints on their own actions through a process of self-regulation and, second, their willingness to exert influence over social issues such as drug use and underage drinking and smoking, an application of influence that has come to be known as **social marketing.**

Self-Regulation

Will marketing organizations accept their responsibilities to protect consumer rights through a process of self-regulation, or will they abdicate their responsibilities to government in the expectation of further legislation, more controls, and the establishment of more regulatory bodies?

The preference in a marketing society, on both pragmatic and ideological grounds, is for self-regulation rather than additional government regulation. However, the record of corporate performance cited previously is not encouraging. The failure of large companies to recall unsafe products, the willingness to use "green" claims to mislead consumers, the inability of "smokestack" industries to establish adequate controls over air pollution, and the targeting of younger smokers by cigarette companies are all indications of the need for continued government controls.

However, marketing organizations have been moving toward more responsible self-regulation. We have seen some companies take voluntary action to protect the environment. According to a study by *Fortune* magazine, companies such as Dow Chemical, IBM, and Xerox have effectively integrated environmental performance into their corporate goals.[105] Others such as Monsanto and DuPont have made major efforts to contain air and water pollution. Many companies have also accepted self-imposed industry standards for labeling, product safety, and children's advertising.

Of equal importance, many organizations have recently attempted to ensure consumer rights by providing better means to redress complaints through toll-free numbers and consumer service representatives. For example, Whirlpool was one of the first to establish a 24-hour "cool line" to handle consumer complaints and inquiries, Marriott hotels have data terminals at the checkout desk to provide immediate service to complainants, and Johnson & Johnson's 22 subsidiaries each have representatives on call at all times.

Companies have also sought to improve communications with consumers through consumer affairs offices that formulate policies for handling consumer complaints. JCPenney, Eastman Kodak, and Giant Foods were among the first to establish such units.

Companies have also used consumer affairs offices to educate consumers by disseminating information on nutrition, product content, and product safety. JCPenney was also one of the first to establish a concerted effort in consumer education. It published *forum,* a publication for teachers of consumer education; *Insights Into Consumerism,* a magazine providing teaching modules on consumer issues; and numerous buying guides containing factual product information.

Ultimately, companies must realize that it is in their self-interest to protect the consumer rights cited in this chapter. One indication of the importance of recognizing such corporate responsibility is a poll that found that 88 percent of consumers would be more likely to buy from a company that is socially responsible and a good corporate citizen.[106]

Social Marketing

Marketing organizations can also demonstrate social responsibility by attempting to influence consumers to behave in a more socially responsible manner. Drinking and driving, smoking excessively, taking drugs, and refusing to recognize "safe sex" as a precaution against AIDS are four examples of behavior that is not in the best interests of the consumer.

Social marketing is the use of marketing tools by organizations to try to influence such behavior, generally on a pro bono basis, that is, at no cost for their services. An example is the formation of a group of advertising agencies and media companies into the Partnership for a Drug-Free America to develop a communications campaign to reduce drug use. Social marketing also involves sponsorship of events to assist causes. The advertising firm of Kirshenbaum Gond & partners developed the ad in Exhibit 2.7 to sponsor a race to benefit God's Love We Deliver, an organization that feeds homebound people with AIDS. An offshoot of social marketing is **cause-related marketing,** which in-

▶EXHIBIT 2.7
An example of social marketing

volves a firm sponsoring a charity or a cause that it then links to its name. For example, Avon Products sponsored a national teleconference on breast cancer with the Centers for Disease Control. In a more commercial vein, Nabisco has sponsored the World Wildlife Fund and, in return, won the right to run a sweepstakes for its endangered species Animal Crackers tied into the Fund. Similarly, General Motors' sponsorship of the Nature Conservancy has given it the right to cite its contribution to that organization in its advertising (see Exhibit 2.8).

It is estimated that American companies spent $600 million in 1996 on cause-related events and advertising.[107] One reason is that a 1994 study showed that 80 percent of consumers said they have a better image of a company if it is involved in making the world a better place. And two-thirds said they would switch brands to support a cause-related marketing effort.[108]

▶EXHIBIT 2.8
An example of cause-related marketing: GM promotes its trucks and The Nature Conservancy

SUMMARY

Our marketing economy does not always afford the consumer an environment for making an optimal or even an adequate choice. The necessity to promote consumer rights relative to the powers of big business is known as the *consumer movement* or *consumerism.*

Consumerism is the set of activities of consumer organizations, government, and even business to promote the rights of the consumer. Consumerism is a global phenomenon, with strong consumer movements in Western Europe protesting environmental pollution. The consumer movement in the United States is not new. Three distinct periods in the last century have been marked by increased activities to protect consumer rights: 1890–1915, 1933–1940, and 1962–1977. Each of these periods was marked by increased prices and exposés of business practices leading to legislation protecting consumer rights. The 1980s saw a marked decrease in government activities to protect consumer rights as a result of the Reagan Administration's emphasis on self-regulation.

The 1990s is seeing a rebirth of the consumer movement under the Clinton Administration with a particular focus on four issues: (1) protection of the environment, (2) health and nutritional claims for food products, (3) the influence of advertising on children, and (4) the right to nondisclosure of private consumer information without their consent.

Four consumer rights spelled out by President Kennedy in the early 1960s are of central concern to consumerists:

1. The right to safety protects consumers against the marketing of hazardous goods.
2. The right to be informed means protection from misleading information and the need for a sufficient amount of accurate information to make an informed choice.
3. The right to choose requires access to a variety of products and services at competitive prices.
4. The right to be heard requires provision of the channels of communication to permit consumers to register complaints to business.

An additional right is:

5. The right to be in the minority without disadvantage; that is, assurance that being a minority or low-income consumer does not mean deprivation of the foregoing rights.

Marketing organizations have a role in ensuring these rights. Some organizations have accepted their responsibilities by improving the means for registering complaints and by establishing consumer advisory boards and consumer affairs offices. However, there is still much to be done to encourage self-regulation to ensure consumer rights.

Having set the stage for the study of consumer behavior by considering consumer rights, in the next few chapters, we turn our attention to the process consumers use to make purchase decisions.

QUESTIONS

1. What are the reasons for the increasing awareness of consumer rights and greater current interest in the consumer movement?
2. What are the roles of the three groups in Figure 2.1 to ensure consumer rights?
3. Consumerism is a global movement. In what ways?
4. The 1980s did not see the emergence of another period of consumer activity parallel to that of the 1970s. Why not?
5. What is the difference in the role of the FTC in regulating advertising under the Reagan and Clinton Administrations?
6. What are the causes of the new environmentalism? How have governmental agencies reacted to this development?
7. What have been some of the more constructive responses of corporate America to the new environmentalism? Some of the less constructive responses? Provide examples.
8. Why do most consumers express increasing concern about the environment, yet show greater reluctance to buy "green" products?
9. Why have consumers been confused over health claims on food products? What is the government doing to control these claims? What is business doing?
10. What are the pros and cons of advertising to children? What are the findings from studies that support concerns about advertising to children?
11. What has been the role of the three forces in consumerism—consumer organizations, government, and business—regarding advertising to children?
12. Why has there been increasing concern about the privacy of consumer information in the 1990s?
13. What is the distinction among fraudulent, false, and misleading advertising? Cite an actual or hypothetical example of each. Clearly, the FTC should require advertisers to cease using fraudulent and false advertising. Should the agency require advertisers to cease using misleading advertising? Why or why not?
14. Why do most dissatisfied consumers fail to complain to manufacturers about products? Why should manufacturers encourage such complaints? How can they do so?
15. Why did R. J. Reynolds withdraw Uptown, a cigarette positioned to African Americans, but continue to use Joe Camel ads in the face of criticism that the character appeals to children?
16. What role do socially responsible companies have in marketing social causes?

RESEARCH ASSIGNMENTS

1. Go to the Internet sites for the Federal Trade Commission (http://www.ftc.gov) and the Consumer Product Safety Commission (http://www.cpsc.gov). How do these sites relate to consumerism? Are these sites for individual consumers or are they for businesses? Scan newsgroups on the Internet and find three locations where a newsgroup is discussing a product. How could/should

the companies who make these products interact with members of the newsgroups?

2. Conduct a survey among 40 to 50 consumers and identify those consumers who have taken some environmentally relevant action in the past month (for example, purchased recycled paper or brought materials to a recycling center). Identify the demographic and lifestyle characteristics of these consumers and their media habits.
   - What are the differences in demographics, lifestyle, and media habits between the more environmentally conscious consumers and the rest of the sample?
   - What are the implications for a campaign by the federal government to influence people to buy products that safeguard the environment?
3. Identify three companies that have consumer affairs departments.
   a. Determine the organization and objectives of the each department.
   b. Determine the mechanisms for processing consumer complaints.
   c. What are the differences between these organizations regarding the purpose and operation of their consumer affairs departments?

PART II

CONSUMER DECISION MAKING

In Part II of the text, we consider how consumers decide what products and services to buy and where to buy them. The way consumers make these decisions directly influences marketing strategies. If consumers want certain benefits in a brand, marketers should emphasize those benefits in the product and in advertising. Thus, criteria consumers use in choosing brands should provide management with guidelines for developing marketing strategies.

In the next few chapters, we recognize that consumer decision making is not a uniform process. There are distinctions between (1) decision making and habit and (2) high-involvement and low-involvement decisions. Chapter 3 considers complex, high-involvement decisions; Chapter 4 describes habit; Chapter 5 reviews low-involvement decision making; and Chapter 6 discusses how the situation in which consumers purchase and consume products and services influences what they buy. These chapters introduce behavioral concepts used throughout the text. They also set the stage for a consideration of market segmentation, product positioning, marketing communications, and marketing strategy applications in succeeding chapters.

COMPLEX DECISION MAKING: THE PURCHASE PROCESS AND CONSUMPTION EXPERIENCE

Chapter 3

SATURN ESTABLISHES AN EMOTIONAL BOND WITH ITS CONSUMERS

This chapter presents a model of complex decision making. A detailed example of a couple deciding on the purchase of a new car is used to describe this process.

The process of complex decision making includes many of the important behavioral concepts used throughout the text. For example, it involves an active search for information; therefore, consumer information processing is introduced. It also involves the evaluation of alternative brands; therefore, the process consumers use to assess products in light of their needs is also considered. Finally, complex decision making involves the consumers' evaluation of the brand after purchasing it; therefore, concepts of consumer satisfaction and postpurchase evaluation are formulated.

Since the basis for evaluating the product after the purchase is consumption, this chapter considers not only the purchasing process, but the consumption experience. It highlights the fact that products can be purchased and consumed for both utilitarian and emotional reasons.

http://www.saturncars.com/

General Motors' introduction of its Saturn car, designed to compete with lower-priced Japanese compacts, illustrates the importance of complex decision making for marketers. General Motors made a basic mistake in the 1980s: it did not pay sufficient attention to the needs of compact car buyers for quality at reasonable prices. When consumers evaluated alternative brands, many found GM's compacts inferior to the imports.

GM designed the Saturn to lure Honda and Toyota buyers by "slashing costs and boosting quality."[1] In so doing, its initial objective was to convince consumers that GM could make a quality compact and thus change consumer beliefs and attitudes toward GM cars. But after GM introduced Saturn in 1991 and saw the enthusiasm for the car among some early buyers, it decided that Saturn should stand alone without trying to establish a close association with GM in consumers' minds.

TV spots and magazine ads featured the enthusiasm for the car among Saturn employees and buyers rather than the usual ads touting economy, prestige, or performance. Each ad ended with the tagline, "A Different Kind of Company. A Different Kind of Car" (see Exhibit 3.1.) The uniqueness of the car and enthusiasm portrayed in the ads were reinforced by the experiences of Saturn owners. One national survey of customer satisfaction placed Saturn highest among compacts and third among all cars, after the higher-priced Infiniti and Lexus. By 1994, there was widespread reference to Saturn owners as being cult-like.[2] Saturn attempted to reinforce this image by inviting all 700,000 owners to a "home-

▶ **EXHIBIT 3.1**
Saturn attempts to establish an emotional bond with potential buyers

coming" at its Spring Hill, Tennessee, plant to "seek a taste of the American value mystique the car's advertising has helped create."[3] By 1995, the number of Saturns sold surpassed the one million mark.

Saturn's success portrays both the utilitarian and emotional side of complex decision making. Saturn succeeded in convincing baby boomers, a prime target, that the car represents value. The strong attachment of many buyers to the car shows that car buying goes beyond strictly utilitarian criteria. The identity with Saturn and formation of owners' clubs suggests a strongly emotional context for ownership. Saturn reinforces this emotional context by forging a strong relationship with owners after the purchase. Saturn dealers communicate with recent buyers to insure they are satisfied after a sale and mail anniversary cards commemorating the original date of purchase. Some organize weekend events such as car-care seminars and camping trips.[4]

It is clear that Saturn has succeeded in convincing compact car buyers that a domestic car is a viable alternative to the Japanese imports.

TYPES OF CONSUMER PURCHASING DECISIONS

The process by which consumers make purchasing decisions must be understood in order to develop strategic applications. Consumer decision making is not a single process. Deciding to buy a car is a different process from deciding to buy toothpaste. Figure 3.1 presents a typology of consumer purchasing decisions based on two dimensions: (1) the extent of decision making and (2) the degree of involvement in the purchase.

The first dimension represents a continuum from decision making to habit. Consumers can base their decisions on a cognitive (thought) process of information search and evaluation of brand alternatives. On the other hand, little or

FIGURE 3.1
Consumer decision making

	HIGH-INVOLVEMENT PURCHASE DECISION	LOW-INVOLVEMENT PURCHASE DECISION
DECISION MAKING (information search, consideration of brand alternatives)	COMPLEX DECISION MAKING (autos, electronics, photography systems) Chapter 3	LIMITED DECISION MAKING (adult cereals, snack foods) Chapter 5
HABIT (little or no information search, consideration of only one brand)	BRAND LOYALTY (athletic shoes, adult cereals) Chapter 4	INERTIA (canned vegetables, paper towels) Chapter 5

no decision making may take place when the consumer is satisfied with a particular brand and purchases it consistently.

The second dimension depicts a continuum from high- to low-involvement purchases. **High-involvement purchases** are those that are important to the consumer. Such purchases are closely tied to the consumer's ego and self-image and involve some financial, social, or personal risk. In such cases, it is worth the consumer's time and energies to consider product alternatives carefully. **Low-involvement purchases** are not as important to the consumer, and the financial, social, and psychological risks are not nearly as great. In such cases, it may not be worth the consumer's time and effort to search for information about brands and to consider a wide range of alternatives.

Decision making versus habit and low versus high involvement produce four types of consumer purchase processes. The first process, called **complex decision making,** takes place when involvement is high and decision making occurs (upper left-hand box). Examples might be the decision to buy a home computer, a car, or even clothing if the purchase is sufficiently important to the consumer. In such cases, consumers have the time to search for information and process it in more detail. They use this information to evaluate and consider alternative brands by applying specific criteria such as economy, durability, and service for an automobile.

When a consumer makes a decision in a low-involvement condition, it is likely to be characterized by limited decision making (upper right-hand box). Consumers sometimes go through a decision process in buying, even if they are not highly involved, because they have little past experience with a product. For example, a new line of microwaveable snacks may be introduced. Not aware of or involved with the product category, the consumer examines the package in the store and purchases the product on a trial basis to compare to regular snack foods. Information search is limited and few brands are evaluated.

Limited decision making is also likely to take place when consumers seek variety. When involvement is low, consumers are more likely to switch brands out of boredom and in a search for variety.[5] Since the brand decision is not important enough to be preplanned, the consumer is likely to make the decision inside the store. For example, a consumer may decide to try a new brand of cookies or an adult cereal for variety's sake as there is little to lose.

Complex or even limited decision making will not occur every time the consumer purchases a brand. When choice is repetitive, the consumer learns from past experience and with little or no decision making buys the brand that is most satisfactory. Such brand loyalty is the result of repeated satisfaction and a strong commitment to a particular brand (lower left-hand box). Examples might be the purchase of Nike basketball sneakers or one of Kellogg's adult cereals. In each case, the purchase is important to the consumer (basketball shoes because of involvement in the sport; adult cereals because of the importance of nutrition).

Notice that adult cereals appear as products that could be characterized by both brand loyalty and limited decision making. This shows that the decision processes in Figure 3.1 are consumer-specific rather than product-specific. That is, the degree of involvement and decision making depends more on the consumer's attitude toward the product than on the product's characteristics. One consumer might be involved with adult cereals because of their nutritional value; another might regard them as pretty much the same and switch brands in a search for variety.

The fourth choice process in Figure 3.1 is inertia (lower right-hand box), or low involvement with the product and no decision making. **Inertia** means the consumer is buying the same brand, not because of brand loyalty, but because it is not worth the time and trouble to search for an alternative. Robertson states that under low-involvement conditions "brand loyalty may reflect only the convenience inherent in repetitive behavior rather than commitment to the brand purchased."[6] Examples might be the purchase of canned vegetables or paper towels.

CONSUMER INVOLVEMENT AND COMPLEX DECISION MAKING

The two conditions for complex decision making in Figure 3.1 are (1) a decision process requiring extensive information processing and (2) a high degree of consumer involvement with the product. Therefore, to understand complex decision making, we will first consider the nature of consumer involvement and then describe the nature of the decision process.

Involvement and Information Processing

The reason that involvement is linked to complex decision making is that, generally, the higher the level of involvement, the greater the search for information (see top branch of Figure 3.2). Such information processing defines complex decision making.

FIGURE 3.2 Involvement and information processing

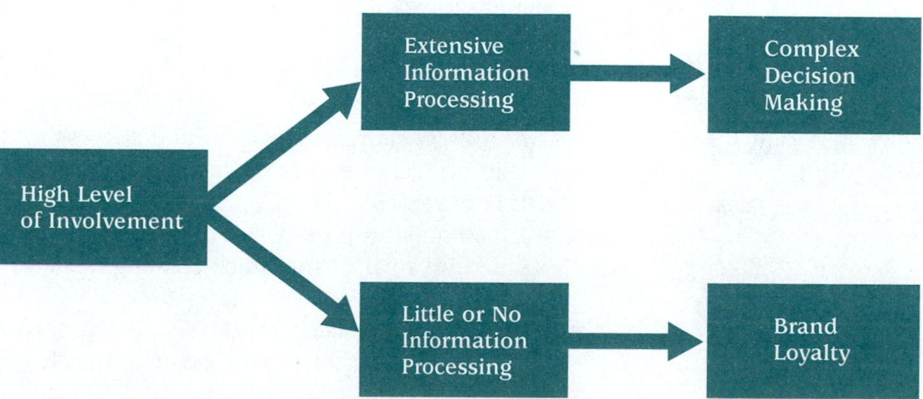

In a study of involvement with tennis and tennis equipment, Celsi and Olson found that people who are more involved devote more attention to ads for tennis products and process the product information in the ads more extensively.[7] Similarly, Gensch and Javalgi found that farmers who were more involved with learning about farming methods were likely to use more attributes in evaluating alternative suppliers. Among involved farmers, 47 percent used three or more attributes in evaluating alternative retail stores. Among uninvolved farmers, only 15 percent used three or more attributes.[8] Both studies confirm that greater involvement results in consumers making choices by complex decision making.

But as Figure 3.1 shows, a high level of involvement does not always lead to complex decision making. In some cases, consumers may be involved with a product and consider only one brand (see bottom branch of Figure 3.2). As we will see in the next chapter, such brand-loyal consumers are satisfied with a brand based on repeat purchases and do not feel the need to engage in extensive information processing. The committed Saturn or Harley owner may not engage in extensive information processing and consider alternative brands in the next purchase. The only choice may be the model and options.

Even when decision making does take place, involved consumers are likely to vary greatly in the extent of information processing. Some may evaluate just a few brands on one or two attributes. Others might evaluate a larger number of brands on many attributes. This means that the extent of information processing should be regarded on a continuum from high to low, and the degree of decision making should be regarded on a continuum from complex to limited. (We will consider the factors that motivate more extensive information processing in Chapter 7.)

Conditions for Involvement

The level of consumer involvement is also a continuum from high to low. The position of the consumer on this continuum will depend on several factors. Generally, a consumer is likely to be more involved with a product when it:

- *Is important to the consumer.* A product is most likely to be important when
  - The consumer's self-image is tied to the product (for example, the Gitano ad in Exhibit 3.2 portrays a relaxed and casual self-image).
  - It has symbolic meaning tied to consumer values, as when ownership of a BMW represents power and success to baby boomers or ownership of Nike sneakers represents athletic prowess to teenagers.
  - It is expensive.
  - It has some important functional role such as the transportation provided by a car or the quick cooking facilities provided by a microwave oven.
- *Has emotional appeal.* Consumers do not only seek functional benefits in products. They often seek benefits that trigger an emotional re-

http://www.bmwusa.com/

http://www.Nike.com/

EXHIBIT 3.2
Ads reflecting product involvement

A Product Associated with Self-Image

The Badge Value of a Cartier Watch

http://www.harley-davidson.com/

sponse. For many buyers, the very ownership of a Saturn car or Harley-Davidson motorcycle produces a kinship with other owners. This kinship produces the cult-like following frequently referred to for these two brands. Clearly, any such kinship goes beyond functional benefits and is a more emotional response to the product.

- *Is continually of interest to the consumer.* The fashion-conscious consumer, for example, has an ongoing interest in clothing; the car buff an ongoing interest in cars.
- *Entails significant risks.* Among these risks would be the financial risk of buying a house, the technological risk of buying a personal computer, the social risk of changing one's wardrobe, or the physical risk of buying an unsafe car or the wrong medication.
- *Is identified with the norms of a group.* That is, the sign or "badge" value of a product.[9] The ad for a Cartier watch in Exhibit 3.2 is an example; it depicts the brand as a mark of status in an understated way.

These conditions are more likely to result in complex decision making. As most brands lack significant self-identity, interest, risk, emotion, or badge value, it is not surprising that buying by inertia is more widespread than purchasing by complex decision making.

Types of Involvement

Behavioral researchers have identified two types of involvement with products: situational and enduring.[10] **Situational involvement** occurs only in specific situations and is temporary, whereas **enduring involvement** is continuous and is more permanent. Situational involvement generally occurs when a purchase decision is required. For example, an MBA graduate may not be particularly fashion-conscious but she must buy a suit for job interviewing. This graduate will be highly involved with clothes only in that particular situation but not afterward. Another MBA graduate may be very fashion-conscious. She may also be looking for a suit for job interviews but her interest in clothes is enduring, not situational. Such enduring involvement requires an ongoing interest in the product category, whether a purchase is required or not. According to Celsi and Olson, "The emphasis is on the product itself, and the inherent satisfaction its usage provides, rather than on some (situational) goal."[11]

Both situational and enduring involvement are likely to result in complex decision making. Whether the graduate is interested in clothes because of a job interview or on a more enduring basis, he or she will be aware of fashion information, consider alternative lines of clothing, and evaluate them carefully before making a decision.

http://www.godiva.com/

Marketers take a very different approach in targeting those with enduring versus situational involvement. The deep-seated nature of enduring involvement means that symbols and images are more likely to be used to connect the consumer with the product. In targeting the situationally involved, more specific appeals to the particular context of the purchase will be made. The first ad for Godiva chocolates in Exhibit 3.3 targets those who believe the "rhythmic beauty of nature" can be preserved in a chocolate and presents an image of refinement for "the most cultured of palates." The second ad focuses on a particular situation, gift giving for Christmas, without the rich symbolism of the first. Whereas the former individual may be a chocoholic who buys chocolates all year, the latter consumer is involved only on gift-giving occasions.

The Multidimensional Nature of Involvement

The five conditions for involvement suggest that consumers can be involved with a product on several dimensions. In their study, Kapferer and Laurent[12] confirmed the multidimensional nature of involvement. They asked 800 women to agree or disagree with statements about 20 product categories. The statements were closely related to the five components of involvement: product importance,

EXHIBIT 3.3
Enduring versus situational involvement

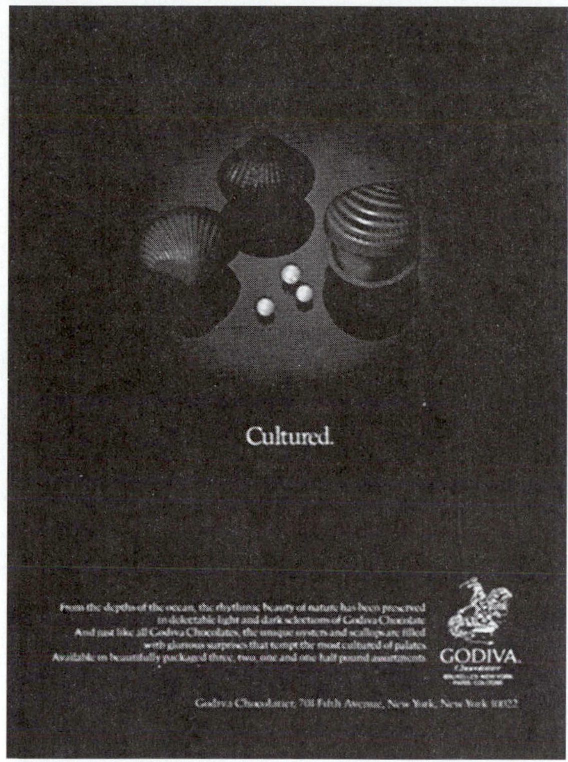

Enduring Involvement

Situational Involvement

interest, risk, emotion, and badge value. Scales were developed for each component of involvement.

The scores for 10 of the products are shown in Table 3.1 (with 100 as an average score). Clearly, for this sample of women, clothing and perfume were involving across all components, except for risk. This suggests that consumers are more likely to be involved with these items on an enduring rather than a situational basis. Champagne was involving for all components except continuous interest, suggesting that consumers are involved with champagne on a situational basis (that is, for special occasions). Chocolate was involving only in its emotional appeal, suggesting possible pleasurable childhood associations with the product. Detergents and facial soap were not involving in any respect.

This study is important because it shows that products can be involving in different ways. For example, washing machines and vacuum cleaners were high in product importance, possibly because they serve a support role in the household. However, neither product had pleasure (emotional) or badge value because they were associated with housework.[13] If the promotional objective is to create consumer involvement, advertisements for both washing machines and vac-

TABLE 3.1
Product categories by components of involvement

Product	Components of Involvement				
	Interest	*Emotion*	*Budget Value*	*Product Importance*	*Risk*
Clothing	123	147	166	129	99
Perfume	120	154	164	116	97
Champagne	75	128	123	123	119
Washing Machine	130	111	104	136	102
Vacuum Cleaner	108	94	78	130	111
Detergent	80	44	77	75	94
Facial Soap	88	91	99	78	85
Shampoo	99	78	93	94	102
Yogurt	95	105	73	72	73
Chocolate	94	130	86	76	91

Source: Jean-Noel Kapferer and Giles Laurent, "Consumer Involvement Profiles: A New Practical Approach to Consumer Involvement," *Journal of Advertising Research* 25 (December 1985–January 1986), p. 51.

uum cleaners might emphasize their time-liberating value to increase their emotional appeal.

The Cross-Cultural Nature of Involvement

The level of involvement with a product varies by individual. Some individuals may be highly involved with the purchase of toothpaste because they associate the product with personal appearance and social acceptance. However, most consumers are not highly involved because they view brushing their teeth as a necessary chore and see little difference between brands.

Differences in product involvement also occur on a cross-cultural basis. For example, bicycles are more important in China, where they are the primary means of transportation, than they are in the United States. A Chinese consumer might be as involved in buying a bicycle as an American consumer is in buying a car. Zaichkowsky and Sood surveyed business students in 15 countries to determine involvement levels for eight product categories.[14] Involvement in the purchase of beer among English and American students was significantly higher than that for students from South American countries. This difference probably reflects the cultural role of beer in these countries. English and American students associate beer with relaxation and social occasions, whereas no such association exists for students from South America. Students' involvement with soft drinks was uniformly low for all countries except China. Apparently, soft drinks in China are a more valued commodity, particularly with the introduction of Western brands in the last 10 years. Involvement with blue jeans was fairly uniform across countries, probably as a result of similar perceptions of the product among students worldwide.

These findings suggest that international marketers must adjust their strategies on a country-by-country basis, depending on the cultural role and importance of certain products.

COMPLEX DECISION MAKING

In **complex decision making,** consumers evaluate brands in a detailed and comprehensive manner. More information is sought and more brands are evaluated than in other types of decision-making situations.

Conditions for Complex Decision Making

As we saw, complex decision making is most likely when consumers are involved with the product. Therefore, complex decision making is most likely for:

- High-priced products.
- Products associated with performance risks (medical products, automobiles).
- Complex products (compact disc players, personal computers).
- Products associated with one's ego (clothing, cosmetics).

The nature of the product is not the only condition for complex decision making. Certain *facilitating* conditions need to exist. The most important is adequate *time* for extensive information search and processing.[15] Complex decision making will not occur if a decision must be made quickly. If a washing machine breaks down in a family with eight children, it is unlikely the parents will spend several weeks establishing purchasing criteria and evaluating alternative brands. Also, consumers may not have the time to devote to extensive information processing because business or social obligations may have a higher priority. A recent law school graduate working 14-hour days is unlikely to spend a great deal of time replacing a broken-down stereo system.

A second condition for complex decision making is the availability of *adequate information* to evaluate alternative brands. A study by Greenleaf and Lehmann found that consumers sometimes delay a decision because of insufficient or inaccurate information. The same study also found that decision making is delayed when there are too many product characteristics and features to consider. Such confusion means that complex decision making also requires a consumer's *ability to process information.*[16]

A Model of Complex Decision Making

Research on decision making has identified five phases in the decision process: (1) problem recognition, (2) search for information, (3) evaluation of alternatives, (4) choice, and (5) outcome of the choice.[17] For a consumer engaging in complex decision making, these steps can be translated into (1) need arousal, (2) consumer information processing, (3) brand evaluation, (4) purchase, and (5) postpurchase evaluation. A model of complex decision making representing these five steps is presented in Figure 3.3.

Each of these five processes is considered in more detail to introduce some of the important behavioral concepts that will appear in later chapters. The model of complex decision making is illustrated by another example, that of a couple purchasing an automobile.

NEED AROUSAL

Need arousal is outlined in Figure 3.4. A consumer's recognition of a need is a function of various input variables: (1) the consumer's past experiences, (2) consumer characteristics, (3) consumer motives, (4) environmental influences (face-to-face groups, culture, social class, and the buying situation), and (5) marketing stimuli (seeing advertising, noticing the product on the shelf, hearing about it from salespeople).

Recognition of a need represents a disparity between a consumer's current situation and some desired goal (need for a more economical means of transportation, desire for more stylish clothing). Such a disparity produces a motivation to act. Need recognition shapes the benefits consumers seek in a brand and brand attitudes. Desired benefits and brand attitudes determine the consumer's **psychological set,** that is, the mindset of the consumer toward various brands prior to seeking and processing information.

Input Variables

Consider the following example. Rob and Linda Greene are a couple in their late 20s with a three-year-old daughter; they live in a middle-class suburban neigh-

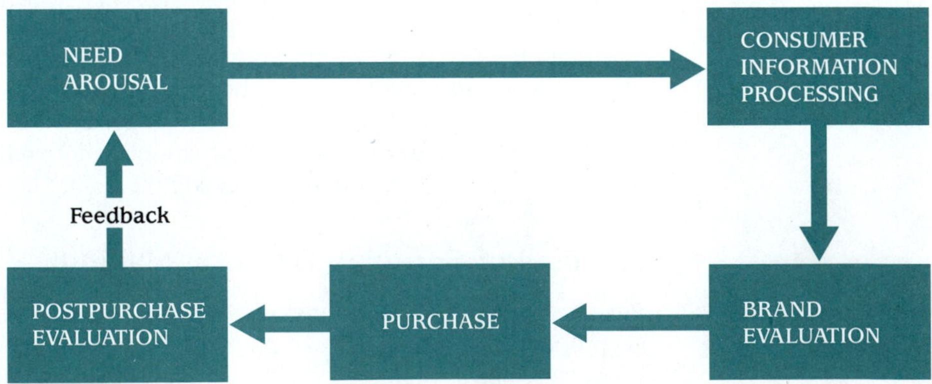

FIGURE 3.3
A basic model of complex decision making

FIGURE 3.4
Need Arousal

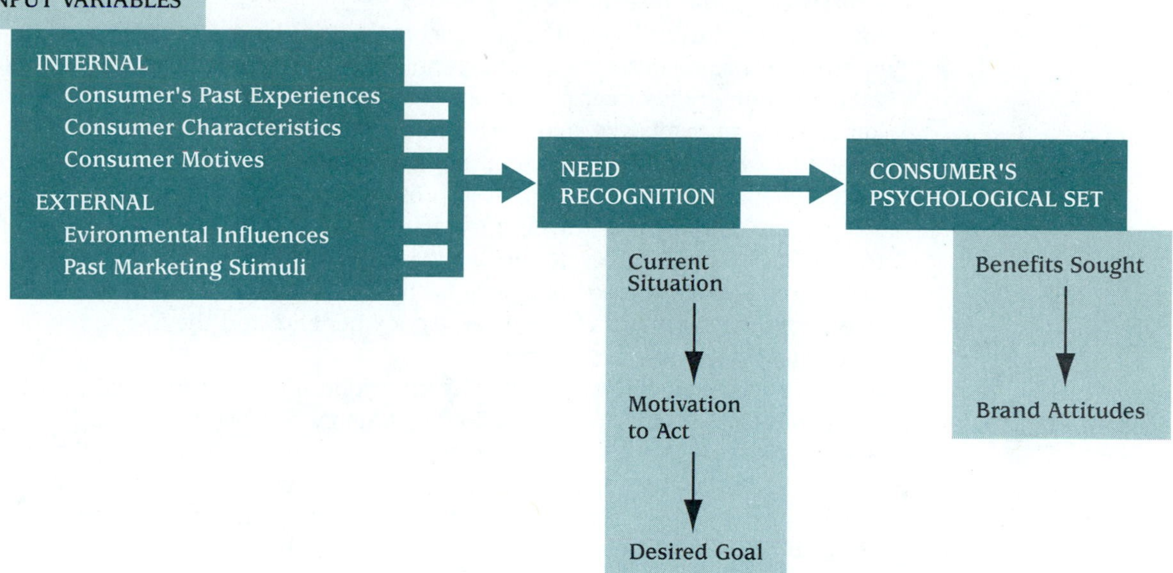

borhood of a large metropolitan area. They both work and use public transportation to get to their jobs. Their daughter is in a day-care center during the week. They are a one-car family.

Consumer's Past Experiences

Rob inherited his parents' Oldsmobile when he married Linda five years ago. No longer satisfied with the economy or styling of their current model, both Rob and Linda are in the market for a new car. As a result, they recognize a need.

Rob and Linda are not involved in cars on an enduring basis. Their high level of involvement arose as a result of the situation—dissatisfaction with their current car. The status communicated by a car (badge value) is not very important to them. Since they are both starting out in careers—Rob as a financial analyst and Linda as a product manager for a food company—they see substantial financial and performance risks in buying. Highly involved in the purchase decision, they place more importance on economy, service dependability, performance, and comfort, in that order. They use their Olds primarily on weekends and for shopping needs, and it has served them well according to these benefit criteria. As a result, their past experiences with the car have been positive.

Rob and Linda have also developed a set of expectations regarding a car. They have come to expect good service and a car that performs consistently over time. Any deviations from these expectations might cause them to consider alternative models.

Consumer Characteristics

The benefits consumers seek and their brand attitudes are partially conditioned by their characteristics—their demographics, lifestyles, and personalities. Income may affect the type of car purchased—compact, standard, or luxury. Age, marital status, and number of children may affect the class of car—sports car, sedan, or station wagon. Lifestyle may affect the make. A socially oriented, outer-directed couple may want a car that impresses others and may stress styling and size of car. A family that travels a lot may emphasize the benefits of comfort at the expense of styling. Even personality has an influence. The power-oriented, aggressive individual may want a car with a great deal of acceleration. The compulsive individual may stress regular service benefits and the alleviation of anxieties with better warranty terms.

http://www.avon.com/

Consumer characteristics can play an important part in marketing strategy. We saw that Avon adjusted its marketing strategy because of the move of many women from the home to the workplace. Tupperware—famous for selling housewares through at-home "Tupperware parties"—saw its market shrink in the 1980s for the same reason. By the mid-1990s, the company was on the ropes because of its failure to adjust to this significant demographic shift and was a candidate for divestment.[18]

Consumer Motives

Motives are general drives that direct a consumer's behavior toward attaining his or her needs. The greater the disparity between a consumer's current situation and desired goals, the greater the motivational drive to act to satisfy consumer needs.

The motivational drive directly affects the specific benefit criteria consumers use to evaluate brands. If Rob and Linda are motivated by a drive to meet the need for status, two important benefit criteria will be the size and styling of the car. If the need for economy drives the motivation to act, then benefit criteria may be gas mileage, service costs, and sticker price.

Environmental Influences

Consumers purchase and use many products in a social setting. The purchase of a car is frequently a family decision, and each member of the family influences the decision. Neighbors and business associates may also be important sources of information and influence.

A car is also a symbol as well as a means of transport. As a result, social and cultural norms influence the purchase of a car and the way it is used. Teenagers are more likely to use a car as a means of socialization, adults as a symbol of socioeconomic status.

A study by Vinson, Scott, and Lamont found a marked difference in the perception of automobiles among college students from liberal and conservative universities.[19] Students from the liberal university emphasized performance and engineering, whereas students from the more conservative university emphasized prestige and luxury. Apparently, cultural norms at the two universities affected students' perceptions of automobiles.

Past Marketing Stimuli

Past information about brand characteristics and prices will also affect consumers' needs. Consumers obtain such information from advertising, in-store stimuli, and sales representatives.

Need Recognition

The various input variables in Figure 3.4 determine a consumer's current state. Consumers recognize a need when there is a disparity between their current state and some desired end state. This disparity creates tension and arouses a *motivation to act*.

http://www.gm.com/

Rob and Linda were motivated to act because of their current state of affairs. They learned that the Oldsmobile needed a transmission overhaul. This fact, in addition to poor gas mileage, caused them to begin considering alternative makes. One additional factor prompted them to act. Both Rob and Linda believed the Olds had a stodgy image and agreed they should consider getting a sportier, more modern-looking car. Rob remembered an ad campaign meant to counteract the Olds' image based on the theme "This is not your father's car." Rob found that campaign amusing since the Olds used to be his father's car. The ad had done little to counter Rob and Linda's perception of the Olds.

A Hierarchy of Needs

Abraham Maslow developed a motivational theory based on a *hierarchy of needs*.[20] According to Maslow, consumers are motivated to act by first satisfying the lowest level of needs before the next higher level of needs becomes activated. Once these have been satisfied, the individual then attempts to satisfy the next higher level, and so on. Thus, the unfulfilled needs lead to action. Maslow defined five levels of needs, from lowest to highest:

1. Physiological (food, water, shelter, sex).
2. Safety (protection, security, stability).
3. Social (affection, friendship, acceptance).
4. Ego (prestige, success, self-esteem).
5. Self-actualization (self-fulfillment).

Marketers can appeal to a range of needs within Maslow's five levels. For example, they can appeal to:

- Physiological needs through sexual appeals, as in ads for personal grooming products.

- Safety needs, as in messages advertising safer cars or promoting a safer environment.
- Social needs, by showing group acceptance as a result of wearing certain types of clothing or using a brand of soap or deodorant.
- Ego needs, by linking a product to success in business (credit cards) or in sports activities (athletic shoes).
- Self-actualization needs, by showing self-fulfillment through travel, education, or cultural pursuits.

According to Maslow, few people satisfy their social and ego needs and move to the fifth level. In fact, most advertising appeals focus on social and ego needs, whether it is an appeal for the status of a luxury car or the more mundane appeal for the social protection a deodorant affords.

One researcher equates Maslow's theory to three stages in a family's life cycle.[21] In the first stage, young adults acquire material possessions primarily to gain acceptance and to emulate their peers (Level 3). Having established themselves in their middle years, consumers view possessions as a means of demonstrating success and gaining self-esteem (Level 4). As adults reach older age, possessions are no longer important. They now seek experiences that provide emotional satisfaction and self-realization (Level 5).

Utilitarian versus Hedonic Needs

In addition to Maslow's classification, needs can be classified even more basically as utilitarian or hedonic. So far, Rob and Linda's purchase of a car assumes that they make decisions objectively by collecting information on utilitarian product attributes such as service costs, gas mileage, repairs, and performance. This is not always the case. As we all know, we sometimes make decisions based on emotional factors that are the result of our more innate desires and fantasies.

Utilitarian needs seek to achieve some practical benefit such as a durable car, an economical computer, or warm clothing. Such needs are identified with functional product attributes (durability, economy, warmth) that define product performance. **Hedonic needs** seek to achieve pleasure from a product. They are more likely to be associated with emotions or fantasies derived from consuming a product. In being more closely identified with the consumption process, hedonic needs are more experiential. A hedonic need might be the desire to appear more masculine or feminine, to be associated with a winning sports team, or to feel at one with nature.

In satisfying hedonic needs, consumers frequently use emotional rather than utilitarian criteria in evaluating alternative brands. (We use the term *emotional* rather than *irrational* and the term *utilitarian* rather than *rational* because emotional criteria such as "feel behind the wheel" could be as rational as utilitarian criteria such as "service costs.") Buying a Gucci scarf for twice as much as the same scarf with a store label cannot be justified based on the functional benefits of a scarf, but it can certainly be justified based on its hedonic benefits.

The marketing strategies used to appeal to utilitarian and hedonic needs are very different. Advertising that appeals to utilitarian needs tends to be more informative and rational. An ad for a bicycle might advertise durability, a comfortable ride, and ease in shifting gears. Advertising that appeals to hedonic needs tends to be more symbolic and emotional. The ad for Schwinn bicycles in Exhibit 3.4 is more symbolic and emotional because it appeals to the challenges of bike riding. As the creator of the ad said, "The audience considers every scar a tattoo. You either win or crash, and those are two goals worth achieving." Given the experiential and emotional tone of the ad, functional benefits do not have to be cited.

http://www.schwinn.com/

Consumer's Psychological Set

The consumer's psychological set is his or her state of mind at the time needs are recognized and motives are aroused. In the context of consumer decision making, the consumer's psychological set is directed to brand, product, or store evaluations. The psychological set is made up of two components: benefits sought and brand attitudes.

Benefits Sought

Benefit criteria are the factors consumers consider important in deciding on one brand or another. Rob and Linda's most important criteria are economy and service dependability; but other criteria such as road performance, comfort, styling, and safety are also relevant. Marketers identify **benefit segments** by

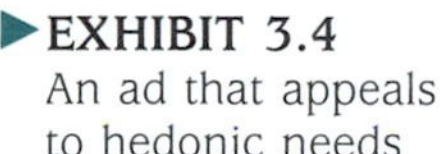

EXHIBIT 3.4
An ad that appeals to hedonic needs

consumers who emphasize the same benefit criteria. In identifying consumer segments who emphasize benefits such as economy, performance, and style, marketers try to develop product characteristics that satisfy these benefits. The car manufacturer that appeals to a performance segment might advertise product characteristics such as quick acceleration and a smooth ride.

Consumers regard product characteristics as goal objects that may or may not satisfy desired benefits. Thus, the goal object consumers use to evaluate economy may include gas mileage and service costs.

The distinction between hedonic and utilitarian needs also applies to benefits and goal objects. Hedonic needs will lead to defining pleasure-oriented benefits and goal objects in satisfying these needs. The relationship between needs, motives, benefits, and goal objects for both utilitarian and hedonic needs are provided in the examples below:

Needs	*Motivation*	*Benefits Sought*	*Goal Objects*
Utilitarian:			
Adequate transportation	Drive to act to meet needs	Economy	Gas mileage Service costs Sticker price
Hedonic:			
Pleasure in driving	Drive to act to meet needs	Good feeling behind wheel	Purring engine Smell of the car Smooth ride

Brand Attitudes

Brand attitudes are consumers' predispositions to evaluate a brand favorably or unfavorably. They are represented by three factors: beliefs about brands, evaluation of brands, and tendency to act.[22] The assumption is that these components operate in sequence as follows:

1. Beliefs are formed about the brand that influence
2. attitudes toward the brand, which then influence
3. an intention to buy (or not to buy).

That is, if brand beliefs result in positive attitudes, there is a greater chance the consumer will buy the brand.

This sequence has been referred to as a **hierarchy of effects** model of consumer decision making. It stipulates the sequence of stages consumers go through in purchasing, a sequence involving thinking (beliefs), feelings (evaluations), and actions (the intention to buy the brand).[23] Interestingly, the first person to theorize this decision-making sequence of thinking, feeling, and acting was Plato in ancient Greece.

The hierarchy of effects is particularly important to marketers because it provides a basis for defining the factors that influence consumer behavior. The sequence was implicit in the description at the beginning of the chapter of the strategic issues related to the Saturn. In this case, GM knew that a large segment of car buyers emphasizes economy because of budgetary constraints and wants value for their money as defined by quality and dependability. These desired benefits (economy, quality, dependability) drive their decision process. Compact car buyers will evaluate alternative makes primarily on these criteria. Beliefs about the extent to which cars have these attributes will determine their evaluation of the car. Thus, the belief that a Saturn is economical, dependable, and of high quality will result in a positive evaluation of the car, which in turn will increase the likelihood that consumers will decide to buy it. That is, needs influence the nature of beliefs about the Saturn, and these beliefs determine how consumers will evaluate it and whether they are likely to buy.

Returning to the Greenes, Rob and Linda believe their Olds provides performance and comfort but question its economy because of the increasing costs of maintenance. Consumers attribute characteristics to brands whether they have used them or not. Because of advertising and comments from friends, Linda suggests they consider a Toyota Corolla and a Saturn because both are nicely styled, provide comfort, and are not expensive to maintain.

An important link exists between benefits and attitudes. When beliefs about a brand conform to the benefits consumers desire, consumers will evaluate the brand favorably. Favorable brand evaluation is more likely to lead to an intention to buy the brand. Given that Rob and Linda's primary benefit criteria are economy and service dependability, they will prefer a car (brand evaluation) that has these characteristics (their beliefs) and will probably plan to buy such a car (their tendency to act).

CONSUMER INFORMATION PROCESSING

Consumer information processing involves the exposure to and perception of information and its retention in memory. These processes are represented in Figure 3.5 and are summarized here. They are considered in detail in Chapters 7 and 8.

Stimulus Exposure

Once a need is recognized, consumers are more likely to search for and process information relevant to that need. Rob and Linda are more likely to notice stimuli related to cars such as advertisements, comments friends make about their cars, and cars in showrooms and on the street. They are also more likely to be aware of information that affects the cost of owning and operating a car such as sticker prices, trade-in allowances, gasoline, and service and parts.

Consumers' exposure to stimuli is often selective. People tend to choose friends who support their views, reinforce their egos, and parallel their lifestyles.

FIGURE 3.5
Consumer information processing

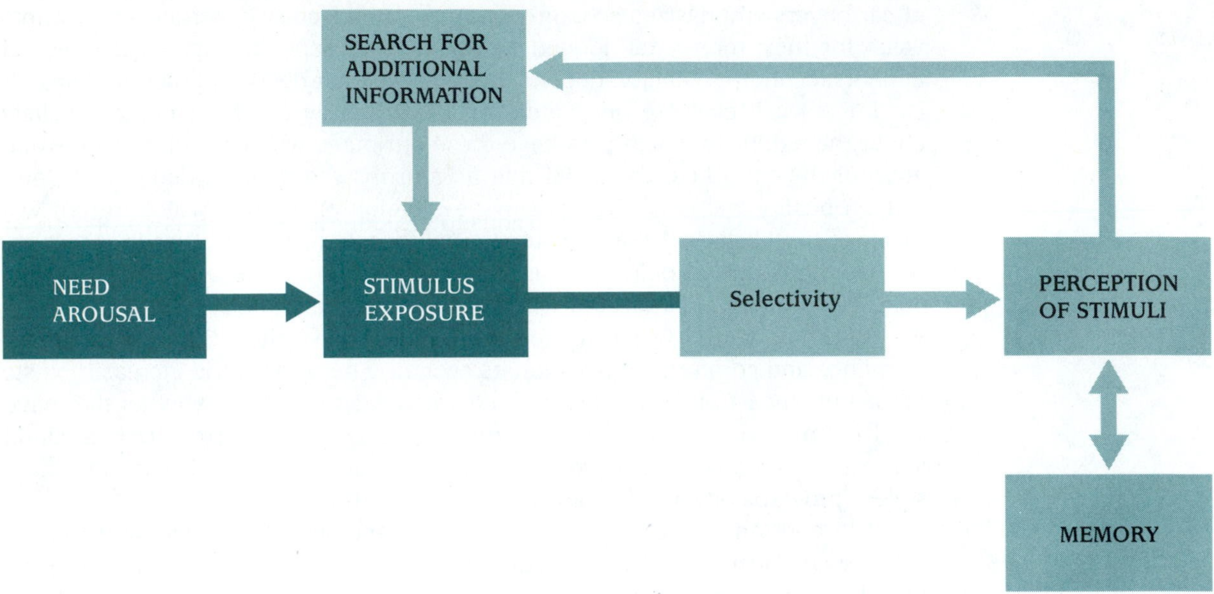

They often seek commercials that support recent purchases in an attempt to justify them. They also frequently tune out information that conflicts with their needs or beliefs. The recent car buyer may ignore the negative experiences of a friend with the same make or may rationalize poor performance by thinking the car is not yet broken in.

Therefore, stimulus exposure is a selective process that is directed by the need to reinforce existing brand attitudes and perceptions and to seek additional information.

Perception of Stimuli

Perception is the process by which consumers select, organize, and interpret stimuli to make sense of them. Stimuli are more likely to be perceived when they:

- Conform to consumers' past experiences.
- Conform to consumers' current beliefs about a brand.
- Are not too complex.
- Are believable.
- Relate to a set of current needs.
- Do not produce excessive fears and anxieties.

It is clear that consumers' perceptions of stimuli, as well as their exposure to stimuli, are selective. Ads that reinforce consumers' beliefs and experiences are more likely to be noticed and retained. Also, consumers are more likely to dismiss or reinterpret those ads that contradict past experiences and current beliefs about a brand. By perceiving stimuli selectively, consumers attempt to achieve a state of psychological equilibrium, namely, a state that lacks conflict and avoids contradictory information.

Memory

Retained information is stored in consumers' **memory,** which is composed of past information and experiences. Once stored in memory, information can be recalled for future use, as shown by the double arrow in Figure 3.5 between memory and perception of stimuli. (Memory processes are described in Chapter 8 as part of a detailed discussion of consumer information processing.)

Search for Additional Information

Consumers may not have enough information to make adequate decisions. In such cases, they will search for additional information. Such a search is most likely when consumers:

- Believe that alternative brands being considered are inadequate.
- Have insufficient information about the brands under consideration.
- Receive information from friends or media sources that conflicts with past experiences and current information.
- Are close to deciding on a particular brand and would like to confirm expectations regarding its performance.

Studies have shown that consumers do not engage in an extensive information search unless they consider the value of any additional information collected worth the cost of obtaining it. One study found that when consumers were presented with information on 16 alternative brands, they used only 2 percent of the information available in making a decision.[24] Another study found that one-half of all consumers studied visited only one store or showroom when buying cars and major appliances.[25] A limited search does not necessarily reflect consumers' lack of concern about the purchase. It may mean that many consumers rely on past experience in deciding on a brand or believe they have enough information at the time of purchase.

About two weeks after deciding to purchase a new car, Rob and Linda visited several showrooms and obtained figures from dealers on gas mileage, service costs, and resale value of various makes of cars. Linda took several copies of *Consumer Reports* out of the library to determine ratings of various makes from an impartial source. On occasion, Rob and Linda asked friends who owned one of the makes under consideration about their experiences. On the basis of this information search, they narrowed their choice to three cars—Toyota Corolla, Honda Accord, and Saturn.

Figure 3.5 shows that the search for additional information feeds back to stimulus exposure, as additional information may stimulate further search. This process illustrates the dynamic nature of consumers' decision-making process. The components of information processing and brand evaluation are not discrete; they occur on an ongoing basis until consumers reach a final decision.

BRAND EVALUATION

Brand evaluation is illustrated in Figure 3.6. As a result of information processing, consumers use past and current information to associate brands they are aware of with their desired benefits. Consumers prefer the brand they expect will give the most satisfaction based on the benefits they seek.

Benefit Association

In benefit association, one must develop a priority of desired benefits and relate a brand's characteristics to these benefits. Rob and Linda's priorities are, in order of importance, economy, service dependability, performance, comfort, safety, and styling. Rob and Linda use these benefit criteria to evaluate the characteristics of the three makes they are considering. While they give greater weight to benefits they regard as most important, they also include other benefits in

FIGURE 3.6
Brand evaluation

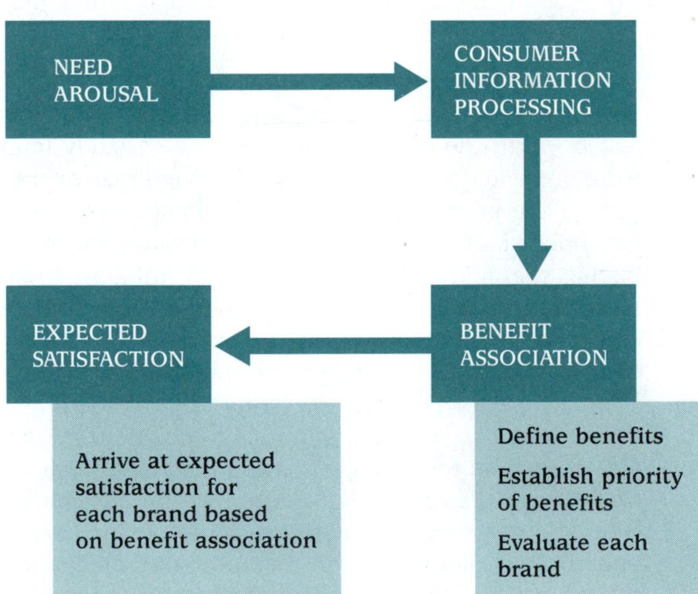

assessing the relative merits of each car. On this basis, Rob and Linda determine that the Saturn and Corolla do best on economy, the Saturn and Accord score best on service dependability, and all three makes are rated close to equal on performance. However, the Saturn scores worst on styling. Rob and Linda select the Saturn, despite the negative rating on styling, because it scored highest on the most important benefits.

Rob and Linda used utilitarian criteria in selecting a car. As we saw, consumers can also use more *hedonic* criteria such as the feeling of freedom in driving or the pleasurable feeling of being behind the wheel. As we saw earlier, Saturn's advertising appealed more to emotional than utilitarian benefits by portraying Saturn owners as free spirits with pride in ownership.

The procedure Rob and Linda used to evaluate alternative cars is known as a **compensatory method** of evaluation because a negative rating on one criterion can be made up by a positive rating on another. Thus, even though the Saturn scored lowest on styling, its high ratings on economy and service dependability resulted in Rob and Linda choosing the car.

In the compensatory method, consumers evaluate each brand across all benefit criteria. The alternative is a **noncompensatory method** of evaluation in which consumers evaluate brands one criterion at a time across all brands. For example, Rob and Linda might first evaluate the three cars by service dependability and might eliminate the Accord on this basis. They would then evaluate the two remaining cars by the next most important criterion, performance, and eliminate the Corolla, leaving the Saturn as the choice. Thus, consumers may use different decision rules in evaluating brands.[26]

Two factors are likely to determine which method of evaluation is used: the nature of consumer needs and the level of involvement. When consumers are driven by functional needs, they are more likely to use a compensatory system. Consumers are likely to use multiple criteria in evaluating a car's economy, dependability, or comfort. In evaluating economy, reasonable service costs and good gas mileage may counterbalance a higher sticker price. When consumers are driven by hedonic needs, a "one strike and you're out" decision rule is more likely. If a car does not give the consumer a pleasurable feeling behind the wheel and a sense of driving enjoyment, it would be immediately out of the running.

Consumers are also more likely to use noncompensatory decision rules for less involving decisions such as those for detergents and toothpaste. In such cases, it may not be worth the time and effort to choose a brand by the more extensive processing requirements of a compensatory method.

Expected Satisfaction

Both the compensatory and noncompensatory models agree that consumers develop a set of expectations based on the degree to which a brand or product satisfies the benefits consumers desire. The brand that comes closest to satisfying the most important benefits is expected to provide the most satisfaction. For Rob and Linda, the Saturn had the highest expected satisfaction because it did best on their most important benefit criterion, economy.

PURCHASE AND POSTPURCHASE EVALUATION

The outcome of brand evaluation is an intention to buy (or not to buy). The final sequence in complex decision making involves purchasing the intended brand, evaluating the brand during consumption, and storing this information for future use (that is, feedback). These steps are outlined in Figure 3.7.

Intention to Buy

Once consumers evaluate brands, they intend to purchase the one achieving the highest level of expected satisfaction. Purchasing in complex decision making is not likely to be immediate. Rob and Linda may still have some shopping to do to obtain the best trade-in value on their present car, and they may have to obtain financing. Therefore, some time will pass before Rob and Linda purchase the Saturn. To purchase the car, they must do several things called **instrumen-**

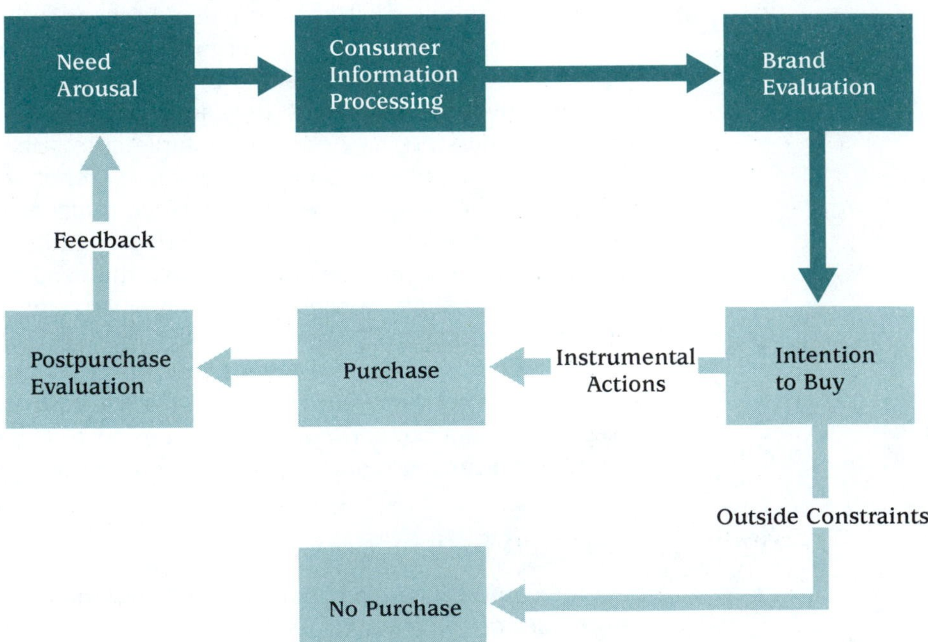

FIGURE 3.7 Purchase and postpurchase evaluation

tal actions: select a dealer; determine when to purchase; go to the place of purchase; and, as is often the case with an automobile purchase, arrange for financing. Moreover, they may have to decide on options such as air conditioning or a CD player.

No Purchase

The consumer decision-making model shows that a decision might be made to delay purchase or not to buy. Rob and Linda may decide not to buy a new car because they estimate that, in the long run, it would be cheaper to fix the Olds. Or, having evaluated the various brands, they may decide to wait and see if some additional options may be introduced in next year's models.

The study by Greenleaf and Lehmann cited earlier found a number of reasons why consumers might delay a decision, namely that they:

- Are too busy to devote time to the decision.
- Do not like shopping for the item.
- Are concerned that the purchase may make other people think less well of them (social risk).
- Are concerned that they might have made the wrong decision or that the product might not work (ego and performance risk).
- Need more information about the item.
- Believe that the product's price may soon decrease or that a better item may soon become available.

Figure 3.7 demonstrates that the decision-making process may be terminated or delayed at any stage because of such outside constraints. For example, the Saturn may not be available when expected, or the price of the Saturn may increase unexpectedly due to cost overruns in production.

Purchase

Figure 3.7 demonstrates that the link between intention to buy and actual purchase requires instrumental action. The time lag between intention and purchase is likely to be greater in complex decision making because of the greater number of actions required for a purchase to take place.

Of the instrumental actions required for a purchase, store selection is most important. In fact, store selection may require a decision-making process of its own. Where to purchase a suit or dress may be more critical than what brand to buy. The act of purchasing may also require Rob and Linda to negotiate to get the best terms regarding price, used car allowance, and financing. Rob and Linda will select the dealer that gives them the best terms.

In this case, Rob and Linda made their decision to buy a certain car prior to the purchase. For many goods, decision and purchase are almost simultaneous because consumers make the brand decision in the store. For example, by a glance at the supermarket shelf, a consumer may be reminded of a need for canned peas. With no strong brand loyalties, the consumer may just select the lowest priced brand.

Postpurchase Evaluation

Once the product is purchased, the consumer will evaluate its performance in the process of consumption.

Purchasing versus Consuming

It is important to distinguish between purchase and consumption for three reasons. First, the product may be purchased by one person and consumed by another. The consumer, not the purchaser, determines product satisfaction. Second, the purchase depends on consumer expectations of the degree to which brands are likely to satisfy needs. Consumption determines whether these expectations are confirmed. Third, a consumer's postpurchase evaluation determines whether the brand is likely to be repurchased. It is unlikely that any brand can survive over time without some degree of loyalty. The consumer's dissatisfaction will lead to no further purchases, negative word-of-mouth communication about the brand, and lost sales.

Satisfaction versus Dissatisfaction

Satisfaction occurs when consumer expectations are met or exceeded and the purchase decision is reinforced. Such reinforcement is represented in Figure 3.7 as feedback from postpurchase evaluation. Satisfaction reinforces positive attitudes toward the brand, leading to a greater likelihood that the consumer will repurchase the same brand. Dissatisfaction results when consumer expectations are not met. Such **disconfirmation of expectations** is likely to lead to negative brand attitudes and lessens the likelihood that the consumer will buy the same brand again.

Postpurchase Dissonance

In many cases, a decision involves two or more close alternatives and could go either way. Having made their decisions, consumers may feel insecure, particularly if substantial financial or social risks are involved. Any negative information about the chosen product causes **postpurchase dissonance,** that is, conflict resulting from two contradictory beliefs.

Assume in Rob and Linda's decision-making process that the Toyota Corolla was a close second to the Saturn. The likelihood of postpurchase dissonance increases. The financial risks of purchasing the car make dissonance even more likely. There are also the social risks of buying a car that may not conform to the norms of friends and neighbors, and there is the psychological risk that the wrong decision may have been made.

Suppose that shortly after the purchase, Linda meets a friend who also purchased a Saturn and who relates some negative experiences such as lower than expected gas mileage and mechanical failures. At about the same time, Rob learns that Toyota will be introducing a more economical model next year. This information produces postpurchase doubt, as Rob and Linda believe that perhaps they should have delayed the purchase. Such doubt is psychologically uncomfortable. The tendency is to reduce doubt by confirming the purchase. Consumers do this in several ways:

1. By ignoring the dissonant information.
2. By selectively interpreting the information, saying, for example, that any brand will have an occasional lemon.
3. By lowering the level of expectations, saying that even if there are a few problems with the car, it still is an acceptable choice.
4. By seeking positive information about the brand.
5. By convincing others they made a good choice, and in doing so convincing themselves.

In each case, dissonance is reduced.[27]

Now assume that after six months, Rob finds the Saturn's gas mileage is about 20 percent lower than dealer and advertising claims. Linda determines that service costs are somewhat higher than expected. In other respects (styling, comfort, performance), the car meets expectations. The theory of postpurchase dissonance says that Rob and Linda will focus on the positive performance and tend to dismiss or rationalize the negative performance. If, as is true with Rob and Linda, the disparity between prior expectations and subsequent product performance is not great, an **assimilation effect** occurs. That is, consumers ignore the product's defects and their evaluation of the product remains positive.

If there is a great disparity between prior expectations and performance, however, a **contrast effect** is likely to take place in which consumers recognize and magnify poor performance.[28] Thus, if the Saturn's gas mileage is half of that claimed in the advertising, it is unlikely that Rob and Linda would focus solely on the positive aspects of performance. They would probably be extremely dissatisfied, have negative attitudes toward the selected brand, and be unlikely to consider that brand next time.

This description of complex decision making has focused on the individual consumer. The complexities of group decision making were not emphasized in this chapter. For example, what occurs when spouses have different objectives, different sources of information, or different preferences? What is the nature of word-of-mouth influence from friends and relatives in the decision process? What is the impact of differing roles such as influencer, information gatherer, purchasing agent, decision maker, and consumer in the process of group decision making? These considerations will be incorporated into the model of complex decision making in Part VI of the text.

THE CONSUMPTION EXPERIENCE: HEDONIC CONSUMPTION AND PRODUCT SYMBOLISM

So far, we have focused on the consumer's purchasing process. But as we saw, consumption determines the level of satisfaction and repeat purchasing behavior. Therefore, the consumption experience is at the center of future purchase decisions.

Two distinctions are important to better understanding the consumption experience: first, the difference between consuming products versus services and, second, the difference between consumption that satisfies hedonic versus utilitarian needs.

Product versus Service Consumption

Products are tangible entities that are produced by manufacturers, purchased, and then consumed. Services are intangible offerings that are produced and consumed simultaneously. An airplane flight, a college course, or a financial service are being consumed as they are being offered by the marketer. The consumption experience involves direct interaction with a service provider—the airline attendant, the college professor, the financial consultant, a symphony orchestra.

The intervention of a service provider means that the consumption experience is likely to be much more variable for services than for products. A shopper may find salespeople helpful and courteous on one trip and rude on another; a traveler may have a flawless flight on one occasion, but have her baggage lost on the next. Such variability makes it more difficult for consumers to assess services than products, and the level of dissatisfaction is likely to be higher because prior expectations are not as likely to be met.

How can marketers try to reduce the potential for dissatisfaction with the consumption experience? They can minimize service variability and establish a longer-term customer relationship. Companies attempt to minimize service variability by trying to instill a customer-oriented focus in service providers and insuring constancy in service. McDonald's attempts to control the operations of its franchises by insisting on uniform training and facilities; FedEx ensures on-time delivery through a rigid adherence to routine.

http://www.mcdonalds.com/

http://www.fedex.com/

Service marketers have also relied on **relationship marketing,** that is, an attempt to establish a one-to-one relationship with consumers over time. As we saw, Saturn dealers have successfully established a bond with many of their customers through owner clubs and car-care seminars. Such one-to-one contacts are becoming more feasible through the establishment of databases that identify users of services. American Express, for example, has been able to target specific promotional offerings to card users based on their spending patterns. For example, a frequenter of Italian restaurants could be offered a reduced price coupon to several neighborhood Italian restaurants.

http://www.americanexpress.com/

Hedonic Consumption

The same distinction between hedonic and utilitarian needs in the purchasing processes apply to the consumption experience. Utilitarian consumption involves using a product for some functional purpose—detergents to wash dishes or clothes, cereals for a nutritious breakfast, a car as transportation to work. The cognitive processes of postpurchase evaluation cited earlier work fairly well in assessing satisfaction in these cases. Satisfaction is determined by the degree to which the product meets prior expectations on functional attributes such as softness and whiteness for a detergent or gas mileage and comfort for a car.

Hedonic consumption involves use of a product to fulfill fantasies and satisfy emotions. Level of satisfaction cannot be determined in the same orderly manner in hedonic as in utilitarian consumption. It is more likely to be based on the pleasurable experiences and emotions that result from using the brand rather than on the brand's utilitarian performance and economic value. As a result, the consumer is likely to arrive at some overall judgment of satisfaction based on the totality of the consumption experience. Satisfaction is assessed on a simple like/dislike (or in a more emotional context, love/hate) dimension.

The same product can be consumed in both a hedonic and utilitarian manner. Rob and Linda purchased the Saturn based on utilitarian criteria. But after buying it, they got caught up in the mystique of the car among owners, would blow their horn at other Saturn drivers and be tooted in return, and even took the company up on its offer to host a weekend for Saturn owners in Spring Hill, Tennessee. They used the car for shopping trips, but they also found themselves taking more outings with their daughter partly because of the sheer pleasure of driving the car.

Product and Service Symbolism

Products and services that satisfy hedonic needs are often purchased for their symbolic value. As Hirschman and Holbrook note, products so purchased "are viewed not as objective entities but rather as subjective symbols."[29] Putting it another way, "People buy products not only for what they can do, but also for what they mean."[30] As a result, many of our purchases are a reflection of who we are—our values, aspirations, and social connections. A study of motorcycle owners found that many buy not because of the bike's performance, but because of the feeling of independence and power they get while riding and the feeling of kinship with fellow riders at bike rallies.[31] Similarly, rather than buying a pair of Nikes based on comfort or durability, a consumer might buy them because he or she feels the product enhances self-image (see Exhibit 3.5).

The marketer's perspective is very different when products are purchased more for pleasure and fantasy. In these cases, marketing research is concerned not so much with what the product is as with what it means to consumers.[32] As a result, advertising tries to associate the product with the symbols that generate positive emotions and fantasies. Kawasaki was successful in developing

http://www.kawasaki.com/

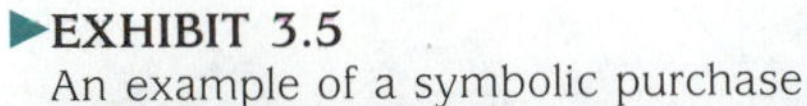

EXHIBIT 3.5
An example of a symbolic purchase

such symbolism for its motorcycles with an ad showing a lone rider rounding a bend on a deserted country road with his knee almost touching the ground. The ad captured the feeling of freedom, speed, danger, and contact with the elements—in short, emotion, not performance.

A viewing of television advertising on any given day demonstrates the importance of product symbolism in purchasing behavior. Advertisements for cars, cosmetics, clothing, sports equipment, and a range of other products frequently use symbols meant to evoke positive emotional associations.

Services are also often associated with emotions and pleasure. Their intangibility makes it harder for marketers to communicate specific benefits, so many service advertisers use symbols that reinforce feelings of security or pleasure. Prudential uses the symbol of a rock to convey security; Merrill Lynch uses a bull to convey financial success.

Specific product or service characteristics become less important elements in marketing strategy for such products. The overriding concern is establishing a brand image that is linked to positive consumer emotions. As we shall see in the next chapter, if product symbols become strongly linked with positive emotions, consumers may eventually purchase by habit rather than by decision making.

Even when utilitarian product characteristics dominate in brand evaluation, as was the case with Rob and Linda's purchase of a car, symbols are likely to influence purchases. Although Rob and Linda selected the Saturn primarily on performance criteria, an important symbolic factor was its "new wave" image among many of their friends. As such, the Saturn was a symbol of innovativeness and independence from traditional alternatives for Rob, Linda, and their peer group.

At times, advertisers attempt to appeal to both the symbolic motives of consumers through emotional themes and the more utilitarian motives through product information. The ad for Saab, shown in Exhibit 3.6, is an example. The first page is clearly informational; the second page relies on a direct appeal to the car buyer's emotions.

In summary, complex decision making should incorporate consumer evaluations of brands as both objective entities and subjective symbols. Since consumers frequently employ products as symbols in a social setting, the role of product symbolism in consumer behavior will become more evident in Chapters 11 and 13, which cover consumer lifestyles and cultural values.

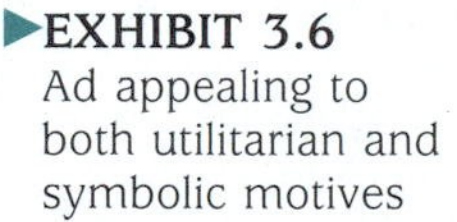

EXHIBIT 3.6
Ad appealing to both utilitarian and symbolic motives

STRATEGIC APPLICATIONS OF CONSUMER BEHAVIOR

► From Heavy Metal to Cologne: Harley-Davidson Changes Its Symbols

Harley-Davidson has long recognized that bikers choose motorcycles for their symbolism as much as for their performance. Until the 1980s, Harley's symbols were the heavy metal and black leather associated with big bikes—a throwback to the days of James Dean and Marlon Brando. Harley had a virtual monopoly of the big bike market. However, by the 1980s, the black leather crowd was dwindling and Harley knew it would have to look to a new customer base.

The new customer base Harley went after—baby boomers—was a complete reversal of form. By the mid-1980s, many baby boomers were heading toward midlife crises and were looking for some escape from everyday cares. The stock market crash of 1987 further fueled the search for fantasy. Harley felt big bikes might provide it.

But the symbolism would have to change, and with it Harley's image. Harley changed its image to appeal to a more affluent, white-collar market in several ways. Out went the heavy metal look in its advertising; in came a softer approach. One ad featured a baby in a Harley T-shirt with the tag line, "When did it start for you?" Harley also began to use celebrities such as Kurt Russell and Elizabeth Taylor in its advertising. The company even began to sell items such as cologne and wine coolers with the Harley name in its dealerships.

Harley's success in attracting baby boomers was reflected in the fact that over 60 percent of its buyers attended college and had a median income of $45,000, and the company could boast of a threefold rise in revenues and earnings. By 1994, it owned 63 percent of the U.S. market for large motorcycles.

Buying a Harley may still be a good example of symbolic purchasing behavior, but the symbolism has certainly changed.

Sources: "Cult Followings," *Advertising Age* (March 28, 1994), p. S-12; "The Power of Cult Brands," *Adweek's Marketing Week* (February 24, 1992), pp. 18–21; "After Nearly Stalling, Harley-Davidson Finds New Crowd of Riders," *The Wall Street Journal* (August 31, 1990), pp. A1 and A6; "Bikers Ride into Middle Age," *American Demographics* (December 1991), p. 15.

COMPLEX DECISION MAKING AND STORE CHOICE

Until now, we have focused on decision making for brands. However, consumers also make decisions regarding the stores in which they will shop. In buying a car, consumers will determine the make of car first and then choose the dealer to buy from. But frequently, consumers' choice of a store comes first and influences their choice of the brand. For example, we generally make a decision regarding the store first and then the brand when we shop for clothes. Similarly, we often make a brand decision in the store when we shop for appliances or electronics. In these cases, store choice conditions brand choice.

A Model of Store Choice

Consumers' decision making process for a store is similar to that for a brand. The model of store choice in Figure 3.8 is an adaptation of the basic model of complex decision making in Figure 3.3. Consider the business school student who is purchasing a notebook computer. One of the first decisions she has to make is what stores to visit to gather information about alternative brands. The model in Figure 3.8 shows that there are two components to need arousal in store choice: first, a purchasing need (recognition of a need to buy a computer) and, second, a shopping need (need to search for alternatives in various stores). Shopping needs can be complex. Some consumers consider the process of shopping time-consuming and not particularly enjoyable. Others like to search for bargains and enjoy interacting with salespeople.

Need arousal will establish certain priorities as to the store or stores that consumers will select. Assume our student is time-oriented and does not enjoy shopping. Based on her purchasing and shopping needs, she is looking for conveniently located stores with knowledgeable salespeople and competitive prices. Information search involves asking friends which stores are reliable and searching for store ads with information on prices and models.

On this basis, our consumer will evaluate stores and choose several to visit. In the process, she will develop an image of each store. The closer the store is to her needs (knowledgeable and helpful salespeople, good service, competitive prices), the more likely she will buy the computer from that store. Therefore,

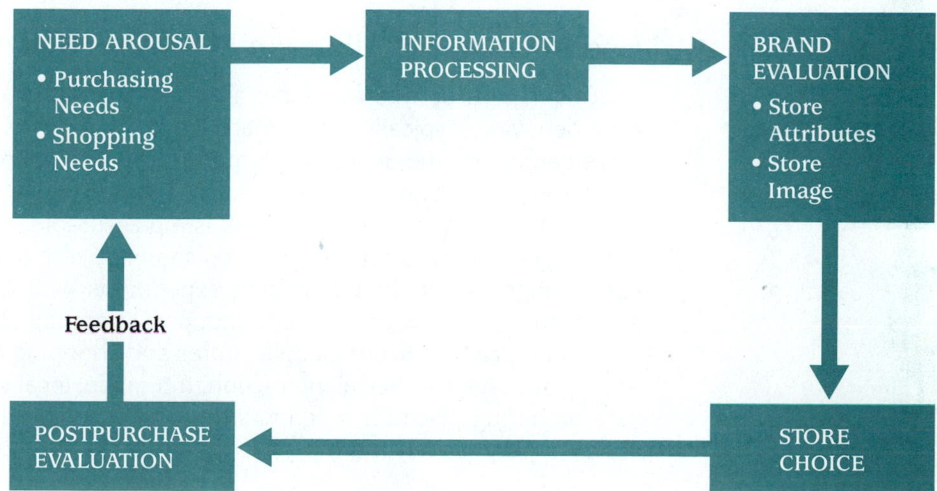

FIGURE 3.8 A model of store choice

store choice depends on the degree to which the consumer's image of the store is related to his or her purchasing and shopping needs.

Say our consumer decides to purchase a Toshiba. Having made the brand decision, she selects the store based on price, service, and convenience. In postpurchase evaluation, she will evaluate both the brand and the store. The two are closely related; satisfaction with the brand will lead to satisfaction with the store. However, some components of postpurchase evaluation are specific to the store; for example, a car buyer who is satisfied with the purchase but dissatisfied with the service the dealer offers.

Store Choice and Brand Choice

In the preceding example, our consumer selected the brand first and then the store. It is possible that a consumer might make a computer decision in the store (that is, store choice preceded brand choice).

Under what circumstances is store choice most likely to influence brand choice?

- *When store loyalty is high.* Consumers loyal to a particular department store are more likely to shop there first for desired items.
- *When brand loyalty is low.* Consumers with no strong loyalties to a particular brand are more likely to select the store first and make a brand decision within the store.
- *When brand information is inadequate.* Consumers who have little brand experience or information are more likely to rely on sales personnel for assistance. Brand choice is, therefore, more likely to be made in the store.

Hedonic versus Utilitarian Shopping Behavior

The distinction between hedonic and utilitarian consumption applies to shopping behavior. Typically, consumers view shopping as a necessary task to acquire goods. For the utilitarian shopper, shopping is not inherently pleasurable. It is simply a means to an end.

But for many, the shopping task is a pleasurable event. The thrill of finding a bargain or the satisfaction of beating someone else out to the last item in stock can be highly rewarding. Shopping expeditions with friends are regarded as a social experience for the hedonic shopper. Shopping also offers an opportunity to communicate with salespeople. Stores and shopping malls are viewed as gathering places for such social interaction. In France, local shops traditionally served as a gathering place for neighbors and tradespeople. In these cases, shopping serves a purpose beyond the selection of goods.

SUMMARY

The purpose of this chapter was to present a comprehensive model of complex decision making. Complex decision making occurs when consumers are involved with the product and go through an extensive decision process to arrive at a choice. Other types of decision processes are (1) limited decision making (decisions in low-involvement conditions); (2) brand loyalty (repetitive behavior in high-involvement conditions); and (3) inertia (repetitive behavior in low-involvement conditions).

To better understand the nature of complex decision making, consumer involvement with products and purchases was discussed. Two types of involvement are enduring (involvement with the product on a continuing basis) and situational (involvement with the product only during the purchase situation). Consumers are involved on an enduring basis if the product is important, has emotional appeal, and has badge value. Situational involvement is likely to occur when consumers see risk in purchasing the product.

Complex decision making not only requires an involved consumer, it also assumes that adequate information is available for a decision and that the consumer has the time and ability to process information extensively.

A model of complex decision making has several phases:

1. *Need arousal* initiates a decision process. Consumers are prompted to act by a disparity between their current situation and a desired goal. Such a disparity results in tension and a motivation to act. Several factors influence the consumer's current situation and desired goals—namely, the consumer's lifestyle, demographics, and personality characteristics, as well as environmental influences such as group norms and family needs.
2. *Consumer information processing* involves exposure to and perception of information from various sources. Information processing is selective; consumers choose information that is (1) most relevant to the benefits they seek and (2) likely to conform to their beliefs and attitudes. Processing of information involves a series of steps: exposure, attention, comprehension, retention in memory, and search for additional information.
3. In the process of *brand evaluation,* consumers evaluate the characteristics of various brands and choose the brand that is most likely to fulfill their desired benefits.
4. Consumers *purchase* the brand most likely to satisfy their desired benefits. In so doing, various instrumental actions are required such as selecting a store, determining when to purchase, and possibly obtaining financing.
5. Once consumers have made purchases, *postpurchase evaluation* occurs. If performance has met the consumers' expectations, they are likely to be satisfied with the product. If not, dissatisfaction will occur, reducing the probability that consumers will repurchase the same brand. In cases in which consumers had difficulty making up their minds, dissonance is likely. Dissonance, or postpurchase conflict, results from doubts about the decision. As dissonance is not a desirable state, consumers may seek to reduce it by ignoring negative information or by seeking positive information about the brand.

Central to the decision-making process is the consumption experience. Consumption determines the level of satisfaction with the product or service and influences future decision making. Two distinctions were drawn in understanding consumption: the difference between consuming products and services and the difference between consuming products for utilitarian and hedonic purposes. Since services are intangible and more variable, they are more difficult to evaluate. Consumers are more likely to be dissatisfied. As a result, marketers try to follow strategies to decrease variability and increase the tangibility of services.

Hedonic consumption is driven by emotional and pleasure-seeking criteria. Consumers consume products for what they mean rather than for what they can do. Examples are motorcycles, perfume, and clothing. Marketing strategies attempt to associate products with symbols that generate positive feelings for such products.

Although most of the chapter was devoted to brand decision making, we noted that consumers also make store decisions. At times, the store decision may determine brand choice. A model of store decision making is essentially the same as that for brands, except that consumers are evaluating store attributes and selecting stores according to shopping as well as purchasing needs.

The next chapter shifts the focus from complex decision making to habit.

QUESTIONS

1. In what ways does Saturn appeal to both utilitarian and emotional car-buying needs with its marketing strategy?
2. An auto manufacturer is trying to distinguish between consumers who are involved with cars and those who are not. What conditions would identify a consumer who is involved with cars? What are the strategic implications of these conditions?
3. The auto manufacturer further distinguishes between consumers who are involved with cars on an enduring basis and those involved on a situational basis. Cite an example of a consumer who is involved with cars on an enduring basis and one who is involved on a situational basis. What are the distinctions between the two types of involvement?
4. Use the model of complex decision making in this chapter to describe the steps in the decision-making process for the following cases:
   - A businessperson considers purchasing a new Picturephone for communication between branches of the firm.
   - A college student considers purchasing a laptop computer.
   - A consumer considers purchasing a headache remedy that is advertised as stronger and more effective.
5. What are the implications for marketing strategy based on your description of the decision-making process for each of the three cases in Question 4, particularly implications for (a) market segmentation, (b) advertising, (c) pricing, (d) distribution, and (e) development of new products?
6. Of what use might the model of complex decision making be to a marketing manager in the following situations?
   - Kellogg's introduces a new line of adult cereals.
   - General Motors introduces its new line of Saturn cars.
   - Procter & Gamble introduces an improved version of Pampers disposable diapers with better absorbency.
7. What differences in the decision-making process might exist for Rob and Linda Greene in the following situations?
   - They have never purchased a car before.
   - They are in a lower-income group.
   - They are buying a car for business purposes.
8. What are the distinctions between utilitarian and hedonic needs? What are the implications for marketing strategy of targeting consumers who purchase a car to fulfill hedonic versus utilitarian needs?
9. In some cases, consumers buy almost immediately after reaching a decision. In other cases, there might be a gap between intention and purchase. What are the possible reasons for such a delay? What are implications for advertising and selling strategies?
10. What types of products are consumers most likely to purchase because of their symbolism? Why?
11. Select a product category that consumers are more likely to purchase on a utilitarian basis and a product category that consumers are more likely to purchase on a hedonic basis.
    - What types of attributes are consumers likely to use in evaluating alternative brands for the utilitarian product? For the hedonic product?
    - What are the implications for advertising the utilitarian product? The hedonic product?
12. A large retailer of sports equipment in an urban area finds sales slipping. As a result, the retailer wishes to conduct a study to determine (a) how consumers decide on a store for sports equipment and (b) the image of the store relative to that of the competition. Specify how the model of store choice in Figure 3.8 might help in determining the required information.

RESEARCH ASSIGNMENTS

1. Log onto an Internet search engine (for example, http://www.yahoo.com) and search the word "automobile."
   - What types of sites are retrieved?
   - What is the difference between manufacturer and dealer sites?
   - How does the information presented vary among sites?

- Is there any way that dealer sites could be integrated into manufacturer sites (for example, http://www.gm.com)?
- How would you improve the communication to facilitate the complex decision-making process?

2. Select a product that is more utilitarian in nature (washing machine, refrigerator, vacuum cleaner). Conduct a focus group interview* with 6 to 10 consumers who bought the item in the last year and focus the discussion on how they decided on what brand to buy. Now select a product that is more hedonic in nature (perfume, designer clothes), conduct a focus group interview with consumers who bought the item in the last year (or less, depending on the product), and ask them how they decided on the brand.
   - What are the differences in the nature of information search, the attributes used for evaluation, and the way the brands were evaluated?
   - What are the implications of these differences for advertising strategy?
3. Select an electronics product that is likely to cost several hundred dollars or more (a video cassette recorder, compact disc player, or personal computer, for example). Conduct focus group interviews with consumers who have purchased the item within the past year or who are currently considering purchasing.
   - Describe the decision-making process for both the decision to buy the product and the particular brand to be purchased.
   - Does the decision-making process conform to the model in Figure 3.3?
   - What are the implications of the decision-making process for (a) market segmentation, (b) product positioning, and (c) advertising strategy?
4. Now select an electronics product that is likely to cost under $100 (portable headphones, telephone answering machine, calculator). Conduct in-depth interviews with consumers who have purchased the item within the past year or who are currently considering purchasing.
   - How does the decision-making process differ from that described in the first assignment?
   - What are the implications of the decision-making process for (a) market segmentation, (b) product positioning, and (c) advertising strategy?
5. Select a product category in which the choice of a store is particularly important (for example, clothing, furniture, rugs and carpets). Identify consumers who have bought an item in the category within the past six months. Conduct seven or eight in-depth interviews with the consumers to identify the process of store choice.
   - Describe the decision process.
   - Does the process of store choice conform to the model described in Figure 3.8?
   - What are the strategic implications of the decision process for the retailer?

*Many of the research assignments proposed in this text will involve conducting focus group interviews among a group of 6 to 10 consumers. The researcher does not ask specific questions; rather, he or she acts as a moderator or passive listener. The researcher may develop a list of areas to be covered in the discussion and may steer the conversation to these topics. (See Chapter 1 for a further description of focus group interviews.)

CONSUMER LEARNING, HABIT, AND BRAND LOYALTY

Chapter 4

THE REBIRTH OF BRAND LOYALTY: COKE IS IT, AND SO ARE MCDONALD'S, TIDE, AND INTEL

This chapter describes the opposite of complex decision making—habit. A consumer's prior satisfaction with a brand results in purchasing it on a routinized basis. For such purchases, the consumer finds little need to evaluate brand alternatives. Recognizing a need leads directly to a purchase. Therefore, habit is a way of ensuring satisfaction based on past experience and of simplifying decision making by reducing information search and brand evaluation.

Understanding habit requires understanding the principles of consumer learning because learning theory focuses on the conditions that produce consistent behavior over time. Such consistent behavior can be the result of brand loyalty or inertia. **Brand loyalty** is repeat buying because of commitment to a brand, whereas *inertia* is repeat buying without commitment. For unimportant brands, if a brand is reasonably satisfactory, a consumer may buy again because it is not worth the time and trouble to go through a decision process.

http://www.cocacola.com/

The strategic importance of brand loyalty is demonstrated by one of the leading brands in the world—Coke. Coca-Cola executives estimate that the name of their flagship brand is worth close to $100 billion, independent of all the manufacturing, bottling, and distribution facilities.[1] This figure represents the value of the brand in the consumer's mind—known as **brand equity.** How did Coke achieve this equity? First, the brand has been available on a widespread basis since the turn of the century, giving satisfied consumers a constant opportunity to buy again. Second, it uses symbols such as the hourglass-shaped bottle and the red and white can that resulted in consumers *learning* to associate these symbols with past brand satisfaction. Third, its constant advertising *reinforces* these positive associations. And fourth, by establishing such learning, reinforcement, and brand equity on a global basis, today Coke is considered an American icon.

The hue and cry that arose when Coca-Cola announced a change in the formula of its flagship brand in 1985 and its reversal in bringing back the original formula attests to the depth of commitment for a brand, even when it is typically purchased on a routine basis. Had the company insisted on the introduction of New Coke, for many satisfaction would have turned to dissatisfaction and reinforcement to extinction, that is, the elimination of the positive association between past experience and the brand.

Brand loyalty is not a constant in marketing. In the 1980s and early 1990s, many marketers thought brand loyalty was in permanent decline (see Strategic Applications box). Lower-priced private brands were making substantial inroads into the sales of national brands because many national brands were overpriced and because consumers were more price-sensitive as a result of steep recessions in the early 1980s and 1990s. But national brands are experiencing something of a renaissance because marketers recognize the consumer's desire for quality at reasonable prices. Many national brands lowered their prices to become more competitive with private brands and to better satisfy the consumer's need for value. Led by Procter & Gamble in the early 1990s, many packaged goods marketers have instituted a policy of everyday low prices (EDLP) for national brands to assure consumers that lower prices are permanent rather than just a temporary promotion. Leading brands in diverse categories such as McDonald's, Tide, and Levi have lowered prices, maintained quality, and seen their market shares rise. As a result, growth of private brands plateaued after 1992. These national brand manufacturers are also spending more on advertising to maintain brand equity.[2]

http://www.pg.com/

http://www.intel.com/

Even high-technology brands are developing substantial brand equity. Although consumers do not directly buy an Intel computer chip, Intel is still able to command loyalty through product quality and advertising awareness. Witness the positive association in consumers' minds between the brand and its advertising tagline, "Intel Inside" (see Exhibit 4.1). In all these cases, brand loyalty is back as a result of price and advertising appeals to a value-driven consumer.

In this chapter, we elaborate on many of the terms used above: learning, habit, reinforcement, extinction, and brand loyalty. We first describe learning

▶EXHIBIT 4.1
Establishing brand equity for a high-technology product

as a process leading to repetitive behavior. Then, we describe habit and consider two possible outcomes of habitual purchase behavior: brand loyalty and inertia.

✦ CONSUMER LEARNING

Consumers learn from past experience, and their future behavior is conditioned by such learning. In fact, **learning** can be defined as a change in behavior occurring as a result of past experience. As consumers gain experience in purchasing and consuming products, they learn not only what brands they like and do not like, but also the features they like most in particular brands. They then adjust their future behavior based on past experience. After wearing the brand repeatedly, a consumer might determine that a pair of Reebok running

http://www.reebok.com/

shoes is the most comfortable and provides the best support. Continued satisfaction with the brand leads this consumer to buy Reeboks every time he needs new athletic shoes. Thus, continued satisfaction reinforces past experience and increases the probability that the consumer will buy the same brand next time.

There are two schools of thought in understanding the process of consumer learning: the behaviorist and the cognitive. The **behaviorist school** is concerned with observing changes in an individual's responses as a result of exposure to stimuli. Behaviorist psychologists have developed two types of learning theories: classical conditioning and instrumental conditioning. Classical conditioning views behavior as the result of a close association (contiguity) between a primary stimulus (social success) and a secondary stimulus (a brand of toothpaste, deodorant, or soap). Instrumental conditioning views behavior as a function of the consumer's assessment of the degree to which purchase behavior leads to satisfaction. Satisfaction leads to reinforcement and to an increase in the probability of repurchasing.

The **cognitive school** views learning as problem solving and focuses on changes in the consumer's psychological set (the consumer's attitudes and desired benefits) as a result of learning. In this respect, the cognitive school more closely describes learning within a framework of complex decision making. However, the concepts are relevant to habit since complex decision making may lead to routinized purchases when the consumer is satisfied with the brand and repurchases it over a period of time.

Figure 4.1 illustrates the cognitive and the behaviorist schools of learning and, within the behaviorist school, classical and instrumental conditioning. These three theories of learning will be considered next.[3]

►FIGURE 4.1
Types of learning theories

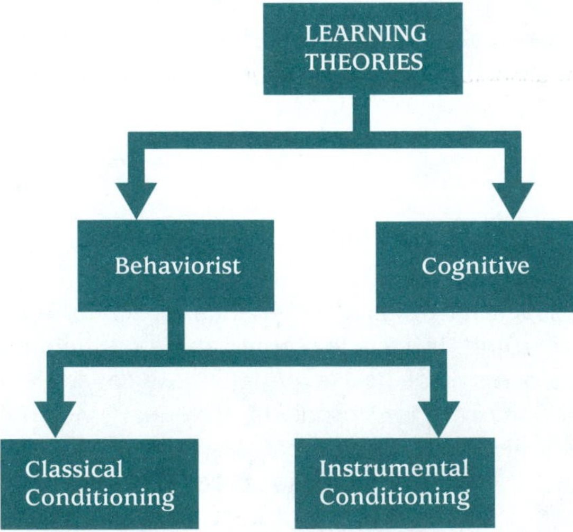

Classical Conditioning

In **classical conditioning,** a secondary stimulus is paired with a primary stimulus that already elicits a particular response. As a result of this pairing, an association is formed. Eventually, the secondary stimulus will elicit the same reaction as the primary stimulus. An effective advertising campaign may link a product to a stimulus that evokes a positive feeling. A good example is one of the most successful and longest-running advertising campaigns in history, the Marlboro cowboy campaign. Although some might rightfully object to cigarette advertising, there is no denying that the campaign is highly effective. The basis for the Marlboro cowboy campaign was the fact that many people viewed a cowboy as conveying strength, masculinity, and quiet security. The cowboy is the **primary** or **unconditioned stimulus.** The positive feeling that the cowboy evokes (strength, masculinity) is the **unconditioned response.**

Consumers associate Marlboro cigarettes with the cowboy through (1) repetitive advertising and (2) contiguity between the unconditioned and conditioned stimulus (cowboy always linked to Marlboro). The product then becomes a **secondary** or **conditioned stimulus** because it will evoke the same positive feeling as does the cowboy. The Marlboro campaign was successful because of this positive link. As a result, the cowboy influenced smokers to buy Marlboro and reminded Marlboro smokers to repurchase. The brand purchase is the **conditioned response.**

Theories of classical conditioning[4] are reflected in Pavlov's famous experiments.[5] Pavlov reasoned that because his dogs salivated (unconditioned response) at the sight of food (unconditioned stimulus), a neutral stimulus such as a bell could also cause the dogs to salivate if it was closely associated with the unconditioned stimulus (food). To test his theory, Pavlov rang a bell when presenting food to the dogs. After a number of trials, the dogs learned the connection between bell and food; and when they heard the bell (conditioned stimulus) even in the absence of food, they salivated (conditioned response).

These associations are represented at the top of Figure 4.2. The association between the conditioned stimulus and the unconditioned stimulus is represented as a dotted arrow because it is a learned association. The association between the conditioned stimulus and the conditioned response is also learned. The two key concepts are repetition and contiguity. To establish a conditioned response, the conditioned stimulus must be frequently repeated in close contiguity to the unconditioned stimulus.

Classical conditioning can be applied to marketing in an effort to associate a product with a positive stimulus. For example, Miller Lite Beer is frequently advertised during exciting sports events. Because of the repetitive pairing of the product with sports events, the excitement the sports event produces may eventually carry over to Miller Lite. This association may influence people to buy the brand. Similarly, companies frequently use celebrities who have some legitimate link with the product as spokespersons to es-

FIGURE 4.2
Summary of three learning theories
Source: Reprinted with the permission of Macmillan College Publishing Company from *Consumer Behavior and the Practice of Marketing,* 3/e by Kenneth E. Runyon and David W. Stewart. Copyright © 1987 by Macmillan College Publishing Company, Inc.

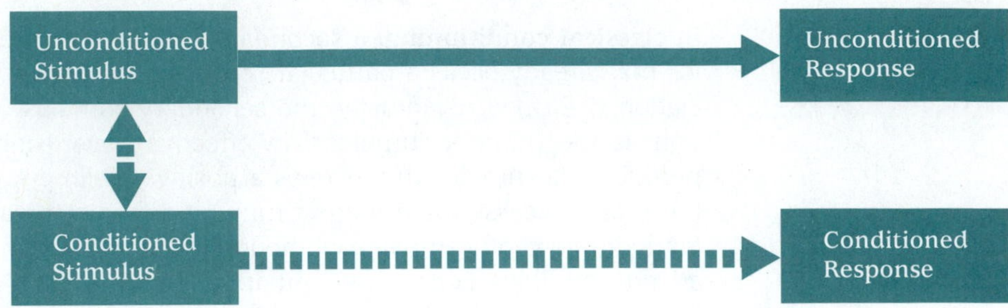

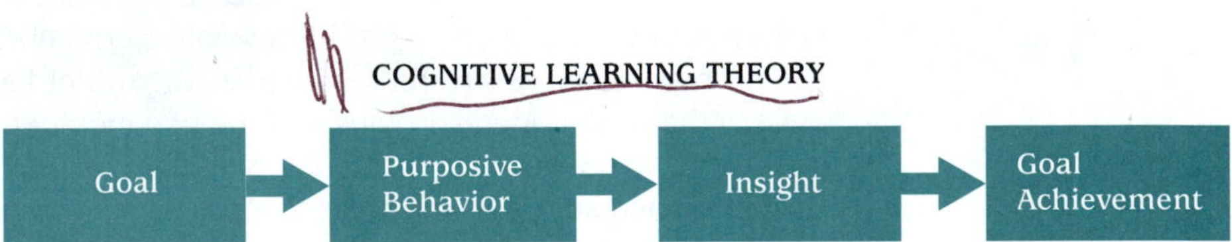

http://www.nike.com/

tablish positive associations—for example, Andre Agassi for Nike apparel (see Exhibit 4.2).

Associative Learning: Beyond Pavlov's Dogs

When consumers establish a link between an unconditioned and conditioned stimulus, they are engaging in learning through association. If we take Pavlov's

▶EXHIBIT 4.2
Using a spokesperson to establish a positive link with the product

experiments as our frame of reference, such *associative learning* is based on contiguity between the unconditioned and conditioned stimulus and requires no thought. But consumers rarely act on such a mindless basis. They go through a thought process in linking a cowboy to Marlboro or a doughboy to Pillsbury. This link is stronger if consumers recognize that it is associated with their needs. Therefore, contiguity must be coupled with relevance or need recognition if consumers are to establish a strong connection between an unconditioned and conditioned stimulus.

A study by Janisewski and Warlop found that consumers considered the link between an unconditioned and conditioned stimulus informative and that such a link often leads to the search for additional information.[6] Sports enthusiasts might value Miller Lite more highly compared to other beers because of its association with sports events in advertising, and they might pay more attention to ads for Miller Lite as a result. Such associative learning is not mindless; it is consciously developed.

As a result, it is not enough for marketers to rely on repetitive advertising showing the association between the unconditioned and conditioned stimulus. They must do so in some meaningful way that relates to consumer needs, whether it is the need for masculinity associated with the cowboy or the need for a vicarious identification with a winning team associated with Miller Lite.

Requirements for Utilizing Classical Conditioning

If advertisers are to use classical conditioning concepts to influence consumers, several conditions must occur. McSweeney and Bierley cite four conditions:[7]

1. *There should be no other stimuli that could overshadow the unconditioned stimulus.* For example, assume the Marlboro cowboy was always portrayed on a white horse. It is possible the white horse might have overshadowed the cowboy as a stimulus, thus weakening the association between the cowboy and the product. This is known as the **overshadowing effect.** The overshadowing effect purposefully occurs in advertising Marlboro cigarettes in Hong Kong, where the cowboy is shown in a white hat on a white horse to create an association with the positive cultural significance of the color white in the Far East.
2. *Unconditioned stimuli should have no previous associations to other brands or product categories.* Assume a beer company decides to use a cowboy in its advertising to convey a macho image to its target group. The campaign would be ineffective because of the association already established by the Marlboro cowboy. This is referred to as the **blocking effect.**
3. *The unconditioned stimulus should not be overly familiar and should be presented alone.* Consumers could become oversaturated with certain stimuli that frequently appear in the mass media (known as a **preexposure effect**). Such stimuli are unlikely to be effective as the unconditioned stimulus. For example, the tuxedo has been shown so often as a symbol of luxury that it has probably lost its effectiveness. Similarly, Michael Jordan appearing as a spokesperson for Nike may wear thin as a result of his frequent exposure. He has also served as a spokesperson for McDonald's, Hanes, Wheaties, and Gatorade, and a new Michael Jordan cologne introduced by Bijan Fragrances (see Exhibit 4.3).
4. *Classical conditioning is more effective when the conditioned stimulus is new.* Consumers have established associations for well-known products. Given Pillsbury's strong association with the doughboy, it would be difficult for the company to link its products with a new unconditioned stimulus. When Philip Morris introduced the Marlboro cowboy, it repositioned the brand as a new product entry. First introduced in the 1920s as an elite cigarette aimed at women smokers, Marlboro had a rose tip so the red imprint of women's lipstick would not show;

http://www.pillsbury.com/

EXHIBIT 4.3
An example of the preexposure effect

its advertising slogan was "Mild as May." Performance was lackluster.[8] In repositioning the brand, Philip Morris wanted to make a clean break with these past associations.

Additional support for the greater effectiveness of new stimuli comes from research by Shimp, Stuart, and Engle. They associated colas with various background scenes and found that conditioning was strongest for relatively unknown cola brands with names like Elf, Cragmont, and Target. When it came to Pepsi and Coke, they "are so well-known that little opportunity remains for additional learning."[9]

Strategic Applications of Classical Conditioning

Advertisers accepted classical conditioning concepts of repetition and contiguity on a more widespread basis before 1950. At that time, advertisers frequently used jingles and themes in radio commercials. The advent of television lent a new dimension to advertising by providing more variability through the video component. In addition, a more consumer-oriented approach to advertising resulted in greater variation as advertisements were directed to particular consumer segments. A mass advertising approach based on a single repeated theme was not as viable a strategy. As a result, advertisers rarely attempt to establish associations solely through repetition.

The shift in advertising emphasis away from classical conditioning also implied a shift toward principles of cognitive learning. Measures of recall are still used in evaluating ads to determine whether basic brand associations have been established. However, measures of attitude change (changes in brand beliefs, preferences, and intention as a result of advertising) are also used as criteria for advertising effectiveness. This change means that criteria of effectiveness have shifted from measures of association (such as recall) to measures of change in the consumer's psychological set (for example, brand perceptions and attitude change).

Today, advertisers still recognize the importance of principles of classical conditioning and attempt to associate products with positive symbols and images. One such application is the recent swing back to using past advertising themes and symbols that were so successfully bonded to the product that consumers still associate the brand with the theme. Examples of past campaigns that have been brought back are Timex ("It takes a lickin' and keeps on tickin'"); Memorex tapes ("Is it live or is it Memorex?"); Campbell's Soup ("Mmm, Mmm, Good!") (see Exhibit 4.4); and Wonder Bread ("Helps build strong bodies twelve ways").[10]

http://www.timex.com/

http://www.cambellsoup.com/

Instrumental Conditioning

Instrumental conditioning also requires the development of a link between a stimulus and a response. However, the individual determines the response that

▶**EXHIBIT 4.4**
An example of classical conditioning: using oldies but goodies

provides the greatest satisfaction. That is, no previous stimulus-response connection is required; response is within the conscious control of the individual. In classical conditioning, the unconditioned stimulus is already linked to a response and response is more reflexive. Instrumental conditioning can best be illustrated by a hypothetical experiment. Suppose Pavlov had provided his dogs with two levers instead of one. When pushed, one lever would produce food; the other, a shock. The dogs would have quickly learned to press the lever that produced food and to avoid the lever that produced a shock. Learning occurs because the same act is repeatedly rewarded or reinforced.

The foremost proponent of instrumental conditioning was B. F. Skinner. In Skinner's experiments, the subject was free to act in a variety of ways.[11] The consequences of the act (degree of satisfaction or dissatisfaction) will influence future behavior. These associations are summarized in the middle of Figure 4.2. Behavior results in an evaluation of degree of reward or punishment obtained from past behavior. Reward will increase the probability of repeating the behavior; punishment will decrease that probability.

Antismoking commercials rely on principles of instrumental conditioning by linking smoking to a shortened life span. This link, which is meant to create avoidance, would be analogous to the lever producing an electric shock. In contrast, Philip Morris was relying on principles of classical conditioning by trying to condition smokers' responses based on the positive association of the cowboy with the product.

Reinforcement

Instrumental conditioning comes closer than classical conditioning to describing the formation of habit in consumer purchasing. The consumer has control over his or her purchasing behavior. Continuous **reinforcement** (repeated satisfaction) resulting from product usage increases the probability that the consumer will purchase the same brand. Initially, the consumer undergoes a decision process; but with continuous reinforcement, the probability of buying the same brand increases until the consumer establishes a habit and buying is routinized.

The role of reinforcement in producing habit is illustrated in a study by Bennett and Mandel.[12] They asked a sample of recent car buyers to recall the cars they had purchased in the past and to determine the amount of information seeking in their most recent purchase. Although Bennett and Mandel found that information seeking did not decrease with the number of car purchases made in the past, it did decrease if the consumer purchased the same car repeatedly. In other words, past experience alone will not reduce information seeking. Rather, it is reduced only by past experience that leads to satisfaction and repeat purchase of the same brand. Therefore, a necessary condition for the formation of habit is reinforcement of past purchase behavior.

The purchase of a car or other high-priced item by habit may seem questionable. We might assume that consumers would want to maximize value and reduce risk through extensive information search and brand evaluation. But in a study of French car buyers, Lapersonne et al. found that 17 percent of consumers engaged in little or no search behavior and considered only their current make for purchase. The researchers concluded that these buyers were so satisfied with their current model and dealer that the value of collecting additional information and considering other brands was small.[13]

http://www.saturncars.com/

Stimuli other than the product can also be positive reinforcers. In the Lapersonne study, French consumers strongly identified the dealer as well as the car as a basis for satisfaction. French consumers tend to have stronger personal relationships with local retailers. But as we saw in the last chapter, Saturn owners experienced the same positive reinforcement from dealers. Other reinforcers may be a special sale on the consumer's regular brand, a new, improved version of it; or positive word-of-mouth communication about the brand from friends and relatives.

Extinction and Forgetting

Theories of instrumental conditioning also help us understand the events that may lead a consumer to cease buying by habit. If a consumer is no longer satisfied with the product, a process of **extinction**—that is, the elimination of the link between stimulus and expected reward—takes place. Extinction leads to a rapid decrease in the probability that the consumer will repurchase the same brand. Successful antismoking commercials will create extinction by elimi-

STRATEGIC APPLICATIONS OF CONSUMER BEHAVIOR

▶ The Marlboro Cowboy: Still Riding Tall in the Saddle?

It was Friday, April 2, 1993, and Philip Morris had just announced a steep price cut for its flagship brand, Marlboro. The reaction on Wall Street was immediate, an almost 15-point drop in Philip Morris's stock price, representing a loss of $13 billion in market value. In the coming week, other producers of packaged goods would experience a similar drop in their stock prices—PepsiCo, Coca-Cola, P&G, Gillette.

What happened? Investors were reacting to a change in consumer buying habits that had been building for a decade. The 1991–1992 recession hit the bastion of brand loyalty—the middle class—hardest. In moving from the free-spending 1980s into the 1990s, this group became more price- and value-conscious. Higher-priced national brands were out. Lower-priced private brands (that is, brands sponsored by retailers or wholesalers) and lower-priced manufacturers' brands were in because they were often of equal quality to the national brands. (In a 1993 survey, 50 percent of consumers said private brands equalled national brands in quality, up from 31 percent in 1985.)

Marlboro was particularly hard hit by the shift. The brand lost five share points from 1989 to 1993, representing a loss of close to $2 billion a year in sales. Lower-priced brands such as Doral, Viceroy, and Bucks were stealing Marlboro loyalists in droves because these brands cost as much as a dollar a pack less. By 1993, 39 percent of cigarette sales were going to private brands.

Once the company decided to satisfy the consumer's greater price sensitivity, the Marlboro cowboy began to be downplayed. Philip Morris began relying more on coupons, price promotions, and special offers than on advertising to sell Marlboro. As one analyst said, "Today a campaign [such as the Marlboro cowboy] won't have much impact on puffers who want to snag a bargain" [*The Wall Street Journal* (June 23, 1992), p. B1.]

The prevailing view was that brand equity was on the skids, but skeptics were downplaying its power. All it took was a price decrease to increase Marlboro's market share by 5 percent, back to where it was in 1989. Consumers recognized the value of national brands once prices were decreased.

Today, the Marlboro cowboy isn't what he used to be. Philip Morris's price promotions are a more dominant part of its marketing strategy. And the company recognizes that, occasionally, it has to get the cowboy out of his saddle. Recent ads have him riding a chopper, and in Japan boarding the bullet train rather than a horse.

Philip Morris is not dispensing with the image of the cowboy; it is still dominant in its advertising. But the result of the consumers' value orientation in the 1990s is a clear weakening of the power of the Marlboro cowboy. The conditioning effect has been weakened. The company realizes that if it is to appeal to value-oriented consumers, the Marlboro cowboy's days in the saddle may be numbered.

Sources: "Whoa Horse," *The New York Times* (March 21, 1995), p. D5; "Up in Smoke," *Adweek* (June 21, 1993), pp. 24–32; "Brands on the Run," *Business Week* (April 19, 1993), pp. 26–28; "Marlboro's 2-Fisted Pitch," *The New York Times* (April 6, 1993), pp. D1, D22; and "More Shoppers Bypass Big-Name Brands and Steer Carts to Private-Label Products," *The Wall Street Journal* (October 20, 1992), pp. B1, B5.

nating the link between a cigarette and the pleasure of smoking (see Exhibit 4.5).

Forgetting differs from extinction. **Forgetting** occurs when the stimulus is no longer repeated or perceived. If a product is not used or if its advertising is discontinued, consumers may forget that product. At the turn of the century, Sapolio soap was on a par with Ivory as a leading brand. When the company decided that Sapolio was so well known that a reduction in advertising was warranted, both the company and the product began their demise. In this case, extinction did not occur because the brand still satisfied consumers. Rather, the company's action resulted in forgetting and a long-term decline in sales. Another cause of forgetting is competitive advertising, which causes interference with receipt of the message. The consumer may become confused by advertising clutter, and the link between stimulus and reward weakens.

Marketers can combat forgetting by repetition. By simply maintaining the level of advertising expenditures relative to competition, a company can generally avoid any serious forgetting on the consumer's part. However, repetition in itself is of limited use because showing the same ad again and again may merely irritate the consumer. It is more important to avoid extinction since lack of sufficient reward can mean the quick end of any brand. The most important method of avoiding extinction is to deliver sufficient benefits to a defined target segment.

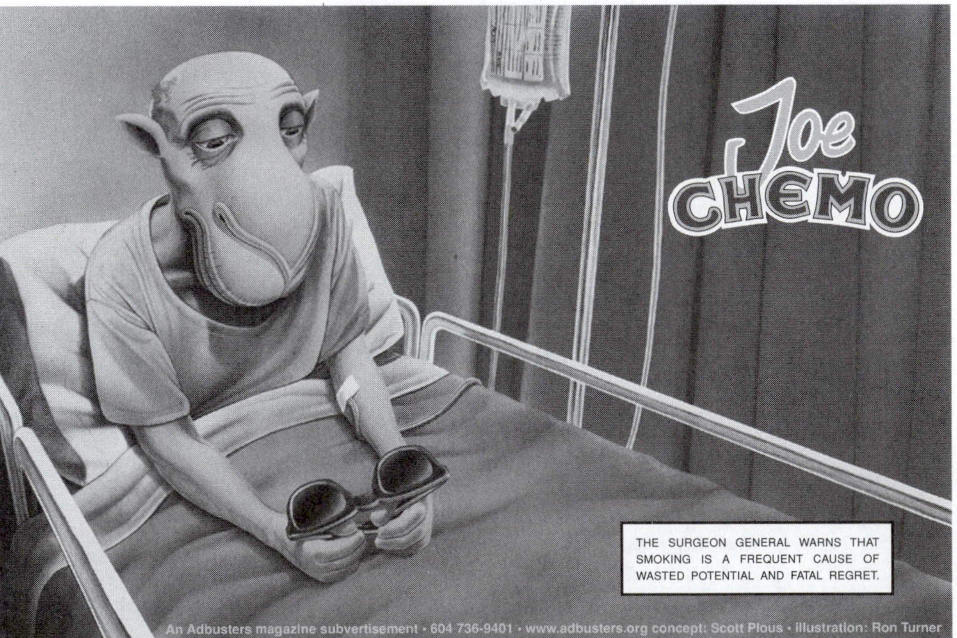

EXHIBIT 4.5
An attempt to extinguish the link between cigarettes and pleasure

Figure 4.3 presents learning curves that reflect processes of reinforcement, extinction, and forgetting as related to advertising exposure. Reinforcement occurs if repetitive exposures to an ad campaign increase the probability of repurchase. Extinction quickly decreases that probability because of a negative stimulus, even if the consumer continues to see the ad campaign for the product. Forgetting results in a longer-term decline in the probability of repurchase due to a decrease in advertising frequency.

An unforeseen potential for extinction occurred in 1990 when Perrier found traces of benzene, a possible carcinogen, in its bottled water. The company recalled its inventory (representing 72 million bottles in the United States) and immediately launched a $25 million marketing campaign to avoid product extinction and to reestablish the product's credibility. The tag line "Perrier. Worth waiting for" was meant to reassure loyal users that the link between the product and customer satisfaction would be maintained once the product returned.[14]

http://www.kraftfoods.com/

http://www.nabisco.com/

The importance of the effects of forgetting is illustrated by an antitrust action against Kraft Foods, owners of Post cereals, for its acquisition of Nabisco Shredded Wheat in 1994. The government argued that the acquisition would extinguish the link between Nabisco and Shredded Wheat, thus destroying the brand's equity and lessening competition in the cereal market. Kraft (which was allowed to use the Nabisco and Post name on Shredded Wheat until 1997 when it became Post only) successfully argued that consumers would be on the forgetting rather than the extinction portion of the curve in Figure 4.3. Kraft won

FIGURE 4.3 Reinforcement, extinction, and forgetting

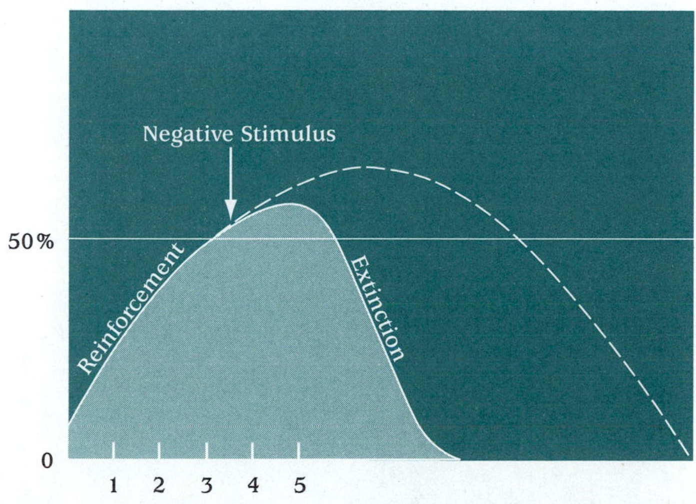

its case because it convinced the court that it would be many years before consumers stopped associating Shredded Wheat with Nabisco (see Exhibit 4.6).

http://www.ftc.gov/

Another application of the principle of forgetting is the Federal Trade Commission's decision to force Listerine to undertake corrective advertising to counter its long-advertised claim that its mouthwash helped stop colds. The FTC could have merely asked Listerine to stop making the claim, but it chose corrective advertising because of the cumulative effects of past reinforcement. As the campaign had run for many years, consumers' memories of it would die slowly, and positive association between stimulus and response would continue. In other words, the consumer would be on the forgetting portion of the curve. Corrective advertising, however, would force extinction between the stimulus and response. As *Ad Age* reported, "The FTC said it believed it had ample evidence to demonstrate that the effects of Listerine advertising will carry over into future consumer buying decisions unless corrective advertising is implemented."[15]

Applications of Instrumental Conditioning to Marketing

Instrumental conditioning is important in marketing because the theory focuses on reinforcement. Quite simply, consumers will repurchase when they are satisfied. Therefore, the objective of all marketing strategy should be to reinforce the consumer's purchase through product satisfaction. This thesis is the very basis of the marketing concept: develop marketing strategies that deliver known consumer benefits. Only in this manner can a brand achieve repeat purchases and a core of loyal users.

Principles of instrumental conditioning can be applied to advertising and sales promotional strategy. The role of advertising is to increase consumers' expectation of reinforcement. This can be done by communicating product bene-

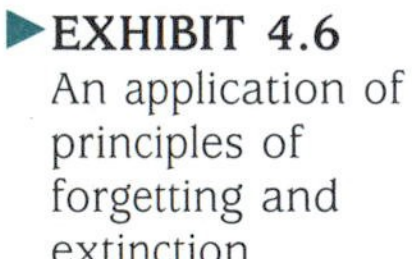

EXHIBIT 4.6
An application of principles of forgetting and extinction

fits to convince consumers that they will be satisfied if they buy the product. The role of sales promotion is to create an initial inducement to try the product by offering free samples, coupons, or price deals. If the product is satisfactory, many consumers will continue to buy even if the incentives are withdrawn. Coupons and price deals should be withdrawn gradually, however.[16] These strategies can be successful only if the product is a source of satisfaction and reinforcement. Advertising and price inducements cannot support a poor product for very long.

Cognitive Learning

Cognitive psychology views learning as a problem-solving process rather than as the development of connections between stimulus and response. Cognitive learning for consumers is a process of perceiving stimuli, associating stimuli to needs, evaluating alternative brands, and assessing whether products meet expectations. Learning is equated to a process of complex decision making because of the emphasis on problem solving.

Cognitive Learning Theory

Markin compares the cognitive orientation to learning with the behaviorist orientation:

> The behaviorist is inclined to ask, "What has the subject learned to do?" The cognitivist, on the other hand, would be inclined to ask, "How has the subject learned to perceive the situation?" The cognitivist is interested in examining a learning situation in terms of such factors as motivation, the perceived goals, the overall nature of the situation, and the beliefs, values, and personality of the subject—in short, the entire range of the subject's psychological field. The cognitivist, as opposed to the behaviorist, contends that consumers do not respond simply to stimuli but instead act on beliefs, express attitudes, and strive toward goals.[17]

In other words, cognitive theory emphasizes the thought process involved in consumer learning. Classical and instrumental conditioning emphasize the results based on the stimulus associations.

Cognitive learning theory is an outgrowth of Kohler's experiments on apes conducted in the early 1920s.[18] In one experiment, Kohler placed a chimpanzee in a cage with several boxes, and bananas were hung from the roof. After trying to reach the food and failing, the chimp solved the problem by placing a box under the bananas. Learning was not a result of contiguity between stimulus and response or reinforcement; it was the result of insight. The cognitive approach to learning is presented at the bottom of Figure 4.2 as recognition of a goal, purposive behavior to achieve the goal, insight as to a solution, and goal achievement. Reinforcement is a recognized part of cognitive learning as there must be an awareness of goal achievement for learning to take place. However, the nature of the goal is understood from the beginning, and the reward (such as eating the bananas) is anticipated. In instrumental conditioning, the reward is not apparent until after behavior takes place.

Vicarious Learning

http://www.nfl.com/

http://www.nhl.com/

A type of cognitive learning that has important marketing applications is **vicarious (observational) learning.** Through vicarious learning, people imitate the behavior of others as a result of observing them. To be effective, the consumer should have the ability to perform the behavior and it should appear useful to him or her. Starter jackets are officially licensed by the National Football and Hockey Leagues. Starter advertises its jackets by showing sports stars wearing them. A sports enthusiast can emulate the behavior of a Charles Barkley, for example, by wearing a Phoenix Suns jacket made by Starter.

Marketers frequently show the positive results of using their products; for example, attractive models are shown using cosmetics or perfumes that result in social success or wearing clothes that result in business success. Sometimes typical consumers are portrayed providing testimonials for the product as in Saturn car ads. In each case, the consumer learns by associating the actions of others to some positive consequence and emulating those actions.

In these examples, the consumer sees the positive consequences of imitating the behavior of others. The other side of the coin is seeing the negative consequences of another's actions and avoiding them. The social embarrassment of not using a deodorant or a denture adhesive stimulates negative vicarious learning.

Marketing Applications of Cognitive Learning

Cognitive learning is relevant in understanding the process of consumer decision making. The model of complex decision making in Chapter 3 describes a process of cognitive learning. Consumers recognize a need, evaluate alternatives to meet that need (purposive behavior in Figure 4.2), select the product they believe will most likely satisfy them (insight), and then evaluate the degree to which the product meets the need (goal achievement).

A study of the purchasing patterns of recent residents of a community reflects a process of cognitive learning. Andreasen and Durkson studied the purchasing patterns of three groups of households selected according to the time they had been living in the Philadelphia area: less than three months, one and a half to two years, and three years or more.[19] The researchers believed there would be little difference among the three groups for national brands. However, for local brands, they predicted that the longer a family lived in the area, the closer brand awareness and purchasing would be to those of established residents. Results confirmed their hypothesis. The families living in the area one and a half to two years were closer to the purchase patterns of the established residents than were families living in the area three months or less.

CONSUMER BEHAVIOR AND THE NEW TECHNOLOGIES

► Learning on the Internet: Purposeful or Incidental?

Cognitive learning is particularly important in understanding the adoption process for an innovation. Consumers learn of innovations from advertising, friends and relatives, and impartial sources such as *Consumer Reports* magazine. To consider a new product, the consumer goes through a series of cognitive stages—awareness, interest, evaluation, and, if possible, trial—before deciding whether to adopt the product. The current adoption of Internet access services is an example. Widespread availability of on-line services such as Netscape and America Online has spurred Internet usage, with 10 million subscribers to on-line services in 1995.

Trial is a key component of adoption of Internet services. Many current Internet users are accepting free trial offers to assess usefulness. A process of cognitive learning is taking place through such trial in millions of homes. (With 50 million households having home computers, the base for future growth is tremendous.) One study found that in just seven months, from August 1995 to March 1996, the proportion of consumers accessing the Internet jumped by one-third. But the same study also found that 20 percent of users did not maintain Internet access.

Learning on the Internet is taking place in two ways. Browsing is one mode of learning by discovering Web sites at random. But such learning is largely *incidental* and discovery often serendipitous. The key issue is whether learning on the Internet will become more *purposeful.* That is, will users learn to go directly to Web sites of interest with a minimum of effort? Loss of current subscribers is probably due to discouraging results from incidental rather than purposeful learning. Many subscribers or temporary triers decided that the Internet is simply not worth the time and money. Internet access is sometimes slow, search processes cumbersome, and the amount of information provided disappointing. That is why purposeful rather than incidental learning is more likely to fuel future expansion.

Purposeful learning is also more likely to lead to a diffusion process that spreads knowledge about an innovation across groups. Such a diffusion process is necessary if an innovation is to be adopted on a widespread basis. The Internet lends itself to the diffusion of information since users can chat with other users and provide information on Web sites. More importantly, the Internet user base will expand as users communicate with nonusers and demonstrate access and usefulness.

Marketers have a keen interest in encouraging more purposeful learning and a diffusion process since many are beginning to advertise on Web sites to encourage consumer interaction.

Source: "Follow-Up Survey Reports Growth in Internet Users," *The New York Times* (August 14, 1996), p. D2.

Andreasen and Durkson identified three learning tasks in a new market environment: (1) brand identification, (2) brand evaluation, and (3) establishment of regular behavioral patterns with respect to the evaluated brands. This perspective clearly reflects a cognitive orientation to learning.

Relevance of the Cognitive versus Behaviorist Perspective

It is apparent that the cognitive and behaviorist approaches to learning are very different. Therefore, it is reasonable to ask in what marketing situations one is more likely to be relevant than the other.

As the behaviorist approach places little emphasis on thought processes and consumer attitudes, it might be most relevant when the consumer's cognitive activity is minimal. As we will see in the next chapter, this is most likely to occur when the consumer is not involved with the product. Taking an instrumental conditioning perspective, consumers in a passive, uninvolved state may be more receptive to buying what they purchased before as long as it is reasonably satisfactory. Perhaps if they spent more time searching for information on soap, toothpaste, or paper towels, they might find a better brand. However, for many products, it is simply not worth the effort. Positive reinforcement produces a satisfactory but by no means optimal choice.

Principles of classical conditioning can also be applied to low-involvement purchasing behavior. According to Allen and Madden, when the consumer is in a passive state, it is easier to establish a link between a product and a positive stimulus.[20] For example, a brand of toothpaste might be linked to a nice smile or a brand of disposable diapers to a contented baby, with little thought on the part of the consumer. If the link is repeated frequently enough, the consumer may see the brand in the store and buy it based on these positive associations.

Cognitive learning theory is more relevant for important and involving products. In these cases, a consumer's problem solving takes place through a process of information search and brand evaluation. Goal achievement through purposive behavior is more descriptive of decisions for buying cars, clothing, or furniture than those for buying toothpaste, paper towels, or detergents.

✦HABIT

Habit can be defined as repetitive behavior resulting in a limitation or absence of (1) information seeking and (2) evaluation of alternative choices. Learning leads to habitual purchasing behavior if the consumer is satisfied with the brand over time. After repetitive purchases, the consumer will buy the brand again with little information seeking or brand evaluation. Such an absence of cognitive activity can also be described as *routinized decision making* to distinguish it from the more extensive information processing in complex decision making.

In this section, we consider the nature of habit or routinized decision making. We then consider brand loyalty as a likely result of habitual purchasing behavior.

A Model of Habitual Purchasing Behavior

A model showing the process of habitual purchasing behavior is presented in Figure 4.4. The consumer has settled on a regular brand, for example, Coca-Cola Classic (hereafter, Coke), based on past experience and has become a loyal purchaser. Need arousal may occur simply because the consumer is out of stock or may be due to a simple stimulus such as thirst.

Information processing is limited or nonexistent. That is, recognition of a need is likely to lead directly to an intention to buy. Being out of the brand may be sufficient reason to add Coke to the shopping list, or perhaps the loyal consumer will be reminded by seeing Coke on the store shelf. The consumer evaluates the brand after purchase and expects to receive the same satisfaction from the brand as experienced previously. This is very likely since prepackaged products generally ensure standardization. Continued satisfaction results in a high probability that the consumer will repurchase the brand.

However, the possibility exists that the product will not meet the consumer's expectations, resulting in extinction of the link between brand usage and positive rewards. For example, the consumer may find a box of cereal is half empty

FIGURE 4.4 A model of habitual purchasing behavior

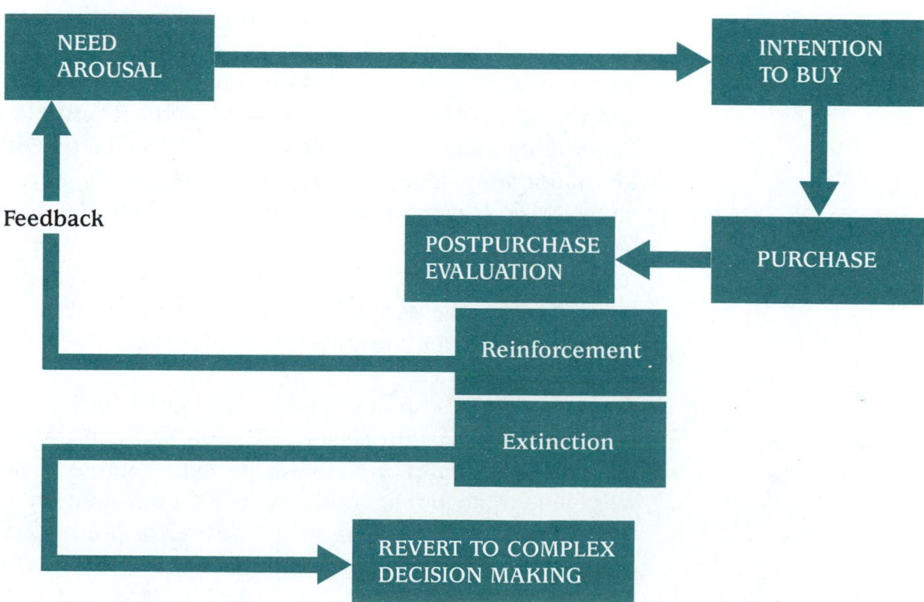

when purchased or may not like the taste of a reformulation of a brand of toothpaste. As a result, the consumer considers alternative brands, initiating a process of decision making.

Other factors besides dissatisfaction may cause extinction and a change from habit to complex decision making. For instance, a new product comes on the market; the consumer becomes aware of it and considers purchasing. Information search and brand evaluation result. In another case, additional information may cause a change in needs and may result in decision making. Information on the negative effects of smoking might cause a smoker to reassess the favored brand of cigarettes.

Also, boredom with a brand may prompt the consumer to look for something new. Howard and Sheth state that at times consumers get tired of buying by habit: "The buyer, after attaining routinization of his decision process [habit], may find himself in too simple a situation. He is likely to feel monotony or boredom associated with such repetitive decision making. . . . He feels a need to complicate his buying situation by considering new brands."[21] The result, once again, is a move away from habit to more complex decision making.

Finally, extinction may result because of constraints on purchasing the same brand. For example, if the store was out of the preferred brand, the consumer then considers other brands and finds a preferred alternative. There may also be a change in price. If the price of a less-preferred brand is reduced or that of the regular is brand increased, the consumer may consider other alternatives.

Habit and Information Seeking

Several studies have examined the relationship between habit and information seeking. Newman and Werbel evaluated habitual purchasing according to information sought and classified purchases as (1) habit, (2) approaching habit, and (3) decision making.[22] They used this scheme to analyze the purchase of major appliances. One would assume the incidence of habit would be very low for major appliances as they are infrequently purchased and carry high financial risk. Newman and Werbel found that 15 percent of the purchases could be characterized as habit and another 12 percent as approaching habit. Therefore, over one-fourth of the purchases of major appliances are routinized despite the potential risks. Interestingly, this figure is close to the 17 percent of French car buyers found to have purchased based on habit in the study cited earlier.

A study by Lehmann, Moore, and Elrod further illustrates the link between habit and information seeking. They asked consumers to choose five different types of bread over a six-week period.[23] Before making a choice, consumers were able to acquire as much or as little information as they desired. The study found a decline over time in the desire for information. In fact, for a substantial number of respondents, choice became so routinized that they selected no information at all.

Functions of Habit

Purchasing by habit provides two important benefits to the consumer. First, it reduces risk; second, it facilitates decision making. When consumers are highly involved with the product, habit is a means of reducing purchase risk. Buying the same brand again and again reduces the risk of product failure and financial loss for important purchases. Frequently, when information is limited, consumers buy the most popular brand as the safest choice. Several studies cite such brand loyalty as a means of reducing risk. Roselius questioned consumers on ways of reducing purchase risk and found that brand loyalty and buying a well-known brand were mentioned most frequently.[24]

Habit also simplifies decision making by minimizing the need for information search, resulting in routinized decision making. When consumers are not involved with a product, they try to minimize search because it is not worth the time and energy involved. A typical shopping list may easily include 20 items or more, many of which are relatively unimportant. Consider the amount of time the consumer would spend in prepurchase deliberation or in-store selection if each item required an examination of brand alternatives.

A study by Kass examined the role of habit in new mothers' purchases of baby products.[25] As mothers became more experienced and knowledgeable, the number of information sources they used in evaluating alternative baby products and the amount of information they sought decreased. Clearly, habit formation was taking place. The findings also showed that as purchases become more routinized, not only is information reduced, but the type of information also changes. For example, purchasing by habit resulted in:

1. A shift in the type of information sought from general product information to specific brand information.
2. More reliance on information on price or availability, with less reliance on product-specific information such as freshness and vitamin content.

Consumers were learning to be more efficient purchasers by selecting a favorite brand. However, they were also watching for price specials on competitive brands and for the appearance of new brands.

Habit versus Complex Decision Making

Complex decision making and habit (routinized decision making) are two extremes on a continuum. In between is what might be described as limited decision making. The top of Figure 4.5 presents complex decision making, limited decision making, and habit on a continuum based on the probability of repurchase. Consumers purchase products bought by habit more frequently. With each successive purchase of the same brand, the chances of buying again increase until there is a high probability consumers will continue to repurchase. As the probability of repurchasing increases, the time consumers spend on information search and prepurchase deliberation decreases, as shown on the bottom half of Figure 4.5.

The curve at the top of Figure 4.5 is a learning curve because it shows that over time consumers learn which brand satisfies them. The result is an increase in the probability that consumers will continue to purchase the brand.

Table 4.1 further distinguishes between complex decision making and habit. Consumers are more likely to use complex decision making for more expensive products and products they are more likely to be involved with on an emotional level. Low-cost products purchased frequently with little commitment are more likely to be subject to routinized behavior. Consumers are more likely to use compensatory decision rules in purchasing by complex decision making, that is, evaluating brands by many product attributes simultaneously so as to reduce risk. Simpler, noncompensatory decision rules involving one criterion at a time are more likely to be used for routinized purchases because it is not worth the time and effort to engage in more extensive brand evaluations.

▶FIGURE 4.5 As the probability of purchasing the same brand increases, the amount of information search and prepurchase deliberation decreases.

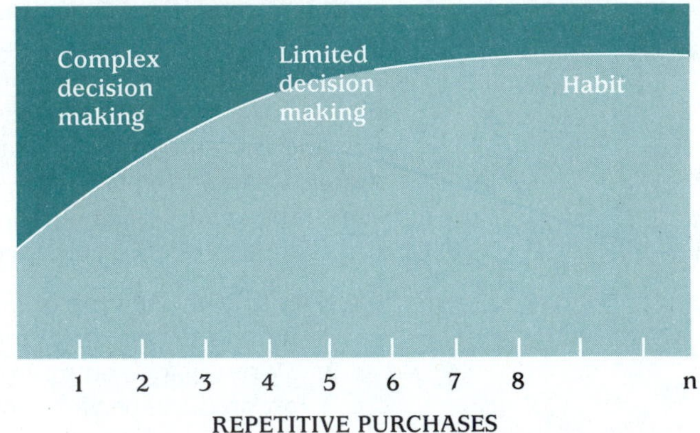

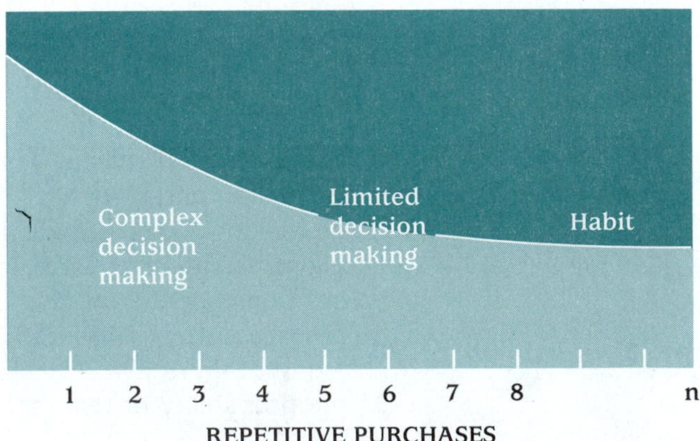

TABLE 4.1
Characteristics of complex decision making versus habit

Complex Decision Making	Limited Decision Making	Habit (Routinized Decision Making)
Little or no information processing		Extensive information processing
Frequently purchased products		Infrequently purchased products
Lower-priced products		Higher-priced products
Low level of consumer involvement		High level of consumer involvement
Noncompensatory decision rules		Compensatory decision rules
Strategic implications		
Extensive distribution		Selective distribution
Few service requirements		Service often required
Personal selling important		Personal selling unimportant
Sales promotions important		Sales promotions unimportant
Advertising used for reminder effect		Advertising used to provide information
Greater price sensitivity		Less price sensitivity

Strategic Implications of Habit versus Complex Decision Making

It is important for marketing management to identify the position of a brand on the continuum from habit to complex decision making. The strategic implications of this position apply to every facet of marketing strategy and are summarized on the bottom of Table 4.1.

Distribution

As brands consumers purchase by habit are likely to be high-turnover, low-margin items, they should be distributed extensively. Widespread distribution is important for those consumers who purchase by habit because seeing the item reminds them to buy. The classic example is Hershey's sole reliance, until the early 1970s, on intensive distribution rather than on advertising to promote its chocolate bar. Manufacturers are more likely to distribute products purchased by complex decision making selectively or exclusively.

http://www.hersheys.com/

Product

Products consumers purchase by complex decision making, primarily appliances and durables, tend to be technically more complex. Personal selling is more important for these products, and service is more likely to be required. Products consumers purchase by habit are generally packaged goods involving few service requirements and little direct selling.

Advertising and In-Store Promotions

The nature of advertising and promotions differs according to the product's position on the decision-making continuum. Products consumers purchase by habit are more likely to use advertising as a reminder. Repetitive advertising is more important. The Czech ad for Coke in Exhibit 4.7 uses the symbol of a yo-yo to remind consumers that they should return the bottle, and in so doing reminds them to buy. In-store promotions are also more effective for low-involvement products because consumers often make the purchase decision once they are in the store.

In contrast, products consumers purchase by complex decision making are more likely to use advertising selectively to convey information to specific audiences, for example, the Apple ad in Exhibit 4.7.

Pricing

Pricing policies are also likely to differ. When consumers purchase brands by habit, frequently the only way a competitor can get a brand-loyal consumer to try an alternative brand is to introduce a price deal or special sale. Another method of inducing trial among brand loyalists is to provide free samples in the hope the loyal consumer will consider buying the alternative brand. Price deals or free samples are less effective in influencing consumers purchasing by complex decision making because the risks of buying just to save money may be too great. In addition, the marketer's costs for free samples or price deals for specialty items may be prohibitive.

Inducing a Switch from Habit to Decision Making

Generally, consumers are more likely to purchase the market leader in a product category by habit. This is because many consumers buy the leading brand to avoid risk and the need to search for information. Buying the market leader is a safe way to routinize purchase behavior.

Marketers who want their brands to challenge the leading brand must induce consumers to switch from habit to decision making. Various marketing strategies can induce consumers who buy by habit to consider other brands:[26]

http://www.mci.com/

http://www.att.com/

- Creating awareness of an alternative to the leading brand. MCI advertises "800 reasons to leave AT&T" to create awareness of an alternative for long-distance service.
- Advertising a new feature in an existing brand. Plaque-fighting properties in toothpaste or hexachlorophene in soap may induce consumers to switch brands.

▶**EXHIBIT 4.7**
Advertising used to inform versus to remind consumers

Advertising to inform

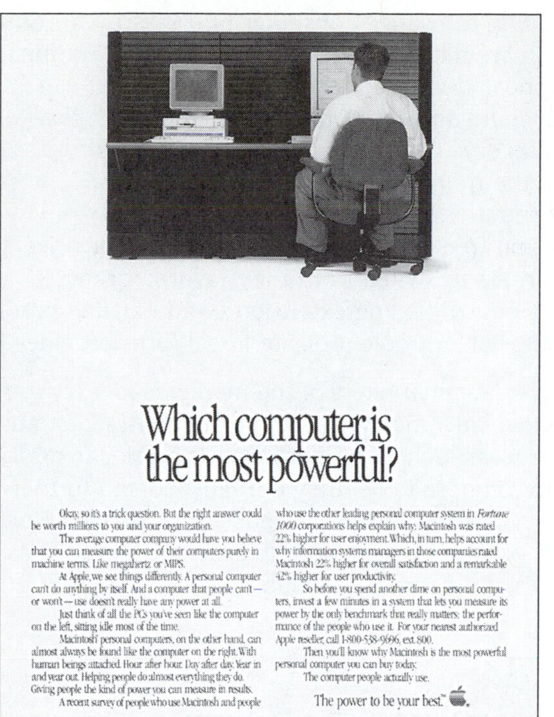

Advertising to remind

- Trying to change consumer priorities by introducing a feature consumers had not previously considered. Toothpaste in pump dispensers appealed to many consumers.
- Encouraging consumers to use the product as a substitute for another category. Trying to convince consumers to drink Pepsi instead of coffee in the morning or to eat Special K cereals instead of cookies in the afternoon are examples.
- Using free product samples, coupons, or price specials to get consumers to switch from their favored brand.
- Introducing a line extension of an existing brand that offers a new benefit. For example, Colgate in gel form provides better taste.

http://www.colgate.com/

Conversely, marketers of the market leader try to retain habitual purchasers by repetitive advertising that reinforces satisfaction and attempts to simplify the choice process. Coke's former advertising slogan "Coke Is It" implied that once consumers choose Coke, they are satisfied and further information search is not necessary. One reason the introduction of a new Coke formula was a mistake is that it prompted many habitual Coke users to reassess their choice (that is, to switch from habit to decision making).

BRAND LOYALTY

A close link exists among learning, habit, and brand loyalty. **Brand loyalty** represents a favorable attitude toward a brand resulting in consistent purchase of the brand over time. It is the result of consumers learning that one brand can satisfy their needs.

Two approaches to the study of brand loyalty have dominated the marketing literature. The first, an instrumental conditioning approach, views consistent purchasing of one brand over time as an indication of brand loyalty. Consumers' repeat purchasing behavior is assumed to reflect reinforcement and a strong stimulus-to-response link. Research that takes this approach uses probabilistic models of consumer learning to estimate the probability of consumers buying the same brand again, given a number of past purchases of that brand. The shape of the learning curve in Figure 4.5 determines this probability. Thus, 10 consecutive purchases of Minute Maid frozen orange juice might mean a 92 percent probability that the consumer will buy the same brand again on the next purchase. Since the prediction is always in probability terms, this is a **stochastic model** of consumer behavior.

The second approach to the study of brand loyalty is based on cognitive theories. Some researchers believe that behavior alone does not reflect brand loyalty. Loyalty implies a commitment to a brand that may not be reflected by just measuring continuous behavior. A family may buy a particular brand because it is the lowest-priced brand on the market. A slight increase in price may cause the family to shift to another brand. In this case, continuous purchasing does not reflect reinforcement or loyalty. The stimulus (product) and reward links are not strong. An attitudinal measure combined with a behavioral measure is required to identify true loyalty.

Cognitive theorists are more likely to develop deterministic models of consumer choice. **Deterministic models** demonstrate the linkages between variables that influence behavior and attempt to predict behavior based on these linkages. The models of complex decision making in the previous chapter and habitual purchasing behavior in this chapter (Figure 4.4) are examples of deterministic models.

The differences between a behavioral and a cognitive orientation in defining brand loyalty and habit are best illustrated by the statements of two researchers. Tucker takes a strong behavioral position: "No consideration should be given to what the subject thinks or what goes on in his central nervous system; his behavior is the full statement of what brand loyalty is."[27] Jacoby takes a clear cognitive position: "To exhibit brand loyalty implies repeat purchasing behavior based on cognitive, affective, evaluative and predispositional factors—the classical primary components of an attitude."[28] And, "brand loyalty is a function of psychological (decision-making, evaluative) processes."[29] In this discussion, behavioral (instrumental conditioning) and attitudinal (cognitive) approaches to understanding brand loyalty will be considered.

Behavioral Approach to Brand Loyalty

Recent developments in data collection have given more spur to the behavioral as opposed to the cognitive school in measuring brand loyalty. The availability of electronically recorded purchases through in-store scanners has made it possible to provide managers with quick information on what people do. As a result, marketers are relying more on behavioral data generated through scanners and less on attitudinal and perceptual data generated through surveys.

The problem with relying primarily on behavioral data in developing and assessing marketing strategies is, in the words of one marketing expert, that "what people do does not say anything about why they do it. There is no surrogate available for talking to the consumer."[30]

Behavioral Measures of Loyalty

Behavioral measures have defined loyalty by the sequence of purchases (purchased Brand A five times in a row) and/or the proportion of purchases (Brand A represents 80 percent of all purchases of frozen orange juice). In one of the earliest studies in this area, Brown defined *brand loyalty* as five purchases in a row of the same brand. He analyzed a panel of consumers for frequently purchased items such as coffee, orange juice, soap, and margarine and found that from 12 to 73 percent of the families studied were loyal to the same brand, depending on the product.[31] Tucker defined *loyalty* as three purchases in a row,[32] while Lawrence defined *loyalty* to a new brand as four purchases in a row.[33] Blattberg and Sen used proportion of purchases, rather than sequence, as the behavioral measure of loyalty and identified consumers loyal to national and private-label (retailer-owned) brands.[34]

These varying definitions illustrate the fact that no consistent measure of behavioral loyalty has been accepted in consumer research.

Limitations of Behavioral Measures of Loyalty

Several limitations of a strictly behavioral approach to identifying brand loyalty should be recognized. First, measurement of loyalty based on past behavior may be misleading. Consider the consumer who buys one brand of coffee for personal consumption, another brand for the spouse, and occasionally a third, higher-priced brand to have available for guests. The purchase sequence would not indicate loyalty; however, the consumer may be highly loyal to the preferred brand.

Second, consumer purchases may not reflect reinforcement. Lawrence studied the sequence of purchases after a consumer switched his or her regular brand.[35] He found four patterns of purchasing:

1. Reversion (switching back to the original brand).
2. Conversion (remaining loyal to the new brand).
3. Vacillation (random switching between brands).
4. Experimentation (further systematic trial of other brands).

Only the reversion and conversion patterns would conform to instrumental conditioning since, in both cases, previous purchases are clearly increasing the probability of buying the same brand again. For vacillation and experimentation, no specific sequence is established, making it difficult to predict behavior from past purchases. However, Lawrence found that over 50 percent of the consumers studied conformed to a pattern of vacillation or experimentation.

Third, brand loyalty is not merely a function of past behavior. It is a multidimensional concept that must incorporate the consumer's commitment to the brand. The very term *loyalty* implies commitment rather than just repetitive behavior, which suggests that there is the need for a cognitive as well as a behavioral view.

Cognitive Approach to Brand Loyalty

Some of the limitations of a strictly behavioral approach in measuring brand loyalty are overcome when loyalty includes both attitudes and behavior. Day states that to be truly loyal the consumer must hold a favorable attitude toward the brand in addition to purchasing it repeatedly.[36] Day recognizes that consumers might continue to buy the same brand because other brands are not readily available, a brand offers a long series of price deals, or consumers want to minimize decision making. Day defines these conditions as *spurious loyalty* because they do not reflect commitment.

Evidence suggests that utilizing both the attitudinal and behavioral components provides a more powerful definition of brand loyalty. In his study, Day found that when he attempted to predict brand loyalty, the predictive power of the model using both attitude and behavior measures was almost twice as good as the model using behavior alone. Furthermore, if the behavior measure alone were used, over 70 percent of the sample would have been defined as brand loyal. Adding the attitudinal component reduced the proportion of brand-loyal consumers to under 50 percent. In other words, defining loyalty based only on repeat purchasing overstates the degree of loyalty.[37]

The Brand-Loyal Consumer

Several researchers have attempted to define the characteristics of a brand-loyal consumer. Their studies have uniformly shown that there is no general, brand-loyal consumer, that is, a consumer who tends to be loyal regardless of product category.[38] Brand loyalty is product-specific. Consumers will be loyal to brands in one category and will have little loyalty to brands in other categories.

Despite the product-specific nature of brand loyalty, some generalizations can be made about those who tend to be brand loyal:

1. The brand-loyal consumer tends to be more self-confident in his or her choice. Both Day[39] and Carman[40] found this relationship to be true in separate studies of consumer packaged goods.

2. Brand-loyal consumers are more likely to perceive a higher level of risk in the purchase and use repeat purchasing of a single brand as a means of reducing risk.[41]
3. The brand-loyal consumer is more likely to be store-loyal. Carman states that the consumer who restricts the number of stores visited thereby restricts the opportunity to be disloyal to the brands the store sells. Therefore, "store loyalty is a regulator of brand loyalty."[42]
4. Minority-group consumers tend to be more brand loyal. Some studies have found that African-American and Hispanic-American consumers tend to be more brand loyal.[43] Loyalty may be the result of greater financial risk in purchases and a desire to "play it safe."

Brand Loyalty and Product Involvement

The cognitive definition of brand loyalty means that loyalty represents commitment and, therefore, involvement with the purchase. (See Exhibit 4.8 for the ultimate example of commitment resulting in brand loyalty.) A study by J. Walter Thompson, a large advertising agency, found that brand loyalty is highest when consumers are personally involved with the brand and find the purchase risky.[44] In these cases, the brand is a source of self-identification (cosmetics, automobiles, cigarettes).

EXHIBIT 4.8
An example of commitment and brand loyalty
Source: © Bill Whitehead

"Brand loyalty isn't just an empty phrase to Arthur!"

Inertia—that is, repeat purchasing of a brand without commitment—represents habitual purchasing with a low level of involvement. In this case, the consumer has no strong opinions or feelings about the brand. The consumer bases purchasing on what is most familiar. Repeat purchase of a brand does not represent commitment; it merely represents acceptance.

STORE LOYALTY

Consumers are loyal to stores just as they are to brands. At times, store loyalty may be stronger than brand loyalty. A young lawyer may religiously shop at one particular department store because it conforms to his self-image as being upwardly mobile and achievement-oriented. Given this link between his self-image and his image of the store, our shopper's loyalties to this department store are likely to be stronger than his loyalty to any of the items of merchandise it carries.

As with brand loyalty, store loyalty may also reflect inertia. Our young lawyer may shop at a particular department store not because of any strong commitment to the store, but because his time is limited and it is simply easier to shop in one place for clothing and accessories.

The Store-Loyal Consumer

In the previous section, we noted that brand-loyal consumers also tend to be store-loyal. It is possible that consumers who wish to reduce the time and effort in brand selection also seek to minimize time and effort in store selection. Another possibility is that shopping in the same store fosters loyalty for brands carried by that store, particularly private (retailer-controlled) brands.

Reynolds, Darden, and Martin related lifestyle characteristics to store loyalty.[45] They identified store loyalty by the willingness of a sample of women to shop in the same stores and to avoid the risk of shopping in new stores. They found that the store-loyal woman tends to be older and more downscale (lower income, less educated) than one who is not loyal.

Goldman supported these findings in his study.[46] He found that store-loyal consumers engaged in less prepurchase search, knew about fewer stores, and were less likely to shop even in stores known to them. Goldman concluded that store-loyal behavior appears to be "part of a low search, low knowledge and low utilization level shopping style" and that this shopping style is more likely to exist among low-income consumers because they are constrained by their inability to shop much.[47] The clear implication is that store loyalty is an inefficient mode of shopping and is more likely to exist among low-income consumers because of limited information and less discretionary income.

The two studies just cited also found that store-loyal consumers see more risk in shopping.[48] The lower income and educational level of the store-loyal consumer may heighten the sense of risk in shopping behavior. The careful and conservative nature of these customers suggests that store loyalty may be a means of reducing the risk of shopping in unknown stores. One obvious strategy in reducing risk in store choice is to shop in one or a select number of stores.

Level of Store Loyalty

Consumers' greater price sensitivity as a result of the two recent recessions has led to an erosion of store loyalty. A study by Yankelovich, Skelly, and White, a marketing research firm, found that almost 50 percent of all shoppers said they switched from their favorite supermarket to one with lower prices during the 1980–1982 recession.[49] The 1991–1992 recession promoted comparison shopping and further discouraged store loyalty.

But the Yankelovich study also found a countervailing trend. The increase in the number of working women increased the premium on convenience and reduced the time for comparison shopping. The greater number of single-parent households has also limited the amount of time available for shopping. For these consumers, the additional cost of being store- or brand-loyal is worth the time saved.

As a result, store loyalty is likely to be pulled by two opposing trends. Consumers' greater value orientation is likely to cause them to comparison shop, eroding store loyalty. But demographic trends such as more working women and single-parent households are likely to put a premium on time, encouraging store loyalty.

SOCIETAL IMPLICATIONS OF BRAND AND STORE LOYALTY

The preceding description of brand and store loyalty suggests that it may not be the most efficient mode of decision making for consumers. On the positive side, brand and store loyalty save consumers time and effort in evaluating alternatives. However, such loyalty may lead consumers to repurchase the same brand even if it is higher priced or of inferior quality.

Implications for Brand Loyalty

Name brands often trade on their national reputation and frequent advertising to charge higher prices. Many consumers are swayed by the name appeal alone and establish strong brand loyalties based on image. Blind taste tests have shown that many consumers cannot tell the difference between Pepsi and Coke or Miller and Budweiser. However, when the name is revealed, the consumers exhibit strong preferences. Clearly, loyalty is a function of brand name and image rather than any functional brand attributes. Similarly, bleach is a fairly standardized product; however, Clorox can charge more than other brands because it is a known commodity.

http://www.clorox.com/

Consumers have a right to develop brand loyalties based on image alone. However, the fact that brand and store loyalties tend to be higher for minority consumers and older, downscale consumers is disturbing. These consumers are often the ones who can least afford the higher prices of national brands.

In this respect, the recent move to every day low prices (EDLP) for national brands may be beneficial from a societal standpoint. Increasingly, consumers are showing more willingness to shop around for value. Shopping for value could mean trying a lower-priced brand of toothpaste or a private brand of disposable diapers. As a result, we are witnessing the development of more efficient and economical consumers.

Unfortunately, this move to more effective modes of brand choice is more characteristic of middle-income consumers, not lower-income consumers. Because lower-income consumers are less likely to be aware of brand and price alternatives, a key question is whether there should be a governmental role in increasing price and brand awareness for these consumers.

Implications for Store Loyalty

The same considerations apply to store loyalty. Store loyalty may be a convenient mode of shopping and does save time and effort, but it inhibits comparisons of brand alternatives by restricting choice to one store.

From a societal viewpoint, any erosion of store loyalty may be beneficial in encouraging consumers to shop for alternatives. As a result, consumers are more likely to be aware of lower-priced alternatives. Here again, the problem is that older, downscale consumers and disadvantaged minorities continue to be the most store loyal. As noted in Chapter 2, low-income consumers often lack the mobility to engage in comparison shopping. Goldman's description of store-loyal consumers as exhibiting a low knowledge and low utilization style of shopping most applies to downscale consumers.[50] However, these are the consumers who can most benefit by increasing their range of alternatives.

In this regard, government could have a role in increasing the mobility of lower-income, disadvantaged consumers through improved modes of transportation to facilitate comparison shopping.

SUMMARY

Consumer learning, habit, and brand loyalty are closely linked concepts. Habitual purchasing behavior is the result of consumer learning from reinforcement. Consumers will repeatedly buy what satisfies them best. This behavior leads to brand loyalty.

Concepts of learning are necessary to understanding habit. The distinction is made between behavioral and cognitive approaches to learning. Behavioral learning focuses on the stimuli that affect behavior and on behavior itself. Cognitive learning focuses on problem solving and emphasizes the consumer thought variables that influence learning. Within the behavioral school, the distinction is also made between classical and instrumental conditioning. Classical conditioning explains behavior based on the establishment of a close association between a primary and a secondary stimulus. Instrumental conditioning views behavior as a function of the consumer's actions. Satisfaction leads to reinforcement and to an increase in the probability of repurchasing.

Learning leads to repetitive buying and habit. In a model representing habitual purchasing behavior, a consumer's need arousal leads directly to an intention to buy, a subsequent purchase, and postpurchase evaluation. Information search and brand evaluation are minimal.

Habit serves two important functions. It reduces risk for high-involvement purchases and saves time and energy for low-involvement products.

Habit frequently leads to brand loyalty, that is, repetitive buying based on a commitment to the brand. The different learning theories describe two views of brand loyalty. An instrumental conditioning approach suggests that a consumer's consistent purchase of a brand is a reflection of brand loyalty. But such loyalty may lack commitment to the brand and reflect repeat buying based on inertia. The cognitive school believes that behavior is an insufficient measure of loyalty. Attitudinal commitment to the brand is also required.

Brand-loyal consumers also tend to be store-loyal. But store loyalty is an inefficient mode of shopping since it is likely to result in the consumer paying more because of a lack of search for alternatives.

Chapter 5 focuses on the low-involvement conditions that encourage inertia, often in the form of brand and store loyalty.

QUESTIONS

1. How can principles of classical conditioning be applied to advertising? What are the shortcomings of such applications?
2. What conditions are necessary for classical conditioning to work in advertising? Provide examples.
3. The implication in this chapter is that the emphasis in advertising strategy has shifted from an adherence to classical learning theory before 1950 to an adherence to cognitive theories of learning after 1950.
   - How would such a shift be reflected in advertising strategy?
   - Do you agree that such a shift has taken place in advertising in the past 30 years?
4. Why was the Marlboro campaign less effective in the early 1990s compared to its success in previ-

ous years? How can learning theory explain this development?

5. How can principles of instrumental conditioning be applied to advertising? In what ways do applications of instrumental conditioning differ from those of classical conditioning?
6. What are the implications of extinction and forgetting on the antitrust case brought against Kraft for its acquisition of Nabisco Shredded Wheat?
7. As a member of the Federal Trade Commission, what principles of conditioning would you use in deciding whether a company engaging in misleading advertising should either correct its advertising or simply stop it? If corrective advertising were ordered, what principles of conditioning would you use to determine if this action had the desired effects?
8. A good example of the operation of cognitive learning is to determine how new residents in a community learn about new products not available in their previous community. What evidence might demonstrate that a process of learning is taking place among new residents of a community?
9. What are the marketing strategy implications of positive and negative vicarious learning?
10. If habit is based on reinforcement and an increased likelihood of consumers buying the same product, why have certain dominant brands, once purchased by habit, become extinct or experienced a substantial loss in market share (for example, Sapolio soap)?
11. This chapter suggests that consumers' boredom and desire for variety may result in a change from habit to decision making.
    - Is this more likely for certain product categories than for others?
    - Is this more likely for certain consumers than for others? That is, is there a "stick-with-it" type as opposed to a "novelty-seeker" type?
12. Habit serves two different purposes for high- and low-involvement situations.
    - What are they?
    - Can you cite examples of habit in a high-involvement situation? In a low-involvement situation?
13. A brand manager for a brand with frequent deals and coupons assumes that consumers who repeatedly buy the brand are loyal purchasers.
    - What are the dangers of such an assumption?
    - What marketing errors might result in (a) advertising strategy, (b) pricing, and (c) in-store promotions?
14. What are the strategic implications of the erosion of brand loyalty in the 1990s?
15. Under what circumstances are brand and store loyalty inefficient models of consumer choice? What are the societal implications?

RESEARCH ASSIGNMENTS

1. Visit Pepsi's Internet site at http://www.pepsi.com. Then visit Coca-Cola's site at http://www.cocacola.com.
    - In what specific ways do each of the manufacturers build brand loyalty?
    - Which site is more effective? Why?
    - Do you think this effectiveness differs by target market?
2. Develop an experiment in which you ask consumers to evaluate three brands in a product category. Each brand should be placed in a separate room with background music. Make sure the brands are in the same price range and of the same quality. Play rock music in one room, classical in the second, and country and western in the third. Ask consumers to state their preference for one of the three brands. Ask consumers their musical preferences as well.
    - Are brand preferences related to preferences for the background music played?
    - What learning theories could you use to explain your results?
    - What are the implications of your results for marketing strategy?

    References for this assignment: M. Elizabeth Blair and Terence Shimp, "Consequences of an Unpleasant Experience with Music: A Second-Order Negative Conditioning Perspective," *Journal of Advertising* 21(March 1992), pp. 35–43; and Gerald Gorn, "The Effects of Music in Advertising on Choice Behavior: A Classical Conditioning Approach," *Journal of Marketing* 46 (Winter 1982), pp. 94–101.
3. Develop a measure of brand loyalty using either a behavioral or a cognitive approach. Interview a sample of from 30 to 50 consumers of a frequently purchased packaged product (coffee, toothpaste, frozen orange juice). Identify those who are loyal to a brand versus those who are not.
    - Are there any differences between the two groups in terms of (a) demographic characteristics, (b) importance placed on need criteria in selecting brands, (c) brand attitudes, (d) advertising recall, and (e) price paid?

- What are the implications of the differences between loyalists and nonloyalists for (a) attempts at increasing the number of loyal users, (b) product positioning, and (c) utilization of deals and coupons?

4. Develop a measure of loyalty incorporating both behavior and brand attitudes. Interview a sample of consumers of a frequently purchased packaged good. Distinguish between true loyalists and those who buy regularly out of inertia.

- What are the differences between the two groups according to the criteria in Assignment 2?
- According to your findings, should marketers try to influence consumers who buy their brand out of inertia to become truly loyal? What are the advantages and disadvantages of such a strategy?
- What other marketing implications emerge from your findings?

LOW-INVOLVEMENT DECISION MAKING

Chapter 5

KELLOGG'S INCREASES INVOLVEMENT WITH CEREALS

In describing complex decision making and brand loyalty in the last two chapters, we assumed that consumers are involved with the purchasing decision. However, when we consider the variety of more mundane products purchased on an everyday basis—toothpaste, detergents, cereals, deodorants—it is not surprising that most purchases are low in consumer involvement.[1] A **low-involvement purchase** is one in which consumers do not consider the product important and do not strongly identify with it.

Marketers like to think that consumers are involved with their products because involved consumers are more likely to pay attention to their advertising, to evaluate their brands carefully, and to become brand-loyal. Where consumer involvement is lacking, marketers try to create it by introducing new product attributes that are important to consumers or by linking uninvolving products to involving situations and issues.

For example, when 7-Up advertised its flagship brand as having no caffeine ("Never http://www.7up.com/

http://www.kelloggs.com/

Had It, Never Will"), it touted an attribute which the product had all the time but never appeared important to the company until consumers became more health-conscious. Advertising a "new" attribute was designed to increase consumer involvement and create brand loyalty.

Kellogg's followed a similar strategy in the 1980s with more profound consequences for the cereal industry when it created the adult cereal market. Until then, cereals were primarily a children's product; but by 1980, the market was stagnating because of a declining birth rate. Kellogg's saw an opportunity for targeting cereals to nutritionally oriented baby boomers. To do so, however, it would have to get these consumers more involved in cereals by convincing them that they are not just kid stuff.

Kellogg's did so in the most direct way. In 1984, it began touting the high-fiber content of its All-Bran cereal as helping to prevent cancer (see Exhibit 5.1). It followed by targeting a new line of cereals—Common Sense, Just Right, Mueslix—to diet-conscious, health-oriented, and fitness segments. As a result, adults

EXHIBIT 5.1
Kellogg's increases the level of involvement with cereals

began seeing cereals as part of a healthier lifestyle, a highly involving issue (see Exhibit 5.1). Kellogg's success in transforming cereals from a less to a more involving product doubled the growth rate for cereals. Today, adult cereals represent one-third of the company's sales.

http://www.fda.gov/

However, Kellogg's might have gone too far when it introduced Heartwise as a cereal that helped reduce cholesterol. When the Food and Drug Administration forced Kellogg's to withdraw the claim as insupportable, the company reintroduced Heartwise as Fiberwise to avoid the connotation that the product fights heart disease.[2]

Marketers accept the fact that consumers are not involved with their products and try to attract them through price promotions and other incentives. The proliferation of coupons and price promotions for products such as paper towels, household cleaners, coffee, and detergents attests to the low-involvement nature of these product categories.

This chapter focuses on purchase decisions in which consumers are not highly involved. The importance of a low-involvement perspective is considered first. Next, consumer decisions are classified by level of product involvement. Several theoretical bases for low-involvement purchase behavior are described. Strategic implications of high- versus low-involvement situations are considered, with special emphasis on advertising strategy.

IMPORTANCE OF A LOW-INVOLVEMENT PERSPECTIVE

Most consumers' purchases are not involving. Kassarjian supports the view that most purchase decisions do not greatly involve consumers: "Subjects just do not care about products; they are unimportant to them. Although issues such as racial equality, wars and the draft may stir them up, products do not."[3]

Although dated, a 1970 study comparing the importance of political issues to products lends support to Kassarjian's low-involvement perspective. College students were asked to rate 20 issues and 20 products on a seven-point scale from very important (7) to not important at all (1).[4] Some of the relative ratings are listed in Table 5.1. Although students rated some of the products as fairly important (automobiles and houses), it is apparent that in most cases students considered the product categories as relatively unimportant when compared to the issues. Vietnam and Watergate dominated the early 1970s, and the importance of products paled in comparison to these issues. Product choice was not one of the most important concerns in consumers' lives then, and it is probably not now.

Involvement and the Hierarchy of Effects

If low involvement characterizes so much of purchasing, why have marketers focused on high-involvement decisions (that is, complex decision making and

TABLE 5.1
Relative importance of products and issues

Product or Issue	Rating	Product or Issue	Rating
The draft	6.71	Coffee	2.61
Vietnam War	6.28	Fraternity membership	2.38
World peace	6.17		
Automobiles	4.52	Toothpaste	1.95
Houses	4.17	Bicycles	1.39
Beer	3.00	Facial tissues	1.19

Source: Nancy T. Hupfer and David M. Gardner, "Differential Involvement with Products and Issues: An Exploratory Study," in David M. Gardner, ed., Proceedings of the 2nd annual conference of the Association for Consumer Behavior (College Park, MD: Association for Consumer Research, 1971), pp. 262–269.

brand loyalty)? There are two reasons. First, since marketers are highly involved with their products, they easily assume consumers are also highly involved. Tyebjee notes the reluctance of product and advertising managers to consider an uninvolved consumer:

> These individuals [product and advertising managers] spend a major part of their waking hours thinking about their brand. Therefore, when they evaluate the advertising strategy they do so as highly involved individuals, unlike the target consumer. Highly cluttered, complex advertising copy is often a result of agency and brand group decision makers who are unable to view the product from the perspective of the [uninvolved] consumer.[5]

Exhibit 5.2 is a good illustration of the marketer's assumption that consumers are involved with mundane products.

A second reason why marketers tend to focus on high-involvement decisions is that it is easier for them to understand and influence consumers if they assume consumers employ a cognitive process of brand evaluation. Complex decision making assumes a sequence in the consumers' choice process (referred to as a **hierarchy of effects**), which stipulates that consumers think before they act. That is, they first form brand beliefs (the cognitive component of attitudes), then evaluate brands (the affective component), and then make a purchase decision (the behavioral or conative component). The beliefs/evaluation/behavior hierarchy assumes involved consumers. The assumption that such a high-involvement hierarchy of effects describes consumer choice has dominated marketing thought since consumer behavior became an integrated field of study.

Low-Involvement Hierarchy

Consumer behavior researchers are directing more attention to a low-involvement hierarchy of effects. This hierarchy stipulates that consumers may act without

EXHIBIT 5.2
The involved marketer and the uninvolved consumer

Source: Drawing by H. Martin; © 1983 The New Yorker Magazine, Inc.

"And now a message of importance to those of you who have been giving serious thought to the purchase of a new tube of toothpaste."

thinking. For example, when purchasing table salt, it is unlikely that the consumer will initiate a process of information search to determine brand characteristics. Nor is the consumer likely to evaluate alternative brands to identify the most favored one.

Rather than searching for information, the consumer will receive information passively. The consumer sits in front of the television and sees an advertisement for Morton salt that describes it as "easy to pour." Stifling a yawn, the consumer is thinking about anything but salt. The consumer is not really evaluating the advertisement. Rather, in just seeing the ad, the consumer is storing information in a few bits and pieces without any active cognitive process. However, over time, the consumer establishes an association of Morton salt with ease in pouring. Lastovicka refers to this process as information catching rather than information processing.[6]

A need arises simply because the amount of salt in the house is running low. The consumer buys Morton salt because of the familiarity that repetitive advertising produces. The consumer sees the brand on the store shelf, associates it with the advertising theme, and has sufficient stimulus to purchase Morton salt. Under these conditions, the consumer does not form an attitude toward the brand and has no favorable or unfavorable reaction. Instead, the consumer regards the brand as relatively neutral since it is not associated with any important benefits tied to self or group identification.

TABLE 5.2
A comparison of low- and high-involvement hierarchies

Low-Involvement Hierarchy	High-Involvement Hierarchy
1. Brand beliefs are formed first by *passive* learning.	1. Brand beliefs are formed first by *active* learning.
2. A purchase decision is made.	2. Brands are evaluated.
3. The brand may or may not be evaluated afterward.	3. A purchase decision is made.

Therefore, the hierarchy of effects for low-involvement products is quite different from that for high-involvement products, as indicated in Table 5.2. Consumers become aware of the product and form beliefs about it passively. They make a purchase decision with little brand information and then evaluate the brand after the purchase to determine the level of satisfaction. At this point, consumers may develop weak attitudes toward the brand—for example, if a new feature such as a convenient spout is introduced (favorable evaluation) or if the brand performs poorly (sticks to the container, producing an unfavorable reaction). If such attitudes develop, they occur after the purchase and are weakly held.[7]

http://www.time.com/

Several studies have supported the distinction between a high- and a low-involvement hierarchy. Joseph E. Seagram & Sons and Time, Inc., jointly conducted a study of consumer choice of liquor brands and found that an increase in brand awareness was related to a subsequent purchase of the advertised brand. However, there was no change in attitudes toward the brand as a result of brand evaluation. The study concluded that the findings "tend to contradict the long-accepted belief that first you change people's attitudes, then you change their buying habits."[8] The findings supported a beliefs/behavior/attitude hierarchy.

In a later study, Beatty and Kahle distinguished between consumers who are and who are not involved with soft drinks. The more involved consumers tended to make choices based on favorable attitudes toward the preferred brands. Attitudes did not play an important role in the decision for less involved consumers.[9]

Low Involvement and Brand Evaluation

The Morton salt example cited previously suggests that in low-involvement decision making, consumers do very little brand evaluation and information processing. This is because consumers are generally governed by a principle of **cognitive economy**—they search for only as much information as they feel is necessary to adequately evaluate brands.[10] In low-involvement conditions, consumers are not motivated to actively evaluate brands. The product being evaluated is not particularly risky, expensive, important, or personally relevant. This lack of motivation to process information is why brand beliefs are formed in a passive state.

Research supports the lower levels of brand evaluation and information processing for low-involvement conditions. The study by Beatty and Kahle examined the scope of brand evaluations and found that more involved consumers evaluated brands more extensively than uninvolved consumers (that is, more brands are evaluated and more attributes used in evaluating them).[11] Similarly, Mulvey et al. examined consumers' evaluation of tennis rackets and found involved consumers used more complex means of evaluation. For example, less involved consumers thought of the quality of a tennis racket in the abstract, whereas more involved consumers could articulate what makes a high-quality tennis racket using criteria such as head size, grip, and materials.[12] Park and

GLOBAL APPLICATIONS OF CONSUMER BEHAVIOR

▶ What Is Low Involvement at Home May Be High Involvement Abroad

Many products that are taken for granted by consumers in more advanced economies may be valuable items in other countries. Whereas hair spray is a low-involvement product for most consumers in the United States, in Poland it is more likely to arouse intense consumer interest. The product was almost unknown during the Communist years. When Poland converted to a free market system, the novelty and initial scarcity of the product aroused consumer interest. Polish consumers attached badge value to the product—a well-groomed look enhanced social status. They also became personally involved as a result. And, they were willing to pay more for the product on a relative price basis than American consumers.

In other cases, many products that are regarded as commonplace in the United States are assigned more importance abroad because they are regarded as American icons. McDonald's is an example. Considering the poor service in Eastern European countries and those of the former Soviet Union, McDonald's standards of uniformity, tasty food, and child-friendly tables created instant involvement with fast-food establishments. As one executive said, "The world is becoming a service society, but in many countries they don't get any except at McDonald's." But the novelty of good service is not the only reason Eastern European and Russian consumers are more involved with McDonald's. The price of a meal for a family of four often equals a week's pay.

Hair spray in Poland and McDonald's in Russia demonstrate that involvement is consumer, not product, related. Differences in a consumer's economic and cultural environment mean that a low-involvement product in one country can be totally absorbing in another.

Hastak investigated another dimension of brand evaluation, reaction time, and found that the time involved in making brand evaluations was greater for involved compared to uninvolved consumers.[13]

Low-Involvement Decision Criteria

If brand evaluation is minimal in low-involvement conditions, then how do consumers make decisions? They follow relatively simple decision rules that follow principles of cognitive economy by minimizing the time and effort in shopping and decision making.

One rule cited in the Morton salt example is to pick the most familiar brand. Our consumer saw Morton salt on the shelf, recognized the name, associated it with the advertising, and picked it because it was most familiar. A study by Hoyer and Brown supports this type of decision making in low-involvement purchases. They found that consumers who are aware of one brand in a product category will repeatedly choose it even if it is lower in quality than other brands.[14]

Another simple decision rule is to pick the brand purchased the last time if it was adequate. A study by Lynch, Marmorstein, and Weigold found that uninvolved consumers make decisions on this basis by recalling previously formed brand evaluations.[15] Finally, if uninvolved consumers have few prior associations with brands, the simplest expedient is to pick the least expensive alternative.

In each of these cases, consumers are making quick decisions (generally in the store) with little or no brand evaluation.

FOUR TYPES OF CONSUMER BEHAVIOR

In Chapter 3, we described four types of consumer choice processes based on the level of involvement and decision making: complex decision making, brand loyalty, limited decision making, and inertia. Figure 5.1 shows that each of these processes is described by a different hierarchy of effects.[16] The high- and low-involvement processes are also described by different learning theories based on these decision hierarchies.

Complex Decision Making and Brand Loyalty

The upper left-hand box of Figure 5.1 represents the process of complex decision making described by the traditional "think before you act" hierarchy. The learning theory that best describes this process is cognitive learning, that is, a process that requires consumers to develop brand attitudes and evaluate brand alternatives in detail.

The lower left-hand box describes brand loyalty; that is, consumers make purchases with little deliberation because of past satisfaction and a strong com-

FIGURE 5.1
Four types of consumer behavior

	HIGH INVOLVEMENT	LOW INVOLVEMENT
DECISION MAKING	DECISION PROCESS Complex Decision Making HIERARCHY OF EFFECTS Beliefs Evaluation Behavior THEORY Cognitive Learning	DECISION PROCESS Limited Decision Making HIERARCHY OF EFFECTS Beliefs Behavior Evaluation THEORY Passive Learning
HABIT	DECISION PROCESS Brand Loyalty HIERARCHY OF EFFECTS (Beliefs) (Evaluation) Behavior THEORY Instrumental Conditioning	DECISION PROCESS Inertia HIERARCHY OF EFFECTS Beliefs Behavior (Evaluation) THEORY Classical Conditioning

mitment to the brand as a result. The learning theory that best describes brand loyalty is instrumental conditioning (positive reinforcement based on satisfaction with the brand leading to repetitive behavior). Both high-involvement processes are described by a beliefs/evaluation/behavior hierarchy, except that forming beliefs and evaluating brands are not a necessary part of the choice process in brand loyalty. Complex decision making was described in Chapter 3 and brand loyalty in Chapter 4. In this chapter, we focus on the two low-involvement processes shown in Figure 5.1: inertia and limited decision making.

Inertia

The lower right-hand box represents the Morton salt example—buying based on **inertia.** As we saw, when a low-involvement hierarchy operates, a consumer forms beliefs passively, makes a decision with little information processing, and then evaluates the brand after the purchase. As inertia involves repetitive buying of the same brand to avoid making a decision, the consumer does not make a subsequent brand evaluation until after the first few purchases. If the brand achieves a certain minimum level of satisfaction, the consumer will repurchase it on a routinized basis. This process is sometimes referred to as **spurious loyalty** because repetitive purchases may make it appear that the consumer is loyal to the brand when actually no such loyalty exists.

The learning theory that best describes inertia is classical conditioning. When the consumer is not involved with the product, contiguity between a stimulus and a response could be established more easily through repetitive advertising because the consumer is in a passive state. The consumer forms the association without thinking. When the consumer goes into a store, the association may be triggered by seeing the product; and the easiest thing to do is to buy the product with little deliberation. Thus, repetitive exposure to a theme like "The quicker, thicker picker upper" for Bounty paper towels might create an association between absorbency and the product for a low-involvement product category.

Various studies have demonstrated the effectiveness of repeating advertising themes in low-involvement conditions. Batra and Ray showed that repeating an advertising message will result in more favorable brand attitudes for low-involvement purchases.[17] In the high-involvement case, repetition had an initial favorable impact; but after a while, repetition became counterproductive. Similarly, Hawkins and Hoch found that for low-involvement purchases, repetition resulted in greater acceptance of the truth of advertising claims.[18] In both cases, repetition created familiarity, allowing consumers to more easily associate known claims with a particular brand.

The study by Hoyer and Brown supports these findings by reinforcing the importance of creating brand awareness for low-involvement products.[19] The study found that if consumers were aware of a particular brand of peanut butter (a low-involvement product), this awareness was sufficient to make a brand choice. Consumers would choose the known brand of peanut butter even if taste tests suggested it was of lower quality. These consumers were not motivated to process information on alternative brands of peanut butter. They demonstrated inertia by simply selecting the brand they knew best. Such brand awareness is best created by repetitive advertising.

Because of the dominance of low-involvement products, inertia is probably much more common than most marketing managers would like to admit. Product managers and advertisers sometimes use marketing strategies that assume consumers care. Most consumers do not.

Limited Decision Making

Occasionally, low-involvement purchases warrant some decision making (upper-right box in Figure 5.1) in contrast to the process of routinized decision making that characterizes inertia. The introduction of a new product, a change in the existing brand, or a desire for variety might cause a consumer to switch from routinized to limited decision making. For example, assume a new, thicker paper towel is introduced and is advertised as being so strong it can be reused. A consumer who consistently buys Bounty notices the ad. Involvement with the category is low, but introduction of the new product is enough to arouse mild interest and curiosity. The decision process conforms to a low-involvement hierarchy as there is little information seeking and brand evaluation. The consumer forms beliefs about the brand (thick, strong, can be reused), purchases the brand, and then evaluates it based on initial trial.

Although limited decision making involves cognitive processes, the relevant learning process is described as passive rather than cognitive learning because no active information search and brand evaluation takes place. The consumer receives information about the new paper towel passively and puts it in the back of his or her mind. Seeing the brand in the store triggers recall; the consumer examines the package and purchases the product for trial.

An important form of limited decision making is variety seeking. Consumers often try a variety of brands out of boredom simply because many low-involvement products are ordinary and mundane. It is unlikely that consumers develop strong preferences for a brand of salad dressing. However, a consumer may consciously experiment by buying a variety of brands. Purchases are made without brand evaluation or changes in brand attitude. The chosen brand will be evaluated while being consumed.

In their study, R. H. Bruskin, a large marketing research firm, found evidence of variety-seeking behavior. Bruskin found that for certain low-involvement products such as toothpaste, potato chips, and salad dressing, most consumers who switched to other brands continued to have favorable attitudes toward their former brand. The study concluded that consumers do not switch to other brands because of dissatisfaction but "just to try something new."[20] Since the level of involvement is low, the consumer is not likely to be seriously dissatisfied. Rather, the motivation to switch brands is a desire for change and a search for novelty.

UNPLANNED PURCHASING BEHAVIOR

When consumers are not involved with the product, they often make a purchase decision inside the store. There is insufficient motivation to preplan a purchase. Such unplanned decisions are generally made by inertia or by limited decision making. In contrast, complex decision making assumes a preplanning process. There are two basic reasons for an **unplanned purchase.** First, the time and effort involved in searching for alternatives outside the store may not be worth the trouble, and consumers buy largely on a reminder basis (that is, by inertia). Second, consumers may seek variety or novelty and thus buy on impulse (that is, by limited decision making).

The influence of in-store stimuli such as displays, shelf position, packaging, and price becomes more important for unplanned purchases than for preplanned purchase decisions. This does not mean that advertising and in-store stimuli are separate. As we know, advertising can reinforce in-store stimuli by reminding consumers of the brand once they see it on the shelf. Conversely, displays and good shelf position are a necessity if advertising is to be effective. As a result, the role of advertising will differ markedly depending on the type of purchase. For preplanned purchases, advertising attempts to create demand beforehand. For unplanned purchases, advertising is meant to tie in with in-store stimuli that influence consumers at the point of sale.

Types of Unplanned Purchases

Unplanned purchasing is often **impulse buying,** which is a tendency to buy on whim or an action based on a "powerful and persistent urge."[21] However, there are other types of unplanned purchases. By seeing the product on the supermarket shelf, a parent may be reminded that there is no breakfast cereal in the house. The parent then decides to examine nutritional information on various packages and selects that cereal judged to be most nutritious. This is an unplanned purchase, not an impulse purchase, as the parent did not make it on whim or base it on some persistent urge.

There are five types of unplanned purchases:[22]

1. *Pure impulse* purchases are made for variety or novelty. This type of behavior represents a departure from the normal set of products or brands purchased.
2. *Suggestion effect* purchases are made for a new product based on in-store stimuli. For example, a consumer was not aware of a nondetergent laundry product. Seeing it on the shelf or in a counter display, the consumer purchases it because the product is related to his or her needs.
3. *Planned impulse* refers to a consumer's intention to go to a specific store because of a sale but with no plan to buy particular products. Buying on special sale or by coupon is planned, but purchasing the item itself is not.
4. *Reminder effect* purchases are made because the consumer needs the item but did not include it in shopping intentions prior to entering the store. The trigger is seeing the product on the shelf or on display.
5. *Planned product category* refers to a consumer who plans to buy a particular product category (for example, paper towels) but does not preplan the brand decision. This consumer conducts an in-store search to decide on the brand and then selects the brand that is often the lowest price option.

Scope of Unplanned Purchases

http://www.dupont.com/

Several studies document the scope of unplanned purchases. DuPont Inc. conducted a study of consumer purchasing of toiletry, health care, and pharmaceutical products in supermarkets.[23] Among consumers' decisions for health care and beauty aid items, 61 percent were unplanned. Among their decisions for pharmaceuticals and vitamins, 51 percent were unplanned. A more recent study of supermarket items found that from 65 to 70 percent of consumers' purchases of dinners, entrees, and soups were unplanned.[24] Even purchases consumers make outside of supermarkets and drugstores are frequently unplanned. Prasad found that 39 percent of department store shoppers and 62 percent of discount store shoppers purchased at least one item on an unplanned basis.[25]

The last two recessions have probably increased unplanned purchases but have reduced pure impulse buying. The decrease in store loyalty, cited in the last chapter, has caused more consumers to shop for bargains. Most of these purchases are unplanned and are frequently based on price. On the other hand, pure impulse purchases (that is, purchases for variety or novelty) have probably decreased as a result of the last two recessions. A study by Yankelovich, Skelly, and White, the marketing research firm, found that almost one-fourth of the shoppers surveyed after the 1980–1982 recession said they made fewer impulse purchases.[26] The recession in the early 1990s probably reinforced this trend since impulse purchases are largely discretionary and shoppers are generally more price-sensitive.

THREE THEORIES OF LOW-INVOLVEMENT CONSUMER BEHAVIOR

A better understanding of low-involvement choice has evolved in marketing because of three theories: the theory of passive learning developed by Krugman,[27] the theory of social judgment developed by Sherif,[28] and the elaboration likelihood model developed by Petty and Cacioppo.[29]

Krugman's Theory of Passive Learning

One of the first perspectives on low-involvement consumer behavior was provided by Krugman's theory of passive learning. Studying the effects of television as a medium in the 1960s, Krugman sought an answer to why TV ads produced high levels of brand recall yet little change in consumers' brand attitudes. He hypothesized that television is a low-involvement medium that results in **passive learning.** The viewer is in a relaxed state and does not pay attention to the message. In this low-involvement environment, the viewer does not link the message to his or her needs, brand beliefs, and past experiences (as is assumed in the high-involvement case). The viewer retains information randomly because of repetition of the message. As a result, a respondent can show a high level of recall for a particular television advertisement, but the advertisement has little influence on brand attitudes.

Why is television a low-involvement medium? First, television advertising is animate while the viewer is inanimate (passive). Second, the pace of viewing is out of the viewer's control, and the viewer has little opportunity for reflection or making connections.[30] In contrast, print media (magazines and newspapers) are high-involvement media because advertising is inanimate while the reader is animate. The pace of exposure is within the reader's control because the reader has more opportunity to reflect on the advertising.

Krugman predicted that television would be more effective for low-involvement cases and print advertising for high-involvement cases. In their study, Grass and Wallace confirmed this view.[31] They found that for unmotivated consumers television was more effective in conveying a message than print ads were. For motivated consumers, print ads were somewhat more effective. A study by Childers and Houston concluded that verbal messages (such as print ads) are best for high-involvement audiences, and visual messages (such as TV ads) are best for low-involvement audiences.[32]

Krugman summarized his view of television by saying,

> The public lets down its guard to the repetitive commercial use of television. . . . It easily changes its ways of perceiving products and brands and its purchasing behavior without thinking very much about it at the time of TV exposure.[33]

In other words, consumers can change beliefs about a brand, leading to a purchase decision with very little thought and deliberation involved.

Krugman's theory of passive learning also has implications for the nature of advertising. If consumers are passive and disinterested, brand evaluation is unlikely to occur. Therefore, conveying product benefits through an informational approach is unlikely to work. Advertising must use noninformational means such as symbols and imagery to convey the message.

Consumer Behavior Implications of Passive Learning

Krugman's view of a passive consumer has stood many of the traditional behavioral concepts in marketing on their heads. Table 5.3 lists the traditional behavioral concepts associated with an involved, active consumer and the parallel concepts of an uninvolved, passive consumer.

The newer, low-involvement view holds that:

1. *Consumers learn information at random.* Krugman views uninvolved consumers as those who learn from repetitive advertising, much as children learn nonsense syllables, by just picking up random stimuli and retaining them. The traditional view is of involved consumers who actively process information in a cognitive manner by going through stages of awareness, comprehension, and retention. Hollander and Jacoby's study supports the low-involvement view of nonsense learning. They overlaid the audio portion of one commercial on the video portion of another, producing a nonsense TV commercial. Recall of the nonsense commercial was higher than the recall of the normal commercial.[34]

2. *Consumers are information catchers.* In the low-involvement case, consumers are information catchers, that is, passive receivers of information. High-involvement consumers are regarded as information seekers, actively searching for information from alternative sources and engaging in shopping behavior. Studies by Celsi and Olson and by Gensch and Javagali have confirmed that less involved consumers seek less information and consider fewer product alternatives in evaluating brands.[35] The limited amount of information search for most consumer products is demonstrated in studies that show that many consumers typically visit one store and consider only one brand.[36]

TABLE 5.3
The low-involvement, passive consumer versus the high-involvement, active consumer

Newer, Low-Involvement View of a Passive Consumer	Traditional, High-Involvement View of an Active Consumer
1. Consumers learn information at random.	1. Consumers are information processors.
2. Consumers are information gatherers.	2. Consumers are information seekers.
3. Consumers represent a passive audience for advertising. As a result, the effect of advertising on the consumers is strong.	3. Consumers represent an active audience for advertising. As a result, the effect of advertising on the consumer is weak.
4. Consumers buy first. If they do evaluate brands, it is done after the purchase.	4. Consumers evaluate brands before buying.
5. Consumers seek some acceptable level of satisfaction. As a result, consumers buy the brand least likely to give them problems and buy based on a few attributes. Familiarity is the key.	5. Consumers seek to maximize expected satisfaction. As a result, consumers compare brands to see which provide the most benefits related to needs and buy based on multiattribute comparisons of brands.
6. Personality and lifestyle characteristics are not related to consumer behavior because the product is not closely tied to the consumer's identity and belief system.	6. Personality and lifestyle characteristics are related to consumer behavior because the product is closely tied to the consumer's identity and belief system.
7. Reference groups exert little influence on product choice because products are unlikely to be related to group norms and values.	7. Reference groups influence consumer behavior because of the importance of the product to group norms and values.

3. *Consumers represent a passive audience for advertising.* The low-involvement perspective views advertising as most effective when it deals with unimportant matters. Under these conditions, advertising is a much more effective medium for inducing purchasing behavior in low-involvement conditions. In Krugman's view, just being exposed to a commercial is persuasive and may lead consumers to purchase without the intervening step of comprehension.

The traditional active audience view is tied to the assumption that consumers are involved information seekers with strongly held brand attitudes. Under such conditions, consumers are likely to resist advertising that does not conform to prior beliefs (selective perception). This view logically leads to the conclusion that advertising is a weak vehicle for changing people's minds and is better suited to confirming strongly held beliefs. Bauer summarizes the active audience view in describing advertising as a "most difficult business. . . . Typical communication experiments, including advertising tests, show that only a few percentages of the people exposed to the communication ever change their mind on anything important."[37]

On balance, when consumers are passive and the message is relatively unimportant, the low-involvement view considers advertising a more powerful medium than does the traditional active audience view.

4. *Consumers evaluate brands after buying.* Krugman states that uninvolved consumers may buy simply due to a reminder effect since most such purchases are unplanned. As a result, consumers often make the connection between a

need and the brand in the store. Brand evaluation occurs after the purchase. For example, consumers select a lower-priced brand of paper towels in the store and then evaluate the brand after using it. The traditional view holds that consumers evaluate alternative brands before purchasing them.

5. *Consumers seek an acceptable rather than an optimal level of satisfaction.* In the low-involvement case, consumers do not seek to maximize brand satisfaction. The energy required in search of the best product is not worth the expected benefits. A lower level of satisfaction is acceptable. Active consumers seek to maximize satisfaction by extensively evaluating brands. Comparing brand attributes, consumers select the brand that best meets their needs.

6. *Personality and lifestyle characteristics are not related to consumer behavior.* There is no reason to assume that personality variables such as compulsiveness and lifestyle variables such as sociability are related to behavior for uninvolved consumers. Most products consumers purchase are not central to their beliefs or self-identity. As Kassarjian said, "Personality variables may be related to racial prejudice, suicide, violent crimes, or the selection of a spouse. But turning to unimportant, uninvolving, low-commitment consumer products such as brands of beer, chewing gum, t-shirts, and magazine exposure, the correlations [of personality to behavior] are extremely low."[38]

In contrast, the traditional view assumes that the consumer's personality and lifestyle will be related to the purchase decision. Such relationships are assumed to exist because a high level of involvement assumes the product is important to the consumer's belief system and self-identity. Since self-identity is reflected in the consumer's personality and lifestyle, it makes sense to relate these characteristics to products with high consumer involvement.

7. *Reference groups exert little influence on consumers.* The low-involvement perspective holds that reference groups have little influence on consumers. A study by Cocanougher and Bruce supports this view.[39] Products such as salt, toothpaste, paper towels, and plastic wrap have little visibility and are not relevant to group norms. Since reference groups are not very important for low-involvement products, much of the advertising portraying social approval in the use of products such as floor wax or room deodorizers may be misplaced. The more relevant approach may be to portray the problems such products can eliminate.

Involved consumers are more likely to be influenced by reference groups because a high-involvement product is likely to reflect the norms and values of the group. Products such as automobiles, homes, and stereo sets are visible and have important status connotations.

Sherif's Theory of Social Judgment

A second theory that sheds additional light on uninvolved consumers is Sherif's **social judgment theory.** Sherif described an individual's position on an issue according to his or her involvement with the issue.[40] He identified a latitude of acceptance (the positions the individual accepts), a latitude of rejection (positions the individual rejects), and a latitude of noncommitment (positions toward which the individual is neutral). A highly involved individual who has a definite opinion about an issue would accept very few other positions and would reject a wide number of positions (narrow latitude of acceptance and wide latitude of rejection). An uninvolved individual would find more positions acceptable (wide latitude of acceptance) or would have no opinion about the issue (wide latitude of noncommitment).

A highly involved individual who agrees with a message (within his or her latitude of acceptance) will interpret it more positively than it actually is. This reaction represents an **assimilation effect.** A message that the individual disagrees with (within the latitude of rejection) will be interpreted as more negative than it actually is. This reaction represents a **contrast effect.** For example, a car buff who just bought a Chevy Blazer and is very satisfied with the car might recall some comments a friend made about it as more positive than they were (assimilation). However, if very disappointed with the Blazer, the car buff may recall the same comments by the friend as more negative than they actually were (contrast). Therefore, the highly involved individual is more likely to perceive messages selectively based on his or her preconceptions and biases. The uninvolved individual is less likely to perceive the message selectively, and an assimilation or contrast effect is less likely to occur.

http://www.chevrolet.com/

Sherif's theory as applied to consumer behavior is illustrated in Figure 5.2. Active, involved consumers would find fewer brands acceptable and would actively process information, whereas less involved consumers would find many brands acceptable and would engage in less information processing.

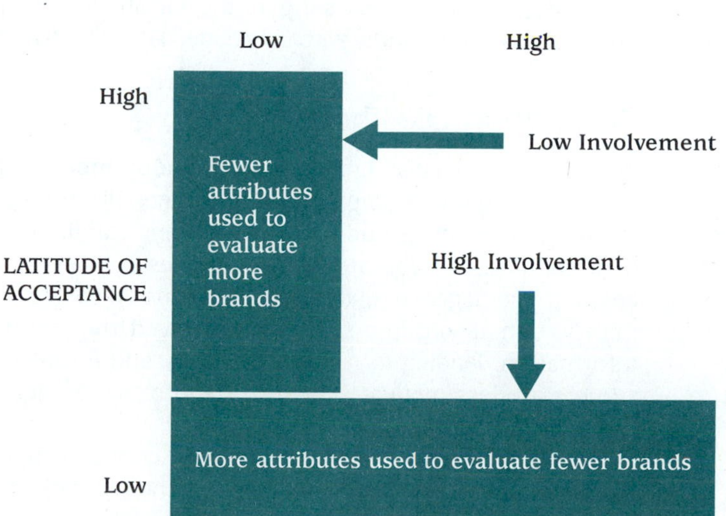

FIGURE 5.2 Social judgment theory applied to consumer behavior

Sherif's theory conforms well to Krugman's concept of passive learning and provides more insight into passive consumers. Uninvolved consumers are willing to consider a wider number of brands because of a lack of commitment to one or several brands, but they do not search for alternatives. Given a lack of commitment, they are less willing to spend time interpreting advertising messages and evaluating brands. As a result, they perceive advertising with little cognitive activity and purchase brands in the easiest way possible: they purchase the most familiar brand and buy the same brand repetitively. On this basis, social judgment theory and the theory of passive learning agree that uninvolved consumers seek a satisfactory solution to problem solving, whereas involved consumers seek a more optimal solution.

Rothschild and Houston extend Sherif's theory to predict that highly involved consumers will use more attributes to evaluate fewer brands (horizontal bar in Figure 5.2), while less involved consumers will use fewer attributes to consider more brands (vertical bar in Figure 5.2).[41] This assumption makes sense since more involved consumers' latitude of acceptance is narrower (fewer brands considered) and level of information processing is greater (more attributes used in evaluation), while the reverse is true for less involved consumers.

Several studies have supported Sherif's social judgment theory. Rothschild and Houston applied Sherif's measures of involvement to political choice.[42] They identified two types of political choices: a presidential election (high involvement) and a state assembly race (low involvement). They found the latitude of acceptance of issues was narrower and the number of issues used to evaluate the candidates was greater for the presidential race than for the state assembly race.

A study by Gensch and Javagali of farmers' selection of sources of supply found that less involved farmers evaluated more suppliers and did so on fewer attributes.[43] Both studies support the likelihood that less involved consumers process less information with a broader latitude of acceptance.

Elaboration Likelihood Model

Petty and Cacioppo's **elaboration likelihood model (ELM)** is a third theory that provides insight into uninvolved consumers. Illustrating how consumers process information in high- and low-involvement conditions,[44] the model presents a continuum from elaborate (central) processing to nonelaborate (peripheral) processing. The degree of elaboration depends on consumers' motivation to process information. If consumers are more involved, they are more motivated to process information, leading to more elaborate (central) processing. Less involved consumers are less motivated to process information, leading to nonelaborate (peripheral) processing.

Motivation to process the message is closely related to its relevance in meeting consumer needs. The more relevant the message, the more likely consumers will be to develop thoughts in support of or counter to its content (that is, the more consumers will elaborate on the message). Thus, the arthritic consumer viewing a commercial for a pain reliever that claims to relieve the pain of arthritis is more likely to elaborate on the message by injecting his or her thoughts (such as, "This product might help me" or "This product could upset my stomach") compared to the consumer who rarely encounters such pain. Uninvolved consumers are unlikely to develop such message-relevant thoughts. Elaboration is minimal because consumers are not motivated to process the information. They act as passive recipients of information.

Petty and Cacioppo's distinction between high and low elaboration is similar to Krugman's distinction between active and passive consumers, shown in Table 5.3. The difference is that ELM focuses on the consumers' response to the message (in support of or against) and the nature of the stimuli that are most likely to persuade the active or passive information processor, whereas Krugman's model focuses on message exposure and comprehension.

Several studies support the elaboration likelihood model. Petty, Cacioppo, and Goldman found that involved consumers are more likely to be influenced by the quality and strength of the message (central cues). In contrast, less involved consumers are more likely to be influenced by stimuli that are peripheral to the message—for example, the use of color in the ad, the nature of the background, or the use of an expert spokesperson.[45] Such peripheral cues had little influence on involved consumers.

Schumann, Petty, and Clemons found that less involved consumers are likely to be influenced by cosmetic variations in the ad (print type, layout, a picture of a spokesperson), whereas more involved consumers are likely to be influenced by substantive variations (changes in message content regarding product attributes and benefits).[46] Here again, less involved consumers were engaging in peripheral processing, and more involved consumers were engaging in central processing.

Another study supports the use of message cues with involved consumers and nonmessage cues with uninvolved consumers. Gardner, Mitchell, and Russo found that involved consumers are more likely to retain and organize advertising messages that help them in their brand choice.[47] On the other hand, uninvolved consumers view advertising more for form than content. They are more likely to notice elements of the ad such as music, characters, and scenery without linking these elements to the brand.

These studies imply that advertising to involved consumers should emphasize central message cues dealing with performance. Advertising to uninvolved consumers should use peripheral cues that might create a positive environment to stimulate the passive receipt of information. The ad in Exhibit 5.3 for Bauer in-line skates, a highly involving product, focuses on message cues closely related to the product's importance and consumer's self-image. The ad for Miracle Whip, an uninvolving product, relies on a story line dealing with a cop in the kitchen that is peripheral to the product. The danger is that product benefits might get lost if such peripheral cues dominate.

EXHIBIT 5.3
Use of central versus peripheral cues in advertising

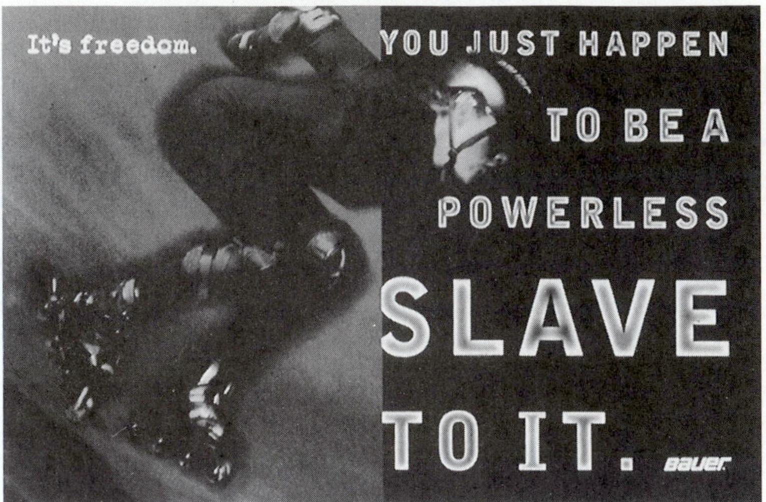

Central message cues for a high-involvement product

Peripheral message cues for a low-involvement product

STRATEGIC IMPLICATIONS OF LOW-INVOLVEMENT DECISION MAKING

The low-involvement perspective and the theories of Krugman, Sherif, and Petty and Cacioppo have implications for every facet of marketing strategy. This section reviews the strategic implications of low-involvement decision making and some strategic issues that arise from this perspective.

Marketing Strategy

The most important implications of a low-involvement perspective are for advertising strategy. Important implications apply to other facets of marketing strategy as well.

Advertising

Advertising strategy should be very different for a low-involvement product than for a high-involvement product. Differences in advertising approaches, as reflected in the theories cited, suggest the following strategies for low-involvement products:

1. *Advertising dollars should be spent in a campaign of high repetition and ads should provide short-duration messages.*[48] As Krugman notes, repetition is necessary to gain exposure, even though processing of the message may be minimal.[49] High repetition and short messages encourage passive learning and ensure brand familiarity.

These principles apply concepts of classical conditioning. Repetition is required to create consumers' contiguity between advertising theme or symbol and brand use. An example is the constant repetition of Diet Pepsi's theme over a two-year period; Ray Charles sang "You Got the Right One, Baby," which was followed by an "Uh Huh" refrain. The message was short, did not require the consumers' attention, and could, therefore, be processed passively. However, consumers remembered and easily linked it to the brand once they were in the store. In-store promotions and print ads with the same theme reinforced the television campaign.

http://www.pepsi.com/

In the high-involvement case, advertising should do more than create awareness and contiguity. It should influence consumers by communicating a persuasive message. Repetition is not the key; rather, it is the content of the message. Messages are likely to be more complex and varied and are likely to deal more directly with desired product benefits. Such ads can utilize an emotional or an informational appeal. The ads for car stereos in Exhibit 5.4 illustrate both approaches. The ad for the Coustic car radio takes an informational approach by detailing the characteristics and performance of the product. The Clarion ad in Exhibit 5.4 creates involvement through emotion but has little informational content.

http://www.clarion.com/

2. *Advertising should focus on a few key points rather than on a broad-based information campaign.* Where there is little consumer interest or attention, there is limited ability to process and assimilate information. A proper campaign in the low-involvement case "utilizes short messages emphasizing a few key points."[50]

3. *Visual and nonmessage components should be emphasized.*[51] Since uninvolved consumers learn passively and forget quickly, it is important to keep the product visually in front of them. In-store displays and packaging are important communications tools. Television advertising is more likely to be effective than print media because of the active visual component in television commercials. Where print is used, the product should be in the foreground and any peripheral cues in the background. The Miracle Whip ad in Exhibit 5.3 is illustrative.

▶EXHIBIT 5.4
Two approaches for high-involvement products

This Coustic ad for car stereos reflects consumer involvement by supplying detailed information on product performance.

This Clarion ad, also for car stereos, reflects consumer involvement by showing emotional attachment to the product.

4. *Advertising should be the primary means of differentiating the product from that of the competition.* Because there are no substantial brand differences for many low-involvement products, advertising becomes a primary means of competitive differentiation. Advertisers use symbols and imagery as substitutes for actual product differences and to maintain interest in undifferentiated brands. In this respect, symbols that can be positively identified with the brand, such as the Pillsbury doughboy, should be used. As Tyebjee states, "Communication differentiation rather than product differentiation is the strategic role of the sales proposition of low involvement advertising."[52]

5. *Television rather than print media should be the primary vehicle for communication.* If less product information is required, a low-involvement medium such as television is more suitable. This is because television does not require consumers to evaluate the content of the communication as closely as they do print communication. Print media are more suitable if the audience is active in seeking information and evaluating it.

Product Positioning

Low-involvement products are more likely to be positioned to minimize problems, whereas high-involvement products are more likely to be positioned to maximize desired benefits. This is true because uninvolved consumers seek acceptable, not optimal, products.

Taking a high-involvement view, a product such as plastic wrap might be positioned to stress benefits such as extra strength and the protection it affords food. A low-involvement positioning might emphasize problem minimization such as a wrap that is less likely to shred or one that prevents freezer burn. Frequent reference to avoiding problems such as dirty floors, stained glasses, or "ring around the collar" suggests the prevalence of a problem minimization approach for low-involvement products.

Price

Consumers buying low-involvement products are likely to be more price-sensitive. They frequently purchase on the basis of price alone, since brand comparisons are unimportant and there are few differences between brands. Therefore, a decrease in price or a coupon offer may be enough to influence the consumer to buy.

A study by Gotlieb, Schlacter, and St. Louis confirmed the greater price sensitivity of less involved consumers.[53] They found that it took smaller decreases in the price of competitive products to get uninvolved consumers to switch from their current brand. In his study of margarine purchasers, Lastovicka also demonstrated the importance of price for uninvolved consumers. Among those who said the purchase was unimportant, 52 percent said price was the determining factor. Among those who thought the purchase important, only 22 percent said that price was the determinant.[54]

STRATEGIC APPLICATIONS OF CONSUMER BEHAVIOR

▶ Advertising Agencies Utilize the Involvement Concept

Several advertising agencies have begun to utilize the concept of involvement in developing advertising strategy. Foote Cone & Belding (FCB) classifies products on two dimensions: level of involvement (high versus low) and motives for purchasing (think versus feel). Think (or cognitive) motives are utilitarian and are related to product performance. Feel (or affective) motives are more self-expressive and sensory. They are related to a product's badge value and its ability to arouse emotion. A consumer buying a car based on criteria such as handling and acceleration reflects utilitarian motives and would be in the "think" category. A consumer who buys a car based on style and status criteria would reflect self-expressive motives and would be in the "feel" category.

The matrix shown in Figure 5.3 classifies products into four categories. Products in Quadrant 1 are generally high in involvement, and consumers evaluate them based on utilitarian motives. Examples are life insurance, cameras, and credit cards. Products in Quadrant 2 are high-involvement categories that consumers evaluate based on more emotional criteria. Examples are sports cars, perfume, and wine. Products in Quadrant 3 are low in involvement, and consumers evaluate them based on utilitarian criteria. Examples are razors, liquid bleach, and suntan lotion. Products in Quadrant 4 are unin-

▶**FIGURE 5.3**
The FCB involvement grid

INVOLVEMENT LEVEL	MOTIVES FOR PURCHASING: Think	MOTIVES FOR PURCHASING: Feel
High	1 • Insurance • Economy Cars • Tires • Credit Cards • Analgesics	2 • Sports Cars • Perfume • Wine
Low	3 • Suntan Lotion • Liquid Bleach • Razors • Paper Towels	4 • Pizza • Beer • Soft Drink

volving, and consumers usually buy them based on sensory criteria. FCB describes these products as "life's little pleasures." Examples are beer, soft drinks, pizza, and cigarettes.

Foote Cone & Belding has developed advertising strategies for each of these four categories. Products in Quadrant 1 should be advertised using an informational approach that emphasizes performance, while products in Quadrant 2 should be advertised through emotional appeals linked to the consumer's self-image. Quadrant 3 products should be advertised by repetitive appeals that maintain brand awareness and encourage repeat buying. Quadrant 4 products should be advertised by utilizing principles of classical conditioning: repetitive appeals that develop contiguity between a symbol or theme (such as the Marlboro cowboy) and the product.

As stereo components straddle the think-feel dimension, there is probably a place in Figure 5.3 for both the informationally oriented Coustic car stereo ad and the emotionally oriented Clarion ad in Exhibit 5.4. The two products probably appeal to different segments of the car stereo market—Coustic to performance-oriented consumers and Clarion to consumers who view the product as an extension of their self-image.

Another advertising agency, Lintas USA, has adopted a remarkably similar classification. The only difference is that instead of think versus feel, they classify products into those that consumers purchase for negative versus positive motives. Negatively motivated products are almost always in the think category—credit cards and insurance for high-involvement products; razors and suntan lotion for low-involvement products. These are products designed to solve problems. Positively motivated products are almost always in the feel category. They are related to taste (soft drinks, wine) or self-enhancement (perfumes, sports cars). Advertising for less involving, negatively motivated products should demonstrate clear solutions to a problem, for example, controlling tartar build-up by using a certain toothpaste. Ads for less involving, positively motivated products should emphasize positive sensory experiences, for example, a refreshing soft drink.

Sources: "What's in a Brand?" *American Demographics* (May 1993), pp. 26–32; Brian T. Ratchford, "New Insights About the FCB Grid," *Journal of Advertising Research* 27 (August-September 1987), pp. 24–38; and Richard Vaughn, "How Advertising Works: A Planning Model Revisited," *Journal of Advertising Research* 26 (February-March 1986), pp. 57–66.

In-Store Stimuli

Since most low-involvement purchases are unplanned, in-store stimuli such as coupons, displays, or price deals are more likely to be important when consumers are not involved. Consumers may purchase the brand at eye level or the one with the largest shelf space simply because of the reminder effect. The package may be more influential for low-involvement goods because it is encountered in the store.

Distribution

Widespread distribution is particularly important for low-involvement products because consumers are not motivated to search for a brand. If a favored brand is not in the store, consumers are likely to make another choice. Marketing strategy must ensure in-store availability to discourage the likelihood of a brand switch.

Product Trial

Attempts at inducing trial are particularly important for low-involvement products since consumers may form a favorable attitude toward the brand after the purchase.[55] For instance, a consumer may try a free sample of toothpaste, like the taste, and purchase it. Not seeking to maximize satisfaction, the consumer may continue to purchase the toothpaste just because the brand is adequate.[56] Information search and further brand evaluation are not warranted. Due to inertia, trial may be sufficient to induce the consumer to continue purchasing the brand.

What strategies can the marketer use to encourage trial under low-involvement conditions? Free samples, deals and coupons, joint promotions with other products, in-store displays, and intensive distribution are all useful. Under high-involvement conditions, consumers are unlikely to switch brands because of a price deal or coupon incentives, so these strategies are not likely to induce trial. Trial under high-involvement conditions can be encouraged only by demonstrating that the brand can deliver desired product benefits.

Strategic Issues

Several strategic issues dealing with low-involvement decision making remain to be considered:

- Should marketers attempt to get consumers more involved with a low-involvement product? If so, how?
- Given low involvement, should marketers attempt to shift consumers from a pattern of repetitive buying that reflects inertia to variety-seeking behavior?
- Should marketers segment markets by degree of involvement so that different strategies are directed to high-involvement and low-involvement consumers for a particular product category?

Shifting Consumers from Low to High Involvement

It would make sense for a marketer to try to get consumers more involved in a product. Because involvement means commitment, involved consumers are more likely to remain loyal to the marketer's brand in the face of competitive activity. What strategies can the marketer use to involve consumers with the product?

1. *Link the product to an involving issue.* Rothschild and Houston use Sherif's theory in citing one strategy as an attempt to widen the latitude of rejection of competitive brands. This can be done by linking the advertised brand to an involving issue.[57] Motorola links its cellular phones to an involving issue:

bringing mobile communications to World Wildlife Fund teams working to save endangered species in remote parts of the world. Ajax links an uninvolving product to a highly involving issue—youth employment in minority neighborhoods (see Exhibit 5.5).

2. *Create a problem and solve it.* Madison Avenue has tried to increase involvement in mundane products by attempting to convince consumers that they have problems they never knew about. In the 1940s and 1950s, it was halitosis and body odor; in the 1960s and 1970s, it was coffee nerves and dishpan hands; in the 1980s it was vaginal yeast infections. Pepsi-Cola tried a similar strategy in 1994 when it tried to convince consumers of the importance of dating cola cans. Stale cola never occurred to most consumers as a problem, and for good reason: most colas are consumed before they lose their fizz. As a result, Pepsi's attempt to create awareness of a problem fell flat.[58]

3. *Link the product to an involving personal situation.* Another strategy is to associate a low-involvement product with an involving situation. Tyebjee suggests relating the product to an activity in which the consumer is engaged.[59] He cites examples such as an early morning coffee commercial, advertisements of automobile products on radio during rush hours, and messages about sleep aids on nighttime television shows. In each case, involvement with the product increases because of the situation's relevance.

4. *Link the product to involving advertising.* A third strategy is to create involvement with the advertising in the hope that consumers will establish some link with the product. Lutz said that just because "some products may be inherently low in involvement, their advertising need not be."[60] He cites two types of ads that may create involvement. An ego-defensive ad would help consumers defend themselves against inadequacy (for example, Marlboro smokers are masculine). A value-expressive advertisement expresses the consumers' values and beliefs. The Brazilian ad for Parmalat in Exhibit 5.5 appeals to mothers everywhere, but particularly in South American countries, by linking the product to family values. It tries to create an emotional attachment for an uninvolving product.

A third approach is to give an uninvolving product badge value through advertising. A Häagen-Dazs ad, for example, shows the product in the middle of an elegant table setting with the statement, "It is now socially acceptable to eat Häagen-Dazs ice cream with your fingers." The ad tries to increase involvement with an uninvolving product category by a tongue-in-cheek attempt at creating snob appeal.

5. *Change the importance of product benefits.* A more difficult strategy is to try to change the importance consumers attach to product benefits. We saw that 7-Up began advertising its flagship brand as having no caffeine even though this was not a new attribute. With the greater health-consciousness of American consumers, 7-Up felt it could increase the importance attached to caffeine content in soft drinks and thereby increase the involvement with its product.

EXHIBIT 5.5
Two strategies to increase involvement for uninvolving products

Linking the product to an involving issue

Linking the product to involving advertising

6. *Introduce an important characteristic in the product.* Boyd, Ray, and Strong cite the possibility of introducing an attribute into a product that had not been considered important or that did not previously exist.[61] Examples include using additives in gasoline, adding bran to cereals, and introducing automatic rewinds in cameras.

These five strategies would assist the marketer in creating more product involvement—but involvement is relative. Creating greater involvement for toothpaste or ice cream does not mean that consumers are likely to engage in complex decision making when they evaluate brands. It means only that a moderate amount of cognitive activity may be stimulated through advertising and product policies.

Shifting Consumers from Inertia to Variety Seeking

Under a condition of low involvement, another question is whether marketers should encourage consumers to switch brands in a search for variety or to avoid product search and stay with the same brand (inertia) because of familiarity. (See Exhibit 5.6 for an example of switching from inertia to variety seeking.)

EXHIBIT 5.6 Switching from inertia to variety seeking

Source: © Bill Whitehead.

"I've been faithful to this brand for 27 years. . . . Maybe it's time for a little fling!"

If a brand is a market leader, it would be in the brand's best interest for the marketer to encourage inertia. If it is a less-known brand, the marketer should encourage variety seeking. In a low-involvement situation, consumers may purchase the market leader because of familiarity. In such conditions, the marketer should use advertising as a reminder. In-store conditions would also be important to maintaining brand familiarity. To keep the brand in front of consumers, the market leader would place the brand in the dominant shelf space in the store. For less familiar brands, the marketer would attempt to encourage variety seeking by using deals, lower prices, coupons, and free samples to encourage trial. The objective is to induce consumers to switch brands and gain wider experience. Sherif's theory would support this view. In a low-involvement condition, the consumer has a wide latitude of acceptance, which suggests a greater willingness to try a diversity of brands.

http://www.cambellsoup.com/

Campbell's Soup is a good example of a market leader in a low-involvement category. Campbell's strategy has consistently been to advertise frequently to maintain familiarity and to dominate shelf space within the store. Other canned soups have occasionally been introduced. Competitors' strategies have reflected attempts to induce trial by lower prices, free samples, and appeals to variety in advertising. However, Campbell's high-frequency advertising campaigns and in-store dominance have made entry into the canned soup market difficult for other brands.

Segmenting Markets by Degree of Consumer Involvement

The concept of involvement is consumer-related, not product-related. It is defined in terms of consumers' evaluation of the importance of and identity with the product. Although most consumers may have little involvement with toothpaste, some consumers may be more highly involved.

Because involvement can be measured on an individual level, markets can be segmented by consumer involvement. Purchasers of toothpaste can be categorized as high-, medium-, and low-involvement consumers. Therefore, should marketing strategies for a given product category be differentiated by the degree of consumer involvement? Is it feasible to direct different advertising strategies to a high- versus a low-involvement segment for the same product? Such an approach would be expensive and could confuse consumers. A more realistic approach would be to differentiate the product rather than the advertising strategy.

A good example is cereal. Ordinarily, cereal is regarded as a low-involvement product; however, to consumers concerned with nutritional and health benefits, it is more involving. A company would introduce a cereal brand to more involved consumers through print as well as TV advertising by communicating the benefits of the brand in an informationally oriented campaign. Deals and coupons would not be emphasized, but nutritional information would be prominently displayed in the ads and on the package.

To direct a brand to the low-involvement segment, marketers would use deals and coupons to induce trial and place less emphasis on nutritional information. The marketer would also seek in-store displays and eye-level shelf space for the brand to encourage impulse buying.

In short, where it is possible to identify high- and low-involvement segments, marketers should consider differentiating their strategies by offering different brands.

SOCIETAL IMPLICATIONS OF LOW-INVOLVEMENT DECISION MAKING

Consumers are involved with issues as well as with products. Some consumers are more highly involved than others with issues such as environmental protection, drug abuse, teenage drinking, and prevention of AIDS. Whereas it would not necessarily benefit society to increase consumer involvement with bleach, toothpaste, or cars, it would be of benefit to increase involvement with these societal issues.

The problem is that consumers who are not involved reflect Krugman's profile of the passive consumer: low awareness of the issues, little processing of information regarding these issues, and little or no consideration of alternative solutions. What kind of consumers are least likely to be involved with societal issues? There have been few studies to identify these consumers. Webster's study of the ecologically conscious consumer found that those least likely to be involved with ecological issues were older, less educated, and less likely to be upwardly mobile.[62] Studies of political involvement indicate that those least involved have the exact same profile: older, less educated, lower income.[63] Reinforcing this profile of the low-involvement consumer is Hyman's study of involvement with the selection of a phone company after the deregulation of telephone service. Hyman found that the least involved consumers had essentially the same profile.[64] These studies suggest that those least likely to be involved with key societal issues and perhaps even with their own well-being may be older, downscale consumers.

A key question is how to increase involvement with societal issues among those least involved. The three groups cited in Chapter 2—business, government, and consumer groups—have a role. At times, companies have played a constructive role. For example, Anheuser-Busch has run ads in magazines such as *Parenting* to increase awareness of problems of teenage drinking and driving (see Exhibit 5.7). Consumer groups have played an active role in trying to increase awareness of and involvement in key issues. For example, the Environmental Defense Fund has mounted advertising campaigns to increase awareness of recycling; the Association for a Drug-Free America has run a nationwide

http://www.edf.org/

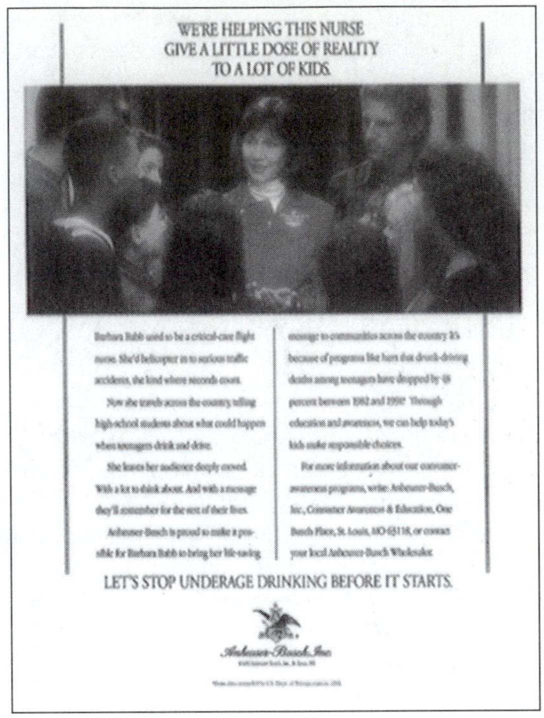

▶EXHIBIT 5.7 The role of business in increasing involvement with a societal issue

campaign to increase awareness of drug abuse; and organizations such as Momentum have been instrumental in increasing awareness of AIDS prevention.

Government plays an indirect role in increasing involvement by trying to encourage participation in the political process and by publicizing legislation and activities at the federal, state, and local levels regarding issues such as pollution control. A key question is whether the federal government should do more to provide information to those who might be most at risk—for example, providing more effective information on AIDS prevention to drug abusers or increasing awareness of the dangers of drinking and driving among teenagers.

SUMMARY

This chapter focused on consumer choice in low-involvement situations. Four types of consumer behavior were identified using two dimensions: level of consumer involvement and level of decision making.

1. Complex decision making requires high consumer involvement and extensive information processing. Consumers form beliefs about brands, evaluate them, and then choose. This think-before-you-act model conforms to a traditional hierarchy of effects.
2. Brand loyalty requires high involvement but little information processing. Positive reinforcement results in the consumers' repetitive purchase of the same brand.
3. Inertia assumes a low level of involvement and little information processing. The consumer has found a reasonably satisfactory brand and will stick with it. There is little incentive to search for information

and to evaluate alternative brands. Brand switching may be induced by price deals and coupons.

4. Limited decision making assumes a low level of involvement but a moderate amount of information processing. Consumers may switch from inertia to limited decision making because of the introduction of a new product or changes in the existing product. Variety seeking because of boredom is an important example of limited decision making.

Unplanned purchases are an important manifestation of low-involvement purchasing behavior since consumers make most unplanned purchase decisions in the store. As a result, in-store stimuli such as displays, coupons, and price specials are more likely to be influential.

Three theories were presented as a basis for understanding low-involvement decision making. Krugman's *theory of passive learning* suggests that when consumers are not involved, they do not cognitively evaluate advertising messages. Exposure to advertising could occur without recall and comprehension. Sherif's *theory of social judgment* suggests that in conditions of low involvement, consumers are willing to consider many brands; however, they are likely to use only a few attributes to evaluate them. Petty and Cacioppo's *elaboration likelihood model* suggests that uninvolved consumers are more likely to react to nonmessage stimuli in communications than they are to the message itself.

The implications of low-involvement decision making for the development of marketing strategy were described. Several important strategic questions were raised:

- How can marketers get consumers more involved with low-involvement products?
- How can marketers of less-known brands get consumers to switch from inertia to variety-seeking behavior?
- Should marketers segment markets by consumers' degree of involvement?

The chapter closed by considering the societal implications of a lack of involvement in key issues such as environmental control, teenage drinking, and drug abuse and the role of business, consumer agencies, and government in increasing awareness and involvement.

QUESTIONS

1. What is the strategic value of companies such as Kellogg's and 7-Up increasing consumer involvement with their products?
2. This chapter suggests that many consumers are not involved with the brand purchased and that they frequently make decisions based on inertia.
   - If this is true, why do most marketing strategies assume an involved consumer?
   - Why is it hard for a marketing manager to believe that most consumers are not involved in the purchase of the company's brand?
3. Design a general marketing strategy for a new brand of paper towel that is positioned as more economical because it has more sheets at the same price, yet has the same level of quality as other towels. (In most cases, consumers would regard paper towels as a low-involvement product.)
   - Now assume that the same manufacturer has identified a segment of paper towel users who are more involved with the product because they recognize many usage situations that require a high-quality towel. The company decides to introduce a heavier-weight/high-quality towel to this involved segment. How would this marketing strategy differ from the previous strategy?
4. What is meant by the principle of "cognitive consistency?" How is it related to low-involvement purchasing behavior?
5. One group of consumers usually determines what cereal it will buy in advance and then goes to the store and buys it. Another usually makes its decision in the store. What differences might be employed in marketing to each group?
6. Develop a profile of the involved consumer for paper towels (the segment in the second part of Question 3) versus the uninvolved consumer (the segment in the first part of Question 3). Use Table 5.3 as a basis for profiling these two segments.
7. Why is variety seeking considered a form of low-involvement consumer behavior?
8. What strategies can a retailer use to encourage the five types of unplanned purchasing behavior specified in the chapter?
9. What is the FCB grid? What are the advertising implications of the FCB grid for each of the following product categories: (a) life insurance, (b) detergents, (c) beer, and (d) perfume?

10. The elaboration likelihood model suggests that nonmessage cues in advertising are more influential in low-involvement conditions.
    - Why is this true?
    - How can nonmessage cues be used in advertising strategies?
11. Discuss the following two arguments: (a) Advertising is a weak communications medium because consumer involvement results in selective exposure (the active audience view). (b) Advertising is a strong communications medium because a lack of consumer involvement results in retention of the message with little cognitive activity (the passive audience view).
    - What is the predominant view in advertising today? Why?
    - Can you cite advertising examples that tend to support advertisers' recognition of a passive audience?
12. Pick a low-involvement product category. Assume you are introducing a new brand in this category. Devise a strategy for attempting to create higher involvement with the brand by utilizing the five strategies for shifting consumers from low to high involvement described in the chapter.
13. Consider the product you selected in Question 12.
    - Under what conditions would a marketer of a brand encourage variety seeking?
    - Under what conditions would the marketer encourage inertia?
14. Is it realistic to develop separate brand and marketing strategies for high- and low-involvement segments of a product category?
15. Should business, government, and consumer groups have a role in increasing consumer involvement with societal issues such as pollution control or teenage drinking? If so, what should that role be?

RESEARCH ASSIGNMENTS

1. Find Web sites for a high-involvement, expensive product and a low-involvement, inexpensive product. Compare the two sites.
    - How is the different involvement level represented in site development?
    - Is there any reason for you to visit these sites more than once?
    - Do you think the sites are consistent with the type of decision making the consumer employs?
2. Select what you regard as a high-involvement and a low-involvement product category. Develop a means of measuring degree of consumer involvement for these two product categories using a consumer's rating of (a) the importance of the product, (b) the risk associated with the product, and (c) the emotional appeal of the product. Applying this measure, interview a small sample of consumers.
    - Was your assumption correct? That is, are significantly more consumers involved in what you identify as the high-involvement category compared to the low?
    - Determine the following information for each consumer:
        - Number of brands considered.
        - Number of attributes cited as important in evaluating brands for each product.
        - Advertising recall for key brands.

    Now categorize the sample into those above and below average on level of involvement for each product category.
    - Are there differences in characteristics between those more and less involved according to the three areas of information listed above?
    - Do your findings conform to the theories of (a) passive learning, (b) social judgment, and (c) elaboration likelihood?

SITUATIONAL INFLUENCES

Chapter 6

TIMEX POSITIONS ITS WATCHES BY USAGE SITUATIONS

In the previous three chapters, we described how consumers go about making decisions and how, at times, their decisions become routinized. Since purchasing and consuming are the objectives of consumer decisions, the situation in which consumers purchase and consume products and services influences what they buy.

Regarding the purchase, the type of store (small boutique or department store), the purpose of the purchase (as a gift or for oneself), and the context of the purchase (shopping alone, with friends, assisted by a salesperson) are likely to influence the consumer. Regarding consumption, a consumer could easily say, "The brand I select depends on how, when, where, and why I'm going to use it." A consumer may prefer one brand of paper towels for heavy-duty cleaning and another for wiping, one brand of coffee to have alone and another to serve guests, and one make of automobile for long business trips and another for local shopping trips. These consumption situations directly affect purchasing behavior.

In this chapter, we consider three types of situations—the purchase situation, the consumption situation, and the communication situation—as influences on consumer decisions. We will consider

- The nature of these situational influences.
- A model of consumer behavior based on situational effects.
- Recent studies that account for consumption and purchase situations.
- The use of situational variables in developing marketing strategies.

http://www.timex.com/

The consumption situation can be the basis for introducing and positioning a product. Timex has positioned its watches based on the consumption situation in appealing to the fitness segment. It switched from plain, low-priced watches to more stylish models positioned to younger, sports-oriented con-

EXHIBIT 6.1
Positioning Timex watches by sports situations

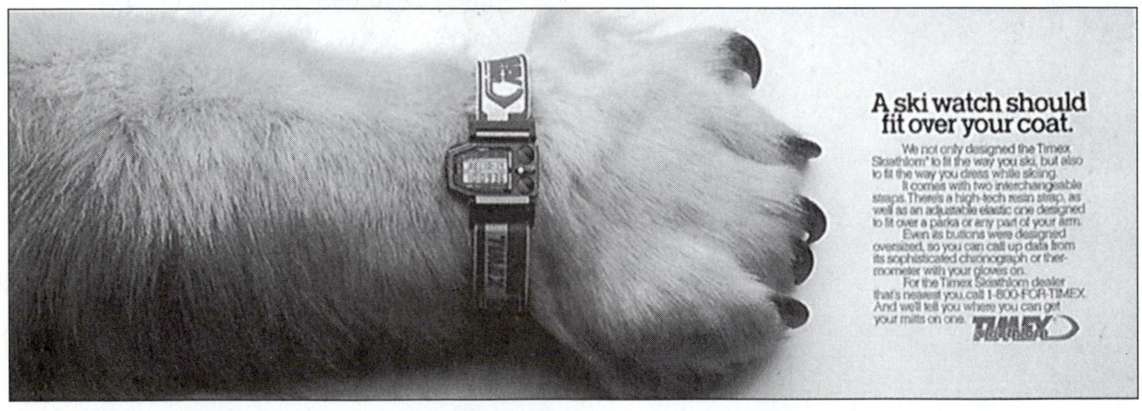

sumers and geared to specific situations. One watch, the Ironman, is designed for joggers and has features such as a stopwatch to count time and laps. Another, the Skiathlom, can fit over a parka and gloves and records temperature as well as time (see Exhibit 6.1). As a result of Timex's repositioning to focus on particular sports situations, sales soared.

Leveraging on this success, in 1994 Timex introduced a new line of watches, Timex Data Link watches, specifically geared to busy executives. These watches provide users with the ability to upload appointments and phone numbers from an electronic day-planner on a personal computer to the watch's memory. This upload occurred by simply pointing the watch at the computer screen. By 1996, the watch had won numerous awards and was compatible with a popular electronic day-planner, Schedule+ for Windows 95. This is yet another example of Timex introducing a watch based on a consumption situation, scheduling and planning day-to-day activities.[1]

Purchase situations can also be central to marketing strategies. For example, the gift-giving situation is often the basis for advertising products such as watches, electronics, and toys. Manufacturers frequently advertise products for Father's or Mother's Day and for holidays, particularly Christmas. In many retail businesses, 50 percent of sales occur between Thanksgiving and Christmas and most are for gift-giving occasions.

NATURE OF SITUATIONAL INFLUENCES

Situational influences are temporary conditions or settings that occur in the environment at a specific time and place. Examples are shopping for a gift, going skiing, or jogging.

If marketers consider the situation in developing their marketing strategy, they must understand the nature of situational variables. To gain such an understanding, we will consider the:

- Types of situations that influence consumers' decisions.
- Characteristics of these situations.
- Development of an inventory of situations to measure how they influence consumer attitudes, preferences, and purchasing behavior.

Types of Situations

Three types of situations are relevant to marketers: the consumption situation, the purchase situation, and the communication situation.[2]

Consumption Situation

The consumption situation is the one in which consumers use the brand. A consumer may use a particular brand of perfume or cologne for special occasions and another brand for everyday wear. Another consumer may consider different brands of personal computers for home versus business use. A consumer might serve regular coffee to guests but drink instant coffee when alone. Each of these consumption situations affects brand choice.

Marketers must identify consumption situations relevant to the product category. Bearden and Woodside identified the following consumption situations for beer:

- Entertaining close friends at home.
- Going to a restaurant or lounge on Friday or Saturday night.
- Watching a sports event or a favorite TV show.
- Engaging in a sports activity or hobby.
- Taking a weekend trip.
- Working at home on the yard, house, or car.
- Relaxing at home.[3]

Consumers can anticipate situations like these. That is, most of the time, consumers know in advance that they will be entertaining friends or going to a restaurant. Some situations are unanticipated, however—for example, having friends drop in unexpectedly or deciding to go away for the weekend on the spur of the moment. These situations may prompt consumers to buy certain items quickly and to pay more than they ordinarily would because of a lack of time to shop around for lower prices.

The consumption situation is also likely to affect consumers' choice of services. Gehrt and Pinto identified the following consumption situations for health care services:

- Wether the health problem is major or minor.
- Whether the health problem affects the consumer or another member of the family.
- Whether the health problem occurs at home or away from home.[4]

These situations directly affect the type of health care consumers choose. For example, going to a hospital's emergency room for a major health problem is more likely when consumers are away from home than it is when they are at home.

Purchase Situation

The purchase situation may also affect consumer decisions. Three factors are particularly important in affecting marketing strategy based on the purchasing situation: (1) the in-store purchase situation; (2) whether or not the purchase situation is for a gift-giving occasion; and (3) whether or not the purchase situation is unanticipated.

In-Store Situations. We saw the importance of store influences on shopping behavior when we discussed store choice in Chapters 3 and 4. In-store stimuli such as product availability, shelf position, pricing promotions, displays, and ease of shopping are important in influencing consumer purchasing decisions, especially for unplanned purchases.

The importance of the purchase situation has been documented in many studies that demonstrated the effects of price changes, displays, and salesperson influences on consumer behavior as a result of the in-store environment.[5] One such study of beauty aids found that the following situational factors were instrumental in influencing unplanned purchases:[6]

- *Price promotions.* Fifty-six percent of respondents bought more unplanned items because of these in-store stimuli.
- *Free samples.* Thirty-five percent of respondents bought more unplanned items because of free samples.
- *Displays.* Twenty-seven percent of respondents bought more unplanned items because of displays.

The importance of in-store stimuli is further demonstrated by the fact that expenditures on sales promotions have risen more rapidly than those on advertising. In 1988, total expenditures on sales promotions exceeded those for advertising for the first time, and they have continued to increase at a more rapid rate. The majority of such expenditures are for in-store stimuli such as price promotions, displays, and coupons.[7]

Because of these influences, it is important for marketers to identify various in-store situations and ask consumers how they would respond. For example, assume a manufacturer of a leading line of cereals conducts a survey and asks a sample of consumers how the following purchase-related situations may affect brand choice:

- You are in the store and find your favorite brand of cereal is not in stock. (Do you go to another store, buy a substitute brand, or delay the purchase?)
- Your favorite brand of cereal is five cents more than it was last time.
- A brand of cereal that you have used occasionally has a price deal.
- You need cereal, but there is a long line at the checkout counter as you come into the store.
- You have some difficulty finding your favorite brand of cereal. (Do you ask a clerk for help or buy a competitive brand?)

Responses to these in-store situations may affect brand strategies. One essential indicator of brand loyalty, for example, is whether consumers will stick to their favorite brand, regardless of in-store stimuli, or whether such stimuli may influence them to try a competitive brand.

Gift-Giving Situations. A second purchase-related situation is whether consumers buy the product as a gift or for themselves. Marketers target a wide range of products from candy to clothing to electronics for holidays and other gift-giving occasions. The first ad in Exhibit 6.2 shows a product advertised for

▶EXHIBIT 6.2
Advertising for gift-giving situations

a holiday occasion—Easter. The second shows a product targeted to a more personal occasion, a birthday.

Purchasing a gift is likely to be more involving for consumers than purchasing a product for themselves. As Belk notes, when consumers give gifts, they are giving not only the physical product, but also a symbolic message with it.[8] They want to ensure that they are sending the right message in terms of the type of gift, its price, and the brand name. As a result, they frequently spend more time selecting products for gifts than selecting products for their own use. Consumers use different criteria in evaluating brands and are likely to select a different brand than if the purchase were for themselves.

Even if the products themselves are uninvolving, when placed in a gift-giving context consumers are likely to be more involved. Clarke and Belk found that when buying uninvolving products such as bubble bath or blankets, consumers visited more stores and spent more time in information search when the purchase was for a gift.[9]

One result of this greater involvement in gift-giving is that consumers are likely to see more risk in the selection. As a result, they are more likely to buy brand names and to shop in well-known stores. A study by Ryan found that consumers are more likely to purchase small appliances for gifts from stores with a high-quality image.[10]

The gift-giving situation has been described as a *cultural ritual.* Gift giving requires a sequence of events that often entails symbolic behavior. The consumer acquires a gift, removes the price tag, wraps the item, delivers it, awaits a reaction, receives a gift in return in some circumstances, and conveys a reaction. This process of exchanging gifts creates bonds of trust and dependence between the parties.

Sherry describes the gift-giving ritual in more detail by dividing it into three stages.[11] In the first stage, the consumer identifies a gift-giving situation. The situation might be identified by society, as in a holiday, or might be more personal, as when a parent rewards a child for some achievement. The donor determines an appropriate price and product category for a gift and makes a selection. The second stage is the process of gift giving and possibly exchanging gifts. The donor determines the time, place, and mode of giving the gift and assesses the recipient's response. In the third stage, the gift is disposed of by being consumed, displayed, stored away, or returned. The nature of disposition will strengthen the bond between donor and receiver (as when the gift is displayed) or weaken it (as when the gift is returned).

The nature of the gift-giving ritual is also culturally bound. In Japan, for instance, gift-giving rituals are more prescribed than they are in the United States. The Japanese view gifts as part of the process of bonding in a highly group-oriented society, and they define more gift-giving occasions and give gifts to a much wider network of friends, acquaintances, and family.

Although gift giving has generally positive connotations, Sherry and his colleagues also describe a *darker side of gift-giving* in the context of rituals. Using depth interviews and ethnographic techniques (see Chapter 1), Sherry et al. found that many consumers considered gift giving and receiving anxiety producing, creating interpersonal conflicts. Consider the following narrative between husband and wife during a gift-giving occasion:[12]

John: Mabel, why did your brother send me this plaid shirt?

Mabel: Billy called and asked if you liked the way he dressed. I couldn't hurt his feelings.

John: Isn't it funny how your gift is so pretty and mine looks like a roving used car salesman's loungewear?

Mabel: John, just throw it away or give it to the Goodwill and let the whole matter drop.

John: I don't want to let it drop. I paid good money to buy Bill and Nancy a gift that we thought was nice. We got them a set of very expensive wine glasses from Neiman Marcus.

Mabel: I told you what to do with the shirt once. Plus last year they got us both a really nice gift.

John: Yeah, you can talk. Your gift is great. Mine is really garbage. Next year nothing, nothing. The damn cheapskates.

Mabel: Let me tell you something. That's my brother. I don't complain when your mother gives me a pair of Kmart stockings which no one wears. (etc. etc.)

This narrative certainly reflects the negative dimensions of gift giving: invidious comparisons of gifts, resentment of the gift-giving process, and basic interpersonal conflicts that are laid bare as the result of the wrong gift. Most gift-giving occasions do not approach this negative effect, but in many cases there is underlying resentment at the obligatory nature of gift giving, the shopping task required, and the time deadlines involved. As Sherry et al. note, "Gift giving frequently becomes a contest, even an ordeal. Both giver and receiver may be caught in the snares of temporal deadlines and unattainable expectations."[13]

Unanticipated Purchase Situations. Purchase situations can sometimes be unanticipated. For example, if unexpected guests arrive, consumers may have to make a special shopping trip and may be willing to pay higher prices to obtain needed items quickly. Cote, McCullough, and Reilly studied several unanticipated purchase situations such as an unexpected price change, bumping into friends who might influence choice, and being short of time.[14] Among the products studied, unanticipated situations were particularly important in explaining the purchase of hamburgers, beer, and potato chips, items that typically can serve as last-minute fill-ins for unexpected situations. The study also found that consumer behavior for most of the food items studied could be better predicted when unexpected situations were included as variables.

Two unanticipated situations—out-of-stock products and product failures—are particularly important because they precipitate the need for making a choice. Consumers finding a food item out of stock may have to make a special purchase trip if the item is important enough. Product failures for durable goods like appliances and automobiles require consumers to make decisions to repair or replace the item. One study found that 60 percent of purchases of major home appliances resulted from breakdowns or the need for repairs.[15]

Communication Situation

The communication situation is the setting in which consumers are exposed to information. It can be person-to-person (word-of-mouth communications between friends and neighbors or information from a salesperson) or impersonal (advertising, in-store displays). The communication situation could determine whether consumers will notice, comprehend, and retain the information. Three types of situations may affect consumer response: the exposure situation, the context of the communication, and the consumers' mood state while receiving the communication.

Regarding the first factor, the following define various situations for advertising exposure:

- Did consumers hear a radio commercial while riding in the car or while sitting in the living room?
- Did consumers read a magazine inside or outside the home?
- Did consumers read the magazine as a pass-on issue?
- Did consumers see a TV commercial alone or with a group of people?
- Did consumers see the TV commercial in the middle of an involving program?

All of these situations are likely to influence the effectiveness of the advertisement, independent of its content.

A second situational variable that is likely to affect reaction to the communication is the context in which it appears—for example, the type of programming during which a TV commercial appears. One study found that "happy" programming, in contrast to "sad" programming, led consumers to have more positive thoughts during exposure to the commercial and a higher level of recall.[16] Program content led a number of advertisers to withdraw from the TV miniseries "The Day After" during the Cold War. The program dealt with the aftermath of a Soviet-American nuclear war, and advertisers did not want to be associated with the program's depressing content.

A third situational variable is the consumers' mood state when receiving the communication. Research has shown that whether consumers are happy or sad affects the processing and recall of brand information.[17] As a result, consumers' mood state is also likely to affect comprehension and retention of the advertising message.[18]

We will consider the consumption and purchase situation in the remainder of the chapter. Communication situations are explored further in Chapter 11, "Marketing Communications."

Characteristics of Consumption and Purchase Situations

It is necessary to identify not only specific types of consumption or purchase situations, but also to consider the more general characteristics of such situations. Belk identified five characteristics:[19]

1. *Physical surroundings*. For example, a store's decor and shelf layout, being indoors or outside when using a product, being in a noisy room when watching TV.
2. *Social surroundings*. Whether guests are present, the social occasion, the importance of friends and neighbors who are present when purchasing or consuming a product.

3. *Time.* Breakfast, lunchtime, between meals; seasonal factors such as winter versus summer relative to clothing; the time that has passed since the product was last consumed.
4. *Task definition.* Shopping for oneself or for the family; shopping for a gift; cooking for oneself, for the family, or for guests.
5. *Antecedent states.* Momentary conditions such as shopping when tired or anxious, buying a product on impulse, using a product when in an excited state. The consumer's mood when buying or using a product would be an antecedent state. Antecedent states such as people's moods are internal to consumers because they are determined by the consumer's state of mind. The four other situational characteristics are determined by the environment and are, therefore, external to consumers.

Situations are likely to be made up of several of these characteristics. For example, the purchase situation "shopping for a snack that the family can eat while watching television in the evening" is made up of the physical surroundings (at home), the social surroundings (family), time (evening), and task definition (consumer is doing the shopping and family will do the eating).

One study of attitudes toward do-it-yourself auto maintenance examined situations that might influence these attitudes, such as physical surroundings (convenient area to work, tools available), time availability, and antecedent states (knowledge of maintenance procedures before starting work). These characteristics were found to affect willingness to engage in auto maintenance.[20]

Development of Situational Inventories

To determine the influence of situations on behavior, marketers must develop an inventory of purchase and consumption situations. Such inventories must be product-specific because the situations that affect the choice of a snack food, for example, differ from those that affect the choice of a cosmetic.

To develop a situational inventory, consumers are brought together in focus groups for an open-ended discussion of the purchase and usage of a certain product category. From these discussions, marketers identify a large number of purchase and consumption situations. They can then reduce the number of situations by eliminating any redundancy between situations (for example, a between-meal snack and an afternoon snack frequently represent the same situation) and by selecting those situations that seem to be most closely related to brand choice.

Once the situational inventory is developed, consumers can be asked the frequency with which the situation arises and how likely they are to buy a particular product or brand in that situation. Table 6.1 presents a situational inventory used in a snack food study. Ten situations were identified based on preliminary focus-group interviews with consumers. The 10 situations were factor-analyzed (a statistical technique used to eliminate redundancy between variables) to reduce them to four situational dimensions:

1. Informal serving situations (represented by Items 5, 7, and 8 in Table 6.1).
2. Nutritive situations (Items 4, 9, and 10).
3. Impulsive consumption situations (Items 3 and 6).
4. Planned purchasing situations (Items 1 and 2).

These situations were related to the purchase of three types of snack foods: substantial snacks (sandwiches, cheese, crackers), light/salty snacks, and sweet snacks. Consumers were not homogeneous in the types of snack foods they purchased for the four situations. One segment bought substantial snacks for all occasions, except unplanned purchases. For unplanned purchases, they tended to buy light/salty snacks. A second segment bought light/salty snacks primarily for informal serving situations. A third segment bought sweet snacks primarily for impulsive situations.[21]

Although dated, the study has implications for marketing strategy. Marketers of light/salty snacks such as potato chips and pretzels would do best to portray these products in informal or party situations. Ads for Frito-Lay's line of salty snacks show children and adults in party situations. Marketers of sweet snacks

http://www.fritolay.com/

TABLE 6.1
Examples of situational inventories for snack foods and for beer

Snack Food Inventory
1. You are shopping for a snack that you or your family can eat while watching television in the evenings.
2. You are planning a party for a few close friends and are wondering what to have around to snack on.
3. Snacks at your house have become a little dull lately and you are wondering what you might pick up that would be better.
4. You are going on a long automobile trip and are thinking that you should bring along some snacks to eat on the way.
5. You suddenly realize that you have invited a couple of friends over for the evening and you have nothing for them to snack on.
6. You are at the grocery store when you get an urge for a between-meal snack.
7. You are at the supermarket and notice the many available snack products; you wonder if you should pick something up in case friends come by.
8. You are thinking about what type of snack to buy to keep around the house this weekend.
9. You are at the store to pick up some things for a picnic you are planning with friends and are trying to decide what kind of snack to buy.
10. You are thinking about a snack to have with lunch at noon.

Source: Russell W. Belk, "An Exploratory Assessment of Situational Effects in Buyer Behavior," *Journal of Marketing Research* 11 (May 1974), p. 160. Reprinted with permission from *Journal of Marketing Research*.

such as cookies could emphasize the impulsive nature of consumption—the urge to buy and to liven up a snacking occasion. Marketers could link such a situation to the pleasure of eating sweets.

Limited Use of Situational Variables

Because the usage situation is so important to brand choice, it is surprising that most marketing studies do not account for the situation. Consumers are asked to rate brands on nutrition, taste, convenience, and other variables without reference to the usage situation. The assumption seems to be that brand attitudes, brand preferences, and consumer choice are the same regardless of the situation.

It is clear that if marketing strategy is to be geared to consumer needs and preferences, marketers must measure these needs and preferences for a particular usage situation.

A MODEL OF SITUATIONAL INFLUENCES

The simple model of consumer behavior in Chapter 1 described three possible influences on purchasing behavior: (1) the consumer, (2) environmental influences, and (3) marketing strategy. A model of situational determinants on consumer behavior would describe behavior as a function of the same three basic forces, except that the consumers' environment would be represented by the consumption, purchase, or communications situation and marketing strategy would be represented by the product being consumed.

This model of situational influences is presented in Figure 6.1. The two outside forces acting on consumers are the product and the situation. Consumers react to the product and the situation and decide on the brand to be purchased. The interaction between the consumer's psychological set (needs, attitudes, and preferences), the situation, and the product results in a process of choice leading to behavior. The situation and the product can also be viewed in terms of the cognitive principles of *context,* which states that consumers organize stimuli into *figure* (foreground) and *ground* (background) by distinguishing stimuli that are prominent from those that are less prominent. This distinction is clear in viewing almost any print advertisement. The product generally appears in the foreground and the situation in the background. The ads in Exhibit 6.3 are examples. The French ad for Sprite shows the product in the foreground with a consumption situation, quenching one's thirst after exercising, in the background, and the tagline, "Forget what you see. Think of what you will drink. Listen to your thirst." The ad for Baccarat also shows the product in the foreground with a usage situation, a New Year's gala party, in the background. In both cases, the background is fairly indistinct compared to the product.

http://www.cocacola.com/

FIGURE 6.1
A model of situational determinants of consumer behavior

Source: Adapted from Russell W. Belk, "Situational Variables and Consumer Behavior," *Journal of Consumer Research*, 2 (December, 1975), p. 158. Reprinted with permission from The University of Chicago Press.

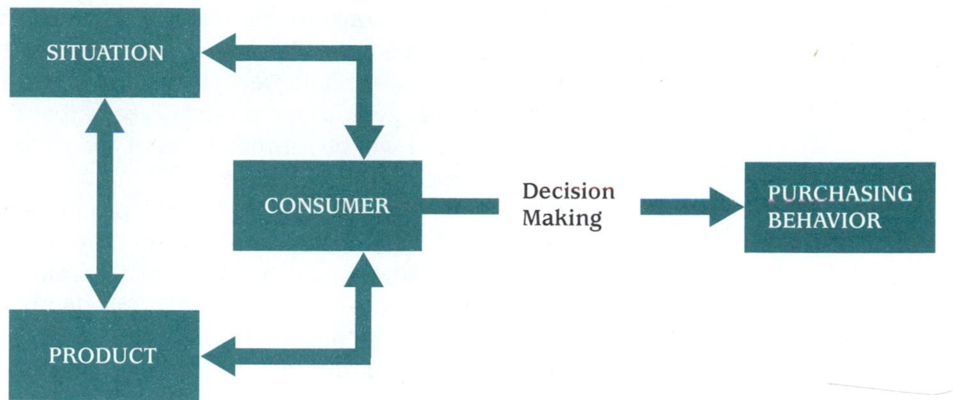

EXHIBIT 6.3
Advertising with the situation as background

Although the situational model may seem simple compared to the descriptions of decision making in Chapters 3 through 5, it is not as simple as it appears. Do consumers attribute behavior to the situation, to the product, or to both? Attributing behavior to the product means that the consumer is loyal to a particular brand and will buy it regardless of the situation. Attributing behavior to the situation means that consumers will purchase different brands for different situations. The situation rather than the product is the determining factor.

As a result, behavior may be due primarily to loyalty to the product regardless of the situation or to the situation regardless of the product. But it is more likely that behavior is due to some interaction between product, situation, and the consumer. (The possibility of such interactions is represented in the model by the two-way arrows between situation, product, and consumer.)

Consumer Attributions to Situation versus Product

A key consideration in the situational model is whether consumers attribute their behavior to the product's characteristics or to the situation. Consumer researchers have used attribution theory to answer this question. **Attribution theory** states that people attribute a cause to their prior behavior.[22] If consumers attribute behavior to the product rather than to the situation, attitudes toward the product will be more positive, increasing the likelihood that consumers will purchase the product again.[23] Thus, if consumers attribute the purchase of a cereal to its nutritional content (a product attribute) rather than to the fact that it was on sale (a situational determinant), their attitudes toward the cereal are likely to be positive and they are likely to repurchase it. On the other hand, if attribution is to the situation ("I purchased because it was on sale"), their attitude toward the product is not likely to be as positive.

Several principles can be stated in determining whether the product or the situation is a more important influence on consumer behavior.

1. *The greater the degree of brand loyalty, the less important are situational influences.* For example, the loyal Michelob beer drinker makes no distinction between drinking Michelob when alone, with guests, while watching TV, with meals, between meals, or at any other time. This consumer happens to like Michelob, and the consumption situation will not influence purchasing behavior. The product, not the situation, is paramount in determining this consumer's behavior. Conversely, when loyalties are not strong, the consumption situation may be the determining factor in brand choice. A consumer may prefer a certain brand of beer because it is adequate and less expensive than most beers. For social occasions, this consumer may purchase a higher-priced beer. The consumption situation will determine what brand the consumer buys.

2. *The higher the level of enduring product involvement, the less likely it is that situational factors will determine behavior.* This principle relates to the dis-

tinction between enduring and situational involvement cited in Chapter 3. Enduring involvement is an ongoing interest in the product, whereas situational involvement is interest in the product triggered by a need to purchase it. In cases of high enduring involvement, consumers' interest in the product itself influences behavior. In cases of low enduring involvement, consumers' need to purchase the product is the motivator for their brand evaluation. Clarke and Belk studied situational and enduring involvement for four product categories.[24] They found that when enduring involvement in the product is low, the situation tends to determine behavior. When enduring involvement is high, the situation is not as important.

3. *When a product has multiple uses, situational factors will be less important in determining brand choice.* Conversely, products purchased for a single use are more likely to be influenced by the situation. Such products are most likely to be packaged goods. Studies of soft drinks,[25] snack foods,[26] beer,[27] meat products,[28] and breath fresheners[29] all have shown that the consumption situation directly affects behavior. Consumers tend to purchase these products for particular occasions—for meals, between-meal snacks, or social occasions. Products that consumers purchase for multiple uses are more likely to be durable goods. It is unlikely that consumers will own different television sets for different viewing occasions or different stereo sets for different listening occasions. In some cases, however, situational effects may be important. For example, many two-car families use one car primarily for work purposes and another for local shopping or evening entertainment. Some camera buffs may have several cameras for different types of situations. Belk concluded that even though situational effects are less likely to be important for durable goods, "there are few if any product and service purchases which are devoid of potential consumption situation influences."[30]

In summary, situational factors tend to be less important when consumers are loyal to a brand, when consumers are involved with the product category on an ongoing basis, and when the product has multiple uses.

Studies of Situational and Product Effects

Studies have considered the influence of the situation and the product on the purchasing behavior of at least eight product categories. These are:[31]

- Beverage products
- Meat products
- Snack products
- Fast foods
- Leisure activities
- Motion pictures
- Financial services
- Health care services

Meat products were most subject to situational influences. That is, consumers purchase meats depending on the situation. For example, hamburgers might be viewed as appropriate for informal meal occasions and steaks and roast beef for more formal occasions.

Health care services and motion picture choices were least likely to be subject to situational influences. Individuals generally select health care options independent of the situation. For example, individuals selecting emergency room care would do so whether at home or away from home and whether it was for themselves or another member of the family. As for motion pictures, consumers are likely to see a film regardless of the situation. For example, some people may see every Michelle Pfeiffer or Tom Hanks movie that is released.

Health care and motion pictures may be less subject to situational influences because they may be more involving. For meat products, loyalty to a certain product regardless of the situation is much less likely.

For the remaining product categories—beverages, snack and fast foods, leisure activities, and financial services—consumers were influenced by both the situation and the product. For example, consumers may buy certain snack foods for guests and others when snacking alone. This effect would represent an interaction between the situation (party versus snacking alone) and the product (different brand preferences for each occasion).

Contiguity Between Situation and Behavior

Another issue relevant to the situational model in Figure 6.1 is the contiguity between the situation and behavior. If the purchase and the situation are close in time, then the situation is likely to influence brand choice.[32] A consumer who is shopping for food for a big dinner party that evening may buy items not ordinarily purchased. A consumer who sees a sharp reduction in price for a particular brand (a purchase situation) may buy it even though it is not among those brands regularly purchased. In both cases, behavior is situation-specific. On the other hand, the consumer buying food items for normal usage may just be "stocking up" for the future. Situational requirements are not apparent, and the consumer will purchase preferred brands. Under such conditions, behavior is due to preferences for the product rather than to the urgency of any situation.

✦ SITUATIONAL INFLUENCES ON CONSUMER BEHAVIOR

http://www.kraftfoods.com/

The research cited in the previous section has shown that consumers frequently purchase products for particular situations. Research on situational influences has tended to focus on the influence of situations on (1) product attitudes (Shake 'n' Bake chicken may be rated as convenient to prepare for lunch but not for dinner), (2) product choice (Coca-Cola may be purchased for parties rather than for meal occasions), and (3) the consumer's decision process (more product attributes are considered when selecting a hair dryer as a gift than when selecting it for oneself).

Influence of Situation on Product Attitudes

http://www.budweiser.com/

A number of studies have shown that consumers' attitudes toward products vary depending on the situation.[33] That is, consumers vary their beliefs about brands depending on the situation. For example, a consumer may rate Budweiser as refreshing "when I'm thirsty" but not "at mealtime." In evaluating fast-food chains, a consumer may rate "convenience" more important for lunch or snack occasions than for dinner, and "good for the family" more important for dinner occasions than for lunch or snacks.

One study of transportation alternatives found that the value consumers placed on certain attributes varied by situation.[34] For example, individuals who avoided riding buses put more emphasis on shorter travel time and comfort when going to work than did bus riders. Such differences in needs and attitudes by situation have important implications for marketing strategy. Encouraging more people to use buses than cars to get to work would require convincing them that the bus can be as fast and as comfortable as a car.

Differences in attitudes by situation might indicate strengths and weaknesses of brands. If consumers rate a certain snack food particularly low on taste for parties and social occasions, the marketer would want to correct this potential weakness: Is it a problem with the product formulation or with the brand's image? Furthermore, if a brand is stronger in a particular situation, this strength should be exploited. For example, if consumers regard Budweiser as a good beer to have alone rather than on social occasions, perhaps marketers should emphasize taste benefits for situations when beer drinkers are alone.

Miller and Ginter undertook one of the most comprehensive studies of the situational determinants of product attitudes.[35] They asked consumers to rate eight fast-food restaurants on attributes such as speed of service, variety, cleanliness, and convenience for four situations:

1. Lunch on a weekday.
2. Snack during a shopping trip.
3. Evening meal when rushed for time.
4. Evening meal with the family when not rushed for time.

Convenience and speed of service were considered most important for lunch on a weekday and for evening meals when rushed. Variety of menu and popularity with children were most important for evening meals with the family when not rushed for time. Thus, consumers do differentiate product benefits by situation.

Consumers also rated various fast-food outlets by situation. They saw Arby's and Burger King as more convenient for snack occasions during a shopping trip. Burger Chef and McDonald's were more convenient for evening meal occasions.

Influence of Situation on Product Choice

The final element in Miller and Ginter's analysis was to evaluate the ability of the four situations in the study to predict consumers' restaurant choices. The results are in Table 6.2. Miller and Ginter predicted consumers' choices of fast-food restaurants with and without the benefit of knowing the situation. When the consumption situation was included in the prediction, the model correctly predicted a greater proportion of consumers' restaurant choices than a model that did not take account of the situation. For example, the situational model predicted the right choice for lunchtime occasions 41.3 percent of the time, compared to 30.5 percent of the time for the nonsituational model. This result shows the importance of situation in explaining consumer behavior.

Other studies have also found that situational variables better predict product choice. Stanton and Bonner found that situational variables outperformed demographics and attitudes in predicting the choice of a food item.[36] Similarly, Umesh and Cote found that they could better predict choice of soft drinks by including situational variables.[37]

Influence of Situations on Decision Making

Studies have focused on the effects of different situations on decision making. It is likely that the number of brands considered, the extent of the search, the type of information sought, and the sources of information will vary by the consumption and purchase situation. For example, one study found that when a shopper is with friends, he or she visits more stores and makes more unplanned purchases than when shopping alone.[38]

TABLE 6.2
Prediction of choice of fast-food outlets using a nonsituational model versus a situational model

	% Correct Predictions	
Situation	***Nonsituational Model***	***Situational Model***
Lunch on a weekday	30.5	41.3
Evening meal when rushed for time	38.6	44.0
Evening meal with family when not rushed for time	45.9	49.5
Snack during a shopping trip	31.6	34.7

Source: Kenneth E. Miller and James L. Ginter, "An Investigation of Situational Variation in Brand Choice Behavior and Attitudes," *Journal of Marketing Research*, 16 (February, 1979), p. 121. Reprinted with permission from the *Journal of Marketing Research*.

Several studies have examined differences in decision making when consumers buy a product as a gift or for themselves. We saw that consumers' purchase decisions for gifts tend to be more involving than when buying for themselves. As a result, as Clarke and Belk note, shopping for a gift "increases the overall level of arousal and causes more effort to be expended."[39] As a result, consumers' information search is more extensive when purchasing a gift than when purchasing for themselves.

Studies have found other factors that characterize decision making for gifts:

- Consumers are more likely to use in-store information sources (such as salespeople) than out-of-store sources (such as advertising).[40]
- Consumers are likely to set a price limit beforehand.[41]
- Consumers are likely to shop in higher-quality stores and to buy prestige brands.[42]
- Consumers consider stores' policies on return merchandise to be more important.[43]

The studies cited evaluated differences in decision making for purchasing situations. Ptacek and Shanteau focused on differences in decision making for consumption situations. They defined four situations in the use of paper towels:[44]

1. Heavy-duty jobs.
2. Lighter jobs.
3. As napkins and for cleaning up at a barbecue.
4. Just to have on hand.

They divided decisions into simple strategies in which consumers evaluated brands by one or two criteria and more complex strategies in which consumers used more criteria that varied by brand. When consumers purchased paper towels for light-duty jobs, their decision strategies were more complex. When they purchased towels for heavy-duty jobs, consumers used simpler strategies based on one or two criteria, probably because the selection of a towel for heavy-duty use rests on a simpler evaluation based on strength and durability. For light-duty work, consumers probably needed more attributes to evaluate the towels, thus requiring a more complex decision strategy. The findings suggest that consumers are likely to vary their method of selecting brands depending on the consumption as well as the purchase situation.

USE OF SITUATIONAL VARIABLES IN MARKETING STRATEGY

Marketers can use situational variables in marketing strategy in two ways: by introducing new usage situations or by targeting existing ones.

Introducing New Usage Situations

An effective marketing strategy is to influence consumers to use the product for new usage situations. Car wax was introduced in the 1930s when Johnson Products discovered consumers using their furniture wax on cars. Similarly, Arm & Hammer expanded the uses for baking soda by first advertising it as a refrigerator deodorizer and then suggesting it can also be used to brush your teeth. The company took the next logical step by introducing separate products in these categories: a toothpaste product and a room deodorizer with baking soda as a basic ingredient.

Wansick and Ray examined how advertising can effectively encourage consumers to use a brand in new situations in the context of *usage expansion* strategies.[45] They found that advertising is effective in proposing new uses for a brand as long as the new usage occasion is congruent with the consumer's existing notion of how to use the product. For example, if Campbell's soup proposes drinking soup for breakfast, the question is whether this usage is consistent with eating hot cereals for breakfast. Consumers who see little difference between eating hot cereal and drinking soup for breakfast are likely to accept such a usage expansion strategy.

http://www.campbellsoup.com/

In this context, Johnson's Wax could have advertised using furniture wax on cars ("Get your car as shiny as you get your dining room table") because consumers obviously saw this usage extension as congruent. But Pepsi failed in trying to get consumers to drink Pepsi AM at breakfast because the usage situation was not congruent with the consumers' existing notion of carbonated soft drink usage.

Targeting Existing Usage Situations

Marketers can target existing usage situations by (1) segmenting users by product usage, (2) developing new products to appeal to specific usage situations, (3) using advertising to position products to particular usage situations, and (4) distributing products to satisfy situational needs.

Market Segmentation

Market segmentation often depends on consumers' use situation. A snack food company, Great Snacks, conducted a study to define consumer segments by similarity in needs. It identified six segments: nutritional snackers, weight watchers, guilty snackers, party snackers, and indiscriminate snackers.

The consumption situation was important in defining five of the six segments. Both nutritional snackers and weight watchers were less likely to eat snacks between meals. Guilty snackers tended to eat snack foods between meals. Party snackers obviously ate and served snacks primarily at social occasions. Price-oriented snackers bought based on the purchase situation rather than on the consumption situation, buying snacks primarily when they were promoted by price deals and coupons. The only segment for which situational factors were not important was the indiscriminate snackers who tended to eat snacks in most usage occasions.

The importance of the situation was evident when Great Snacks considered introducing a new chip-type snack made of only natural ingredients. The fact that the target market—nutritional snackers—was unlikely to consume the product during the prime time for snacking (between meals) caused the company to reevaluate the viability of targeting the product to this segment.

http://www.viad.com/

http://www.dole5aday.com/

STRATEGIC APPLICATIONS OF CONSUMER BEHAVIOR

▶ Lunch Bucket: A Product Developed for a Situation

In September 1987, Jewel Food Stores set up microwave ovens at its 135 outlets in the Midwest. Employees spent the next two days giving out samples of a new microwaveable product called Lunch Bucket. The result? Within two days, the chain sold 420,000 containers of the new product.

The product was introduced after seven years of product development by Dial Corp., the $870 million Phoenix-based packaged goods company. Dial Corp. saw several developments that spelled opportunity. First was the increasing proportion of working women. Second was the greater number of microwave ovens in the workplace. (About two-thirds of workers now have access to a microwave at work, and four out of five of these workers use it.) Third was the trend among younger career-conscious workers to work longer hours and eat at their desks to save time. The company put these trends together and saw an opportunity to develop a product for a specific situation: a line of microwaveable food products designed for the workplace. In the process, Dial developed a brand new food category, shelf-stable microwaveable meals.

On introduction, the line included 15 varieties of foods, including 9 entrees ranging from beef stew to scalloped potatoes flavored with ham chunks. The line is positioned to upscale working women ages 25 to 54.

Surprisingly, Lunch Bucket is not advertised on a situational basis. According to the line's advertising director, "We've found that people don't need to be told where to use it." Rather, the main theme of the campaign is convenience.

Success breeds competition; Hormel, Chef Boy-Ar-Dee, and Campbell have also introduced shelf-stable microwaveable food lines aimed at the workplace. Also, other nonmicrowave lunch products began to appear in 1996. For example, the Dole Foods Company launched "Lunch for One," a precut, bagged salad meal positioned to the same target group as Lunch Bucket. However, Dial, being the first one in, has the edge. Dial Corp. has shown that a new product can be developed for a particular situation.

Sources: "Dole Segments Salads with Packed Lunch Kits," *Brandweek* (February 19, 1996), p. 3; "Dial's Hearty Office Meal," *Adweek* (June 27, 1988), pp. 20–23; and "Canned Goods," *Supermarket Business* (September 1991), p. 129.

New Product Development

Companies can develop new products for specific situations. Dickson distinguished between product benefits geared to consumer types and benefits aimed at specific situations.[46] We saw in the beginning of the chapter that Timex developed new line extensions of its watches for various sports situations and extended new product introductions to include watches designed for specific business purposes.

http://www.pepsi.com/

Pepsi targeted Pepsi AM to a particular situation, the need for a "pick-me-up" at breakfast. It advertised the brand to baby boomers as a healthier substitute for coffee to provide that caffeine boost in the morning. But the product flopped because consumers could not accept a carbonated cola drink for breakfast.

Product Positioning

A large food manufacturer undertook a study to determine consumers' association of a broad range of food products to four types of occasions:

1. Special meal occasions.
2. Family meals.
3. Regular day-to-day meals.
4. Snacks and quick meals.

The purpose of the study was to determine whether consumers link products or groups of products to these meal occasions. For example, do consumers associate a roast with special meals, family meals, or day-to-day meals? If it is a special meal, do they associate potatoes or vegetables with the roast?

A sample of consumers was asked to associate 16 products with these occasions. Results of the analysis are shown in Figure 6.2. Each quadrant in the figure represents one of the four mealtime occasions.[47] For example, cold cuts, grilled cheese, and English muffins are associated with snacks and quick meals; hamburgers and hot sandwiches with regular meals; and roasts and fresh cooked vegetables with special meals. The study provides guidelines for advertising in a situational context. For example, a marketer may have assumed that hamburgers are associated with quick meals; but the study showed that hamburgers and accessory products should be advertised in a regular meal situation. The findings also provide a rational basis for grouping products in a situational context. A logical product grouping would be cold cuts and cheeses for snacks.

The study of paper towel usage cited earlier also shows the importance of situational variables in positioning products. Heavy-duty uses included cleaning ovens, washing windows, and cleaning cars; light-duty uses involved wiping hands, wiping kitchen counters, and wiping dishes; and decorative uses were for napkins or placemats.[48] Positioning a paper towel requires recognition of the usage situation. A positioning toward heavy-duty usage should dictate the product's characteristics (multi-ply), the target segment to which the product should be positioned (the heavy-duty user), the promotional appeals (strength and dura-

FIGURE 6.2
Positioning products by four meal situations

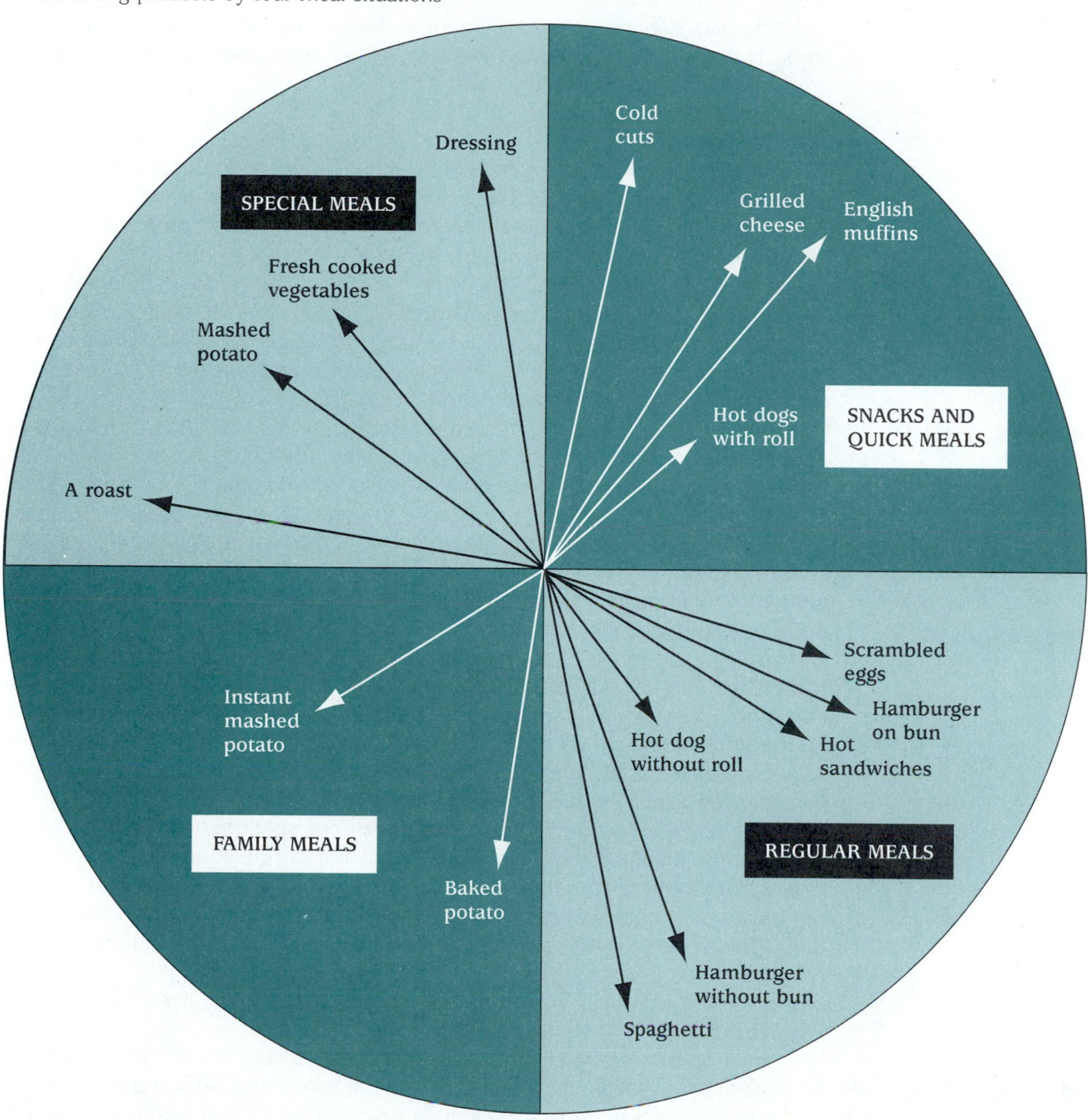

bility), and possibly the media to be used (based on the demographic characteristics of the heavy-duty segment).

American Can identified a segment of heavy-duty paper towel users on this basis. It then introduced Bolt, a multi-ply towel, and positioned it as a strong product suitable for heavy-duty uses.

Advertising

The usage situation can also dictate promotional appeals. If consumers purchase a soft drink primarily for social occasions, then marketers should advertise it in this context. Similarly, if a certain segment purchases a food processor primarily for cooking for guests, marketers should advertise it in the context of meal preparations for guests rather than for the family. Deighton, Henderson, and Neslin referred to the practice of advertising products in the context of the usage situation as **framing;**[49] that is, the usage situation frames the product in a relevant context for consumers. On this basis, the ad "tells the consumer what to look for in the product-usage experience."

http://www.mot.com/

The two ads in Exhibit 6.4 frame products in usage situations. The Motorola pager is shown as a means of staying in touch with loved ones in various situations. The ad for Swatch's waterproof watch shows it being worn during a game of water polo.

http://www.gatorade.com/

http://www.agf.co.jp/

Two other bases for advertising products by situation are gift giving and seasonal usage. Exhibit 6.2 showed products advertised in a gift-giving context. An advertising campaign may also reflect seasonal usage—for example, iced tea during the summer and hot soup in the winter. While consumption of Gatorade is heavier in the summer, the company tries to smooth out demand by advertising Gatorade not only as a summer thirst quencher during active sports activities, but also as a winter fluid replacement for consumers with colds and the flu. General Foods follows a similar strategy for Sanka coffee, but with reversed seasons. Since coffee consumption is heavier in the winter, the company advertises iced Sanka for the summer.

Advertising on a situational basis requires not only a portrayal of the situation, but also a link between product benefits and the situation (see Exhibit 6.4). The Motorola pager ad emphasizes the freedom to "do the things that are important to you" once you have the peace of mind of staying in touch with loved ones. The ad for WD-40 cites the benefits of the product for getting people out of "sticky situations."

Distribution

http://www.7-11.com/

The situation may also influence distribution strategies. One of the competitive advantages of 7-Eleven, the largest chain of convenience food stores in the country, is that it stays open late to cater to unanticipated situations food shoppers face when most supermarkets are closed.

http://www.perrier.com/

Perrier's distribution strategy is also a function of situational influences. As a carbonated mineral water, Perrier tends to be taken at mealtimes. As a result, more than a third of its bottles are shipped to restaurants, hotels, and bars.[50]

EXHIBIT 6.4
Ads that frame products in usage situations

SUMMARY

The usage situation is an important factor that directly influences consumers' decisions. However, marketers have largely overlooked this factor. It should influence marketing strategy by affecting the manner in which markets are segmented, products are positioned, and brands are advertised and distributed.

Three types of situations have important implications for marketing: the consumption situation, the purchase situation, and the communication situation. The consumption situation refers to the circumstances in which consumers use the product. The purchase situation refers to the conditions under which consumers make a decision (for example, whether purchasing as a gift or for themselves) and the in-store conditions at the time of the purchase. The communication situation refers to the conditions in which advertising exposure occurs (for example, a radio commercial heard in a car or at home, or TV watched alone or with friends).

Gift giving was cited as a particularly important purchase situation since gifts represent a substantial portion of retail sales. Consumers buying gifts tend to be more involved with the purchase and, as a result, are more likely to see the purchase as risky.

An important part of using situational variables to explain consumer behavior is the development of a situational inventory. Situational inventories require the identification of relevant usage, consumption, or communication situations specific to the product category.

The chapter described a simple model of the decision process incorporating situational factors. The model recognizes that a consumer's decision can be a function of the brand, the situation, the consumer's own predispositions, or, more likely, some combination of these factors. Various studies were cited demonstrating that, for many products, the most important factor in explaining behavior is the interaction between situation and product. That is, choice of brands is likely to vary by situation. However, the situation will not be important in all cases. When a high level of brand loyalty exists or there is enduring involvement with the product, consumers may buy a particular brand regardless of the situation.

Studies have examined the effects of situational influences on product attitudes, product choice, and the nature of consumer decision making. In most cases, situational variables led to a better understanding of consumer attitudes and a better prediction of consumer choices. The chapter concluded by describing applications of situational variables to market segmentation, product positioning, new products, advertising, and distribution strategies.

The next section of the book considers what the consumer brings to the decision process, namely his or her own individual predispositions in the form of perceptions, attitudes, and needs.

QUESTIONS

1. A manufacturer of instant coffee considers introducing a new line of continental flavors to be advertised for special occasions. The objective is to gear marketing strategy to the situations that warrant distinctive coffee that can be conveniently prepared.
   - For what types of situations should the coffee be positioned?
   - What are the implications for (a) defining a target segment and (b) developing an advertising strategy?
2. A product manager for a leading brand of paper towels notices substantial variation in sales performance for the brand among stores in the same trading area. The manager hypothesizes that marked differences in the in-store purchase situation may be causing variation in sales. What differences in in-store purchase situations could be causing differences in sales?
3. A manufacturer of hair dryers identifies two types of purchase situations that lead to differences in brand evaluation: (a) purchase for oneself and (b) purchase as a gift.
   - What are the marketing implications for positioning a product to appeal to each of these purchasing situations?
   - What may be the differences in brand evaluation in each condition?
4. How might a large department store try to counteract some of the negative aspects of gift giving cited in the Sherry et al. study cited on p. 181.
5. Develop a list of communication situations that may affect a consumer's awareness and comprehension of (a) print advertising and (b) television advertising.
6. Under what conditions is brand choice more likely to be influenced by the situation than by product

characteristics? Under what conditions is the reverse likely to be true?

7. Why did several studies find that situational influences were less important for health care services and motion pictures than for other product categories studied.
8. A company marketing a leading brand of yogurt has always focused on yogurt's nutritional benefits without considering the possibility of varying its appeal to depend on the usage situation.
   - Could the product benefits consumers see in yogurt vary by the usage situation? Specify.
   - What are the marketing implications of variations in perceived benefits by usage situation?
9. Why are situational influences more important when they are contiguous to behavior? Cite some examples.
10. What are the marketing implications of the Wansick and Ray study (p. 194) for advertising existing products in new usage situations?
11. Market segments can be defined by usage situation for snack foods; for example, there are between-meal snackers and party snackers. What market segments could be identified by usage situation for (a) deodorants and (b) paper towels?
12. What marketing opportunities led Dial Corp. to introduce Lunch Bucket? How were these opportunities situation-specific?
13. What do we mean by the framing effect in advertising? Cite two examples of the framing effect other than those shown in Exhibit 6.4.
14. What are some purchase and consumption situations that might influence distribution strategies?

RESEARCH ASSIGNMENTS

1. Find examples of World Wide Web sites for the consumption situation, purchase situation, and communication situation.
   - How are marketers overcoming initial consumer reluctance and fostering purchases over the Internet?
   - Are marketers tailoring the Internet communication situation to each individual user? How?
2. Select two product categories that are frequently given as gifts: one that is higher in price (for example, hair dryers or watches) and one that is lower priced (compact discs or books). Select a sample of about 50 respondents and ask them (1) how much time they would spend and (2) what information sources they would consult in choosing a particular alternative for:
   a. Themselves.
   b. A birthday gift for a close friend.
   c. A wedding gift for a close friend.
   d. A thank-you gift to repay someone for watching their home or apartment while they were away.
   e. A birthday gift for a casual friend.[51]
   - Did respondents spend more time in selecting a product for themselves (a) or as a gift (b–e)?
   - Did respondents spend more time in selecting a gift in a high-involvement gift-giving situation (b and c) or in a low-involvement gift-giving situation (d and e)?
   - How did sources of information differ for buying for themselves versus buying as a gift? For giving a gift in a high- versus a low-involvement situation?
   - Were there any differences in the amount of time respondents spent in searching for a high-priced gift versus a low-priced gift? In the sources of information used in evaluating the higher- versus the lower-priced gift?
3. Select a product category that you believe is likely to be affected by the usage situation (soft drinks, paper towels, coffee, snacks, and so on). Conduct several depth interviews with consumers to define:
   a. The most frequent usage situations for the category.
   b. A vocabulary of evaluative product attributes.
   - Develop a questionnaire in which consumers are asked to rate:
   a. The importance of each of the attributes by the four most important situations you defined in the depth interviews (for example: How important is a soft drink that is refreshing when drinking it alone? When drinking it at a party?)
   b. The three leading brands by the vocabulary of product attributes for the four most important situations (for example, rate Pepsi on "refreshing" when drinking it alone, drinking it at a party, and so on).
   - What is the variation in importance ratings by situation?
   - What is the variation in brand ratings by situation?
   - What are the implications of variations in importance ratings and brand image by situation for (a) positioning a new product, (b) repositioning an ex-

isting product, (c) advertising strategy, and (d) definition of a target group?

4. Do a series of depth interviews with consumers to develop a comprehensive situational inventory for snack products. Make sure the inventory contains the five elements Belk defined: physical surroundings, social surroundings, time, task definition, and antecedent states. (See Table 6.1 as an example.) Submit the inventory to a small sample of consumers (10 to 20) and determine the frequency with which various snack foods (potato chips, pretzels, cheese, crackers, fruit, cookies) are considered for each usage occasion. What are the implications of your findings for (a) product line strategy, (b) new product development, and (c) advertising?

PART III

THE INDIVIDUAL CONSUMER: COGNITIVE AND EXPERIENTIAL PROCESSES

In this section and the next, we focus on the individual consumer's cognitive (mental) processes and how they influence purchasing decisions. In Chapter 7, we consider perceptions, that is, the consumer's interpretation of advertising, price, and product stimuli in the context of his or her own needs. Chapter 8 delves more deeply into how consumers acquire, organize, and process these stimuli. In Chapters 9 and 10, we consider another key cognitive variable: attitudes. Attitudes are the evaluative component of the consumer's thought processes. They lead consumers to judge whether a service or product should be viewed favorably and whether it is likely to meet their needs. We will be referring to perceptions and attitudes as the consumer's *thought variables* because they represent the mental processes by which the consumer makes decisions.

In Chapter 11, we focus on the strategic implications of these thought variables in the context of how marketers can effectively communicate information to consumers. A communication model is presented that considers the transmission of information from marketer to consumers and receipt and processing of the information by consumers.

Although the focus in this section is on cognitive processes, this view is juxtaposed with a more experiential perspective, one that does not emphasize systematic processing of information but rather a more global reaction to marketing stimuli based on feelings, emotions, and fantasy. Such a view does not negate cognitive processing; it takes a somewhat different perspective on the nature of such processing. In most cases, consumers will process at various points on the continuum from systematic to experiential, processing some products and services more systematically and other on a more hedonic and experiential basis.

CONSUMER PERCEPTIONS

Chapter 7

CAN MCDONALD'S EXPAND ITS MARKET BY CHANGING CONSUMER PERCEPTIONS?

One of the key elements of a successful marketing strategy is the development of product and promotional stimuli that consumers will perceive as relevant to their needs. In Chapter 3, we defined consumer **perceptions** as the selection, organization, and interpretation of marketing and environmental stimuli into a coherent picture. In this chapter, consumer perceptions are considered in more detail.

Consumer perceptions are the reason why McDonald's is attempting to broaden its base to appeal to adults as well as kids. The company did such an effective job in appealing to children with Ronald McDonald, on-site playgrounds, promotional tie-ins with Disney, and kid-friendly Happy Meals that Mom and Dad *perceived* the chain as kid-oriented. In 1996, McDonald's introduced a new Arch Deluxe sandwich targeted specifically to adults and backed by a $500 million marketing budget.[1]

McDonald's strategy stems from the assumption that it has built up enough brand equity with kids to welcome adults under its

http://www.mcdonalds.com/

arches. And there is precedent for this strategy. Disney established Epcot as an adult alternative to Disneyland. And Coca-Cola introduced adult-oriented Diet Coke to balance its flagship brand's appeal to youngsters.

But McDonald's is taking a risk. The strategy for the Arch Deluxe seems like it is trying to undermine traditional adult perceptions of McDonald's as kid- and family-oriented. One print ad shows a sneering youngster rejecting the new entry. A TV ad shows a bunch of cute kids turning suddenly gloomy at the mere mention of the Arch Deluxe sandwich. As one marketing expert said, "The idea of children turning up their noses at something coming from McDonald's is horrific."[2] And, as a McDonald's franchisee said, "I know we have to get the adults, but I don't want to lose the kids."

This last statement reflects the basic quandary McDonald's is facing in trying to influence consumer perceptions. In attempting to broaden its consumer base to adults, it might also be undermining its strong association with kids.

In this chapter, we first focus on what consumers are perceiving: stimuli. Next, we consider the three processes by which consumers perceive stimuli—selection, organization, and interpretation—and their strategic implications for marketing. We then focus on one of the most important applications of perceptions: consumer perceptions of prices and association of price with product quality.

MARKETING STIMULI AND CONSUMER PERCEPTIONS

Stimuli are any physical, visual, or verbal communications that can influence an individual's response. The two most important types of stimuli influencing consumer behavior are marketing and environmental (social and cultural influences). In this chapter, we consider marketing stimuli. Environmental stimuli are considered in Parts V and VI.

Marketing stimuli are any communications or physical stimuli that are designed to influence consumers. The product and its components (package, contents, physical properties) are **primary** (or **intrinsic**) **stimuli.** Communications designed to influence consumer behavior are **secondary** (or **extrinsic**) **stimuli** that represent the product either through words, pictures, and symbolism or through other stimuli associated with the product (price, store in which purchased, effect of salesperson).

To survive in a competitive market, manufacturers must constantly expose consumers to secondary marketing stimuli. Continuous advertising would not be profitable, however, unless enough consumers were to buy again. Therefore, the ultimate determinant of future consumer actions is experience with the primary stimulus, the product. At times, manufacturers attempt to introduce such product experience prior to a purchase by giving consumers free samples. Before introducing their products to the general market, some manufacturers may offer samples to provide consumers a direct and risk-free product experience. However, distributing free samples as a primary stimulus to influence consumers to buy products is the exception. The dominant element in marketing strategy is communication about the product.

The key requirement in communicating secondary stimuli to consumers is the development of a product concept. A **product concept** is a bundle of product benefits that can be directed to the needs of a defined group of consumers through messages, symbolism, and imagery. The product concept represents the organization of the secondary stimuli into a coordinated product position that can be communicated to consumers. For example, Nestlé developed the concept for its freeze-dried coffee entry, Taster's Choice, as a product that provides the convenience of instant but the taste and aroma of regular coffee. Nestlé geared the secondary stimuli to the intended concept. The brand name implied taste, and the advertising demonstrated the taste benefits of a good instant coffee. Nestlé even tested the shape of the jar and determined that a deep square jar would provide more of an image of hefty taste than would the traditional cylindrical jar. Clearly, definition of the product concept must precede development of the secondary stimuli in the marketing plan.

http://www.nestle.com/

Two key factors determine which stimuli consumers will perceive and how they will interpret them: the characteristics of the stimulus and the consumers' ability to perceive the stimulus. These two influences interact in determining consumer perceptions. Assume a company producing a leading deodorant subtly changes ingredients to give the deodorant a "cleaner" smell (a stimulus characteristic). If many consumers cannot distinguish between the new and the old smell (a consumer characteristic), the change in stimulus will be ineffective. We will consider stimulus and consumer characteristics in the following sections.

Stimulus Characteristics Affecting Perception

Several characteristics of marketing stimuli affect the way consumers perceive products. These characteristics can be divided into sensory elements and structural elements. Both have implications for product development and advertising.

Sensory Elements

Sensory elements are composed of color, smell, taste, sound, and feel.

Color. *Color* has important sensory connotations. Consider the preponderance of red logos or names on packages in the supermarket aisle—Coca-Cola, Nabisco, Campbell's Soup, Colgate, Jell-O, Kellogg's. Evidence suggests that red is regarded as warm, sensual, and not intimidating. On a more basic level, red is the lifeblood.[3] Blue is seen as comforting, which may be one reason why IBM's logo is blue; it is an attempt to convey a more friendly image from a company that is often seen as cold and distant.[4]

Research shows there is a close link between color preferences and brand choice. One study tested the same roll-on deodorant packaged in three differ-http://www.marykay.com/

http://www.pg.com/

ent colors.[5] Respondents said the product in one color scheme dried quickly and was effective, the product in the second had a strong aroma, and the product in the third was irritating and ineffective. Differences in consumers' reactions to the identical product were caused solely by differences in the color of the packaging. Mary Kay, the second largest direct seller of skin care products in the United States, has always associated its products and logo with pink, a color that reinforced an old-fashioned image. In an attempt to appeal to the contemporary woman, the company has begun to use a more sophisticated off-white.[6] Even in Spain, a more traditional country, Mary Kay uses new color schemes to depict a contemporary woman but retains its basic pink as background.

The importance of color perceptions is further illustrated by P&G's attempt to change Prell shampoo from its traditional green to blue. An outcry arose

GLOBAL APPLICATIONS OF CONSUMER BEHAVIOR

► Purple and Gray Are One Thing in the U.S. and Another in China

Color perceptions are likely to differ among countries because of cultural associations. A study by Jacobs et al. of consumers in the Far East and in the United States found that consumers in China and Japan associate purple with expensive products and gray with inexpensive products. The associations are exactly the opposite for American consumers, who associate purple with inexpensive products and gray with expensive ones. In Hong Kong, Marlboro uses cross-cultural differences in color perceptions by depicting the Cowboy in a white hat on a white horse because white is culturally significant in China.

Cultural differences also affect color preferences for cosmetics. In Latin American countries, women prefer more strongly accented hues of lipstick and powders because of the cultural association of femininity with these hues. In Mexico, for example, women are willing to pay a premium for nail polishes with names like "Orange Flip."

The cultural trend in America is the reverse; consumers prefer more subdued hues. This trend is partially the result of the increasing proportion of working women, many of whom regard excessive makeup as unprofessional. It is also partially due to the merging family and occupational roles of men and women. Cosmetics still retain a sensual role, but in a more understated fashion.

Sources: Laurence Jacobs, Charles Keown, Reginald Worthley, and And-Il Ghymn, "Cross-Cultural Colour Comparisons: Global Marketers Beware!" *International Marketing Review* 8(1991), pp. 21–30; "Cost No Object for Mexico's Makeup Junkies," *The Wall Street Journal* (June 7, 1994), p. B1.

among loyal Prell users, forcing the company to change Prell back to its traditional green. One analyst concluded, "Challenging [long-standing] consumer perceptions is very tricky and is generally a mistake."[7]

Taste. *Taste* is another sensory factor that will condition consumers' brand perceptions. When PepsiCo introduced Crystal Pepsi to appeal to consumers' desire for light, natural flavorings, it immediately captured 2 percent of the soft drink market, making it a $1 billion brand (see Exhibit 7.1.) But sales quickly slid. Why? Because many consumers expected it to taste like regular Pepsi, whereas it has a distinctly lighter taste. Reinforcing the taste problem was the lack of color. Whereas some consumers associate clear with natural and healthy, others simply associate it with water.[8] PepsiCo tried to recoup by advertising "You've never seen a taste like this," but to no avail. The expectation of a cola taste was too strongly ingrained in consumers' minds.

http://www.pepsi.com/

The importance of taste is also illustrated by P&G's blunder when it first introduced Pringles potato chips. Its main focus was the novel packaging in an easy-to-stack cylindrical can that avoided content breakage. Not only did the package look like a tennis ball can, but the chips also tasted like tennis balls. P&G had to spend hundreds of millions of dollars to reformulate the product and successfully reintroduce it.

Taste can be an elusive perception. A study by Allison and Uhl found that when consumers were asked to taste three unlabeled brands of beer (known as a *blind taste test*), they rated all three brands similarly, and most consumers could not identify their regular brand.[9] However, when shown the labels, consumers had a strong preference for their regular brand. The result shows that taste is not an objective criterion. It is inextricably linked to the brand's image in the consumer's mind. Without brand identification, the consumer's taste experience is entirely different. This fact was illustrated when Coca-Cola tried to change the formula of its flagship brand. Blind taste tests showed that New Coke

http://www.cocacola.com/

►**EXHIBIT 7.1** Crystal Pepsi: Taste perceptions did not meet expectations was superior to the original. When the company tried to change the formula, consumer resistance was so great it had to bring back the original as Coca-Cola Classic. The strong association with a brand that was part of many consumers' heritage went beyond taste.

Smell. *Smell* is particularly important for cosmetics and food products. In one study, two different fragrances were added to the same facial tissue. Consumers perceived one facial tissue as elegant and expensive and the other as a product to use in the kitchen.[10] Smell can be a factor even in car purchases. Car dealers have been known to use a spray inside cars so they smell "new." Rolls-Royce included scent strips in advertisements in *Architectural Digest* to convey the smell of its leather upholstery. In another application, Procter & Gamble used scratch-and-sniff stickers on its detergent packaging so consumers could more easily smell the products in the store.[11]

http://www.rolls-royce.com/

Smell also has cross-cultural dimensions. The social role of perfumes and colognes in Western society was never established in Japan. Because of crowding and small living spaces, Japanese consumers value cleanliness and never felt the need for using these products as a means of avoiding body odor. In fact, many Japanese regard perfumes and colognes as intrusive to other people's privacy.

Sound. *Sound* is another important sensory stimulus. Advertisers have traditionally used English accent voice-overs to convey status and authority. This was one reason why Commander Whitehead was an effective spokesperson for Schweppes beverage mixers. Advertisers also frequently use music through jingles or as background themes to create positive associations with brands. Marketers must pretest such stimuli to ensure that they will create positive associations with a brand. Gorn demonstrated the importance of such associations in an experiment. Consumers were asked to choose among several pens, one of which they saw advertised with background music. Consumers were more likely to choose the pen if they liked the background music.[12]

Feel. The *feel* of certain products will also influence consumers' perceptions. Softness is considered a desirable attribute in many paper products. The former theme "Don't squeeze the Charmin" suggests the importance of feel. Feel is also a means of determining quality. Consumers often use the feel of textile fabrics, clothing, carpeting, or furniture to evaluate quality. For example, a smooth, velvety feel in textile fabrics is considered an indication of quality.

Structural Elements

A number of findings have emerged from studies of structural elements applied primarily to print advertising. For example:

- The larger the size of the ad, the more likely it is to be noticed.[13]
- A position in the first 10 pages of a magazine or in the upper half of a printed page produces more attention.[14]

- Contrast—for example, the picture of a product on a stark white background—is likely to produce attention.
- Novelty is another attention-getting device. An example is the Panasonic ad in a Saudi Arabian magazine (Exhibit 7.2) under the heading "Mood music on the move."

Consumer Characteristics Affecting Perception

Two characteristics are important in determining consumers' perception of stimuli: ability to discriminate between stimuli and propensity to generalize from one stimulus to another.

Stimulus Discrimination

One of the basic questions regarding the effect of marketing stimuli on perceptions is whether consumers can discriminate among differences in stimuli. Do

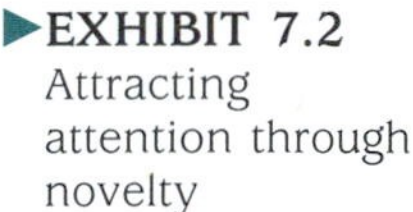

►EXHIBIT 7.2
Attracting attention through novelty

consumers perceive differences between brands in taste, feel, price, and the shape of the package?

The ability to discriminate among stimuli is learned. Generally, frequent users of a product are better able to notice small differences in product characteristics between brands. However, in many cases, the consumers' ability to discriminate sensory characteristics such as taste and feel is small. As a result, marketers rely on advertising to convey brand differences that physical characteristics alone would not impart. They attempt to create a brand image that will convince consumers that one brand is better than another.

Threshold Level. The ability of consumers to detect variations in light, sound, smell, or other stimuli is determined by their **threshold level.** Some consumers are more sensitive to these stimuli than others. Arthur D. Little, a management consulting firm, has identified expert taste testers for products such as cigarettes and coffee. Since their level of sensory discrimination is much greater than the average consumer's, these experts can detect subtle differences in coffee or cigarette blends and are used by marketers to evaluate various test products and to screen out potential losers. Once these experts identify the best prospective blends, the products are then tested on consumers in standard taste tests.

Just-Noticeable Difference. A basic principle in determining a consumer's threshold level is that a differential threshold exists in comparing two stimuli. The consumer will not be able to detect any difference between stimuli below his or her differential threshold. The differential threshold, therefore, represents the **just-noticeable difference (j.n.d.).** For example, if a private-label detergent costs five cents less than the consumer's regular brand, the consumer may not notice the difference. However, if the private-label brand costs ten cents less than the regular brand, the consumer is likely to notice the difference. Therefore, ten cents is the differential threshold, or j.n.d., for this consumer.

Marketers sometimes seek to make changes in marketing stimuli that will not be noticed (a decrease in package size or an increase in price). A good example of the need to change a marketing stimulus without notice is the periodic updating of existing packaging. For instance, General Mills has subtly changed one of the most enduring symbols in advertising, Betty Crocker, who was first introduced in 1921, to give her a more contemporary look (see Exhibit 7.3).

http://www.genmills.com/

Most consumers would not notice the more subtle changes (for example, the ones between 1965 and 1980) because they are below their j.n.d. But the company departed from an attempt to stay below the j.n.d. with its 1986 version of Betty Crocker. This portrayal was an attempt to show a professional working woman with family responsibilities. The most marked departure from the traditional portrayal occurred in 1996 when, to mark her 75th birthday, the company decided to develop a composite to represent American women across ethnic and age groups. It selected pictures of 75 women and developed a composite representation. The new Betty Crocker "will look more like the growing market of blacks and Hispanics. This will let [General Mills] straddle their conservative core and their emerging market."[15] The new Betty Crocker is the last picture in Exhibit 7.3.

Of even more direct application to marketing strategy is the need to differentiate a brand from that of the competition so it will be noticed. In this case, the marketer seeks to develop product characteristics and advertising messages that are easily detectable (differences in size, taste, color, ingredients, and so on).

Weber's Law. As most consumers cannot detect small changes in a product's price, package size, or physical characteristics, a relevant question for marketers is the degree of change required for consumers to take notice. A principle developed by a German physiologist over a hundred years ago, known as Weber's law, provides some insight into this question. **Weber's law** says that the stronger the initial stimulus, the greater the change required for the stimulus to be seen as different. In marketing terms, this would mean that the higher the

EXHIBIT 7.3
Changes in Betty Crocker's appearance below the just-noticeable difference

price, the greater the change in price required for consumers to take notice. The price of a $500 stereo set would have to increase more significantly than that of a $100 tape deck in order to be noticed. Moreover, Weber's law says that the increase in the difference required to reach the differential threshold (the j.n.d.) is constant. That is, if price had to increase by a minimum of $10 to be noticed for a $100 tape deck, it would have to increase by a minimum of $50 to be noticed for a $500 stereo set. In both cases, the j.n.d. is a constant 10 percent.

http://www.ftc.gov/

The Federal Trade Commission implicitly recognized the nature of Weber's law when it required that the surgeon general's warning in cigarette advertising had to be a certain size.[16] The bigger the ad, the bigger the warning's typeface had to be to be noticed. If the typeface size fell below the specifications the FTC set, it might fall below the j.n.d. for many consumers who would thus not perceive it.

The most direct applications of Weber's law are in regard to price. One important implication is that the higher the original price of an item, the greater the markdown required to increase sales. The required markdown on a designer suit would be greater than that on a regular suit.

Subliminal Perceptions. The differential threshold was identified as the minimum difference between two stimuli that consumers can detect. Thus, a consumer may be able to tell the difference between two cordials of 40 proof and 60 proof, but if the difference between the two is smaller, a consumer will not detect it (60 minus 40, or 20 proof, is the j.n.d.). There is also an **absolute threshold** below which consumers cannot detect the stimulus at all. Thus, a consumer can detect alcohol in a cordial that is 10 proof, but below that, a consumer can detect no alcoholic content in the beverage. Therefore, the differential threshold is 20 proof, and the absolute threshold is 10 proof.

One of the major controversies regarding consumer perceptions is whether consumers can actually perceive marketing stimuli below their absolute threshold. **Subliminal perception** means perception of a stimulus below the conscious level.[17] The absolute threshold level at which perceptions occur is referred to as the **limen.** Thus, perception below the absolute threshold is subliminal. It may seem contradictory that consumers can perceive a message below their minimum level of perception, but experiments conducted in the 1950s suggested that exposure may actually occur without attention and comprehension. That is, consumers do not see the message, but they register it.

Vicary conducted a test in 1957 in which two messages, "Eat popcorn" and "Drink Coca-Cola," were shown in a movie theater for 1/3,000 of a second (well below the absolute threshold) at five-second intervals.[18] Popcorn sales in the theater increased by 58 percent and Coca-Cola sales by 18 percent compared to periods in which there was no subliminal advertising. These results immediately raised serious ethical questions, as consumers could be influenced by messages without their approval or knowledge. The *New Yorker* magazine said that "minds had been 'broken and entered.'"[19]

http://www.fcc.gov/

The controversy over subliminal advertising proved shallow because there was little proof that it influenced consumer actions.[20] Subsequent attempts to replicate Vicary's findings did not succeed.[21] Although the Federal Communications Commission took an immediate interest in the implications of subliminal advertising, it could not confirm the conclusion that subliminal advertising influences the receiver's responses.[22] Later studies by Moore and Saegert found little influence resulting from subliminal advertising.[23] However, at least one study by Janiszewski did find that consumers process advertising information on a subliminal level and that such processing may in fact interfere with communication of the intended advertising message.[24]

The controversy over subliminal advertising has extended to print as well as to TV advertising. Some writers have claimed that print ads use **subliminal embeds,** that is, tiny figures inserted into magazine ads by high-speed photography or by airbrushing.[25] As evidence, a Gilbey's Gin ad was cited in which the ice cubes spell out the letters SEX. However, a study by Rosen and Singh found little evidence that such embeds exert a subconscious influence on unaware consumers.[26]

Overall, the evidence suggests that it would be extremely difficult at best to exert influence through subliminal stimuli. Variations among consumers in perceptual ability, the difficulty of implementing advertising themes at low threshold levels, and the lack of evidence of any effect of subliminal advertising on purchasing behavior have effectively eliminated subliminal advertising as a marketing tool.

Adaptation Level. **Adaptation level** is the level at which consumers no longer notice a frequently repeated stimulus. An individual walking into an air-conditioned room, a kitchen full of fragrances, or a noisy party will not notice these stimuli after a period of time. **Advertising wearout** is the consumers' adaptation to an advertising campaign over time due to boredom and familiarity. Consumers reduce their attention level to frequently repeated ads and eventually fail to notice them.

Consumers differ in their level of adaptation. Some tune out more quickly than others. Certain consumers have a tendency to be more aware of the facets of information and communication, even if they are repeated frequently. Because of the advertiser's desire to gain attention and maintain distinctiveness, the objectives of the typical advertising campaign are to decrease the adaptation level by introducing attention-getting features. Novelty, humor, contrast, and movement are all stimulus effects that may gain consumers' attention and reduce their adaptation. The most effective means of reducing the adaptation level, however, is to ensure that the message communicates the benefits consumers desire.

Stimulus Generalization

Consumers develop not only a capacity to discriminate between stimuli but also a capacity to generalize from one similar stimulus to another. The process of

stimulus generalization occurs when two stimuli are seen as similar (contiguous), and the effects of one, therefore, can be substituted for the effects of the other.

Discrimination allows consumers to judge brands selectively and to evaluate one brand over another. Generalization allows consumers to simplify the process of evaluation because they do not have to make a separate judgment for each stimulus. Brand loyalty is a form of stimulus generalization. The consumer assumes that positive past experiences with the brand will be repeated. Therefore, a consumer does not need to make a separate judgment with each purchase. Perceptual categorization is also a form of stimulus generalization.

As new products are introduced, consumers generalize from past experience to categorize them. When the automobile was first introduced at the turn of the century, it was called the "horseless carriage." People generalized from their experience with the best-known mode of transportation, the horse and carriage, and put the automobile in the same general category.

Strategic Applications of Generalization

It may appear that marketers seek to avoid consumers' generalization because they are attempting to distinguish their brands from those of the competition. However, in some cases, generalization may be a conscious and productive strategy. Heinz uses a strategy of generalization by advertising "57 varieties." The hope is that consumers will generalize the positive experience with one of the company's brands to its other brands. General Electric also follows this policy of family branding. On the other hand, Procter & Gamble avoids a policy of generalization, preferring to position each brand in a unique way without reference to the company name. Whereas Heinz and General Electric employ stimulus generalization, Procter & Gamble employs stimulus discrimination.

http://www.heinz.com/

http://www.ge.com/

A related form of stimulus generalization is **brand leveraging.** (See the Strategic Applications box.) Companies often use a successful brand name on a product-line extension (Diet Coke and Ivory Liquid, for example) or on a different product category (Arm & Hammer detergents, Jell-O Pudding Pops).

Advertisers also use generalization in positioning brands to compete with the market leader. A brand may be introduced with the same basic benefits but at a lower price or in a larger package. The hope is that consumers will generalize the known benefits of the leading brand to the new entry and thus accept it. Some private (retailer-controlled) brands use a principle of generalization by making their package look as similar as possible to that of the leading brand in the category. One problem with these attempts at generalization is that they may be infringing on the trademark of the better-known brand. Companies zealously guard their package design and brand name, and they can sue imitators. For example, Toys R Us successfully sued a children's clothing chain called Kids R Us for trademark infringement and then introduced its own line of children's clothing under that name.

http://www.toysrus.com/

Principles of generalization can also be used to encourage new uses for a product such as eating cold cereals as a snack or using bleach as a cleanser. Wansick found that such usage generalizations are most likely to be accepted by consumers if common attributes are advertised—for example, the desirability of a nutritious cereal and a nutritious snack.[27]

STRATEGIC APPLICATIONS OF CONSUMER BEHAVIOR

▶ Brand Leveraging: An Application of Stimulus Generalization

Brand leveraging is one of the most direct and popular applications of stimulus generalization in marketing. Companies have utilized the strategy with increasing frequency because of the growing expense of introducing new products and the fact that such introductions are 40 to 80 percent less expensive when a product is given an existing name. A study by Aaker and Keller found two perceptual requirements for brand leveraging to work. First, consumers must associate the brand with high quality. Second, there must be a perception of fit between the two products—that is, a logical transference from the old to the new product—for stimulus generalization to take place. A quality name and positive transference through stimulus generalization led Eastman Kodak to introduce a battery line. Research showed that a significant number of consumers thought the company already sold batteries, even before it introduced them.

There are two types of brand leveraging: a simple line extension (Diet Coke) and a transference of the name from one product category to another (Bic pens to Bic disposable lighters). Park, Milberg, and Lawson studied these types of brand leveraging and found that successful line extensions require product feature similarity, whereas successful category extensions require concept consistency. That is, Coca-Cola could leverage its flagship brand to Diet Coke because both brands had similar features to permit name transferability (for example, carbonation, colas, color, and so forth). Bic was able to leverage its name from pens to disposable lighters despite a lack of similarity in product features because there was concept consistency between the two categories—disposability.

When concept consistency is lacking, brand leveraging will fail because consumers will not be able to generalize from one product category to another. When Bic attempted to introduce perfumes, it failed. Consumers could not generalize the Bic name to perfume because the category was not consistent with disposability.

Sources: C. Whan Park, Sandra Milberg, and Robert Lawson, "Evaluation of Brand Extensions: The Role of Product Feature Similarity and Brand Concept Consistency," *Journal of Consumer Research* 18 (September 1991), pp. 185–193; David A. Aaker and Kevin Lane Keller, "Consumer Evaluations of Brand Extensions," *Journal of Marketing* 54 (January 1990), pp. 27–41.

PERCEPTUAL SELECTION

Having described the nature of stimuli and the factors that affect stimulus perception, we can now turn to describing the process of perception. The steps in the perceptual process—selection, organization, and interpretation—are shown in Figure 7.1.

The first component of perception, **selection,** requires consumers to be exposed to marketing stimuli and to attend to these stimuli. Consumers will pick and choose marketing stimuli based on their needs and attitudes. The car buyer will be more attentive to car ads; the fashion-conscious consumer will be more attentive to ads for clothing; the consumer who is loyal to Budweiser beer will be more attentive to Budweiser advertising. In each case, the consumer is processing stimuli selectively by picking and choosing them based on his or her psychological set.

This process of perceptual selection is increasingly difficult because of the greater clutter of advertising messages. By one estimate, consumers are bombarded by an average of 300 to 600 messages a day, and the number of ads aired has more than tripled in the last 25 years, creating significant *advertising clutter.*[28]

For such perceptual selection to occur, the consumer must first see or hear the stimulus and then respond to it. Therefore, three processes define selection: exposure, attention, and selective perception.

Exposure

Exposure occurs when consumers' senses (sight, hearing, touch, smell) are activated by a stimulus. Exposure to a stimulus either occurs or it does not. Con-

FIGURE 7.1
The perceptual process

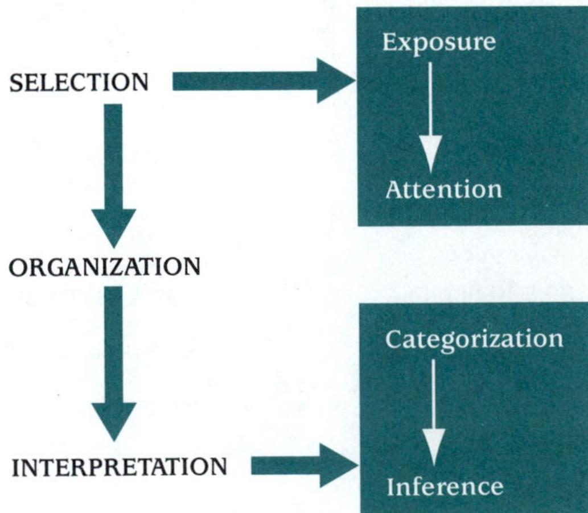

sumers' interest in and involvement with the stimulus is reflected in the level of attention they devote to it.

Consumers will pick and choose the stimuli they are exposed to. A consumer in the market for a new car is more likely to look for car ads. The consumer shopping for a laptop computer is more likely to ask friends and business associates about their experiences with various brands.

Consumers are also likely to avoid exposure to stimuli that are unimportant and uninteresting. The advent of remote control devices for TV sets has permitted "zapping" of TV commercials by switching channels. Consumers also employ "zipping" (as opposed to zapping) by fast forwarding through commercials while playing recorded tapes. Some VCRs even remove the need for zipping by automatically removing commercials while recording. Another manifestation of stimulus avoidance is known as the *flush factor.* When the first Superbowl game was held between the Green Bay Packers and the Kansas City Chiefs in 1967, at halftime the water pressure in Kansas City reached a record low.

Attention

Attention is the momentary focusing of a consumer's cognitive capacity on a specific stimulus. When consumers notice a TV ad, a new product on a shelf, or a car in a showroom, attention has taken place.

Advertisers can use many of the structural factors described previously to get consumers' attention—for example, size through larger ads, position by placing an ad in the upper half of a page, and novelty by using eye-catching photos or illustrations. These factors apply to in-store stimuli as well. For example, one study found that brands on the upper shelf in a supermarket received 35 percent more attention than those on the lower shelf and that increasing the number of packages for a particular brand on the shelf from two to four increased attention by 34 percent.[29] Sensory factors can also increase consumers' attention—for example, sound such as the use of a jingle or voice-overs of famous people in a commercial, or smell such as scratch-and-sniff print ads for perfume.

An important principle of attention is that the greater the consumers' adaptation level, the less likely it is that attention will take place. Many consumers have become so adapted to repetitive TV commercials that they "tune out"; that is, they are exposed to the commercial but do not notice it.

The opposite of adaptation is **contrast,** a change from the constant conditions consumers are used to. Advertisers try to achieve contrast by varying their campaigns, by using attention-getting stimuli, or by introducing new stimuli. This reduces advertising wearout. Brand repositioning is an example of moving from adaptation to contrast by introducing new stimuli. When Philip Morris bought Miller Brewing Co., it changed the theme of its leading brand, Miller High Life, from "The champagne of bottled beers" to a "Miller Time" campaign targeted to the heavy beer drinking segment. The contrast between the elite beer drinking group in the older campaign and the male-oriented, blue-collar group pictured in the later ads was sharp and drew attention to the campaign. As time passes, consumers adapt to any campaign and further attempts at introducing contrast to maintain consumer attention are required.

Selective Perception

Consumers perceive marketing stimuli selectively because each individual is unique in the combination of his or her needs, attitudes, experiences, and personal characteristics. **Selective perception** means that two consumers may perceive the identical advertisement, package, or product very differently. One consumer may believe a claim that Clorox gets clothes whiter than other bleaches; another may regard such a claim as untrue and may believe that all bleaches are the same.

http://www.clorox.com/

Selective perception occurs at every stage in the perceptual process as illustrated in Figure 7.1. *Selective exposure* occurs because people's beliefs influence what they choose to listen to or read. *Selective organization* occurs because people organize information to be consistent with their beliefs. Also, *selective interpretation* occurs so that perceptions conform with prior beliefs and attitudes. For example, Arm & Hammer's claim that its baking soda toothpaste is healthier for teeth and gums was consistent with consumers' beliefs that the kind of toothpaste makes a difference, even though it usually does not. As a result, many consumers chose to believe the claim, despite statements from dentists that baking soda does not affect dental hygiene one way or the other.[30]

Such selective perception operates for both high- and low-involvement purchases. In the high-involvement case, consumers selectively choose information that (1) helps them evaluate brands that meet their needs and (2) conforms to their beliefs and predispositions. In the low-involvement case, consumers selectively screen out most information in an attempt to avoid cognitive activity and informational clutter.

There is ample evidence of selective perception of marketing stimuli. We noted the research by Allison and Uhl that found consumers perceived taste differences between brands of beer only when they were shown the brand label. These consumers' perceptions were based on brand-name associations derived from advertising and social stimuli, associations that tended to conform to the consumers' current knowledge and past experiences.

Functions of Selective Perception

Selective perception ensures that consumers will receive information most relevant to their needs. This process is called **perceptual vigilance.** In a marketing study demonstrating the operation of perceptual vigilance, Spence and Engel found that consumers recognize names for preferred brands more quickly than they do names for other brands.[31] Individuals were more likely to perceive preferred stimuli.

In high-involvement purchases, perceptual vigilance guides consumers to necessary information. Consumers are directed to information that is instrumental in attaining desired benefits. In low-involvement purchases, perceptual vigilance acts by screening out information because consumers want to minimize information processing. Therefore, the less involved consumer must be selective in screening out information.

Consumers sometimes perceive information to conform to their beliefs and attitudes. This second function of selective perception is called **perceptual defense** because it protects the individual from threatening or contradictory stimuli. For example, the cigarette smoker may avoid antismoking advertisements or play down their importance. Accepting the message may mean recognizing that the smoker's actions are detrimental to his or her health. The recent purchaser of a poorly insulated home may ignore unexpectedly high fuel bills or rationalize the situation by saying fuel costs are high for everyone.

Perceptual defense tends to operate when consumers are involved. Involved consumers have strong beliefs and attitudes about a brand. In terms of Sherif's social judgment theory, firmly held beliefs reflect a narrow latitude of acceptance.[32] Messages in agreement with the consumers' beliefs will be accepted and distorted in the direction of those beliefs (an assimilation effect). Messages that do not conform to the consumers' strongly held beliefs will be rejected or distorted to contrast with the consumers' opinions (a contrast effect).

Perceptual defense is more likely in anxiety-producing situations because it leads consumers to avoid stimuli that produce fears and anxieties. For example, the heavy smoker avoids the anxiety of viewing an antismoking commercial. A current example of perceptual defense is the many misconceptions people have formed about AIDS. The ad in Exhibit 7.4 tries to break down these perceptual defenses by correcting misconceptions and educating individuals about the realities of AIDS.

Perceptual Equilibrium

The underlying principle in the operation of selective perception is that consumers seek **perceptual equilibrium,** that is, consistency between the information they receive about a brand and their prior beliefs about that brand. Such consistency ensures that the consumers' psychological set is in equilibrium. Three cognitive theories are based on principles of selective perception and perceptual equilibrium.

- *Sherif's social judgment theory* (discussed in Chapter 5) states that consumers process information to ensure consistency by either rejecting contradictory information (contrast) or by interpreting acceptable information to fit more closely with their views (assimilation).[33]
- *Heider's balance theory* states that when information about an object conflicts with consumers' beliefs, they will achieve balance by changing their opinion about the object, about the source of information, or both.[34] The result is a balance in beliefs about the information and the object. For example, if a close friend expresses the view that your fa-

▶EXHIBIT 7.4
An attempt to break down perceptual defense

You won't get AIDS from everyday contact.
You won't get AIDS from being a friend.
You won't get AIDS from a mosquito bite.
You won't get AIDS from a kiss.
You won't get AIDS by talking.
You won't get AIDS by listening.
You won't get AIDS from a public pool.
You won't get AIDS from a pimple.
You won't get AIDS from a toilet seat.
You won't get AIDS from a haircut.
You won't get AIDS by donating blood.
You won't get AIDS from an airplane.
You won't get AIDS from tears.
You won't get AIDS from food.
You won't get AIDS from a hug.
You won't get AIDS from a towel.
You won't get AIDS from a telephone.
You won't get AIDS from a crowded room.
You won't get AIDS from an elevator.
You won't get AIDS from a greasy spoon.
You won't get AIDS from a bump.
You won't get AIDS by laughing.
You won't get AIDS by watching a movie.
You won't get AIDS from a cat.
You won't get AIDS from a schoolyard.
You won't get AIDS from going to a party.
You won't get AIDS from taking a trip.
You won't get AIDS from a dog bite.
You won't get AIDS from visiting a city.
You won't get AIDS from a cab.
You won't get AIDS from a bus.
You won't get AIDS at a play.
You won't get AIDS by dancing.
You won't get AIDS because someone is different from you.
You won't get AIDS from a classroom.

Stop Worrying About How You Won't Get AIDS. And Worry About How You Can.

You *can* get AIDS from sexual intercourse with an infected partner.
You *can* get AIDS from sharing drug needles with an infected person.
You *can* get AIDS by being born to an infected mother.

1-800-342-AIDS
Deaf access:
1-800-AIDS-TTY
1-800-342-7889

U.S. DEPARTMENT OF HEALTH AND HUMAN SERVICES/PUBLIC HEALTH SERVICE/Centers For Disease Control

vorite camera takes poor pictures, you can doubt the credibility of your friend as a source of information about cameras, form a more negative attitude toward your favorite camera, or do a little bit of both to obtain balance between information and object.

- *Cognitive dissonance theory* states that when postpurchase conflicts arise, consumers will look for balance in the psychological set by seeking supporting information or by distorting contradictory information.

Each of these theories results in consistency between consumers' perceptions of marketing stimuli and their beliefs and attitudes.

Perceptual Disequilibrium

Consumers not only accept information that is consistent with their beliefs, but they will also accept discrepant information about a selected product. If they did not, it would mean that every time a consumer was dissatisfied, he or she would make some attempt to rationalize the purchase and would never switch brands. Both learning and cognitive dissonance theories predict different outcomes from dissatisfaction.

- *Learning theory* says that when a brand does not meet expectations, consumers learn from the negative experience and adjust beliefs and attitudes accordingly. The result is a reduction in the probability of repurchase. For example, even though 80 percent of nonsmokers accept the link between smoking and cancer, over half of heavy smokers also accept this link. These smokers must be in a state of perceptual disequilibrium. Many will accept this dissonant information and attempt to stop smoking to change their behavior to conform to the information.
- *Cognitive dissonance theory* says that when a brand does not meet expectations, consumers will discount the negative information; for example, heavy smokers may discount the link between cancer and smoking and rationalize their smoking behavior.

Selective Perception and Marketing Strategy

Marketing messages can be clear-cut or ambiguous. If consumers engage in perceptual defense, then ambiguous messages are more likely to be effective because the marketer is giving consumers latitude to interpret the message to accord with their beliefs about the brand. If consumers engage in perceptual vigilance, then clear-cut messages are more likely to be effective because it is apparent whether the information is supportive of or contradictory to the consumers' beliefs.

Using Perceptual Defense. Ambiguity should be used in advertising when the product is important to consumers but its benefits are not clear-cut. Since consumers are utilizing beliefs that are consistent with their needs, the operating principle is perceptual defense. The ad for Microsoft in Exhibit 7.5 illustrates this principle. The tagline "Where do you want to go today?" enables the consumer to project almost any motive for using Microsoft products. The theme can mean many different things to different people. As a result, consumers can selectively perceive a range of applications with a minimum of informational content. Ambiguity, therefore, permits different consumers to selectively perceive a message in line with their needs.

http://www.microsoft.com/

Generally, a moderate amount of ambiguity is optimal. If the message is too explicit, consumers have little room for projecting, and the marketer may be un-

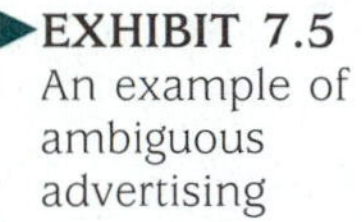

▶EXHIBIT 7.5
An example of ambiguous advertising

necessarily restricting the potential market. On the other hand, if the message is too ambiguous, consumers will have difficulty understanding it or relating to it.

Using Perceptual Vigilance. Marketers should be explicit in their advertising if the product's benefits are clear-cut and if the product is targeted to a well-defined segment. In such cases, the informational content of the advertisement dominates and ambiguity is held to a minimum. Industrial advertising tends to be less ambiguous because it is more heavily balanced toward informational content than toward symbolism. Since consumers are seeking information directed to their needs and avoiding unnecessary information, the operating principle is perceptual vigilance.

Performance-oriented autos use unambiguous ads with straightforward informational content. An ad for the Pontiac Grand Prix refers to a turbocharged V6 engine creating over 200 horsepower, a cross-ram intake, GT + 4 radial tires, and so on. There is little left to the imagination. The information is clear and readily perceived. It is also easily filtered out by those who are not interested in the intricacies of a car's performance.

PERCEPTUAL ORGANIZATION

In being exposed to 300 to 600 commercials a day, the typical consumer uses some form of perceptual organization of disparate, and at times conflicting, stimuli. **Perceptual organization** means that consumers group information from various sources into a meaningful whole to comprehend it better and to act on it.

The basic principle of organization is **integration,** which means that consumers perceive various stimuli as an organized whole. Such an organization simplifies information processing and provides an integrated meaning for the stimuli. These principles have been derived from **Gestalt psychology.** (*Gestalt* is roughly translated from German as total configuration or whole pattern.) Since they provide a framework for interpreting advertising messages as an integrated whole, principles of Gestalt psychology apply directly to marketing strategy. The advertising campaign, price level, distribution outlet, and brand characteristics are not disparate elements of the marketing plan. They are viewed in concert and produce an overall brand image. In short, the whole is greater than the sum of the parts.

The principles of perceptual integration are based on Gestalt psychologists' basic hypothesis that people organize perceptions to form a complete picture of an object. Perceptual integration is a process of forming many disparate stimuli into an organized whole. The picture on a television screen is a good example. In actuality, it is made up of thousands of tiny dots, but we integrate these dots into a cohesive whole so that there is little difference between the picture on the screen and the real world.

The most important principles of perceptual integration are those of closure, grouping, and context.

Closure

Closure refers to a perceiver's tendency to fill in the missing elements when a stimulus is incomplete. Consumers have a desire to form a complete picture and derive a certain amount of satisfaction in completing a message on their own. This principle operates when consumers develop their own conclusions from moderately ambiguous advertisements. A study by Heimbach and Jacoby showed that an incomplete ad may increase attention to and recall of the message.[35] They presented one group of consumers with a complete commercial and another group with a commercial cut at the end. The incomplete commercial generated 34 percent more recall than did the complete version.

Grouping

Consumers are more likely to perceive a variety of information as chunks rather than as separate units. They integrate various bits and pieces of information into organized wholes. **Chunking** or **grouping information** permits consumers to evaluate one brand over another by using a variety of attributes. Principles of grouping that have emerged from Gestalt psychology are proximity, similarity, and continuity. These principles are represented in Figure 7.2.

The tendency to group stimuli by **proximity** means that one object will be associated with another because of its closeness to that object. Because of their vertical proximity, the 12 dots in Figure 7.2 are seen as three columns of four dots rather than four rows of three dots. Most advertising uses principles of proximity by associating the product with positive symbols and imagery that are close to the product. For example, an L.A. Gear ad positions sneakers in prox-

FIGURE 7.2 Principles of organization

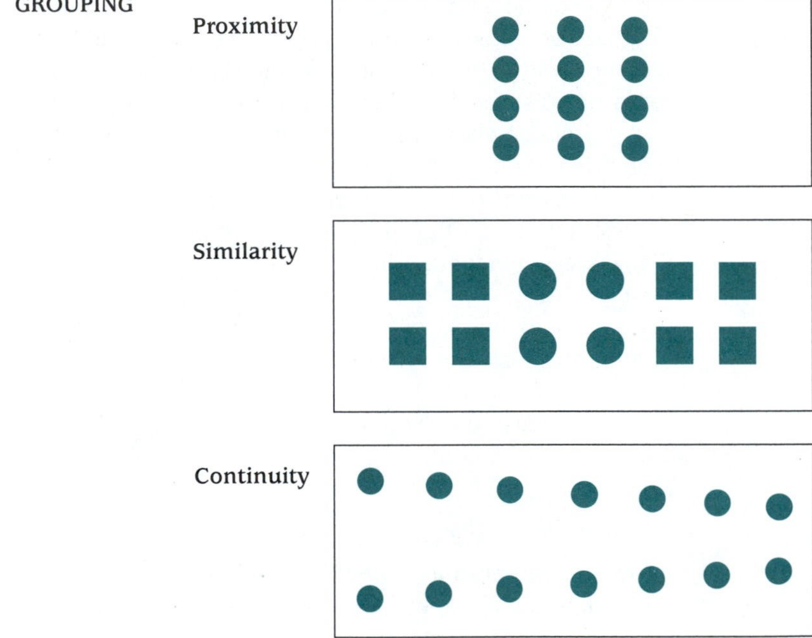

imity to a guitar and a picture of James Dean. The attempt is to associate the product with rock music and with a symbol of anti-establishment culture.

Consumers also group products by **similarity.** The eight squares and four circles in Figure 7.2 are grouped in three sets because of their similarity—two sets of four squares and one set of four circles. The ad for Look cosmetics in Exhibit 7.6 illustrates the concept of similarity by grouping various products by shades and distinguishing product lines by using different shapes. The intention is to view each product line as an integrated whole.

Consumers also group stimuli into uninterrupted forms, rather than into discontinuous contours, to attain **continuity.** The dots in the third part of Figure 7.2 are more likely to be seen as an arrow projecting to the right than as columns of dots. Applying continuity to a retail store means that there should be no sharp breaks from one sales station to the next by type of merchandise. The transition should be reasonably continuous.

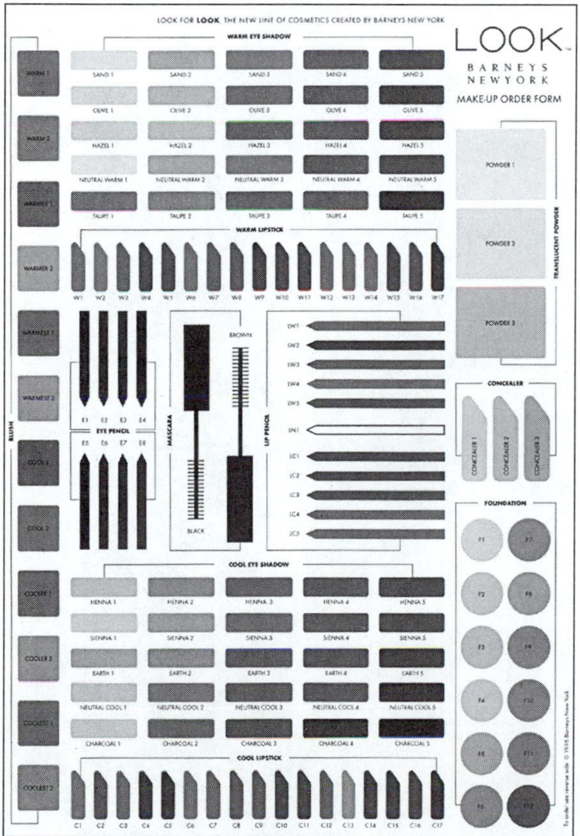

EXHIBIT 7.6
Use of the principle of similarity in advertising

Context

Consumers tend to perceive an object by the **context** in which it is shown. The setting of an advertisement will influence the perception of a product. For example, consumers may perceive one advertisement quite differently in two different media. In a study by Fuchs, identical advertisements were placed in high-prestige magazines (*Harper's, New Yorker*) and in low-prestige magazines (*True, Detective*). Not surprisingly, consumers rated advertisements in the high-prestige magazines much higher than the identical ads in low-prestige magazines, showing that media context will directly influence the perception of the ad.[36]

The most important principle of context is **figure and ground.** Gestalt psychologists state that in organizing stimuli into wholes, individuals will distinguish stimuli that are prominent (the figure that is generally in the foreground) from stimuli that are less prominent (those in the ground or background). The lower part of Figure 7.2 illustrates the principle of figure and ground. The picture can be seen as a goblet (figure) with a dark background or as two profiles (figure) with a lighter background. Advertisers seek to ensure that the product is the figure and the setting is the background.

▶EXHIBIT 7.7 The use of figure and ground in advertising http://www.metlife.com/

The determination of what part of the whole is the figure and what part is ground will greatly affect the way consumers perceive stimuli. Utilizing the Snoopy cartoon figure, MetLife's advertising campaign used figure and ground (see Exhibit 7.7). The Snoopy campaign was successful in changing MetLife's image from a faceless and friendless company to a warmer and friendlier one. The campaign has not increased sales, however.[37] The campaign should convey the product, MetLife, as the figure and the Snoopy characters as the ground. However, the advertisement in Exhibit 7.7 raises the question of whether Snoopy is the figure and the company is the background. If so, the campaign may be placing too much attention on Snoopy at the company's expense.

PERCEPTUAL INTERPRETATION

Once consumers select and organize stimuli, they interpret them. Two basic principles help consumers interpret marketing information. The first principle involves a tendency to place information into logical categories. **Categorization** helps consumers process known information quickly and efficiently. ("This is another ad for Bounty. I know what they are going to say, so I don't have to pay much attention.") Categorization also helps consumers classify new information. ("This is an ad for a new breakfast food that is probably like Carnation Slender.")

Inference involves the development of an association between two stimuli. For example, consumers might associate a high price with quality or blue suds in a detergent with cleansing power.

Perceptual Categorization

Marketers seek to facilitate the process of perceptual categorization. They want to make sure consumers recognize a brand as part of a product class, but do not want their brand to be a direct duplicate of other brands. Product positioning attempts to establish both product categorization and product uniqueness.

http://www.monsanto.com/

Monsanto's Starch-Eze is an example of a new product that failed because it was not correctly categorized. A starch concentrate, Starch-Eze had to be diluted and was meant to be used only every 10 or 12 washings.[38] The product was advertised as a starch, and the name implied it was easy to use. Consumers categorized it as another brand of starch and used it in every wash cycle. The result was a cardboard shirt. According to Day, "Once a new object is placed in an existing category, it becomes the focus of the existing repertory of behaviors which are appropriate to the overall category."[39] The problem was not with Starch-Eze itself but how consumers placed the product in the traditional category of starch. The existing repertory of behaviors required using the product frequently, which resulted in the product's failure.

Category Levels

When consumers first learn about a product, they classify it at the most basic level. As they process more information, they then develop a capacity to use refined classifications.[40] For example, when computers were first introduced in the 1950s, they were one category. By the 1970s, consumers could distinguish between mainframes, microcomputers, and later, personal computers (PCs) (see Figure 7.3). By the 1980s, PCs could be categorized into desktops, portables, and laptops. Then, by the 1990s, as laptops became more widespread, they could be further categorized as notebooks, pen computers, and personal assistants.

The more involved the consumer, the greater the likelihood that he or she will classify stimuli at more refined levels. Thus, the typical consumer might say, "I rode to work in my neighbor's car," whereas the car buff might say, "I rode to work in my neighbor's new Chevy Blazer." Categorization based on usage will also vary across cultures. Chinese consumers are likely to have many more categories for bicycles, but they may view computers as one category. Conversely, most American consumers view bicycles as one category but recognize several categories for computers.

http://www.chevrolet.com/

Process of Categorization

The process of establishing subcategories within a broader product category can be better understood by introducing two concepts: schema and subtyping.

▶ FIGURE 7.3 Category levels for computers

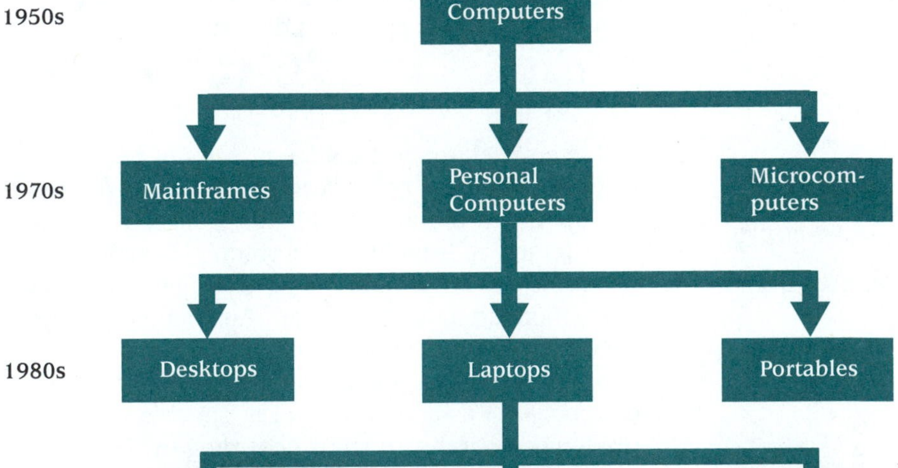

Schema. When consumers first gather information about a new product such as computers, they store bits and pieces of information about the category in their memory.[41] As they gain more knowledge of the category, they recall information in clusters of thoughts, ideas, and symbols known as a **schema.**[42] The consumers' original schema for computers in the 1950s might have equated them to desk calculators and more generally to business machines. By the 1960s, their schema for computers was more detailed, probably involving ideas and objects such as "punch cards," "mainframes," and "automatic processing."

Subtyping. As the computer industry developed new technologies and consumers gained more information, a process of subtyping began. **Subtyping** involves developing a subcategory of a broader category. By the 1970s, consumers could distinguish between mainframes and microcomputers based on characteristics such as size, speed, interfaces, terminals, and so forth. The schema (that is, words, ideas, and symbols) associated with microcomputers became the definition of a subcategory of computers in consumers' minds. By the 1980s, personal computers became the dominant subtype based on a schema that included hard disks, floppies, memory, portability, and other features.

When marketers offer unique benefits in a new product they encourage consumers to subtype.[43] If successful, marketers have established a dominant position in a new subcategory. When PepsiCo introduced Slice, it was successful in establishing a new schema in consumer minds: fruit-based soft drinks. It did so with the campaign theme "We've Got the Juice" and with the name Slice. The entry of Coca-Cola and P&G with juice-enriched products firmly established the subcategory.

Research on Categorization

Several studies have considered the role of schema and subtyping in the process of categorization. Stayman, Alden, and Smith found that schema tend to be more important for consumers who are not highly knowledgeable about product categories.[44] A typical consumer buying a computer might first determine the category of computer to be purchased and then think of the schema associated with the category (memory, speed, hard drive capacity) to determine the criteria by which to evaluate brands. Computer buffs tend to think more in terms of what they want from computers across categories.

Another study by Meyers-Levy and Tybout also sheds some light on the process of subtyping.[45] They found that consumers subtype products that are moderately different from existing products. Slice had common attributes with the soft drink schema, but the fruit-based feature warranted developing a subcategory within the broader category of soft drinks. If PepsiCo were to introduce a calcium-based breakfast drink, it is likely consumers would establish a totally new schema to incorporate this product.

Perceptual Inference

Consumers develop inferences about brands, prices, stores, and companies.[46] These inferences are beliefs consumers form about objects from past associations. Consumers may associate a Rolex watch with quality. This inference is based on word-of-mouth communications from friends and on advertising for the watch.

Perceptual Inference and Product Symbols

The symbols we see in ads and packages are socially and culturally derived. For example, the cowboy has been a symbol of masculinity since frontier days; the predominance of red, white, and blue on many packages is implicitly associated with patriotism.

There is a close relationship between the role of product symbols and the nature of the consumption process. Symbols associated with fantasy and emotion are linked to *hedonic consumption,* that is, a more experiential and emotional interaction with the product on the part of the consumer. The emotional link between a Harley owner and his or her bike means that the Harley logo may be enough to trigger an imaginary ride down a lonely road.

Despite the generality of symbols such as a cowboy, consumers will perceive them selectively. The Mercedes symbol may connote wealth and prestige to some and mere ostentation to others. The Marlboro cowboy may represent strength and masculinity to some and an invidious attempt to reinforce an addiction to others.

Semiotics

A field of study called **semiotics** examines the role signs and symbols have in assigning meaning to objects.[47] In a marketing context, semioticians see the symbols in packaging "as a kind of culture/consumption dictionary; its entries are products, and their definitions are cultural meanings."[48]

Semiotics attempts to determine the meaning consumers assign to symbols through three components: (1) the *object* (a product such as Crystal Pepsi), (2) the symbol associated with the object (a clear product), and (3) the interpretant or meaning of the symbol (light and natural).[49] These associations, shown in the top of Figure 7.4, are the ones that PepsiCo hoped to promote by introducing a clear product. But as we saw, many consumers associated clear with weak and watery (bottom of Figure 7.4). That is, the meaning many consumers associated with the symbol was not the one that the company hoped to elicit, defeating the purpose of using the symbolism of a clear cola.

An example of the application of semiotics is a study of the association consumers make with corporate logos.[50] The study found little association between the level of advertising and the strength of the logo's association with the company, suggesting that consumer perceptions vary widely depending on how they interpret these signs and symbols. For example, the heavily advertised Centu-

FIGURE 7.4 The three components of semiotics

Symbolic Product Associations Desired by Pepsi

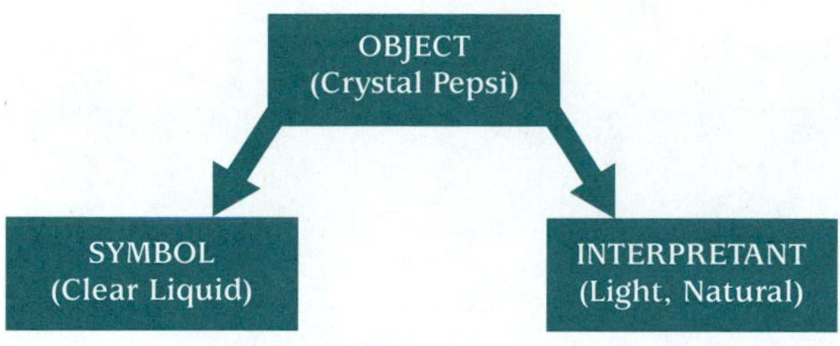

Symbolic Product Associations Held by Many Consumers

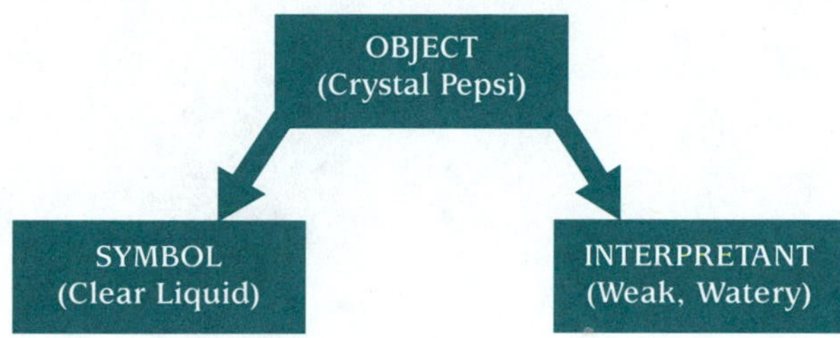

rion American Express used was not strongly associated with the company. However, the much less advertised Michelin man had a stronger and more positive association with the company.

http://www.michelin.com/

http://www.pillsbury.com/

Symbols like the Michelin man or the Pillsbury doughboy are clearly related to the products the company produces, thus facilitating inferences of quality and reliability. However, since the Centurion is not a clear symbol of anything that American Express does, making positive inferences is difficult.

Marketing Implications of Perceptual Inference

Consumers tend to form images of brands, stores, and companies. An **image** is a total perception of the object that consumers form by processing information from various sources over time. Gestalt psychology suggests that forming an image is a natural process of developing a total perception of the object. Consumers form images in two ways: (1) They draw inferences about brands and products from environmental stimuli such as ads or word-of-mouth communication with friends and neighbors. (2) They draw these inferences internally by developing *fantasies,* that is thoughts that are not based on reality. For example, teenage girls and young women may fantasize about becoming basketball star Lisa Leslie in the Nike ad (see Exhibit 7.8).

Brand Image. Brand images represent the overall perception of the brand and are formed based on the inferences consumers make about the brand, whether based on external stimuli or fantasies. Brand image is closely tied to a

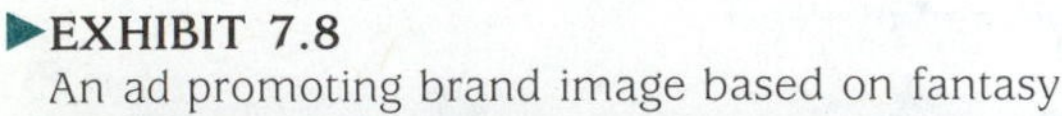

EXHIBIT 7.8
An ad promoting brand image based on fantasy

brand's equity, as reflected in the record $25 billion purchase price for RJR Nabisco. This figure was based primarily on the value of the company's brand names rather than on its physical facilities.

The key ingredient in influencing consumers' brand image is **product positioning.** Marketers try to position their brands to meet the needs of defined customer segments. They do so by developing a product concept that can communicate the desired benefits through advertising and by utilizing media that will reach the target segment. When Schweppes first came on the market in the United States, it could have been positioned as a soft drink or as a mixer. Positioning it as a mixer guided the promotional direction. The use of Commander Whitehead as the dapper Englishman referring to "Schweppervescence" produced an image of prestige for a product category that consumers might have otherwise regarded as commonplace. This positioning also required the selection of media for an older, more conservative, and more upscale (higher socioeconomic) group than the group that Schweppes would have targeted to position the product as a soft drink.

Store Image. Consumers develop store images based on advertising, merchandise in the store, opinions of friends and relatives, and shopping experiences. Store image often influences brand image.

Consumers will perceive the identical product quite differently in Woolco or Kmart than in Neiman Marcus or Bloomingdale's. In one study, four identical samples of carpet were given to consumers to evaluate.[51] Each sample was labeled with a more or less prestigious store. Even when prices were identical, consumers rated the same samples higher in a prestigious store than those in a less prestigious one. A positive store image thus produced a positive brand image, even though product and price were identical.

Retailers have a particular stake in establishing a positive store image, as their image is directly tied to sales results. JCPenney has upgraded its image by repositioning its line to higher-quality merchandise.[52] It deleted appliances, garden supplies, and automotive products and put more emphasis on designer clothing.

Corporate Image. Consumers also organize the variety of information about companies and experiences with a company's products into corporate images. Companies spend millions of dollars to improve their images with the public for several reasons. First, a positive corporate image will reinforce positive perceptions of the company's products. Such a link between corporate and brand image is particularly important when the brand name is closely associated with the company. General Electric advertises itself as innovative and forward-looking in the hope that consumers will carry over the association to its brands. Such advertising is not as important for Procter & Gamble because it does not link its brands closely to the corporate name.

http://www.toyota.com/

Companies also seek to maintain a favorable image regarding public issues that may directly affect consumers. For example, Toyota advertised that it invested $5 billion in the American economy by building manufacturing facilities in Kentucky and California and creating 16,000 U.S. jobs. The purpose was to show that Toyota's presence in America is having a positive effect.[53]

PRICE PERCEPTIONS

One of the most important applications of consumer perceptions to marketing strategy is in the area of price. Consumers' price perceptions directly influence their perceptions of brand quality and frequently determine their purchasing behavior.

Companies must establish pricing strategies based on consumer price perceptions. In the early 1980s, Parker Pen repositioned its pens based on price. It decided to move away from its line of expensive, hand-finished pens to low-priced pens because of the explosive growth of cheap ballpoints. The results were disastrous because the company's image was not consistent with its price. In 1989, it moved back to its strength, high-priced fountain pens, with an ad campaign featuring style and luxury. The shift made the company profitable once again.[54]

Consumers' price perceptions may appear to be a simple matter of determining a product's price based on an ad or on observation in a store. However, it is not that simple because (1) consumers have certain expectations about what prices are or should be; (2) these expectations may or may not reflect the actual price; and (3) consumers frequently associate price level with the product's quality. We will consider each of these components of consumer price perceptions.

Price Expectations

When deciding whether to replace an old 19-inch color TV set, a consumer may expect to pay about $400 for a comparable set. This price is the consumer's **reference price** (also known as a **standard price**), that is, the price the consumer expects to pay for a certain item. The reference price serves as a standard or frame of reference by which consumers compare prices for alternative brands.[55]

Consumers do not have just one price point when they consider buying a product. Generally, they are willing to accept a range of prices, known as an **acceptable price range,** for a particular product. The reference price and the acceptable price range for the consumer buying a TV set are shown at the top of Figure 7.5. The acceptable price range is from $250 on the lower end (a set priced below $250 might arouse suspicions about its quality) to $500 on the higher end. The higher end of the acceptable price range is known as the **reservation price** and is the "upper limit above which an article would be judged too expensive." The lower end of the acceptable price range is the "lower limit below which the quality of the item would be suspect."[56]

The acceptable price range is likely to vary widely, depending on consumer characteristics and attitudes toward a brand. For example, Rao and Sieben found that when consumers were not knowledgeable about a product, they put a lower limit on the acceptable price range.[57] These consumers had lower price expectations because they had little basis for making quality judgments.

One other measure of price expectations is shown in Figure 7.5. The **expected price range** is the range of prices the consumer expects to find in the

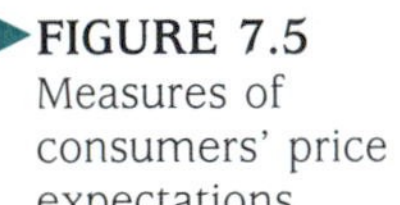
FIGURE 7.5
Measures of consumers' price expectations

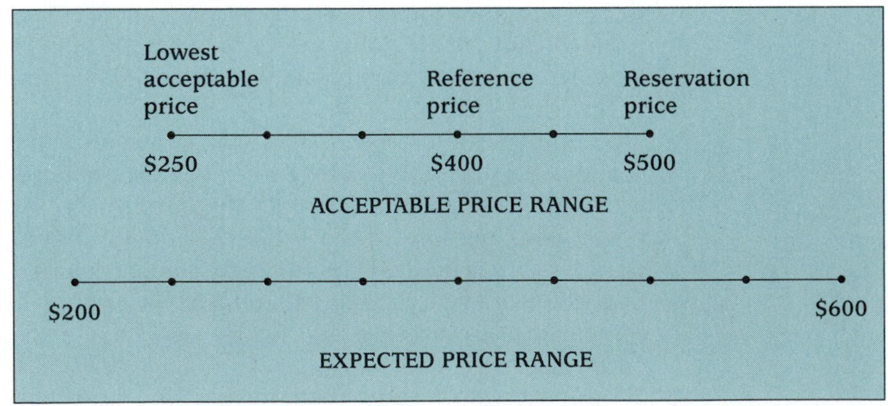

marketplace.[58] This range is almost always wider than the acceptable price range. In our example, the consumer expects to find 19-inch color TV sets priced as high as $600 and as low as $200, but anything above or below the acceptable price range is unlikely to influence the consumer's behavior.

Research has found that consumers typically understate actual prices.[59] That is, if the consumer's expected price range for color TVs is $200 to $600, the actual price range might be from $300 to $750. But when consumers are actively involved in the decision and are collecting product information, the expected and actual price ranges converge.[60]

Actual versus Reference Prices

An important consideration for marketers is the relationship between consumers' reference prices and the actual prices they encounter in the marketplace. Consumers' reference prices are rarely exactly the same as the actual prices of items. How do consumers react to a difference between their reference price and the actual price?

Researchers have used assimilation-contrast theory (see Chapter 5) to explain consumer reactions. If the difference between actual and reference price is within the consumer's acceptable price range, an assimilation effect occurs. Suppose our consumer evaluates three TV brands and finds that 19-inch sets are priced at $299, $320, and $350. These are within the consumer's acceptable range. Our consumer is likely to shift her reference price from $400 down toward the actual price of one of these brands (say $320) as a result of comparing alternatives.

Urbany, Bearden, and Weilbaker confirmed such a shift. They found that a difference between reference and actual prices resulted in a move by reference prices closer to actual prices as long as the actual prices were acceptable. What happens when actual prices are not in the acceptable price range? For example, our consumer encounters brands at prices of $550 and $600. In such a case, a contrast effect is likely to occur. That is, our consumer will reject brands priced higher than the acceptable price range.[61]

Price-Quality Relationship

An important question for marketers is whether consumers perceive a price-quality association. Generally, when consumers do not have sufficient information about product quality, they use price as an indication of quality. Since these consumers know little about the product, they are less likely to be involved. Conversely, consumers with information about product characteristics are less likely to make price-quality inferences. These consumers are more likely to be involved with the product category.[62]

Various studies have supported this view. Rao and Monroe found that price-quality associations are strongest for consumers who have less product information.[63] Similarly, Monroe found that when respondents had experience with a brand, that experience overcame price as the dominant factor in brand choice.[64]

Price is more likely to be a reflection of quality if consumers have confidence in the source of the price information. Gotlieb and Sarel found that when consumers felt the source of price information was trustworthy and credible (for example, an electrical engineer evaluating a VCR), they were more likely to associate a higher price with quality.[65]

Price is also more likely to be a surrogate for quality when consumers believe that quality and price differences exist between product alternatives. Such variations allow for price-quality inferences. Consumers are unlikely to attribute higher quality to products that are standardized or that differ by only a few cents. A price range permits quality inferences. In support of these views, Obermiller found that price-quality associations are more likely for product lines than they are for single brands because product lines are more likely to have a wide range in prices.[66] Similarly, Zeithaml found that when products are standardized (salt or gasoline), consumers view prices as reflecting cost rather than quality.[67]

On this basis, if the consumer shopping for the 19-inch color TV set believes there are significant price and quality differences among brands and has little knowledge about TV sets, she will tend to use high price as an indicator of quality.

SUMMARY

A product's success depends largely on the way consumers perceive and process marketing stimuli designed to promote it. In this chapter, we considered the nature of marketing stimuli and how consumers perceive them.

Marketing stimuli were classified into the primary stimulus (the product) and the secondary stimuli (symbols, imagery, and information representing the product). A key question is the degree to which consumers can discriminate between marketing stimuli. Marketers attempt to create such discrimination by informing consumers about the differences between their brands and competitors' brands. Consumers also generalize from one similar stimulus to another. By using existing brand names for new products, marketers use strategies of stimulus generalization through brand leveraging. Positive associations with the existing brand help launch the new product. The chapter also recognized that consumers differ in their ability to perceive marketing stimuli.

Selection, organization, and interpretation are the three basic processes underlying consumer perceptions. Selection involves being attentive to stimuli and selectively perceiving them. Selective perception serves two purposes: (1) It guides consumers in selecting information that is relevant and in screening out information that is not relevant to their needs. This process is known as perceptual vigilance. (2) It permits consumers to select information that conforms to their beliefs and predispositions about brands, products, and companies. This function is known as perceptual defense.

The organization of marketing stimuli depends on the principle of integration. Integration permits consumers to perceive many different stimuli and to organize them into a cohesive whole. Consumers are able to integrate information by processes of closure, grouping, similarity, continuity, and context.

Interpretation of stimuli also depends on two processes: categorization and inference. Categorization simplifies information processing by permitting consumers to classify brands into product categories. Inference is a belief about objects that consumers develop from past associations. Consumers often make product inferences based on the symbols associated with products. The science of semiotics analyzes the meaning consumers give symbols and their association to objects such as brands and products.

Consumers form total perceptions or images of brands, stores, and companies based on inferences. Marketers try to influence brand image by communicating desired product benefits through positioning strategies. The store image will also influence the brand image, particularly for brands that are distributed in selective stores. The corporate image affects consumers' purchasing behavior, particularly for brands that are tied to the company name.

Consumer perceptions of prices are particularly important to marketers because they often influence perceptions of quality. Consumers also form expectations regarding price levels that influence their behavior.

The next chapter focuses on how consumers process the information they perceive.

QUESTIONS

1. What risks does McDonald's face in changing adult perceptions of its stores?
2. Can you cite applications of the differential threshold to changes in (a) package size and (b) advertising duration and intensity?
3. Some studies have shown that sensory perceptions (taste, smell, and so on) play a minimal role in the selection of major national brands in such categories as tea, coffee, cigarettes, and perfumes. How does Coca-Cola's experience with reintroducing old Coke relate to this finding?
4. What are the implications of the concept of stimulus discrimination for changes in the packaging of Ivory Soap in the 100-plus years it has been in existence?
5. What are the implications of the concept of stimulus generalization for (a) using the GE name on refrigerators, (b) Colgate introducing cold tablets and antacids under its name, and (c) Bic introducing perfumes?
6. What is the distinction between perceptual vigilance and perceptual defense? Which is most likely to operate when (a) a consumer buys the same brand of frozen orange juice because of inertia and (b) a consumer buys the same perfume because of brand loyalty?
7. What are the implications of principles of proximity and similarity for (a) product-line policies and (b) in-store product organization?
8. What are some of the implications of principles of context for (a) media selection, (b) advertising layout, and (c) positioning of brands to specific usage situations?
9. Do consumers have a schema for brands such as the Macintosh computer as well as categories such as PCs? What is the purpose of a brand-related schema? What might be some logical components of a Macintosh schema?
10. Cite a product category and trace the subtyping that has occurred over time for the category. Why does such subtyping take place?
11. How can a semiotician help a marketer in developing an advertising campaign for a BMW motorcycle in an attempt to challenge Harley-Davidson's dominant position?
12. Why are certain companies that do not sell directly to the final consumer concerned with the corporate image they project to the consuming public?
13. Apply the concept of reference price and acceptable price range to explain a rationale for the decrease in the price of Macintosh computers in 1993.
14. How are consumers' price perceptions likely to change if there is a difference between their reference price and the actual price for a product? How can assimilation-contrast theory explain consumer reactions to such a difference?
15. Under what conditions is price likely to be used as an indicator of quality? Are consumers more likely to establish a price-quality association for certain products? If so, what products?

RESEARCH ASSIGNMENTS

1. Pick two closely competing brands in two product categories: a high-involvement category (such as cars) and a low-involvement category (such as toothpaste). Identify a number of consumers who own or regularly use each brand. Ask consumers to rate the two competing brands (their own and the close competitor) on a number of need criteria (for cars it might be economy, durability, and style). If consumers perceive brands selectively, they are likely to rate their own brand much higher than they do

the competitive brand. This selective perception is more likely for the high-involvement than it is for the low-involvement category.

- Do your findings show this to be true? That is, (a) are brand ratings for the consumer's own brand much higher than those of the competitive brand, and (b) are the differences in ratings between the regular and competitive brands greater for the high-involvement product category?
- Do consumers rate their own brand much higher on certain attributes but not on others?
- Do these differences reflect a process of selective perception?

2. Test consumers' ability to discriminate between the taste of alternative brands in one of the following product categories: soft drinks, coffee, or tea. Run the following experiment: Identify three leading brands in the category. (Make sure the brands tested are in the same class for the product; for example, colas or noncolas for soft drinks, regular or instant for coffee.) Select an equal number of respondents who pick one of the three brands as their regular brand. Ask all respondents how often they purchase their regular brand. Then have each respondent taste the three unidentified brands. (Make sure to rotate the order of tasting so the same brand is not always presented first.) Ask the respondent to identify his or her preferred brand. On the basis of chance, one would expect one-third correct identification.

- Was the proportion of correct identification significantly more than chance?
- Were those who correctly identified their preferred brand different from those who did not? Were they more frequent users of the category? Did they use a certain brand?

3. Select two advertising campaigns that are informationally oriented and two that rely on symbolism and imagery and can be regarded as more ambiguous. Select a sample of consumers and measure (a) unaided advertising awareness for the four brands and (b) awareness of key points in the advertising message.

- Was awareness of the informationally oriented campaign more accurate than that of the more ambiguous campaign?
- Were consumers more likely to project themes and messages not actually in the ads into the more ambiguous communications? If so, what was the nature of these projections?
- Did you detect any misperception or misinterpretation of the advertising messages? Did these misperceptions reflect perceptual defense?

4. Select a frequently purchased consumer good (such as toothpaste, detergents, or analgesics). Select a sample of 50 consumers who buy the product. Determine each consumer's acceptable price range by identifying a standard size and by asking consumers the price below which they would not trust the product's quality and the price above which they would not buy. In addition:

a. Ask consumers to identify their regular brand. Then ask them to assume there is a price increase in their regular brand. At what price increase would they switch to a competitive brand?

b. Determine the strength of the consumer's preference for the regular brand by asking if it is the best brand on the market, one of the best brands, or the same as other brands.

c. One would expect that the higher the price required for the consumer to switch to another brand, the greater the degree of brand loyalty. Was this confirmed in your study?

CONSUMER INFORMATION ACQUISITION AND PROCESSING

Chapter 8

THE ENERGIZER BUNNY: CONSUMERS WIND UP PROCESSING THE WRONG MESSAGE

To make purchasing decisions, consumers acquire and process information from advertising, from friends and neighbors, and from their own experiences with products. Processing requires that consumers perceive information by selecting, organizing, and interpreting it. However, processing requires that consumers go beyond the perceptual processes described in the last chapter. Consumers must also retain information in memory and retrieve it when evaluating brands.

Marketers have a direct interest in the way consumers process information. If consumer information processing does not result in positive brand evaluation and purchase behavior, companies can lose millions of dollars on ineffective advertising. Eveready learned this lesson when it introduced the Energizer Bunny to sell batteries. The campaign was designed to poke fun at Eveready's main competitor, Duracell, whose ads showed toys with Duracell batteries winning endurance contests. The series of Eveready ads (launched in 1989) developed into a parody of typical TV

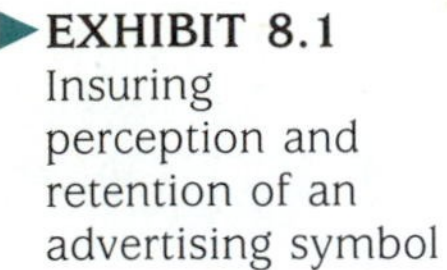

EXHIBIT 8.1
Insuring perception and retention of an advertising symbol

commercials, with each commercial being interrupted by the drumming Energizer Bunny and a voice-over saying "Still Going."

Consumers loved the ads, and their recall of the Bunny was very high. In fact, it became something of a cultural icon. It was featured hopping through an actual Diet Coke ad, Jay Leno made jokes at the Bunny's expense on the "Tonight Show," and the Bunny even got a Web site on the Internet. However, there was one problem. In one study, fully 40 percent of consumers recalled seeing a Duracell ad.[1] Why? Since the ads parodied prior Duracell commercials, they appeared to be an extension of Duracell's theme of endurance. There was another problem. The Bunny, rather than the product, was the centerpiece of the ad. The humor of the ad seemed to be dominating the message. Worst of all, the campaign did not seem to be affecting sales. By 1993, four years into the campaign, Duracell's sales of alkaline batteries grew 10.2 percent, more than double Energizer's 4.7 percent increase.[2]

http://www.eveready.com/

But Eveready feels the Bunny is now ingrained in the consumer's memory bank and should just keep going. After six years, consumers have finally learned to associate the Bunny with Eveready. As a result, in 1995 the company sank another $20 million in the campaign and has extended it to print ads (see Exhibit 8.1) to insure that this association will be maintained.

In this chapter, we extend our discussion of perception by focusing on how consumers process information. We first discuss how information is acquired from marketing and nonmarketing sources. We then consider information processing, with particular emphasis on the role of memory, and conclude by considering limitations consumers face in processing information.

CONSUMER INFORMATION ACQUISITION

Consumers must acquire information before they can process it. The role of information acquisition in consumer decision making is shown in Figure 8.1.

FIGURE 8.1
Role of information acquisition in consumer decision making

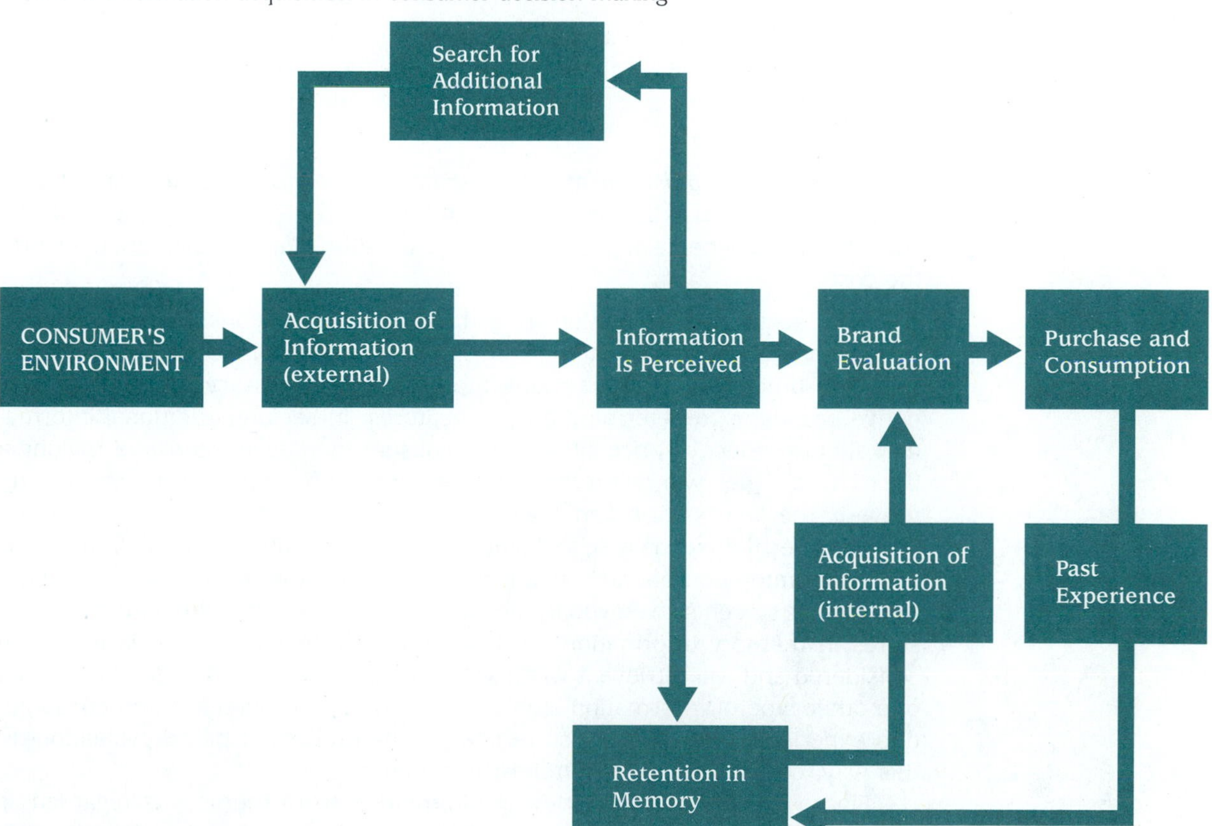

TABLE 8.1
Processes for acquiring external information

Acquisition Process	Type of Involvement
1. Ongoing Search	Enduring Involvement
2. Purchase-Specific Search	Situational Involvement
3. Passive Acquisition	Low Involvement

Consumers acquire information from their environment—from ads, salespeople, word-of-mouth communications with friends and neighbors, impartial sources such as *Consumer Reports,* and so forth. These are *external* sources of information. Table 8.1 shows that consumers use three different processes for acquiring such external information, each process being related to the consumer's involvement with the product.

1. *Ongoing search* might characterize the consumer with enduring involvement in the product. For example, the computer buff who subscribes to computer magazines is aware of a wide variety of options.

2. *Purchase-specific search* is characteristic of the consumer with situational involvement who collects information when making a purchase decision (for example, visiting a retail store or asking a friend about personal computers).

3. *Passive acquisition of information* characterizes the uninvolved consumer. Information is acquired in passing, with little effort on the part of the consumer. The benefits of actively acquiring additional information are not worth the cost.

After acquiring information from the environment, consumers perceive it, that is, they organize and interpret it. In the course of processing the information, consumers may believe more information is necessary to evaluate alternative brands or to determine product features. In seeking additional information about product or price alternatives, consumers reduce the risk of making a poor choice. They will retain the more important information in memory to retrieve in the process of brand evaluation.

Consider the business school student cited in Chapter 3 who is in the market for a laptop computer. You will recall that she was most concerned about the laptop's screen size, keyboard flexibility, and capacity on the hard drive. She stores in memory information on these three attributes for each brand being considered and will retrieve it when she compares the brands. Figure 8.1 shows one other type of information stored in memory: past purchase and consumption experiences. These are also recalled in the process of brand evaluation. In this way, consumers learn from past experience.

Figure 8.1 shows that retrieving information from memory is regarded as *internal information acquisition* because the source of information is the consumer. (We further discuss internal acquisition later in the chapter, when we discuss memory processes.)

Several studies have found that, other things being equal, consumers tend to rely more on external than memory-related sources of information. For example, Biehal and Chakravarti found that consumers are more likely to choose a brand that they can see in a store (external information source) rather than one they might remember from a previous shopping trip (internal source).[3] However, Alba and his colleagues found this to be true only if recall about brands is poor.[4] For example, our student will tend to rely more on external sources of information about computers if she has little recall about her past experiences with computers (that is, internally derived information). If her past experiences are memorable and persuasive, then these experiences might outweigh the influence of advertising, salespeople, or even friends and relatives.

Determinants of Information Search

A key component of information acquisition in Table 8.1 is whether the process is active or passive. Several factors encourage consumers to actively acquire more information:

1. *High consumer involvement.* As we saw in Chapter 3, the higher the level of involvement, the greater the amount of information acquired. That is, information search is greater if consumers' self-images are tied to the product, if the product has emotional appeal or badge value, or if consumers have ongoing interest in the product.

2. *High perceived risk.* The higher the perceived risk in purchasing, the greater the amount of information search. Locander and Hermann found that when risk was high, consumers searched for more information from neutral sources such as *Consumer Reports* and from personal sources such as friends and neighbors.[5] Murray also found that perceived risk increases information search, particularly for services as compared to products. This is because services tend to be harder to evaluate and collecting more information on them is instrumental in reducing risk.[6]

3. *Little product knowledge and experience.* In a study of purchases of TVs, VCRs, and home computers, Beatty and Smith found that consumers with less knowledge of these products were more likely to search for information.[7] Conversely, Srinivasan and Ratchford found that past experience with a product reduces information search because consumers with experience learn how to search for information more efficiently.[8] However, if past experience is negative, it may increase the search for information.[9]

4. *Clear goals.* Information search is likely to be greater when consumers have clear goals that identify the features they want; for example, a goal of auto safety can be promoted with air bags and shatterproof glass. Huffman and Hous-

ton found that such clear goals direct a consumer to acquire specific information on product attributes.[10]

5. *Less time pressure.* Time pressure to make a decision will discourage information search. Beatty and Smith found that if consumers have more time available, their information search will increase.[11] This is probably true for high- rather than low-involvement products.

6. *High price.* The higher the price, the greater the information search. This was found to be true for women's apparel, appliances, and cars.[12] A higher price means that the economic benefits of information search are greater; therefore, consumers are more likely to devote more effort to search.

7. *More product differences.* There is a higher payoff in searching for information when substantial differences exist between brands. Claxton, Fry, and Portis found that furniture and appliance buyers who saw more differences between brands visited more stores.[13]

8. *Cost-effectiveness of information search.* Another determinant of information search is its cost. There are monetary and nonmonetary costs associated with information search. Information search frequently involves the monetary costs of traveling to various retail stores. Another cost is the time involved in traveling, shopping, reading advertisements, asking the advice of friends, and so on. Consumers must weigh search time against alternatives such as leisure or business pursuits. A third cost is psychological. Information search may not be desirable to individuals who dislike shopping.

If costs are too high, consumers will avoid information search, even if the six conditions encouraging search are operating. As we saw in Chapter 5, consumers are "cognitive misers." They operate on a principle of cognitive economy so that they search only for the information they need. They make this assessment by evaluating the cost of information relative to its benefits. One economist suggested that consumers use principles of cognitive economy at the margin; that is, they will continue to collect information until the incremental benefits of the additional information no longer exceed the incremental cost of collecting that information.[14] Although consumers may not consciously operate at the margin, they do choose information sources with some cost-benefit principle in mind.

Sources of Information

Consumers can utilize several sources of information from their environment. Figure 8.2 shows these sources categorized on two dimensions: personal versus nonpersonal sources and marketer-controlled versus non-marketer-controlled sources.

In evaluating alternative laptop computers, our student utilizes all four types of sources shown in Figure 8.2. She talks to salespeople in retail stores about al-

FIGURE 8.2
Sources of consumer information

Source: Adapted from CONSUMER BEHAVIOR by Thomas S. Robertson, Joan Zielinski, and Scott Ward. Copyright © 1984 by Scott, Foresman and Company. Reprinted by permission of HarperCollins College Publishers.

	PERSONAL	IMPERSONAL
MARKETER-CONTROLLED SOURCES	• Salespeople • Telemarketing (telephone information lines) • Trade Shows	• Advertising • In-Store Displays • Sales Promotions • Packaging
NON-MARKETER-CONTROLLED SOURCES	• Word-of-Mouth from Friends and Family • Professional Advice • Experience from Consumption	• Editorial and News Material • Neutral Sources such as *Consumer Reports* Magazine

ternatives, prices, and peripherals (personal marketer-controlled sources). She is aware of advertising in magazines for laptops (nonpersonal marketer-controlled sources). She also talks to friends and business associates about their experiences with laptops (personal non-marketer-controlled sources). Finally, she uses neutral sources such as *Consumer Reports* magazine, a publication that impartially tests and rates products, to determine its evaluation of laptop brands (nonpersonal non-marketer-controlled source).

Figure 8.2 shows the sources of information for external search. As we noted, consumers also undertake a process of internal search by retrieving information from memory. In trying out several laptop models her friends owned, our consumer stored her past experiences in memory and retrieved them in the process of brand evaluation.

The consumers' stage in the decision process affects their use of information sources. Marketer-controlled sources tend to be more important in the early stages of decision making when consumers are obtaining information on product alternatives. The opinions of friends and associates and the consumers' own experiences become more important as they move closer to the final decision because they regard these sources as more trustworthy.

Use of information sources also varies according to the conditions for information search. In their study of VCRs, TVs, and home computers, Beatty and Smith found that consumers with little product knowledge are more likely to rely on friends and associates for information because they are regarded as more credible than a salesperson.[15] On the other hand, more knowledgeable consumers are likely to rely on their past experiences because they are confident of their evaluations and judgments.

CONSUMER BEHAVIOR AND THE NEW TECHNOLOGIES

▶ P&G Encourages Information Acquisition Through Cyber-Surfing

Procter & Gamble is betting that it can get women to go on-line to find out if Tide detergent will remove a raspberry jelly stain or if Cover Girl makeup looks better on brunettes.

As of 1996, over two-thirds of Internet users were men, yet the bulk of purchasers of P&G products are women. So the company anticipates an expansion of Internet users to cover its primary target group.

P&G has a growing commitment to the Internet. In March 1996, it opened two new Web sites for Sunny Delight orange drink (http://www.sunyd.com) and for the controversial new fat substitute olestra (http://www.olean.com). Additional brands slated to have their own Web sites are Tide, Pampers, and Cover Girl cosmetics. The company already has 80 Web sites registered, although not all are on line yet.

P&G anticipates that the Internet will be accepted as an additional source of nonpersonal marketer-controlled information. But, contrary to advertising or sales promotions, consumers must seek out information from the Internet. Therefore, this new medium is likely to appeal to more involved consumers engaged in active information search. For those interested in olestra, for example, P&G's site addresses questions regarding the product's safety and benefits.

P&G has often taken a leadership role in determining the direction of marketing strategies. As a result, its move onto the Internet means others are likely to follow. One estimate is that marketers' spending on the Web will increase from $74 million in 1996 to $2.6 billion in 2000, a thirty-five-fold increase in four years. A new dimension is opening up for consumer information acquisition.

Source: "P&G Steps Up Ad Cyber-Surfing," *The Wall Street Journal,* April 18, 1996.

Amount of Information Search

Despite consumers' reasons for undertaking a search for information, their amount of information search for all but the most expensive products is very limited.[16] In subscribing to principles of cognitive economy, consumers often consider the search for additional information simply not worth the time and money.

The limited nature of consumer search is illustrated in an experiment by Jacoby and his colleagues.[17] They presented consumers of breakfast cereals with information in a matrix of 16 brands by 35 product characteristics—560 pieces of information in all. On average, consumers selected 11 pieces of information, or less than 2 percent of the information available, before making a decision.

Capon and Burke studied appliance purchasers and found that consumers used 24 percent of available information.[18] The higher level of information utilization is due to the higher price and greater risk of purchasing appliances compared to those of cereals. Even so, information use was low.

Other studies have focused on the number of retail stores consumers visited.[19] Most purchasers of toys and small appliances visit only one store. Purchasers of refrigerators and furniture are more likely to visit three or more stores. Half of the purchasers of cars and major appliances, however, visited only one showroom. The amount of shopping for these products is not as great as one might expect, given the risks involved.

Studies have also considered the number of alternative brands. One study[20] found the following proportions of consumers considering more than one brand:

- 59 percent for refrigerators
- 53 percent for cars and household appliances[21]
- 39 percent for washing machines
- 29 percent for vacuum cleaners

These figures suggest that the number of brands consumers consider is typically small. Although the evidence points to limited information search, this does not mean buyers are uninvolved. A prospective consumer may be entering the decision-making process with a large amount of past experience and purchase information stored in memory.[22] Therefore, for such consumers, the necessity for extensive information search may be low.

Limits of Information Acquisition

Some consumer advocates and government agencies assume that consumers should be supplied with as much information as possible to permit a comparison of brand alternatives. The same assumption underlies economic theory: optimal choice requires access to information on all alternatives. The reality, however, is that consumers rarely seek all of the available information. They find the cost of search and the complexity of processing just too great to attempt to consider all brand alternatives. Therefore, more information is not necessarily better. In fact, too much information may create **information overload,** that is, confusion in the decision task resulting in an ineffective decision.

Jacoby, Speller, and Kohn found that information overload exists.[23] They provided consumers with a range of 8 to 72 items of information on alternative laundry detergents by varying the number of brands consumers could consider and the number of pieces of information per brand. They then related the amount of information to the effectiveness of brand choice. Effectiveness of choice was determined by the degree to which consumers chose brands that were similar to their ideal laundry detergent. If consumers used up to 24 pieces of information, the "more is better" notion seemed to hold. However, more than 24 pieces of information seemed to cause consumers to choose brands that were not similar to their ideal. Thus, having too much information and too many brands to choose from complicated the consumers' decision task and resulted in less effective choices.

A more recent study by Hutchinson and Alba provides further confirmation of information overload. They varied the number of comparisons consumers had to make to evaluate stereo speakers. They found that when comparative brand information increased, the consumers' ability to classify and evaluate brands correctly was reduced.[24]

The possibility that at some point too much information may have negative consequences on decision tasks suggests that both advertisers and public agencies must be careful not to provide consumers with irrelevant information. The problem is aggravated by the sheer number of commercials on the air. Simplifying information on complex decisions would be a step in the right direction.

Another factor contributing to information overload is the large number of alternative brands available to consumers. A decade ago, the average supermarket carried 9,000 items; today, it carries an average of 25,000. American consumers buying cereal face a choice of over 200 products. Further, the number of variations of existing products (known as *brand extensions*) has increased tremendously because marketers are finding it safer and cheaper to rely on such extensions rather than on new products.

Increasing evidence suggests that many consumers see little added value from such brand extensions and regard them as sources of confusion. One survey found that 44 percent of consumers agree that the increasing number of product introductions makes selection more difficult, not easier.[25] As Alvin Toffler concluded in his book *Future Shock,* "We are racing toward 'overchoice'—the point at which the advantage of diversity and individualization are canceled by the complexity of the buyer's decision-making process."[26]

Information Acquisition for Utilitarian versus Hedonic Products

http://www.harleydavidson.com/

In Chapter 3, we saw that consumers can view products as primarily utilitarian (serving some functional purpose) or hedonic (creating pleasure and encouraging fantasy). A Saturn car or a Harley-Davidson motorcycle can be a utilitarian product for one consumer and a hedonic product for another.

The nature of information acquisition is likely to differ in each case as shown in Table 8.2. In evaluating utilitarian products, consumers will logically seek information on product performance. Product attributes will, therefore, be the focus of a consumer's information search. In evaluating hedonic products, consumers will seek out sensory stimuli that might trigger pleasure or fantasy. In such cases, symbols and imagery may be more important than hard information on product performance. The consumer buying a Harley for transportation will seek information on acceleration, gas mileage, comfort, and other product

TABLE 8.2
Information acquisition for hedonic versus utilitarian products

Hedonic Products	Utilitarian Products
1. Sensory stimuli dominate	Product attribute information dominates
2. Ongoing information search	Purchase-specific information search
3. Personal sources most important	Nonpersonal sources most important
4. Symbols and imagery most effective	Product information most effective

attributes. The consumer buying a Harley as an extension of his or her self-image will be more sensitive to images and symbols in ads that connote the "feel" of the product or the "pleasure" of sitting on one. These consumers do not ignore performance information. Rather, performance is a requirement for considering the product. The basic decision will hinge on more emotive criteria. As a result, when we talk of information acquisition, consumers may be acquiring information regarding the product's potential for sensory stimulation as well as information on product attributes.

Table 8.2 also suggests that when consumers are evaluating hedonic products, information search is likely to be ongoing, whereas when they are evaluating utilitarian products, information search is likely to be purchase-specific. This is because products purchased for pleasure and fantasy are likely to be involving on an ongoing basis. Products purchased for utilitarian purposes are likely to be relevant to the specific purchase situation.

In addition, consumers purchasing products for pleasure and fantasy are more likely seek the advice of those with similar experiences because of the emphasis on the experiential aspects of the product. As a result, they rely on personal nonmarketing sources—friends, relatives, and owners of the product, as well as their own past experiences. The prospective Harley owner is likely to rely on the experiences of others in evaluating the potential for the bike to be an extension of his or her self-image. Consumers purchasing utilitarian products are more likely to rely on nonpersonal sources for product attribute information.

Strategic Implications of Information Acquisition

The way consumers acquire information has direct implications for marketing strategy.

Determinants of Information Acquisition

The distinction between hedonic and utilitarian products has a direct bearing on the type of information marketers convey. Information for hedonic products is

►EXHIBIT 8.2
Hedonic versus utilitarian appeals in advertising

Hedonic Appeal

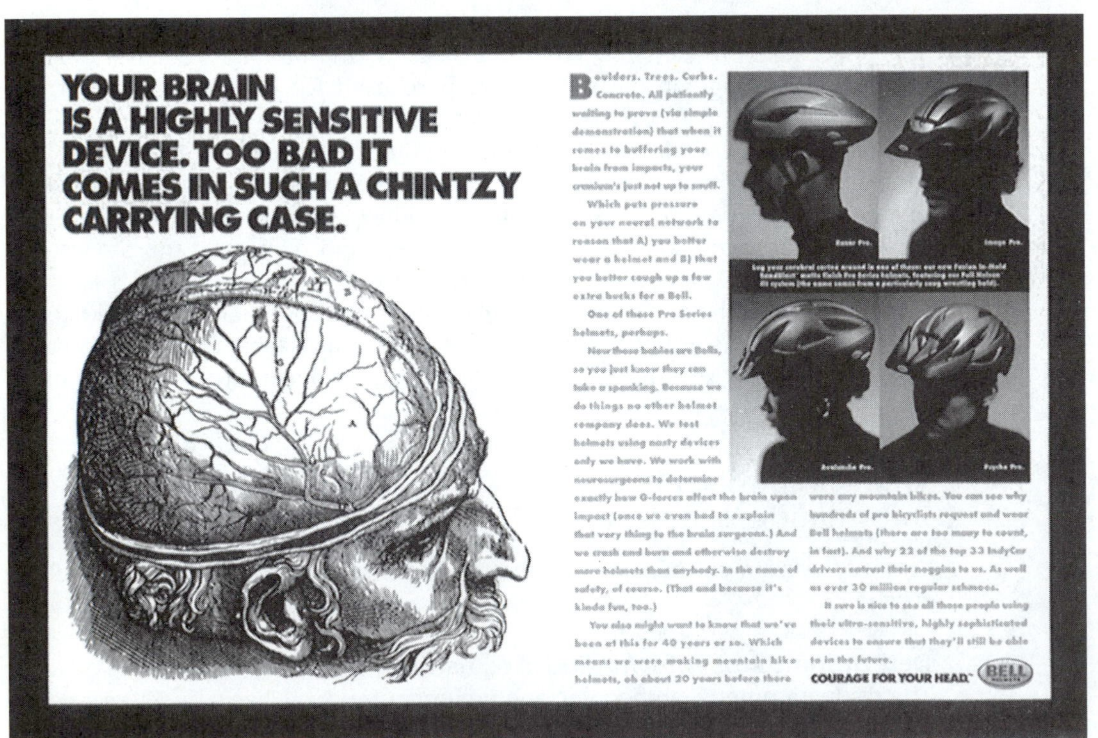

Utilitarian Appeal

►**EXHIBIT 8.3**
An example of a strategy to reduce information search

likely to be conveyed through symbols and imagery, whereas information for utilitarian products is more likely to rely on the written word.

http://www.schwinn.com/

The ad for Schwinn bicycles in Exhibit 8.2 was meant to reestablish the company's image with bike enthusiasts after it emerged from bankruptcy. The symbol of a biker challenging cars on the road is likely to hit an emotive chord with this group. The ad is nearly all image, with little text.

In contrast, the ad for bicycle helmets is almost all text. A bicycle helmet is unlikely to arouse pleasure and fantasy. It is a product designed for a utilitarian purpose, protection. As a result, the ad is designed to communicate product information.

Cost of Information Acquisition

http://www.apple.com/

Marketers must consider ways to reduce the costs of information search for consumers. Offering free samples is one method of reducing search by providing consumers product experience. Apple Computer's offer to "test drive a Macintosh" in a past ad campaign (see Exhibit 8.3) had a similar objective: to provide consumers with direct experience to reduce the need for additional information. Intensive distribution of products is also a means of reducing information search, as consumers do not have to travel as far to inspect products. For marketers who can identify prospects and provide relevant information directly, direct mail is another means of reducing the costs of information search. In-store information can also reduce search costs. Unit pricing has helped some consumers reduce the time spent on in-store brand comparisons.

Marketers might also try to direct product information more effectively to groups who have higher costs of information search. For instance, AT&T real-

TABLE 8.3
Strategic implications of passive versus active information search

Passive Information Search	Active Information Search
1. Use repetitive advertising	Vary message content frequently
2. Use TV	Use print
3. Emphasize price promotions	Emphasize advertising
4. Emphasize in-store marketing stimuli	Emphasize marketing before entering store

ized that the groups who were taking the best advantage of off-peak rates were higher-income, better-educated consumers. As a result, AT&T attempted to direct its message to the lower-income groups to facilitate information acquisition. Because the marginal cost of information is higher for low-income consumers, AT&T's strategy was designed to lower the cost of search by directing information to this segment more effectively.

http://www.att.com/

Type of Information Search: Passive versus Active

The type of information search—whether it is passive or active—also has important ramifications for marketers. The strategic implications of passive versus active information search are summarized in Table 8.3.

If the product is in a low-involvement category, marketers realize that consumers will acquire information passively and must encourage such passive receipt of information. For example, in introducing a new product, they might use repeat advertising on TV to establish a sufficient level of awareness. Television is the best medium to ensure passive acquisition because consumers' exposure to TV commercials does not require information search.

Passive acquisition points to the importance of trial as a means of obtaining information.[27] It may actually be cheaper for consumers to buy an inexpensive product for trial than it is to search for additional information. Marketers who recognize the limits of information search may decide to put more money into inducing trial than into trying to convey information to consumers. That is, it might be more cost-effective to put additional dollars into free samples and price promotions than to increase advertising budgets.

Passive information search also means that in-store stimuli will be more important. Consumers are unlikely to have searched for information before entering the store. Displays, shelf position, and price promotions are likely to make consumers take notice of the brand and serve as a reminder effect.

If information search is active, marketers are likely to change message content more frequently to provide fuller information. Print ads are more likely to be used than TV because of the importance of communicating product features. Dollars are more likely to be spent on advertising than in-store promotions because consumers are more likely to search for information prior to entering the store.

CONSUMER INFORMATION PROCESSING

Once they acquire information, consumers must process it. Marketers are interested in information processing because it determines which information consumers remember, which information they use in the process of brand evaluation, and how they use it.

An Information Processing Model

Figure 8.3 presents a model of information processing as an extension of Figure 8.1. Let us pursue the example of the business school student in the market for a laptop computer. Figure 8.3 shows that processing takes place as in-

FIGURE 8.3
A model of information

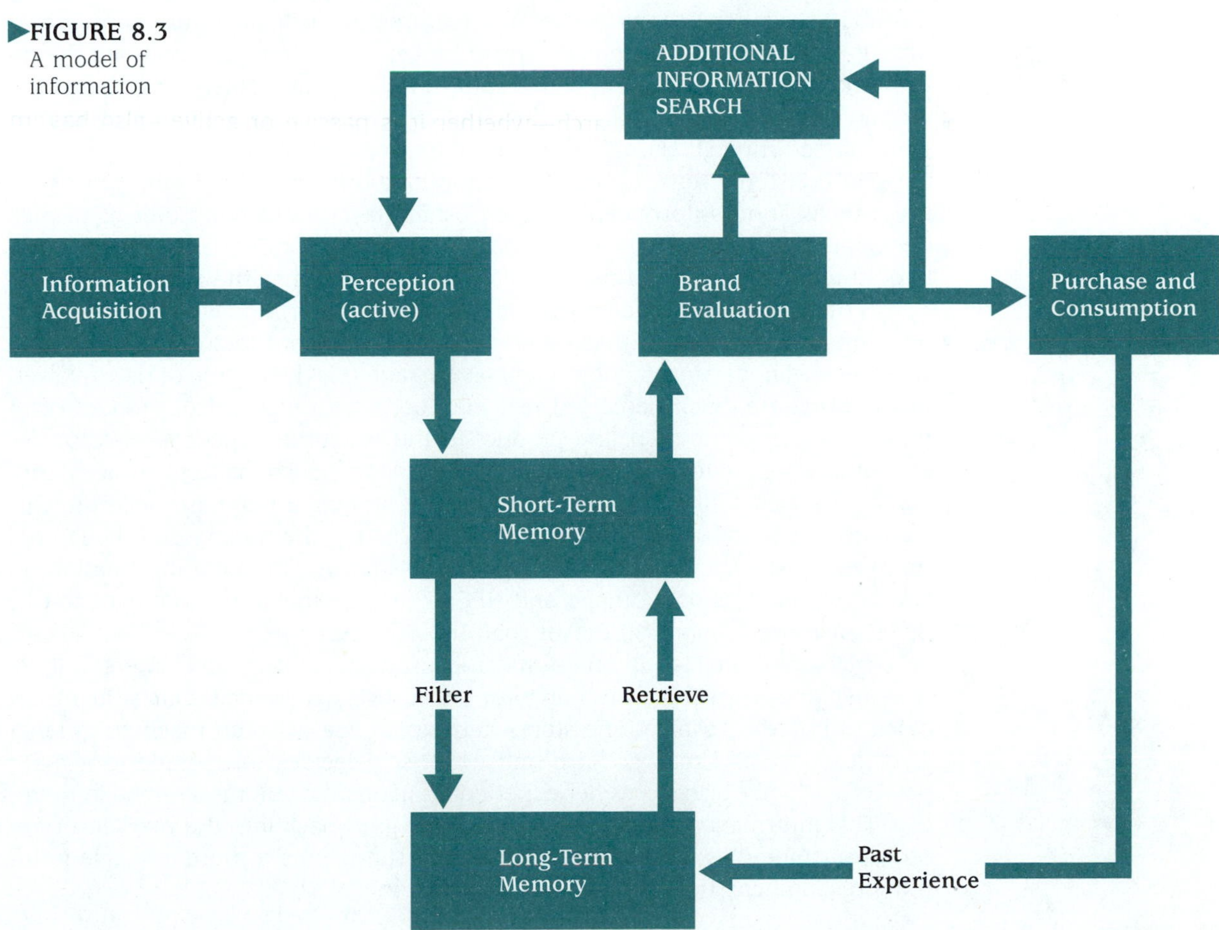

http://www.toshiba.com/

formation is acquired. In the process of information search, our consumer has noticed an ad for a Toshiba, decides to visit several stores to try one out, and realizes that the speed of the machine is faster than anticipated. This information is perceived, that is, it receives the consumer's attention and is then organized and interpreted.

The next step in processing is to determine what information will be retained in memory to be retrieved in the process of brand evaluation. Our consumer first processes information in her **short-term memory,** which acts as a filter to determine the information she will store and the information she will ignore. Such a filter is necessary because no consumer can retain everything that is seen (and no consumer would want to). The principle of selective retention states that only the most important and relevant information to the brand decision will be stored in long-term memory.

Our consumer was interested in information obtained on the Toshiba from advertising and from several salespeople. She organized information on the Toshiba and other laptops by product features to facilitate future comparison (that is, she compared brands by speed, price, and so on). She retained the information on the Toshiba's speed in **long-term memory.** However, other information such as the size of the screen and necessary attachments to the printer were passed through short-term memory and not retained.

Our consumer retrieves information in long-term memory in the process of brand evaluation. Information on the Toshiba causes our consumer to change her beliefs about the characteristics of the brand and to develop a more positive attitude toward it and thus increases the chance that she may select it.

In the process of brand evaluation, consumers determine whether they need additional information to make a decision. An important factor in determining whether additional information search is warranted is the degree of risk involved in the purchase. Such perceived risk may be due to high price, product complexity, the importance of the product to the consumers' peer groups, or the consumers' emotional attachment to the product. Such risk encourages consumers to seek additional information before making a purchase decision. Our student sees both financial and performance risks in the purchase of the laptop. As a result, she continues her information search by obtaining information on two additional brands, Compaq and NEC, to ensure that she is not overlooking better or more economical makes than the Toshiba.

Once the purchase is made and the product is used, consumers will remember and learn from the purchase and usage experience. Our student decides to buy the Toshiba. She stores her experience with the machine in long-term memory and may use it if and when she decides to upgrade to a more powerful PC. She also stores her experiences in deciding on the Toshiba in memory. This information will be useful when she goes back into the market for another machine. Based on these experiences, she will be a more effective information searcher, shopper, and brand evaluator.

Involvement and Information Processing

The way consumers process information depends largely on their level of involvement with the product decision. As we saw, when consumers are involved in a product, they actively search for information and analyze it to assess alternative brands effectively. For low-involvement products, consumers are more likely to receive and process information passively.

Our business school student processed information actively. She carefully interpreted the information and evaluated it in the context of her needs. Brand evaluation was fairly extensive. Further, since perceived risk was high, our consumer actively searched for additional information.

Low-involvement information processing differs in at least four respects, as shown in Table 8.4. First, since consumers process information passively, they can store this information in memory with little attention to it.[28] For instance, the consumer seeing an advertisement for Diet Pepsi may remember two things: the brand name and a theme such as "You got the right one, baby." However, the theme is almost like a series of nonsense syllables and has little immediate meaning, although the message that Diet Pepsi is the right choice may sink in eventually. The consumer organizes the ad and places it in the category of information relating to soft drinks. However, the message is not interpreted. Instead, the consumer filters it through short-term memory and stores some part of it, probably just the basic theme, in long-term memory. Diet Pepsi promotions in supermarkets with the same theme provide an in-store context for the consumer to link the ad to the product. The next time the consumer goes to the store, the sight of Diet Pepsi on the shelf may evoke an association with "You got the right one, baby" and may remind the consumer of a need to purchase a diet soft drink.

A second contrast with the high-involvement model is that here brand evaluation is minimal. The consumer's belief that Diet Pepsi is the right choice may lead to a decision to buy without formation of any strong brand attitudes. The sequence is consistent with the low-involvement hierarchy in Chapter 5: beliefs leading to behavior with the possible development of brand attitudes after the fact.

TABLE 8.4
High- versus low-involvement information processing

High Involvement	Low Involvement
1. Active processing	Passive processing
2. Extensive brand evaluation	Minimal brand evaluation
3. Additional information seeking is likely	Additional information seeking is unlikely
4. Rely more on product information	Rely more on past experience
5. Focus on message content for influence	Focus on peripheral cues for influence

The third difference is that since perceived risk is low, it is unlikely that consumers will seek additional information to make a brand choice. It is not worth the time and effort to do so.

A further contrast is that less involved consumers are likely to be satisfied with relying on their past experiences to make brand judgments. More involved consumers are likely to seek and use product information. Park and Hastak found that as the level of consumer involvement increases, the use of specific product information also increases.[29]

Information Processing and the Elaboration Likelihood Model (ELM)

The elaboration likelihood model (ELM), described in Chapter 5, provides a further distinction in Table 8.4 between high- and low-involvement processing. ELM says that in high-involvement cases, consumers are more motivated to process information because of the importance of the product and the risk associated with its purchase.[30] The model refers to such high-involvement processing as "taking a central route"; that is, consumers process information that directly links product features and benefits to their needs.

In low-involvement cases, consumers have little motivation to search for and process information because product interest and perceived risk are low. In such cases, consumers are likely to process information by a peripheral route. Such a route means focusing on elements in the communication that may not be central to the message—for example, the music, the voice of the announcer, the attractiveness of a spokesperson, or the background in an ad.

The strategic implication is that message cues related to product benefits should be the primary means of persuasion in high-involvement communications; nonmessage (peripheral) cues should be the primary means of persuasion in low-involvement communications.

Memory Processes

In both the high- and low-involvement cases, processing information requires that it, first, be filtered through short-term memory; second, stored in long-term memory; and, third, retrieved for purposes of brand evaluation.

Filtering Information Through Short-Term Memory

When consumers perceive information, they briefly evaluate it in short-term memory to determine whether to store it in long-term memory or to filter it out as unimportant or undesirable information. Consumers decide whether to retain information or to filter it out by relating it to information they already have stored in memory. If the information is important enough, then consumers will store it.

Short-term memory has a limited capacity to process information. In terms of time and pieces of information, short-term memory capacities can be measured in seconds (certainly less than one minute) or an average of seven pieces of information at any one time. Individuals react to this restriction by **chunking** information. For example, a Social Security number is composed of nine figures, but people usually chunk it into three groups of figures to recall it more easily. A brand image represents the beliefs consumers associate with a brand and is an information chunk. It may be composed of 20 different components but it can be retrieved as one general impression.

Once they filter the information through short-term memory, consumers will either store it in long-term memory or choose not to retain it. Most information is not retained for a variety of reasons. It might be irrelevant, not important enough, confusing information that is difficult to interpret or undesirable information that consumers choose to ignore.

Storing Information in Long-Term Memory

Information in long-term memory is stored as images that reflect our memory of past events (**episodic memory**) or as words and sentences that reflect facts and concepts we remember (**semantic memory**).[31]

http://www.mcdonalds.com/

Consumers' memories of brands are in the form of both words and images. The word *McDonald's* may evoke other words such as *fast food* and *Big Mac*. It also may evoke images learned from advertising and from past experience such as golden arches and the Ronald McDonald character. Words and images in long-term memory are linked to other words or images in an information network. Each word or image in long-term memory is called a **node.** For example, a consumer may link McDonald's (a node) to other nodes such as fast service, good for the family, good food, clean surroundings, Ronald McDonald, and Big Mac (see Exhibit 8.4). These nodes represent beliefs about McDonald's in the consumer's mind.

As we saw in the last chapter, such a cluster of beliefs is called a **schema.** In the context of memory processes, a schema occurs when a certain node (such as a brand) elicits a cluster of other nodes such as in Exhibit 8.4.[32] In marketing terms, such a schema is a consumer's brand or company image. McDonald's is a schema because when the word *McDonald's* is activated by either an ad, a food outlet, or in conversation, a group of associated nodes is elicited in the consumer's mind.

Marketing strategy has two important objectives in the context of long-term memory: first, it establishes linkages between the brand and other positive nodes, and, second, it activates these linkages once they are established. As we saw in Chapter 4, positive associations are established through consumer learning. The most important element in establishing associations in memory is consumers' experience with the product, but advertising has a key role in maintaining positive linkages over time.

Repetitive advertising for McDonald's has been successful in establishing such linkages. Its past theme, "It's a good time for the great taste of McDonald's," was the basis for communicating an image of good food and family val-

►EXHIBIT 8.4
The images (or nodes) that are associated with the McDonald's schema

ues, important nodes in McDonald's schema. The high level of awareness of the campaign and the positive associations it produced meant that consumers were likely to retain it in long-term memory.

http://www.burgerking.com/

Until recently, Burger King had a long-standing problem with establishing a positive brand image. Illustrative is a past campaign, "Where's Herb?" that was designed to encourage consumers to find a character called Herb who had never tasted a Whopper. Most consumers never comprehended the message. The focus on Herb as a balding eccentric in glasses, white socks, and gaudy plaids did little to promote retention in long-term memory. The campaign turned out to be a $40 million fiasco. As a result of its problems in establishing a strong brand image, nodes associated with Burger King were weak.

Retrieval

Once consumers filter information through short-term memory and store it in long-term memory, it is available for retrieval. When retrieving information from long-term memory, consumers briefly store it in short-term memory and use it to evaluate brands (see Figure 8.3). In evaluating a brand, consumers will activate some key pieces of information. The activation of the schema for McDonald's and its related nodes will determine how consumers evaluate McDonald's relative to Wendy's or Burger King.

Factors Encouraging Retrieval

Three factors are required for retrieval of information from long-term memory: activation, transfer, and placement. The linkages between nodes must be **activated** for retrieval to take place. For the consumer in Figure 8.4, McDonald's advertising will activate various nodes associated with the McDonald's schema. Sales promotions also play an important role in activation. McDonald's frequently runs sweepstakes that provide an incentive for consumers to visit a McDonald's outlet. Such an incentive will also activate the McDonald's schema. More indirectly, any of the nodes in the McDonald's schema—for example, the words *Big Mac*—might activate it. Keller found that when consumers were provided with cues related to a brand (such as a picture of a Big Mac or of Ronald McDonald), recall for the brand was increased.[33] The brand's schema could be activated by these related nodes without the brand name.

By constantly reminding consumers of the positive linkages related to a brand, repetitive advertising plays an essential role in encouraging activation. Such repetition strengthens the linkages between nodes over time and reinforces positive brand images (schema).

A second process necessary for retrieval is **placement,** which determines which other nodes consumers will connect the activated node to. The student buying a laptop computer may connect Toshiba to processing speed based on new information.

A third factor required for retrieval is a **transfer** process that determines the information consumers will retrieve from long-term and place in short-term memory. Generally, consumers will transfer information that is most important in making a decision—that is, information with the highest potential utility.

Factors Inhibiting Retrieval

Certain factors inhibit retrieval. The three most important are forgetting, interference, and extinction. The student buying a laptop may retrieve information such as the quoted prices for several models, the capacity of these models, and screen and keyboard facility. At one time, she remembered data on processing speed of alternative models; but after a few days, she could no longer retrieve that information. She had forgotten it. **Forgetting** is the inability to retrieve information from long-term memory. If a consumer does not retrieve information for a period of time, any subsequent attempt to do so may fail.

Interference occurs when a related information node blocks the recall of the relevant information. An advertisement by Burger King for a Whopper may cause a consumer to lose the connection in long-term memory between Big Mac and McDonald's because of the strength of the Burger King-Whopper connection. Competitive advertising often causes consumers to be unable to recall ad-

STRATEGIC APPLICATIONS OF CONSUMER BEHAVIOR

▶ Advertising Repetition Can Work For or Against You

One proven method for increasing retention of messages in consumers' long-term memory is repetition. Long-lasting symbols such as Betty Crocker and the Pillsbury doughboy are examples of the benefits of repetition.

When companies lose sight of the benefits of repetition, they can run into trouble. Heineken is an example. It slashed its advertising budget from $13.2 million in 1985 to $2.9 million in 1987 in the face of intense competition from brews such as Corona. Ads on network radio and television were cut entirely. The result? Market share went from 38 percent to 23 percent. The moral? "Out of sight, out of mind." The company has since increased advertising expenditures to remain competitive.

However, there are several risks to repetition. One risk is that consumers learn to expect an advertising theme after many repetitions and pay less attention to it. Such advertising wearout takes its toll by decreasing consumers' attention level to repetitive ads.

A second risk of repetition is that it creates such strong linkages in consumers' long-term memory (that is, the schema associated with the brand node) that any subsequent attempt to change these linkages will be difficult. An example is *Rolling Stone* magazine. Its image, originally reinforced by repeated advertising and editorial content, was that of a magazine for "hippies." This image began to inhibit marketers from placing ads in the magazine. However, the magazine's readership changed over the years to a younger and more urbane group. *Rolling Stone* launched an effective campaign, titled, "Perception/Reality," to change its image (see Exhibit 8.5). The ad pictured a stereotypical "hippie" and, in contrast, a hip-looking young man to characterize the magazine's true readership. The campaign was effective in changing consumers' image of *Rolling Stone* by effectively communicating the change in readership.

Sources: Ronald C. Goodstein, "Category-Based Applications and Extensions in Advertising: Motivating More Extensive Ad Processing," *Journal of Consumer Research* 20 (June 1993), pp. 87–99; "The Message, Clever as It May Be, Is Lost in a Number of High-Profile Campaigns," *The Wall Street Journal* (July 27, 1993), pp. B1, B4; "Heineken Learns the Pitfalls of Cutting Advertising Expenditures," *Forbes* (February 8, 1988), pp. 128–130; and "Defamiliarization," *Marketing Insights* (Fall 1990), pp. 87–90.

vertising for a related brand. At times, consumers confuse one brand with another. Some consumers may even recall an advertisement for a Whopper as a McDonald's ad because of the strength of the McDonald's schema in their long-term memory. In the first case, interference helped Burger King; in the second case, interference hurt it.

Three studies have shown how interference effects inhibit retrieval of information from long-term memory. Keller[34] and Burke and Srull[35] found that the greater the number of competitive claims, the less the recall was for the advertised brand. Keller also found that advertising the target brand at the same time as competitive brands reduces such interference by increasing consumers' recall of correct claims for the advertised brand.[36] The logical conclusion is that interference from competitive advertising is partially offset if the target brand continues to advertise. Such repetitive advertising ensures continued activation of the linkages consumers associate with the brand in long-term memory, despite competitive advertising. (See the Strategic Applications box.)

EXHIBIT 8.5
An attempt to counteract the effects of repetitive advertising: *Rolling Stone* changes its image

Whereas forgetting and interference result in consumers' inability to recall linkages in long-term memory, **extinction** is a change in these linkages. Assume that a consumer reads that McDonald's hamburgers have been criticized for being fatty and having little nutritional value. For this consumer, the linkage between McDonald's and "good for the family" is broken. The McDonald's schema also changes. As we saw in Chapter 4, the FTC may order corrective advertising to correct past erroneous linkages that misleading advertising establishes, such as Listerine's former claim that it fights colds.

Brand Evaluation

The final step in information processing in Figure 8.3 is brand evaluation. Information on brands comes from many sources. As a result, consumers need a set of guidelines or decision rules for evaluating brands. These decision rules are the information-processing strategies consumers use in evaluating brands.

Consumers use a variety of such strategies, depending on the level of involvement with the brand, amount of knowledge about the brand, and whether the information is new or already stored in memory. These strategies are classified in Figure 8.4.

Evaluative versus Nonevaluative Processing

The most basic distinction is whether or not an evaluative process takes place. **Evaluative strategies** require the organization of information about alternative brands. **Nonevaluative strategies** involve the use of a simple decision rule to avoid the necessity of evaluating brands—for example, buying the most popular brand, the cheapest brand, the same brand as your best friend, or the brand a salesperson recommends. In each case, brand evaluation is avoided.

Gardner and her colleagues found that consumers most likely use evaluative strategies when involvement is higher and nonevaluative strategies when involvement is lower. People using a nonevaluative strategy try to avoid the effort involved in active information processing. They do not actively seek brand information. When they view ads, they do not focus on message content; rather, they might view ads for enjoyment or curiosity.[37] As a result, peripheral cues such as color or music might be more effective in influencing consumers who use nonevaluative strategies, whereas message cues communicating product attributes and benefits are most effective in influencing consumers who use evaluative strategies. On this basis, evaluative strategies closely parallel the central processing route in the ELM model and nonevaluative strategies parallel the peripheral route.

Category-Based versus Attribute-Specific Processing

Evaluative strategies can be divided into category-based strategies and those that are attribute-specific.[38] A **category-based strategy** involves evaluation of a brand as a totality rather than on specific attributes. Such brand evaluation requires

▶FIGURE 8.4
Processing strategies for brand evaluation

development of a schema for the brand so that consumers can retrieve a set of associations as a whole from long-term memory. On this basis, they can quickly compare brands and establish a preference. On the other hand, **attribute-specific strategies** require comparison of each brand alternative on specific attributes such as quick service, good taste, or nice atmosphere; then consumers decide which brand to choose.

When are consumers most likely to use category-based processing? They use it when they have some knowledge about the brand and, therefore, have a brand schema that they can call up readily from memory. For example, consumers who objected to Coca-Cola's withdrawal of original Coke did not base their objections on an analysis of specific attributes but on an overall feeling about the brand.

Attribute-specific processing is required when a new product is introduced or when new information is provided about existing products. When consumers started becoming aware of the effects of tartar and plaque on teeth, they began to move from category to attribute processing in evaluating toothpaste. This processing shift is one reason why new tartar- and plaque-fighting toothpastes were successful.

Attribute-specific processing is also more likely when the consumer is (1) involved with the brand[39] and (2) knowledgeable about the product category.[40] Involved consumers are unlikely to be satisfied with an overall judgment of brands based on past information. They are likely to seek additional information about brands and to evaluate them based on specific attributes. A consumer in the market for a new car, personal computer, or stereo system is unlikely to make a decision based on an overall brand image formed from past experience and information. This consumer will seek additional information and specifically evaluate it. Similarly, knowledgeable consumers do not have to rely on an overall schema to make brand judgments. They have the ability and confidence to evaluate brands on an attribute-by-attribute basis.

If consumers use category-based processing, marketers should emphasize the brand name and positive symbols associated with it such as McDonald's arch or Pepsi-Cola's red and blue logo. In doing so, they trigger the schema associated with the brand. If processing is attribute-specific, marketers should focus more on communicating specific information on product characteristics.

Compensatory versus Noncompensatory Processing

The bottom of Figure 8.4 shows that if consumers use an attribute-specific evaluation strategy, two additional strategies are possible. Consumers can evaluate brands one at a time across a range of attributes (compensatory evaluation) or evaluate specific attributes across the range of brands being considered (noncompensatory evaluation).

The student comparing various laptop models could consider a Toshiba by evaluating its processing speed, memory capacity, screen display, keyboard, and other attributes and come up with an overall evaluation. Such a compensatory

TABLE 8.5
Noncompensatory processing strategies

	NEC	Toshiba	Compaq	AST
Processing speed	2	7	7	5
Storage capacity	6	6	4	6
Keyboard/display	7	5	3	7

Conjunctive Processing

- NEC is eliminated because of poor rating on processing speed.
- AST is eliminated because of poor rating on keyboard/display and on storage capacity.
- Select between Toshiba and Compaq.

Lexicographic Processing

- Assume most important attributes are listed in same order as in table above.
- Toshiba and AST are tied for first. Go to next most important attribute and select Toshiba on this basis.

method of evaluation is additive. The evaluation of the Toshiba is the sum of all the attributes, and a good rating on one attribute such as processing speed can compensate for a poor rating on another attribute such as screen display.

The student could also consider one attribute at a time and evaluate all brands being considered by each attribute. In this case, the student will compare the Toshiba, NEC, and Compaq models on processing speed, then on price, then on memory capacity, and so on until she has evaluated each brand on all important attributes. This strategy is noncompensatory because a consumer can eliminate a brand as a result of a deficiency on one attribute. For example, if the student finds the NEC to be significantly more expensive than the Compaq or Toshiba, she might rule it out even before she considers the brands on other attributes. In the compensatory approach, the student would consider the NEC on all attributes before making a decision.

Use of compensatory strategies requires marketers to communicate a broad set of product attributes to allow consumers to make comparisons between brands. If consumers use noncompensatory strategies, the marketer can focus on a few key attributes that consumers are likely to use in brand evaluation.

Figure 8.4 shows two types of noncompensatory strategies. These are further described in Table 8.5. Assume our consumer rates four laptop brands on three attributes. She uses a seven-point scale, with seven being the best rating. Using a **conjunctive strategy,** a consumer considers a brand only if it meets acceptable standards on key attributes. Assume an acceptable rating is one that scores 5 or higher. In this case, NEC is eliminated because our consumer rated it below the acceptable level on processing speed, and Compaq is eliminated because of a poor rating on keyboard/display features and storage capacity. The choice is then between the Toshiba and the AST.

Using a **lexicographic strategy,** consumers first evaluate brands on the most important attribute. If there is a tie, consumers next evaluate brands on the second most important attribute, and so on until a brand is selected. Assume the most important attributes are listed in the same order as in Table 8.5. Toshiba and Compaq are tied for first based on ratings on the most important criterion, processing speed. The consumer then goes to the second most important criterion, storage capacity, and chooses Toshiba over Compaq on this basis.

Several studies have examined the use of compensatory and noncompensatory strategies. Lussier and Olshavsky found that consumers frequently use a combination of both noncompensatory and compensatory approaches.[41] They use noncompensatory strategies to screen out certain brands and then use compensatory strategies to evaluate the final candidates. This is a good strategy for reducing the number of brands under consideration and ensuring that the amount of information to be processed is manageable. In the preceding example, using a conjunctive strategy, our consumer eliminated NEC and AST because of poor ratings on processing speed. The selection between the Toshiba and Compaq then might have been made on a compensatory basis by evaluating each brand across all attributes. The consumer selects the make that is rated best.

A study of the strategies consumers use in selecting stereo systems supported this dual strategy.[42] Consumers first eliminated systems that were not competitively priced and did not have a knowledgeable sales force to back them up. Consumers then evaluated the remaining makes by considering attributes such as quality, style, warranty, and other product features on a compensatory basis.

Information Processing for Utilitarian versus Hedonic Products

As with information acquisition, information processing will vary depending on whether the product is regarded primarily as utilitarian or hedonic. The nature of both information retrieval and brand evaluation will vary on the continuum from hedonic to utilitarian products.

Information Retrieval

The nature of the information retrieved from long-term memory will differ depending on whether the product is viewed as functional or pleasure seeking and emotive. Information for utilitarian products is likely to be based on actual experiences and past events. Consumers may recall information they have seen regarding a motorcycle helmet or remember their experiences in wearing a particular brand.

Information for hedonic products may be based on past experiences, but they may also be based on fantasy. As Hirschman and Holbrook note:

> The colors and shapes that are seen, the sounds that are heard, and the touches that are felt have never actually occurred, but are brought together in the particular configuration for the first time and experienced as mental phenomena.[43]

The prospective purchaser of a Harley-Davidson may visualize himself as the modern version of the lonely rider of frontier days; the prospective purchaser of a Starter jacket may see himself in the batting lineup for the Tigers. In both cases, the imagery has little to do with reality but may directly influence the purchase.

Brand Evaluation

The processing strategies used to evaluate brands will also differ for utilitarian versus hedonic products. Consumers evaluating utilitarian products are likely to use attribute-specific strategies. Product information will be sought to allow the consumer to evaluate a brand's performance. Consumers might evaluate alternative makes of cars on gas mileage, interior roominess, trunk space, acceleration, durability, and price.

Consumers are likely to evaluate hedonic products by category-based strategies, that is, as a totality rather than on particular product attributes. Consumers are likely to associate the product with a set of experiences or fantasies. In this respect, the Harley motorcycle may conjure up a set of images, moods, or emotions that are foreign to utilitarian products. In such cases, marketers should emphasize symbols and imagery that will encourage positive emotional associations with the product. Such symbols and imagery are meant to create an overall impression rather than to impart specific product information.

Perceived Risk

One important component of information processing not shown in Figure 8.3 is **perceived risk.** The perception that a purchase might be risky is actually an outcome of information processing that could lead consumers to acquire additional information.

When consumers see potential risk in a purchase, they may be uncertain about the outcome of the decision (What are the chances my new car will break down in the first six months?), or they may be concerned about the consequences of the decision (What will the results of a breakdown be in terms of cost, inconvenience, and some personal anxiety?). Thus, the two components of perceived risk are uncertainty about the outcome of the decision and concern about the consequences of the decision.

Factors Associated with Perceived Risk

Several factors are likely to increase the risk consumers see in purchasing. Perceived risk is likely to be greater when:

- There is little information about the product category.
- The product is new.
- The product is technologically complex.
- Consumers have little self-confidence in evaluating brands.
- There are variations in quality among brands.
- The price is high.
- The purchase is important to consumers.[44]

Perceived risk in purchasing a laptop is high because most of the listed criteria will be met. As the product category is still relatively new for many consumers, they have little experience with alternatives. Moreover, the product is technologically complex, making evaluation more difficult. As a result, consumer confidence in selecting one brand over another is low. Furthermore, substantial variations among brands and incompatible systems heighten risk. A high price will also contribute to perceived risk. Finally, such a purchase is probably important to consumers.

Perceived risk is also likely for well-established products. Self-confidence in purchasing products such as cameras, stereo equipment, and carpeting is low because most consumers lack knowledge of the criteria by which to judge variations among brands and price. To reduce risk, consumers tend to rely on sources of information with a high degree of credibility such as friends who have purchased the brand or impartial sources such as *Consumer Reports.*

Types of Risk

Consumers may face several different types of risk in purchasing decisions:

1. *Financial risk* is a function of the cost of a product relative to consumers' disposable incomes. For example, the consumer who has saved for four years to buy a high-priced car runs a greater risk than the individual who can buy the same car out of discretionary income every two years.

2. *Social risk* means that a purchase may not meet the standards of an important reference group. Visible items (clothing, cars, household furnishings) and items designed to enhance social attractiveness (cosmetics, mouthwash) are particularly subject to social risk.

3. *Psychological risk* is the loss of self-esteem when the consumer recognizes an error—for example, buying a product and seeing it at a cheaper price a week later or having difficulty in operating a product like a VCR timer.

4. *Performance risk* is associated with the possibility that the product will not work as anticipated or may fail. It is greatest when the product is technically complex or when ego-related needs are involved.

5. *Physical risk* is the risk of bodily harm as a result of product performance; for example, faulty brakes that could lead to a car crash or an adverse reaction to a pharmaceutical product.

Consumer Strategies to Reduce Risk

Consumers use various strategies to try to reduce risk, as shown in Table 8.6. These strategies are designed either to increase the certainty of the purchase outcome or to reduce the consequence of failure.

The most direct means of increasing the certainty of the purchase outcome is to acquire additional information that will allow consumers to better assess risk. Another strategy to increase certainty is to engage in more extensive information processing to better evaluate alternatives. More detailed brand evaluation can ensure that consumers will avoid products that fail.

A third strategy is brand loyalty. Buying the same brand repeatedly increases the certainty of the purchase outcome because consumers know what to expect from the product. The best way to avoid the possibility of dissatisfaction is to stay with a reasonably acceptable alternative. This strategy is apparent in industrial as well as consumer buying behavior. Risk reduction frequently results in staying loyal to the same vendor for years, even though other sources of supply may be less costly. For instance, a purchasing agent perceives the risk of change that involves associations with new vendors and greater uncertainty.

http://www.jnj.com/

Buying the most popular brand is also a safe strategy. For consumers who lack information, purchasing the most popular brand is the best means of increasing the certainty of the outcome. Johnson & Johnson relies on the recognition of its name as the leading producer of baby products. In so doing, it seeks to reduce any uncertainty new parents may have in buying baby products (see Exhibit 8.6). Consumers purchasing appliances, television sets, or stereos also may lack confidence in comparing brands. Claims that a certain brand is the largest seller or a leading brand are attempts to influence prospective buyers by assuring them that millions of fellow consumers cannot be wrong.

Less involved consumers are also likely to use strategies that involve buying the same or the most popular brand because these strategies minimize the time and effort involved in information processing.

Other strategies attempt to reduce the consequences of failure. Consumers' most common means of reducing the consequence of product failure is to buy the lowest-priced item or the smallest size. Obtaining a warranty or guarantee

TABLE 8.6
Consumer strategies to reduce risk

Increasing the Certainty of the Purchase Outcome	Reducing the Consequence of Product Failure
• Acquire additional information	• Buy lowest-priced item
• Undertake more extensive information processing	• Buy the smallest size
• Remain brand-loyal	• Obtain warranty or guarantee
• Buy most popular brand	• Reduce level of expectations

EXHIBIT 8.6
Johnson & Johnson reduces the uncertainty of buying baby products

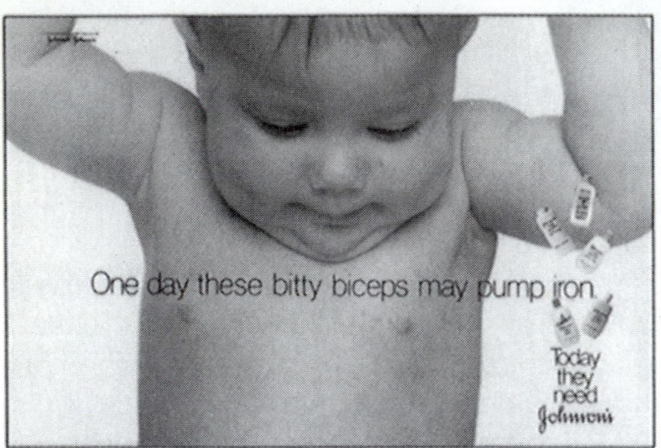

on the product also reduces the consequence of failure. These strategies reduce the financial risk but not the psychological risk. A strategy to reduce the psychological risk of making the wrong decision is to reduce the level of expectation before making the purchase. Consider a purchaser who decides that cars are a necessary evil that inevitably produce mechanical failures and repair bills. This purchaser is not going to be terribly disappointed if his or her car does not perform well; he or she expects it.

In his study, Roselius found that the most common strategy consumers use to reduce risk is brand loyalty.[45] On this basis, it appears that increasing the certainty of the outcome is more important to consumers than reducing the consequences of failure. Such brand loyalty might mean buying a higher-priced item just because it is a known commodity. If this is the case, consumers are merely trading off one risk for another—that is, increasing financial risk to reduce psychological risk.

The various strategies consumers use to reduce risk suggest two types of consumers. Risk avoiders are more likely to buy the lowest-priced brand, the same brand, or the most popular brand. This type of consumer is willing to forego taking a chance on a riskier alternative that might or might not provide better performance in favor of the "safe bet." A second type of consumer is more of a risk taker. He or she will search for more information and will process information in more detail to find the best product. The risk taker is more likely to buy new products before they are well established. Studies have found that risk takers are likely to be higher-income consumers, to have upward social mobility, and to exhibit personality traits such as need for achievement, dominance, and change.[46]

STRATEGIC IMPLICATIONS OF INFORMATION PROCESSING

This chapter has described two key components of information processing: storing information in memory and evaluating brands. An important outcome of information processing, perceived risk, was also described. Important marketing implications emerge in each of these three areas.

Memory Processes

A primary objective of advertising strategy is to ensure that consumers will retain the message in memory. The most obvious means of increasing retention is through repetition of the advertising message. A study by Ray and Sawyer found that advertising recall almost tripled as the number of repetitions went from one to six.[47] The study also shows the diminishing returns of additional repetitions. As advertising is repeated, the incremental gains in consumer retention become smaller.

There is another problem with frequent advertising repetition: a wearout effect. Consumers may become so familiar with an ad campaign that they no longer notice it. The campaign can be revitalized only by introducing new and fresher ideas to communicate product benefits. Constant repetition, in fact, may start irritating consumers. Another important implication of memory processes is for marketers to develop sets of associations with a brand that will lead to a positive and consistent brand image. In establishing a positive image, advertising must link the brand to nodes with positive associations in consumers' memory.[48]

Once consumers establish a strong brand image, marketers should reinforce it by all elements of marketing strategy. This is best achieved by a marketing campaign that coordinates advertising, packaging, and in-store stimuli. McDonald's marketing strategy promotes a strong image because various elements of its campaign such as Ronald McDonald, playgrounds, sales promotions, and in-store decor promote the image of good service and family values. Elements at variance with an established image cause confusion and a weakening of associations in consumers' memory, as when Cadillac introduced a medium-sized car.

Brand Evaluation

The manner by which consumers evaluate brands also has strategic implications. Evaluative processing, which suggests a more involved consumer, requires the marketer to develop a message closely related to consumer needs. Nonevaluative processing suggests a less involved consumer. Here, advertisers can use simpler themes and peripheral cues and rely primarily on TV to communicate them.

There are also strategic implications for the types of evaluative processing consumers use. If consumers evaluate brands on an attribute-specific basis, advertising should be informational and present product characteristics that consumers can evaluate easily. As we saw, category-based evaluation lends itself more to image-oriented advertising since consumers evaluate the brand as a whole. Symbols and images such as the Marlboro cowboy or the Apple Computer logo can be used as a shorthand for the brand. These symbols evoke the brand image without having to specify particular attributes of the brand.

Perceived Risk

Marketers often seek competitive advantage by reducing consumers' risk of purchasing their brand. In all cases, marketers attempt to reduce risks by (1) lowering the consequences of a loss or (2) increasing the certainty of the outcome.

Marketers can reduce the consequences of failure by offering warranties, money-back guarantees, and liberal return policies for defective merchandise. Offering products at lower prices or in smaller packages also minimizes consumers' risk in trying a product for the first time. Shimp and Bearden found that these strategies tended to reduce the perception of financial risk but not the perception of performance risk.[49] Apparently, consumers must have experience in using the product to reduce perceived performance risk.

Marketers can attempt to increase the certainty of the purchase outcome in several ways. Endorsements by experts might assure consumers of the certainty of product performance when consumers are not sure of the purchase. Free samples give consumers the opportunity to try new products before a purchase commitment. One reasonable strategy to increase certainty is to convey sufficient information to provide consumers with a sound basis for choice. Technical specifications on performance, complete labeling of ingredients, and nutritional information are all means of providing consumers with more information to judge product performance better.

SOCIETAL IMPLICATIONS OF INFORMATION PROCESSING

As we saw in Chapter 2, consumers have the right to adequate information to give them the capability to make reasonable decisions. Three societal issues emerge in this regard. First, should consumers be given more information? This is what consumer activists propose. Or, in some cases, should consumers be given less? Some researchers who have found that consumers are subject to information overload have proposed this. Second, do consumers sometimes use poor strategies to process complex brand information and, if so, can anything be done to encourage them to use more optimal strategies? Third, evidence of less efficient information processing among younger and older consumers raises the question of whether government and/or business organizations have a role in increasing the information-processing capabilities of these two groups.

More or Less Information?

Several studies have found that, for some product categories, more information increases consumer confusion and leads to less efficient choices. This may suggest that product information should be limited and kept simple.

Consumer activists would argue that product information such as ingredients, nutritional content, performance, and price should be made available to consumers on a uniform basis, and consumers should then decide how much information to use. These activists believe it is better to run the risk of too much information and consumer confusion than too little information and a poor choice.

http://www.fda.gov/

As we saw in Chapter 2, government is taking an increasingly activist view in supporting additional information. The Food and Drug Administration has established rules requiring more information on ingredients and nutritional value and clearer warning labels on packaging. More states are requiring unit pricing information in stores and open dating of perishable items. Business organizations are also showing more willingness to supply detailed product information in ads, brochures, and direct-mail advertising. Some retailers, such as Jewel and Shop-Rite stores, have introduced in-store consultants to inform shoppers of price and brand alternatives.

There are several compelling reasons to support this trend toward more information. First, some consumers will use such information. Unfortunately, older and less-educated consumers are least likely to use product information. Government and business can do more to increase information acquisition by these groups—for example, by providing comparative price information for key product categories such as pharmaceuticals and improving transportation to shopping areas.

Second, when consumers use information, they often make more efficient purchases. Several studies have found that consumers who use unit pricing information shift their purchases toward lower-priced goods.[50] Third, providing more information increases consumer confidence. One study found that although only 10 percent of consumers used credit information in buying a durable good, 54 percent said they felt better about knowing the rates and charges.[51]

Compensatory or Noncompensatory Processing?

A second issue is whether consumers use adequate processing strategies, regardless of the amount of information available. Hutchinson and Alba found that in selecting stereo speakers, most consumers used only two or three criteria, despite the availability of a full complement of product information.[52] Similarly, we noted a study by Capon and Burke that found consumers using only 24 percent of available information in buying appliances.[53] Unless consumers are knowledgeable about the product category, such noncompensatory strategies may lead to suboptimal decisions, particularly for expensive and high-risk items such as stereo speakers and appliances.

A strong case could be made for encouraging consumers to use a wider set of criteria in making decisions for expensive, high-risk products, particularly if they lack knowledge and confidence in their choices. Companies can do more to educate consumers about criteria for comparing brands by product features. For example, a computer company could provide prospective buyers with an informational brochure explaining how to use criteria such as memory, capacity, and speed in selecting a computer.

Age-Related Information Processing

Sufficient evidence of reduced processing capacities among the very young and very old raises some serious societal issues. The information capabilities of preschoolers are limited and improve by the early elementary school years.[54] Chapter 2 noted that young children generally fail to understand the purpose of commercials and often cannot distinguish between TV programming and commercials. The focus was on ensuring responsible actions by business to avoid taking advantage of children based on their reduced processing abilities.

A related issue is whether responsible advertising strategies can be geared to improving children's acquisition of information. For example, Peracchio studied the ability of kindergarten children to learn how to return defective merchandise. She found that their acquisition of information regarding the procedures for such returns was as efficient as older children's when the younger children (1) were repetitively exposed to a single story line, and (2) the information was very explicit.[55] The study suggests that advertisers could use repetitive and explicit information to improve children's acquisition of information as long as there is some assurance that such information is accurate and responsible.

There is also evidence that older consumers process information less efficiently. Studies have found that older consumers cannot retain as many alternatives in memory as can younger consumers and tend to use fewer attributes in evaluating brand alternatives.[56] A study by Cole and Balasubramanian found that when elderly consumers were instructed to select a cereal according to specific nutritional criteria, they were less likely than younger subjects to search for information and to select a cereal based on their needs.[57]

The latter study also found that when elderly consumers were asked to write down information, their processing abilities improved. Further, visual symbols that integrated information such as a Good Housekeeping seal of approval improved the elderly's information processing abilities. The implications are that stores can provide checklists of information that should be considered in buying nutritional or drug items to facilitate information processing by the elderly. Further, companies can develop symbols to connote chunks of information. For example, they could develop a symbol for cholesterol-free food products or use a common symbol to indicate a generic drug item.

SUMMARY

An important part of any consumer's decision process is the acquisition and processing of information. Consumers will acquire more information about products if they are involved in the purchase, see risk in purchasing, have little product knowledge, and see differences among products. Information acquisition is limited by the amount of information consumers can reasonably process. Studies have shown that consumers sometimes are subjected to information overload—that is, too much information—which results in confusion.

Once consumers acquire information, they must process it. To process information, consumers must be able to retain it in and retrieve it from memory. The memory process has short-term and long-term components. Short-term memory acts as a filter to determine what information will be retained in long-term memory. Information stored in long-term memory is organized into schemas, which represent the sets of associations consumers have with brands, products, or companies. Such schemas are the basis for brand or company images.

Consumers retrieve information from long-term memory to evaluate brands. Brand evaluation requires a set of decision rules for comparing brands. Using category-based processing, consumers evaluate brands as a whole and make judgments based on associations in long-term memory. Attribute-specific processing requires consumers to compare brands on specific attributes. A possible outcome of the brand evaluation process is the perception that the purchase will involve financial, social, or performance risks. Consumers seek to reduce risks by buying the same brand, a low-priced brand, or the most popular brand. They can also reduce risk by seeking more information to increase the certainty of a purchase outcome.

A distinction was drawn between information acquisition and processing for hedonic versus utilitarian products. Consumers buying hedonic products are more likely to seek symbols and imagery rather than specific product information. They are also more likely to retrieve fantasy-like imagery from memory rather than actual experiences and will process information as a whole rather than on an attribute-by-attribute basis.

Strategic applications were developed from the two key components of information processing: storing information in memory and evaluating brands. Strategic applications from perceived risk were also described.

The chapter concluded by considering the societal implications of information processing. Three issues were considered. First, should more information be provided to consumers and, if so, what should be the role of government and business in providing such information? Second, can consumers be encouraged to use processing strategies that evaluate brands on a wider set of criteria? Third, given the reduced processing abilities of the very young and very old, can business or government play a role in improving their abilities?

In the next two chapters, we consider the results of information processing; namely, the formation of consumer attitudes toward brands and products.

QUESTIONS

1. Which of the following situations would you describe as either (a) ongoing search, (b) purchase-specific search, or (c) passive information acquisition? Why?
   - A consumer listening to a radio ad for life insurance
   - A consumer shopping for a suit to wear to a job interview
   - A consumer reading several magazines dealing with antique furniture
2. What types of sources of information are most likely to be important for each of the following consumers and why?
   - A business school student close to a final decision in purchasing a laptop computer
   - An industrial buyer purchasing electrical cable

- A consumer first considering various alternatives in selecting life insurance

3. What are the limits of consumers' ability to acquire and process information?
4. How can marketers attempt to overcome the limits you cited in Question 3?
5. Consider the following purchasing situations:
   - A consumer regards cereals as a source of bran and other nutritional ingredients and is aware of brand alternatives and their ingredients. This consumer regards the brand decision for cereals as important as it is related to health and fitness.
   - Another consumer sees little difference among brands of cereal and buys primarily for taste. This consumer has a low level of information regarding brand alternatives and ingredients and does not associate the purchase of cereals with health and fitness.

   A new brand of cereal containing raisins and nuts and advertised as a product with all-natural ingredients is introduced. What differences might occur between the two consumers in acquiring and processing information on the new cereal?
6. How does short-term memory operate for:
   - The prospective car buyer who first becomes aware of GM's Saturn line?
   - The consumer who sees an ad for Pampers disposable diapers while watching an early evening quiz show?
7. What are the differences in information acquisition and processing for products consumers regard as hedonic versus utilitarian? What are the strategic implications of these differences?
8. What strategies have you used in buying a car and in selecting a college or business school to:
   - Reduce the consequences of failure?
   - Increase the certainty of the outcome?
9. What are the differences between risk takers and risk avoiders in the ways they deal with perceived risk in the purchasing process?
10. What are the pros and cons of providing consumers with more information? Under what circumstances should business and government be encouraged to provide consumers with more information?
11. What are the societal issues regarding age-related differences in acquiring and processing information? What are the public policy implications of these differences?

RESEARCH ASSIGNMENTS

1. Log onto AT&T's Web site at http://www.att.com. Compare it to Sprint's site at http://www.sprint.com.
   - What is the target market for each site?
   - What specific recommendations would you make to improve the way the sites are building each brand name?
   - How do the sites affect brand beliefs, brand attitudes, and brand behavior for each of the companies?
2. Develop an information board for automobiles and another information board for cereals. The boards should list at least four brands or models across the top and eight attributes down the side. Show the boards to about 10 consumers for each product category. Ask consumers to describe aloud their process of evaluating the brands on each board. On this basis, try to determine if processing is by category or by attribute and, if by attribute, whether it is compensatory or noncompensatory processing.

   At the end of the process of evaluation, ask consumers to complete a short questionnaire to determine (a) demographics, (b) selected lifestyle items, (c) brand or model used, and (d) frequency of usage or number of miles driven in a year.
   - What are the differences in evaluation between the cereals and the autos? Specifically, are consumers more likely to evaluate autos and cereals by category-based or by attribute-based processing? If the latter, are consumers more likely to evaluate each product category by compensatory or noncompensatory processing?
   - Are there differences in evaluation between types of consumers? That is, are certain consumers more likely to evaluate by category and others by attribute? If so, are there differences in the characteristics of category versus attribute evaluators?
3. Some studies have compared perceived risk across product categories. For example, Jacoby and Kaplan studied the risk college students perceive in the purchase of 12 product categories such as cars, life insurance, color TV sets, clothing items, and pharmaceutical products.[58] Using the references in this chapter, develop a measure of perceived risk that incorporates (a) the uncertainty of product performance and (b) the consequences when a product

does not meet consumer expectations. In addition, measure the respondents' self-confidence in selecting a brand in the product category. Select a sample of college students and apply the measure of perceived risk and self-confidence to four or five product categories.

- What are the variations in perceived risk among product categories?
- What are the variations in perceived risk among students? That is, do certain individuals (risk takers) see less risk than others? If so, are there any differences in characteristics (for example, frequency of use of the product categories, brands purchased, needs emphasized) between those who tend to see more risk and those who tend to see less risk?

ATTITUDES

Chapter 9

CHANGING ATTITUDES: CAN AT&T REDEFINE ITSELF AMONG YOUNGER CONSUMERS?

The last two chapters dealt with how consumers perceive and process information. In this chapter, we explain how consumers develop beliefs about and preferences for brands based on the information they have processed. These beliefs and preferences define consumers' attitudes toward a brand. In turn, their attitudes toward a brand often directly influence whether they will buy it.

We will consider brand attitudes from the perspectives of the consumer and the marketing manager. In so doing, we will consider:

- The nature, function, and development of brand attitudes.
- Research that establishes a relation between brand attitudes and purchasing behavior.
- Attitude models that provide a basis by which marketers can evaluate a brand's strength or weakness relative to consumer needs.
- Strategic implications of attitudes to develop guidelines for advertising and product positioning.

The strategic importance of attitudes is illustrated by marketers' attempts to reposition their brands. Such repositioning requires a change in attitudes on the consumers' part. In past chapters, we saw how difficult it can be to reposition a brand when consumer attitudes are fairly entrenched. Oldsmobile's attempt to reposition itself as a car for the younger generation with the theme "This is not your father's Olds" only succeeded in alienating its older customer base. There have also been classic success stories in repositioning brands—for example, repositioning Miller High Life from an elite beer to a product with a mass-market appeal targeted to heavier beer drinkers with the theme "It's Miller time."

http://www.oldsmobile.com/

More recently, AT&T is repositioning itself among its younger consumers. Whereas older consumers still view AT&T as the phone company, attitudes of younger consumers (those under 40) are not nearly as positive. Many have flocked to alternative providers such as Sprint and MCI because they view AT&T as less innovative with fewer service options. AT&T's objective is similar to that of Oldsmobile's: to improve attitudes among the younger set without alienating its older customer base. The stakes in repositioning itself are particularly high, because AT&T's share of the long-distance market has slipped from more than 90 percent in 1984 to about 60 percent in 1996, a sales decrease of $10 billion per year![1]

http://www.att.com/

The key thrust in changing attitudes among the under-40 group is an advertising campaign that defines AT&T as an innovative computer and communications company. Whereas past advertising took a very soft image approach in positioning AT&T (consumers shown using the phone in meaningful, personal moments), the newer ads are more modern, emphasizing new technologies that appeal to younger consumers. Through new home entertainment technologies, Internet access, and mobile communications, AT&T will better focus on the needs of younger consumers. Whether AT&T will be successful in improving attitudes among the younger set while maintaining its loyal customer base remains to be seen.

Consumers develop attitudes toward social issues as well as brands. Marketers have a role in influencing consumer attitudes toward issues such as smoking, drinking, drugs, and AIDS protection. For example, a group of advertising agencies and media companies formed the Partnership for a Drug-Free America on a pro bono basis (that is, for free) to combat drug use. The purpose was to create an *attitude* of intolerance toward drugs. (We describe marketing's role in changing social attitudes at the end of the next chapter.)

http://www.drugfreeamerica.org/

NATURE OF CONSUMER ATTITUDES

Over 50 years ago, Gordon Allport formulated the most frequently used definition of attitudes. He wrote: "Attitudes are learned predispositions to respond to an object or class of objects in a consistently favorable or unfavorable way."[2] **Attitudes** toward brands are consumers' learned tendencies to evaluate brands in a consistently favorable or unfavorable way, that is, consumers' evaluation of a particular brand on an overall basis from poor to excellent.

FIGURE 9.1 Three components of attitudes

Brand attitudes are based on the schema of a brand consumers store in long-term memory. A schema of AT&T as being stodgy and old-fashioned has led many younger consumers to choose other long-distance providers. Older consumers are more likely to have a schema of the company associated with reliability, security, and good service. Since these attributes constitute the beliefs many older consumers have of AT&T, they are likely to lead to a positive evaluation of the company and to selection of AT&T as the long-distance provider. As a result, brand beliefs (AT&T provides good service) lead to brand evaluations (I like AT&T) and thus to intended behavior (I plan to use AT&T for long-distance service).

Three Components of Attitudes

The link among brand beliefs, evaluations, and intended behavior will be a main focus of this chapter.[3] Brand beliefs, brand evaluations, and intention to buy define the three components of attitudes shown in Figure 9.1. Brand beliefs are the **cognitive** (or **thinking**) component of attitudes; brand evaluations, the **affective** (or **feeling**) component; and intention to buy, the **conative** (or **behavioral**) component. As these three attitudinal components play such a central role in marketing strategy, it would be helpful to have a fuller understanding of each of them.

Beliefs: The Cognitive Component

Consumers' beliefs about a brand are the characteristics they ascribe to it. Through marketing research, marketers develop a **vocabulary of product attributes and benefits** similar to the vocabulary a large food company develops for a beverage (see Table 9.1). These types of vocabularies are based on the results of a series of **depth** or **focus group interviews** with consumers. Once marketers establish a vocabulary of product attributes and benefits, they include it in a questionnaire and conduct a consumer survey in which they ask respondents to rate brands utilizing the vocabulary. Thus, a study of soft drinks may involve asking consumers to rate various brands on the criteria listed in Table 9.1.

The vocabulary of beliefs for a soft drink in Table 9.1 show both attributes and benefits. Consumers may be asked to rate soft drinks on attributes such as sweetness and carbonation, and on benefits such as nutritional and thirst-quenching. Such ratings provide the marketer with the means to identify the strengths and weaknesses of the company's brand relative to that of the competition. For example, beliefs may show that teenagers regard Pepsi as a sweeter and more carbonated beverage than Coke. If beliefs show weakness, then the marketer might consider a repositioning strategy, similar to what AT&T is doing in attempting to strengthen attitudes among younger consumers.

http://www.pepsi.com/
http://www.cocacola.com/

The vocabulary of attributes and benefits in Table 9.1 provides the marketer with only part of the equation in understanding beliefs. A consumer may rate a soft drink very sweet, but this rating does not mean the consumer wants a sweet drink. Marketers must determine the value consumers place on attributes such as sweet and refreshing and benefits such as nutritional and thirst-quenching. Two consumers can rate a soft drink "very sweet," but one puts a high value on sweetness, whereas the other does not. As a result, the first consumer will have a more positive attitude toward the brand compared to that of the second consumer, despite similar beliefs.

TABLE 9.1
Vocabulary of brand beliefs for a soft drink product

Product Attributes	Product Benefits
Caloric content	Restores energy
Vitamin content	Nutritional
Natural ingredients	Good for the whole family
Sweetness	Gives a lift
Aftertaste	Good at mealtimes
Carbonation	Thirst-quenching

This evaluative component is important in segmenting consumers because it shows what they want. In this case, it would be logical to define a "sweet" segment in the soft drink market.

Overall Brand Evaluation: The Affective Component

The second attitude component, the affective or feeling component, represents consumers' overall evaluation of the brand. Beliefs about a brand are multidimensional because they represent the brand attributes consumers perceive. The affective component, however, is one-dimensional. Consumers' overall evaluation of a brand can be measured by rating the brand from "poor" to "excellent" or from "prefer least" to "prefer most." If we accept the basic attitudinal model in Figure 9.1, brand evaluations result from brand beliefs. Teens have a positive attitude toward Pepsi because they believe that it is a sweeter drink and they place a high value on sweetness.

Of the three components, brand evaluation is central to the study of attitudes because it summarizes consumers' predisposition to be favorable or unfavorable to the brand. Brand beliefs are relevant only to the extent that they influence brand evaluations, which are the primary determinants of intended behavior. In fact, brand evaluation conforms to the definition of brand attitudes as a "tendency to evaluate brands in a favorable or unfavorable way."

Therefore, rather than speaking of three components of attitudes in the remainder of this chapter, *we will refer to brand attitudes as the overall evaluation of a brand.* Brand beliefs influence attitudes, and attitudes influence intention to buy.

Intention to Buy: The Behavioral Component

The third attitude component, the conative dimension, is consumers' tendency to act toward an object, and this is generally measured in terms of intention to buy. Measuring buying intent is particularly important in developing marketing strategy.

Marketing managers frequently test the elements of the marketing mix—alternative product concepts, ads, packages, or brand names—to determine what is most likely to influence purchase behavior. Tests of these alternatives are conducted under artificially controlled circumstances that try to hold all factors constant except the marketing stimuli being tested. Consumers viewing alternative ads or trying various product formulations are asked about their intentions to buy after experiencing these marketing stimuli. Marketers regard the alternative producing the highest buying intent as the best choice. In the absence of actual buying behavior, management uses the closest substitute, intention to buy, to determine the effectiveness of the components of the marketing mix.

Marketers can try to appeal to this third component of attitudes without necessarily influencing the other two—beliefs and brand evaluation. A sharp reduction in price or a special coupon offer may be inducement enough for consumers to try a less-favored brand. Beliefs and attitudes about the chosen brand do not have to change for consumers to establish an intention to buy if the economic inducement is large enough.

Attitudes and the Hierarchy of Effects

The relationship between the three components of attitudes is known as the **hierarchy of effects.**

The High- versus Low-Involvement Hierarchy

In Chapter 5, we referred to the hierarchy of effects as a sequence in the consumer's choice process and distinguished between a high- and low-involvement hierarchy. The high-involvement hierarchy assumed a "think before you act" process, whereas the low-involvement hierarchy described more of an "act before you think" process. Table 9.2 describes these hierarchies based on the three components of attitudes.

When consumers are involved, they will first develop beliefs about the brand through a process of active information search. On this basis, they evaluate the brand, develop definite brand attitudes, and make a purchase decision accordingly. In the low-involvement hierarchy, consumers form beliefs passively. They make a purchase decision with limited information because it is not worth the time and trouble to engage in active information search and processing. Brand evaluations and attitudes are formed after the fact and are likely to be weak. This means that consumers often buy low-involvement products without forming a definite attitude about the brand. As a result, attitudes do not predict behavior as well in low-involvement purchases as in the high-involvement case because well-defined attitudes do not generally precede behavior.

Because attitudes do not have as central a role in low-involvement decisions, much of this chapter assumes an involved consumer. Several studies have found support for a diminished role of attitudes for less involved consumers. Beatty and Kahle identified consumers who were more and less involved with soft drinks. Attitudes influenced behavior for the more involved individuals, but they did not play any significant role in influencing behavior for less involved consumers.[4] In another study, MacKenzie and Spreng motivated consumers to process advertising information and thereby increased these consumers' involvement in the task. They found that attitudes were more closely related to purchase intentions for the motivated group as compared to those of the unmotivated group.[5]

Although the attitudes consumers form after a low-involvement purchase may be weakly held, they may still influence future purchases. A consumer who tries a new paper towel and decides it is not as good as his or her regular brand is unlikely to buy it again. This overall evaluation is important information for the marketer, even if this consumer is not very involved with the brand.

The Experiential Hierarchy

Our focus on hedonic as opposed to utilitarian products in past chapters leads to a third hierarchy of effects, what has been referred to as an *experiential hi-*

erarchy.[6] The experiential hierarchy is based primarily on a consumer's emotional response to the brand.

As Table 9.2 suggests, consumers first evaluate a brand on an overall basis by relying on their feelings, emotions, and fantasies and act on this basis. Beliefs about the attributes and characteristics of a brand may be formed after the fact. The consumer's primary purchase motive is the anticipated *experience* of enjoying the brand, not the projected performance of the brand based on evaluative product criteria. A teen may buy Shaq Attack basketball sneakers because of the feeling of being like Shaquille O'Neal on the basketball court, not because of any specific performance or comfort criteria. He may determine the degree of comfort only after buying them.

In the experiential hierarchy, consumers are likely to be more aware of stimuli such as symbols and imagery that will shape their feelings about a brand. Given their emotional involvement, search for such stimuli is likely to be ongoing. In contrast, consumers buying utilitarian products are more likely to be aware of brand attributes and search is more likely to be purchase-specific.

The experiential hierarchy has important implications for marketing strategy when compared to the traditional high-involvement hierarchy. In a "think before you act" hierarchy, marketers will advertise product features and benefits to influence beliefs. Most marketing strategies adhere to this hierarchy by advertising product features and benefits to influence beliefs. This is the case with AT&T's attempt to convey the belief that it is a progressive and innovative computer and communications company. As we noted, younger consumers adopting these beliefs are more likely to have positive attitudes about the company and to use AT&T.

The experiential hierarchy shows that when a product is perceived as pleasurable or expressive, cognitive processes do not have to be central. As a result, marketers can directly appeal to brand evaluations without necessarily influencing beliefs. They do so by using symbols and imagery to evoke positive feel-

TABLE 9.2
Three hierarchies of effect

Type of Hierarchy	Sequence	Nature of Information Processing
HIGH-INVOLVEMENT	Beliefs Evaluation Behavior	Active, purchase-specific processing
LOW-INVOLVEMENT	Beliefs Behavior Evaluation	Passive, purchase-specific processing
EXPERIENTIAL	Evaluation Behavior Beliefs	Active, ongoing processing

►**EXHIBIT 9.1**
Influencing beliefs and brand evaluations

Influencing beliefs

Influencing brand evaluations

ings and emotions about the brand. In contrast, influencing beliefs tends to be more information based because such strategies focus on product features.

http://www.toyota.com/

Toyota uses both approaches, as shown in Exhibit 9.1. The German ad for Corolla's Starlet is primarily informational and tries to influence beliefs about the brand. There is little attempt to establish an overall mood or image. The American ad for the Celica is strictly image-oriented. It makes no reference to product features. Rather, it tries to influence a consumer's evaluation of the brand by establishing a mood of luxury. In this case, belief formation is not a prerequisite for developing positive feelings and preferences for the brand.

Measuring the Attitudinal Components

The components of attitudes must be measured reliably if they are to form the basis for marketing strategies. Since these are qualitative variables, this is a difficult task. The most common approach is to develop rating scales so consumers can identify the degree to which they think a brand has certain attributes (beliefs), the degree to which they prefer certain brands (brand evaluations), and their intentions.

Using colas as an example, Table 9.3 shows one or more rating scales to measure these attitudinal components.

Brand Beliefs (*b*)

Measuring beliefs first requires determining the attributes and benefits that might make up consumers' schema for soft drinks (such as those in Table 9.1). Typically, 10 to 15 attributes, such as carbonation and sweetness, will be identified in depth interviews.

Three measures of beliefs (b) are shown. Measure b_1 rates brand attributes on a probability basis using a seven-point scale. Measure b_2 is a scaling device known as the **semantic differential.** It uses bipolar adjectives on a seven-point scale to measure brand beliefs. The third scale measures beliefs about the accuracy of a brand's description—for example, whether it is accurate to describe a brand as highly carbonated.

Each of these rating scales approaches the measurement of beliefs differently, suggesting there is no standard measure. The semantic differential scale (b_2) is the most widely used because it is easy to construct and administer. Marketers can quickly determine the image of their brand by how consumers position it on various bipolar adjectives.

Attribute Evaluations (*e*)

Although attribute evaluations are not cited as one of the three components of attitudes in Figure 9.1, they must be measured to understand brand beliefs. As we noted, rating a brand on degree of carbonation must be coupled with measuring the consumer's desire for carbonation. Three scales are shown to rate attribute evaluations. The first (e_1) asks consumers to rate each attribute from "very important" to "not at all important"; the second (e_2) from "very satisfying" to "not at all satisfying." The third scale (e_3) asks consumers to visualize an ideal cola. A semantic differential scale is used to rate this ideal brand.

Overall Brand Evaluations (*A*)

The affective component of attitudes—overall brand evaluations—can be measured in various ways. The first scale measures the likability of the brand (measure A_1). The second ranks the preferences for various brands from most to least preferred (measure A_2). This scale, known as a **rank order of preference scale,** is *nonmetric.* That is, the values have *ordinal* meaning in the sense of "better than" or "more than." The other scales cited have *metric* meaning in the sense that a rating of "2" is equidistant from "1" and "3." As a result, they are known as **equal interval scales.**

The fourth measure of brand evaluations (A_4) asks consumers to assume they will be given 10 free cans of cola and can select any combination of brands they want. The degree to which consumers select a brand is a measure of pref-

TABLE 9.3
Measures of attitudinal components*

Brand Beliefs (b)

b_1: How likely is it that I will get a highly carbonated cola if I buy Brand A?
Very likely ___ ___ ___ ___ ___ ___ ___ ___ Very unlikely

b_2: Rate Brand A by the following characteristics:
Highly carbonated ___ ___ ___ ___ ___ ___ ___ ___ Not at all carbonated

b_3: Indicate how well Brand A is described by the following characteristics:
Highly carbonated
Describes very well ___ ___ ___ ___ ___ ___ ___ ___ Does not describe at all

Attribute Evaluations (e)

e_1: How important is buying a cola that is highly carbonated?
Very important ___ ___ ___ ___ ___ ___ ___ ___ Not at all important

e_2: Indicate the degree of satisfaction you would get from the following:
Highly carbonated
Very satisfying ___ ___ ___ ___ ___ ___ ___ ___ Not at all satisfying

e_3: Think of your ideal brand of cola and rate it on the characteristics listed below:
Highly carbonated ___ ___ ___ ___ ___ ___ ___ ___ Not at all carbonated

Overall Brand Evaluations (A)

A_1: Rate Brand A as follows:
I like it very much ___ ___ ___ ___ ___ ___ ___ ___ I don't like it at all

A_2: Which of the following brands do you prefer most? Which of the brands do you prefer second, third, (and so forth)?
[Key brands of cola would be listed.]

A_3: Rate Brand A as follows:
Very favorable ___ ___ ___ ___ ___ ___ ___ ___ Very unfavorable

A_4: Suppose you could pick ten free cans of cola and had the choice of any combination of brands. Which brands would you pick? How many of each brand? (Make sure the total adds up to ten cans.) (Key brands would be listed and respondents instructed to place any number of cans next to each brand so the total allocated equals ten.)

Intention to Buy (BI)

What is the likelihood you would buy Brand A the next time you purchase cola?

Definitely will buy ____

Probably will buy ____

Might buy ____

Probably will not buy ____

Definitely will not buy ____

(Key cola brands will be listed and respondents asked their intention to buy.)

*Scales for brand beliefs and attribute evaluations are developed for a number of characteristics such as sweet, carbonated, good to serve guests, and so forth.

erence. This scale is known as a **constant sum scale** because the amount selected must always add to the same number—in this case, 10. The constant sum scale is known as a *ratio scale* because it permits ratio comparisons. A consumer who picks six cans of Pepsi and three of Coke has selected twice as much Pepsi as Coke. The question is whether one can assume that this rating means the consumer prefers Pepsi twice as much as Coke.

The constant sum scale, semantic differential, and rank order of preference are the three major categories of scales. The constant sum scale has ratio properties, the semantic differential is an equal interval scale, and the rank order of preference is an ordinal scale.

Buying Intentions *(BI)*

Buying intentions are generally measured on a scale from "definitely will buy" to "definitely will not buy." The percentage of consumers saying they will definitely buy is a closely watched figure because studies have shown a close relationship between this percentage and subsequent trial of a new product.

Behavior *(B)*

Since the attitudinal components are assumed to be related to behavior, it is important to consider how consumers' behavior is measured. In the past, behavior was measured in consumer surveys on a self-reported basis. The question asked was "What brand did you last purchase?" with additional details on quantity and price paid.

The increasing availability of scanner data (bar-coded merchandise that is laser-scanned at the checkout counter) has made it possible to use more objective measures of behavior. Research companies have established scanner panels—that is, a sample of consumers who use an identification card when they purchase. These same consumers can then be asked attitudinal questions like those in Table 9.3, thus linking survey-derived attitudinal questions to scanner-derived background data.

Attitude Development

To understand the role of attitudes in consumer behavior, we must understand how they develop and the functions they play. Attitudes develop over time through a learning process affected by family influences, peer group influences, information, experience, and personality.

Family Influences

The family is an important influence on purchase decisions. Regardless of their tendency to rebel in teenage years, there is a high correlation between children's attitudes and those of their parents. As Bennett and Kassarjian note, "Attitudes toward personal hygiene, preferences for food items, attitudes toward boiled vegetables or fried food, and beliefs about the medicinal value of chicken soup are similarly acquired (from parents)."[7]

http://www.jnj.com/

This influence is demonstrated in some advertising themes. For instance, Johnson & Johnson once advertised its baby powder by portraying a mother using it on her daughter's wedding day and tearfully reminiscing about its earlier use. Parental influence is especially apparent in attitudes toward candy. If parents used candy as a punishment or reward for their children, in later years those children as adults have subconscious guilt feelings about eating candy. Thus, some advertising tries to alleviate guilt feelings by making positive associations with candy.

Peer Group Influences

Many studies have shown pervasive group influence on purchasing behavior. Katz and Lazarsfeld found that peer groups are much more likely than advertising to influence attitudes and purchasing behavior.[8] Coleman found that socially integrated doctors who valued peer group norms accepted a new drug faster.[9] Arndt found that socially integrated consumers accepted a new coffee product sooner.[10] In each of these studies, group norms influenced product attitudes.

Information and Experience

Consumers' past experiences influence their brand attitudes. According to learning theory, such experiences condition future behavior. Information is also an important attitude determinant. For example, knowing that a pain reliever has a newer, faster-acting formula may result in a more favorable evaluation of the brand and may induce consumers to switch.

Personality

Consumers' personalities affect their attitudes. Traits such as aggression, extroversion, submissiveness, or authoritarianism may influence attitudes toward brands and products. An aggressive individual may be likely to be involved in competitive sports and will buy the most expensive equipment in an attempt to excel. In such a case, attitudes toward sports equipment are a function of personality.

Functions of Attitudes

Understanding the **functions of attitudes** means understanding how they serve the individual. Daniel Katz proposed four classifications of attitude functions:[11]

- Utilitarian function.
- Value-expressive function.
- Ego-defensive function.
- Knowledge function.

Utilitarian Function

The utilitarian function of attitudes guides consumers in achieving desired benefits. For example, a consumer who considers safety and immediate relief the most important criteria in selecting a pain reliever will be directed to brands that fulfill these benefits. Conversely, in their utilitarian role, attitudes will direct consumers away from brands unlikely to fulfill their needs. Auto advertising reflects the utilitarian function of attitudes when it features performance characteristics.

Exhibit 9.2 shows examples of advertising's use of each of the four functions of attitudes. The ad for the Nike Sneaker is an example of the utilitarian function. For the active person who values comfort and flexibility while jogging, doing aerobics, or participating in other sports activities, the ad's appeal will enhance the brand's utility.

Value-Expressive Function

Attitudes can express consumers' self-images and value systems, particularly for a high-involvement product. The self-image of an individual purchasing a sports car, for example, may be of a hard-driving, domineering person who likes to gain the upper hand. Aggressiveness may manifest itself in purchasing a car that fits this image. Likewise, the individual who dresses conservatively like everyone else where he or she works has accepted the values of conservatism and wealth as expressions of success.

http://www.reebok.com/

Advertisers often appeal to the value-expressive nature of attitudes by implying that use or purchase of a certain item will lead to self-enhancement, achievement, or independence. In this manner, advertisers are appealing to a large segment who value these self-expressive traits. The French ad for Reebok in Exhibit 9.2 says that the wearer always knows what she is doing and is an involved and spontaneous sports enthusiast, suggesting a confident, self-aware woman.

Ego-Defensive Function

Attitudes protect the ego from anxieties and threats. Consumers purchase many products, such as mouthwashes, to avoid anxiety-producing situations. Most individuals use mouthwashes to avoid bad breath rather than to cure it. Advertising capitalizes on the fear of social ostracism by demonstrating greater social acceptance through use of certain products. As a result, consumers develop positive attitudes toward brands associated with social acceptance, confidence, and sexual desirability. The ad for Retin-A in Exhibit 9.2 is an example. Using Retin-A increases social acceptance by avoiding the embarrassment of pimples and acne.

Knowledge Function

Attitudes help consumers organize the mass of information they are exposed to daily. Consumers sort all of the messages, ignoring the less relevant information. The knowledge function also reduces uncertainty and confusion. Advertising that provides information about new brands or new characteristics of existing brands is valuable for the information it provides. The ad for Depo-Provena in Exhibit

▶EXHIBIT 9.2
Ads depicting the four functions of attitudes

Utilitarian Function

Value-Expressive Function

Ego-Defensive Function

Knowledge Function

9.2 informs teens that if they are serious about birth control, a new contraceptive injection required only four times a year is more than 99 percent effective.

In summary, attitudes have different functions. The function that is served will affect the individual's overall evaluation of an object.[12] For example, two individuals having equally favorable attitudes toward Listerine mouthwash will vary markedly in the nature of these attitudes, depending on whether they reflect a utilitarian function (Listerine freshens my mouth) or an ego-defensive function (Listerine prevents bad breath). Trying to influence the utilitarian consumer that Listerine prevents bad breath would be as ineffective as trying to influence the ego-oriented consumer that Listerine freshens one's mouth.

http://www.oral-care.com/

Further, it is important to realize that attitudes can fulfill more than one function. For example, brand attitudes can help consumers judge the value of information while at the same time guiding consumers to achieve desired benefits. A consumer who evaluates alternative VCR models by the number of events that can be programmed will be guided to such information (the knowledge function) and will evaluate brand attitudes based on this information (the utilitarian function).

ROLE OF ATTITUDES IN DEVELOPING MARKETING STRATEGY

Marketers define and measure attitudes toward their brands because attitudes can help them identify benefit segments, develop new products, and formulate and evaluate promotional strategies.

Define Benefit Segments

Market segments can be defined by the benefits consumers desire. These benefits identify the key product attributes marketers should use to influence consumers. The benefits consumers desire are measured by attribute evaluations (see Table 9.2). For example, consumers who rate nutrition, taste, or economy as most important in buying cereals would belong to one of these three benefit segments. In the car market, segments are defined by economy, performance, and luxury. Marketers attempt to influence consumer attitudes in the performance segment by citing key features such as acceleration, horsepower, and fuel efficiency. Price and service costs are the primary criteria to emphasize for the economy segment.

An example of benefit segmentation for a total product line is provided by Coca-Cola (see Figure 9.2). When it introduced Tab in 1963 as a diet cola positioned to women, Coca-Cola was one of the first to recognize the importance of a diet segment. Twenty years later, it used the magic name Coke on a product other than its flagship brand for the first time by introducing Diet Coke positioned to men. In 1983, it also introduced caffeine-free versions of Coca-Cola, Diet Coke, and Tab positioned to a health-oriented segment. Cherry Coke was a further extension of the Coke name to appeal to teenagers who wanted a sweeter cola drink. The company has also positioned Sprite to those who like lemon-lime and introduced Minute Maid soda as a fruit-based drink that was leveraged from Coca-Cola-owned Minute Maid fruit juice.

Coke's most famous move was the introduction of New Coke to replace the original in an attempt to appeal to teenagers who favored Pepsi because of its sweeter taste. After the consumer outcry, Coca-Cola brought back the original

FIGURE 9.2
Benefit segmentation of Coca-Cola's product line

BENEFIT SEGMENTS / PRODUCTS	Cola	Diet Cola	Caffeine-Free	Fruit-Based	Lemon-Lime
Taste-Oriented: Like sweet-tasting colas	New Coke Cherry Coke				
Taste-Oriented: Like unsweetened colas	Coca-Cola Classic				
Taste-Oriented: Like fruit juice				Minute Maid	
Taste-Oriented: Like lemon-lime					Sprite
Health/Nutrition-Conscious			Caffeine-Free Tab, Coke, and Diet Coke	Minute Maid	
Weight Watchers		Diet Coke, Tab, and Diet Cherry Coke			

brand as Coca-Cola Classic. It reinforced its benefit segmentation strategy by positioning New Coke to those who wanted a sweeter drink and Classic Coke to traditional Coke loyalists who preferred the original formula.

Develop New Products

http://www.nabisco.com/

Attitudes are crucial in evaluating alternative positionings for new products. For example, at one time Nabisco conducted a benefit segmentation study of the snack food market to identify opportunities for a new product. It identified the six benefit segments shown as circles in Figure 9.3 The vectors in Figure 9.3 define the primary benefits sought by each segment. Figure 9.3 is known as a **perceptual map** because it is based on consumers' perceptual ratings of how various brands are related to each other and to the benefits shown. Brands close

FIGURE 9.3
Perceptual map to evaluate a new product

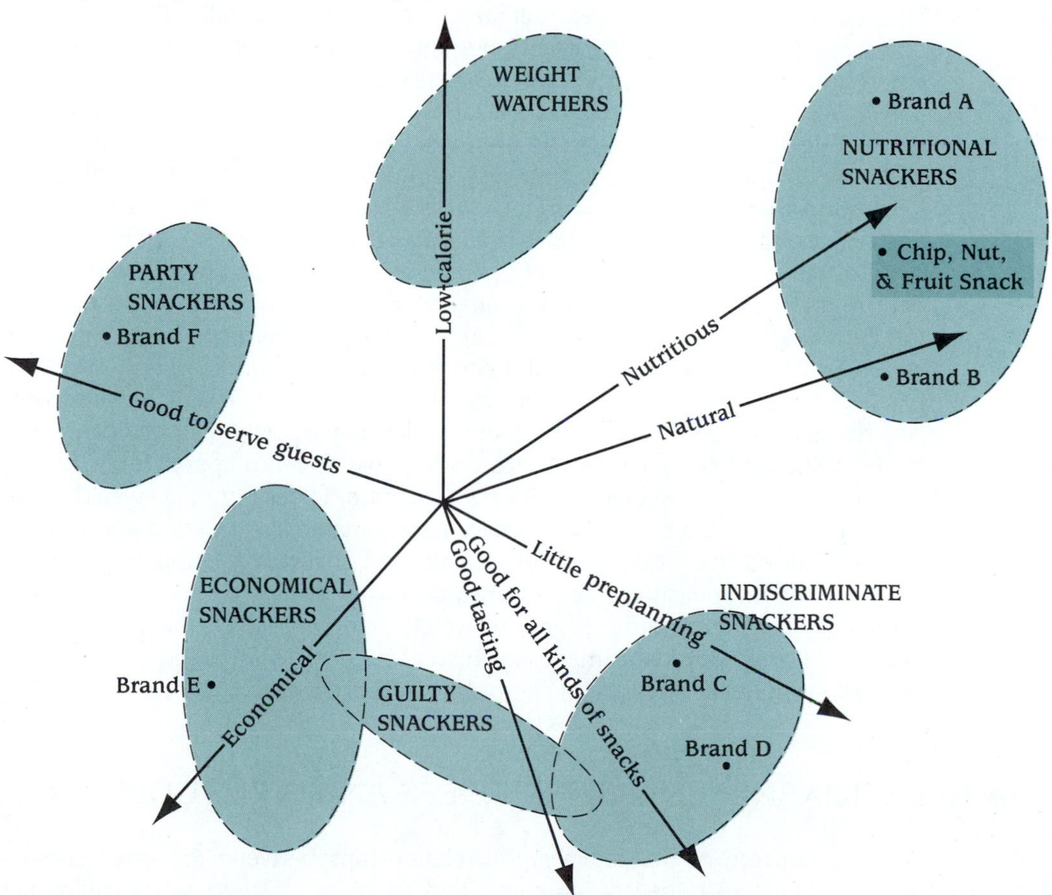

to each other are seen as most similar and are associated with the benefits closest to them. Brands C and D are seen as similar and are associated with little preplanning and good for all kinds of snacks.

On this basis, Nabisco decided to test consumer reactions to a new product intended to be positioned to nutritional snackers: a mixed chip, nut, and fruit snack. It found that nutritional snackers associated the brand with nutrition and natural ingredients and were likely to buy the product as a result. Further, the new product was positioned far enough from Brands A and B so it would not be regarded as a "me too" brand.

Develop and Evaluate Promotional Strategies

Attitudes are important in developing promotional strategies. If snack purchasers emphasize nutrition and natural ingredients as desired benefits, these are the appeals marketers must emphasize in advertising and promotional literature to create favorable attitudes among the target group. Communication of these benefits as well as their subsequent fulfillment by the product will result in positive attitudes toward Nabisco's fruit and nut snack product. Advertising's role is to communicate the benefits the brand can deliver.

Attitudes are also important in evaluating the effectiveness of advertising messages. Television commercials and print ads are frequently judged by how large and how favorable an attitude shift they produce. Brand attitudes are measured before and after exposure to a commercial in a controlled environment. Marketers use any changes in brand attitudes to evaluate the commercial's effectiveness.

Marketers also use attitudes to evaluate advertising campaigns over time to determine whether the attitudes are being maintained or whether they are changing favorably or unfavorably. Advertising campaigns may have attitude change as a specific objective. Consider the perceptual map in Figure 9.4 showing the position of Lord & Taylor department stores. Lord & Taylor is associated with security and tradition. That is a positioning that may be strong among older consumers. But Lord & Taylor recognizes that it must begin to appeal to the under-40 set. As a result, it should consider a repositioning strategy that would move the chain down the vertical axis toward a combination of tradition and innovation (see dotted line for desired attitude shift). An advertising campaign with this objective would measure attitudes toward Lord & Taylor before and after the campaign to determine the degree to which attitudes reflect a shift to a more innovative and up-to-date image. In this case, changes in brand attitudes are used to evaluate an advertising campaign's effectiveness.

RELATIONSHIP BETWEEN BELIEFS AND ATTITUDES

The key concern of marketers is the relationships between the three components in Figure 9.1: beliefs, attitudes, and behavior.[13] These relationships are

FIGURE 9.4
Using attitudes to evaluate a department store's position
Source: "Image and Attitude Are Department Store's Draw," *The New York Times* (August 12, 1993), p. D1.

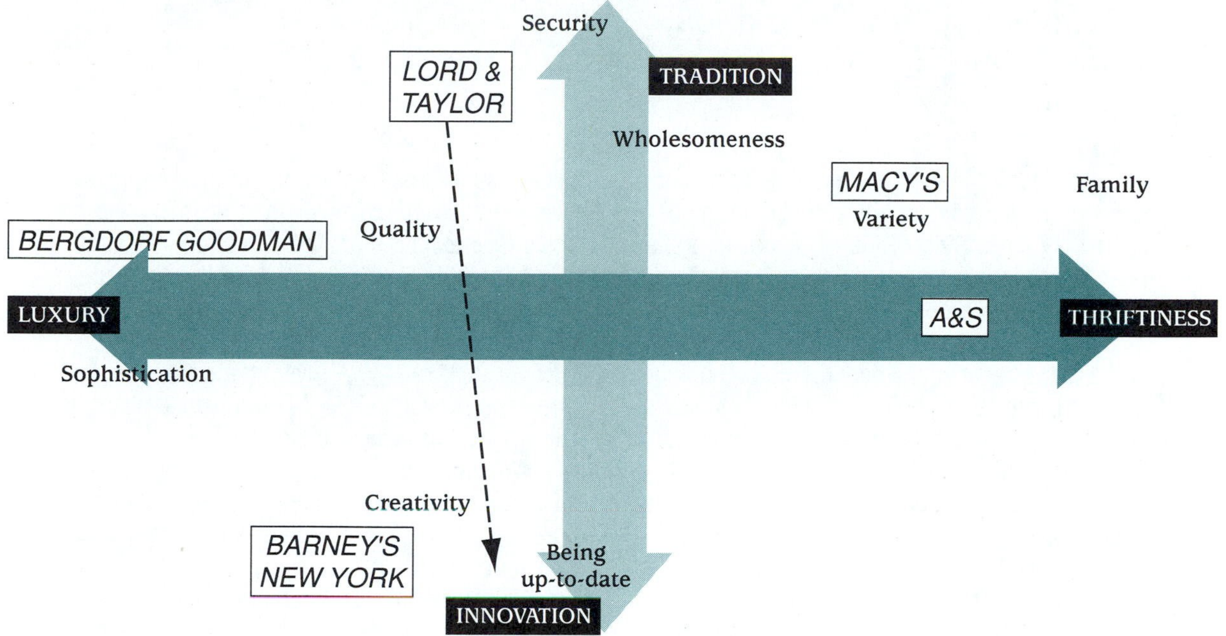

important to marketers because they indicate the success of marketing strategies. If advertising is successful in establishing positive beliefs about a brand, consumers are more likely to evaluate the brand positively and to buy it. Satisfaction with the brand strengthens positive attitudes and increases the probability that consumers will repurchase it.

The remainder of this chapter considers these relationships. In this section, we discuss the relationship between beliefs and brand attitudes by considering two theories that focus on this relationship: Heider's balance theory and Fishbein's multiattribute theory. In the next section, we consider the relationship between attitudes and behavior.

Heider's Balance Theory

Heider's **balance theory** is so named because it maintains that people seek to achieve balance between their thoughts (beliefs) and feelings (evaluations).[14]

http://www.jcpenney.com/

A good illustration of how balance theory operates occurred when JCPenney attempted to upgrade its image by contracting to carry Halston's line of designer clothes. Many consumers had a positive image of Halston but a negative

STRATEGIC APPLICATIONS OF CONSUMER BEHAVIOR

Volvo: Doing Too Good a Job in Forming Consumer Attitudes?

Can a company do too good a job in forming consumer attitudes and molding its brand image? Volvo may have. Since 1968, it has used a singular theme in positioning its cars—safety.

But there is a downside to Volvo's reliance on consumer attitudes toward safety to sell its cars. First, whereas the safety theme was unique to Volvo in the 1970s, this was no longer the case in the 1980s and 1990s. Other carmakers began positioning their models based on safety, particularly with the advent of air bags. Second, Volvo's safety theme has been so persistent that consumers saw little else and began associating Volvo with attributes such as "plodding" and "sluggish." Safety became a two-sided sword in forming consumer attitudes. Partly as a result, Volvo's sales in the United States were halved from 1986 to 1992.

Volvo's answer was to lampoon its safety image. The company introduced its sporty 850 model in 1993 with a commercial showing a couple driving a sturdy tank and the tag line "Driving a Volvo usually inspires a certain sense of safety" (see Exhibit 9.3). But in lampooning its image, Volvo merely reminded consumers of associations with plodding and sluggish. Further, Volvo learned that changing entrenched attitudes is difficult. It just did too good a job in linking its cars to safety.

As a result, the company went back to its safety image in 1994 with an older campaign called "survivors," showing individuals whose lives were saved because they were driving a Volvo (see Exhibit 9.3). But Volvo took the campaign one step further by making it more experiential and hedonic with TV spots featuring the Cambridge singers in a golden light making every survivor look saintly. A reverential voice-over by Donald Sutherland says, "These people share a belief, that a car saved their lives."

Whether this campaign will counteract the plodding, conservative image of Volvo owners is uncertain. So in 1995 Volvo began testing an even more assertive campaign in the United Kingdom with the same safety theme. Ads show drivers in Volvos in risky situations such as driving through a tornado. The tornado ad literally drives the viewer into the eye of the storm. The purpose was to change the image of the Volvo owner from conservative to risk-taker, from sluggish to fashionable. After the campaign broke, Volvo sales in the UK jumped 40 percent.

Volvo has changed its strategy from debunking its safety image to reinforcing it, but with a difference—safety with a new image of a Volvo owner.

Sources: "Middle of the Road," *Adweek* (October 9, 1995), p. 36; "Cinemainminiature," *Adweek* (August 21, 1995), p. 36; "Volvo Seeks to Soft-Pedal Safety Image," *The Wall Street Journal* (March 16, 1993), p. B7.

EXHIBIT 9.3
Volvo moves from debunking to reinforcing its safety image

VOLVO

"McLEODS" :15

(MUSIC UNDER THROUGHOUT)

ANNCR VO: Susan, James and Megan McLeod

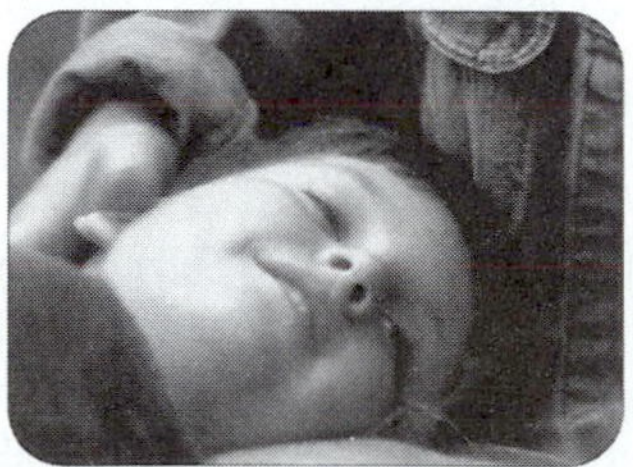

all share

a belief:

that a car saved their lives.

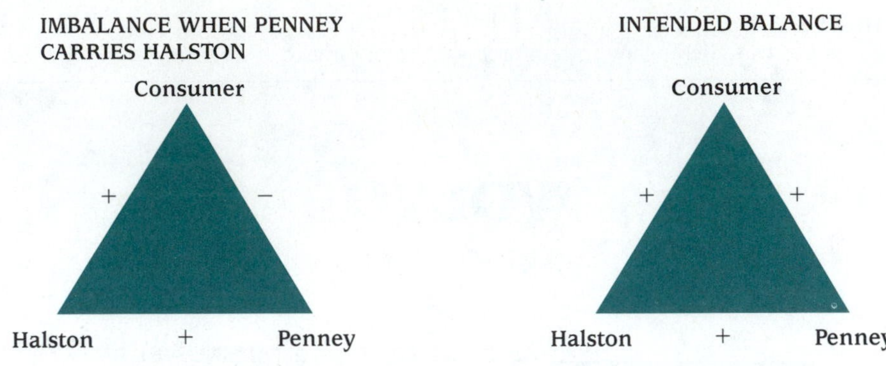

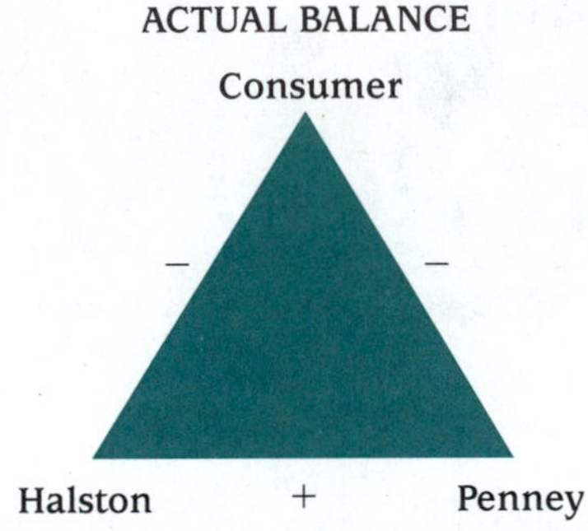

FIGURE 9.5 Illustration of balance theory

image of Penney (as shown in the top left triangle in Figure 9.5). When Halston began selling at Penney's (represented by a plus between Halston and Penney), this relationship created an imbalance (a positive object linked to a more negative object). Two pluses and a minus produce a minus, leaving an imbalance in consumers' minds. Penney hoped that consumers would resolve this imbalance by developing a more favorable image of its stores (the triangle in the upper right). What actually happened was that many consumers maintained their image of Penney but developed a more negative image of Halston (lower triangle). This image shift created balance in consumers' cognitive system (two minuses and a plus produce a plus), but not the balance Penney intended.

One of the problems with balance theory is that it presents attitudes in absolute, rather than relative, terms. What actually happened in the preceding example is that many consumers developed somewhat more positive attitudes toward Penney and much more negative attitudes toward Halston, which created balance. The actual result was similar to the bottom triangle in Figure 9.5.

Balance theory conforms to a basic behavioral principle of **cognitive consistency.** This principle states that consumers value harmony between their beliefs and evaluations. If one is inconsistent with the other, consumers will change their attitudes to create harmony in their cognitive structure. Research supports the idea that consistency exists between beliefs and brand evaluations. In a study of six consumer goods, Sheth and Talarzyck found that brand ratings on specific attributes such as taste, price, nutrition, and packaging were closely related to overall evaluation of the brand.[15] Other studies have also found a link between brand beliefs and overall evaluations.[16]

Fishbein's Multiattribute Model

Fishbein's **multiattribute model** of attitudes[17] describes attitude formation as a function of consumer beliefs about the attributes and benefits of a brand. Fishbein's model allows marketers to diagnose the strengths and weaknesses of their brands relative to those of the competition by determining how consumers evaluate brand alternatives on important attributes. In so doing, marketers can apply multiattribute models directly to vocabularies of attributes used to evaluate specific brands.

Fishbein's model is shown in Figure 9.6. It states that consumers' beliefs (*b*) that the object has certain attributes (*i*), and the evaluation (*e*) of these product attributes (*i*) results in an attitude toward an object (A_o). That is,

$$A_o = \sum b_i \times e_i$$

As shown in Figure 9.6, consumers start with the evaluation of certain attributes (a medicinal tasting mouthwash is good for you). Consumers then form beliefs as to whether an object has that attribute (Listerine has a medicinal taste). Attitudes toward the object are the sum total of beliefs and values for not just one attribute, but for all relevant attributes. Thus, a consumer might rate Listerine more favorably because it has a medicinal taste and gives the mouth a fresh feeling, both of which this consumer considers desirable attributes. At the same time, the consumer might rate Listerine less favorably on certain other important attributes such as irritation to the gums.

As a result, Fishbein's model is a compensatory model of brand attitudes. That is, consumers can compensate the weakness of a brand on one attribute by its strength on another. All of the attributes are summed to determine the favorability or unfavorability of the attitude toward the brand. On balance, the fact that Listerine is rated positively based on its medicinal taste and refreshing feeling but negatively because of irritation to the gums should produce a somewhat positive overall evaluation of the brand.

Fishbein's multiattribute model is linked to the traditional hierarchy of effects shown in Figure 9.1. The sum total of desired attributes (e_i) and brand beliefs (b_i) influence brand evaluations (A_o). Fishbein's model also states a linkage between brand evaluations and intended or actual behavior: a positive (negative) attitude toward a brand will increase (decrease) the likelihood that con-

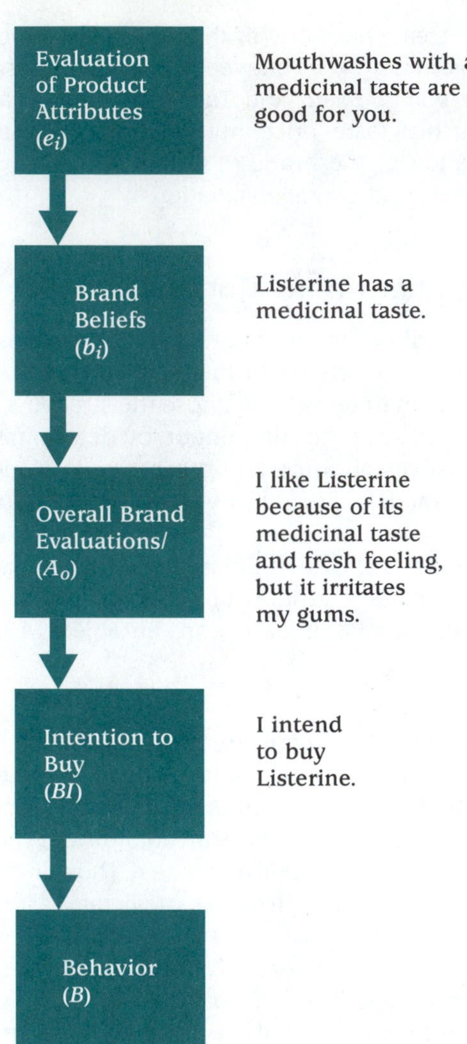

FIGURE 9.6 Fishbein's multiattribute model

sumers intend to buy it. Positive buying intentions are likely to lead to actual behavior. Therefore:

$BI \sim A_o$ That is, buying intentions are a function of brand attitudes (evaluations).

$B \sim BI$ That is, behavior is a function of buying intentions.

Although the attitude-to-behavior link completes the model, the key is not so much this link but, rather, the link between beliefs and evaluations that explains attitude formation. Nonetheless, without a link between attitude and behavior, Fishbein's model would be irrelevant for marketers.

Factors Inhibiting the Relationship Between Beliefs and Attitudes

There are cases when beliefs may not be related to attitudes. If a consumer buys a product on a hedonic basis, overall attitudes will be formed first. Beliefs developed subsequently may not conform to these attitudes. The teen buying Shaq Attack basketball sneakers does so because of the fantasy associated with the basketball star. Subsequently, the teen may find the sneakers are too rigid or do not breathe. But this makes little difference in the overall evaluation of the brand because of the continued association with Shaquille O'Neal, an association reinforced by the brand name and advertising.

http://www.mcdonalds.com/

Another reason why beliefs and overall evaluations may not be related is that beliefs may not be relevant to consumers' decisions. The belief that McDonald's is a good place for the family and has quick service is not particularly relevant for the single consumer who likes leisurely dining. These beliefs may be positive, but they do not enter into this consumer's evaluation of restaurant alternatives.

RELATIONSHIP BETWEEN ATTITUDES AND BEHAVIOR

If attitudinal models are to be strategically relevant, they must show some link between attitudes and behavior. Both the traditional hierarchy of effects and Fishbein's model link attitudes to behavioral intentions. (See the link between the affective and conative components in Figure 9.1.)

Fishbein's Theory of Reasoned Action

In an attempt to better explain the link between attitudes and behavior, Fishbein modified his multiattribute model. The resulting **theory of reasoned action** proposes that to predict behavior more accurately, it is more important to determine the person's *attitude to that behavior* than to the object of behavior.[18] That is, it is more important to determine an individual's attitude toward buying a Pepsi, a Saturn car, or a Sony TV than it is to measure attitudes toward these individual brands. The appropriate attitude measurement should be based on the act of purchasing or using a brand (A_{act}), not on the brand itself (A_o). It is the consumer's act of purchasing and, ultimately, consuming the product that determines satisfaction. The attitude toward the object may not be a valid basis for gauging attitudes. A consumer may have a very positive attitude toward a Rolls-Royce but a negative attitude toward buying one because of the price. In Fishbein's words:

> A woman might believe that "high pile" carpeting is "warm," "comfortable," "luxurious," and "prestigious," and since she positively evaluates those at-

tributes, she is likely to have a positive attitude toward "high pile carpeting." However, what do you think the consequences of buying high pile carpeting are for that woman if she has two dogs, a cat, and three children under nine?[19]

A second modification in the model was to define beliefs as the perceived consequences of an action rather than the perceived attributes of a brand. Rather than rating a toothpaste brand on attributes such as "whitens teeth" and "freshens breath," consumers would rate a brand based on the likelihood that their teeth would be whiter or their breath fresher if they used it. The distinction is subtle—the difference between rating a brand in general and rating it if you use it—but it could be important. For example, a person might rate a certain car as safe. However, if asked if it was safe enough for her to drive with her baby as a passenger, she might say no. Consumers' beliefs are likely to differ when asked to rate a product in the context of their own personal use rather than in general.

Fishbein developed a third modification in his model because of mixed results in relating beliefs and evaluation to behavior. He concluded that other elements must also influence behavior. Since family and peer group norms are so important in shaping attitudes, he introduced social influences into his model. Two social elements were introduced: normative beliefs and the motivation to comply with them. Normative beliefs may be represented by the following measure:

My family thinks I:

Should buy Brand X	Should not buy Brand X

The motivation to comply could be measured by this scale:

I want to do what my family thinks I should do regarding Brand X	I do not want to do what my family thinks I should do regarding Brand X

Figure 9.7 illustrates the theory of reasoned action. Studies have found that it predicts intentions and behavior better than does the original multiattribute model. In a review of these studies, Ryan and Bonfield concluded that attitudes toward purchasing a brand were more highly correlated with behavior than were attitudes toward the brand itself.[20] Wilson, Matthews, and Harvey measured intentions and behavior for toothpaste purchases using the original and extended Fishbein models.[21] They also found that attitudes toward the purchase of a brand were more closely related to behavior than were attitudes toward the brand. A study by Knox and Chernatony of buyers of mineral water confirmed that using attitudes toward purchasing was a good predictor of subsequent behavior.[22]

Relationship Between Intention to Buy and Behavior

In the attitudinal models in Figures 9.6 and 9.7, intention to buy is shown as an intervening variable between attitudes and behavior. Both marketers and economists have used intention to buy to predict future behavior. Marketers use consumer buying intentions to evaluate alternative new product concepts and advertising themes. Economists use consumer intentions to predict future economic trends.

Marketers should confirm the relationship between intention and subsequent behavior if purchase intention is to be regarded as a valid measure of action tendency. In a study of magazine readership, Bagozzi and Baumgarten found that intentions were closely related to behavior for six of the seven magazines studied.[23] McQuarrie's study of purchasers of computer systems found intentions were more closely related to behavior for heavy computer users. The implication was that greater knowledge and higher involvement produce a closer link between intentions and behavior.[24]

In an earlier study of seven product categories, Banks found that 62 percent of respondents who said they would buy actually did so.[25] Among those who did not intend to buy, 28 percent purchased the product. The greatest fulfillment rate (correspondence between intention and actual purchase) occurred for coffee and scouring cleanser. The lowest fulfillment rate was for ice cream, which reflects the impulsive nature of ice cream purchases.

http://www.isr.umich.edu/

The Survey Research Center at the University of Michigan provided the most extensive confirmation of the relationship between intentions and purchase. George Katona, founder of the center, used consumer buying intentions to forecast economic trends. He reported on the close relationship between intentions and behavior for automobiles.[26] Among those consumers who said they planned to or might buy a new car, 63 percent bought in the next year. Among those consumers who did not intend to buy, 29 percent purchased a new car. These fulfillment rates were almost identical to those in Banks's study. Both studies showed that the majority of consumers who intended to buy a product fulfilled their intentions.

Katona conducted his studies before 1970. Since then, consumer intentions have proved to be a less reliable predictor of behavior. Energy shortages and two severe recessions in the early 1980s and 1990s have made the relationship between intentions and behavior less certain. During the energy crisis, most consumers said they would cut back on driving but did not. After the stock market crash of 1987, many consumers said they would cut back on purchases of high-ticket items but did not. Interestingly, the Survey Research Center now asks consumers not what they intend to buy, but what their expectations are regarding their economic situation.[27] The latter measure seems to be more predictive of total consumer expenditures.

Another factor inhibiting the fulfillment of consumer intentions is a long repurchase cycle. The University of Michigan study interviewed consumers to de-

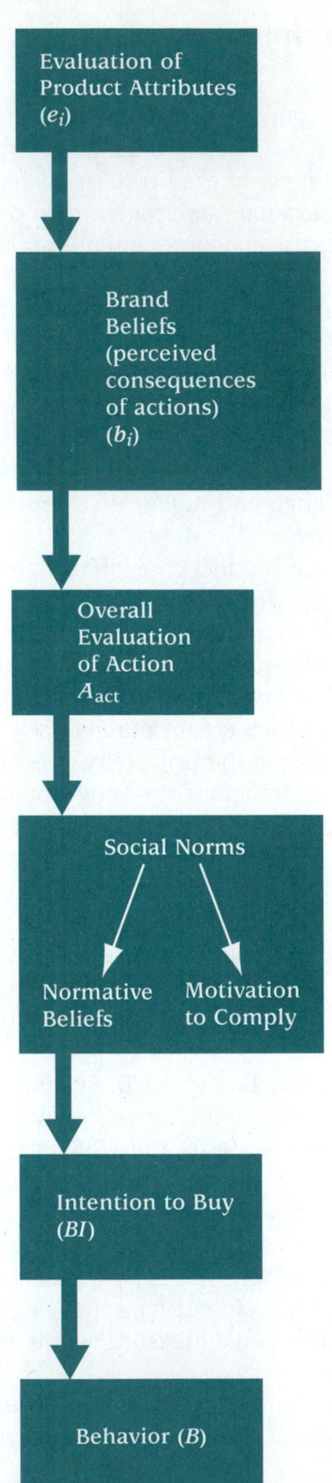

FIGURE 9.7 Fishbein's theory of reasoned action

termine actual car purchases one year after determining intentions. Many factors, such as a change in needs, economic circumstances, or alternatives available, can intervene in the space of a year to change intentions.

Relationship of Behavior to Attitudes

Not only do consumer attitudes influence behavior, but behavior can also influence subsequent attitudes. Three situations are likely to result in behavior influencing attitudes: cognitive dissonance, passive learning, and a disconfirmation of expectations.

Theories of cognitive dissonance, passive learning, and disconfirmation of expectations have reduced the importance of attitudes in explaining consumer behavior by showing that attitude change is not a necessary condition for a change in purchasing behavior.

Cognitive Dissonance

According to dissonance theory, consumer attitudes sometimes change to conform to previous behavior, thus reducing postpurchase conflict. Several studies have confirmed these relationships. For example, Knox and Inkster interviewed bettors at a racetrack before bets on a horse were made.[28] On the average, bettors gave their horse little better than a fair chance of winning. The researchers then interviewed the same bettors after they made their bets but before the race. Predictions about the performance of the horse became substantially more positive after they made the decision. Apparently, bettors sought to reduce the potential for postdecisional conflict by enhancing the evaluation of the chosen alternative. This finding indicates that individuals tend to reinforce their decision after the fact by changing their attitudes in favor of the chosen brand.

Passive Learning

The theory of **passive learning** provides another basis for downplaying the importance of consumer attitudes as determinants of behavior.[29] As we have seen, under conditions of low involvement, a change in attitude is not necessary to influence a change in behavior. The awareness of a new brand may be sufficient reason for consumers to switch in a search for variety, and consumers may form attitudes toward the new brand after using it. Ginter's study of a low-involvement category, household cleaning products, found that consumers tended to rate brands more favorably after they made the purchase.[30]

Disconfirmation of Expectations

When expectations regarding product performance are not met, such **disconfirmation of expectations** may give consumers more negative attitudes toward the product after the purchase. According to **assimilation/contrast theories,** when consumers are only slightly disappointed, attitudes will adjust to expectations since the experience is accepted and assimilated. When consumers are very disappointed, however, a negative change in attitudes is likely to occur after the purchase, and they may exaggerate this change.

Factors Inhibiting the Relationship Between Beliefs, Attitudes, and Behavior

Marketers must recognize occasions when consumer attitudes are unlikely to be related to behavior. The following conditions may cause a lack of association between beliefs, attitudes, and behavior:

1. *Lack of involvement.* As we saw in Chapter 5, consumer attitudes are less likely to be related to behavior for low-involvement products.

2. *Lack of purchase feasibility.* Consumers may have a very positive attitude toward the brand, but it may not be one of the brands consumers can feasibly purchase. For example, a consumer may evaluate a Porsche very positively, but the car is not a realistic alternative for most consumers because of its price. As a result, attitudes are not related to behavior.

3. *Lack of direct product experience.* A study by Berger and Mitchell found that when consumers have direct product experience, their attitudes are more likely to be related to subsequent behavior.[31] Lack of product experience may result in weakly held attitudes that are not related to behavior.

4. *Lack of relation between values and beliefs.* Attitudes are unlikely to be related to behavior if brand beliefs are not tied to consumer values. The fact that consumers believe a brand of cereal has fewer calories is not going to predict behavior if consumers have no interest in losing weight.

5. *Changing market conditions.* An increase in the price of the favored brand may cause consumers to switch with no change in attitudes. Special price promotions or better credit terms for competitive brands may cause consumers to buy a less preferred brand. The unavailability of the preferred brand may lead consumers to purchase a less preferred brand with no change in attitudes.

6. *Poor attitude accessibility.* As we saw in the last chapter, consumers retain brand beliefs in memory as schema representing their associations with the brand. For these beliefs to affect brand evaluations, they must be accessible from memory. Fazio and his associates suggest that lack of a relationship between attitudes and behavior may be due to the fact that some attitudes are so weakly held that they are not accessible.[32] If consumers have strongly held attitudes, they often spontaneously retrieve them when they encounter the object. If a consumer has a strong positive attitude toward McDonald's, the consumer could spontaneously retrieve the McDonald's schema by the mere mention of a Big Mac or by the sight of the golden arches.

SUMMARY

This chapter focused on one of the most important consumer thought variables: attitudes. In a marketing context, attitudes are predispositions toward specific brands, products, or companies that cause consumers to respond favorably or unfavorably toward them. The development and function of attitudes were discussed.

Brand attitudes are composed of consumer beliefs about a brand, an overall evaluation of the brand, and an action tendency. A hierarchy of effects links these three components in a sequence leading to purchase behavior. This sequence will differ depending on whether the purchaser is involved with the product and whether the product is purchased on a utilitarian or experiential basis.

The attitudinal components are important to marketers because they (1) influence consumers' behavior, (2) enable marketers to define attitudinal segments toward which strategies can be directed, and (3) help marketers evaluate strategies.

The focus of this chapter was on the relationships between brand beliefs and brand attitudes and between brand attitudes and behavior. Two theories best describe the link between brand beliefs and attitudes. Heider's balance theory posits that consumers always strive for cognitive balance between beliefs and evaluations. Fishbein's multiattribute model describes attitudes as a function of beliefs that a brand has certain attributes and the desirability of these attributes.

The link between brand attitudes and behavior was also examined. Fishbein's theory of reasoned action proposes that the appropriate focus of research is consumer attitudes toward the purchase of a brand rather than attitudes toward the brand itself. Research suggests that such a focus increases the strength of the association between attitudes and behavior.

The final sections of the chapter considered various factors that might inhibit the relationships among consumer beliefs, attitudes, and behavior and the role of attitudes in developing marketing strategies.

The next chapter focuses on the strategic applications of attitudes; namely, strategies for attitude reinforcement and change.

QUESTIONS

1. What are some of the difficulties AT&T faces in changing the attitudes of younger consumers toward the company?
2. Why are attitudes more closely related to behavior for consumers who are involved with the purchase? Does this mean that consumer attitudes play no strategic role for low-involvement products? Explain.
3. What are the strategic implications of an experiential hierarchy of effects for advertising?
4. Two manufacturers of men's clothing launch a national advertising campaign. One directs the campaign to value-expressive attitudes toward men's clothing. The other directs advertising to ego-defensive attitudes.
   - What differences may result from the two campaigns?
   - To what types of consumers would each campaign appeal?
5. How do the ads in Exhibit 9.2 reflect each of the four functions in Katz's functional theory of attitudes?
6. Why did Volvo do too good a job in shaping consumer attitudes toward the car? Do you agree with its current strategy? Why or why not?
7. A consumer has a positive attitude toward his gas-guzzling car and values environmental protection. Apply balance theory in resolving this apparent conflict.
8. A food company is considering introducing an artificial bacon product that is leaner and has less cholesterol than bacon. How can it use Fishbein's multiattribute model to evaluate the new product? What strategic implications might it derive by applying the model?
9. One study linking attitudes to behavior suggested that an ongoing marketing information system designed to track changes in attitudes may benefit management. Of what use would a system that tracks consumer attitudes be for (a) new product development and (b) evaluating advertising effectiveness?
10. Consider the statement: "Consumer attitudes toward the act of using or purchasing a brand are

more closely related to behavior than are consumer attitudes toward the brand itself." Assume you are a marketer considering repositioning a breakfast food so that it will also appeal to the snack market. What are the implications of the statement for repositioning strategy?

11. Under what circumstances is consumer behavior likely to influence subsequent attitudes? What are the strategic implications of attitude change occurring after behavior?
12. Under what circumstances are consumer brand attitudes unlikely to be related to purchase behavior? If attitudes are not related to behavior, should marketers continue to measure them? Why or why not?

RESEARCH ASSIGNMENTS

1. Given that Kmart is trying to create a more upscale image, how is this goal shown in its Web site (http://www.kmart.com)? Do you think the site is effective at changing consumers' attitudes about the retailer? Compare Kmart's site with those for Sears (http://www.sears.com) and Marshall Field's (http://www.shop-at.com/marshallfields). In your analysis, develop a rationale for how site construction accommodates different target markets.
2. According to the theory of cognitive dissonance, recent purchasers of important items such as cars or appliances are more likely to have positive attitudes toward their brands than those who have owned the brand for a longer period of time. The reason for this is that once they make a purchase, recent purchasers are likely to seek positive information about the brand to reinforce the choice they have made.

   Test this hypothesis by selecting both recent purchasers of a major durable good (car, stereo set, microwave oven) and consumers who have owned the item for a longer period of time. Measure (a) beliefs about the brand utilizing a vocabulary of need criteria and (b) overall evaluation of the brand.
   - Do recent purchasers have more positive attitudes?
   - Are there differences in beliefs about brands between recent purchasers and long-time owners?
   - What are the strategic implications of your findings, particularly for (a) advertising and (b) service policies?
3. Select a particular brand to study (preferably a consumer packaged good). You would like to evaluate the strengths and weaknesses of the brand relative to the competition. To do so, you decide to utilize a multiattribute approach.

   Conduct a number of depth interviews with consumers to develop a vocabulary of attributes that consumers use in evaluating brands. Construct scales to measure (a) how consumers evaluate each attribute in the vocabulary and (b) beliefs about the brand under study and two or three other key competitive brands, based on the vocabulary of attributes. Select a sample of users of the product category so that at least one-third of your sample uses the brand under study.
   - What are the brand's strengths and weaknesses based on a comparison of the brand to (a) desired attributes and (b) competitive brands?
   - How do brand ratings differ between users and nonusers of the brand?
   - What are the implications of your findings for (a) possible repositioning strategies for the brand, (b) identification of unmet needs, and (c) formulation of new product concepts to meet consumer needs?
4. Some marketers believe that a significant proportion of consumers develop images of brands based on advertising rather than on product experience. If this is true, one would expect beliefs about brands to reflect advertising themes. Select a product category in which different advertising themes can be associated with brands (for example, pain relievers, airlines, paper towels). Construct a vocabulary of product attributes, including the advertising themes. Ask consumers to rate the brands in the product category utilizing the vocabulary.
   - Are brands rated higher on criteria used in the brand's advertising?
   - Do both heavy and light users of the product category rate brands in accordance with the advertising themes? Do both users and nonusers of the brand?

ATTITUDE REINFORCEMENT AND CHANGE

Chapter 10

CHANGING ATTITUDES AT KMART: FROM POLYESTER PALACE TO HIGH-FASHION RETAILER

Marketers can use their knowledge of consumer attitudes to develop two types of strategies. One strategy reinforces existing attitudes; another tries to change them.

In this chapter, we show how marketers use consumer attitudes to develop strategies of attitude reinforcement and change. To understand this process, we consider:

- The conditions required to change consumer attitudes.
- Theories that provide guidelines for attitudinal change both before and after a purchase.
- The nature of communications strategies to reinforce attitudes or to change them.
- The application of these strategies to social issues as well as brands.

There is no question that reinforcing existing attitudes is easier than changing them. Most advertising for well-known brands attempts to maintain and reinforce positive attitudes. Successful themes such as Chevrolet's "Heartbeat of America" or Miller Lite's http://www.chevrolet.com/

http://www.kmart.com/

"Less Filling/Tastes Great" reinforced consumer attitudes through long-running campaigns.

Strategies that reinforce attitudes may be easier to implement, but there may be compelling reasons to try to change attitudes. A good example is Kmart, the number-two retailer in the country. In the 1980s, Kmart came up against the baby boom generation. These consumers wanted greater quality and value than Kmart was giving them. Kmart could not afford to ignore this group, given their numbers and purchasing power. The trouble was that many baby boomers viewed Kmart as a purveyor of low-quality merchandise. These negative attitudes earned Kmart the nickname "The Polyester Palace."[1]

In 1987, a new management team embarked on a strategy to reposition Kmart as a high-fashion discount store and thereby change the negative attitudes of baby boomers. The company introduced a high-quality clothing line, the Jacklyn Smith Signature Collection, by using the former star of the TV show "Charlie's Angels" to promote the line. In a further attempt to leave its polyester image behind, Kmart signed on Martha Stewart, a stylish hostess, as its spokesperson in its advertising.

By 1990, flat sales were showing Kmart the difficulty of moving out of its polyester image. So management initiated a five-year, $3 billion chainwide store renovation program to improve its in-store decor. Then, in 1993, it embarked on a new advertising campaign to try to get working women to think of Kmart as a source of fashion.[2] The campaign used a "soft-image" approach to try to show that Kmart is in tune with consumers' feelings. One ad showed a working mother relaxing, with the copy: "You put yourself through a lot. Between the kids, the home, and your job, it seems there's no time left for you."

However, there is little evidence that the company is attracting fashion-oriented baby boomers. From 1987 to 1995, Kmart's share of total discount sales fell from 34.5 percent to 22.7 percent.[3] Not surprisingly, in 1995, the chief architect of Kmart's unsuccessful repositioning strategy, Joseph Antonini, was forced to resign. Kmart's new CEO has yet to articulate a new strategy that will transform its image. Obviously, Kmart still has a long way to go to convince consumers it has transformed itself from polyester to high fashion.

CONDITIONS FOR ATTITUDE REINFORCEMENT AND CHANGE

Several studies show that when communications conform to, rather than contradict, existing brand attitudes, consumers are more easily influenced. McCullough, MacLachlan, and Moinpour found that communicating toothpaste attributes known to be important to consumers was more effective than attempting to change the importance of these attributes.[4] A study by Raj found that reinforcing users' positive attitudes of a brand was more effective in increasing consumption of the brand than trying to change the attitudes of nonusers.[5]

Given that it is more difficult to change consumer attitudes than it is to reinforce them, marketers must know when attitude change is feasible. The conditions for attitude change are particularly important, as there are times when marketers must attempt to change consumer attitudes about their companies or brands. However, a certain irony exists in attempting such changes: attitudes are easiest to change when they are least likely to influence behavior (for example, when product involvement is low and when attitudes are weakly held). As a result, strategies of attitude change may take much longer than expected (for example, Kmart's attempt to develop a more upscale image) or they may not produce the payoff that marketers expect.

Despite the difficulty in changing brand attitudes, a significant portion of advertising expenditures is devoted to such change by providing additional information and persuasive appeals. The question marketers must ask is: "Under what conditions should changes in attitudes be attempted?" A number of conditions reflecting the product category, market environment, and nature of consumers make it easier to produce changes in attitudes through marketing strategies. These principles may change consumers' beliefs about a brand, brand attitudes (evaluations), or intention to buy.

1. *Beliefs are easier to change than desired benefits.* Marketers could seek to change beliefs about a brand. They could also attempt to change the benefits consumers desire by changing the value consumers place on brand attributes. Desired benefits are more enduring, ingrained, and internalized than beliefs because they are more closely linked to consumer values. For instance, a manufacturer of pain relievers produces a brand that consumers regard as significantly stronger and as providing more immediate relief. However, most consumers put more value on the benefits of a mild, safe brand that doctors recommend. The manufacturer could try to convince consumers that pain relievers are nonprescription items that do not need a doctor's recommendation, that safety should be of no concern, and that a stronger product is perfectly acceptable. Alternatively, the manufacturer could tone down the emphasis on strength in the advertising, continue to emphasize quick relief, and point out the safety of the product based on FDA approval. The latter strategy is going to be more effective than the former because the marketer is trying to change beliefs about the brand within the consumers' existing value structure.

Lutz tested the effectiveness of changing beliefs versus benefits. He introduced a fictitious laundry soap to consumers in a test situation.[6] After receiving a description of the brand, consumers were asked to read an article in *Consumer Reports* that was designed to change their beliefs about the brand. A second message attempted to change their values by convincing them that high sudsiness was not a valuable attribute. Lutz found that a change in beliefs changed the overall evaluation of the brand, but an attempted change in values did not cause any change in evaluation. This finding conforms to the principle that changing beliefs about a brand is easier than changing the value of these beliefs.

2. *Brand beliefs are easier to change than brand attitudes.* Cognitions (beliefs) are easier to change than affect (attitudes). The traditional high-involvement hierarchy of effects states that a change in beliefs precedes a change in brand attitudes. Therefore, when consumers are involved, changing their beliefs should be easier than changing their brand attitudes. The information that a car has fast acceleration will change the beliefs about the brand, but the evaluation of the car will not necessarily change unless consumers see a benefit in fast acceleration. Most advertising implicitly follows the principle that beliefs are easier to change because advertising generally communicates the attributes of a brand.

If consumer beliefs inhibit purchase, advertisers sometimes try to change their attitudes without changing their beliefs. For example, the belief that Rolls-Royce is a high-priced car inhibits attitudes toward purchasing the car (A_{act}). As a result, Rolls tried to change consumer attitudes toward purchasing without changing beliefs. It identified its target as affluent consumers who have positive beliefs about the car but who are intimidated by the price and its image. Rolls ran a campaign comparing its cars to other luxury cars such as the BMW, Mercedes, and Cadillac. The campaign does not try to change beliefs, since little is said about the characteristics of the car. Rather, it attempts to change attitudes toward purchasing a Rolls among owners of other luxury cars. The campaign is unlikely to succeed because beliefs about the car have not changed and the initial price resistance has not been overcome.

3. *For hedonic products, attitudes are a more relevant vehicle for change than beliefs.* When consumers buy a product based on emotion or fantasy, they are relying on affect (attitudes) rather than cognitions (beliefs). Therefore, for hedonic products, attitudes are the more relevant strategic vehicle for change. Paradoxically, attitudes are harder to change for involving products, and hedonic products are more involving.

http://www.car.volvo.se/

Volvo attempted to change its image from a somewhat dour, dependable car to one associated with pleasure and fantasy, but with limited success. Volvo had to appeal to attitudes rather than to beliefs in trying to move consumers in a more hedonic direction. Its limited success drove it back to more utilitarian themes that reinforced consumers' prior beliefs.

4. *Attitudes are easier to change when there is a low level of involvement with the product.* Attitudes toward uninvolving products are easier to change because consumers are not committed to the brand. This principle is true for the three key components of involvement; that is, consumer attitudes are easier to change if there is little self-identification with the product, little emotional attachment to it, and no badge value associated with it. Sherif's theory of social judgment supports this view.[7] When consumers have a high level of involvement with a product, they will accept messages only if the messages agree with their beliefs. When involvement is low, consumers are more likely to accept a message even if it does not agree with prior beliefs.

▶EXHIBIT 10.1
Changing attitudes for a low-involvement product

The National Fluid Milk Processor Promotion Board, representing milk dairies across the country, has instituted a campaign to convince adults that milk has nutritional value for them as well as for kids. It has used celebrities such as Pete Sampras, Tina Turner, Danny DeVito, and Rhea Perlman sporting milk mustaches to make its point (see Exhibit 10.1).[8] It has even gone international with ads in magazines such as the Spanish version of Cosmopolitan featuring olympic star Florence Griffith Joyner. The Board has been fairly successful in its campaign, primarily because milk is a low-involvement product. It lacks badge value and is not a source of self-identity.

5. *Weak attitudes are easier to change than strong ones.* If consumer brand attitudes are not strong, marketers can more easily establish new associations with the brand. Lubriderm®, a skin care product, had the image among nonusers of a heavy, greasy product. Nonusers viewed Lubriderm® more as a medicinal product for serious skin problems than as a general cosmetic product, and mar-

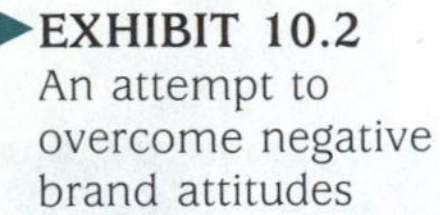
EXHIBIT 10.2
An attempt to overcome negative brand attitudes

keters knew the attitudes of nonusers would have to change if the brand was to increase sales. The company began advertising the brand as an everyday product that softens the skin (see Exhibit 10.2) and tried to put as many free samples in the hands of potential users as possible to prove that Lubriderm® was not greasy. One of the reasons that nonusers were open to the campaign is that their attitudes were weakly formed impressions that were not based on direct product experience.[9] But, weakly held attitudes also make it easier for competitors to convince consumers to switch brands.

When company or brand attitudes are strongly held, as with Rolls-Royce and Kmart, they are much more difficult to change.

6. *Attitudes held by consumers who have less confidence in their brand evaluations are easier to change.* Consumers who are unsure of their evaluation of a brand will be more receptive to the informational content of advertising and more subject to attitude change. Confusion about the criteria to use in evaluating a brand can cause consumers to lack self-confidence in making a decision. A number of years ago, the Carpet Institute hired a research firm to study the purchasing process for rugs and carpets. They concluded, "There is a great deal of confusion and misconception about the characteristics, features and termi-

nology in carpeting. Even the terms *rug* vs. *carpet,* the type of rug construction vs. company names are confused. It would seem on the surface that too wide a variety of features are pressed upon the housewife with her rather simple needs in floor covering."[10]

In a case like this, consumers would be receptive to a brand that provides information on a few key product attributes. The strategy would be to change beliefs about the product category and to capitalize on these attitudinal changes by associating them with the manufacturer's brand name.

7. ***Attitudes are easier to change when they are based on ambiguous information.*** Consumers faced with ambiguous claims about competitive products or with highly technical information they cannot assess seek clarifying information that may produce attitude change. When information is highly ambiguous, any clarifying information may cause a change in attitudes. One study found that high informational ambiguity consistently produced greater attitude change over a wide variety of products.[11]

http://www.apple.com/

In presenting a clear-cut message of the user-friendly nature of its machines, Apple was successful in introducing its personal computers to schools in the late 1970s. At this time, PCs were in a product category that first-time users found highly technical and ambiguous. For many students, the symbolism of the Apple was meant to alleviate uncertainty of using a PC.

ATTITUDE CHANGE BEFORE A PURCHASE

Given the frequency with which marketers attempt to change consumer brand and product attitudes and the difficulty they often have in doing so, a fuller understanding of the process of attitude change is warranted. Marketers can attempt to change consumer attitudes before they make a purchase to influence them to buy, or they can change attitudes after a purchase to reduce any postpurchase dissonance. The attitudinal theories described in the last chapter provide a basis for influencing both pre- and postpurchase attitudinal change.

Two types of theories influence attitude change strategies before a purchase: attitudinal theories and theories of information processing. The processing model with the greatest relevance for attitude change is Petty and Cacioppo's elaboration likelihood model (ELM). Whereas the attitudinal models provide strategic implications primarily for high-involvement conditions, ELM provides separate strategic implications for attitude change for low-involvement purchases.

Attitudinal Theories and Attitude Change

The attitudinal theories described earlier—Fishbein's multiattribute models, Katz's functional theory of attitudes, Sherif's social judgment theory, and Heider's balance theory—provide a good framework for considering strategies of attitude change before a purchase. Each model assumes a link between attitudes and behavior.

Multiattribute Models and Attitude Change

In Fishbein's multiattribute model, consumer beliefs about brands (the b_i component) and the value placed on these beliefs (the e_i component) influence the overall evaluation of the brand (A_o) which, in turn, influences behavioral intent (BI) and, ultimately, behavior (B).

On this basis, marketers can consider four strategies to influence behavior based on the multiattribute models:

1. Change the values placed on particular product attributes (a change in an e_i component).
2. Change beliefs (a change in a b_i component).
3. Change brand attitudes—that is, brand evaluations (a change in A_o) or attitudes toward buying the brand (a change in A_{act}).
4. Change behavioral intentions (a change in BI) or behavior (a change in B).

1. *Change the values placed on particular product attributes.* This strategy requires convincing consumers to reassess the value of a particular attribute—for example, convincing consumers that bad taste is a good quality in mouthwash. Any attempt to change the values placed on product attributes must rely on prior research showing that a certain segment of the market would be receptive to such a change. For example, the packaging component of many products is rarely the most important criterion in selection. Pringles potato chips were introduced in a new cylindrical container as a means of preserving freshness. Such a strategy can be successful only if the company has done prior research to demonstrate that the importance of the package could be increased through advertising an association between the package and freshness. However, Pringles had two strikes against it because most consumers rated its taste poorly. Procter & Gamble's advertising failed to increase the value consumers placed on freshness relative to taste. As a result, poor taste determined consumers' attitudes, and P&G had to reformulate and reintroduce the product.

Values based on deep-seated social and cultural norms are the most difficult to change. The values consumers place on the taste of a mouthwash or the freshness of potato chips may be changed, but it is doubtful that advertising could influence a change in values related to social attractiveness, security, or status.

2. *Change beliefs.* By far the most common strategy is one that attempts to change consumer beliefs about brands through product and advertising strategies. The important point is to ensure that the beliefs being changed will induce favorable changes in consumer brand evaluations and intention to buy. Quaker

http://www.QuakerOats.com/

▶EXHIBIT 10.3
Changing beliefs about rice cakes

Oats is trying to change consumer beliefs about Quaker Rice Cakes.[12] Typical comments from consumers in consumer research indicated that rice cakes taste like styrofoam or cardboard. The introduction of flavored rice cakes brought back some past users. However, Quaker had to attract nonusers who generally had negative attitudes. It did so with an effective campaign showing a foam cup with a piece bitten out and with the headline "If this is what you think of rice cakes, wait till you taste them now" (see Exhibit 10.3).

Marketers can change consumer beliefs by introducing new product attributes as well as by communicating the benefits of existing attributes. Nestlé convinced consumers that large, dark granules were associated with a richer and heftier tasting instant coffee. Similarly, Procter & Gamble convinced consumers that a blue detergent is stronger and cleaner than a white one.

Features that consumers take for granted cannot be the basis for attitude change. For example, advertising good taste for a ground coffee cannot be a basis for changing beliefs about a brand because consumers expect all ground roast coffees to have good taste. On the other hand, taste could be a determining attribute for decaffeinated coffee. Nestlé successfully changed beliefs that decaffeinated coffee was inferior in taste to other coffees by introducing Taster's Choice decaffeinated as an extension of its instant Taster's Choice brand. The name focused on taste. Also, since the brand was the first freeze-dried decaffeinated coffee, advertising was successful in convincing consumers of the brand's taste benefits. Most important, once consumers tried the coffee, most accepted the taste claim.

3. *Change brand attitudes (evaluations).* Marketers also try to influence consumer brand attitudes directly without specific reference to product attributes. This shortcut strategy may involve associating a positive feeling (affect) with product usage. As noted, this strategy can be used to try to establish a more hedonic perception of a brand, one based on emotion and fantasy. Philip Morris was successful in changing attitudes toward Miller High Life from a beer promoted to the elite based on the theme "the champagne of bottled beer" to a more emotion-laden theme depicting blue-collar beer drinkers in interactive sports or social situations. The music and the theme "Miller Time" changed attitudes in a more hedonic direction without referring to specific brand attributes.

As we will see in the next chapter, marketers are putting more emphasis on changing consumer attitudes through symbols and imagery to create uniqueness in increasingly standardized product categories.

4. *Change behavioral intentions or behavior.* Another change strategy is to induce consumers to purchase a brand that is not preferred—that is, to induce attitude-discrepant behavior. The assumption is that some inducement to try an unpreferred brand (possibly by lowering the price or by offering a deal or a coupon) may change consumers' brand attitude after the purchase to conform to their behavior.

For example, an individual may purchase a pain reliever with a 25-cents-off coupon. Assume there is little difference in effectiveness between the regular brand and the new brand. To justify the purchase, the consumer might decide that the new brand provides immediate relief and, therefore, decides to buy it again, even when the price returns to normal. This strategy makes use of the theory of cognitive dissonance. According to Festinger, the magnitude of such inducements to switch should not be large; otherwise, consumers could always say the only reason for a brand switch was the obvious price difference.[13] The tendency then would be to switch back to the regular brand when the price of the less-preferred brand returns to normal. However, if the difference is a relatively small price change, but one sufficient to cause a saving, consumers will have to find a reason other than price to justify the purchase.

Functional Theory and Attitude Change

Another model that has implications for strategies of consumer attitude change before a purchase is Katz's functional theory of attitudes.[14] As noted in the pre-

STRATEGIC APPLICATIONS OF CONSUMER BEHAVIOR

▶ Changing Beliefs: Can Gallo Be Seen as an Upscale Wine?

When they hear the name Gallo, most consumers think of inexpensive wines. In recent years, Ernest and Julio Gallo, founders of the winery, have been trying to change that. They have been moving upscale with the introduction of varietal wines—wines made from a specific variety of grapes. Gallo first started introducing varietals in the mid-1970s at $3 to $5 a bottle. Over time, it then introduced varietals at $5 to $7.

In 1992, they really began moving upscale, introducing a line at the $8 to $10 range with plans to go higher. In 1993, the Gallo name appeared on two new ultrapremium wines, a Chardonnay at $30 a bottle and a Cabernet Sauvignon at $60.

Wait a minute. The Gallo name on a $60 bottle of wine? The move to higher-priced wines has aroused much skepticism among both consumers and the trade. Further, the Gallo brothers are defying conventional wisdom by putting their name on the wine. Most marketing experts would have advised them to use a different name and keep the Gallo label for less expensive wines.

How is Gallo moving upscale? Primarily with a $20 million advertising budget for its higher-priced varietals. One commercial showed baby boomers drinking Gallo sauvignon blanc with their grilled salmon with the theme "It's time to change the way you think about Gallo." And, in a direct application of Heider's balance theory, Gallo hooked up with Waterford crystal for a 1992 holiday ad campaign. Hopefully, consumers with a positive image of Waterford will improve their attitudes toward Gallo to create balance, making it easier to accept Gallo's higher-priced wines. To reinforce this high-priced strategy, Gallo introduced Turning Leaf Chardonnay in 1995. By April 1996, Turning Leaf rocketed from 649th place to number 2 in the sales of Chardonnay wines.

Given the marketing savvy of the Gallo brothers, they should not be counted out in fighting the odds that Gallo can move its image upscale. Some of the skeptics are starting to become believers.

Sources: "Marketing: Grapes of Wrath," *The Wall Street Journal* (April 5, 1996), p. B1; "The Gallos Go for the Gold, and Away from the Jugs," *The New York Times* (November 22, 1992), p. F5; and "A Holiday with Waterford," *Brandweek* (November 30, 1992), p. 3.

vious chapter, Katz believes that attitudes serve four functions: utilitarian function, value-expressive function, ego-defensive function, and knowledge function. Marketing strategies can attempt to change attitudes serving each of these functions.

Changing Attitudes Through the Utilitarian Function. One way to influence a positive change in brand attitudes is to show how the product can solve a utilitarian goal consumers may not have previously considered. For example, Arm

& Hammer began advertising various utilitarian uses of baking soda in an attempt to increase sales. According to the Arm & Hammer package, the product:

- Soothes minor skin irritations (insect bites, sunburn, etc.).
- Absorbs carpet odors ("helps eliminate all types of odors in a safe, effective way").
- Is a pure, natural skin conditioner ("for a relaxing bath and soft, smooth feeling skin").
- Is an antacid (to alleviate heartburn, sour stomach, and/or acid indigestion).
- Is a bleach booster (when using liquid chlorine bleach, add baking soda).

This array of uses for a traditional cooking and baking product may induce a favorable change in consumers' attitudes toward the brand. These uses satisfy a set of utilitarian functions.

Changing Attitudes Through the Value-Expressive Function. Advertising that attempts to influence the value-expressive function deals with personal values that may be difficult to change. For example, advertising retirement communities by extolling the virtues of getting older would be a poor campaign. Rather, advertising should accept the predominant value orientation of youth and vigor by emphasizing the physical activities and facilities these communities provide to help one stay young. The clear principle is that advertising should accept deep-seated values rather than attempt to change them.

By advertising its benefits to baby boomers, Miami Beach, the epitome of retirement communities, attempted to change an image that only the elderly and infirm live there. The campaign did not persuade baby boomers and alienated older residents. The town council would have been wiser to continue to appeal to older residents but to use youthful themes more in accord with the personal values of potential retirees, rather than targeting a new segment with ingrained beliefs about the community.

Changing Attitudes Through the Ego-Defensive Function. Research has consistently shown that the more ego-defensive the attitude, the less subject it is to outside influence. The heavy drug user is likely to ignore information about the dangers of drug use. Avoiding painful information is an ego-defensive reaction. Advertising should accept and adapt to ego-defensive attitudes rather than try to change them. This means that rather than taking a negative approach by showing the dangers of drug use, advertising should instead show what steps the user can take to decrease usage. Such an approach would account for the user's ego-defensive reaction.

Changing Attitudes Through the Knowledge Function. The knowledge function organizes and classifies information, facilitating consumers' information-processing task. It is important for marketers to provide a clear and unambiguous positioning for their product to ensure favorable attitudes.

A good example of a clear and unambiguous positioning is Carnation Instant Breakfast. The company clearly positioned the product as a breakfast food directed to nutritionally oriented consumers who did not have time to prepare a traditional breakfast. The company provided information on the nutritional value and caloric content of the product. In so doing, it tried to counter Kellogg's successful strategy of establishing cereals as the primary source of breakfast nutrition for the adult market.

Had the product tried to reach a broader market by being positioned as a nutritional pick-me-up at any time of the day, it probably would have failed. Although this positioning may be directed to a greater number of usage situations, it would be more likely to confuse the consumer. Consumers could have seen the product as a breakfast food, a nutritional snack, or a dietary supplement. Such an ambiguous positioning might have led to a less-favorable evaluation of the brand.

Social Judgment Theory and Attitude Change

Sherif's theory of social judgment provides direct implications for strategies of attitude change.[15] Two strategies cited earlier—changing consumer beliefs about a brand or changing the values associated with these beliefs—require that consumers accept the advertising message. Sherif's theory predicts that if the change suggested by advertising is too extreme, consumers will reject the message because it will fall into their latitude of rejection. If the message suggests moderate changes, however, consumers will accept it because it is within their latitude of acceptance. Therefore, marketers may be more successful in inducing attitude change with small changes in beliefs over a longer period of time.

More involved consumers are less likely to accept messages proposing a change in beliefs or values. However, consumers are not highly involved with most product categories. Therefore, consumers are more likely to accept advertising suggesting moderate changes in beliefs or values.

http://www.clubmed.com/

Club Med, the worldwide vacation resort firm, attempted to change its image from a firm running resorts for swinging singles to one that also offered married couples and families a carefree environment. It opened resorts targeted to older, more conservative vacationers and advertised accordingly.[16] The target group accepted the change because a Club Med for married couples and vacationers was within their latitude of acceptance. More importantly, the appeals did not fall into the latitude of rejection for swinging singles, as Club Med still ran resorts and ads positioned to this group.

Some evidence suggests that messages attempting to change consumer beliefs and values that are extreme, but not extreme enough to bring about rejection of the message, may create curiosity and lead to product trial.[17] Introducing a high-styled refrigerator (different color and design, possibly even different shape) would represent an extreme change in beliefs for a standard product. However, the change may not be extreme enough to be rejected outright, especially as it does not threaten consumers' basic values or self-identification. An arousal of curiosity, a visit to a store to see the product, and, in some cases, a purchase may result.

Heider's Balance Theory

Heider's balance theory also provides direct implications for attitude change. Balance theory says that attitudes will change to avoid conflict between beliefs and evaluations.[18] Marketers implicitly use balance theory to create attitudinal conflicts in the hope that the resultant change in consumer brand attitudes will be positive. Thus, Gallo's link to Waterford crystal created conflict because of the luxury image of Waterford and the economy image of Gallo. Balance theory would predict that either Waterford's image will suffer because of the linkage or Gallo's image will improve. Both Waterford and Gallo obviously believed the latter to be more likely than the former.

The implication in balance theory is that when attitudes conflict, they are easier to change because of consumers' desire for balance. For example, many consumers' attitudes toward environmental control and toward consumption of certain products are in conflict. An individual may have a positive attitude toward disposable diapers but also be strongly in favor of pollution control. According to Heider, such imbalance will produce tension and lead to a change in one or both attitudes. The consumer may realize that disposable diapers are not fully biodegradable. As a result, the consumer's attitude toward disposable diapers will become more negative. On the other hand, the consumer may maintain a positive attitude toward disposable diapers and decrease his or her emphasis on the environment. In either case, attitudes about disposable diapers and environmental protection have to be modified to achieve balance.

Processing Models and Attitude Change: The Elaboration Likelihood Model

The elaboration likelihood model (ELM) described in Chapter 5 is another theory with strategic implications for attitude change.[19] It states that involved consumers process information through a "central route" in which message cues are more likely to be processed, whereas uninvolved consumers use a more peripheral route in which nonmessage cues are more likely to be processed. As a result, in high-involvement conditions, attitude change can best be accomplished through advertising that conveys product benefits and information on performance. In low-involvement conditions, attitude change can best be accomplished through the use of spokespersons and symbols attached to the product. Because of his likable image that appeals to kids, Bill Cosby was an effective spokesperson for Jell-O Pudding Pops (a low-involvement product). He had little to say about product attributes. All he had to do was appear on TV with a Pudding Pop in his hand.

An important extension of ELM is a consideration of the thoughts consumers have when they process marketing stimuli such as advertisements or sales promotions (referred to as **cognitive responses**).[20] According to cognitive response research, when consumers are involved, they produce thoughts that are more relevant to the message. For example, a nutritionally oriented consumer who becomes aware of advertising citing products with Olestra, the new fat substitute introduced by P&G in 1996, may think "Olestra is a good substitute for saturated fats," or "The FDA approved Olestra so it must be safe." In both cases, these thoughts support the advertising; that is, they are **support arguments.** The consumer might also think, "I have my doubts about this product. No one knows whether it might cause side effects." This would represent a **counterargument** to the advertised claim.

The existence of both support arguments and counterarguments indicates that the consumer is actively processing the ad's information in a high-involvement context. The impact of the ad on the consumer will depend not only on the information in the ad, but also on the interaction between the consumer's thoughts and the ad's message.

In low-involvement situations, when consumers process information, they are likely to react with thoughts that are more related to peripheral cues than to the message itself.[21] One such peripheral cue is the source of the message. Less involved consumers might be more likely to reflect on the motives of the advertiser or on less important components of the ad such as the background or the voice of a spokesperson. For example, a consumer not particularly concerned about fat content in foods seeing the ad for Olestra might react more to the source than to the message. The consumer might think, "P&G sponsored this ad and I like their products." This is an example of **source bolstering.** On the other hand, the consumer might react by thinking, "This ad is sponsored by a company trying to sell the product, so why should I believe its claim?" This would be an example of **source derogation.**

Support arguments and counterarguments, therefore, are cognitive responses to marketing stimuli more likely to occur in high-involvement situations; source bolstering and derogation are cognitive responses more likely to occur in low-involvement situations.

Cognitive Responses and Attitude Change in High-Involvement Processing

Consumers involved with the nutritional content of food will pay more attention to ads citing Olestra. Since involved consumers are more likely to introduce their own thoughts (support arguments or counterarguments) when evaluating ads, there is a greater likelihood that these message-related thoughts will influence beliefs and attitudes about the fat substitute.

To create more positive attitudes, advertisers must discourage counterarguments and promote support arguments. One way to do this is suggested by **inoculation theory,**[22] which proposes that marketers can "inoculate" consumers against negative thoughts about a product by introducing messages that anticipate these negative thoughts and refute them. Such an approach is known as http://www.olean.com/

two-sided refutational advertising. For example, a spokesperson for Olestra in a commercial might say, "You might think products with Olestra cannot taste as good because Olestra is an artificial ingredient. [This portion of the commercial anticipates negative reactions.] "Well, you have a surprise coming because Olestra does not affect taste. *And* it is healthier for you because it has no saturated fats." [This portion is the refutation.] Such an approach might be successful in changing attitudes for involving products. (Two-sided advertising will be considered further in the next chapter when we discuss marketing communications.)

Cognitive Responses and Attitude Change in Low-Involvement Processing

Marketers can also change consumer attitudes by influencing cognitive responses in low-involvement conditions. Just as marketers will attempt to discourage counterarguments and encourage support arguments for involved consumers, they will seek to discourage source derogation and encourage source bolstering for uninvolved consumers.

Two strategies designed to discourage source derogation are to increase the attractiveness of the source and to increase its credibility. If consumers are not involved, an effective way to draw attention to the ad is through an attractive and likable spokesperson. Bill Cosby was used as a spokesperson for Pudding Pops because of his attractiveness, not because of any expertise he had regarding the product. The second strategy to discourage source derogation is to increase the credibility of the source.[23] A testimonial from the American Dental Association for the cavity prevention properties of fluoride in Crest made it the leading toothpaste brand. Expert spokespersons, such as Michael Jordan for Nike basketball sneakers, also enhance the credibility of an ad.

http://www.pg.com/
http://www.nike.com/

Of the two strategies, increasing source attractiveness is more likely to change attitudes for uninvolved consumers because they may not consider product expertise that important in a category for which brand evaluation is minimal. Not surprisingly, marketers use spokespersons to increase attractiveness for less involving products like Pudding Pops, whereas they use experts for more involving products like athletic shoes.

ATTITUDE CHANGE AFTER A PURCHASE

Marketers may seek to change consumer brand attitudes after as well as before a purchase. Such a strategy may attempt to counter competitive advertising that creates doubts in consumers' minds about the purchase, or it may attempt to counteract negative experiences with the product. Three theories provide strategy implications for attitude change after the purchase: dissonance theory, attribution theory, and the theory of passive learning. These theories are briefly reviewed here within the context of attitude change strategies.

Dissonance Theory

Dissonance theory suggests that marketers should seek to reduce dissonance by supplying consumers with positive information about the brand after the purchase. Runyon cites five strategies to provide supporting information after the purchase and, thus, to reduce dissonance:

1. Provide additional product information and suggestions for product care and maintenance through brochures or advertising.
2. Provide warranties and guarantees to reduce postpurchase doubt.
3. Ensure good service and immediate follow-up on complaints to provide postpurchase support.
4. Advertise reliable product quality and performance to reassure recent purchasers of product satisfaction.
5. Follow up after the purchase with direct contacts to make sure the customer understands how to use the product and to ensure satisfaction.[24] A study by Hunt showed that such postpurchase reassurances from a seller were effective in reducing consumer dissonance after purchase of a refrigerator.[25]

All of these strategies are relevant for high-risk, high-involvement product categories. They are designed to change consumer attitudes toward the product by reducing postpurchase doubts.

Attribution Theory

Attribution theory states that consumers seek to determine causes (or attributions) for events, often after the fact.[26] A consumer can attribute product performance to his or her choice (I made a very economical purchase) or to the product (This brand is a good value for the money).

Attribution theory implies that advertisers should give consumers positive reasons for the purchase after they have bought the product. For example, a consumer buys a brand of coffee on sale and attributes the purchase to the fact that the brand is cheaper. Such an attribution is unlikely to win any long-term converts to the brand. However, if the manufacturer's advertising could convince the consumer that the brand makes a richer, heftier brew, the consumer is likely to buy again. The important point is that the manufacturer is trying to convince the consumer of the claim after the purchase.

Based on attribution theory, a marketing strategy for low-involvement products is to demonstrate potentially significant product differences that consumers can use as a postpurchase rationale for having purchased. Such differences give consumers a reason for buying again. Marketers cannot rely solely on price promotions to influence consumers to buy uninvolving products. They must use advertising to provide a nonprice rationale to buy the same brand again.

Passive Learning

Krugman's passive learning theory states that consumers learn about brands with little involvement and purchase with little evaluation of alternative brands.[27] Attitudes are more likely to be formed after, rather than before, a purchase.

Krugman's theory is most relevant for developing strategies to increase the level of consumer involvement after the purchase. Marketers seek to increase involvement with their brand because a higher level of commitment means that true, rather than spurious, brand loyalty is more likely to result. In Chapter 5, we cited the following strategies for increasing involvement:

1. Link the product to an involving issue.
2. Link the product to an involving personal situation.
3. Link the product to involving advertising.
4. Change the importance of product benefits.
5. Introduce an important characteristic in the product.

The first three strategies cited are illustrated in the Kmart ad discussed at the beginning of this chapter. Showing a working woman relishing a relaxing moment between work and family is an involving issue, an involving personal situation, and an involving ad for the target segment. Any increase in involvement with Kmart should result in a more favorable attitude toward the store. As in dissonance and attribution theories, such a favorable shift in attitude often follows behavior.

TYPES OF STRATEGIES FOR ATTITUDE REINFORCEMENT AND CHANGE

Given the preceding principles of attitude change, we can now cite various types of strategies that serve either to reinforce existing attitudes or to change them.

Strategies to Reinforce Attitudes

Marketers can use **reinforcement strategies** to:

1. Reinforce positive attitudes among existing users.
2. Attract new users to an existing brand.
3. Attract new users to a new brand.

In each of these strategies, marketers are reinforcing existing attitudes rather than attempting to change them.

Reinforcing Existing Users Through Advertising

Companies use advertising to maintain users' positive attitudes toward their products. In this way, companies are ensuring the loyalty of their core users. Most advertising by Campbell's Soup is directed to increasing the amount of soup consumed by existing consumers. Because of its dominant position in the

http://www.cambellsoup.com/

canned soup market, Campbell's most effective strategy is to reinforce the attitudes of existing users rather than to try to change the attitudes of nonusers.

In the past, Campbell tried to increase soup consumption by touting the benefits of canned soup with themes such as "Soup for Lunch" and "Soup for One." With nearly an 80 percent share of the canned soup market, increasing canned soup consumption meant increasing Campbell's sales. However, as competition from dried soup cut into Campbell's sales and the market became more value-oriented, simple appeals to eat more soup began to wear thin. So in the early 1990s, Campbell began advertising individual soups to specific targets, often on a regional basis—for example, nacho cheese soup targeted to the Southwest, Creole soup to southern markets, and red bean soup to Hispanic markets.[28] The focus on existing users remains, but the emphasis has shifted from advertising the product category to advertising individual soup flavors.

Reinforcing Existing Users Through Relationship Marketing

Companies have increasingly recognized the value of maintaining an ongoing bond with their customers by turning to what has been called relationship marketing. **Relationship marketing** is a company's effort to build an enduring relationship with each of its customers on a one-on-one basis. Relationship marketing involves an attempt to communicate with individual customers through direct mail, contacts by company representatives, or the Internet.

The key is ongoing communications to maintain positive attitudes toward the company. A senior marketing manager at Sears makes this point:

> You can't just talk with customers once and tell them they're special. You have to constantly reinforce that with communications and privileges. Our rule-of-thumb is that it takes between six and eight communications during the year.[29]

Nestlé has become a key player in the baby food market in France by utilizing relationship marketing. It maintains a database of 220,000 new mothers. Each person on the list receives a direct-mail solicitation and a reply card. Based on the replies, Nestlé sends targeted mailings personalized with the first name of the baby at key stages in the child's life. Each mailing includes sample products. The personalized campaign has led the company to capture a 43 percent share of the baby food market in France, even though it is being outspent seven to one in advertising by its leading rival.[30]

Attracting New Users to Existing Products

Management will attract new users to its existing products by showing that they can better deliver desired benefits than can other alternatives. When Gillette introduced the Sensor razor in 1990, it turned out to be the most successful new product introduction in Gillette's history. But the company did not rest on its laurels. It sought to extend positive brand attitudes for Gillette to other market segments. Women were an obvious extension of the Sensor franchise since they

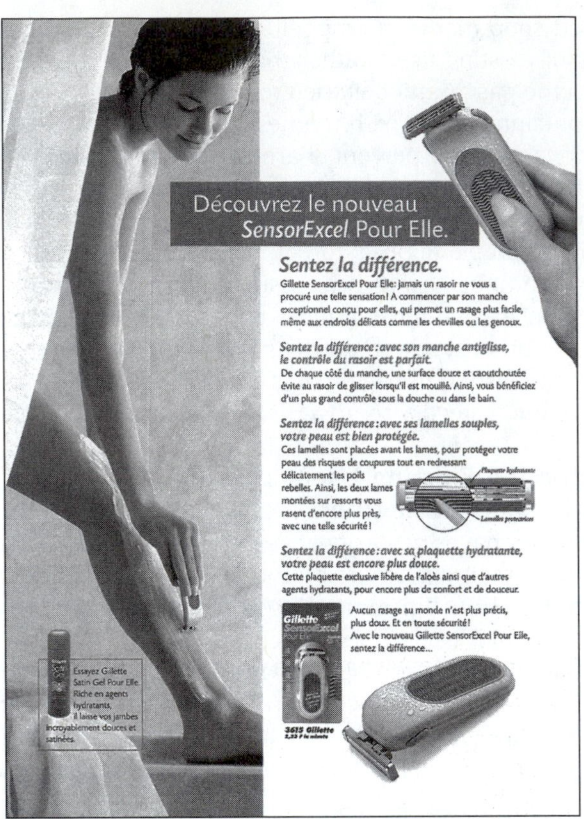

EXHIBIT 10.4
Targeting an existing product to a new market: Sensor for women

represent 29 percent of all razor sales. In 1992, Gillette introduced Sensor for Women on a worldwide basis (see Exhibit 10.4). The flat, wafer-shaped handle and firm grip made it easier for women to shave in the shower. It only took six months for Sensor for Women to be the leading women's shaving product in the country.[31]

Attracting New Users to New Products

Marketers seek opportunities to meet the needs of new and emerging markets. In these cases, the intent is not so much to reinforce existing attitudes but to establish new ones. For example, Motorola's introduction of cellular telephones in the mid-1980s met the need for mobile communications in the business market. Motorola was instrumental in developing in-car and walk-around (hand-held) cellular telephones as well as the regional cells that ensure decreased interference compared to regular portable and car telephones. Motorola's link with mobile communications in customers' minds made it easy for the company to establish positive attitudes toward a new product, cellular telephones.

http://www.mot.com/

Let us consider how Motorola might have established positive attitudes toward this new product by taking the example of the business communications market. Motorola first determines the benefits that managers seek in business communications. It develops a vocabulary of communications benefits (precision, speed, service, walk-around communications, in-car communications, privacy, and so on), then surveys business people responsible for communications and asks them what benefits they emphasize most.

On this basis, Motorola identifies three benefit segments, shown in Figure 10.1. One emphasizes interference-free communications while driving. This group is composed of customers in sales and service-related businesses. Another group emphasizes interference-free walk-around communications. This group is composed primarily of doctors and other medical professionals. A third group emphasizes the greater privacy portable communications affords. This group is composed primarily of corporate executives.

Motorola then produces a few prototype cellular telephones and asks key business people responsible for communications to try the prototype and then rate it in relation to other modes of communication. The perceptual map in Figure 10.2 shows how business people rate the various communications modes. Mail is seen as providing documentation and interference-free communications; fax transmissions as providing speed and precision; and the telephone as providing economy and service. The cellular telephone is associated with the benefits of in-car and walk-around mobile communications.

The circles show what benefits three key segments emphasize in accordance with Figure 10.1. On this basis, the key targets are salespeople for in-car communications and doctors for walk-around communications. Figure 10.2 shows that cellular telephones are seen as delivering the key benefits desired by these two target segments.

FIGURE 10.1
Benefit segments in the cellular telephone market

	Salespeople	**Service Personnel**	**Doctors/ Medical Personnel**	**Corporate Executives**
In-Car Mobile Communications	*	* *		
Walk-Around Mobile Communications			*	
Privacy				*

*** = Primary market**
*** * = Secondary market**

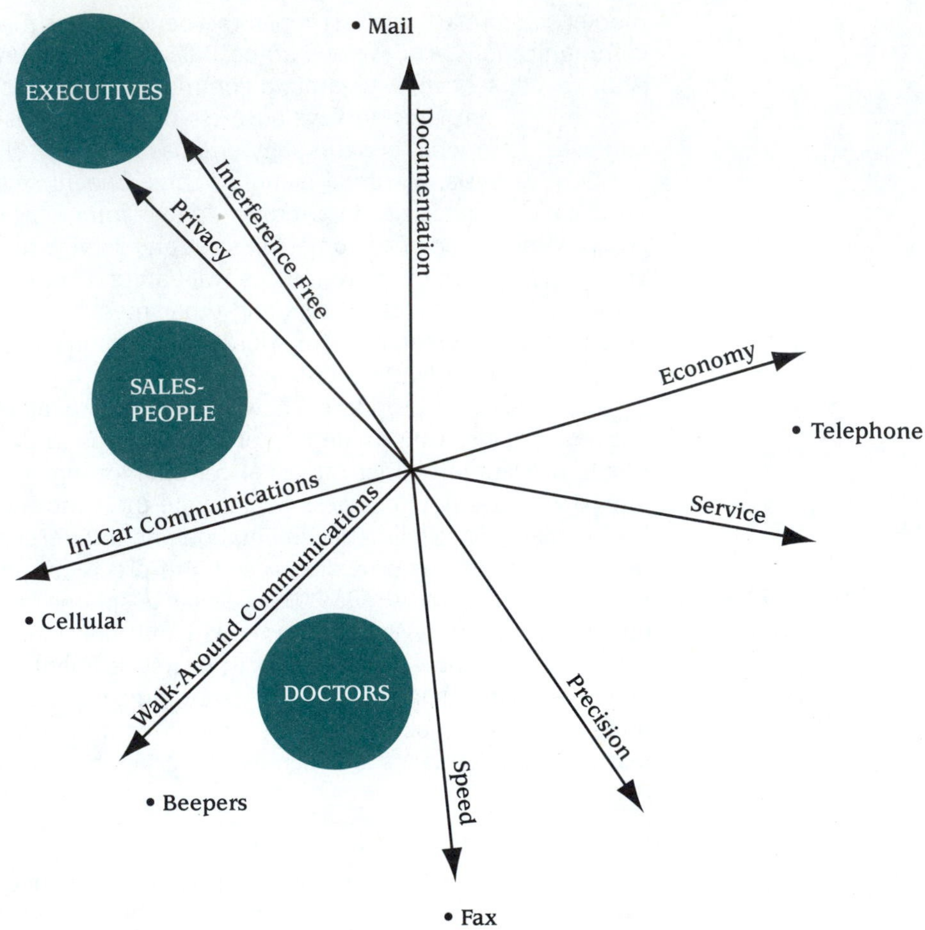

FIGURE 10.2 Beliefs regarding alternative communications modes

Strategies to Change Attitudes

Strategies that attempt to change consumer attitudes generally require repositioning an existing brand, that is, changing the set of attributes and benefits communicated to consumers to influence them to buy. Marketers can direct such repositioning strategies to existing users to improve the brand's image or target them to nonusers to influence them to switch to the brand.

Changing Attitudes of Existing Users

Companies faced with declining sales often attempt to reposition their offerings to existing users. Arrow Shirts has been successful in repositioning itself. The company's image as a purveyor of conservative white shirts was restricting sales in an increasingly fashion-oriented market; so, Arrow expanded its offerings with a wider line of sports shirts and casual wear. Its innovative campaign to change its image is shown in Exhibit 10.5.

Very often, attempts at repositioning to reverse downward demand trends are undertaken on an industrywide basis through a cooperative advertising effort. The campaign of the National Fluid Milk Processor Promotion Board in Exhibit 10.1 is an example. The industry has been successful in positioning milk as the fitness drink of the 1990s because its appeals conform to the current emphasis on health and nutrition.

►EXHIBIT 10.5
Changing attitudes to conform to an expanded product line

In the past, cooperative campaigns to reverse downward demand trends were run for men's hats and for sterling silverware. Both campaigns failed because they were swimming against, rather than with, the consumer tide. The campaign for men's hats tried to bring back a conservative look that contradicted the trend toward youth and vigor. The campaign for sterling silverware failed because it tried to bring back the custom of giving sterling silverware as a wedding present. The campaign contradicted the trend toward greater informality.

Changing Attitudes of Nonusers

http://www.att.com/

In an attempt to appeal to new segments of the market, companies often attempt to change attitudes among nonusers. Often these changes are necessary for the company to ensure future sales. We saw that AT&T is trying to change its image among younger consumers who are using alternative services. Kmart is having difficulty changing its image among more fashion-oriented, affluent working women. In both cases, younger consumers view these companies as conservative and old-fashioned.

By appealing to married couples and families, Club Med was successful in changing the attitude that the resort chain is for swinging singles. Avon is changing attitudes toward its offerings by advertising higher-priced lines for more affluent women.

SOCIETAL APPLICATIONS OF ATTITUDE CHANGE

So far, we have discussed changes in consumer attitudes regarding brands and companies. Marketing also has a role in changing consumer attitudes toward social issues. An example is the advertising campaign cited in Chapter 6 (Exhibit 6.5) to correct the many misconceptions about AIDS. The campaign, sponsored by the U.S. Department of Health, was designed to eliminate some of the fears about contracting AIDS and, in so doing, to encourage the public to become less fearful of and more tolerant toward those who have contracted the disease.

Changing attitudes toward social issues such as AIDS is a difficult task because such attitudes are almost always deep-seated. Very often people reject the message because it conflicts with strongly held beliefs. Another factor creating difficulty is that such attempts are generally public-service campaigns that rely on free media time. As such, TV time is relegated to off-peak hours and exposure is minimal.

There have been some successes in changing consumer attitudes through marketing communications. Both the American Cancer Society and the American Heart Association have used advertising to increase awareness of the risks of smoking. Such advertising has been successful over the years in a supportive role in conjunction with information from government sources (for example, the Surgeon General's Office).

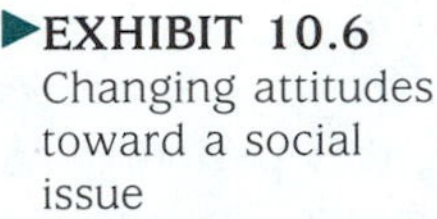

EXHIBIT 10.6
Changing attitudes toward a social issue

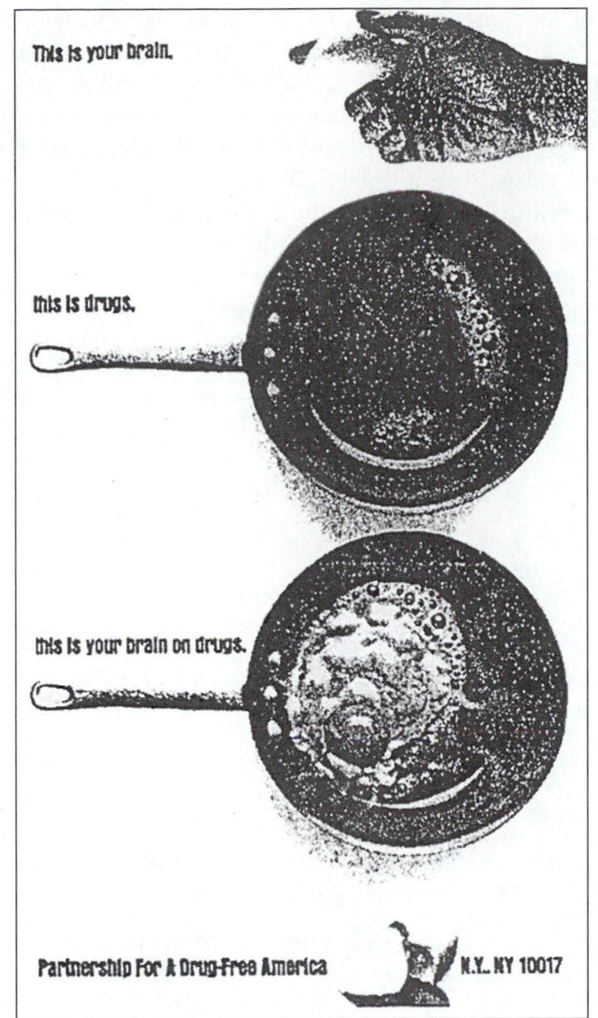

One of the most successful campaigns to change attitudes toward a social issue is the Partnership for a Drug-Free America. As noted, it is composed of advertising agencies and media companies that want to reduce drug use. The target is nonusers and occasional drug users. If attitudes toward drug use can be changed among this broad-based group, then peer group and family pressure might discourage drug use among heavier users.[32]

Unlike other social issue campaigns, this one was intensive. Some 300 ads were created for all the major media and run without charge (see Exhibit 10.6). Had a product been advertised, the equivalent expenditures would have been $900 million. Because of this intensive effort, the campaign has been highly successful. In markets where the ads were run most frequently, more teens said there is a greater risk in using marijuana and more preteens spoke to teachers about drugs. Further, the use of cocaine went down during this period.[33] Although these changes cannot be solely attributed to the campaign, the greater improvement in attitudes and decreased use in markets with more advertising suggest the ads were highly effective.

The efforts of the consortium of companies making up the Partnership shows that business can play a constructive role in changing consumer attitudes toward social issues. Similarly, the campaign the Department of Health ran regarding AIDS shows that government also has a role in such attitude change. Obviously, business, government, and charitable agencies can do more on a host of social issues, from environmental protection to health care.

SUMMARY

This chapter described principles of attitude reinforcement and change. Attitudes are easier to change when they are weakly held, when consumers are not involved with the product, when consumers have little confidence in evaluating the brand, and when information is ambiguous. Certain components of attitudes are easier to change: Beliefs are easier to change than desired benefits, and beliefs are easier to change than evaluations of the brand.

Various attitudinal theories were described as a basis for changing consumer attitudes before and after a purchase. The attitudinal theories most relevant for changing attitudes before a purchase are multiattribute models, Katz's functional theory of attitudes, Sherif's social judgment theory, Heider's balance theory, and the elaboration likelihood model. Multiattribute models suggest changing desired benefits, beliefs about a brand, the overall evaluation of the brand, or behavior directly without attempting to change attitudes. Functional theory provides guidelines for strategies to change utilitarian, value-expressive, and ego-defensive attitudes and to change attitudes by providing knowledge. Social judgment theory suggests that attitude change should take place within consumers' latitude of acceptance. Balance theory says that attitudes change to avoid conflict between beliefs and evaluations.

The elaboration likelihood model distinguishes attitude change in high- and low-involvement conditions. It suggests using message cues to influence consumer attitudes in high-involvement situations and peripheral cues such as use of spokespersons or the layout of an ad to change attitudes in low-involvement conditions.

Marketers may also seek to change consumer attitudes toward a brand after a purchase. Three theories provide strategic guidelines. Dissonance theory suggests that, to reduce dissonance, advertisers should provide consumers with positive information after they purchase. Attribution theory suggests that marketers supply consumers with a reason for purchasing after the fact. The theory of passive learning suggests that inertia can be translated into brand loyalty by increasing consumers' commitment to the brand.

The chapter also discussed various strategies to reinforce or change consumer attitudes. Strategies to reinforce consumer attitudes are designed to:

- Reinforce positive attitudes among existing users.
- Attract new users to existing products.
- Attract new users to new products.

Strategies to change attitudes are designed to reposition products to strengthen the brand among existing users or to attract new segments.

The chapter concluded by considering attitude change for social issues. Marketing has an important role in changing consumer attitudes toward key issues such as preventive health care, perceptions of AIDS, smoking, and environmental protection.

In the next chapter, we consider marketing communications as a means of influencing consumer perceptions and attitudes.

QUESTIONS

1. Why is it easier to implement strategies that reinforce rather than change attitudes?
2. Which of the following companies might find it most difficult to change consumers' attitudes toward its products and why?
   - Manufacturer of breakfast cereals trying to attract the adult market.
   - Specialty retailer introducing a line of designer clothes.
   - Low-priced, no-frills airline that decides to expand its routes, add services, and increase fares.
   - Fast-food outlet that decides to open a chain of low-priced restaurants.
3. Which of the companies cited in Question 2 do you think would find it easiest to change consumer attitudes? Why?
4. What problems might the Department of Transportation face in mounting an advertising campaign to influence people to switch from automobiles to mass transit?
5. When Cadillac introduced a medium-sized car, it could have developed a reinforcement or a change strategy in communicating this basic change in its line. What focus could advertising have taken in following (a) a reinforcement strategy and (b) a change strategy?
6. A manufacturer of high-priced stereo components finds that attitudes toward the company's line of products are very positive, but many stereo purchasers are uncertain of the criteria to use in selecting components and, therefore, reduce risk by buying the lowest-priced or the best-known brand. The company would like to increase consumers' confidence in the purchase process. By doing so, it believes it will increase the likelihood consumers will buy its products. What strategies can the company use to increase consumers' self-confidence in the purchasing process?
7. Consider this statement: "Attitudes are easier to change when there is a low level of ego involvement." In view of this statement, why might it be particularly hard to change attitudes toward a consumer's regular perfume, baby food, and clothing store?
8. Values based on deep-seated social and cultural norms are the most difficult to change. Can you cite examples of advertising campaigns that have attempted to change such deep-seated norms? Were they successful? Why or why not?
9. What are the differences among (a) dissonance theory, (b) attribution theory, and (c) the theory of passive learning in explaining attitude change after a purchase?
10. A producer of ready-to-eat cereals conducts a survey and finds that consumers who rate the company's brand high on nutrition are more likely to buy it. These consumers tend to be younger and more affluent. The advertising manager decides to direct a major portion of the advertising budget to nonusers (older, less affluent consumers) to try to convince them of the cereal's nutritional content. The manager reasons there will be a higher payoff in attempting to change attitudes of nonusers than in reinforcing attitudes of users. What are the pros and cons of this argument?
11. If Motorola found that mobile communication was a relatively unimportant attribute of cellular phones, one option would be to try to change benefit criteria by demonstrating the importance of mobile communication to businesses through an advertising campaign.
    - What are the pros and cons of such a strategy?
    - Under what circumstances is such a strategy most likely to succeed?
12. What role can marketing play in changing consumer attitudes toward social issues? Why are such attempts more difficult than changing attitudes for products and brands?

RESEARCH ASSIGNMENTS

1. Companies sometimes use the Internet for one-way communication and at other times to obtain feedback. Give examples of sites where the goal is to obtain feedback from consumers. Choose one of the sites and provide feedback.
   - Was this a one-time communication or did you have ongoing dialogue with the company?
   - Did the company respond directly to you?
   - Do you know if or how your feedback was used?

   Repeat this process with another company and compare the experiences.

2. Select a frequently purchased product (such as soft drinks, coffee, detergents) for study. Select a sample of about 100 product users.
   a. Develop a description of a fictitious brand and give it to consumers. The description should come from a neutral source such as a government agency.
   b. Ask the consumer to rate the brand from poor to excellent.
   c. Split the sample into three groups:
      - Group 1 receives an ad reinforcing the prior brand description (a reinforcement strategy).
      - Group 2 receives an ad meant to change beliefs about the brand ("Brand X is much tastier or much more effective than previously described").
      - Group 3 receives an ad attempting to change values (for example, an ad saying brands with low sudsing ability are more effective).
   d. Ask consumers to rate the brand again after they see one of these three ads.

   If a reinforcement strategy is more effective, one would expect the first ad to produce the most positive attitudes. Furthermore, of the two change strategies, one would expect the ad attempting to change beliefs to produce more positive effects than the ad attempting to change values. Do your findings conform to these expectations?
3. Principles of attitude change suggest that attitudes are easier to change when consumers are less confident in their evaluations of a brand. Pick a product category and ask consumers to rate three of the leading brands on (a) an overall basis and (b) a vocabulary of product attributes. In addition, ask consumers to (c) rate their degree of confidence in making judgments about brands in the category and (d) rate the degree to which they think the product is important to them. Present consumers with ads for each of the three brands in a dummy magazine format. Have consumers rate the brands once again on an overall basis and on the vocabulary of product attributes.
   - Do overall brand ratings for those consumers who have less confidence in their brand evaluations shift more than those of consumers who have a greater degree of confidence?
   - Do ratings shift in the direction of the advertised claims?
   - Attitude theory also suggests that those who rate the product category as less important are more likely to change attitudes. Do your findings support this?
4. Marketers sometimes seek to induce a behavior change without appeals to attitudes by offering brands at a lower price. The theory of cognitive dissonance would predict that if the consumer bought a brand other than the regular brand at a much lower price, the attitude toward the brand would be more negative than if the brand were bought at a price only slightly lower than the regular brand.
   - Select a heavily dealed product category such as coffee, paper towels, or detergents. Identify a sample of consumers who recently bought a brand other than their regular brand on a price deal or by coupon. Determine attitudes for the brand purchased.
   - Do your data confirm the hypothesis that the greater the price differential between the regular and the dealed brand, the more negative the attitude toward the brand purchased on deal?

INFLUENCING ATTITUDES THROUGH MARKETING COMMUNICATIONS

Chapter 11

MCDONALD'S COMMUNICATES BENEFITS WHILE BURGER KING FLOUNDERS

In the last four chapters, we considered how consumers' attitudes and perceptions influence their behavior. Marketers attempt to influence consumers through communications—primarily advertising, sales promotions, personal selling, and packaging. In this chapter, we will

- Describe a marketing communications model.
- Discuss the key components of this model, namely the source of the message, the message itself, and the media used to communicate it.
- Describe the role of the consumer in evaluating marketing communications.
- Consider societal and ethical implications of the process of marketing communications.

Marketing communications have two primary purposes, to inform and to persuade: to inform consumers of product attributes and benefits and of new product introductions; to persuade them to buy. Without information, consumers cannot act.

Through marketing communications, consumers learn about new products, the prices and availability of existing products, and the characteristics of alternative brands. But marketing communications are clearly partisan in favoring the advertised brand, so influencing consumers is a consistent objective. As a result, the marketers' *communication* of information and influence and consumers' *receipt* of marketing information are key elements in the study of consumer behavior.

To be effective, marketing communications must convey how products and services can meet consumer needs. The one constant in effective communication is conveying product benefits. Product benefits can be communicated through words, symbols, and imagery. As we have seen before, the hedonic or utilitarian nature of a product is likely to influence the communication approach, with symbols and imagery more likely to dominate when consumers are motivated to buy based on pleasure and fantasy.

http://www.mcdonalds.com/

A good example of the effects of marketing communications is McDonald's promotional strategy. Consumers have associated McDonald's symbols such as the golden arches and the Ronald McDonald character with food, fun, and family values. Past campaigns, such as "You deserve a break today" showing a family enjoying a Big Mac, have reinforced this image. McDonald's communication prowess is partly a function of a $1 billion promotional budget that eclipses those of its competitors.[1] However, it is also a function of McDonald's ability to change its message to prevent it from becoming stale.

In the mid-1980s, the company quickly shifted from a lackluster "McDonald's and You" advertising campaign to a more effective and upbeat "It's a good time for the great taste of McDonald's." The theme associated McDonald's with fun and pleasure. Then, with the advent of a recession in 1990, the company switched to a more utilitarian emphasis on economy with the theme "Good Food, Good Value." In 1995, it returned to a hedonic theme with a takeoff on its classic "You deserve a break today." The new slogan, "Have you had your break today," implies that a break no longer needs to be deserved, it is a given. Going to McDonald's should now be guilt-free. As one advertising expert put it, the campaign gives consumers "a waiver of dietary correctness."[2]

McDonald's communications strategy does not rely solely on advertising. Sales promotions such as sweepstakes, contests, and coupons support the benefits that advertising conveys. For example, McDonald's used a Monopoly game promotion that gave away $40 million in prizes based on "deeds" to Monopoly board locations. And in 1995, McDonald's launched its first interactive site on America Online called McFamily. The site is designed to give parenting advice and to obtain data from participants so they can be reached for future promotions.[3]

http://www.burgerking.com/

In contrast to McDonald's, Burger King has had trouble staying on track and communicating product benefits. The company floundered in the mid-1980s with a "Search for Herb" campaign, a $40 million fiasco based on a search for a mythical figure called Herb who had never tasted a Whopper. The focus on

Herb as a balding eccentric in glasses, white socks, and gaudy plaids did not get any particular message across regarding the benefits of visiting a Burger King rather than a McDonald's. Burger King then changed its slogan to "Sometimes you've got to break the rules." Again, customers could not understand what benefits the slogan was trying to convey. One Burger King franchisee asked, "Are we telling kids to go out and buy drugs?"[4]

Having gone through eight campaigns since 1976, Burger King finally hit on a campaign in 1991 that communicated a consistent benefits-oriented message, "Your way. Right away." The slogan communicated satisfaction and quick service at Burger King outlets. To reinforce the message, the company began touting value-oriented sales promotions in a "Your Way" in-store campaign. But in 1995, the company again seemed to have lost its way with a bland campaign, "Get Your Burger's Worth." The campaign "eavesdropped" on people citing the product and price benefits of Burger King, but fell flat on emotion.[5] Whereas Burger King's campaign was focusing on people's minds, McDonald's, with a market share over twice that of Burger King's, seems to be the winner in the contest over people's hearts.

MARKETING COMMUNICATIONS PROCESS

The primary means of marketing communications are advertising, personal selling, and sales promotions. We will be focusing mostly on advertising in this chapter. Regarding other components of marketing communications, we considered in-store sales promotional effects in Chapters 3 and 5 and will consider salesperson influences in Chapter 18.

Advertising is one of the most important forms of marketing communications. Yearly advertising expenditures in the United States are over $200 billion and are expected to be close to $500 billion by the turn of the century.

A detailed model of marketing communications is presented in Figure 11.1. There are five components in any communications process:

1. A source of the message that develops communications objectives and identifies a target for its communications. Marketing organizations develop objectives for their advertising and promotional campaigns and target these campaigns to defined target segments.
2. A process of ***encoding,*** which requires translating these objectives into a message. Advertising agencies develop messages that are encoded into ads. Salespeople encode messages in developing a sales presentation for customers.
3. ***Transmission*** of the message through media designed to reach the intended audience. Transmission of marketing communications might involve mass media, word-of-mouth communications from salespeople, or direct-mail literature sent to targeted households.

FIGURE 11.1
The marketing communications process

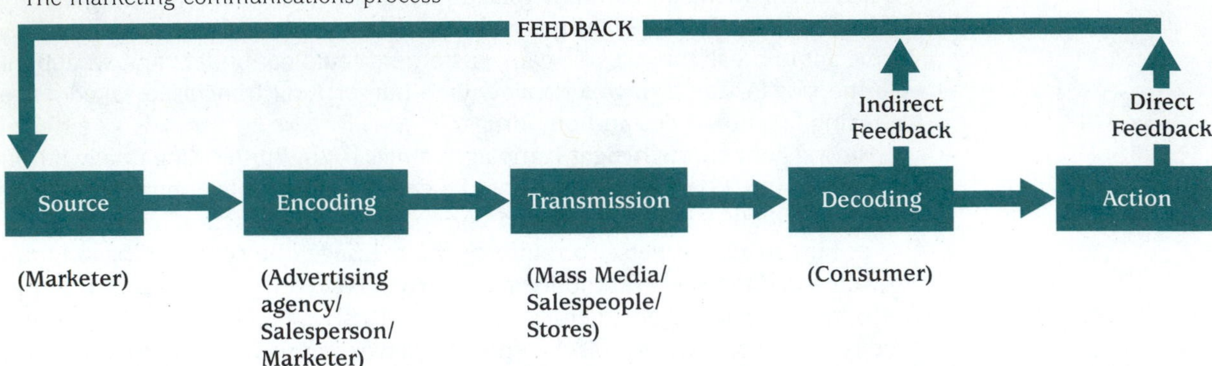

4. ***Decoding*** the message by the recipient in order to understand it and possibly retain it in memory. Two key questions are whether consumers interpret the message in the manner intended by the advertiser, and whether the message positively influences consumer attitudes and behavior.
5. ***Feedback*** on the effectiveness of the communications process to the source.

Figure 11.2 cites these five components in the context of the results of the marketing communications process. The figure also shows possible barriers to effective communication from advertiser to consumer.

http://www.ralston.com/
http://www.duracellusa.com/

In the first step, the source (the marketer) *defines communications objectives.* For example, when Ralston Purina bought Eveready in 1986, it found Duracell closing in on Eveready's 52 percent share of the $2.5 billion U.S. battery market.[6] Duracell's campaign showing battery-powered toys outlasting the competitor's in endurance contests was effective in conveying product benefits, while Eveready's spokesperson, Robert Conrad, was lackluster. Eveready's management realized it would have to do a more effective job in communicating key benefits: durability and a steady power source.

Next, the advertising agency encodes messages to *communicate product benefits.* A good example is the Energizer Bunny campaign cited in Chapter 7. By parodying Duracell's endurance toys, the ads were meant to convey the same benefits that Duracell was communicating—durability and reliability in a power source—but in a humorous way that was also meant to undercut Duracell.

The third step in the communications model, *transmitting the message to a target* segment, requires a cost-effective media plan. An effective media plan achieves a delicate balance between several potentially conflicting objectives. One possible conflict occurs between trying to reach as many people as possi-

http://www.crest.com/
http://www.cocacola.com/

ble versus reaching them as frequently as possible. Given a limited budget, advertisers cannot maximize both **reach** (the number of people exposed to the message) and **frequency** (the number of times an individual consumer or household is exposed). Reaching as many people as possible is more important for broadly targeted products such as Crest toothpaste or Coca-Cola. Frequency is more important when trying to influence a particular target group such as young, upscale car buyers. In this case, the objective is to reach a limited market segment as often as possible within budgetary constraints.

http://www.people.com/

In the Energizer Bunny campaign, the media plan involved a balance between reach and frequency. Initially, Ralston Purina used network television to reach as broad an audience as possible. By 1990, print ads began appearing in magazines such as *Newsweek, People,* and *Sports Illustrated* to ensure greater frequency of exposure among battery purchasers.

The next steps involve consumers—*exposure to the message, decoding it (perception and interpretation), and possible action* based on the message. When the Energizer Bunny campaign was first introduced, many consumers remembered a Duracell, rather than an Eveready, campaign. Why? Because the Bunny's theme, "Still going," was a spinoff of Duracell's earlier endurance theme. Con-

FIGURE 11.2
Results of and barriers to the marketing communications process

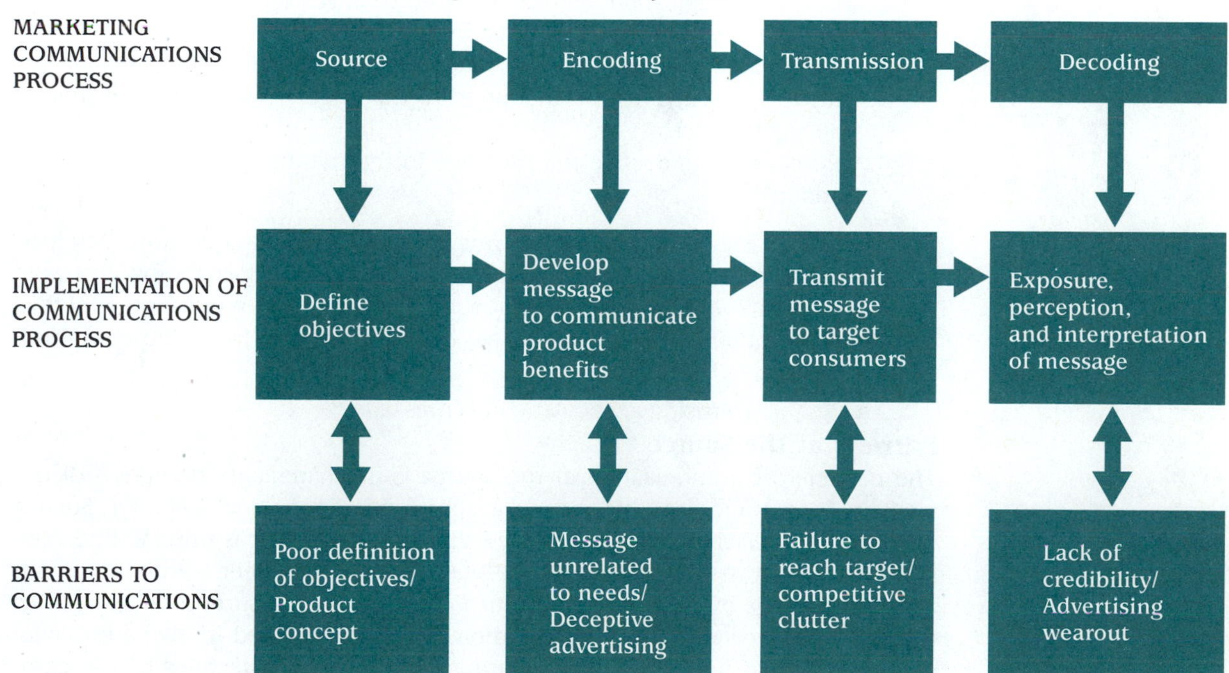

sumers simply did not decode the message correctly. There was evidence that the campaign was boosting Duracell's sales. However, Ralston Purina's management was not deterred. They had faith in the campaign and, eventually, most consumers associated the Bunny correctly with Eveready.

The last step, *feedback,* is designed to determine whether consumers have decoded the message as intended and whether they are likely to translate perceptions of the message into purchasing actions. Such feedback should help advertisers determine whether to continue, change, or cancel the campaign. By 1991, Eveready claimed that brand awareness rose 33 percent from the year before and recall of the advertising message was up 50 percent. The most difficult question to answer is whether such improvements in brand awareness and recall are translated into brand purchases. Apparently they were, because by 1991, Eveready stopped the hemorrhaging of its market and maintained its market position relative to Duracell. By 1995, Eveready was ready to invest another $20 million in the campaign. The Energizer Bunny campaign seems to be still going.

Barriers to Communications

In evaluating the advertising communications process, marketers must ask four questions:

1. Have communications objectives been defined to reflect consumer needs?
2. Have marketers adequately encoded product benefits?
3. Has the message been transmitted to the target segment by utilizing the right media?
4. Did consumers decode the message in the manner the advertiser intended?

Figure 11.2 shows that a negative answer to any of these questions can lead to barriers in the communications process at the source, in encoding, in transmission, or with the receiver in decoding the message. A fifth question, whether the communication leads to a purchase, bears on the results of the communications process.

Barriers at the Source

The barrier to communication at the source is an inadequate definition of objectives. In many cases, this means a poor focus on product benefits. Such a failure is most likely to lead to an advertising message that is unrelated to consumer needs. A number of years ago, a popularly priced beer wanted to create a prestige image by advertising its beer in status-oriented surroundings such as a country club or a fox hunt. The campaign only succeeded in alienating loyal users who could not relate to the settings. Clearly, the objectives of the campaign—creating a more upscale image—did not relate to consumer needs.

Barriers in Encoding

Failures in marketing communications can also be attributable to the process of encoding. At times, copywriters and artists may be more interested in developing creative, original advertising than in conveying product benefits. The result may be a message that gains attention but does not communicate benefits to the consumer. When Eveready first tried to take on Duracell, it borrowed an Australian campaign for Eveready that used an eccentric square-jawed soccer star named Jacko Jackson who said "Oy" and demanded that viewers "Get Energizer." Eveready's CEO decided that with a little grooming, Jacko could be exported to the United States. Eveready sank $30 million into a campaign doomed to failure.[7] Why? Because Jacko simply did not communicate product benefits. Americans grew to loathe Jacko as a loud-mouthed irritant. The ads were as much of a debacle as Burger King's "Where's Herb?" campaign.[8] Both of the campaigns created barriers to communication by poorly encoding product benefits.

Figure 11.2 shows that deceptive advertising is also a barrier to encoding in misleading the consumer as to the nature of product benefits. As we saw in Chapter 2, the FTC can force companies to undertake corrective advertising. However, most misleading advertising is not an outright fraudulent claim. Many claims are likely to be inflated, leaving it to the consumer to sort out what is accurate and what is not.

Barriers in Transmission

Barriers to communication can occur in the process of transmission. One barrier is failure to use the right media to reach the target group. Advertisers must match the demographic characteristics of their user group to the demographic profile of magazine readers, TV viewers, or radio listeners. For example, when Polaroid introduced its Spectra camera, its target was younger, upscale viewers who might pay $225 to get higher quality instant pictures. As a result, Polaroid advertised on network TV programs whose primary viewers were under 35 and in upscale magazines such as *New Yorker*.

http://www.polaroid.com/

Perhaps the greatest barrier in transmission is *competitive clutter*. The number of commercials and print advertisements has been increasing for several reasons. First, the proliferation of new products demands more commercial time. Second, competitive intensity has caused advertising budgets to rise proportionately faster than sales. Third, TV commercials are getting shorter with a shift from 30- to 15-second spot commercials. *Business Week has* estimated that U.S. adults are "bombarded with 3,000 marketing messages a day."[9] Because of such clutter, it is estimated that in the last 20 years, the likelihood that the consumer remembered the last commercial seen on TV declined from 18 to 7 percent.[10] Clearly, the increase in the number of commercials has inhibited consumers' decoding process. (An illustration of the problem of competitive clutter is shown in Exhibit 11.1.)

http://www.businessweek.com/

EXHIBIT 11.1
An illustration of the problem of competitive clutter
Source: From *The Wall Street Journal*. Permission, Cartoon Features Syndicate.

"We'll return to our commercials in a moment, but first this program . . ."

Several studies have documented the fact that more frequent advertising has resulted in less consumer attention to messages. Webb found that attention and recall dropped off as the number of ads increased.[11] Burke and Srull found that more exposure to competing ads inhibits consumers' ability to remember the advertised brand.[12] They concluded that greater similarity between brands and between advertising themes creates confusion and makes retrieval of specific brand information from memory more difficult. As a result, consumers are more likely to confuse ad themes for Pepsi and Coke, for Crest and Colgate, and as we saw, for Eveready and Duracell.

What can marketers do to combat the confusion competitive clutter creates? An easy answer is to increase the frequency of advertising to make a more lasting impression on consumers. However, this can be a solution only if the message is closely tied to consumer needs (that is, the message has no source or encoding barriers). Increased frequency rescued Eveready's Energizer Bunny campaign because greater exposure caused consumers to correctly identify the source as Eveready rather than Duracell. However, success depended on the Bunny commercials' ability to convey the key benefits of durability and dependability.

Barriers in Decoding

Barriers can also occur in the decoding process. A failure to develop a product concept or to create an advertising message related to consumer needs is likely to lead to such barriers. Consumers will selectively ignore messages of no interest to them, as they did with Burger King's "Where's Herb?" and Eveready's Jacko campaigns, because of their failure to communicate benefits. Furthermore, if consumers find that the source of the message is not credible, they will reject the message. For example, consumers may reject an advertisement from a large utility company justifying higher prices to finance nuclear energy for lack of credibility. However, consumers are more likely to accept a similar message from the Environmental Protection Agency.

http://www.epa.gov/

Barriers to decoding may occur because of lack of attention to the message. Competitive clutter is a barrier not only in transmission, but also in the decoding process because it encourages inattention. The continued use of an ad for a long period of time is another cause of inattention. **Advertising wearout** may occur; that is, advertising effectiveness may decrease because of consumer boredom and familiarity with the campaign.

Results of Communications

Consumers may avoid exposure to a message or, if exposed, may accept or reject it. *Message acceptance* is due to an effective process of communicating product benefits that are important to a target segment. *Message rejection* may be due to lack of message credibility or believability, or it may be independent of message content and reflect consumers' attitudes, past experiences, and beliefs. For example, a consumer who has had consistently poor performance from a certain automobile make is unlikely to accept the validity of a claim that the car is well engineered and durable and provides maximum performance on the road.

From the advertiser's standpoint, the most desirable result of the communication process is a purchase as a result of message acceptance. Message acceptance may lead to a purchase, or consumers may decide not to purchase for reasons other than the information in the communication. Price and availability are obvious restrictions to purchase. Another is lack of an immediate need. Consumers may be attracted to a car because of the advertising but may not be in the market for one.

Regardless of the outcome, marketers would like to assess the effect of the marketing communication on the purchase. Evaluation of the communication by marketing and advertising research provides marketers with feedback. Figure 11.2 shows that **direct feedback** is provided when a marketing communication can be directly linked to consumer actions, that is, sales. Marketers can judge retail advertising announcing a sale on a given day by the number of shoppers, and they can evaluate the effects of in-store displays by comparing sales with and without displays. Also, marketers can relate coupon returns to the advertising source. However, the sales effectiveness of an advertising message in the mass media is harder to judge. Marketers have difficulty determining the degree to which an advertising campaign is instrumental in brand choice because so many other factors enter into the purchase decision. As a result, indirect feedback assumes more importance in evaluating ad campaigns. **Indirect feedback** is provided when the marketing communication is evaluated on the basis of the consumers' process of decoding the message. Indirect criteria of effectiveness relate to the advertisement's ability to produce exposure, awareness, comprehension, and retention of the advertising message.

In the rest of this chapter, the primary components of the advertising communications process are considered in detail: (1) source, (2) message (encoding), (3) media (transmission), (4) consumer (decoding), and (5) feedback.

SOURCE EFFECTS IN MARKETING COMMUNICATIONS

The source of information (advertisers, salespersons, friends) directly influences consumers' acceptance and interpretation of a message. It is important to consider the *credibility* and *attractiveness* of the source to consumers to understand the effects the source has on consumer behavior.

Source Credibility

Source credibility is the level of expertise and trustworthiness consumers attribute to the source of the message.[13] *Expertise* is the ability of the source to make valid statements about the product's characteristics and performance. Few would question the ability of a Pete Sampras or a Martina Navratilova to make valid assessments of tennis equipment. *Trustworthiness* is the perception that a source has made a valid statement about the product. Some spokespersons may be regarded as experts in their field, but consumers may question the trustworthiness of their product endorsements because the advertiser is paying them.

Consumers frequently question the trustworthiness of ad claims because advertisers have a vested interest in selling the brand. The use of puffery (inflated claims in advertising) reinforces this view. When nearly all toothpastes claim to do the best job of eliminating cavities or controlling tartar and when nearly all detergents claim to do the best job of getting clothes cleaner, consumers naturally wonder what they can believe.

Consumers regard neutral sources such as *Consumer Reports* magazine as trustworthy because these sources have no vested interest in the brand and they make no attempt to change attitudes or influence behavior. Newscasters and editorial sources also have a high degree of credibility. Walter Cronkite, the former newscaster, has been cited in polls as the most credible individual in the eyes of the American public. In addition, consumers are likely to accept the brand judgments of family and friends, particularly those with particular knowledge of the product category.[14]

Some researchers have used attribution theory to explain why consumers view advertising as less credible than personal and neutral sources. Attribution theory states that receivers attribute certain motives to a communication source. When all ads consumers see are making uniformly positive claims (the best-tasting coffee, the most reliable airline, the best performing car, and so on), consumers begin to doubt the advertiser's motives. Uniformly positive claims lead consumers to attribute the message to the advertiser's desire to sell the product rather than to a desire to transmit valid information about product performance.

On the other hand, if a message provides some variation in the claim (for example, headache remedy A is stronger and provides quick relief, but it is more likely to upset the stomach), consumers are more likely to accept the source as credible. As we will see, consumers are more likely to attribute such two-sided advertising appeals to the product's actual characteristics than to the advertiser's desire to sell.

Credibility and Message Acceptance

http://www.coned.com/

http://www.dps.state.ny.us/

Studies have concluded that the greater the perceived credibility of the source, the greater the likelihood that receivers will accept the message.[15] For example, Craig and McCann studied the effects of messages from Con Edison and the New York State Public Service Commission asking consumers to save money by reducing the consumption of electricity used for air conditioning.[16] The message was enclosed in the monthly utility bill. The group receiving the message from the Public Service Commission—perceived as a more credible source—consumed substantially less electricity than the group receiving the message from Con Edison. The authors concluded that "the effectiveness of a communication advocating energy conservation can be enhanced by using a source of greater credibility."[17]

Source credibility in itself does not ensure message acceptance. Source credibility is not likely to increase message acceptance if:

- Consumers rely on their past experiences rather than on the ad in evaluating a brand.[18]
- The message conflicts with consumers' best interests.[19]
- The message is threatening.[20]

http://www.cancer.org/

An ad on the risks of smoking from a credible source like the American Cancer Society will not increase message acceptance by many confirmed smokers because they see the message as a threat and want to avoid it.

Increasing the Credibility of the Source

Because a lack of credibility is a major limitation to consumers' acceptance of advertising messages, advertisers should consider how they can increase their credibility. The implication from attribution theory is to vary the claim so that it is not uniformly positive. If advertisers present both positive and negative information about the product (a two-sided message), consumers are more likely to attribute the claim to the product's actual characteristics rather than to the advertiser's desire to sell. However, marketers have rarely used such two-sided advertising because they are reluctant to present negative information about their product, even on relatively unimportant attributes. Research has demonstrated, however, that consumers have more confidence in claims that cite the pros and cons of a brand.[21]

There are two other strategies to enhance the advertiser's credibility. First, utilize expertise. Salespeople who are viewed as experts seem more credible in sales situations than do nonexpert salespeople. Advertising that uses spokespersons whom consumers accept as experts (for example, Lee Iacocca for Chrysler cars, based on his past role as CEO) increases credibility. In evaluating the impact of celebrity spokespersons on consumers, one study found that the expertise of the spokesperson is a more important influence than his or her trustworthiness or attractiveness.[22]

A second strategy to enhance credibility is to increase trustworthiness. Marketers often utilize neutral sources to encourage trustworthiness. Ads that cite neutral sources such as ratings from *Consumer Reports* or *Good Housekeeping* Seal of Approval are more likely to gain trustworthiness.

http://www.homearts.com/

Source Attractiveness

Another basis by which consumers evaluate the source is its attractiveness, which is determined by its likability and its similarity to consumers.[23] Research has shown that when consumers see salespeople as similar to themselves, they are more likely to accept and be influenced by the sales messages.[24]

Since source attractiveness increases message acceptance, marketers try to emphasize similarity and enhance likability to increase attractiveness. Advertisers have emphasized the similarity between the source and the consumer by portraying "typical consumers" using and endorsing products. When consumers see others similar to themselves using the product, they are more likely to react positively to it. Brands as diverse as Subaru cars and Tylenol analgesics have used this approach. Salespeople often emphasize similarity with consumers because a salesperson who is seen as a peer becomes more attractive as a source of information.

http://www.subaru.com/
http://www.tylenol.com/

Marketers can use spokespersons in advertising to increase credibility and/or attractiveness. Two types of spokespersons are used in advertising: **expert spokespersons** to increase credibility and **referent spokespersons** (those to whom consumers can easily relate) to increase source attractiveness. For example, James Garner was successful as a referent spokesperson for Polaroid's regular line of instant cameras; he was likeable but had no particular credibility as an expert in photography. Conversely, the late John Houseman was effective in conveying expertise as a spokesman for the brokerage house, Smith Barney, based on his role as a law professor in the TV series "The Paper Chase." However, he was not particularly likeable as he intoned "Smith Barney makes money the old-fashioned way. They earn it!"

http://www.smithbarney.com/

When should advertisers emphasize attractiveness or expertise? Mazursky and Schul found that if consumers are involved in the purchase, expertise should be emphasized; if consumers are not involved, attractiveness should be emphasized.[25] In the high-involvement case, consumers will focus on the message, and an expert best presents credible information. In the low-involvement case, consumers are not that focused on the message, and the source will have more of an impact. As a result, the attractiveness of the spokesperson may be effective in gaining attention. Thus, Deion Sanders may be effective as an expert spokesperson for an involving product like athletic shoes, given that he is a leading National Football League receiver (see Exhibit 11.2). In contrast, Bill Cosby could be an effective referent spokesperson, given his likeability, for an uninvolving product like Jell-O.

Source versus Message Effects

Source credibility does not always operate to increase message acceptance. As the research by Mazursky and Schul showed, involved consumers are likely to focus primarily on the message's content rather than its source. This finding conforms to the elaboration likelihood model (ELM) discussed in Chapter 5. According to ELM, involved consumers process messages through a central route that focuses on message content, while less involved consumers process messages through a peripheral route that focuses on factors extraneous to the message (peripheral cues). The source of the message is a peripheral cue. Therefore, according to ELM, source credibility is most important in influencing message acceptance in low-involvement conditions. Message effects are most important in high-involvement conditions.

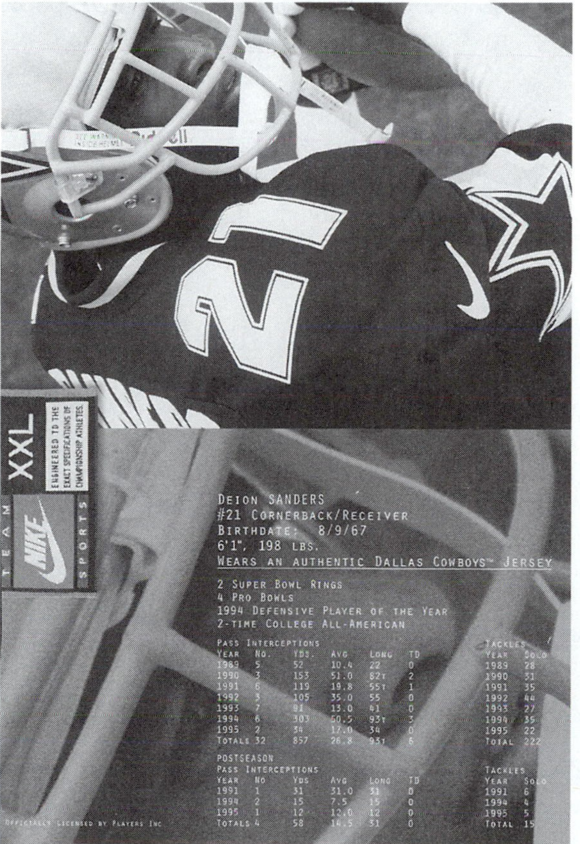

▶EXHIBIT 11.2 Deion Sanders: An effective expert spokesperson for Nike

Research supports this contention. Petty, Cacioppo, and Schumann found that use of celebrity spokespersons in ads had little influence when consumers were involved. However, such spokespersons exerted a strong influence on less involved consumers.[26] Similarly, Ratneshwar and Chaiken found that consumers who processed information more fully (and were, therefore, more involved with the situation) were less likely to be influenced by the source of the message.[27] They also found that source credibility was more important if consumers had little knowledge of the brand or product category. In such cases, it would be natural for consumers to rely on an expert spokesperson.

Miniard and his colleagues found that source credibility is also important when brands with similar claims are advertised.[28] In such cases, consumers may have difficulty distinguishing one claim from another and rely on the credibility of the source. For example, consumers evaluating advertising claims among three or four analgesic brands may find they are making similar claims regarding safety and efficacy. In such cases, use of a credible spokesperson may be decisive. Miniard et al. also found that source credibility may be important when brands make conflicting claims. If one analgesic says aspirin can irritate the stomach and another says it does not, consumers may throw up their hands and decide to believe the claim an expert spokesperson backs.

In summary, source credibility is likely to be most influential when:

- Consumers are not involved.
- Consumers have little knowledge of the appropriate characteristics by which to evaluate brands.
- Brands with similar claims are being evaluated.
- Brand claims are conflicting.

EFFECTS OF THE MESSAGE

The advertising message is meant to inform and persuade. Informational objectives may be directed toward announcing new products or changes in existing products, informing consumers of product characteristics, or providing information on price and availability. Persuasive objectives may be directed toward convincing consumers of product benefits, trying to induce trial, or reducing uncertainty about buying the product. The methods used to develop and present advertising messages are beyond the scope of this text, but certain aspects of message content bear directly on the likelihood that consumers will accept and act on the message. Consumer researchers have considered five questions:

1. Should the message take a more hedonic (emotional and fantasy-oriented) or a more utilitarian approach?
2. Should the message be one-sided or two-sided?
3. Is comparative advertising (naming a competitor in the ad) an effective means of communicating product benefits?

4. What are the advantages of using fear appeals?
5. What is the appropriate role of humor in advertising?

Hedonic versus Utilitarian Appeals

An important issue for advertisers is whether the message should appeal to the emotions of consumers or be more directed to transmitting information about product features. We have seen in past chapters that advertisers frequently use appeals directed to pleasure seeking, sentiment, and fantasy. Such appeals are most likely for:

- Involving products that are more likely to arouse emotions.
- Products that consumers often view as part of their self-image (clothing, cars, athletic shoes).
- Products that do not require communication of features and information (nontechnical products).

An example of an appeal to pleasure, excitement, and fantasy is the ad for Bauer's in-line skates in Exhibit 11.3. Although the taste of the ad is questionable in citing a "near death experience," it clearly appeals to the consumer's fantasies and emotions.

▶EXHIBIT 11.3
An appeal to excitement and fantasy

▶EXHIBIT 11.4
Increasing product involvement through emotional appeals

http://www.michelin.com/

Emotionally based advertising has also been used in an attempt to increase involvement for less involving products. The ad for Michelin tires in Exhibit 11.4 is an example. Tires are a product that consumers view as a necessity for driving with little emotional context. Michelin tried to increase involvement by equating tires with the safety of loved ones. The ad makes the point that anyone worried about their child's safety should be willing to pay a premium price to buy a Michelin tire.

The attempt to portray uninvolving products in a more hedonic context has increased since the mid-1980s. As one advertising agency executive observed, "emotion [is] playing a greater role in advertising [by becoming] less product-feature oriented and much more nonverbal."[29] Why this trend toward emotional themes for uninvolving products? First, many products have become more standardized. When a tire advertiser has no unique product claim, what better approach than to develop an emotionally based position? Second, the intensity of competition has increased in many categories. More product alternatives make it harder for any one product to be noticed. What better way to stand out from http://www.nestle.com/

the crowd than to take an emotional approach? Taster's Choice instant coffee—certainly a product that's hard to get steamed up about—has leapfrogged Folgers and Maxwell House to become the nation's number-one soluble brew with an emotional ad campaign centered around a budding romance between a couple who meet as new neighbors.

One-Sided versus Two-Sided Appeals

Two-sided messages are those that provide both positive and negative information about a product. The negative information is usually relatively unimportant compared to the positive information. Such messages are effective because they increase source credibility and reduce resistance to the message among skeptics.

Refuting Negative Information

Two-sided ads can be refutational (the negative information is presented and then refuted) or nonrefutational. A two-sided refutational ad might say that a car

STRATEGIC IMPLICATIONS OF CONSUMER BEHAVIOR

► Can Computers Be Sold Based on Emotional Appeals?

For most of the 15 years that personal computers have been readily available, computer ads have tended to be aimed at high-tech users, people who can truly get misty eyed at the size of a hard drive or the amount of a machine's random access memory. That was fine when the market was relatively open and computer companies advertised almost exclusively in computer magazines.

But now that the computer has reached the mature stage of its life cycle and the market has become highly competitive, high-tech companies have found themselves in a pitched battle not for the brains of consumers, but for their hearts and souls. The new reality has computing companies scrambling to create emotional bonds with their customers. Computer advertising has now taken a turn toward the hedonic.

"Almost all of the advertising in the PC field today has really missed the mark," says IBM's marketing maven C. Ray Freeman. "It's all technical specs—my machine's faster than yours—and price." Freeman says that IBM is now using its advertising to try to build a strong, positive bond with consumers.

And so are IBM's main competitors. Apple began a campaign in 1994 called "Contrasts," in which unlikely duos such as a prelaw student and an established attorney peek at each other's Powerbook in voyeuristic fashion to answer the question "What's on your PowerBook." (see Exhibit 11.5). Compaq found a simple way to improve what it calls its "likeability." Hewlett-Packard introduced a campaign for its Pavilion PC using the nontechnical appeal of "Real life made simple." And Compaq advertises its machine's versatility through a series of lifelike commercials. In one TV spot, a father struggling to get his preschool daughter to brush her teeth bribes her with the promise that he'll use his Compaq laptop to read her a CD-ROM bedtime story. In another, several male execs sweat out a traffic jam that may make them lose a major contract and are bailed out when one of their female underlings pulls out her Compaq laptop and uses the car phone to calmly fax their proposal from the center of the freeway.

"It's critical that we not distract consumers with a lot of information about bits and bytes," says Mark Rosen, Compaq's ad director. "We've got to show how and why computers will help them do things better and smarter."

Computer firms are placing their ads on primetime network TV because computers have now penetrated into one-third of America's 90 million households. IBM, Intel, and Microsoft are spending about $100 million in an advertising binge on shows like "Seinfeld," "Frasier," and even the "Late Show with David Letterman." In the fourth quarter of 1994 alone, Compaq spent about $20 million on its image-oriented TV advertising.

The goal, it seems, is no longer to get Americans to buy computers because they're highly efficient technical marvels. Now the idea is to get people to feel warm and fuzzy about their computers and the companies that make them.

Sources: "H-P Sets Pavilion PCs in 'Real Life'," *Brandweek,* (March 11, 1996), p. 4; "Computer Selling Moves into 'Warm, Fuzzy' Phase," *Advertising Age* (November 14, 1994), p. S4; "Computer Companies Try TV Ads' Mass Appeal," *The Wall Street Journal* (September 20, 1994), p. B1; "IBM's Flawed Advertising Strategy to Get an Overhaul," *The Wall Street Journal* (October 22, 1993), p. B1.

EXHIBIT 11.5 Selling computers by hedonic rather than utilitarian appeals

▶EXHIBIT 11.6
Example of a two-sided message

**Avis is only No.2.
But we don't
want your sympathy.**

Have we been crying too much? Have we overplayed the underdog?

We didn't think so till David Biener, 11 years old, sent us 35¢, saying, "It may help you buy another Plymouth."

That was an eye-opener.

So now we'd like to correct the false impression we've made.

We don't want you to reserve Avis cars for your clients because you feel sorry for us. Give us a chance to prove that a No. 2 can be just as good as a No. 1. Or even better. Because we have to try harder.

Maybe we ought to eliminate the negative and accentuate the positive.

Instead of saying "We're only No. 2 in rent a cars," we could say "We're the second largest in the world."

is relatively small; but for the young professional just starting out, economy is more important than comfort, and this car is the most economical on the market. A nonrefutational ad would simply present the pros and cons of the car in a straightforward fashion.

http://www.avis.com/

Presenting negative information about the company's product is an infrequent strategy in advertising. Advertisers are fearful that it could point out product deficiencies and discourage consumers from buying, even if the negative information is refuted. However, such a strategy can be quite effective if refuting a negative factor actually reinforces the benefits of the product. For example, for years Avis used a two-sided refutational strategy by first stating that it was not the largest company and then discounting that by saying, "We try harder" (see Exhibit 11.6). The Avis campaign actually turned an unimportant negative into a positive benefit by convincing many consumers that being number two prompted the company to pay more attention to its customers.

Defusing Objections to the Product

Another reason for favoring two-sided appeals is that they may defuse nonusers' objections to a product. Consider the consumer who believes that food cooked in microwave ovens is tasteless. The consumer sees a one-sided ad for a microwave oven claiming that it not only cooks food faster, but also actually enhances the taste of certain foods. We saw in Chapter 10 that when consumers obtain information that is discrepant with their beliefs, they often develop counterarguments (thoughts that counter information in the ad). The consumer develops counterarguments to the claims in the ad (How can a microwave oven cook better-tasting food than a regular oven?) and rejects the message.

Counterarguing is most likely to occur in high-involvement situations when consumers see discrepant information as a threat.[30] If a two-sided ad is presented, one in which possible arguments against the brand are presented first and then refuted, the objections of consumers with discrepant beliefs are defused, as the ad has already stated the counterarguments. The consumer seeing a two-sided ad for microwave ovens may be told that microwaves improve taste in certain kinds of cooking situations but not in others and that the company's brand is most effective in retaining taste for these types of foods. The consumer is more likely to accept this type of refutational ad.

Research has shown that two-sided appeals lead to less counterarguing and greater message acceptance by consumers because their concerns have already been stated in the ad.[31] Kamins and Assael found that two-sided appeals produced significantly less counterarguing than one-sided appeals in advertising a new product and led to higher intentions to buy.[32] Similarly, Szybillo and Heslin found that when messages were presented to consumers supporting the use of air bags (one-sided) and both supporting and rejecting their use (two-sided), the two-sided ads were more effective in convincing consumers of the air bags' merits.[33] They used *inoculation theory* (see Chapter 9) to posit that the two-sided ad "inoculated" consumers against counterarguing by preempting any of their negative thoughts. The conclusion in both studies is that two-sided advertisements are more effective in introducing a new product that must overcome some consumer objections.

Two-sided ads are less effective when consumers are not involved with the product because less involved consumers are not as attentive to the pros and cons stated in two-sided advertising.[34] Evidence also suggests that one-sided ads produce greater message acceptance when:

- Consumers are less educated.[35]
- There is agreement with the advertiser's position.
- Consumers are loyal to the advertiser's brand.[36]

In today's environment, advertisers should consider increasing their use of two-sided advertising in an attempt to enhance their credibility in the eyes of a doubting public.

Comparative Advertising

Another type of advertising that has experienced increased usage is comparative advertising, that is, naming a competitor in the ad. The use of comparative advertising has increased since the networks removed a ban on its use in 1976.

http://www.mci.com/
http://www.att.com/
http://www.nissan.com/
http://www.toyota.com/

Most comparative advertising is one-sided; that is, it presents the strengths of the advertised product and the weaknesses of the competitive product. For example, MCI names AT&T in its ads and claims it provides better service, Nissan compares its price to that of the Toyota Camry, and Almay moisturizer claims that Cliniqe can cost twice as much. At times, the use of comparative ads can get heated. In 1992, Coors introduced a TV campaign claiming that its Extra Gold tasted more like the "real beers" of the past than Budweiser. A few months later, Anheuser-Busch (makers of Budweiser) retaliated by claiming that Coors dilutes the vaunted Rocky Mountain spring water it uses for its beers with water from one of its Virginia breweries. Coors then sued Anheuser for false advertising.[37]

http://www.ftc.gov/

Despite this potential for undermining other brands and being undermined in turn, evidence suggests that comparative ads can be highly effective in influencing consumers. The arguments in favor of comparative advertising are that (1) users of competing brands are more likely to notice the ad and are, therefore, more likely to consider the advertiser's brand, and (2) claims made in comparative ads provide consumers with more information and a more rational basis for choice (an advantage cited by the Federal Trade Commission).[38]

However, studies have questioned the effectiveness of comparative advertising. Swinyard found that when it is one-sided, comparative advertising loses credibility and generates sympathy for the brand being attacked.[39] A study by Ogilvy-Mather, a large ad agency, found that consumers frequently confuse the sponsor for the competitor in many comparative ads. Furthermore, there was no difference in the persuasiveness of comparative and noncomparative ads.[40]

However, other studies have found that if the source is credible, comparative advertising is effective. Gotleib and Sarel found that credible, comparative ads were more likely to be noticed and were more likely to influence intentions to buy the advertised brand compared to noncomparative ads. They also found that credible comparative ads were particularly effective for new products.[41] Swinyard found that credibility can best be achieved by making a comparative ad two-sided—that is, a comparative ad that names a competitor, cites some of the advantages of the competitive brand, and then points out the arguments for the advertised brand.[42] Although they may be effective, these types of ads are rare because advertisers are reluctant to cite the advantages of a competitive brand, even in the context of comparative advertising.

Another study by Pechmann and Stewart went further in exploring the effectiveness of comparative advertising by showing it is best used for brands with lower market share.[43] Consumers like underdogs and are more likely to accept comparative ads from smaller challengers. Also, a comparison to the market leader may elevate the low-share brand to the same level of quality and popularity in the consumers' eyes. That is probably why MCI compares itself to AT&T. Conversely, if a market leader compares itself to a lower-share brand, it may enhance the competitor's underdog status. When AT&T retaliated by naming

MCI in its ads, one MCI executive said, "AT&T made this a two-horse race. They are Goliath taking on David."[44]

Fear Appeals

Most marketing communications attempt to inform consumers of the benefits of using a product. Fear appeals do the opposite: they inform consumers of the risks of using a product (such as cigarettes) or of not using one (such as deodorants). The importance of fear appeals is reflected in the finding that an estimated 17 percent of all TV commercials are fear-oriented.[45]

Fear appeals are likely to be ineffective if they are too threatening. In the past, the American Cancer Society demonstrated the harmful effects of smoking with appeals from terminal cancer patients. The messages were so stark that consumers ignored or dismissed them because of a natural process of perceptual defense to reduce dissonance. Acceptance of these messages meant facing the possibility of death because of the individual's action (or inaction). A Federal Trade Commission report illustrated people's avoidance of such anxiety-producing information; it found that the average number of cigarettes consumed did not change after health warnings became public.[46]

At the other extreme, fear appeals are likely to be ineffective when consumers associate little or no anxiety with the message. A fear appeal for floor cleaners picturing neighbors commenting on a dirty floor is not likely to work these days because homemakers are just not very concerned. Fear appeals, therefore, are most likely to influence consumers when anxiety is moderate.

Research has confirmed the effectiveness of moderate fear appeals. One study tested the effects of high-, moderate-, and low-level fear appeals on attitudes toward drinking. Moderate-level warnings, which consumers considered most truthful, were most effective in changing attitudes toward drinking.[47] Similarly, Keller and Block found that both low- and high-level fear appeals tend to be ineffective: low-level appeals because there is insufficient evaluation by the consumer of the harmful consequences of the behavior; high-level appeals because there is too much elaboration of these consequences. Increasing elaboration for low-intensity appeals and decreasing it for high-intensity appeals makes fear appeals more effective in changing behavior.[48]

When are fear appeals most likely to succeed? Tanner, Hunt, and Eppright investigated the effectiveness of fear appeals in changing behavior toward socially transmitted diseases (for example, the effectiveness of fear appeals in getting individuals to practice safe sex to prevent AIDS).[49] They found that fear appeals were most effective when:

- Consumers recognized the severity of the threat (AIDS can kill).
- Consumers recognize they can be affected by the threat (I could be exposed to AIDS).

- The ad shows how to deal with the problem (the threat of AIDS can be reduced by using condoms).
- The proposed course of action is easily implemented (one can just walk into a drugstore to buy condoms).

The most important finding is that fear appeals must show consumers how to deal with the problem. The ad for bicycle helmets in Exhibit 11.7 shows a survivor who wore a helmet. It is probably more effective than the adjacent ad because (a) it is more moderate in its appeal, and (b) it shows the positive results of wearing a helmet rather than the negative results of not wearing one.

Humor in Advertising

Marketers use humorous messages because they attract attention and because advertisers believe that humor can be persuasive. One source estimates that up to 25 percent of all television commercials contain some element of humor.[50]

There are pros and cons for the use of humor in advertising. On the positive side, humor is likely to increase attention[51] and memorability.[52] It is also likely to enhance the advertiser's credibility.[53] Humor may create a positive feeling toward the advertiser and, thus, increase the persuasiveness of the message. It also may distract consumers who use competitive products from developing arguments against the advertiser's brand and may lead them to accept the message.[54]

The ad in Exhibit 11.8 is attention-getting, memorable, and likely to create positive feelings for the product. Most important, it conveys product benefits—a necessary condition for a humorous ad to be successful—by citing the effectiveness of Halls cough drops for children.

However, there is a risk in using humor. If humor is too dominating, it may have a negative effect on message comprehension and may fail to communicate product benefits.[55] A good example of the ineffective use of humor was the "Where's Herb?" campaign for Burger King, cited earlier. The focus on Herb was attention-getting but did not convey any particular message regarding the benefits of visiting a Burger King. If humor is to work, it must have a natural association with the product.[56]

When is the use of humor most effective? Researchers have found that humor is more effective in gaining message acceptance when:

- ***Consumers are not involved:***[57] Since humor is peripheral to the message, it is more likely to influence consumers who are not involved with the product.
- ***For existing products:***[58] Advertising new products requires conveying information. Humor is more effective in establishing a mood than in conveying information.
- ***Consumers have a positive attitude toward the brand:***[59] Humor can reinforce positive feelings toward a brand, but it is unlikely to reverse negative feelings.

EXHIBIT 11.7
Use of positive and negative fear appeals for bicycle helmets

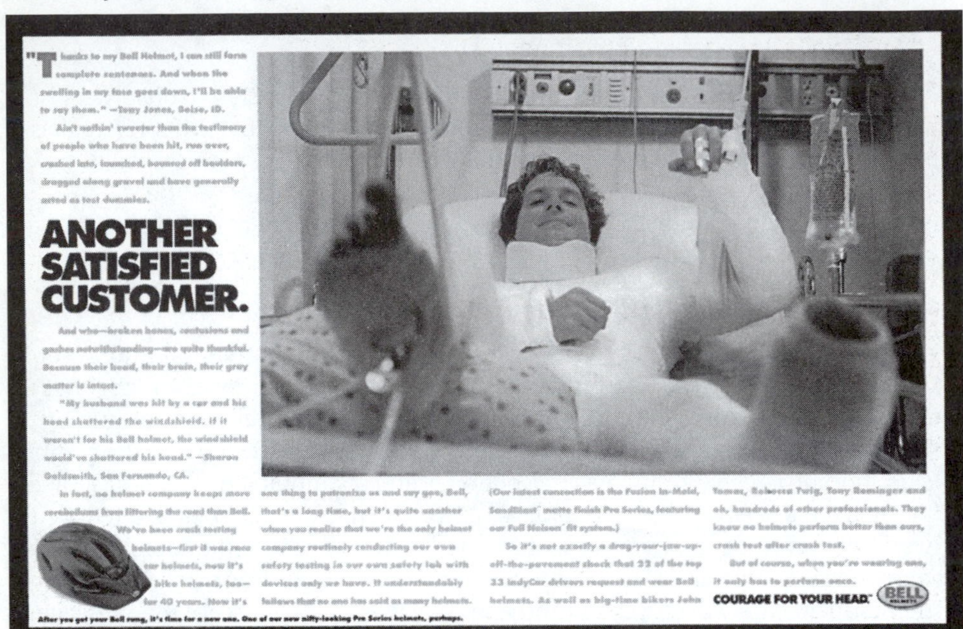

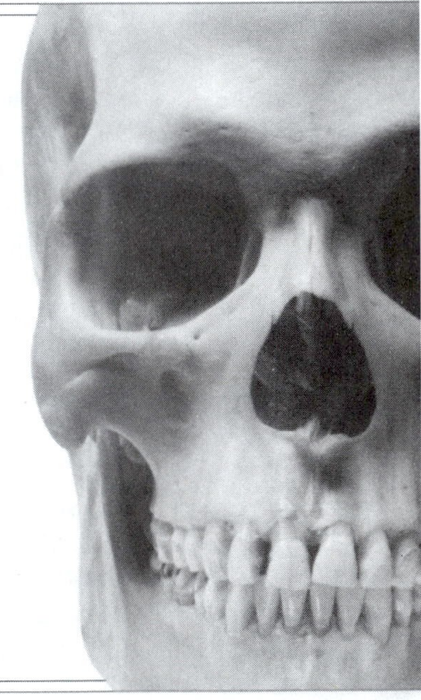

▶**EXHIBIT 11.8**
The use of humor to communicate product benefits

- *The message is incongruous:* Alden, Hoyer, and Lee studied the use of humorous ads in four countries—the United States, Korea, Thailand, and Germany.[60] They found that in all four cultures, a majority of humorous ads had incongruous themes. The ad in Exhibit 11.8 is certainly incongruous in coupling a young child in the guise of a sophisticated adult with the benefits of having a cough drop.

✦ MEDIA EFFECTS

http://www.new-yorker.com/
http://www.readersdigest.com/
http://www.playboy.com/

The third component in the communications model is message transmission. Marshall McLuhan's statement, "The medium is the message," implies that the medium communicates an image independent of any single message that is being transmitted.[61] The media environment influences consumers' reaction to a communication in two ways. First, particular types of media such as magazines may influence message evaluation. Magazines such as the *New Yorker, Reader's Digest,* and *Playboy* have different images based on different editorial content, reputation, and subscribers. Second, different types of media (magazines versus television, for example) influence consumers' reaction to the message.

Differences Within Media

The role of a particular medium in communications is illustrated by the fact that the same advertisement results in different communications effects when run in different magazines or when aired on different TV shows. For example, Aaker and Brown placed identical ads in two contrasting magazines, the *New Yorker* (a prestige magazine) and *Tennis World* (a specialty magazine).[62] The *New Yorker* was more effective in persuading nonusers to consider a product when the ad stressed product quality. *Tennis World* was more effective when the ad stressed reasons for usage. The findings suggest that the medium's environment conveys a message. Specialty media were more effective as vehicles for conveying information, and prestige media were more effective as vehicles for conveying image.

Differences Between Media

Different types of media also influence reaction to a communication. The most important distinction between media types is broadcast (TV and radio) and print (newspapers and magazines). Broadcast media are better at communicating imagery and symbolism, but they are not as effective as print in communicating detailed information. As a result, TV is more suitable for developing a mood or establishing a good feeling about the product, whereas print is more effective in communicating information.

Broadcast media, particularly television, have been described as low-involvement media because the rate of viewing and understanding is out of the viewer's control. That is, the viewer has little opportunity to dwell on a point in television advertising. In contrast, magazines allow the reader to set the pace.[63] The reader has more opportunity for making connections and dwelling on points of interest. The result is that the print media allow for a more traditional learning environment in which information can be absorbed and integrated.

Other environmental factors also distinguish media categories. Television is a good medium for products that require a demonstration of usage or action (such as automobiles or children's toys). Radio is an effective medium for products requiring sounds: records, theater productions, and political candidates. Magazines are important as sources of information on product performance because of the ability to present messages in print. Newspapers are a particularly effective source of information on local sales and merchandise; consumers are able to preshop and to carry them around as sources of shopping information. Product samples are another type of medium that marketers can use to communicate. In this case, the message is direct product experience rather than the symbolism and imagery provided in advertising. Product samples are particularly useful in introducing a new product since they provide immediate experience in an attempt to encourage further trial.

CONSUMER PROCESSING OF MARKETING COMMUNICATIONS

The fourth step in the communications model in Figure 11.1 is consumer decoding of marketing communications. Decoding requires consumers to acquire and process marketing information. The acquisition and processing of information were described in Chapter 8. Here, we are concerned with the process of decoding in the context of marketing communications.

The communications model in Figure 11.1 assumes there is one source of marketing information. When consumers process marketing communications, they are evaluating (1) the *source,* (2) the *message,* and (3) the *media* by which information is transmitted. In this section, we consider consumers' evaluation of each of these three components of marketing communications.

Source Evaluation

When consumers receive a marketing communication, they evaluate the source of information. In Chapter 10, we saw that consumers develop cognitive responses (thoughts developed by consumers in response to a communication) to the source. For example, a consumer viewing an ad for E. F. Hutton featuring Bill Cosby as a spokesperson might think, "Why should I accept an actor's advice on investment" (*source derogation*)? Or the consumer might think, "If Bill Cosby is willing to sponsor E. F. Hutton, it must be reliable" (*source bolstering*). These source-oriented responses are important to marketers because they indicate the acceptability of the source.

Advertisers try to avoid source derogation by enhancing their trustworthiness and credibility. As we saw, one strategy is to link the product to a spokesperson with expertise regarding product performance. A second strategy is to use two-sided nonrefutational advertising as evidence that the advertiser is presenting a balanced view of the product. A third strategy is to cite an impartial source, for example, findings from *Consumer Reports* magazine or an established medical organization. Crest became the leading toothpaste because its claim that fluoride in the brand helps fight cavities was endorsed by the American Dental Association. A fourth strategy to reduce source derogation is to moderate claims to avoid any attribution that the advertiser is biased. Claims such as "gets clothes whiter than new" or "best gas mileage of any car on the road" encourage source derogation because consumers have doubts about the veracity of the claim.

Message Evaluation

In evaluating the message, consumers arrive at a judgment regarding the relevance, believability, and likability of the message. These responses can be divided into two types of general reactions: cognitive and affective. Cognitive responses evaluate acceptability of the claims (supportive of or counter to prior beliefs). Affective responses reflect consumers' positive or negative attitudes toward the message.

Cognitive Response

In Chapter 10, we saw that when consumers evaluate messages, they develop thoughts that support or counter the claims made in ads or other communications. These *cognitive responses* are formed based on consumers' prior beliefs.[64] For example, a consumer viewing an ad making a claim for gas economy and low service costs might think, "This claim is consistent with what some of my friends have told me. The car is one of the most economical on the market" (a *support argument*). Or the consumer might think, "In the long run, the car is not going to be very economical because I hear it has a lot of mechanical problems" (a *counterargument*). Cognitive responses are important to marketers because support and counterarguments indicate consumers' acceptance or rejection of the advertised claim.

Message-oriented cognitive responses (support and counterarguments) are more likely to occur for high-involvement products, and source-oriented responses (source enhancement and derogation) are more prevalent for low-involvement products.[65] Involved consumers are more likely to process messages related to product performance. Less involved consumers are more likely to focus on cues that are peripheral to the message, such as the source or background scenery. The strategic implication for high-involvement products is that advertisers should focus on gaining acceptance of the message by generating support arguments. For low-involvement products, communication strategies should increase credibility and acceptance of the source.

Affective Response: Attitude Toward the Ad

Cognitive responses are the way consumers think about an advertisement; attitudes toward the ad (that is, affect) are the way consumers *feel* about it. **Attitude toward the ad** is the consumer's predisposition to respond favorably or unfavorably to a particular ad.[66] Positive cognitive responses (support arguments and source bolstering) are likely to produce positive consumer attitudes toward an ad; negative cognitive responses (counterarguments and source derogation) are likely to produce negative attitudes.

Cognitive and affective responses to an ad have different strategic implications. Cognitive responses are reactions to message content. Consumers' attitudes toward an ad are influenced by a wider range of peripheral factors such as color, music, symbols, and imagery. The key question is how consumers' attitudes toward an ad affect their evaluation of the advertised brand.

Effects of Positive Attitudes. Studies have found that positive attitudes toward an ad create two desirable effects. First, positive attitudes are likely to increase attention directed to the ad. Olney, Holbrook, and Batra found that positive feelings about a TV ad increase viewing time of the ad and, by implication, increase attention to and comprehension of the ad.[67] Second, most studies have found that when consumers have a positive attitude toward an ad, they are more likely to have a positive attitude toward the advertised brand.[68] These findings suggest the desirability of creating a positive mood or feeling so that a positive attitude toward the ad will carry over to the brand.[69]

If the attitude toward the ad carries over to the brand, it can create a **transformational effect** in which the experience of using the brand becomes even more positive due to the positive feelings the ad evokes.[70] The transformational effect explains in part why consumers who cannot tell the difference between soft drinks when the cans are unlabeled nevertheless still have strong brand preferences. Consumers link the advertising to the usage experience so that even though they cannot tell the difference in taste between brands, they remain loyal to a particular brand once they can identify it.

Effects of Negative Attitudes. The studies cited in this section suggest that advertisers should try to create positive consumer attitudes toward the advertising. Some of the most successful ad campaigns, however, have been the most disliked—for example, Wisk's "Ring around the collar," Ajax's "White Tornado," and "Don't squeeze the Charmin." As a result, several researchers have suggested a more complicated relationship between consumers' attitudes toward the ad and the brand—namely, that the most successful ads are those that produce either very positive or very negative attitudes.[71] Thus, a disliked ad can produce a positive consumer response because it creates attention and retention. Even though consumers disliked the Wisk ad, it created greater brand awareness. Thus, the key to influencing consumers is to create *arousal* (a direct positive or negative response to the ad), which results in brand familiarity and recognition once consumers are in the store.[72]

The problem with this conclusion is that it could lead advertisers to create purposefully irritating ads and negative attitudes toward the ad to gain attention and brand recognition. Irritating ads may be effective in creating arousal for certain products, but advertisers run the risk of creating negative brand evaluations. Furthermore, the American public does not particularly like advertising. A study by a large advertising agency found that 73 percent of consumers considered advertising to be exaggerated, 64 percent thought it was misleading at times, and 51 percent viewed it as not believable.[73] Given a general negative attitude toward advertising, it would be dangerous to encourage a negative attitude toward a specific campaign as a means of gaining attention and recognition.

Consumer Mood States. An important determination of consumers' attitudes toward the ad is their mood state at the time of exposure.[74] **Moods** refer to passing feelings that occur at a point in time (feeling happy, sad, silly, anxious, sexy, and so forth). Studies have shown that positive moods can create positive reactions to the ad; negative moods, negative reactions.[75]

Studies have also shown that program and advertising content can influence consumers' moods. Goldberg and Gorn found that "happy" TV programs induced happier moods; unhappy programs, sadder moods.[76] Holbrook and Batra found that TV ads have evoked feelings of pleasure, arousal, and domination, and that these feelings influence attitudes toward the ad and toward the brand.[77]

There are two strategic implications of this research. First, advertisers should try to create a desired mood state. In most cases, advertisers try to create happy moods by showing the benefits of product use or by portraying the product in a positive context. Advertisers can also try to create anxious moods through fear campaigns. In both cases, the advertiser is trying to create the desired mood state.

The second implication of mood research is that advertisers can influence a desired mood state through program or readership content. This requires placing advertising with happy themes on "happy" TV shows. However, the converse does not necessarily apply. Burnkrant, Unnava, and Lord found that if the advertising has a sad theme, program content does not affect reactions to the ad.[78] The conclusion is that ads with sad themes (an insurance ad showing a family that lost its home) should not necessarily be linked to sad programs.

Media Evaluation

Consumers evaluate an advertising message in the context of the medium in which it is transmitted. They develop images of media that influence message acceptance.

Programs or editorial content may vary in a given medium; therefore, advertisers must consider whether the specific environment in which a print ad or commercial is placed may influence message acceptance. One study by Kennedy found that the effectiveness of TV commercials varies depending on the type of show (for example, situation comedies versus suspense thrillers).[79] Another by Soldow and Principe found that when consumers are involved in a TV program, commercial effectiveness is likely to be lower because consumers are focused on the program rather than on the commercial. Frequently, consumers see the commercial as an irritant. When consumers are not involved in the program, they are likely to see the commercial as part of the program material and are more likely to accept the message.[80]

The effects of the program environment can be applied to print ads as well as to TV commercials. The nature of the story in which a print ad is placed may influence message acceptance. One study found that for most products, placing an ad next to an upbeat story has a positive effect on message acceptance. An exception was advertising for cookies, candy, or other products that may be used to cope with anxieties. Placing ads for these types of products next to anxiety-producing stories may be more likely to promote message acceptance.[81]

COMMUNICATIONS FEEDBACK

The final step in the communication process is feedback to the marketer to evaluate the effectiveness of the marketing communication. Figure 11.1 shows that marketers can obtain direct feedback by establishing a link between message effectiveness and purchase behavior or indirect feedback by evaluating the way consumers decode the message. As we saw, it is difficult to determine the effect of advertising on consumers' purchasing behavior, so advertisers have relied on indirect feedback in evaluating advertising. That is, they determine whether the ad results in consumer exposure, attention, comprehension, and retention.

McGuire summarized the types of feedback provided in each of these steps[82] (see Figure 11.3). In addition to exposure, attention, comprehension, and retention, McGuire added message acceptance to measure the effect of the ad on changes in brand attitudes. These steps reflect a hierarchy of effects leading to a purchase. The assumption is that as consumers move from exposure to attention, comprehension, message acceptance, and retention, the probability that they will buy the advertised brand increases with each step. We consider the measurement of each of these steps in the following decoding process:

http://www.nielson.com/

1. *Exposure* can be measured by circulation for print media and by reach for broadcast media. Circulation figures are generally available for magazines and newspapers and are usually broken out by demographic characteristics to allow advertisers to determine the best media to reach their target audience. Determining consumers' exposure to TV is more difficult. In the past, research companies such as A. C. Nielsen have determined TV exposure using electronic meters attached to a sample of TV sets that record the programs consumers watch. These devices, however, could not determine who was watching the set. Recently, "People Meters" have been installed in TV sets in a sample of households. These devices, which require viewers to "punch in" when they are watching TV, record who is watching as well as what is being watched.

2. *Attention* can best be measured by recognition of an advertisement. The Starch service computes a "seen-associated" measure for print ads in which consumers are asked whether they have seen the ad and whether they can associate it with a brand or manufacturer. Advertising agencies have developed a similar measure for TV ads in which households are called the day after a TV commercial appears and are asked what commercials they remember seeing ("day-after recall" measures). With this measure, advertisers can determine

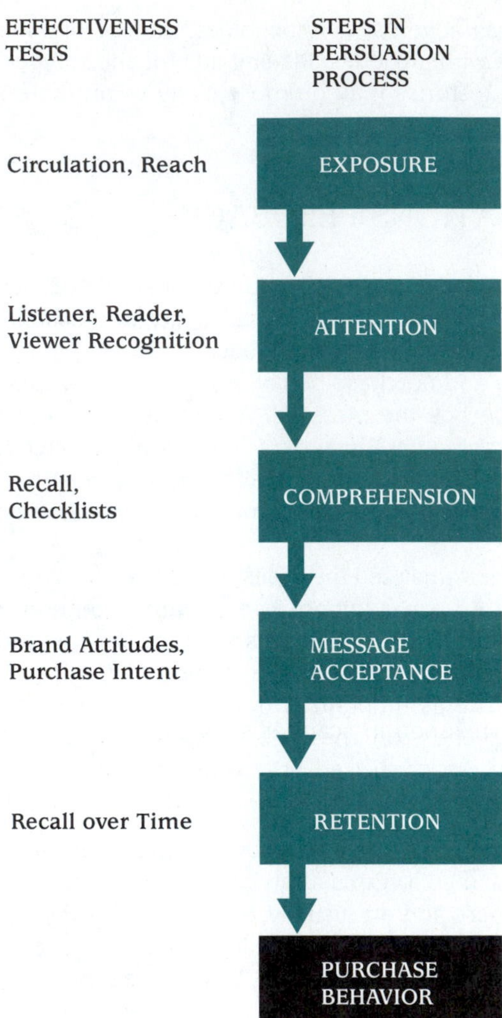

FIGURE 11.3 Methods of obtaining feedback in the decoding process

Source: Adapted from William J. McGuire, "An Information-Processing Model of Advertising Effectiveness," in H. L. David and A. J. Silk, eds., *Behavioral and Management Sciences in Marketing* (New York: Ronald/Wiley, 1978), p. 161. Reprinted with permission from J. Wiley & Sons and William J. McGuire.

whether consumers recalled a commercial and associated it with the brand. Such an association provides some assurance that consumers were attentive to the ad at the time of exposure.

3. *Comprehension* is measured primarily by tests of recall of specific points in the ad. The Gallup and Robinson readership service asks respondents to recall and describe sales messages of specific print ads. Similarly, advertisers use "day-after recall" tests to measure comprehension of TV commercials by probing consumers who recalled the ad to play back specific points in the commercial. In this manner, advertisers can evaluate comprehension of the ad's theme.

4. *Message acceptance* is best measured by its impact on brand attitudes or purchase intent. For example, consumer attitudes toward the brand can be measured prior to and after exposure to print or TV ads. Comparisons of matched groups of consumers exposed to the message and those not exposed can show the effect of the message on attitude change. The Partnership for a Drug-Free America measured message acceptance by comparing attitudes in areas with heavy and light exposure to the campaign. Significantly greater shifts in attitudes against drug use in high-exposure areas indicated acceptance of the campaign's message.

5. *Retention* is measured by consumers' recall of the advertising message after a period of time. Consumers are likely to forget messages over time unless they are repeated. The most effective messages are those that are likely to be retained longest.

The measures in Figure 11.3 assume indirect feedback, that is, no direct link among the five steps involved in the decoding process and purchase behavior. In other words, when marketers obtain sales results, they do not know if consumers who purchased were exposed to the advertising campaign, comprehended it, or retained its messages. Recently, technology has created the possibility of establishing a link between consumers' exposure to advertising and subsequent behavior. The link is **scanner data;** that is, recording sales at checkout counters through electronic scanners. Research companies have identified households who shop in scanner stores and have installed TV meters in these households to record television exposure. In this way, researchers know if consumers who bought, for example, Diet Coke watched a Diet Coke commercial during the previous week. Such direct feedback is promising in trying to evaluate the impact of advertising on consumers' purchasing behavior.

Despite these advances, advertisers are a long way from determining with any precision the effects of marketing communications on purchasing behavior. Advertisers still have difficulty separating their communications strategies from the many other variables that influence consumers' purchasing behavior. The problem remains much as John Wanamaker, the famous Philadelphia retailer, described it over a century ago: "I know half my advertising is working, but I don't know which half."

SOCIETAL IMPLICATIONS OF MARKETING COMMUNICATIONS

Most marketing communication is socially responsible. Unfortunately, however, some strategies violate the public trust. Two types of communication are of concern: deceptive advertising and irresponsible advertising.

Deceptive Advertising

Deceptive advertising is advertising that gives false information or that willfully misleads consumers about the brand's benefits. Deception occurs when consumers acquire false beliefs because of exposure to advertising. For example, in 1990, Volvo ran an ad showing one of its station wagons being run over by a "Monster Truck." The Volvo survived, but the competing cars were crushed. The problem was that the Volvo had been reinforced with metal and wooden struts before the test, and the other cars had been weakened by having their roof supports cut. Volvo then withdrew the ad, blaming its advertising agency for the deception, and ran letters of apology in *The Wall Street Journal* and *USA Today*.[83]

http://www.volvo.se/

As we saw in Chapter 2, the Federal Trade Commission monitors deceptive advertising by either ordering a company to cease its campaign or by ordering the advertiser to correct deceptive claims through new advertising. The Food and Drug Administration also has a role in controlling deceptive advertising. It can order manufacturers of foods and drugs to change claims in advertising or on packages. For example, the FDA ordered several marketers of fiber cereals to stop claiming that they reduce the risk of heart disease.

http://www.fda.gov/

Irresponsible Advertising

An advertising claim does not have to be deceptive to violate the public trust; it can be irresponsible. **Irresponsible advertising** depicts or encourages irresponsible behavior or portrays groups in an irresponsible manner.

An example of encouraging irresponsible behavior was an ad for Reebok sneakers in which two bungee-cord jumpers are shown diving from a bridge. The final shot shows only the Reebok jumper connected to his bungee cord; the other cord has a pair of empty Nike's attached to it. The campaign was meant to combine comparative advertising and humor, but it gave the unfortunate impression that the Nike wearer plunged to his death. *Adweek* magazine editorialized that "this is the sort of [advertising] that gives bad taste a bad name."[84] The ad for Bauer in-line skates in Exhibit 11.4 verges on the irresponsible by seeming to encourage dangerous skating actions in the photo and the tagline, "It's fun in the same twisted way that having a near death experience is fun."

http://www.reebok.com/

http://www.nike.com/

At time, advertising has also been irresponsible in its portrayal of women and minorities. Women have often been portrayed as stupid or dominated by men. African Americans have often been stereotyped in roles as athletes, musicians, or recipients of charity. Fortunately, there are fewer differences in depictions of African Americans and whites.

Advertisers are also more aware in dealing with female target audiences and are portraying women in more realistic purchasing roles. Saturn, for example, has changed the traditional image of women as being interested only in the styling and interior of a car. The company's ads feature actual women who have bought Saturns, including a former airplane pilot (see Exhibit 11.9).

http://www.saturncars.com/

▶EXHIBIT 11.9
Portraying women in more realistic purchasing roles

Deceptive and irresponsible advertising is unlikely to disappear. The FTC and FDA will continue an important monitoring role. However, ultimately, marketers must regulate themselves. A positive sign is the greater awareness that marketers have of their responsibility to society. An example is advertising by some beer companies to discourage underage persons from drinking.

SUMMARY

The chapter first presented a model of the marketing communications process in five steps: (1) development of an idea to be communicated by the marketer, (2) encoding the idea by the advertiser, (3) transmission by the mass media, (4) decoding the message and action by the consumer, and (5) feedback to the advertiser to evaluate the effectiveness of the campaign. Marketers must consider the following questions in evaluating the effectiveness of advertising and other marketing communications:

1. Have communications objectives been formulated to reflect consumer needs?
2. Have marketers adequately encoded product benefits?
3. Has the message been transmitted to the target segment by utilizing the right media?
4. Did consumers decode the message in the manner the advertiser intended?
5. Does exposure to and acceptance of the message lead to a purchase?

The remainder of the chapter discussed the primary components of communications: source, message, media, receiver (consumer), and feedback.

Source effects focus on the credibility and acceptance of the source of the message. The greater the credibility of the source, the greater the likelihood consumers will accept the message. Source credibility is most important when consumers are not involved with the purchase. Involved consumers are more likely to focus on the message rather than on the source. Consumers regard reference groups, family, and impartial sources such as *Consumer Reports* and government agencies as more credible than commercial sources of information. Methods by which marketers could increase their credibility were considered.

The main issues considered in evaluating message effects were the merits of (1) hedonic versus utilitarian appeals, (2) one-sided versus two-sided appeals, (3) comparative advertising, (4) fear appeals, and (5) humor in advertising.

Studies of media effects demonstrate the importance of the media environment in affecting consumers' perception of an ad and acceptance of the message.

The consumers' role in the communication process was also considered. Consumers evaluate the source of a communication, the message, and the media in which the message is transmitted. In evaluating the message, consumers develop cognitive responses that determine message acceptance. They also develop attitudes toward ads that might influence their attitudes toward the advertised brand.

In the last step of the communications process, we considered certain key issues in feedback: the measurement of indirect feedback through consumer thought variables and the desirability yet difficulty of evaluating advertising based on direct consumer purchase response.

The chapter concluded by considering societal issues in marketing communications—namely, the need to monitor and control deceptive and irresponsible advertising.

QUESTIONS

1. Cite an example of an advertising campaign by describing:
   - Advertising objectives and product concept established by the source.
   - How these objectives were encoded into an advertising campaign.
   - Media plan used to transmit the message to the target group.
   - Criteria the company will use in evaluating consumers' process of decoding the message.
2. Using the illustration of barriers to communication cited in Figure 11.2, describe the problems marketers face in developing effective marketing communications.
3. What criteria could Eveready use in evaluating the effectiveness of the Energizer Bunny campaign?
4. Use attribution theory to explain why consumers are more likely to consider advertising less credible than personal or neutral sources of information.
5. Why are source effects more important in gaining message acceptance for low-involvement compared to high-involvement consumers?
6. Assume Exxon initiates a campaign to convince the public that high gas prices are justified as a means of encouraging domestic exploration for oil. What principles could Exxon use to increase its credibility?
7. What strategies can companies use to increase their attractiveness as sources of marketing communications? Provide examples.
8. One use of emotional advertising is to try to increase the consumer's involvement with a product. Why has use of this type of advertising increased since the mid-1980s?
9. Two-sided advertisements were described as means of increasing both credibility and message acceptance.
   - What are the advantages of using two-sided ads?
   - Why are so few advertisements two-sided?
10. Assume state and local agencies in California wish to undertake an educational campaign to alert the public to the dangers of earthquakes. They use several ads to show the severe devastation that earthquakes can produce to convince the public of the importance of the educational campaign. What factors are likely to encourage and discourage the acceptance of the message?
11. What are the risks of relying on an advertising campaign based on (a) comparative advertising and (b) humor?
12. How can advertisers discourage counterarguments when consumers are viewing an ad?
13. Given the difficulties in evaluating the effects of an advertising message on consumers' purchase deci-

sion, advertisers have used measures of consumer attention, comprehension, and retention of advertising as criteria of effectiveness.

- What are some of the limitations of using these measures as criteria of advertising effectiveness?
- What approaches to advertising evaluation hold promise for providing direct feedback to establish the link between the advertising message and consumer behavior?

14. Provide examples of deceptive and irresponsible advertising. Who should be responsible for monitoring and controlling such advertising?

RESEARCH ASSIGNMENTS

1. Show consumers an ad for a high-involvement product (such as a car or investment service) and a low-involvement product (toothpaste, paper towels). As consumers are looking at each ad, ask them to express their thoughts. Classify their comments into those that are related to message content versus those that are related to nonmessage (peripheral) elements in the ad (the use of a spokesperson, scenery, and so on).

   Based on research cited in the text, we would expect consumers to express more message-related thoughts when viewing high-involvement ads and more nonmessage thoughts expressed when viewing low-involvement ads. Did your study confirm this hypothesis?

2. Develop three advertising messages:

   a. One-sided ad (for example, "Avis is great").
   b. Two-sided refutational ad ("Avis is number 2, but we try harder [than Hertz]").
   c. Two-sided nonrefutational ad ("Avis may be smaller and may not have as many locations, but Avis is best in terms of price, the reliability of its cars, and service").

   Ask 50 consumers to rate all three ads on (a) believability, (b) trustworthiness, and (c) expertise of the source. Ask consumers how likely they would be to buy the product or service after seeing each ad.

   - Do the results conform to the findings on credibility and the effects of two-sided and comparative advertising cited in the text?
   - What are the strategic implications of the findings?

PART IV

THE INDIVIDUAL CONSUMER: CHARACTERISTICS AND LIFESTYLES

In the last section, we considered the individual consumer's thought processes leading up to a purchasing decision. Consumer perceptions and attitudes are likely to be conditioned by their demographic characteristics and lifestyles. A working woman in her early 50s with grown children is likely to emphasize a very different set of attributes in buying a car compared to a working woman in her early 30s with two children in day care. The attitudes and perceptions of these two consumers will vary in accordance with their needs. Similarly, a couple that describes themselves as "couch potatoes" may react very differently to ads for products from furniture to electronics compared to a couple that is cosmopolitan and outgoing.

In this section, we consider three key sets of consumer characteristics that are likely to condition the consumer's thought processes: demographics, lifestyles, and personality. We consider key demographic trends in Chapter 12, such as the aging of the baby boomers and the increasing importance of generation Xers. We also consider social class as an offshoot of demographics since one's status in society is largely determined by income, occupation, and education.

In Chapter 13, we review important lifestyle trends such as the greater time pressure on American consumers, the move away from the prevailing emphasis on nutrition and fitness to a more self-indulgent lifestyle, and a decrease in differentiation of purchasing roles between men and women. We also consider the effects of personality variables on purchasing decisions in this chapter. Traits such as dominance, compulsiveness, and aggressiveness are more deep-seated than demographics or lifestyles and are likely to affect purchases of involving products.

Chapters 12 and 13 also emphasize the use of demographics, lifestyles, and personality in developing marketing strategies.

DEMOGRAPHICS AND SOCIAL CLASS

Chapter 12

BMW TARGETS AN EMERGING DEMOGRAPHIC GROUP:

PROFESSIONAL WOMEN

Demographic characteristics such as age, income, family size, and employment status are the objective descriptors of individuals and households. The consumer thought variables we considered in the last five chapters—primarily perceptions and attitudes—are cognitive processes that are specific to a product. Perceptions and attitudes are formed in consumers' minds regarding brands and products. In contrast, demographics are objective characteristics (age is age; income is income) that are not product-specific. One's age and income can affect purchases of everything from autos to deodorants. **Social class,** that is, one's ranking in society based on power and prestige, is defined primarily by demographic characteristics, namely occupation, income, and education.

In this chapter, we focus on the nature of demographics and social class and their applications to marketing strategy. Specifically, we consider demographic trends that have changed the shape of American society, namely:

- Population growth.
- The changing age distribution of the American marketplace.

- Socioeconomic changes affecting purchasing power and patterns of consumption.
- Changes in household composition.

We then discuss the nature and importance of social class distinctions in American society and how they help shape consumer purchases. The chapter also considers applications of demographics and social class to marketing strategy in two areas: defining target segments and *micromarketing,* that is, using demographic information to reach individual consumers rather than broader market segments.

In discussing strategic applications, we will see that marketers are defining more specific demographic segments than in the past. Whereas 10 years ago marketers might have defined the increasing proportion of working women as a target for autos or clothing, today they might split that group by occupation (professional, white collar, and blue collar) or more broadly by social class (upper, middle, lower). For example, many marketers are now targeting the growing number of professional women because of their increased earning power. The prerequisite is understanding their needs and attitudes. Cosmetic companies such as Revlon and clothing manufacturers such as Donna Karan have been successful in such efforts, partly because these are product categories that have targeted women all along.

http://www.revlon.com/
http://www.donnakaran.com/

On the other side of the coin, the luxury auto market has stumbled terribly in its attempts to target professional women because the market has been traditionally male-dominant. It had spent so many decades using scantily clad models to entice men that it seemed to have no idea what the professional woman wanted. At first, some car makers tried placing women in the same product ads they had always produced for men. However, it quickly became clear that a more dramatic approach was needed, especially when the automobile showroom remained a place where women were treated like second-class citizens. With women responsible for 46 percent of car sales and spending $65 billion annually on cars, companies such as BMW began a large-scale effort to better understand them.[1]

http://www.bmwusa.com/

The new demographic research was revealing. BMW, for example, had thought that professional women wanted a car designed specifically for them, but focus groups showed that they share the same desires as men: they want a car that is safe, reliable, and durable. Likewise, conventional wisdom held that women tended to buy with their children in mind. However, a survey conducted by the Condé Nast magazine group found that women are "more likely to purchase cars for themselves" while men are "more likely to buy cars for the family."[2]

While BMW has shied away from creating a "woman's commercial," it has used this data to stress style and performance in its appeals to women. In 1993, for instance, the company invited women journalists to view video testimonials from female BMW owners discussing road feel and driving excitement. The hope was that the writers would convey the testimonials to their audience, thereby creating interest among prospective women customers. In 1994, BMW started seminars for women on subjects such as traction control and braking systems and invited them to take a BMW out for a test drive.[3] In explaining why car companies must stop talking down to women drivers, one BMW executive said: "Women under 40 grew up driving, not sitting in the passenger seat." To reach the 25- to 50-year-old professional woman with an active lifestyle who it believes is its ideal customer, BMW underwrites rock climbing competitions, biking events, marathons, and even triathalons.

The 1980s and 1990s have seen many other major demographic changes that have had an impact on American society. Baby boomers (the group born in the two decades after World War II) are now reaching 50, the mature market (those over 50) is growing rapidly, and nontraditional households are becoming the norm as a result of later marriages, more divorces, and more singles.

One caution regarding this chapter: it considers demographic trends in the U.S. market. Worldwide demographic trends have also affected marketing strategies of international companies. Global aspects of consumer behavior are considered in Chapter 15. Also, there are major differences in demographic characteristics between whites, African Americans, Hispanic Americans, and Asian Americans. These differences are also considered in Chapter 15 in a discussion of subcultures in the United States.

THE DEMOGRAPHIC FRAGMENTATION OF THE AMERICAN MARKET

Demographics have long been used to target consumers. We can refer to three periods in which demographics have been used, representing three distinct approaches: the *mass market era* (pre-1970), the *market segmentation era* (post-1970) and the *micromarketing era* (post-1990.) In the mass market era, marketers targeted broad demographic groupings because consumer needs and purchases tended to be more similar. GM could rely on its traditional socioeconomic division of the market by targeting Chevrolet to lower-income consumers and move up the income scale from Chevrolet to Pontiac to Oldsmobile to Buick to Cadillac in broad socioeconomic sweeps. Pepsi could target teens with its flagship brand without having to worry about expanding its product line to compete with New Age beverages. Campbell's Soup could simply target families with children. Levi could target a broad youth market for its jeans.

http://www.gm.com/

http://www.pepsi.com/

http://www.levi.com/

After 1970, several changes began to occur that made such a mass market approach infeasible. The proportion of working women increased, the traditional family of a married couple with children under 18 began to fragment, increased immigration from Asia and Latin America began to develop regional clusters of Asian and Hispanic Americans, and age groups such as baby boomers and generation Xers (those born between 1965 and 1977) began to be defined as subgroups with distinct norms and values. These changes resulted in differences in needs, attitudes, and purchasing behavior that marketers could not ignore. One could no longer talk about a youth market without distinguishing between specific age categories; one could no longer refer to the needs of working women without considering socioeconomic differences; and one could no longer talk about families without distinguishing between married couples and unmarried couples with and without children.

This fragmentation gave rise to a focus on market segmentation. GM could still position Chevrolet as its lowest priced cars, but now needed to target different models to younger consumers with families, singles, or white-collar working women with the common denominator being price consciousness. Campbell's would begin targeting its soups to specific ethnic groups on a regional basis with new flavors such as nacho cheese soups in Texas and Creole soups in the South, a far cry from selling tomato and chicken soup to a mass market. Levi introduced different jeans to older baby boomers, younger baby boomers, generation Xers, teens, and even preteens.

After 1990, marketers began to recognize the feasibility of going even further than market segmentation and began to talk about **micromarketing,** that is, reaching individual consumers based on their demographic characteristics. Micromarketing is an extension of market segmentation in that it breaks the market down into more finite components. Whereas market segmentation was brought about by the demographic fragmentation of the marketplace, micromarketing is the result of technological developments that make it easier for marketers to reach these fragments.

Three technological and data-related developments make micromarketing feasible. First, interactive technologies such as the Internet and Smart TV will make it possible for advertisers to target individual consumers with messages. Second, databases have been established through credit card usage or car registration that can identify the individual's demographic characteristics, allowing targeting through direct mail. Third, as we will see later, *geodemographic analysis* has allowed marketers to identify the demographic characteristics of zip code areas (or even zip code plus four areas). Research companies such as Claritas have grouped together zip code areas with common demographics such as the suburban elite, upwardly mobile young influentials in urban areas, and single-parent families in inner cities. Claritas has identified 62 such segments, allowing marketers to target them with direct mail or by regional promotions.

DEMOGRAPHIC TRENDS IN THE AMERICAN MARKETPLACE

Marketers define users and prospective users of their brands by demographic characteristics so as to target them with promotional, product, pricing, and distribution strategies. Developing such profiles requires an understanding of the nature of demographic trends in the marketplace. The increasing proportion of working women on professional career paths was a trend that led BMW to realize that this group was a natural target market for luxury cars.[4]

In this section, we consider the demographic trends that define the American marketplace. We start with the broadest demographic trend: changes in population growth.

Population Growth

The U.S. population has increased steadily since this country was formed, although this growth was interrupted from 1970 to 1990. In the 1990s, the United States is expected to experience its biggest population jump since the 1950s.[5]

Population growth is determined by three factors: birthrate, life span, and immigration. Immigration was instrumental in fueling growth until 1920. A high birthrate has fueled growth at various periods in our history, often tied to economic prosperity. For example, the birthrate was at a low during the Depression and World War II, and then it more than doubled after the war in what is known as the baby boom period. More recently, a rise in the birthrate, increased life expectancy, and increases in immigration have fueled population growth. Let us consider these three factors further.

Birthrate

Substantial swings have occurred in the birthrate since World War II (see Figure 12.1). The birthrate increased by 50 percent from 1940 to its highest point in 1957 and then decreased to a historic low in 1976. The period from 1946 to 1964 is known as the baby boom period, a term that reflects the higher birthrate at the time. From 1965 to 1976, the birthrate steadily decreased. Some called this period the "baby bust" period. From 1976 to 1985, the birthrate increased slightly, largely as a result of the baby boom generation entering its childbearing years. As a result of this "baby boomlet," by 1991 there were 15 percent more preschoolers than there were in 1980.[6]

The somewhat higher birthrate held steady through the mid-1990s, as 30-something baby boomers, new immigrants, and professionals in their 40s who delayed having families began having babies. However, the birthrate is expected to drop sharply again by the turn of the century as the baby boomers leave their childbearing years and the smaller baby buster group enters theirs.

http://www.gerber.com/

Gerber illustrates the impact of variations in the birthrate on marketing strategy. Declining baby food sales in the late 1960s and 1970s led the company to seek growth elsewhere. It unsuccessfully tried to diversify into foods for the elderly, life insurance, and transportation. The current increase in the birthrate provided an opportunity for the company to revert to the business it knows best—baby products. In 1993, after lending its name to children's clothing and toys, it introduced a microwaveable line of foods for toddlers called Gerber's Graduates. It financed this growth by selling off some of its ventures into adult products.[7]

FIGURE 12.1
Birthrate in the United States: 1940 to 2000

Sources: U.S. Department of Health and Human Services, *Monthly Vital Statistics Report* (June 7, 1990), Table I-1, pp. 1–7; U.S. Department of Commerce, Bureau of the Census, *Statistical Abstract of the United States, 1990* (Washington, D.C.: Government Printing Office, 1990), Table 821, p. 63; U.S. Department of Commerce, Bureau of the Census, *Statistical Abstract of the United States, 1996,* (Springfield, VA: National Technical Information Service, 1996), Table 109, p. 83.

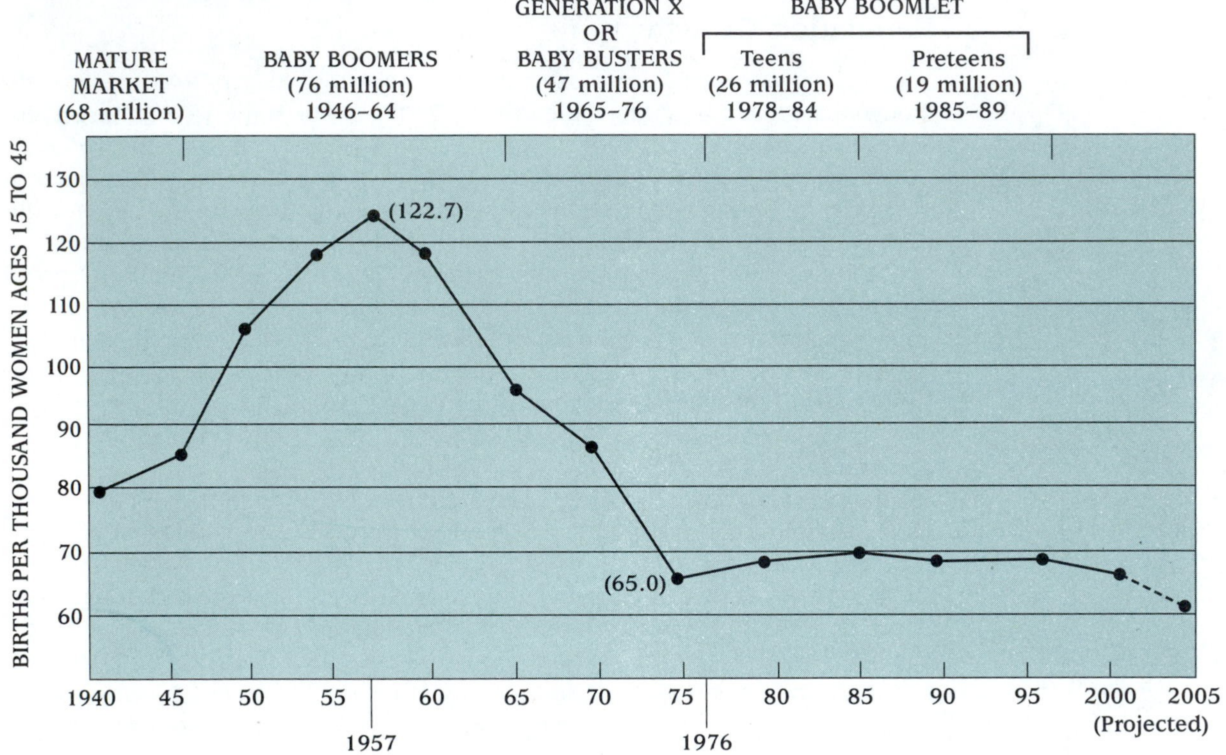

Gerber's move from food to a larger array of baby products reflects the baby boomers' willingness to spend more on their children. Since many marry and have children relatively late in life, they are willing to spend more on baby clothes and toys, thus creating a more lucrative market.

Life Expectancy

Due to medical improvements, life expectancy has been constantly increasing in recent years. Advances in combating heart disease and cancer have been instrumental in increasing longevity. Of equal importance has been the American people's awareness of how to care for themselves better. The proportion of smokers has declined steadily since the Surgeon General first linked smoking to can-

http://www.kraftfoods.com/

cer in 1965. The fact that Philip Morris makes substantially more money from cigarettes than from its ownership of General Foods, Kraft, and Miller combined is due to overseas cigarette sales. (Greater health awareness seems to be more of an American and Western European phenomenon than it is a worldwide trend.)

Americans are also more conscious of what they eat. The desire to reduce cholesterol intake has caused a shift away from red meat and dairy products. The trend was substantial enough to cause beef producers to band together and mount an educational campaign to convince consumers that beef is healthful. The trend to healthier foods has primarily affected product, rather than promotional, strategies. Producers of dairy foods are coming out with lines of low-cholesterol products, cereal companies with high-fiber products, and liquor manufacturers with lower-alcohol lines to reflect the trend away from hard liquor.

The combined effects of better medical care and greater health awareness have resulted in increased longevity in the past 20 years. From 1970 to 1995, the life expectancy of the average American went from 70 to 76 years. The number of people age 85 and older, meanwhile, will grow from 3.7 million in 1996 to 6.5 million by the year 2020 and to 18.2 million by 2050. By then, the number of Americans aged 100 and older will rise to 1 million, from 45,000 today.[8]

It should be noted that there are substantial differences in longevity by race and social class. Longevity for African Americans, which averages six years less than for whites, reflects poorer health care and less access to health care facilities.

Immigration

The third factor affecting population growth is immigration. With successive waves from the English-speaking countries, Western Europe, China, and Eastern European countries up to 1920, immigration was a significant factor in creating the American "melting pot." More recently, it has had an equally significant effect on the nation's population growth. The greatest immigration has occurred from Mexico and Central America, as well as from such Asian countries as Korea and Vietnam. In fact, it is estimated that by the middle of the next century, the U.S. population will include 82 million people who arrived in this country after 1991 or who were born to parents who did. This group will account for one out of every five Americans.[9]

Given this recent pattern, marketers are asking themselves how they can best target the Hispanic-American and Asian-American markets. Gerber, for one, has responded by introducing a line of foods made from tropical fruits such as papayas and mangos for the Hispanic-American market, which buys more prepared baby food than any other ethnic group.[10] Other marketers may target these markets with the same products and promotional strategies but will use media they are more likely to see or read. We will consider marketing to these groups when we discuss subcultures in Chapter 15.

Changing Age Composition

Figure 12.1 identifies three age groups that are the focus of most marketing strategies: (1) **baby boomers,** born between 1946 and 1964 and representing about 76 million consumers; (2) **baby busters,** also known as generation Xers, born between 1965 and 1976 and representing about 47 million consumers; and (3) the baby boomlet (**teens** and **preteens**) born from 1976 to 1990 and representing about 52 million consumers. Because they are not independent purchasers, children born after 1990 are generally not included as a segment, even though they are part of the baby boomlet. However, as we will see in Chapter 17, they can directly influence the parent's decision for items such as candy, cereals, or fast-food outlets.

A fourth group that has become increasingly important but is not shown in Figure 12.1 is the mature market (those born before 1946 and representing 56 million consumers).

Figure 12.1 presents age by generational groups. We can refer to the Depression Era generation (born before 1935), the World War II generation (born 1935–1945), the Woodstock generation (the older baby boomers), and the Vietnam generation (the younger baby boomers). These labels represent the defining moment for each generation in their youth. As such, these groupings are known as **age cohorts,** that is, people of similar ages who have gone through similar experiences.

As a result of these experiences, many individuals in age cohorts also share common values and needs that have not changed much since adolescence. Baby boomers have been described as independent types who see themselves stretching society's bounds.[11] Generation Xers (the baby busters) have been described as cynical, pessimistic, and alienated as a result of a bleak economic outlook and resentment for having to pay the future bill for an unbalanced budget and a polluted environment. Although a generalization that may not accurately reflect the views of many Xers, such descriptions may be useful in painting age groups in broad strokes. Levi's strategy reflects an age cohort perspective as it followed the aging baby boomers by moving them from jeans to Dockers to adapt to their expanding waistlines, and more currently by introducing Slates, a new line of slacks to meet their growing need for casual wear in the office.

Another important perspective on age is to project future age distributions. Figure 12.2 effectively portrays the future "graying of America." It shows that the fastest-growing age group will be the 65+ group (the older mature market). In 1970, this group represented one out of every 10 Americans. By 2030, one out of five Americans will be over 65. This increase represents the weight of baby boomers moving into the mature market and increased life expectancies. By 2010, the first baby boomers will be 65+ with steady growth in this segment thereafter. The marketing implications of the graying of America are enormous. Marketers generally do not target this segment, but as it grows, they will have to. Everything from autos to furniture to clothing will have to be designed

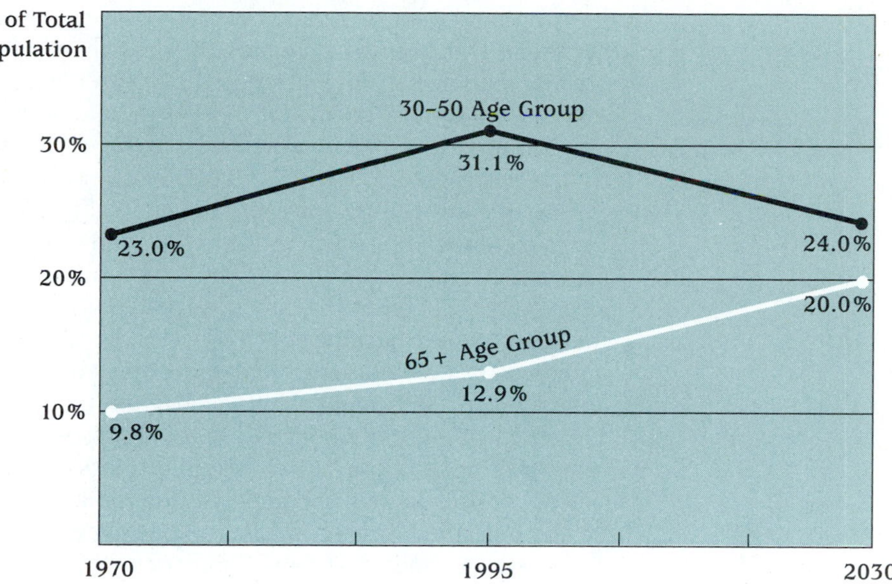

FIGURE 12.2 Projections for two key age groups: 1970 to 2030

Sources: U.S. Bureau of the Census, *Statistical Abstract of the United States, 1996* (Springfield, VA: National Technical Information Service, 1996), Tables 14 and 16; and "Rise and Fall of Generations," *American Demographics* (July 1996), p. 6.

with the 65+ group in mind. Further, there will be a major redistribution in purchasing expenditures as more money goes to health care.

In contrast, the proportion of Americans that are 30 to 50 will decline significantly from 1995 to 2050. This group grew rapidly from 1970 to 1995, reflecting the weight of the baby boomers, but the graying of America will mean proportionately fewer consumers in this broad age group.

Given the importance of the age cohorts in Figure 12.1, we will consider each in turn.

Baby Boomers (33 to 51 years old)

Marketers have focused on the baby boom generation more than any other group. The reasons are not hard to find: they are 75.7 million strong, or 29 percent of the U.S. population. Most are in their prime spending years and have $985 billion in income.[12] As these baby boomers age, their spending power is increasing. Over the next 10 years, average income for all U.S. households should increase by about one-half. However, income for baby boomers should double.[13] Baby boomers will represent the largest chunk of purchasing power in the country as they move into their 50s.

The greater purchasing power of baby boomers is also a result of their high level of education. They are less likely to marry, but if they do, they are more likely to be in dual-income households and to delay parenthood. These factors combine to create higher discretionary income.

The values of the baby boom generation have largely shaped marketing strategies to this group. Once rebellious as a result of the Vietnam War and Watergate, baby boomers then became more acquisitive, materialistic, and conservative. Their leading-edge assertiveness defined fashion trends, identified the popular auto makes, and introduced computer literacy as the norm. By the early 1980s, they were spending far more on furniture, cars, and electronics than the average American.[14] The term *yuppies* (young, urban professionals) was coined to describe these acquisitive and self-indulgent boomers.

By the late 1980s, however, a subtle shift began taking place. Middle-aged introspection combined with the stock market crash in 1987 caused many to step back and question the easy affluence and acquisitiveness of the 1980s. As a result, baby boomers became less materialistic. Focusing on issues outside of themselves, they became more concerned with the environment, social issues, and personal development. In addition, they became more concerned about their children and the society they would grow up in. These former free-spenders turned more serious about quality-of-life issues, earning them the nickname *grumpies,* for grown-up urban mature professionals.

As a result, advertising appeals to materialism and acquisitiveness began to be less relevant. Michelob Light's campaign, asserting "You can have it all," failed because it assumed that baby boomers were, in the words of one writer, motivated by "the compulsive compilation of more and more achievement-oriented activities."[15] The theme simply did not link the product to the needs of grumpies, since most realized that you simply cannot have it all. By 1993, the beer company had shifted its strategy to appeal to the values of an older audience.

Most marketers have come to believe that their products' success will depend on how they adapt to this generation's transition to middle age. That is why American Express has tried to portray boomers in family situations; one ad shows a father on the beach with his son under the slogan "You have your own view of what's important." Similarly, Varilux began a campaign to attract aging baby boomers who need bifocals with the tag line, "Erase the line between youth and middle age."

Changes in values will also cause baby boomers to spend more money on home improvements, travel, education, recreation, and other facets of self-development. As a result, companies developing new products and services in these areas are likely to benefit most from the growing affluence of baby boomers.

Younger versus Older Baby Boomers. Given the 18-year span defining the baby boom market, it would be misleading to treat it as one age cohort with similar tastes and values. Broadly speaking, there are two cohorts of baby boomers: the older baby boomers (those born in the first half of the baby boom generation from 1946 to 1954) and the younger boomers (those born from 1955 to 1964).

The older boomers are the ones who have caught the attention of marketers and shaped the definition of what baby boomers want and value. The defining moment for this group was on January 1, 1996, when the first boomers reached 50. Marketers have begun to direct their attention to a mature baby boomer, for example, the ads in Exhibit 12.1 for skin cream to eliminate wrinkles and

EXHIBIT 12.1
Ads directed to the aging baby boomer

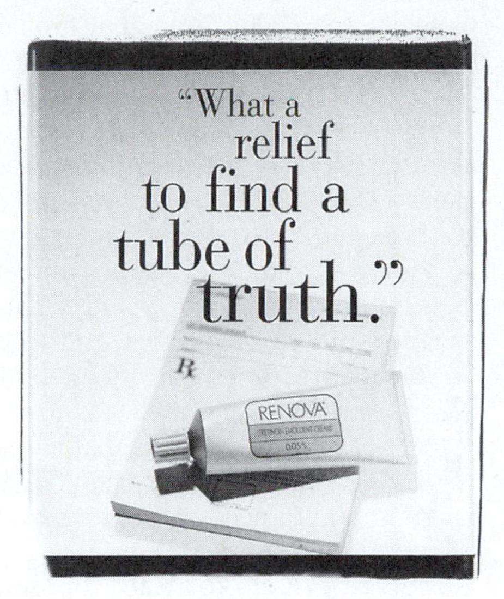

the need for a checkup among baby boomers old enough to remember the first landing on the moon. But as more boomers reach 50, they are likely to redefine the meaning of aging just as they have redefined every other life stage they have been through.[16] And, they are unlikely to accept the tendency of marketers to ignore consumers over 50. The older boomers always got attention from the marketplace, and they will continue to do so.

Younger baby boomers represent the majority of boomers. They are not the antiestablishment generation that was molded by the Vietnam War and Watergate.[17] They tend to be more conservative than their older siblings and did not go through the change from materialism to personal development described earlier. Appeals to the older baby boomers do not always catch the attention of the junior group. If anything, younger baby boomers resent the older group because as 30- to 40-year-olds, they had to compete in a tight job market during the 1990–1991 recession and often found their way blocked by older boomers. Marketers must fine-tune their ads to distinguish between the older and younger groups or develop a theme that is relevant to all. The KinderCare ad in Exhibit 12.2 is geared to younger baby boomers since they are likely to have younger children and to need child care services.

Generation Xers (or Baby Busters) (20 to 32)

Generation Xers (the baby bust generation) are composed of 47.4 million consumers born from 1965 to 1976. Since this was a period of the lowest birthrate in this century, there are fewer young adults today than there were 10 or 15 years ago. However, consumers in their 20s and early 30s are responsible for $125 billion in spending each year.[18] About a quarter of their annual spending comes from discretionary income, making baby busters prime customers for restaurants, alcoholic beverages, clothing, and electronics.[19]

Xers are a varied lot, from college seniors to young executives. In general terms, they have been described as more multicultural, media-savvy, tech-oriented, and cynical about their future than baby boomers. They are also more self-reliant and save a larger proportion of their incomes than baby boomers, anticipating an old age with no Social Security and soaring health costs. They are coming of age in an economically depressed time (the median income for households headed by adults in their age group was $24,500—a 21 percent decline from 1973 in constant dollars), and busters blame their elders for leaving them the check after a decade of free spending. They also tend to feel neglected by a marketing establishment that has been distracted by the higher-profile boomers, leading to their designation as the anonymous "generation X."[20] All of this has made busters more conservative than their elders and more concerned with environmental issues, drugs, and the AIDS epidemic.

http://www.7up.com/

Although described as cynical and full of doom and gloom, research by 7-Up found this to be an exaggerated profile of Xers. Many actually prefer to think positively about life and take a more practical and pragmatic approach to purchasing decisions than baby boomers. As a result, 7-Up targeted Xers in a 1996 campaign that combined upbeat visuals with rhythmic music to show a positive spirit.[21]

Marketers have tried targeting Xers by appealing to their pragmatism and by creating ads that are stripped of glitz and self-deprecation."[22] For example, Liz Claiborne's Curve perfume was developed from focus groups that showed that Xers are

> facing situations that previous generations didn't have to go through, but they have a very positive attitude. They don't know what's around the corner, but they're willing to accept the challenge and embrace it.[23]

http://www.ibm.com/

The tagline of the ad, "See where it takes you," reflects this attitude. The IBM ad in Exhibit 12.2 shows an Xer who is comfortable with the detailed computer specs for an IBM Think Pad. The tagline "Lighten Up" is a play on the sometimes serious self-absorbed focus of Xers. IBM's purpose is to reverse its stodgy image among Xers who think the company is geared exclusively to corporations.[24]

Teens (13 to 19)

They are not easily hyped and hard to shock. They are more environmentally aware and health conscious than past youths. They are concerned not only about

EXHIBIT 12.2
Targeting Baby Boomers and Generation Xers

everyday woes like acne and bad hair, but by real-world problems like AIDS and gang violence. They love sports but are disillusioned by sports and celebrity scandals. They are more cyberliterate than even Xers and are comfortable with any new technology.[25]

There are 25.6 million teenagers aged 13 to 19 who were born in the early baby boomlet period from 1977 to 1983 (some have started calling them generation Y). Their combined spending is over $50 billion a year on products and services, and they influence another $200 billion in spending.[26] They are more materialistic and self-confident than their parents as shown by the following survey conducted by *American Demographics* magazine in 1971 and in 1993:[27]

GLOBAL APPLICATIONS OF CONSUMER BEHAVIOR

▶ In Japan the Xers, Not the Boomers, Are the Movers and Shakers

Whereas in the United States, the baby boomers were the defining generation for styles and fashion, in Japan they were something of a yawn. Japan also had a postwar baby boom, but it peaked in 1949, eight years earlier than in the United States. As a result, boomers were a smaller part of the population.

But it is not smaller numbers that define the lack of impact of boomers in Japan. Boomers accepted the norms and values of their parents. There was no hint of rebellion in their attitudes toward family or institutions. As a result, marketers took them for granted, correctly assuming that what worked for their parents would work for their boomer children.

Boomers' attitudes toward cars is an example. Growing up in a devastated postwar Japan, they saw a car as a status symbol rather than an expression of self and wanted a fancy sedan, a reflection of their parents' tastes.

The group that played the role of change agents in Japan were the equivalent of generation Xers, young adults in their late 20s and early 30s. They have broken the old rules and established new ones. They were the first to break with the traditionalism and male dominance of Japanese society. In the car market, they were the first to lead the move out of sedans and into minivans and sport-utility vehicles. They are the first group in which more than 50 percent of women have a driver's license. And, they are the first group to show the beginnings of a feminist movement as younger women begin demanding some semblance of equality in the workplace.

If generation Xers have the same impact in Japan as boomers had in the United States, that tradition-bound country is going to change in a big way.

Source: "Thirtysomethings dominate Japan's Market Direction," *Advertising Age* (April 1, 1996), p. S18.

	1993	*1971*
I am going to college so I can make more money.	75.1%	49.4%
It is important to be very well off financially.	74.5	40.1
I am above average in leadership ability.	55.9	34.9
I am above average in popularity.	45.6	29.2

Because these were the *latchkey* kids (young children whose parents work and have to fend for themselves when they come home from school) of the older baby boomers, teens have spent more hours outside their parents' influence than any generation before. They have taken on more family responsibilities such as food shopping. Not surprisingly, advertisers such as General Foods, Castle & Cooke, Kraft, and Lipton have begun targeting magazines such as *Seventeen.* Fortune 500 companies such as AT&T have used a number of other teen market magazines—from *Details* to *YM* to *Sassy*—to get their messages across in the hopes that teens will be able to influence their parents' behavior.

http://www.lipton.com/

Teens are also major consumers of media. They watch 5.25 hours of MTV a week, see 2.5 motion pictures a month, are heavy FM radio listeners, and are the largest group of regular prime time TV viewers.[28] Because of their media consumption and the fact that they are willing to experiment with new products, teens form a very attractive market for manufacturers looking to establish long-term loyalty. As the publisher of *Teen* magazine remarked, "Teens may sample extensively as they struggle with forming their own identities, but brand loyalty sets in by age 18."[29]

http://www.mtv.com/

Among the companies trying to build long-term loyalty is Kodak. The film company made a commitment to the teen market in 1992 after its survey data showed that teenagers like taking photos of one another and consider it a bonding experience. Kodak reacted by creating commercials for its Kodacolor film that show a teenage girl's room with photos of her friends strewn across it.[30] Levi Strauss & Co. is another company targeting teens by introducing its 900 Series® of "Real Jeans." The Polaroid ad in Exhibit 12.3 shows the ambivalence of today's teenagers who want to demonstrate independence yet still have strong ties to the home.

http://www.kodak.com/

The youth experience has been one of America's most successful exports, making teen demographic marketing a global phenomenon. Like their American peers, Japanese teens are ruggedly individualistic and have rebelled against the flashy advertising of the 1980s. In fact, they have come to be called the *shinjinrui,* or "new breed of man," because they are so different from their elders.[31] As a result, the environmentally sensitive cosmetics The Body Shop makes sell better in Japan than those from Chanel, and value-oriented products such as L. L. Bean are popular.[32]

http://www.the-body-shop.com/
http://www.llbean.com/

Preteens (8 to 12)

The 18.8 million 8- to 12-year-olds are also mostly children of baby boomers and form the later component of the baby boomlet. They are important to mar-

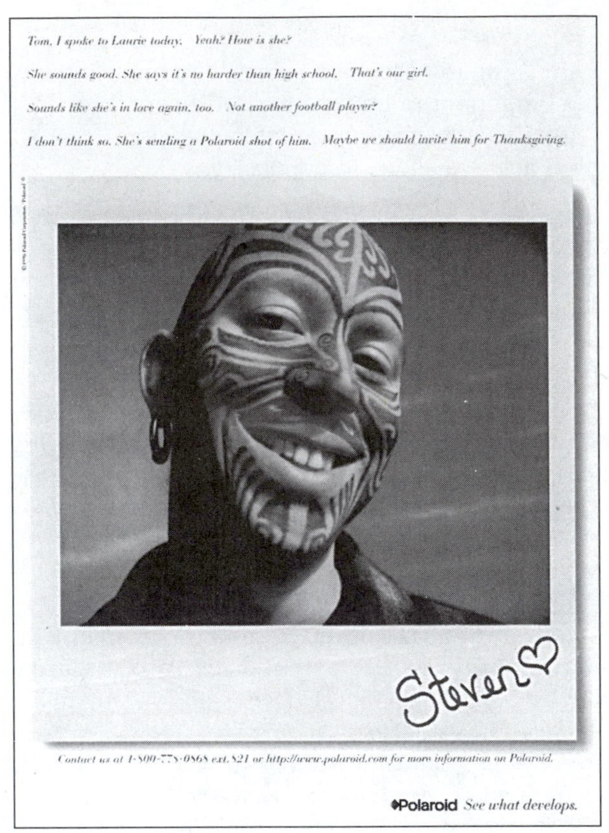

▶EXHIBIT 12.3
Polaroid targets teens

keters as much for their potential as future consumers as for their current purchasing power. Estimates of their pocket money range from $6 billion to $30 billion per year.[33] However, parents are an even greater source of purchasing power for this group. Most preteens live in dual-earning households. Between 1970 and 1993, the number of dual-earning married couples with children increased from 12.7 million to 16.3 million.[34] Further, preteens are increasingly likely to live in nontraditional households—single-parent households or with step-parents. For example, the number of children living with single parents more than doubled from 7 million in 1970 to 15.5 million in 1995.[35]

Many baby boom parents feel guilty for not spending more time with their children and assuage this guilt by being more willing to buy what children want. The combination of parents' expenditures plus their own money makes preteens an area of opportunity for many product categories. One survey found that children influenced $132 billion in purchases in more than 60 categories in the early 1990s.[36] This makes kid-spending one of the fastest-growing sectors of the American economy.

In fact, as retail sales sagged during the 1991–1992 recession, manufacturers looked to the preteen market to boost profits. To keep the refrigerated yogurt category growing in double digits, for instance, General Mills rolled out Yoplait Trix Lowfat, with two colored layers and a third on top. Dannon followed suit with Sprinkl'ins—a fruit-flavored cup doused with rainbow-colored sprinkles.[37] Likewise, Procter & Gamble tried to mine the largely ignored 8- to 12-year-old shampoo set by placing the Pert name on a product for the group.[38] As a result of these types of activities, a new niche of magazines has emerged to cater to children. Two of the best known are Time Warner's *Sports Illustrated for Kids* and the Walt Disney Company's *Disney Adventures*.

http://www.pg.com/

Preteens are almost as cyberliterate as their teenage siblings. Two-thirds of kindergarten kids have used a computer,[39] and by one estimate, in the next five years the number of preteens with access to a computer should triple.[40] Some are beginning to call this group the *Net generation,* given their skills with the Internet and new technologies. As a result, computer companies are beginning to target computers to preteens. Apple, for example, introduced a Macintosh for the whole family called the Performa. Consumer electronics is another traditionally adult category that has been targeted to preteens. Polaroid introduced its Cool Cam instant camera to this group with a sticker price of less than $40 for the camera and expected most purchases to be made by preteens.[41] As Exhibit 12.4. shows, Apple's strategy contrasts with Polaroid's because it is targeting the parent with ads in magazines such as *Better Homes and Gardens*.

http://www.apple.com/

http://www.polaroid.com/

▶EXHIBIT 12.4
Targeting electronic products to preteens and to their parents.

Companies market to preteens as future adults. A McDonald's spokesperson said, "You can see McDonald's appealing to kids to buy hamburgers to create brand recognition and preference so they buy hamburgers for themselves and their children later on."[42] Similarly, in referring to Banquet Kid Cuisine, the president of ConAgra noted, "The appeal isn't simply satisfying kids' needs now, but also developing them as users of our products so that they'll buy as adults."[43]

The Mature Market (50-Plus)

The 68 million Americans who are 50 and over are often divided into four subsegments to distinguish younger and older consumers in the mature market. The four groups are:

- *The bridge generation* (50 to 64), labeled as such because they bridge the attitudes of their parents and baby boom children. This group represents about half of the mature market.
- The elderly (65 to 74).
- The aged (75 to 84).
- The very old (85-plus).

As consumers age, their purchasing power and income decrease. However, discretionary income continues to rise, because they have fulfilled obligations like mortgages and children's education. People age 65 and older have the highest discretionary income of any group.[44]

Overall, the mature market represents the most powerful buying group in the American economy. Although they make up one-fourth of the U.S. population, they control half its discretionary income and 77 percent of its assets. Despite the fact that many in this group are retired, they still earn more than $800 billion in income each year, a figure close to the earning power of baby boomers. Further enhancing the desirability of marketing to this group is the fact that the mature market represents 80 percent of all expenditures for leisure travel, 50 percent of all purchases of domestic cars, and 44 percent of all expenditures for home remodeling.[45]

Given their tremendous purchasing potential, it is curious that marketers target so few products and ads to this group. According to Grey Advertising, a large ad agency, only 6 or 7 percent of TV commercials target the mature market, and only a handful of products or services are tailored to their needs. Of the handful of commercials targeted to older consumers, almost all suffer from what Grey calls the Methuselah Syndrome, that is, portraying the 50-plus consumer as frail, cutesy, and prunelike. As one executive quipped, "Everyone in the world of advertising seems to move straight from 32 to 75-plus."[46]

There are two probable reasons why marketers have not targeted the mature market. First, most marketers are under 50 and do not understand how to appeal to older consumers. Second, older consumers do not like to be reminded of their age. The general approach to the mature market has been to advertise a product to, say, generation Xers or baby boomers using youthful models in the expectation that a portion of the mature market will also buy it. There is some validity to this approach. In general, mature consumers think of themselves as 15 years younger than their actual age. One survey found that consumers aged 50 and older believe old age does not start until age 79; in 1985, they said it began at age 71.[47] As a result, mature consumers prefer to identify with younger spokespersons.

Advertisers are beginning to portray a more vital and involving mature consumer. The most important reason for this change is the fact that baby boomers are starting to qualify for the 50+ label. Since this was the generation that marketers and the media focused on, it is little wonder that their perspective on aging is beginning to change. Baby boomers are starting to redefine the worship of a youth culture in American society by portraying maturing adults in a youthful context. This is illustrated by the change in Quaker Oats' advertising strategy. When Quaker Oats positioned its oatmeal to older consumers, it first used the veteran character actor Wilford Brimley in scenes where he sat stolidly at the dining room table or walked slowly through a park with his grandchildren. However, the image of Brimley as an old geezer backfired in attempting to appeal to mature consumers. So Quaker traded in Brimley for "George," a 60-something model who wears a muscle shirt with bulging biceps.[48]

http://www.QuakerOats.com/

The conclusion is that strategies aimed at the mature market based on negative stereotypes are inappropriate. The ad for Manchester Clinic in Exhibit 12.5 is an example of a negative portrayal of mature consumers. Marketers who emphasize vitality rather than age are more likely to be successful. The ad for Nivea skin care products in Exhibit 12.5 is a conscious attempt by the company to move away from an obsession with the young. It is being targeted to the 60 million women aged 50+ in Western Europe using an attractive and vital 53-year-old model.

This emphasis on youth is targeted primarily to consumers aged 50 to 74. For those over 75, marketers must design products with their age in mind. For example, AT&T has developed phone-receiver amplifiers, automatic emergency dialing attachments, and daytime long-distance discounts for older retired consumers.[49] Choice Hotels has set aside rooms for older customers fitted with TV remote controls, telephones that have large buttons, and wall switches with faint lights so guests can find them easily at night.[50]

http://www.att.com/

Changing Household Composition

The American household is becoming a smaller, less cohesive unit. (A *household* is simply a residential unit composed of one or more people.) Marriage rates are at an all-time low, and Americans are marrying later and having fewer children. In 1995, only 25 percent of American households represented the traditional picture of a married couple with children under 18 living at home, a startling drop from close to 50 percent in this category in 1950. Nontraditional house-

▶EXHIBIT 12.5
Positive and negative portrayals of the mature market

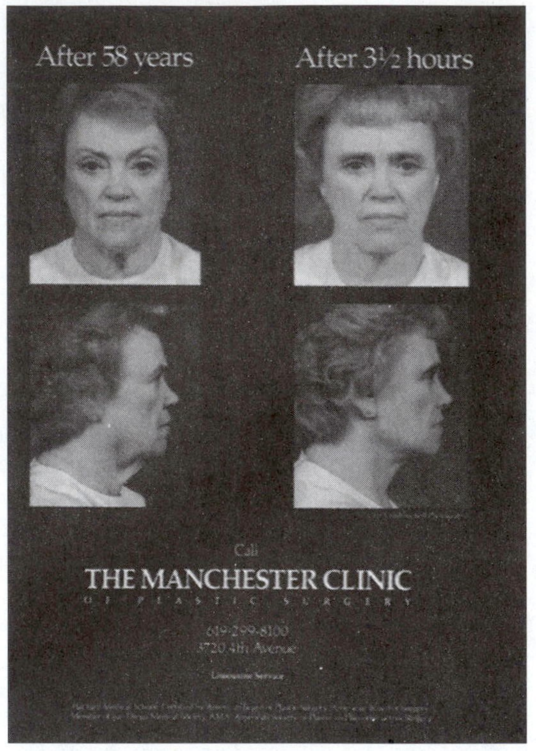

holds (married couples who never had children, single parents, unmarried couples, singles) now represent the majority of all households.

A major factor in the decline of the traditional family is an increasing divorce rate. Half of all marriages today end in divorce, triple the rate in 1970. As a result, today 28 percent of all children live in single-parent households.[51] As one might expect, single-parent homes are likely to have lower incomes. Forty-five percent of households with a female head with children at home live in poverty, as do 19 percent of households headed by a male with children. In contrast, just 8 percent of married couples with children live in poverty.[52]

Another effect of high divorce rates is the number of people living alone. According to the most recent census, 25 percent of households are single persons, and their numbers are growing 2.5 times faster than the overall population. The number of single women living alone has jumped 91 percent since 1970.[53]

The marketing impact of these trends is significant. Singles and childless couples spend more on travel, leisure products, and investments. Unmarried households, for example, spend 50 percent of their food dollars dining out, compared to 37 percent for two-person households.[54] Smaller households also have led some companies to emphasize foods and toiletries in smaller sizes and to introduce kitchen appliances and furnishings in smaller models. Singles are also more willing to buy on credit and to spend more on restaurants and entertainment.

http://www.campbellsoup.com/

http://www.mci.com/

Marketers have been uneven in their understanding of this lucrative market. One example is Campbell's Soup, which decided to sell smaller-portioned cans to singles under the "Soup For One" label. Consumers reacted coolly, believing that the name implied loneliness. "They didn't need to be reminded that they were eating alone," a Campbell's executive later remarked. In 1990, the company removed the Soup For One label and watched sales improve. MCI, on the other hand, has tried to portray the singles market more attractively. The company's strategy plays upon the fact that because singles are not in family situations, they are more emotionally attached to their friends. So the phone company discounts calls to the people its customers call most and advertises the plan with commercials showing adults calling friends.[55]

Some marketers are looking at the changes in family composition outside the United States. With 22 million babies born in China each year (six times the number born in the United States), Heinz, for instance, saw an opportunity for introducing baby products. In 1990, it began marketing an instant rice cereal for babies and almost immediately saw a profit. The cereal is precooked and instant and appeals to the 70 percent of Chinese women who work.[56]

We will be considering changes in household formation and the impact of the increasing number of nontraditional households when we discuss household decision making in Chapter 17.

Regional Differences

One of the most common demographic characteristics marketers use in analyzing purchasing behavior is region. Differences in consumer purchasing habits and tastes by region have led many marketers to vary their marketing strategies on a regional basis. Consider the following regional differences:

- Close to one-half of new car buyers in California purchase foreign cars, compared to one-fourth of new car buyers in the rest of the country.[57]
- In the Northeast, car buyers are more concerned with fuel economy and want front-wheel drive.[58]
- Westerners buy more health foods and exercise machines than consumers in the rest of the country.[59]
- Northeasterners like chicken noodle and tomato soups; Californians like cream of mushroom; Philadelphians like pepperpot soup; and Westerners like cream of vegetable.[60]

How have marketers reacted to these differences? They vary their products and advertising themes on a regional basis. For instance, the auto industry spends http://www.chryslercorp.com/

http://www.kmart.com/

more money on regional and local "spot" advertising than on national campaigns. Much of it has gone to California, where cars are seen as important lifestyle indicators. While Chevrolet advertises its Cavalier as a utility family vehicle in most states, it emphasizes the car's sportiness and excitement in California. Similarly, while Chrysler stresses the luxury of its LeBaron GTS in the Midwest, it hypes the car's acceleration and handling in West Coast ads.[61]

The regional strategy is particularly important to national retailers. Kmart maintains a master database at its Troy, Michigan, headquarters of all the items sold in its 2,300 stores and tailors the stock in each according to local preferences. For instance, peak interest in bowling usually occurs when the weather turns cold. However, not in Phoenix. There, it occurs in the summer, when it is too hot to go outside. So Kmart stores in Phoenix advertise bowling products in the spring, while its stores in Detroit do not do so until fall.[62]

Differences in consumer tastes and purchases can cut across regions and be identified by specific localities. Earlier, we cited **geodemographic analysis** to identify demographic target groups by zip code areas. Claritas, the market research firm that pioneered geodemographic analysis, uses census data to define groups of zip code areas that are similar in age, income, or family composition. It has defined 62 such groupings. One group, identified as "Blue Blood Estates," includes Chappaqua, New York, and Winnetka, Illinois. These groupings are described as "America's wealthiest socioeconomic neighborhoods, populated by established managers, professionals, and heirs to old money."

Such analysis can be used to determine whether similarities in demographic characteristics translate into similarities in purchasing behavior. For example, Dannon Yogurt could determine average yogurt consumption in each of the 62 clusters defined by Claritas based on scanner data (checkout scanners that record in-store sales) tabulated by zip code. Dannon could then use this data to distribute products to clusters that have higher than average yogurt purchases. The company also could distribute coupons or mailers to those clusters that represent the heaviest purchase groups. In a variation of this, GfK Marktforschung of Germany divides European shoppers into 16 "Euro-style" categories by regional similarity, including "Euro-Protest" for neighborhoods with a heavy concentration of purchases of environmentally friendly products and "Euro-Gentry" for affluent areas with established money types and a concentration of purchases of large-ticket items.[63]

Socioeconomic Trends

A key set of demographic variables that defines consumers' current and future purchasing power is socioeconomic factors; that is, consumers' occupational status, income, and education. We will describe the most important occupational trend in the past 40 years, the increasing proportion of working women, and additional trends in income and educational status in the United States.

Occupational Status: Increase in the Proportion of Working Women

Changes in occupational status directly affect purchasing power. For instance, increased unemployment and underemployment (a decrease in time devoted to the job or taking a lesser job to avoid unemployment) during the 1990–1991 recession restricted purchasing power.

The farthest-reaching change in occupational status has been the increasing proportion of working women. Figure 12.3 shows that the proportion of women in the labor force went from 33 percent in 1950 to 59 percent in 1995. The in-

FIGURE 12.3

Percentage of women in the labor force

Sources: "Employed Person with Single and Multiple Jobs by Sex," *Monthly Labor Review* (May, 1982), Table 1, p. 48; "A Portrait of the American Worker," *American Demographics* (March, 1984), p. 19; *Handbook of Labor Statistics* (June, 1985), Tables 1, 6, and 50; *Monthly Labor Review* (February, 1986), Table 1; U.S. Department of Commerce, Bureau of the Census, *Statistical Abstract of the United States, 1990* (Washington, D.C.: Government Printing Office, 1990), Table 625, p. 378; U.S. Department of Commerce, Bureau of the Census, *Statistical Abstract of the United States, 1996* (Springfield, VA: National Technical Information Service, 1996), Table 615, p 393 and Table 624, p. 399.

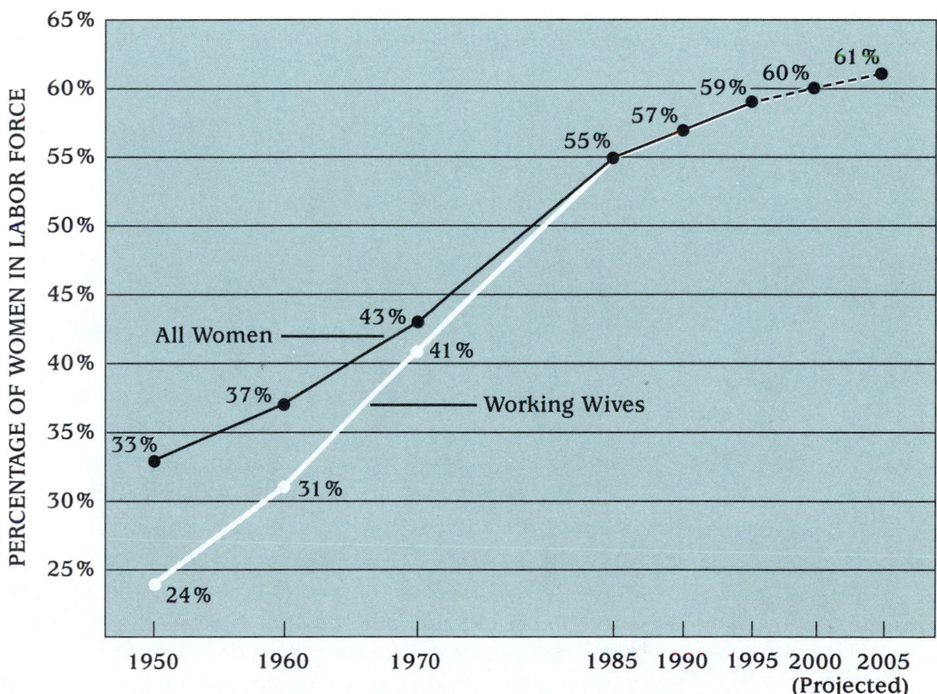

crease in the proportion of working wives has also been dramatic, going from 24 percent in 1950 to 57 percent in 1990. Among mothers with children from ages 6 to 13, close to 70 percent are employed. However, even these figures understate the impact of working women because many women work on a part-time basis. Among women from 18 to 49, fully 90 percent were part of the labor force at some time in the past two years.

The increasing proportion of working women is not just an American phenomenon. It is a global trend that is particularly apparent in Asian and Latin American countries as the stigma against working married women is easing.

Figure 12.3 shows that the rapid rise in the proportion of working women in America is projected to tail off by 2005, with 61 percent of women expected to be in the labor force, representing about half of all workers.

http://www.bls.gov/

An important effect of the greater proportion of working women is the increased affluence of dual-earner households. In 1995, the median income of the family with a working wife was $51,204 compared with $30,218 for families without one.[64] A Bureau of Labor Statistics' study found that differences between families with and without working wives extend beyond income. Dual-earner families are younger, better educated, and less likely to have children. They are more secure about the future and less likely to delay purchases, as evidenced by the fact that they save less.

Another dimension not shown in Figure 12.3 is the even greater rise in professional women. Consider the proportions of women that made up the following professional categories in 1960 and 1990:[65]

	1990	*1960*
Accountants	50.8%	16.4%
Financial managers	44.3	11.9
Lawyers and judges	20.8	3.3
Physicians	19.3	7.0
Architects	18.4	2.5

http://www.toyota.com/

The increasing proportion of working women has also had a dramatic effect on purchasing patterns. In one recent survey, 65 percent of women said they purchased a PC in the last two years and 30% said they installed the software themselves.[66] As we saw in the beginning of the chapter, women are the principal buyers of 46 percent of all cars, and they buy 51 percent of all tires.[67] Computer companies are starting to target women with ads citing detailed specifications, as shown in the ad for IBM in Exhibit 12.2. Automakers have recognized the greater involvement of working women in car-buying decisions. The ad for the Toyota Paseo in Exhibit 12.6 specifically targets the woman car buyer with appeals to safety and reliability. Similarly, office electronics companies have begun to target their products to women executives based on studies that found women own 32 percent of the nation's sole proprietorships and that 75 percent of women managers have a role in buying office equipment.[68]

EXHIBIT 12.6
Depicting women's purchase influence for cars

A direct impact of these trends is the time crunch working women face. Despite their increased job responsibilities, they are still the primary homemaker. In 1975, 45 percent of working women believed they had enough leisure time. By 1990, only 35 percent believed they had enough time. Food companies have adapted to the time crunch working women face by emphasizing easy-to-prepare foods. Campbell's Chunky soups, for example, are advertised as the perfect light meal that even a husband can fix for his working wife.[69] Food concerns have also hedged their bets by buying fast-food outlets. General Mills, General Foods, Quaker Oats, CPC International, and Pepsi-Cola are all mindful of statistics that show working wives average 7.4 meals out per week.[70]

http://www.cpcinternational.com/

Income

A direct correlation exists between income level and the purchasing power of a household. As a result, marketers segment consumers by income level and frequently allocate greater effort to the more affluent segments.

Although most Americans would like to think that their country promotes greater equality, the fact is that in economic terms, the decades of the 1970s and 1980s saw greater inequality in income. Consider the following data:[71]

	Average Income 1970	*Average Income 1993*	*Percentage Change 1970–1993*
Top 5% by income	$87,018	$120,043	+40.0%
Bottom 20% by income	$18,301	17,940	− 2.0%

The data show that the rich have become richer and the poor poorer.

The social consequences of these changes are likely to be significant, particularly in urban areas. The infrastructures of some cities are decaying, with a shrinking tax base and fewer support services available. One reflection of this decay has been the decrease in retail facilities in inner cities. The long-term shift of department stores and mass merchandisers to the suburbs and the development of shopping malls indicate that retailers are "moving to where the money is."

Added to the greater disparities in income are underlying disparities by race and ethnic origin. In 1994, African Americans accounted for only 62 percent of the median income of whites; Hispanic Americans accounted for 69 percent.[72]

Because marketers tend to allocate resources by purchasing power, it is not surprising that they pay more attention to the affluent end of the market. The increasing proportion of working women and the greater number of single-member households have increased purchasing power for many consumers, which further spurs interest in the high-priced end. In 1994, over 30 percent of all households earned more than $50,000, spurring a super-premium price niche in many categories from ice cream to beer.[73]

Education

Education is directly related to purchasing power, as there is a high correlation between education and income. The educational level of Americans has been rising rapidly. In 1940, only 25 percent of American adults completed high school; by 1995, 82 percent had done so. The proportion of college-educated Americans also increased, from 5 percent in 1940 to 23 percent in 1995.[74]

As with income, significant disparities by race and ethnic origin exist. Only 73.8 percent of African Americans and 53.4 percent of Hispanic Americans completed high school in 1991. Restricted educational attainment of minority groups directly constrains their income and purchasing power. Still, educational levels have increased. For example, in 1940, only 1 percent of African Americans completed college; by 1995, 13.2 percent had.[75]

Education affects the way consumers make decisions. Evidence suggests that less educated consumers do not have the same amount of information on brand alternatives and prices as better educated consumers. For example, in making decisions, the less educated are not as likely to use unit price information in stores. However, consumers using such information are more aware of lower-priced alternatives.[76] Furthermore, poor and less educated consumers often do not have the means to comparison shop. As we saw in Chapter 2, the net result is that the underprivileged often pay more than necessary.

USING DEMOGRAPHICS TO DEVELOP MARKETING STRATEGY

The growth of the mature market, the purchasing clout of baby boomers, and the increasing proportion of working women do not mean that every marketer will seek to appeal to these segments. Marketers use demographics to describe and better understand existing and potential users of their products. In this section, we will consider using demographics to *identify market segments* and to identify individual consumers using databases of their characteristics, an application known as **database marketing.**

Identify Market Segments

Marketers use demographics to identify a target group for their brand or product category. A demographic description of a brand's target group can help in media selection, advertising, and product development. It can help in media selection by determining the magazines prospective buyers read or the TV shows they watch. If the professional woman is likely to read *Business Week* or *Vogue* then BMW might advertise in these magazines to target this segment. A demographic profile can also guide advertising strategy by setting the appropriate scene to appeal to a demographic group. Pepsi has targeted teens since the mid-1960s, taking on the mantle of the Pepsi Generation. It typically shows teens interacting in beach scenes or at parties with a Pepsi in hand. Demographics can also be used to identify prospective purchasers of new products. The marketer of a new super-premium ice cream brand would want to determine whether the brand appeals to affluent consumers.

Demographic segmentation is the basis for Kodak's decision to shift from product-driven to age-driven marketing. Now, instead of selling its film to all audiences with a general campaign, the company is creating different commercials for different age groups. One of the ads, for example, aims at baby boom parents by showing how photos provide a good record of their children's adolescent years.[77] Demographics were also the key factor in Levi Strauss & Co.'s decision to advertise its 900 Series® jeans to young women in their late teens and early 20s (see Exhibit 12.3). Levi found that this demographic group has an individualistic streak but has ties to home and tends to be serious about its future. Therefore, the company tailored its ads to reflect those sentiments.

Segmenting with demographic data is also critically important for international marketers. For example, one U.S. bleach firm that was interested in selling to developing countries found that women in Kenya, Bangladesh, Algeria, and Pakistan tended to have five or more children whom they were unable to furnish with proper medical attention. So, it positioned its bleach as a disinfectant and, because literacy rates are low, advertised its use with pictures.[78]

Database Marketing

Whereas marketers typically segment consumers into groups such as higher- versus lower-income or baby boomers versus generation Xers, **database marketing** allows them to identify individual consumers and customize product, service, or promotional offerings to meet their specific needs. The databases used to identify individual consumer characteristics can be sweepstake entries, coupon redemptions, credit card bills, or telephone bills. In each case, demographic data on individual consumers is available, providing the facility for *micromarketing.*

Companies also create their own databases. For example, in 1994 Levi Strauss gave its customers the ability to place alteration instructions in computers that then ordered tailor-made jeans. In so doing, customers provided Levi with demographic information that the company then used to reach these same customers with direct-mail promotions.[79]

In addition to reaching individual customers and customizing offerings, database marketing has been used to solidify the relationship between a company and its customers. For example, Bloomingdale's identifies heavy purchasers in its stores from billing data and provides services such as sending reminders to spouses to buy birthday or anniversary presents or taking orders by fax.[80] Such **relationship marketing** strategies are an attempt to win customer loyalty in an increasingly competitive market.

An issue that arises in the use of databases is the customer's right to privacy. If a customer does not want personal information in credit card or telephone bills used for promotional purposes, he or she should have the right to block the use of this information.

SOCIAL CLASS INFLUENCES

Marketers use three socioeconomic factors—occupation, income, and education—to identify another important dimension of consumer behavior, social class. **Social class** defines the ranking of people in a society into a hierarchy of upper, middle, and lower classes based on their power and prestige. In American society, power and prestige are generally equated to one's occupation, income, and education. Therefore, social class is based on demographic variables.

Nature of Social Class

To understand how social class affects purchasing behavior, we should understand social stratification, status symbols, and social mobility.

Social Stratification

Social class is defined by **social stratification,** that is, "the ranking of people in society by other members into higher and lower positions so as to produce a hierarchy of respect or prestige."[81] The classification of consumers into upper, middle, or lower classes implies that certain members of society rank higher than others in prestige and power. Although contrary to the American creed that all people are created equal, social stratification suggests that some people are more equal than others.

What criteria are used to define this social hierarchy? In addition to income, education, and occupation, other criteria include more intangible factors such as lifestyles, ties and connections, political power, and public service. One study using these criteria found that physicians, scientists, government officials, and college professors rate highest on the social scale.[82] Thus, although a young college professor may be making less than a factory foreman, she may rank higher in social status.

Since the bases for defining power and prestige vary from one society to another, the composition of upper, middle, and lower classes is also likely to vary. Social stratification is dependent on the ideals and values of the society. In Europe, college professors and lawyers probably would be rated lower and artists and writers higher than in the United States.

Social class status does not imply face-to-face influence. This is reserved for peer groups and family who interact on a day-to-day basis. Social class status is likely to indicate common values and similar purchasing patterns. For example, studies have shown that individuals in the upper-middle class emphasize education, are fashion-oriented, and are less likely to be brand-loyal than other groups. Such similarity in norms, values, and purchasing patterns means that social classes serve as a frame of reference for the purchasing behavior of consumers in a particular social class.

Status Symbols

Another indicator of social class is our possessions: the clothing we wear, the houses we live in, and the cars we drive. When Thorstein Veblen wrote of *conspicuous consumption* at the turn of the century, he was referring to the tendency of affluent consumers to demonstrate upper-class membership through their possessions. In other words, homes, clothing, and other visible signs of wealth were signs of achievement or status symbols. Veblen wrote when robber barons were producing unimaginable wealth and class divisions were sharper (the new wealth). Among the aristocratic (old wealth) there was a reverse tendency to take possessions for granted and downplay them as indicators of affluence.[83]

Status symbols do not have to be associated with wealth. A **status symbol** is a symbol of one's status in society. Thus, the policeman's uniform or the CEO's pinstripe suit are status symbols.

Social Mobility

Social mobility refers to the movement of an individual or household from one social class to another. Since the turn of the century, individuals and households have moved up the social ladder, expanding the ranks of the middle class as the American standard of living has increased. More recently, a 1981 study of 800 households supported a pattern of upward social mobility. In almost two-thirds of households, the husband or wife had a higher social status than his or her parents. In only 8 percent of households was the social status lower.[84]

Yet recessions in the early 1980s and 1990s have partially reversed this trend. The recession in the early 1980s was a *blue-collar recession,* thrusting some working-class families into poverty income levels. The recession in the early 1990s was a *middle management recession* due to the effects of the information revolution and corporate downsizing to reduce costs. Managers often had to settle for jobs at half their former salaries. As a result, the social status of many middle-class families declined.

These trends show that social class is a dynamic concept, resulting in changes in social stratification over time.

Social Class Categories and Measurement

As we noted, one's position in the social hierarchy is defined primarily by socioeconomic factors related to occupation, income, and education. These factors are combined into an index of social status that serves to define a consumer's social class.

Warner's Index of Status Characteristics

The most widely used index was W. Lloyd Warner's **Index of Status Characteristics.**[85] Warner developed his index in a study of social class lines in a midwestern city in the early 1940s.[86] The ISC is based on the following socioeconomic indicators:

- Occupation (ranging from unskilled workers to professionals).
- Source of income (ranging from public relief to inherited wealth).
- House type (rated from very poor to excellent).
- Dwelling area (ranging from slums to "gold coast" areas).

Warner identified seven social class categories from low to high based on these four demographic characteristics.

Coleman-Rainwater Social Standing Hierarchy

The fact that Warner's index was developed right before World War II led two sociologists, Richard Coleman and Lee Rainwater, to update it. The resulting

TABLE 12.1
Categories in the Coleman-Rainwater Social Standing Hierarchy

Upper Americans
Upper-Upper (0.3%)—The "capital S society" world of inherited wealth, aristocratic names
Lower-Upper (1.2%)—The newer social elite, drawn from current professional, corporate leadership
Upper-Middle (12.5%)—The rest of college graduate managers and professionals; lifestyle centers on private clubs, causes, and the arts
Middle Americans
Middle Class (32%)—Average pay, white-collar workers and their blue-collar friends; live on "the better side of town," try to "do the proper things"
Working Class (38%)—Average pay, blue-collar workers; lead "working-class lifestyle" whatever the income, school background, and job
Lower Americans
"A lower group of people but not the lowest" (9%)—Working, not on welfare; living standard is just above poverty; behavior judged "crude," "trashy"
"Real Lower-Lower" (7%)—On welfare, visibly poverty-stricken, usually out of work (or have "the dirtiest jobs")

Source: From *Social Standing in America* by Richard P. Coleman and Lee P. Rainwater. Copyright© 1978 by Basic Books, Inc. Reprinted by permission of Basic Books, a division of HarperCollins Publishers Inc.

groupings, shown in Table 12.1 and known as the **Coleman-Rainwater Social Standing Hierarchy,** are similar to Warner's but they more directly reflect the power and prestige associated with each group.

Because it focuses on power and prestige, the Coleman-Rainwater Hierarchy draws social class lines more sharply. Whereas Warner refers to the next to lowest group as on private relief and living in semislum conditions, Coleman and Rainwater describe the group as portraying behavior that is judged by others as "crude" and "trashy," thus reflecting the severe judgments by upper- and middle-class Americans of the lower classes. In so doing, the Social Standing Hierarchy better reflects the tensions between social groups.

Another advantage of the Coleman-Rainwater Hierarchy over Warner's is that it distinguishes between a middle class and a working class. Although the middle class tends to be white-collar and the working class blue-collar, the distinction reflects the values of each group as well as occupation. For example, Coleman describes working-class Americans as "family folk, depending heavily on relatives for economic and emotional support."[87] The values of working-class Americans are reflected in their preference for local rather than national news, for vacationing with relatives at local resorts, and for buying American. In contrast, middle-class Americans tend to buy based on their perception of the norms and values of the upper class. They want to do the right thing and buy what is popular. Their upward mobility distinguishes them from the working class.

TABLE 12.2
Differences in fashions and tastes for three social class groups

CLASS DISTINCTIONS: You are what you choose				
		WORKING CLASS	MIDDLE CLASS	UPPER MIDDLE CLASS
Car	1980s	Hyundai	Chevrolet Celebrity	Mercedes
	1990s	Geo	Chrysler minivan	Range Rover
Business shoe (men)	1980s	Sneakers	Wingtips	Cap toes
	1990s	Boots	Rockports	Loafers
Business shoe (women)	1980s	Spike-heel pumps	Mid-heel pump	High-heel pumps
	1990s	High-heel pumps	Dressy flats	One-inch pumps
Alcoholic beverage	1980s	Domestic beer	White wine spritzer	Dom Perignon
	1990s	Domestic lite beer	California Chardonnay	Cristal
Leisure pursuit	1980s	Watching sports	Going to movies	Golf
	1990s	Playing sports	Renting movies	Playing with computers
Hero	1980s	Roseanne Barr	Ronald Reagan	Michael Milken
	1990s	Kathie Lee Gifford	Janet Reno	Rush Limbaugh

Source: "Class in America," Fortune (February 7, 1994), p. 116.

The values of each of these groups are reflected in what they buy, what they wear, and who they look up to. A survey by *Fortune* magazine of three of Coleman and Rainwater's groups, the working, middle, and upper-middle classes (representing over 80 percent of households) reflected these differences as shown in Table 12.2.

Research into the social classes in Table 12.1 makes it possible to further detail their norms, values, and lifestyles.

***The Old Wealth* (Upper-Upper Class; 0.3 percent of the Population).** The mere presence of wealth is not sufficient to get into this class. This group represents the social elite based on inherited wealth. They dress conservatively and well and avoid ostentatious purchases. They emphasize self-expression, buy quality merchandise, and reflect an ideal of "spending with good taste." Members are part of a closed society of townhouses, country homes, and social gatherings. They are expected to engage in philanthropy and public service.

***The New Wealth* (Lower-Upper class; 1.2 percent of the Population).** This group is likely to be composed of the influentials in society—business leaders and the professional elite. They are self-made individuals who are likely to be active in community affairs and public issues. While not a target for the mass marketer, this group would make an excellent market for specialty items such as expensive clothing, jewelry, furniture, or boats.

Occasionally, members of this group have been derisively referred to as the nouveau riche. The name implies an ostentatious display of new wealth without taste. The phenomenon is apparent in former Communist countries where the transition to capitalism has created a new class of wealthy entrepreneurs who seek the means to display their new-found wealth, but are often frustrated by the lack of availability of luxury goods.

***Upper-Middle Class* (12.5 Percent of the Population).** This group is also comprised of successful professional and business people, but it does not have the wealth or status of the upper class. Combined with the two upper-class categories, the upper-middle class possesses most of the wealth in the United States. These three groups own two-thirds of the securities and almost two-thirds of the real estate in this country, even though they represent only 14 percent of the population.[88] The upper-middle class is career-oriented and achievement-motivated. Members of this group emphasize education; most are college graduates. Because they are well educated, this group is more likely to appraise product alternatives critically. They emphasize quality and value and good taste, rather than status, in their purchases. Women in this group are more likely to be employed, active, and more self-expressive than women in other groups.

***Middle Class* (32 Percent of the Population).** This group is represented by white-collar workers, owners of small businesses, and highly paid blue-collar workers. There is a split in this group between those who emphasize traditional norms and those who subscribe to more modern values.[89] Traditionalists are more home- and family-oriented. Women in this group pride themselves on their role of mother and homemaker. Their orientation is toward traditional, conservative benefits such as pride in meal preparation and satisfaction in the upbringing of their children.

The nontraditional consumers in this group reflect the values of the upper-middle class because they are upwardly mobile. Compared to the traditionalists, wives are more likely to work, husbands and wives are more likely to make joint decisions, and they are more likely to emphasize a college education for their children. Time-saving benefits in food preparation and appliances that are likely to appeal to the nontraditionalist middle-class families are unlikely to appeal to the traditionalists.

Because they seek the trappings of wealth of the upper-middle class, nontraditionalists are more likely to buy based on status considerations. They are more likely to own credit cards, top-of-the-line electronic equipment, and designer clothes.

The middle class is perhaps the most international social class grouping. Middle classes have begun to emerge in developing countries particularly in the Pacific Rim and Latin America. A new prosperity combined with access to global television has communicated Western products from jeans to breakfast cereals and resulted in demands for similar lifestyles. Because of a global outlook and acceptance of American lifestyles, middle-class families are "increasingly looking, living, and even talking more like each other."[90]

***Working Class* (38 Percent of the Population).** The working class consists primarily of blue-collar workers. They depend on friends and relatives for emotional support and escape from uncreative jobs. The narrow dimensions of and lack of self-expression in their jobs lead to a pattern of impulse purchasing to escape from the dull routine. This group would rather buy for today than plan for tomorrow; therefore, advertising appeals to fantasy and escape are likely to be successful.

Their view of life tends to reflect traditional values. The husband is likely to be the breadwinner and the decision maker; the wife, the traditional homemaker. Whereas over one-half of middle-class women work, only about one-third of working-class women are employed.[91]

***Lower Class* (16 Percent of the Population).** This group represents the unskilled, poorly educated, and socially disadvantaged. They earn only one-fifth the income of the average American.[92] Lower-class consumers often live in poverty, frequently on welfare, and are more likely to have a female head of household. Lower-class families often have difficulty moving up the social hierarchy. As a result, they are frustrated and angry about their economic status and inability to share in the "American Dream."

The bulk of the lower-class consumer's income goes to rent and heat. This group also spends a disproportionate amount of their income on food and medicine, reflecting a lower income level. They often pay higher prices for goods than do other groups because they are restricted to poor, inner-city areas and do not have the means or mobility to comparison shop.[93]

Is the United States Becoming a Classless Society?

A key question that may inhibit the use of social class in consumer behavior studies is whether social class lines are becoming more blurred. The universal ownership of television sets means everyone is exposed to the same mass communications. The rise of mass merchandising and the standardization of consumer packaged goods means that most people buy similar brands. The universal ownership of automobiles means greater mobility. In addition, greater access to a college education and, consequently, higher job mobility have created a greater movement up the social scale for many lower-class consumers.

However, recent evidence suggests that social class lines are becoming sharper. The deep recession of 1990–1991 drove many middle-class consumers a notch lower on the social scale. At the same time, opportunities for managers and professionals in high-technology and service areas have provided the means for many middle-class consumers to move into the upper class.[94] The result has been more pronounced distinctions between the upper and lower classes. The information revolution has contributed to these distinctions. Former Secretary of Labor Robert Reich estimates that about 20 percent of American workers have been able to keep up with the new technologies. The other 80 percent—assembly-line workers, data processors, retail salespeople, cashiers, and blue-collar workers—are facing insecure job prospects.[95] This is reflected in surveys that have shown the vast majority of American workers feeling insecure about their current jobs.

As a result of these trends, one writer described an erosion of the American egalitarian spirit and a reemergence of the class system as a result of these trends.[96] Social class in America is still very much a reality and a component to be considered in explaining consumer behavior.

Applications of Social Class to Marketing Strategy

Marketers have found social class measures important because of substantial differences in behavior between classes. As a result, social class characteristics have been related to every aspect of marketing strategy.

Advertising

Social class values can give direction to advertisers. Social class members must understand the language and symbols used in advertising: otherwise, it will fail to communicate. For example, working- and lower-class consumers are more receptive to "advertising that is strongly visual in character, that shows activity, ongoing work and life, impressions of energy, and solutions to practical problems in daily requirements."[97] In contrast, upper-class consumers are more open to subtle symbolism, to approaches that are more "individual in tone . . . that offer the kinds of objects and symbols that are significant of their status and self-expressive aims."[98]

http://www.hud.gov/

The two ads in Exhibit 12.7 are examples of these distinctions. The ad for the Regent Hotel in Beverly Hills is linked to a status symbol—Rodeo Drive and its expensive shops. The ad for HUD-financed homes is directed to working-class consumers who assume they cannot own their own home. It reflects the focus on a solution to a very practical problem, guaranteeing home ownership with financial security.

Power is a frequently used symbol of social class. As the three ads in Exhibit 12.8 show, power themes have been directed to upper-, upper-middle, and working-class values. The ad for the Concorde, targeting professionals and managers, is based on economic power and cites a "power upgrade" to business class. The Motorola ad is directed to the upper-middle-class professional woman who is trying to "successfully balance work and family." The ad for Eureka vacuum cleaners directs a power theme to working-class consumers. It associates a household cleaning tool with a status symbol luxury item.

Market Segmentation

The substantial differences among social classes in the purchases of clothing, furniture, appliances, leisure goods, financial services, and food products provide marketers with a basis for segmenting consumers. For example, upper classes are likely to emphasize style and color in purchasing appliances, whereas lower-class consumers emphasize appliances that work.[99] In each case, different product lines for different social class segments would be appropriate. Some companies are adapting to social class influences abroad. For example, Nestlé recognizes the emerging middle class in developing countries. It has sought to establish manufacturing facilities for many of its packaged goods in countries such as Egypt, India, and Pakistan to facilitate the targeting of its goods to middle-class consumers. Former Communist countries such as Poland are also on the list.[100]

▶EXHIBIT 12.7
Appeals to upper-class values of prestige and working-class values of security

▶EXHIBIT 12.8
Power themes directed to upper, upper-middle, and working-class consumers

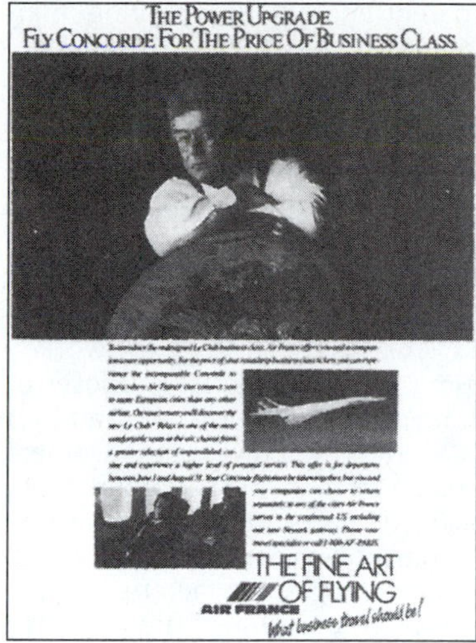

Distribution

Social classes frequently differ in store patronage. Lower-class consumers are more likely to shop in discount stores and in neighborhood stores where they feel most comfortable and can rely on friendly salespeople for information. Upper-class consumers are more likely to shop in regular department stores for products they consider risky and in discount stores for products with little risk.[101]

These findings suggest that social class characteristics can provide guidelines for distribution strategies. If the target market is more likely to be in the lower socioeconomic group, neighborhood stores should be used rather than downtown shopping centers. There should be more emphasis on sales personnel and a friendly store environment. Middle- and upper-class target groups suggest the use of regular department stores, with primary emphasis on the nature and variety of merchandise.

Product Development

Social classes may react differently to product characteristics and styles. A study by AT&T examined the style and color preferences for telephones among various social groups.[102] Lower-class consumers were not interested in a decorative or modern phone; they just wanted one that worked. The working class placed the greatest emphasis on phones of different designs and colors. These findings demonstrate that the lower-class group would be a poor target for decorative phones, but the working class is a surprisingly good target. Had AT&T assumed that higher socioeconomic groups were the best target for high-style phones, it might have missed an important target group.

SUMMARY

Consumers' demographic characteristics influence the markets for most products. Demographics influence whether consumers can buy (based on income) and whether they want to buy (based on factors such as age and household composition).

Marketers segment markets by demographic characteristics to identify the best media to reach prospective users and to give them guidelines for advertising and product strategies. An increasingly important use of demographics is in micromarketing—that is, the use of databases that identify the demographic characteristics of individual consumers, allowing marketers to target these consumers through direct mail and interactive technologies.

Demographic trends in the U.S. market have had a direct impact on marketing strategies. Several basic trends were considered in this chapter:

1. Population growth in the postwar period, resulting in the baby boom, a subsequent decline in the birthrate, and a baby boomlet since 1977 as baby boomers had children.
2. The effect of population growth on the changing age composition of the U.S. population, in particular:
   - The aging of baby boomers.
   - Needs and values of generation Xers.
   - The increasing purchasing power and influence of teens and preteens.
   - The greater population in and importance of the mature market.
3. Socioeconomic trends, particularly the increase in the proportion of working women.
4. Changes in household composition such as increases in the divorce rate, decreases in family size, and increases in single-parent households, resulting in an increase in nontraditional households.

The effects of these changes on purchasing and consumption behavior were also considered. For example, the increase in the proportion of working women has resulted in changing purchasing and consumption roles within the family, less time for shopping, and greater patronage of fast-food establishments.

The chapter also considered the use of demographics in developing marketing strategy in two key areas: (1) identifying market segments for purposes of media selection and advertising development, and (2) the use of databases to identify individual consumers and target them through a strategy of micromarketing.

The chapter concluded by describing social classes. Social class refers to consumers' positions on a social scale based on three key demographic factors: occupation, income, and education. Consumers are classified by these criteria into social class groupings. The most frequently used classification is a five-part designation of upper-, upper-middle-, middle-, working-, and lower-class consumers.

Each of these groups has distinctive norms, values, family roles, and patterns of purchasing behavior. On this basis, social classes vary markedly in the purchase of such items as clothing, furniture, leisure goods, and even food. These differences permit marketers to use social class criteria to identify market segments, select the language and symbols used in advertising, develop in-store strategies, and indicate appropriate product characteristics and styles.

In the next chapter, we consider two key descriptors that further influence purchase behavior: consumer personality and lifestyles.

QUESTIONS

1. What is micromarketing? Why has it become more fesible in the 1990s?
2. What is the relationship between database marketing and micromarketing? Between relationship marketing and micromarketing?
3. What are the marketing implications of the changes in the values of many baby boomers from materialism to personal development?
4. How would you describe the prevalent norms and values of generation Xers? What are the marketing implications of your description?
5. Why is the role of baby boomers and Generation Xers different in Japan compared to the United States?
6. Why are so few ads and products targeted to the mature market? Is this lack of attention to the mature market likely to change in the future? Why or why not?
7. A large food producer is considering directing a wide range of packaged food products specifically to the singles market.

- How do the needs of single-person households differ from those of multiple-person households?
- What are the implications for the marketer?

8. What is meant by geodemographic analysis? How can marketers use it to target geographic segments?
9. What are the marketing implications of the greater emphasis working women put on time-saving conveniences?
10. How have marketers adjusted to the increasingly influential role of working women in buying decisions that men used to dominate? Provide specific examples.
11. Two companies produce different lines of furniture. One directs its line toward upper-middle-class consumers; the other, to working-class consumers. What are likely to be the differences in (a) product styles and features, (b) print media used, and (c) distribution and in-store environment?
12. A magazine publisher decides there are sufficient differences in the orientation, role, and purchasing behavior of working women in different social classes to segment the market by introducing three different magazines: one directed to the working woman in the upper-middle class, another to the working woman in the working class, and a third to the working woman in the lower class.
    - Do you agree with the publisher's premise?
    - Specifically, how might each magazine differ in (a) editorial content and (b) advertising?
13. A company is introducing a new line of instant baking products designed to facilitate the preparation of more complicated recipes for breads, cakes, and pies.
    - Should the company segment its line so that one set of products is directed to higher social classes and another to lower social classes?
    - How would the advertising campaigns to each group differ?
14. Some researchers believe that sports and leisure-time activities serve a different purpose for the upper and lower classes. For the upper class, sports activities may be a compensation for a more sedentary existence as most of these activities involve active movement.[103] For the lower class, sports and leisure-time activities are more of an escape from the dull routine of jobs. What are the implications of this finding for a large producer of sporting equipment such as AMF?

RESEARCH ASSIGNMENTS

1. Give examples of how marketers use surveys and passwords to obtain information about their site's users. What information is typically collected? Do you think marketers are using that information to tailor their site's contents? If so, how?
2. Go to a search engine with banner advertising (for example, http://www.yahoo.com). Conduct two different searches, one with the keyword "computers" and the next with "flowers." What do you notice about the banner advertising? Do you feel that marketers who are targeting their banner advertising are micromarketing?
3. Select a group of working women and nonworking women (approximately 30 to 40 women in each group). Select two food products requiring preparation (for example, cake mix, coffee). Ask respondents to rate various need criteria in selecting brands (such as importance of saving time, ease of preparation, good taste, good for the whole family) and to identify their favorite brand in each category.
    - Do the needs of working and nonworking women differ?
    - Do they prefer different brands?
    - Do the results conform to your expectations about differences between working and nonworking women? In what ways?
4. A study by a large electronics firm determined the demographic characteristics of purchasers of compact discs. These purchasers tended to be in the higher-income group ($40,000 and over) and in professional or managerial occupations.
    - Try to obtain a copy of a Simmons Report or another readership service like MRI. (It is all right if the report is somewhat dated). Analyze 10 or 12 magazines to determine their relative efficiency in reaching the target group identified above. Incorporate cost-per-thousand data for each magazine if they are available. If not, analyze the magazines solely on their ability to reach the target group.
    - If data are also available for TV shows, do the same analysis for a selected number of shows as well.

LIFESTYLE AND PERSONALITY INFLUENCES

Chapter 13

CONAGRA'S SUCCESS IS BASED ON A HEALTHIER LIFESTYLE

The demographic characteristics described in the previous chapters are the surface descriptors of consumers. They answer the *who* of consumer behavior, but not necessarily the *why*. Two higher-income baby boomers living in urban areas may not buy the same brands or have similar possessions. Lifestyle and personality characteristics provide us with a richer understanding of consumer behavior. **Lifestyles** are consumers' modes of living as reflected in their attitudes, interests, and opinions. **Personality** is defined as patterns of individual behavior that are consistent and enduring.

In this chapter, we first discuss consumer lifestyles since they are more directly applicable to marketing strategies than personality. We describe the lifestyle trends that are changing the face of marketing in the 1990s and the measurement of lifestyle variables. We then consider the strategic applications of lifestyle variables. Personality variables are considered next, despite their limited applications, because they are especially relevant when deep-seated purchasing motives are involved. Various personality theories that have been used to understand consumer behavior will be described.

When researchers first began to study consumer behavior, they turned to existing personality theories to explain motivations. First among these theories was Freud's psychoanalytic approach, which stresses subconscious drives. However, theories designed to explain childhood conflicts, adult neuroses, and social disorders are unlikely to explain consumer behavior. As a result, researchers turned to lifestyle variables as factors that more closely reflect consumers' day-to-day interests and, therefore, are more likely to explain consumer purchases.

http://www.healthychoice.com/

Marketers have viewed the lifestyle trends of the 1990s with particular interest because these trends have affected every facet of marketing strategy. ConAgra, for instance, introduced its hugely successful Healthy Choice frozen food line because its lifestyle research found that consumers are increasingly concerned with salt and cholesterol in foods. The idea for Healthy Choice came from ConAgra's CEO, Charles Harper. For most of his 57 years, Harper had not given a second thought to smoking two packs of cigarettes a day, routinely drinking 15 cups of coffee, or eating an artery-hardening diet of beef and fudge. However, that all changed in 1987 when Harper was felled by a massive heart attack and had to change his diet.

While recuperating at home, Harper invited a company executive to a lunch of freshly made chili. Listening to his guest rave about the healthy meal his wife had cooked, Harper realized that there had to be millions of men out there just like him, all desperate for tasty foods that suited their diets.[1] Subsequent research proved Harper's thesis. The only problem was that most consumers believed low-salt, low-cholesterol dinners were tasteless and associated them with "sick people's food."

Agreeing that a tasty product and a strong name would be needed to combat these impressions, ConAgra began a program that eventually resulted in a method of reducing fat and salt in frozen foods while retaining the taste. ConAgra then sent test samples of the new product to national health conferences while drumming up professional interest through direct mailings explaining the product to dieticians. By January 1989, when the first 14-item line was rolled out under the name Healthy Choice, advance word about it was widespread.[2]

Backed by ads that evoked family values (a grandfather with his kids under the tag line "Listen to Your Heart"), Healthy Choice caught on like wildfire, capturing a quarter of the frozen foods market (see Exhibit 13.1). By 1995, Healthy Choice was a 300-item product line representing $1.3 billion in sales.[3] Its success led other companies to request licensing its name—Nabisco, for example, with a Healthy Choice cracker and snack line. And, it established a Web site offering health management programs that track food intake and exercise and the opportunity to exchange e-mail messages with a registered dietician.[4]

ConAgra quickly drew hoards of competitors with their own low-salt, low-cholesterol lines, from Kraft General Foods, which introduced a new product line, to Weight Watchers and Stouffer's, which repositioned old ones. The increased competition was a tribute to the foresight of Charles Harper who recognized an important lifestyle trend and got ConAgra to target it.

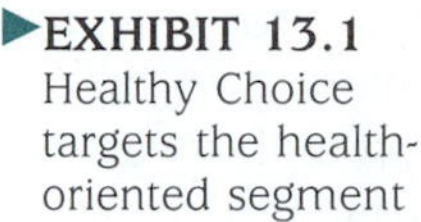

EXHIBIT 13.1
Healthy Choice targets the health-oriented segment

LIFESTYLE

Lifestyle variables are defined by how people spend their time (activities), what they consider important in their environment (interests), and what they think of themselves and the world around them (opinions). Lifestyle variables are also known as **psychographic characteristics** because activities, interests, and opinions are psychologically oriented variables that can be quantified. Some activities, interests, and opinions that define lifestyles are listed here:[5]

Activities	*Interests*	*Opinions*
work	family	personal relations
hobbies	home	social issues
social events	job	politics
vacation	community	business
entertainment	recreation	economics
club membership	fashion	education
community	food	products
shopping	media	future
sports	achievements	culture

Lifestyle factors are relevant to marketers on two levels. First, broad lifestyle trends such as changing male/female purchasing roles have altered the habits, tastes, and purchasing behavior of American consumers. Second, lifestyles can be applied on a product-specific basis. For example, Conagra might develop an inventory of activities, interests, and opinions specifically designed to identify the health-oriented consumer to better understand the needs of this group.

In this section, we first consider the broad lifestyle trends that are changing American consumers in the 1990s, and then we turn to the more product-specific applications of lifestyle variables.

Changing Lifestyle Trends of American Consumers in the 1990s

Changes in the lifestyles of American consumers are due partially to changes in their demographic characteristics and partially to changes in their values. Six broad changes in lifestyles are occurring in the 1990s:

1. Change in male/female purchasing roles.
2. Leveling off of concerns about health and fitness due to a more self-indulgent lifestyle.
3. A more isolated lifestyle as the result of more time spent at home or at both work and play.
4. More self-awareness.
5. A more frugal lifestyle.
6. Greater time pressures and a resulting emphasis on convenience.

Changes in Male Purchasing Roles

The increase in the number of working women and single-parent households has meant a shift away from the traditional roles of a working male and a stay-at-home female. The change in the male's purchasing role is most apparent in increased responsibilities for shopping and child care and in more involvement with cooking and house cleaning—all traditional female roles. One survey found that 35 percent of men buy all the food for their homes, about 30 percent buy all the cleaning supplies and housewares, and about 67 buy all their own personal items.[6] When they do shop, men do not act that differently from women. They tend to spend the same amount of time preplanning purchases, checking prices, and redeeming coupons.[7]

http://www.familiesandworkinst.org/

The participation of males in traditional female roles goes beyond shopping. More men are involved in cooking, cleaning, laundry, and child care. A national study by the not-for-profit Families and Work Institute shows that in households where only the husband works, men do a scant 6 percent of the cooking and 7 percent of child care. However, in homes where both work, the man's role jumps to 20 percent of cooking and 30 percent of child care. These findings must be taken in perspective, however. The fact that men account for about one-third of all homemaking activities means that women still have by far the greatest responsibilities. Also, men are not yet comfortable talking about their role. According to the Institute, some men who depart work early to care for their kids tell co-workers that they are leaving to go to a bar.[8]

http://www.kraftfoods.com/

Companies such as Kraft Foods are shifting a significant proportion of their print advertising budget away from women's magazines to general interest and male-oriented magazines. A recent issue of *Men's Health* magazine had ads for Dannon yogurt, Colgate toothbrushes, Kraft salad dressing, and Nutrasweet.[9] On the other side of the coin, traditionally female magazines such as *Parents* and *Child* are getting more male readership.[10] As a result, ads for men's products such as Calvin Klein's Eternity are starting to appear in these magazines. On television, Kmart has tried making the transition for men easier by showing Mike Starr, a notable movie bad guy, placing shampoo in his shopping cart as he wheels his son down the aisle.[11]

http://www.cambellsoup.com/

The changing male role is not only a function of demographics. It is also a result of changes in male values. In a study, Campbell's Soup found that the men who are most likely to shop view themselves as liberated, considerate, achievement-oriented individuals.[12] These are the types of males who do not feel the need to conform to a "macho" image. As a result, a second change has occurred in male purchasing roles: Males are beginning to buy products that at one time might have been dismissed as too feminine—jewelry, skin care products, moisturizers, and cosmetics. In marketing these products, advertisers have had to depict males in a way that is very different from the traditional strong, masculine image of the Marlboro cowboy or in the typical beer commercial. A new concept of masculinity has emerged: the sensitive male who is as vulnerable in many ways as his female counterpart.

http://www.simmonsco.com/

The ad for Simmons' Beautyrest mattresses in Exhibit 13.2 is a good example. Simmons' ad agency created two versions of the ad, one with the father cuddling a newborn, the other with the mother. The male version of the ad scored higher in consumer tests and was used in the ad campaign.[13] Another example of this trend is an ad for Claiborne, a fragrance for men produced by Liz Claiborne. A man is sitting at a bar watching a woman and is uneasy because he cannot decide if she is smiling or laughing at him. Other variations of the ad show one man wondering if his masculinity is on the wane and another admitting that the future is scary because when he looks in the mirror, he sees his father's face. As the creative director for the campaign explained, "A lot of men today don't want to be seen as strong, silent John Wayne types. Men and women have been thinking about a lot of the same things for a long time. We are only now starting to talk about it."[14]

The net result of the greater involvement of men in shopping and housekeeping activities and their willingness to shed a traditional male image has led to a merger of male and female purchasing roles. Today, it would be as shortsighted for a marketer conducting a survey of paper towels, disposable diapers, or frozen foods to restrict the sample to the "woman of the house" as it would

▶EXHIBIT 13.2
Depicting a changing male image

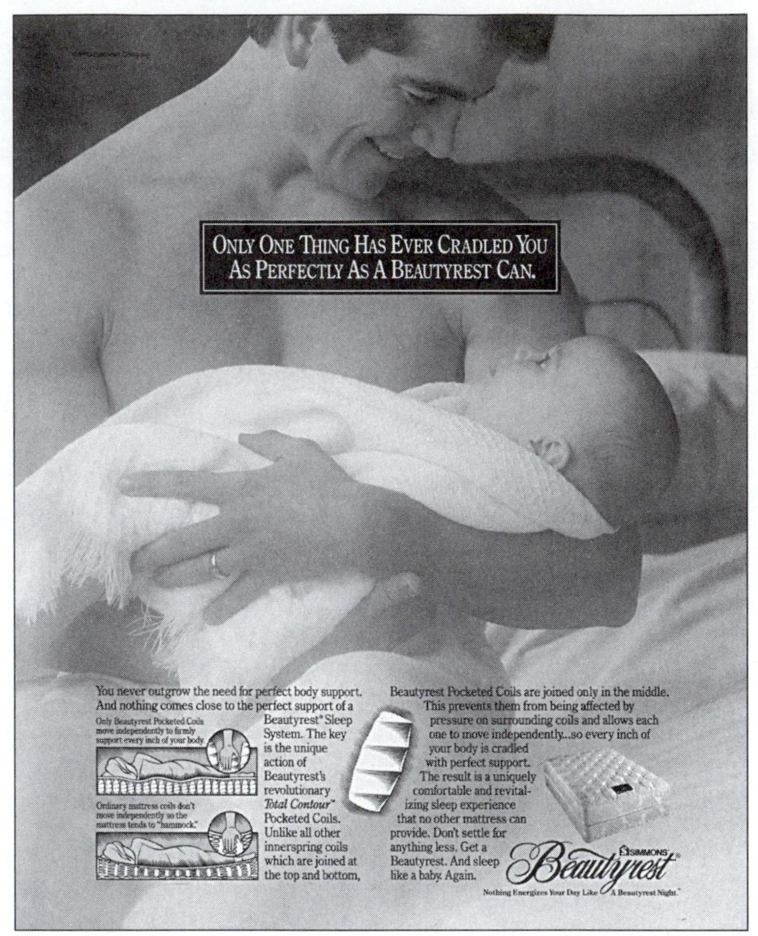

be for a marketer of financial services or automobiles to restrict the sample to the "man of the house."

Changes in Female Purchasing Roles

Working women's greater affluence, independence, and self-confidence have created a substantial change in women's purchasing roles. As their purchasing power has increased, they have flexed more muscle in just about every product category, making almost no enclave a male preserve anymore.[15] As we saw in the last chapter, women spend $65 billion on cars every year.

Women's increasing independence suggests a desire for an identity beyond their traditional roles. A survey of women under 35 found that 90 percent did not aspire to being lifelong homemakers. Three-fourths of these women planned to combine job and homemaking throughout their lives.[16] As a result, most women no longer identify with ads that tell them how to clean their floors or to please their husbands. The problem is creating ads they do identify with. The advertising industry does not have an illustrious track record in this regard. The National Advertising Review Board found that until the late 1970s, women were typically portrayed as "stupid [and] too dumb to cope with familiar everyday chores unless instructed by children or a man."[17] In the early 1980s, many advertisers went to the other extreme, creating a "superwoman" model, which one ad executive described derisively as:

> that disgustingly perfect specimen who serves her family a bountiful, hot breakfast, dashes off to run a corporation all day, and then glides in at 6 P.M. to create a lavish gourmet meal while at the same time changing diapers, leading Cub Scouts, and carrying on stimulating conversation with her husband.[18]

Today, the race is on to win back disgruntled women with campaigns that identify with their professionalism and reinforce their self-esteem. Avon is abandoning its old-fashioned image with appeals to contemporary women such as, "After all, you have more on your mind than what's on your lips. And Avon thinks that's beautiful."[19] The Nike ad in Exhibit 13.3 makes this point by representing a more realistic voice for today's woman, one that is assertive in taking control of her life.

http://www.nike.com/

However, advertisers must be careful not to blur their message in a desire to depict the independent woman. Subaru made a fundamental miscalculation when it aired a TV commercial in 1993 designed to appeal to strong-willed women. The ad began by showing a young woman complaining that "Every guy I know thinks he knows everything about cars and the '69 Mets." After she asserts that she is the one who usually explains the car's ABS brake system and all-wheel drive to her dates, she adds with a wink to the camera: "Oh ya. And the '69 Mets? The Cubs choked." While the ad made the point that women may know more about cars and baseball than men, it obscured Subaru's long-standing slogan, "Inexpensive. And built to stay that way." As a result, sales fell and the campaign was discontinued.[20]

http://www.subaru.cy.net/

EXHIBIT 13.3
More realistic portrayal of women in advertising

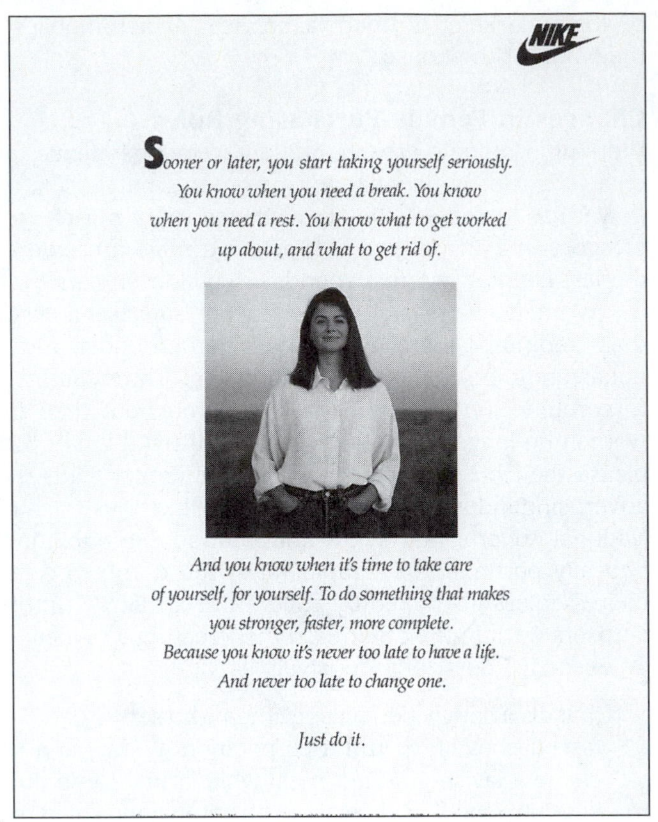

A Global Perspective on Female Roles

Female roles differ greatly between cultures. The relative equality between the sexes in North America and Western Europe is the exception, globally. Most cultures are male-dominant. One extreme example was the Islamic fundamentalism the Taliban guerrillas imposed when they captured Kabul, Afghanistan, in 1996, prohibiting women from working and requiring that they be covered head to foot when seen in public. In Japan, wives are expected to stay home and care for children and traditionally walk two steps behind their husbands. In Latin America, women are frequently portrayed as sex objects or blonde goddesses in advertisements and the media. Hispanic communities in the United States are traditionally bound by a more macho-oriented culture.

The ad for Bijan perfumes in Exhibit 13.4, which appeared in the Spanish edition of *Vogue* magazine, portrays the female roles cited in a cultural context. The first picture shows a woman in Islamic garb with copy saying that women should be quiet, composed, obedient, modest, submissive, and very, very serious. The second shows a woman as more of a sex object and says women should be sophisticated, exotic, mysterious, chic, seductive, and very, very sexy. The

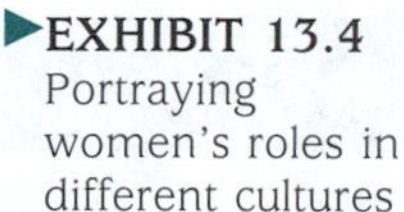

EXHIBIT 13.4
Portraying women's roles in different cultures

third pictures a more independent and liberated woman and says women should be bright, wild, fun, tough, bold, and very, very Bijan. The perfume obviously wants to be associated with this last image of the more independent woman.

Less Emphasis on Health and Fitness

American consumers are among the most devoted in the world to maintaining their health and fitness, as reflected in the success of Conagra's Healthy Choice line. But in the mid-1990s, awareness and concern regarding health and fitness began to level off.

The Health-Conscious American Consumer. American consumers are highly aware of the effects of dietary habits including cholesterol and salt levels, caffeine content, and food additives, on health. According to Food and Drug Administration estimates, 40 percent of consumers are concerned about salt in their diet, while at least one-half of the U.S. adult population is trying to lose weight at any given time.[21]

http://www.fda.gov/

This awareness has been translated into a change in consumer purchasing patterns. A 1989 study found that almost half of consumers surveyed reported

STRATEGIC APPLICATIONS OF CONSUMER BEHAVIOR

Can Anheuser-Busch Build Bridges to Women?

Since they began advertising on television, beer companies have used provocatively clad women to titillate their male customers, the two leading beer companies, Miller and Anheuser-Busch being frequent offenders. So when Stroh's Brewery decided to sell its Old Milwaukee beer by showing a giggling band of blond bombshells called the Swedish Bikini Team parachuting into a campsite of sex-starved men, no one at the company figured it would cause a ripple. However, in December 1991, Stroh's female employees filed a suit against the beer maker claiming the ads were degrading and encouraged sexual harassment.

The Stroh's controversy forced the entire beer industry into a state of reexamination. Though women buy 35 percent of all domestic beer and 45 percent of light beer, few companies have seen a need to talk directly to them. By the time Stroh's pushed the envelope too far, women had become used to macho beer advertising. As a result, they either bought brands *in spite* of their advertising or chose unadvertised selections.

In an attempt to turn that liability into an asset, Anheuser-Busch tried building new bridges. In 1991 it shot ads for Bud Dry from a woman's point of view. They featured five different nightmare date scenarios, including a nerd who talks about his mother's meatloaf and a grating yuppie who keeps interrupting conversation to talk on his cellular phone. The spoofs adopted a gender-oriented slant and used humor to diffuse old hostilities. Anheuser followed with ads for Bud Light showing two women drinking beer in a realistic social context.

In 1992, Anheuser's Michelob brand went one step further with more serious quality-of-life spots. In one, four professional-looking women are seen drinking Michelob inside an upscale neighborhood pub. The copy begins by saying, "They used to call you the Sullivan Sisters." Then, after listing their new married names, the ad conjures a sentimental image of the four enjoying old memories by adding that once again, "Tonight, you're the Sullivan Sisters." With only 1.8 percent of the beer market, it was apparent that, as one analyst wrote, "Michelob certainly wasn't getting anywhere with guys, so its [approach with women was] worth a try." Shortly after the spots appeared, Michelob's sales rose 3.3 percent.

However, when it came to advertising its flagship brand, Anheuser seems to have reverted to its old ways. In 1994, new TV commercials again featured macho men and seductive women. In one commercial, a woman in a tight, sheer top saunters into a bar room turning heads in slow motion. As one observer noted, commenting on the ads:

> The girlie shots are back, to make us fondly associate Budweiser with the "good old days" when a doll in a tight red dress and spike heels could be flailing at pitches in the batting cage, her cleavage bouncing, and nobody would even flinch. Except this is 1994, and we're definitely flinching.

Why the dichotomy between the Bud Light and Michelob ads and the macho-oriented ads for the company's flagship brand? Apparently, beer companies still feel that any time they are targeting a male market, they still have to portray women as sex objects.

Maybe, when it came to learning the lessons from the Stroh experience, Anheuser-Busch really didn't get it.

Sources: "It's Again True: This Bud and Babe Are for You," *Advertising Age* (1994); "Michelob Ads Feature Women—And They're Not Wearing Bikinis," *Marketing News* (March 2, 1992), p. 2; and "This Bud's for You. No, Not You—Her," *Business Week* (November 4, 1991), p. 86.

buying a food product promoting good health in the previous 30 days.[22] It is estimated that almost half of the adult population takes vitamin supplements and over one-third of adults use low-calorie foods and beverages. Consumption of certain products has also decreased. Per capita consumption of cigarettes, liquor, and coffee has steadily decreased since 1980. Consumers have been switching from red meats to poultry because of cholesterol concerns, and their purchase of some dairy products has declined, with a switch to low-fat products such as skim milk and yogurt.

As a result of these concerns, there is hardly a food company that does not have at least one line of diet or nutritionally oriented products. In 1995, over 1,400 new low-calorie or low-fat products were introduced, compared to about 800 in 1993.[23] Companies that repositioned existing products to health-conscious consumers were also able to post strong profits. Tums saw its sales grow by 50 percent when it repositioned itself as a calcium supplement targeted to women concerned about osteoporosis later in life, even though calcium was always part of the product.[24] Bertolli repositioned its olive oil as a means of avoiding saturated oils; its tag line is "Eat well, live long, and be happy."

A More Self-Indulgent Lifestyle. Despite the attention devoted to healthier and more nutritious foods, increasing evidence suggests that this trend has peaked. A 1993 Louis Harris poll of 1,251 adults found that Americans gained more weight and ate less carefully than they did the year before.[25] Susan Powter's antidiet book, *Stop the Insanity!,* sold more copies than any "how-to" diet book. The days of obsessive dieting seem to be fading, and marketers are more willing to appeal to an increasingly indulgent American consumer. The ad for Haagen-Dazs in Exhibit 13.5 is an example with its self-indulgent appeal—"Love It. Need It."

As a result, marketers are positioning fewer products to the health segment. Also, companies introducing light versions of their products have not always fared well. Frito Lay, for example, reported disappointing results after introducing light versions of Cheetos and Doritos. And after consumers rejected its low-fat beef patty, McLean Deluxe, McDonald's introduced the more indulgent Mega Mac, a half-pound burger with cheese and sauce.[26]

http://www.fritolay.com/

http://www.mcdonalds.com/

EXHIBIT 13.5 Appealing to a more self-indulgent consumer

The same trends appear to be occurring in the fitness market. Just as the days of obsessive dieting are fading, so too are the days of obsessive exercising. Americans continue to be concerned about maintaining fitness, but the preoccupation with achieving perfect bodies at all costs has gone the way of the 1980s—a decade known for self-absorption. The more current surveys would seem to suggest that Americans are more willing to accept the bodies they have and resent advertisers who make them feel anxious about it.

As the economy soured in the early 1990s and people had to work longer hours, the amount of time devoted to out-of-home exercising declined. Although the share of adults belonging to health clubs grew from 15 to 24 percent in the five years after 1987, the average member spent 12 percent less time there at the end of the period, according to a time-use research study Reebok conducted.[27]

In a 1992 survey of 2,500 people, Yankelovich Clancy Shulman, the research firm, recorded the sentiments of most Americans. It found most consumers are comfortable with their life choices and, therefore, do not try to impress others when they exercise; they are not attracted by novelty; they are not willing to sacrifice everything for an idealized vision of what a marketer thinks they should look like; and they do not want to give up their occasional indulgences.[28] Food and beverage companies are positioning products to appeal to this ethic. The ad for Evian in Exhibit 13.6 cites water as a means of staying fit by showing a pregnant woman relaxing in the sun. The context of the ad is the farthest thing from a rigorous exercise program.

A More Isolated Lifestyle

Consumers are spending more time at home, resulting in a more isolated lifestyle. There are two dimensions to this trend: staying at home for leisure and working at home.

▶EXHIBIT 13.6
Appealing to fitness in the 1990s

Today, consumers are more likely to stay at home for leisure and entertainment. This trend is particularly apparent for baby boomers and generation Xers. As baby boomers have aged, they have become more traditional stay-at-home types. They are more likely to embrace homespun values and peace of mind as they enter middle age. Some have referred to this trend as *cocooning*. Generation Xers are also staying at home more but for different reasons. They are more likely to be economically strapped and simply cannot afford to go out. Further, many stay home as a form of escapism by eating comfort foods and watching TV and home videos, thereby avoiding issues such as pollution and AIDS.

A second and broader dimension of a more isolated consumer is the greater opportunities for working at home spawned by the information revolution, making it easy for home-based entrepreneurs to operate as if they worked in a corporate office. All that is needed is a fax machine, a copier, and a personal computer.

According to federal estimates, between 10 and 13 percent of the work force is self-employed. Many have taken the freelance route as a lifestyle choice to maximize their personal time and to cut down on commuting. However, the fastest growing group in the segment are 50-something white males with managerial and administrative experience—the prime victims of the corporate layoffs of the 1990s. These highly educated, white-collar executives, whose ranks swelled to 700,000 in the past decade, often find that their skills no longer fetch the price they once did. They find their best course is to become independent operators, even though they are likely to earn less than they did in the corporate world. This was one of the main outcomes of the recession of the early 1990s and a prime reason why most of the new businesses started at home tend to involve consulting, graphic design, computer maintenance, and personnel. These are the areas that have suffered greatly from corporate downsizing, but at the same time require minimal start-up capital.[29]

Not all home-based workers are self-employed, however. Many companies now allow their employees to work from home via computer hookups to save time and to free employees from nonproductive office distractions. Baxter Health Care, American Express, Apple Computer, IBM, Sears, and JCPenney are just a few of the firms with work-at-home policies.

Marketers have responded by trying to serve the rapidly expanding niche of home-based workers. Computer software designers such as Lotus and Borland are leading the way with programs that enable individuals to create elaborate graphics and presentations. However, they are by no means alone. Apple, IBM, Canon, Fujitsu, and other companies are all appealing to the home-based entrepreneur, all through personalized versions of office machines.

http://www.apple.com/

The ad for Apple in Exhibit 13.7 addresses the particular needs of the home office claiming that "you can accomplish a lot more working in your home office if you're working on a Macintosh."

Greater Time Pressures

Time pressures in American society have been increasing in the last 30 years. In 1965, 24 percent of Americans under 50 said they "always felt rushed." By 1992 that figure rose to 38 percent. The share of people claiming they "almost never had excess time on their hands" rose from 46 percent in 1965 to 61 percent in 1995.[31] Interestingly, time-use studies show that Americans in the last thirty years actually have *more* leisure time than before, but feel they have less. The primary reason is increased stress levels. In 1993, 56 percent of Americans reported they experienced "a lot" or "a moderate amount" of stress in the last two weeks, the highest levels ever. Further, Americans are twice as likely to say they have less free time compared to 10 years ago.[32] The American consumer's life has been getting more frenzied.

An ad for Eddie Bauer tries to capture the desire on the part of many American consumers to "Stop the World; I want to get off." It shows a photo of a man skipping a stone across a lake, accompanied by the words, "Deep inside each of us is someone striving to do absolutely nothing." On the other side of the coin, some marketers are reflecting time pressures and the compulsion to do everything. Day Runner, the leader in personal organizers, rec-

▶EXHIBIT 13.7
An appeal to people who work at home

ognizes the penchant for parents to impart time pressures to their kids. It is introducing a new organizer for the young set with Disney cartoon characters on calendars, diaries, and assignment books for those kids who have "a music lesson, a fitness class and two parties this week—on top of your usual hectic schedule."[33]

The most direct effect of greater time pressures is the increasing emphasis consumers are placing on time-saving conveniences. As a result, some marketers have concluded that "time has come to rival money as the commodity people crave most."[34] The focus on time-saving convenience in the 1990s has created two trends in consumption: grazing and refueling.

Grazing is the need to eat on the run. People eat breakfast in the car on the way to work, munch on a sandwich while walking, or eat lunch at their desks. This trend is the result of the demise of sit-down breakfasts and lunches in most households. The need for quick food has led many marketers to repackage their products into smaller sizes and to change them to suit grazers' dietary needs. In 1993, Nestlé reformulated its entire Instant Breakfast line, increasing the vitamin and mineral levels of its Breakfast Bars while cutting the fat content. It also introduced its first granola bars and reformulated the contents of its powdered drink mixes, advertising the change with a campaign that read, "Your breakfast just got more nutritious."[35] Other companies targeting grazers are General Mills, which

http://www.generalmills.com/

introduced Yoplait frozen yogurt in a squeezable paper cone, and Oscar Mayer, which sells Lunchables, packaged meat and cheese slices in plastic trays.[36]

Refueling refers to less time spent in preparing and eating dinner. The primary reflection of this trend is the growing importance of microwave ovens in people's lives. Microwaveable food increases the amount of leisure time available to the harried working woman or the single consumer because it promises independence from kitchen chores. The increase in ownership of microwave ovens during the past decade has been phenomenal. In 1980, 15 percent of homes had microwaves; by 1989, close to 80 percent of U.S. households owned them.[37] Because of this growth, shelf-stable foods account for more than $4 billion in sales annually.[38] Weight Watchers sells sandwiches; Chef Boyardee has a line of Main Meals; Conagra offers Armour Dinner Classics; and Hormell has introduced Kids' Kitchen dinners, all designed for microwave cooking.

http://www.weight-watchers.com/

http://www.crfi.com/

Higher Level of Self-Awareness

The 1990s is seeing an increase in the demand for products and services that offer a sense of personal achievement such as sports equipment, home electronics, and educational products. Two prerequisites for a more self-aware lifestyle are the money required to pursue self-satisfying activities and the time to do so. However, time pressures conflict with a desire for a more self-aware lifestyle. Arthur D. Little, a large consulting firm, sees the resolution of this conflict as an "increasing emphasis on activities that can be mastered easily, can provide high rewards in a short time period, and can be accomplished at or near the home. As a result, such things as home computers, cable TV, and exercisers will be high on consumer shopping lists."[39]

http://www.adlittle.com/

In appealing to self-awareness, many marketers used to focus on high levels of personal achievement. Now, they are using a more relaxed style to focus on improving one's self-image. For example, one of Michelob's print ads depicts headlines torn from other papers admonishing women to "lose fat," "make yourself over," and "have perfect arms in 14 days." The tag line reads: "Relax. You're OK. Improve your beer."[40]

This focus on self with a minimum of anxiety parallels a broader change in the values of many Americans. The 1980s was a decade of obsessive purchasing and a desire for the "good life." As we saw in the last chapter, most baby boomers left that period behind and developed more pragmatic concerns—namely, family, economic security, and the environment. There is a significant increase in products trying to help people address these concerns. *The New York Times Book Review,* a leading indicator of popular reading tastes, became so filled with "how-to" books that the newspaper had to create a separate category for them. Also, late-night television has become crowded with infomercials advising consumers how they can feel better about themselves.

A More Frugal and Value-Oriented Lifestyle

The recession of the early 1990s created a marked trend toward frugality among consumers. Among the signs are fewer expenditures on luxury items, renewed demands for quality, and the loosening of brand loyalties.[41] The market for luxury products has suffered because consumers are framing their lives in terms of survival and security instead of success and acquisition. As one researcher observed:

> In the 1980s, people wanted to make it big; now they just want to make it. People today are more concerned about money, less concerned about "having it all." Needs are more basic—less luxury, less concern with the trendy [and] less faith in their ability to fulfill the American dream.[42]

http://www.waterford-usa.com/

http://www.audi.com/

This placed luxury product marketers in the awkward position of selling high-end products with practical arguments, often using a conservative "family values" theme. Waterford, for instance, used a down-home family setting to sell its fine and expensive crystal: in one ad, a barefoot toddler pulled cherries from a pricey Waterford bowl. However, the campaign failed. As one marketing consultant said of Waterford's attempt, "Who gives two-year-old kids Waterford bowls to eat out of? It's a disaster."[43] Similarly, luxury car makers have attempted to adapt to a more practical orientation. In one campaign, Audi used the theme: "If the 90s are a time of getting more for your money, the new Audi 90 is ideally suited to the times."

The desire for quality has gone hand in hand with the trend toward economy, creating a *value orientation.* Though consumers were buying less expensive products, they sought the same level of quality. This value orientation has resulted in a loosening of brand loyalties and an increase in the purchase of private-label and lower-priced brands. According to a recent study, shoppers are more secure with themselves and no longer need to impress others with expensive purchases. They are more interested in quality merchandise at bargain prices than they are in brand names.

Measuring Lifestyle Characteristics

The previous section described lifestyle trends and their marketing implications. Unlike these general trends, lifestyle characteristics that are specific to certain consumers and product categories must be defined and measured if they are to be useful to marketers. For instance, it would be relevant for a food company to identify a dieter segment or a clothing company to identify a fashion-conscious segment. However, the researcher must define lifestyle characteristics, in contrast to demographics, since there are no fixed definitions such as age, income, or occupation. As a result, marketers must devise methods to measure lifestyles.

AIO Inventories

The most common method for measuring lifestyles is to develop an inventory of activities, interests, and opinions (an **AIO inventory**). Marketers develop two types of AIO inventories. One is a generalized inventory that can be applied across product categories and identifies broad segments such as homemakers, sports enthusiasts, and fashion-conscious consumers. The second is an inventory that is specific to a product category, for example, a lifestyle inventory to describe Internet users, purchasers of new personal care products, or, more generally, users of high-tech products.

In both cases, marketers develop these inventories by formulating a large number of questions regarding consumer activities, interests, and opinions and then selecting a smaller number of questions that best define consumer segments.

Generalized AIO Inventories. An example of a generalized AIO inventory is one developed by Wells and Tigert. They formulated 300 AIO statements and asked respondents to agree or disagree with each one on a six-point scale.[44] Typical statements were "I like to be considered a leader" and "I usually keep my home very neat and clean."

Wells and Tigert then reduced these 300 items to 22 lifestyle dimensions (see Table 13.1) by **factor analysis,** a method for grouping items that are highly correlated. The factor analysis showed, for example, that consumers who agreed with the statement "I shop a lot for specials" also tended to agree with the statements "I find myself checking prices," "I watch advertisements for sales," and "A person can save a lot by shopping for bargains." People who agreed with these statements were called price-conscious consumers. By using responses to the 300 statements, Wells and Tigert could describe certain consumers as price-conscious, fashion-conscious, child-oriented, and so on.

Wells and Tigert then used these 22 lifestyle dimensions in the same manner as demographics to describe and segment consumers. For instance, users of eye makeup tended to agree with the items defining fashion-consciousness, whereas nonusers did not. The heavy user of shortening liked housekeeping, was more child-oriented, and was more of a homebody than was the nonuser.

We must recognize that lifestyles are constantly changing. The financial optimist and the compulsive housekeeper segments in Table 13.1 are smaller today than at the time of Wells and Tigert's study, and the price-conscious segment is larger. Furthermore, new lifestyle trends develop. For example, any AIO inventory developed today would probably identify a health-conscious segment and an environmentally aware segment.

Product-Specific AIO Inventories. An example of a product-specific AIO inventory is one developed by a manufacturer to identify those most likely to buy new personal care products. A group of lifestyle characteristics that were relevant to the purchase of personal care appliances was determined from focus-group interviews with recent purchasers of these items. A sample of women were then asked to rate themselves on these characteristics. Women were then divided into those who were among the first to purchase new personal care appliances (innovators in Table 13.2) versus those who purchased later (noninnovators.)

As Table 13.2 shows, innovators tended to be more style- and appearance-conscious, more self-confident, more likely to communicate about new products, and more likely to look for time-saving products.

TABLE 13.1
Sample lifestyle categories based on perceived activities, interests, and opinions

Price-Conscious
I shop a lot for specials.
I find myself checking the prices in the grocery store even for small items.
I watch the advertisements for announcements of sales.
A person can save a lot of money by shopping for bargains.

Fashion-Conscious
I usually have one or more outfits of the very latest style.
When I must choose between the two I usually dress for fashion, not comfort.
An important part of my life and activities is dressing smartly.
I often try the latest hairdo styles when they change.

Homebody
I prefer a quiet evening at home over a party.
I like parties with lots of music and talk. (Reverse scored)
I would rather go to a sporting event than a dance.
I am a homebody.

Community-Minded
I am an active member of more than one service organization.
I do volunteer work for a hospital or service organization on a fairly regular basis.
I like to work on community projects.
I have personally worked in a political campaign on for a candidate or an issue.

Child-Oriented
When my children are ill in bed, I drop most everything else to see to their comfort.
My children are the most important things in my life.
I try to arrange my home for my children's convenience.
I take a lot of time and effort to teach my children good habits.

Compulsive Housekeeper
I don't like to see children's toys lying about.
I usually keep my house very neat and clean.
I am uncomfortable when my house is not completely clean.
Our days seem to follow a definite routine such as eating meals at a regular time, etc.

Self-Confident
I think I have more self-confidence than most people.
I am more independent than most people.
I have a lot of personal ability.
I like to be considered a leader.

Self-Designated Opinion Leader
My friends or neighbors often come to me for advice.
I sometimes influence what my friends buy.
People come to me more often than I go to them for information about brands.

Information Seeker
I often seek the advice of friends on which brand to buy.
I spend a lot of time asking friends about products and brands.

Dislikes Housekeeping
I must admit I really don't like household chores.
I find cleaning my house an unpleasant task.
I enjoy most forms of housework. (Reverse scored)
My idea of housekeeping is "once over lightly."

Sewer
I like to sew and frequently do.
I often make my own or my children's clothes.
You can save a lot of money by making your own clothes.
I would like to know how to sew like an expert.

Canned Food User
I depend on canned food for at least one meal a day.
I couldn't get along without canned foods.
Things just don't taste right if they come out of a can. (Reverse scored)

Dieter
I drink low-calorie soft drinks several times a week.
I buy more low-calorie foods than the average housewife.
I have used Metrecal or other diet foods at least one meal a day.

Financial Optimist
I will probably have more money to spend next year than I have now.
Five years from now, the family income will probably be a lot higher than it is now.

Source: Adapted from William D. Wells and Douglas J. Tigert, "Activities, Interests and Opinions," *Journal of Advertising Research* 11 (August 1971), p. 35. Reprinted from the *Journal of Advertising Research* © 1971, by the Advertising Research Foundation.

Value and Lifestyle Survey (VALS)

Another approach to measuring lifestyles is to conduct consumer surveys to identify consumer activities, interests, and opinions, and then to develop lifestyle categories on this basis. The Value and Lifestyle Survey (VALS), which the Stan-

TABLE 13.2
Lifestyle characteristics of innovators of personal care products

Lifestyle Characteristics	Innovators (14% of sample)	Noninnovators (86% of sample)
Style- and appearance-conscious/ self-indulgent	39%	28%
Isolate/conservative	25	32
Social/self-confident	44	27
Bargain seekers	28	30
Outdoor types	31	32
New product/social communicators	39	26
Look for time-saving products	39	25
Rely on manufacturer's name	26	20

http://www.sri.com/

ford Research Institute (SRI) developed in 1978, reflects this approach.[45] VALS conducts yearly surveys of 2,500 consumers and has identified groups such as actualizers, strivers, and strugglers based on common lifestyles and values. For example, actualizers have a high level of self-esteem, are open to change, and buy the finer things in life. They would be good targets for laptop computers, adult education courses, or the latest in sound systems. They could best be targeted through upscale magazines rather than television. Such lifestyle profiles help marketers target products to specific consumer groups. That helps explain why the VALS system is the most widely used method of assessing cultural and lifestyle values. Over 150 companies subscribe to its findings on a yearly basis.

The VALS system (known as VALS 2 because it is a revision of an earlier lifestyle grouping known as VALS 1) identifies eight groups, as shown in Figure 13.1. The groups are split on two dimensions. The vertical dimension represents consumers' resources—not only money, but also education, self-confidence, and energy level. Actualizers have the most resources; strugglers, the least. The horizontal dimension represents three different ways consumers see the world. Principle-oriented consumers are guided by their views of how the world is or should be and are represented as either fulfilleds or believers. Status-oriented consumers (achievers and strivers) are guided by the opinions of others. Action-oriented consumers (experiencers and makers) are motivated by a desire for activity, variety, and risk taking. Of the two groups in each sector, one has abundant resources and one minimal resources. The groups in VALS 2 are more fully defined in Table 13.2.

Applications of Lifestyle Characteristics to Marketing Strategies

The most direct applications of lifestyles to marketing strategies have been through the use of the VALS groups shown in Figure 13.1. Marketers have used VALS to develop market segmentation, media, and advertising strategies.

FIGURE 13.1 The VALS 2 consumer segments

Source: "Markets with Attitudes," *American Demographics* (July 1994), p. 25.

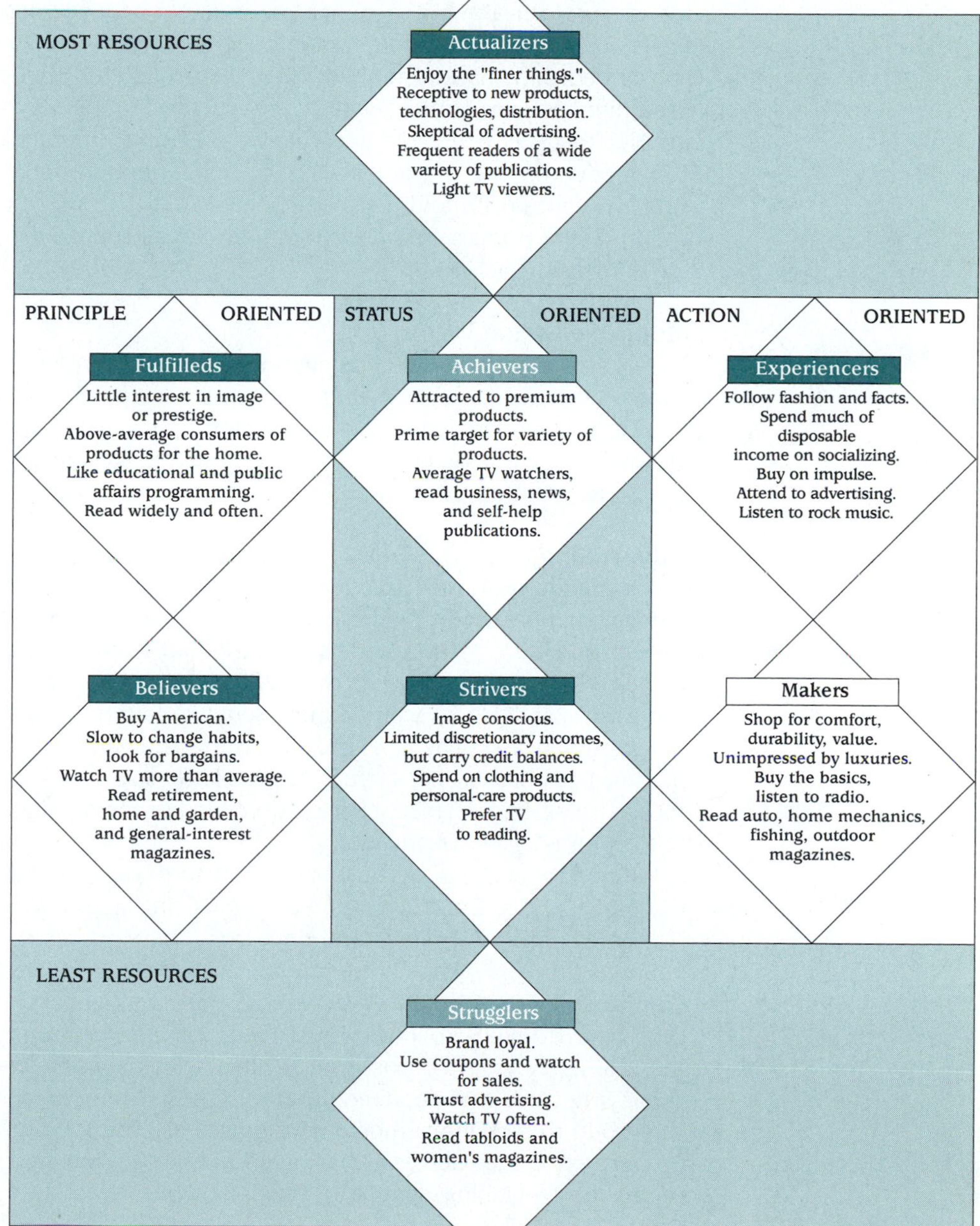

Market Segmentation

http://www.timex.com/

A good example of the application of lifestyles is Timex's use of VALS 2 data to identify segments for a new line of products, a package of three digital instruments for home use (a weight scale, a thermometer, and a blood pressure monitor) under the name Healthcheck.[46] The company believed that consumer attitudes toward health maintenance and home diagnostic products were likely to be value-based and that demographic segmentation would be insufficient. Timex subscribed to VALS and ranked the VALS groups by the degree to which they used high-tech and health-related products. Two target segments were identified for Healthcheck: achievers and fulfilleds. Despite the fact that one group was status-oriented and the other was principle-oriented, both segments showed a concern with health and were better educated than other groups. This identification of the primary target segments drove all subsequent marketing strategy for the Healthcheck line.

Media Selection

Timex also used the VALS typology in media selection for Healthcheck. The data showed that achievers and fulfilleds do not watch much TV; therefore, Timex used print advertising. When these groups do watch TV, it is generally news programs. Timex scheduled its introductory campaign during early and late news programs, with no prime-time or daytime TV advertising.

Advertising

The basic theme Timex used to promote Healthcheck was "Technology—where it does the most good." Models in the ads gave off "the self-satisfied vibes achievers can relate to."[47] The models' clothing had to appear natural looking and be in muted tones to appeal to the fulfilleds, but "statusy enough" to appeal to achievers. Models also were featured outside, often riding bicycles, playing tennis, or doing a similar activity. Both the ads and the package provided information to appeal to the factual needs of the two target groups. As a result of these strategies, the Healthcheck line moved to the top spot in its market within four months of its introduction.

Iron City Beer also used VALS 2 data to develop its advertising strategy. In the early 1990s, Iron City was well known in Pittsburgh but was losing sales. The core drinkers—makers and believers—were aging and drinking less, while younger drinkers were not identifying with the brand. So the ad agency, Della Femina, used VALS data to show that the experiencers were the highest-volume beer drinkers, followed by strivers. Using a technique called *picture sorting,* the agency gave focus groups filled with experiencers and strivers decks of playing cards that depicted different types of people. The agency then asked the group to pick those most like themselves. The focus-group subjects wound up portraying themselves as hard-working but fun-loving, and—much like Pittsburgh itself—gaining economic strength while rejecting a heavy industry image.

Using this data, Della Femina crafted ads mixing images of the Old Pittsburgh with ones of a new, vibrant city and depictions of young experiencers and strivers working hard and having fun. The soundtrack used the song "Working in a Coal Mine," but changed the words to "working on a cold Iron." Partly as a result of this campaign, sales of Iron City increased by 26 percent.[48]

PERSONALITY

An individual's personality represents another set of characteristics that contributes to an understanding of consumer behavior. Personality characteristics can be valuable guides to marketers. For example, knowing that users of a brand of headache remedies are more likely to be compulsive led one company to advertise the product in an orderly setting that described a fixed routine. Another company found that an important segment of users of artificial sweeteners tended to be compliant and to accept guidance from others, especially medical experts, in an attempt to lose weight. This finding suggested advertising these products through an authority figure.

Marketers have used four personality theories to describe consumers: (1) self-concept theory, (2) psychoanalytic theory, (3) social/cultural theory, and (4) trait theory. These four theories vary greatly in their approach to personality measurement. The psychoanalytic and social theories take a qualitative approach to evaluating personality variables; trait theory is the most empirical; and self-concept theory is somewhere in between qualitative and quantitative in its orientation.

Self-concept theory is, arguably, the most relevant for marketers because it focuses on how an individual's self-image affects his or her purchasing behavior. It recognizes that what we buy and own is a reflection of who we are. Extensions of psychoanalytic theory have also been widely used in marketing to develop qualitative insights into why consumers buy. Insights from psychoanalytic theory are particularly relevant when purchase motives are deep-seated. Such motivational research derives from both psychoanalytic concepts related to the resolution of childhood conflicts and from psychoanalytic techniques that rely on in-depth interviews.

We will first describe self-concept theory, then the more qualitatively oriented psychoanalytic and social theories, and conclude with trait theory.

Self-Concept Theory

Self-concept (or **self-image**) **theory** holds that individuals have a concept of self based on who they think they are (the **actual self**) and a concept of who they think they would like to be (the **ideal self**). Self-concept theory is related to two key concepts of psychoanalytic theory: the ego and the superego. Since the ego is a reflection of one's objective reality, it is similar to the actual self. The superego is defined by the way things should be and is therefore a reflection of the ideal self. To determine their self-concept, consumers are asked to describe how they see themselves (actual) or how they would like to see themselves (ideal) on various attributes such as:

happy	serious
dependable	self-controlled
modern	successful
practical	sensitive
energetic	aggressive

Self-concept theory is governed by two principles: the desire to attain self-consistency and the desire to enhance one's self-esteem. Attaining self-consistency means that individuals will act in accordance with their concept of actual self. For example, a consumer may see himself as a practical and self-controlled individual. He buys conservative suits, drives a large four-door sedan, and spends quiet evenings at home. Deep down, however, he would like to be more carefree and reckless. If he were to act more like his ideal self, he might own a small sports car, dress in jeans and sport shirts, and go to rock clubs. Such actions would enhance his self-esteem by drawing him closer to his ideal self.

Actual Self

There is no one actual self. Consumers have various *role identities*—wife, mother, working woman, volunteer for AIDS organizations. One of these roles will be dominant in specific situations; the particular role will affect the individual's style of dress and behavior. The amalgam of the individual's roles make up the actual self.

Applied to marketing, the concept of actual self says that consumers' purchases are influenced by the image they have of themselves. They attain self-consistency by buying products they perceive as similar to their self-concept. That is, there is congruence between brand image and self-image.

Several studies have confirmed that consumers buy products related to their self-concept. Dolich studied this relationship for beer, cigarettes, bar soap, and toothpaste.[49] He found that respondents tend to prefer brands they rate as similar to themselves. Several studies have shown the s ame relationship for automobiles.[50] An owner's perception of his or her car is consistent with self-perception. Furthermore, the consumer's self-image is similar to his or her image of others with the same automobile.

More recently, Burnkrant and Page concluded that the relationship between brand image and self-image is somewhat more complicated because consumers change their self-image with each situation.[51] For example, a consumer may have one self-image in a social situation but another one in a business situation.

Ideal Self

The concept of the ideal self relates to one's self-esteem. The greater the difference between the actual self and ideal self, the lower an individual's self-esteem. In a marketing context, dissatisfaction with oneself could influence purchases, particularly for products that could enhance self-esteem. Thus, a woman who would like to be more efficient, modern, and imaginative may buy a different type of perfume or deodorant or tend to shop at different stores than a woman who would like to be more warm and attractive.

Richins found that advertising themes and images often create greater discrepancy between the real and ideal selves.[52] Advertising that portrays beautiful models or luxurious lifestyles creates an idealized world that is unreachable. As a result, consumers are left with a sense of inadequacy based on a comparison of their real self with these idealized images. For example, the average female fashion model is 5 feet 9 inches and weighs 123 pounds; the average U.S. woman, on the other hand, is 5 feet, 4 inches and weighs 144 pounds.[53] In acting to increase the disparity between the real and ideal selves, advertising tends to lower consumers' self-esteem.

The desire for both self-consistency and self-esteem could be conflicting. Consumers who buy in accordance with their actual self-concept may be achieving consistency but may not be enhancing self-esteem. Generally, consumers buy products that conform to their actual self-image. But if they are low in self-esteem (that is, if there is greater disparity between the actual and ideal selves), they are more likely to buy based on what they would like to be rather than on what they are. As a result, these consumers are more likely to be swayed by appeals to fantasy that portray an idealized self—the alluring woman, the lone biker on his Harley-Davidson, the well-dressed man who attracts women's attention.

http://www.harley-davidson.com/

Buying to achieve an unrealizable self-image can lead to compulsive purchasing behavior. Frequent purchasing is a means to overcome the discrepancy between the real and ideal selves and to relieve a sense of low self-esteem.[54]

Consumption and the Extended Self

Another dimension of self-concept theory is applicable to consumers. Not only does our self-image influence the products we choose (as suggested earlier), but the products we choose frequently influence our self-image.[55] Certain products have symbolic (badge) value. They say something about us and the way we feel about ourselves. For example, when we buy a certain suit or dress, we may anticipate that it will enhance our self-esteem.

On this basis, Belk has identified an **extended self** as distinct from the actual self. The extended self incorporates some of our more important possessions into our self-concept because what we own reflects our personality. In simple terms, we are what we wear, and we are what we use. As Belk notes, "People seek, express, confirm, and ascertain a sense of being through what they have."[56] Belk cites various occasions when it is apparent that possessions are an extension of self. Consider the following statements:

- *A college student whose bike was stolen:* "It hurts to think that someone else is selling something that for me is more precious than money."

- *An elderly consumer pawning possessions to make ends meet:* "I stand in that hock shop, and I tell myself that my entire life is being sold."[57]
- *Saul Bellow after his treasured car was vandalized:* "I felt a . . . rip at my heart . . . I had allowed the car to become an extension of my own self."

This concept of the extended self is related to **symbolic interactionism** because it recognizes the interaction between individuals and the symbols in their environment. It means that consumers buy products for their symbolic value in enhancing their self-concept. It also means that consumers tend to buy *product constellations,* that is, complementary groups of products that are related to each other because of their symbolic association. As Solomon noted, "While the Rolex watch, Brooks Brothers suit, New Balance running shoes, Sony Walkman, and BMW automobile on the surface bear no relation to one another, many consumers would easily group these disparate products together as a symbolic whole."[58]

Research based on the concept of extended self would examine the constellation of products a consumer owns and try to equate these groups of products to the consumer's self-concept. This type of research is very different from looking at a single product and determining if it is related to a consumer's actual or ideal self-concept. It seeks to understand the symbolic role that groups of products play in shaping the consumer's self-concept.

Marketers have understood the symbolic role of product constellations in projecting an image. Advertising for jewelry might show fashionably dressed models or automobiles, and ads for clothing might also show jewelry. The increasing importance of co-branding also reflects an acceptance of the concept of product constellations. Many marketers are finding other products to link up with in joint advertising and promotional efforts. These products must be seen as complementary by consumers. In the car market, for example, the Lincoln Town Car offers a version fitted out by Cartier jewelers; Chrysler's Jeep Grand Cherokee links up with Orvis, the marketer of outdoor gear for fishing and hunting; and VW offers a Trek bike and bike rack to link itself with a rugged, fun lifestyle.[59] In each case, the two products blend together in projecting a consistent image.

http://www.ford.com/

http://www.chrysler.com/

http://www.orvis.com/

http://www.vw.com/

Psychoanalytic Theory

Freud's **psychoanalytic theory** stresses the unconscious nature of personality as a result of childhood conflicts. These conflicts are derived from three components of personality: id, ego, and superego. The **id** (or the **libido**) controls the individual's most basic needs and urges such as hunger, sex, and self-preservation. The source of all innate forces that drive behavior, the id operates on one principle: directing behavior to achieve pleasure and to avoid pain. The id is entirely unconscious, with no anchor in objective reality. A newborn baby's behavior, for example, is governed totally by the id.

The **ego** is the individual's self-concept and is the manifestation of objective reality as it develops in interaction with the external world. As manager of the id, the ego seeks to attain the goals of the id in a socially acceptable manner. For example, rather than manifest a basic need to be aggressive in antisocial ways, an individual may partially satisfy this need by buying a powerful sports car.

The **superego** is the leash on the id and works against its impulses. It does not manage the id but restrains it by punishing unacceptable behavior through the creation of guilt. Like the id, it operates in the unconscious and often represses behavior that would otherwise occur based on the id. The superego represents the ideal rather than the real. It motivates us to act in a moral way.

According to Freud, the ego manages the conflicting demands of the id and the superego. The way the child manages these conflicts (particularly sexual conflicts) determines the adult personality. Conflicts that are not resolved in childhood will result in **defense mechanisms** (strategies that the ego uses to reduce tension) and will frequently influence later behavior in a manner of which the adult is unaware.

Motivational Research

Psychologists applying Freud's theories to marketing believe the id and superego operate to create unconscious motives for purchasing certain products. Although these motives are extremely hard to determine, they might be central to explaining certain purchasing behaviors. Because the focus is on developing means to uncover these unconscious motives, applications of psychoanalytic theory to marketing are known as **motivational research.**

Motivational researchers believe that deep-seated purchasing motives can best be determined through indirect methods by researching a small number of consumers. Two techniques derived from psychoanalytic theory and applied to marketing—depth interviews and projective techniques—have been used frequently in marketing studies.

Depth Interviews. Depth interviews, a technique discussed in Chapters 1 and 9, are interviews with individual consumers designed to determine deep-seated or repressed motives that structured questions cannot elicit.[60] Consumers are encouraged to talk freely in an unstructured interview, and their responses are interpreted carefully to reveal motives and potential purchase inhibitions. An offshoot of the depth interview is the **focus-group interview,** in which 8 to 12 consumers are brought together under the direction of a moderator to discuss issues that may reveal deep-seated needs or unconscious motives. The advantages of focus groups are that they are likely to stimulate discussion because of the group context, and they may elicit thoughts and motives that individual depth interviews will not.

The foremost proponent of depth and focus-group interviews was Ernest Dichter, acknowledged as the father of motivational research. A Freudian psy-

http://www.pg.com/

chologist by training, Dichter came to the United States in the late 1930s and began applying psychoanalytic theory to advertising. One of his first applications was for Procter & Gamble in 1940. The company asked Dichter if there was some way to revitalize Ivory Soap. Based on depth interviews with teenagers, he found that they considered bathing as almost a ritual, especially before a date. It was a means of "getting rid of all your bad feelings, your sins, your immorality, and cleansing yourself."[61] On this basis, Dichter developed the slogan "Be smart, get a fresh start with Ivory Soap . . . wash all your troubles away." Dichter used depth and focus-group interviews in numerous studies that have provided actionable findings; for example:[62]

- Consumers want a sense of freedom and power when they get behind the wheel of a car. They look for that surge of acceleration to free themselves of the mundane aspects of everyday life. If you want to advertise gasoline, go along with this feeling and advertise the "tiger in your tank" (see Exhibit 13.8).
- Men resist giving blood because they equate it with a loss of potency. The Red Cross would be smart to advertise to potential donors that they are lending rather than giving their blood, because blood is regenerated in a short period of time.

http://www.redcross.org/

►EXHIBIT 13.8
An appeal to consumer desires based on motivational research

- Candy consumption is a source of guilt because of childhood associations with reward and punishment. Any attempt to market candy to adults should emphasize the fact that they deserve the rewards associated with candy consumption.

Projective Techniques. Projective techniques are the second set of methods derived from psychoanalytic theory and applied to marketing.[63] Like depth interviews, these techniques are designed to determine motives that are difficult to express or identify. Because consumers may not be aware of their motives for buying, researchers cannot ask direct questions consumers may not be able to answer. Instead, consumers are given a situation, a cartoon, or a set of words and asked to respond. They project their feelings and concerns about products to this less-threatening or involving situation.

In one famous experiment in the late 1940s, Haire used a projective technique to discover why women were reluctant to purchase instant coffee when it was first introduced.[64] He constructed two shopping lists that were identical, except that one included regular coffee and the other instant coffee. Respondents then were asked to project the type of woman most likely to have developed each shopping list. The shopper who included instant coffee in the list was characterized as lazy and a poor planner. These findings demonstrated that many women had a deep-seated fear of buying products such as instant coffee or instant cake mixes because of a concern that their husbands would believe they were avoiding their traditional role as homemakers. As a result of the study, instant coffee was advertised in a family setting portraying the husband's approval. A replication of the study today would produce very different results since this traditional view of a woman's role is not as widespread. The study is a classic example of a psychoanalytically oriented approach to the determination of consumer motives.

Other projective techniques include asking consumers to complete sentences (Someone who buys Brand X is. . . .), to complete bubbles in cartoons (husband changing a diaper with a bubble over his head to designate what he is saying), or to personify brands or products with human or animal traits. In each case, the consumer is projecting his or her feelings regarding a product or situation without being asked a direct question. In one application of personification, when consumers were asked to imagine long-distance carriers as animals, many described AT&T as a lion, MCI as a snake, and Sprint as a puma. Sprint's ad agency used this insight to position the service as the one that could "help you do more business" rather than taking the savings-oriented approach of the other carriers.[65]

http://www.mci.com/

http://www.att.com/

http://www.sprint.com/

Criticisms of Motivational Research. Motivational research has been criticized for relying primarily on the researcher's qualitative judgments without any hard data. Some have also questioned whether advertising could or should influence deep-seated motives. The psychoanalytic approach may be "touchy, feely," but motivational researchers were the first to argue that consumers are "complex, devious, difficult to understand and driven by mighty forces of which they are unaware."[66] In this respect, it has made a significant contribution in understanding behavioral drives for more complex and involving products.

Social/Cultural Theories

A number of Freud's disciples shifted from his view of personality in two respects. First, they thought that social and cultural variables, rather than biological drives, are more important in personality development. Second, Freud's understanding of personality focused primarily on observations of emotionally disturbed people. His disciples subsequently believed that insights into personality development should also rely on observations of people who function normally in the social environment.

Carl Jung and Alfred Adler, the foremost students of Freud, took the psychoanalytic approach in separate directions. Jung believed that one's culture created an accumulation of shared memories from the past—nurturing female, heroic warrior, old wise man. Jung called these commonly shared memories **archetypes.** Jung's archetypes are sometimes depicted in ads that attempt to capitalize on the positive shared meanings in our culture. For example, one advertiser equates Betty Crocker with the Great Mother of ancient myth and the Bud Man as the hero in the Homeric tradition.[67]

Alfred Adler was the foremost proponent of a social orientation. Rather than focus on the importance of sexual conflicts like Freud or culturally shared meanings like Jung, Adler emphasized the individual's striving for superiority in a social context. He stressed that children develop feelings of inferiority, and their primary goal as adults is to overcome these feelings.

Karen Horney was another social theorist. She believed that personality is developed as an individual learns to cope with basic anxieties stemming from parent-child relationships. She hypothesized three approaches to coping with this anxiety: compliance, a strategy of moving toward people; aggressiveness, moving against people; and detachment, moving away from people.

In one of the few studies relying on social theories of personality to explain purchase behavior, Cohen developed a compliance-aggressiveness-detachment (CAD) scale based on Horney's work.[68] Cohen measured CAD using a 35-item inventory. In applying the CAD scale, Cohen found that compliant types used more mouthwash, toilet soaps, and Bayer aspirin; aggressive types used more cologne and after-shave lotion and bought Old Spice deodorant and Van Heusen shirts; and detached types drank more tea and less beer. These findings suggest advertising the use of mouthwash or toilet soap as a means of social approval, advertising colognes and after-shaves as a means of social conquest, and advertising tea in a traditional and subdued context.

http://www.bayer.com/

http://www.old-spice.com/

http://www.van-heusen.com/

Measures such as Cohen's CAD scale are important because they were constructed for marketing applications and have a theoretical base in personality theory. In such cases, the researcher begins a study with defined hypotheses of which personality variables to measure.

Trait Theory

Trait theory states that personality is composed of a set of traits that describe general response predispositions. Trait theorists construct personality inventories and ask respondents to respond to many items, perhaps agreeing or disagreeing with certain statements or expressing likes or dislikes for certain situations or types of people. These items then are statistically analyzed and reduced to a few personality dimensions. This method does not predetermine personality traits and is unlike psychoanalytic and social theories, which have specific hypotheses about the traits that affect behavior (for example, compulsiveness, aggressiveness, and detachment in Horney's theory).

A number of studies have used personality traits to segment markets. A study of smoking behavior found that heavy smokers scored higher on heterosexuality, aggression, and achievement and lower on order and compliance (all personality traits in standard personality inventories.)[69] Heavy smokers are more likely to be oriented toward power and competitiveness and may be more influenced by sexual themes and symbols. They are not as compulsive or submissive as nonsmokers. Because of this emphasis on power and competitiveness, it is not surprising that one of the most successful cigarette campaigns has been the Marlboro cowboy.

When marketers use personality measures specifically developed for consumer behavior applications rather than generalized inventories, they have more strategic applications. For example, Gottleib hypothesized that compulsive and punitive consumers would be more frequent users of antacids.[70]

Compulsiveness and punitiveness were measured by agreement or disagreement with a set of predetermined statements such as, "I like to set up a schedule for my activities and then stick to it" (compulsiveness), and "Discipline is the single most important factor in building children's character" (punitiveness). As expected, high compulsives tended to consume more antacids; but punitive respondents actually consumed less. Because of these results, the advertising for the brand under study emphasized a specific routine and regimen to appeal to the compulsive segment. The results also suggested that it was not necessary to make antacids taste bad to appeal to the punitive segment, as was originally thought.

Limitations of Personality Variables

Consumer behavior researchers have seen drawbacks in using personality characteristics to explain purchasing behavior. Personality theories are meant to describe enduring patterns of behavior. Quite often, the focus is on aberrant, rather than typical, behavior. To apply measures developed for these purposes to consumer behavior assumes that consumers are motivated to buy based on deep-seated drives. As we have seen, however, most consumer behavior is a mundane, day-to-day affair. Kassarjian summarized the limitations of personality measures:

> Instruments originally intended to measure gross personality characteristics such as sociability, emotional stability, introversion, or neuroticism have

> been used to make predictions of the chosen brand of toothpaste or cigarettes. The variables that lead to the assassination of a president, confinement in a mental hospital, or suicide may not be identical to those that lead to the purchase of a washing machine, a pair of shoes, or chewing gum. Clearly, if unequivocal results are to emerge, consumer behavior researchers must develop their own definitions and design their own instruments to measure the personality variables that go into the purchase decision.[71]

The limited capability of personality theories to explain more mundane, day-to-day consumer behavior led researchers to look elsewhere for an understanding of such behavior. The investigation of consumer lifestyles was motivated by these limitations of personality variables.

SUMMARY

Two consumer characteristics of importance to marketers are lifestyle and personality. Lifestyles are the activities, interests, and opinions of an individual that define day-to-day living. Personality characteristics, which are enduring and deep-seated, reflect consistent patterns of response developed since childhood. Lifestyle and personality characteristics make up a richer set of descriptors than do demographics because they represent the psychological makeup of consumers.

The chapter examined the following important changes in lifestyles in American society in the 1990s:

- Change in male/female purchasing roles.
- Leveling off of concerns over health and fitness.
- Greater isolation of the American consumer based on stay-at-home activities.
- Greater self-awareness.
- Greater time pressures resulting in more emphasis on convenience.
- A more frugal lifestyle.
- Greater emphasis on convenience.

Marketers have used lifestyle characteristics in studies by developing inventories to measure consumers' activities, interests, and opinions. Another approach is to conduct consumer surveys to determine lifestyles. The most widely used consumer lifestyle survey—the Value and Lifestyle Survey (VALS)—identifies eight lifestyle segments based on their values and economic resources. Marketers widely use VALS to identify market segments, develop advertising strategies, and provide guidelines for media selection.

Personality variables are more difficult to use in marketing because they are not as closely related to brand usage as are lifestyles and demographics. Because marketers continually use personality variables, several personality theories were reviewed:

- Self-concept theory suggests that individuals have an actual self-image based on who they think they are and an ideal self-image based on who they would like to be. Marketers have applied this theory in the belief that there may be a congruence between consumers' self-image and their image of the brand. An extension of this theory realizes that the symbolic properties of groups of products and brands can influence people's self-image based on the assumption that we are what we use.
- Psychoanalytic theory stresses the unconscious nature of consumer motives as determined in childhood by the conflicting demands of the id and the superego. Marketers have applied psychoanalytic theory by using depth and focus group interviews and projective techniques to uncover deep-seated purchasing motives. These applications are known as motivational research.
- Social/cultural theory emphasizes environmental variables in personality development. It goes beyond psychoanalytic theory in examining conscious, goal-directed behavior and considering individuals who function normally in a social environment.
- Trait theory seeks to measure personality traits by the development of personality inventories. Trait theory is the most widely applied of the personality theories in marketing because specific personality variables can be measured and related to consumer usage.

In the next chapter, we shift our focus from the individual to society as a whole by considering how culture influences consumers.

QUESTIONS

1. What are the marketing implications of a merger of male and female purchasing roles?
2. An ad for a leading detergent manufacturer depicts a woman using the product and being praised by her husband for getting his clothes clean.
   - What are the potential problems with this positioning?
   - What alternative positionings might you suggest to reflect the changing role of women in today's society?
3. An executive for a food company said, "There has been some talk around here about repositioning some of our existing products to promote health and nutritional benefits. I see companies promoting beans as having fiber and tuna packed in spring water. I am against such repositionings because consumers are just going to see them as a ploy to get on the nutritional bandwagon. It is much better to introduce new products for health and nutritional benefits than to reposition existing products."
   - Do you agree with the executive's position? Why or why not?
4. What evidence is there that concerns about health and fitness are leveling off in the 1990s?
5. What is the relationship between the information revolution and a more isolated American consumer? What are the marketing implications of this link?
6. American consumers are feeling more time pressures despite the fact that they have more leisure time than in the past. What are the marketing implications of this trend?
7. What are the marketing implications of a more frugal lifestyle?
8. Define *grazing* and *refueling*. How are these trends reflected in consumers' behavior? What are the marketing implications of each trend?
9. What are the marketing implications in using any of the lifestyle groups cited in Table 13.1 for describing users (or prospective users) of:
   - A new detergent that advertises that it makes washing easier?
   - Personal care appliances such as curling irons or facial care appliances?
   - A new magazine designed to provide up-to-date marketing and financial information to the working woman?
   - A new breakfast cereal for the diet-conscious and active adult?
10. Based on Figure 13.1 and Table 13.2, which VALS group or groups might be the best targets in marketing the following?
    - Ecologically oriented products.
    - Weight-lifting equipment.
    - A new family-oriented magazine.
11. A working woman sees herself as efficient, competitive, and achievement-oriented. Ideally, she would like to combine these traits with greater warmth and understanding. How would her behavior differ if she governed her purchases based on her actual self-image versus her ideal self-image? Under what circumstances might she be more likely to buy based on her ideal self rather than on her actual self?
12. What is meant by the extended self? What is the link between the extended self and symbolic interactionism?
13. Because it deals with deep-seated needs and motives derived from childhood conflicts, psychoanalytic theory has been criticized for having little relevance to marketing.
    - Do you agree?
    - For what types of product categories might psychoanalytic theory provide insights into consumer purchasing motives?
14. How have marketers used depth interviews and projective techniques to understand consumer behavior better? Provide specific examples of marketing applications.

RESEARCH ASSIGNMENTS

1. Give examples of how the following American lifestyle changes are represented on two Web sites of your choice.
   - Change in male/female purchasing roles
   - Greater time pressures
   - A more frugal lifestyle
   - Leveling off of concerns about health and fitness

   Do you consider the growth of Internet usage and the resulting time spent on line an additional American lifestyle change? Do you believe consumers show the same personality traits on line as they do in other "real life" situations?
2. Select a sample of teenagers and generation Xers. Ask consumers in each group to rate the importance

to them of a wide variety of products (life insurance, automobiles, jeans, banking services, do-it-yourself products, phosphate-free detergents, cameras, deodorants, cereal, and so on). Ask respondents for their (a) demographic characteristics, (b) view of their economic future, (c) political preferences, and (d) level of price consciousness (see Table 13.1).

- What are the similarities and differences between the two age groups on the variables you measured? Explain these similarities and differences.
- Can you identify a more and a less price-conscious group in each age segment? Are these differences related to demographics? To economic outlook?

3. Using lifestyle criteria, you would like to distinguish users of natural food products (granola, wheat germ, yogurt, and so on) from nonusers. You plan to use lifestyles to position a new line of natural food products and to develop guidelines for advertising.
   - Conduct a number of depth interviews with users of natural foods. On this basis, develop a lifestyle inventory designed to identify natural food users.
   - Submit the inventory to a sample equally divided between users and nonusers of natural foods. Does the lifestyle inventory discriminate between the two groups? If so, what are the distinctive lifestyle characteristics of natural food users?
   - What are the implications of these lifestyle characteristics for (a) advertising and (b) new product development?
4. Self-concept theory suggests that the disparity between a consumer's actual and ideal self-images could predict the purchase of brands or products related to the consumer's identity.
   - Select 10 or 15 adjectives such as those on page 444. Submit these items to a sample of consumers and ask respondents to rate themselves on both actual and ideal selves. Ask the same respondents to identify brands they regularly purchase for products such as perfume, clothing, magazines, automobiles, or any other items that may be related to self-image.
   - Determine the disparity between actual and ideal self-images by summing across the differences for each item in the scale. Are these differences related to brand or product ownership?

PART V

CONSUMERS AND CULTURAL INFLUENCES

The last two sections of the book deal with environmental influences on consumers. These influences fall into two broad categories: cultural influences, which we consider in this section, and group influences, which we will consider in the next.

Culture influences consumers through the norms and values established by the society in which they live. In Chapter 14, we consider cultural values and the way these values influence marketing strategies through the use of symbolism and imagery.

In talking about culture, we also consider cross-cultural and subcultural influences in Chapter 15. Cross-cultural influences are concerned with variations in norms and values across different societies. A particularly important trend is the increasing globalization of values through influences such as the Internet and cable channels such as MTV. Subcultures have values that distinguish them from society as a whole and influence their purchasing behavior. We all belong to one subculture or another. In Chapter 15, we consider the three most important minority subcultures: African Americans, Hispanic Americans, and Asian Americans.

CULTURE

Chapter 14

MCDONALD'S: A STRATEGY TO REFLECT CULTURAL VALUES

The broadest environmental factor affecting consumer behavior is *culture,* as reflected by the values and norms society emphasizes. Culture affects purchasing behavior because it mirrors the values consumers learn from society—values such as individuality, independence, achievement, and self-fulfillment. As the historian Daniel Boorstin said, twentieth-century Americans affiliate themselves less by their political or religious beliefs than by what they consume. As a result, the purchases and possessions of consumers are a reflection of culture.

In this chapter, we consider:

- The nature and characteristics of cultural values.
- How cultural values are identified.
- How cultural influences manifest themselves through product symbols, myths, and ritual.
- Recent changes in cultural values.
- Societal issues relating to the effects of cultural values on consumer behavior.

Cultural values are more enduring and deep-seated than the lifestyle values described in the previous chapter. For example, describing someone as a sports enthusiast reflects a component of his or her lifestyle. A more deep-seated cultural value that might drive one's interest in sports is the desire for an exciting life or for the self-fulfillment one might feel in being involved in a challenging sports activity. Because cultural values are enduring, attempts to change them have generally failed—for example, the attempt on the part of sterling silver manufacturers to revive the use of formal dinnerware in the face of a general cultural trend toward informality.

http://www.mcdonalds.com/

As a result, marketers almost always attempt to swim with, rather than against, the cultural tide. One company that has successfully done so is McDonald's. In the 1970s, its campaign, "You deserve a break today," implied the deep-seated American belief that the work ethic deserves its rewards. In the early 1980s, the company's advertising theme, "McDonald's and You," reflected a shift away from the work ethic to a "me" orientation, that is, a desire to avoid self-sacrifice and to live for today. By the mid-1980s, there was a general shift to a "we" orientation as reflected in a more traditional focus on family values. McDonald's advertising shifted accordingly by moving from the focus on the individual consumer to family-oriented themes. Its campaign, "It's a Good Time for the Great Taste of McDonald's," was effective in communicating food and fun in the context of family values. The creation of the Ronald McDonald character and the introduction of kiddie playgrounds in many McDonald's outlets further strengthened the family image. The success of McDonald's strategy was confirmed by a study that found that people saw the company as friendly and nurturing. In contrast, its prime rival, Burger King, was described as aggressive, masculine, and distant.[1]

The deep recession in the early 1990s produced another cultural change and a parallel shift in McDonald's strategy. Many consumers became less optimistic about the future, more insecure about the traditional American dream, and more price sensitive—a trend we will refer to later in the chapter as *the new reality*. In 1991, McDonald's began instituting a series of price cuts, introduced numerous price promotions, and began emphasizing value as the dominant theme in its advertising. As the economy came out of recession and economic insecurities lingered, McDonald's adopted a more nurturing theme: "Have You Had Your Break Today?" The slogan reflected a shift to more hedonic values in implying the right to a break.

The one constant in these adaptations to cultural trends has been McDonald's strong focus on attracting kids to its franchise. In a mirror of the times, the company is now trying to attract preteens on the Internet. In 1996, a new Web site was designed to "empower" kids by giving them a chance to create personalized newspaper headlines on the screen so they can develop fantasies like teaming up with Michael Jordan to beat the bad guys.[2] McDonald's knows that the creation of such myths and fantasies helps kids fulfill a basic cultural value—the drive to individualism. Another key cultural value, the work ethic, can wait for later.

McDonald's has not only reflected American culture at home, it has also imported it overseas. The golden arches have been accepted as an American icon of service and good food abroad as the fast-food craze has become global.

NATURE OF CULTURE

Culture is a set of socially acquired values that society accepts as a whole and transmits to its members through language and symbols. As a result, culture reflects a society's shared meanings and traditions.

Culture Influences and Reflects Consumer Behavior

A culture's values are likely to influence its members' purchases and consumption patterns. For example, one consumer may place a high value on achievement and may demonstrate success with symbols of luxury and prestige. Another consumer may have a culturally derived desire to appear young and active, may buy cosmetics that advertise a "younger look," and may enroll in an exercise program. In either case, the marketer must define the consumer's value orientation and determine the symbols that reflect these values.

Culture not only influences consumer behavior, it reflects it. The preponderance of exercise machines, fitness clubs, skin care lotions, diet foods, and low-fat products reflects the emphasis American culture places on youth and fitness. Culture is therefore a mirror of both the values and possessions of its members.

Culture Influences and Reflects Marketing Strategies

Marketing strategies rarely attempt to change cultural values because of the simple fact that advertising, sales promotions, salespeople, and packaging are not sufficiently powerful forces to influence consumers' core values. No matter how much the men's hat industry advertised, it could not reverse the trend toward informality and the demise of the man's business hat. When President Kennedy went around hatless in the early 1960s, the Association of Hat Manufacturers appealed to him and he agreed to walk around with a hat in hand, but never on his head. This did little to help the industry; it was facing an irreversible cultural trend.

Although marketing strategies are unlikely to change cultural values, when viewed in the context of the mass media, marketing does influence culture and culture influences marketing. An advertising agency, a music company, a fashion design house, or a book publisher are all *producers of culture*. In total, they can be regarded as a **culture production system,** that is, the individuals and organizations responsible for creating and producing products designed to meet cultural goals.[3] The products, songs, books, and clothing that emerge from such a culture production system will influence the desire to be slim, independent, beautiful, secure, or socially recognized. Thus, in a broader context, marketing and culture are interactive.

Cross-Cultural and Subcultural Influences

http://www.kelloggs.com/

http://www.gerber.com/

The increasing importance of international trade in the 1990s makes it essential for marketers to understand the value systems of other cultures as well as their own. Such **cross-cultural influences** form the basis for marketing strategies abroad. Understanding that the greater emphasis on health and nutrition was not just an American phenomenon, Kellogg's correctly saw that appeals to health could change breakfast eating habits abroad, thus increasing demand for packaged cereals. On the other hand, Gerber failed to recognize that the strong emphasis on family values in Brazil would cause many mothers to reject processed baby foods. These mothers' attitude was that only they can prepare food for their babies.[4]

The determination of such societal values is essential in applying culture to marketing strategies. For example, it would be logical for a furniture manufacturer marketing abroad to determine the value consumers in each country place on beauty, social recognition, and comfort. The manufacturer would have to develop different product lines and marketing strategies for each market. If beauty is the dominant value, consumers would desire highly styled and pleasurable furniture. Advertising symbols for this market would appeal to environment and to pleasure. A market that emphasizes social recognition would desire furniture that demonstrates status. The furniture might be richer in design, and advertising would use symbols oriented to acceptance in a social environment. Marketing to consumers that emphasizes comfort would require demonstrating product features in an informative campaign.

Not everyone in a particular country holds cultural values to the same degree. While values of comfort and social recognition are widely held in American society, differences in these values between groups provide marketers with a basis for developing different strategies within as well as across countries. Frequently, strategies are targeted to particular **subcultures,** that is, broad groups of consumers with similar values that distinguish them from society as a whole.

Subcultures can be defined by age, region, religious affiliation, or ethnic identity. Older baby boomers might be considered a subculture because many of them experienced a shift in values from acquisitiveness to personal development. Many consumers in New England might constitute a subculture because they demonstrate traditional Yankee values of stubborn individualism. In a broad sense, African-American, Hispanic-American, and Asian-American consumers http://www.harley-davidson.com/

are subcultures because they demonstrate certain similarities in tastes and purchasing behavior. Subcultures can also be defined by common interests and activities. For example, many Harley-Davidson owners can be defined as a subculture based on common activities (biker rallies), dress (some combination of jeans, black boots, T-shirts, and black leather jackets), and membership in Harley Owners' Group (HOG) clubs.

We will be considering subcultural and cross-cultural influences in the next chapter. In this chapter, we focus on the effects of cultural values on consumer behavior in a given culture.

CULTURAL VALUES

Rokeach defined **cultural values** as beliefs that a general state of existence is personally and socially worth striving for.[5] Some cultural values defined by Rokeach are shown in the first column in Table 14.1. **Value systems** are the relative importance cultures place on these values. For example, many Asian cultures might place more emphasis on inner harmony whereas Western cultures might put more stress on individual accomplishment. A value such as world peace is likely to be more universally accepted across cultures.

Rokeach considered these cultural values **terminal values** or goals to be attained and developed. Rokeach also defined another category of values, **instrumental values,** which are the means of achieving the desired goals. A value such as ambition is a guidepost for action to attain a desired end state such as accomplishment; it is not a goal in itself. Other instrumental values might be friendliness, logic, and independence.

Applying Rokeach's classification to purchasing behavior, terminal values are the ultimate purchasing goals, and instrumental values are consumption-specific guidelines to attain these goals. We can go a step beyond consumption-specific values and also cite product attributes and benefits that can attain these values. Thus, in consumer behavior terms (1) product attributes are the means for attaining (2) consumption-specific (instrumental) values which are the vehicle for attaining (3) cultural (terminal) values (see Table 14.1).

http://www.ford.com/

The ad in Exhibit 14.1 is an example of instrumental values: the greater efficiency of a new Maytag washing machine in cleaning clothes. The ad for the Ford Escort is an example of terminal values since it represents an end in itself—family protection, one of Rokeach's key cultural values in Table 14.1.

Few marketing studies have utilized cultural values as descriptors of consumer behavior. One reason for their limited use is that most marketing studies operate on a brand-by-brand basis, whereas cultural values are more likely to influence broad purchasing patterns. But it can be argued that a better understanding of the motivation behind brand purchases can be gained by comprehending culturally derived purchasing values.

TABLE 14.1
Cultural values, consumption, specific values, and product attributes

Cultural (Terminal) Values	Consumption-Specific (Instrumental) Values	Product Attributes
A comfortable life	Prompt service	Service quality
An exciting life	Reliable advertising claims	Reliability
A world at peace	Responsiveness to consumer needs	Performance
Equality	Accurate information	Safety
Freedom	Elimination of pollution	Ease of use
Happiness	Free repair of defective products	Durability
National security	Convenient store locations	Economy
Pleasure	No deceptive advertising	Convenience
Salvation	Courteous and helpful salespeople	Styling
Self-respect	Low prices	
Social recognition	Solutions to urban decay and unemployment	
A world of beauty	Legislation to protect the consumer	
Wisdom	No product misrepresentation	
Family security		
Mature love		
Accomplishment		
Inner harmony		

Sources: Cultural values from Milton J. Rokeach, "The Role of Values in Public Opinion Research," *Public Opinion Quarterly* 32 (Winter 1968), p. 554; Consumption-specific values from Donald E. Vinson, Jerome E. Scott, and Lawrence M. Lamont, "The Role of Personal Values in Marketing and Consumer Behavior," *Journal of Marketing* 41 (April 1977), p. 47. Reprinted with permission from the Journal of Marketing.

Characteristics of Cultural Values

Four characteristics are common to all cultural values:

1. *Cultural values are learned.* Children are instilled with cultural values at an early age. The process of learning the values of one's own culture from childhood is known as **enculturation.** Learning the values of another culture is known as **acculturation.** Cultural learning can occur by informal learning (a foreigner copying local customs), by formal learning (a child taught how to behave by family members), and by technical learning (a child taught in a school environment).

Enculturation takes place through a process of instilling values from key institutions, particularly the family, schools, and religious institutions. The family is particularly important since it is the vehicle for passing values from one generation to the next. Advertising also has a role in enculturating consumers through informal learning. The use of spokespersons (Michael Jordan for Nike sneakers) encourages consumers to imitate these role models or experts and to adopt certain products or styles.

http://www.nike.com/

Consumer acculturation occurs when a person from another country adapts to the consumption values and behavior of his or her adopted country. Such adaptation occurs by observation, by word-of-mouth communication, and through communication from the mass media. The process of acculturation is

▶EXHIBIT 14.1
Examples of instrumental and terminal values

particularly important for business people in foreign markets, since an understanding of the local culture is necessary before they can develop product and advertising plans.

Hair and Anderson studied the process of acculturation among immigrants to America.[6] They found that consumers from developed countries were more quickly acculturated than were those from developing countries. One explanation is that the heritages and lifestyles of consumers from developed countries are closer to those of American consumers. Hair and Anderson also found that acculturation takes place faster for consumer behavior than it does for other forms of behavior. The reason is that material objects are integrated more easily into one's behavior than are more abstract, nonmaterial characteristics.[7] In a study of Mexican immigrants, Penaloza found that their rate of consumer acculturation was rapid because they became familiar with many American products and retail establishments while still in Mexico.[8]

2. *Cultural values are guides to behavior.* Cultural values guide and direct an individual's behavior through the establishment of **cultural norms.** Such norms establish standards of behavior regarding proper social relations, means of ensuring safety, eating habits, and so forth. If behavior deviates from the cultural norm, society may place sanctions or restrictions on behavior.

3. *Cultural values are permanent.* Cultural values gain permanence as parents pass them on to children. Schools and religious groups also are important in maintaining the permanence of cultural values. The emphasis on values such as freedom, self-respect, and individuality has not changed substantially over time in the United States.

4. *Cultural values are dynamic.* Culture is also dynamic; values must change as society changes. Basic changes in values have taken place in American culture during the past 40 years. The Depression, wars, and economic dislocation have drastically changed traditional values such as the work ethic, materialism, and respect for authority figures.

The Monitor Service, a research service that tracks changes in cultural values, found some important differences in values between the 1980s and 1990s, largely as a result of the deep recession in the early 1990s and consequent concerns among younger consumers as to whether they can achieve the same level of well-being as their parents.[9] The service found the following changes:

1980s	*1990s*
Belief in the American dream	A new reality
Live to work	Work to live
Be a winner	Do not be a loser
Family, religion	New alternatives
Home as a cocoon	Home as a resource center
Control the environment	Manage the environment
Control technology	Adapt to technology
Conspicuous consumption	Prudent purchasing

These are important societal changes that we explore later in the chapter. They are rich in their strategic implications. For example, the greater pessimism regarding the future cited above and embodied in the "new reality" suggests that many luxury goods may be on the decline in a more austere 1990s environment. Further, the change in the perspective of the home from a focus on love and nurturing to a resource center for work and entertainment is intriguing. It reflects the extension of work from office to home with the use of cellular phones, fax machines, and personal computers, as well as an increasing proportion of consumers who work at home full time based on this flexible technology.

5. *Cultural values are widely held.* Each culture has certain widely held and commonly accepted values that differentiate it from other cultures. Individuality and youthfulness are widely shared values in the United States, whereas conformity to the group and respect for the aged are widely shared values in many Asian countries.

The sharing of values is facilitated by a common language. In multilingual countries such as Canada and India, the lack of a single cultural bond through language has led to divisiveness. In the United States, the mass media have facilitated the sharing of cultural norms. When two out of three households with television sets view a particular program at the same time, they must share values. As one writer stated shortly after TV ownership became widespread, "Advertising now compares with such long-standing institutions as the schools and the church in the magnitude of its social influence."[10]

Traditional American Values

Four widely held traditional values in American society are materialism, individualism, youthfulness, and a work ethic.

Materialism

Materialism, a reflection of the accumulation of wealth and objects, is manifested in two ways. One is the attainment of goods to achieve a desired goal—for example, buying a new computer to increase storage capacity and speed or acquiring a cellular telephone to provide mobile communication. Using Rokeach's classification, this is known as *instrumental materialism* since the acquisition of such goods is instrumental in attaining cultural values. A second manifestation of materialism is owning items for their own sake. This is known as *terminal materialism* because the acquisition of such goods is directly motivated by cultural values rather than by some intermediate goal. Buying a piece of jewelry for its beauty or acquiring an automobile for its status rather than its functional benefits would be examples of terminal materialism.

Research by Richins suggests that consumers who hold strong material values place their possessions at the center of their lives and value them as a means of achieving happiness.[11] These consumers view their possessions as an indicator of their own success. Such material values are likely to be dominant in the

EXHIBIT 14.2
An appeal to individualism

more advanced economies of North America, Europe, and Japan. Consumers who do not emphasize material values are more hedonically oriented. They are more likely to view their possessions as sources of pleasure and comfort than symbols of status and wealth. In some societies, spiritual as opposed to material values may be emphasized, even to the extent of encouraging members to renounce worldly wealth.

Individualism

American society tends to favor individual initiative, often at the expense of conformity to group goals. Themes focusing on individualism and "standing apart from the crowd" are often seen in advertising. The ad for Tommy Girl cologne in Exhibit 14.2 is a good example of an appeal to individualism. The advertisement represents the spirit of an independent American woman. Clearly, this is an attempt to link the product to independence and freedom of thought.

In Japan there is a greater desire to subjugate individuality in favor of group and societal conformity. Such themes as "McDonald's and You" would not re-

http://www.llbean.com/

flect this dominant value. But recent evidence suggests that the traditional Japanese value system is changing among the young who have a greater desire for American-made goods. For example, L. L. Bean's first retail store outside of its home base in Maine opened in Japan in 1992. Bean's outdoor look is strongly identified with American individualism, reflecting the adoption of key American values by Japanese youth.[12]

Youthfulness

Most Americans are preoccupied with trying to look and act young, regardless of their age. As we saw in Chapter 12, advertising to the mature market has tried to portray older Americans as active, vital, and younger looking than their age. Advertising to baby boomers is also focused on maintaining their youth through face creams, moisturizers, exercise machines, and health clubs.

This penchant for youthfulness is not universal. In Asian countries, the aged are more revered than they are in the United States. Whereas in the United States, youth dominates almost all ads, in Asian countries, the elderly are portrayed more frequently and with greater respect. An elderly spokesperson is more likely to be accepted as an expert or a role model in these countries. But, here again, American values seem to be taking hold abroad. Japanese women are increasingly turning to the same products as American women to keep them looking young. For example, Dior's Svelte and Estee Lauder's Thigh Zone, both creams designed to reduce cellulite and make women's thighs look firmer and thinner, are selling at a rapid rate in Tokyo department stores and being grabbed up by Japanese tourists abroad.[13]

Work Ethic

A work ethic has been a traditional value in American society as a means of personal achievement and attainment of material rewards. Advertisers often seek to promote their products as a reward for work. McDonald's former theme, "You Deserve a Break Today," is an example.

The Monitor Service suggests that the nature of the work ethic in American society may be changing. The "live to work" orientation of the 1980s meant that people saw work as its own reward, a means of personal achievement and self-gratification. However, the demise of the "booming '80s" and the severe recession in the early 1990s promoted a skepticism that has been translated into people's viewing work as a means of acquiring the necessities of life ("work to live"). This means the ethic behind work has changed. Rather than being a terminal goal (work is rewarding), work has become an instrumental goal (work is a means of getting what I want).

Japan has also accepted a work ethic as a traditional value. Interestingly, it seems to be experiencing the same shift to a view of work as a means to an end rather than as an end in itself. One aspect of the desire for L. L. Bean clothes among younger Japanese consumers is to look more relaxed and casual as a manifestation of this trend.

Other Core Values

Other core values in the United States are progress, freedom, and activity. *Progress* is reflected in people's belief in technology and continued improvement in the standard of living. Here again, the Monitor Survey suggests that the belief in progress might have been partially undermined by greater skepticism in the economy. In addition, in the post-cold war period, America's role as the leader of the free world is no longer as compelling. As a result, many consumers no longer see economic progress as a necessary outgrowth of America's world leadership. This perspective has added to the sense of financial insecurity about the future. The result has been a shift from conspicuous consumption and an emphasis on status in the 1980s to more prudent purchasing behavior and a greater emphasis on value in the 1990s.

Freedom, another traditional American value, is reflected in people's ideals of equality and freedom of expression for all. In marketing terms, this value has been translated into the consumer rights described in Chapter 2: the right to choose, the right to be informed, the right to be heard, and the right to safety. This emphasis on freedom has been manifested in the 1990s in an increasingly independent and well-informed consuming public. Consumers are more skeptical of advertising claims and more willing to look at a wider range of product alternatives than in the past.

Activity—that is, the importance Americans attach to being physically active—is another traditional value probably having its genesis in the establishment of frontier farming communities in colonial times. This value seems to have been transformed in an urban setting into a hectic lifestyle that many societies regard as peculiar to American culture. The "grazing" phenomenon cited in Chapter 13 and the popularity of fast-food chains are means of facilitating an active lifestyle.

Identifying Cultural Values

The changes in American values between the 1980s and 1990s demonstrate the need to identify cultural values over time. Researchers have used several methods to track cultural values, namely (1) field studies (known as *ethnographic research*), (2) cultural value inventories such as Rokeach's classification, (3) research services such as the Monitor Service, and (4) content analysis of a society's literature and media.

Ethnographic Studies

An increasingly important method used to identify consumer values is in-depth studies of small groups of consumers by researchers through *participant observation.* As noted in Chapter 1, such in-depth observations are known as **ethnography,** a field borrowed from cultural anthropology. Anthropologists determine cultural values through field studies in which they live with a group or a family in a culture and observe their customs and behavior. Similarly, consumer researchers may spend months living with or observing groups of consumers in their natural environment to study their values and purchasing behavior. The purpose is to understand the role of the product in a cultural context.

In one such ethnographic study, two consumer behavior researchers, John Schouten and James McAlexander, literally became part of the Harley-Davidson bikers subculture by traveling around with Harley owners over a three-year period.[14] They were slowly accepted within the Harley Owners' Group (HOG) they associated with and studied its social structure, values, and behavior. They became acculturated into the HOG social structure by obtaining Harleys and adopting the group's social norms, dress, and behavior. In this process of participant observation, Schouten and McAlexander made some revealing observations about the Harley subculture. For example:

- The Harley experience, captured in the motto "Live to ride, ride to live," reveals a sanctuary for the biker in which he or she can experience a temporary self-transformation from mundane everyday life.
- This experience has a spiritual dimension—the feeling of closeness to nature, a heightened sensory awareness while riding, and the acceptance of risk as the cost of experiencing this spirituality.
- The core cultural value of Harley owners is personal freedom. The motorcycle is a symbol of freedom as embodied in Harley's symbol of a spread-winged eagle. Harley accessories, such as Eagle Iron accessories and Screaming Eagle performance parts, reflect this symbolism.
- Although Harley owners have common values in their motives for riding, reasons for group association among bikers vary widely. There are Harley subgroups that are semiretired Mom and Pop bikers, biker support groups for recovering addicts, and biker groups that verge on outlaw clubs.[15]

Another application of an ethnographic field survey is illustrated in a study by Belk, Sherry, and Wallendorf of the behavior of buyers and sellers at swap meets.[16] Swap meets are markets in which buyers and sellers exchange goods for other goods or for money. A swap meet is distinct from a flea market in that downscale consumers generally frequent swap meets and barter is the more prevalent mode of exchange. The researchers used both observation and open-ended qualitative interviews to try to develop an understanding of the participants' value system and the cultural underpinnings of swap meets.

In studying one swap meet, Belk et al. concluded that freedom is an important motivation for buyers and sellers. Participants enjoy being free from the institutional constraints of buying in retail stores, yet accept the social order inherent in swap meets such as establishing and running stalls, adhering to opening and closing times, and following certain rules such as not allowing dogs. The researchers also found that male-female roles were sharply defined, with men responsible for setting up booths and displays and women acting as clerks and salespersons. Other findings related to the mutual values participants held, the nature of bargaining, and the symbolism associated with what is bought and sold.[17]

Cultural Inventories

Researchers develop cultural value inventories by studying a particular culture, identifying its values, and then determining whether these values are widely held. The best-known inventory is the *Rokeach Value Survey*. The cultural values identified by the survey are based on a study of American culture and are in the left-hand column in Table 14.1.

Kahle, Beatty, and Homer developed another widely used cultural inventory, the *List of Values* (LOV).[18] LOV was developed as an alternative to Rokeach's value inventory because the terminal values identified by Rokeach were too abstract and difficult to apply to marketing situations. The LOV inventory measures nine values:

1. Self-fulfillment.
2. Excitement.
3. Sense of accomplishment.
4. Self-respect.
5. Sense of belonging.
6. Being well respected.
7. Security.
8. Fun and enjoyment.
9. Warm relationships with others.

A study by Homer and Kahle, which utilized the LOV scale, found that purchasers of natural foods are more likely to emphasize self-fulfillment, excitement, and accomplishment.[19] These values reflect a desire to control one's life as reflected in an emphasis on health and nutrition. Consumers who emphasized belonging and security were least likely to buy natural foods because they were more likely to let others control their lives.

Research Services

In an attempt to identify changes in cultural values, several research services conduct periodic surveys of consumers. VALS 2, discussed in Chapter 13, identifies values as well as lifestyles. Categories such as actualizers, achievers, and strivers not only reflect a particular lifestyle, but they also suggest the terminal values driving these groups.

For example, family security is most important to makers, social recognition to strivers, and accomplishment to achievers. These end-state values are manifested in the lifestyles described for each group in the previous chapter.

Like VALS, the Monitor Service interviews 2,500 randomly selected respondents every year in order to determine changes in values measured by a series of multiple-choice questions.[20] The Monitor Service was one of the first to identify the "me" orientation in the early 1980s and a more conservative trend resulting in a shift to a "we" orientation in the mid-1980s. It also identified the greater concern with environmental protection starting in the 1980s.

http://www.ge.com/
http://www.cbs.com/

Over 115 companies have subscribed to the service, including Kraft General Foods, General Electric, and CBS.[21] The trends found in Monitor surveys have direct implications for these companies. For example, General Electric could cite the greater value placed on beauty in the home and concern about the environment (two trends that Monitor identified) to produce more stylish yet energy-efficient appliances. CBS could consider two other trends identified by the service—toward personal creativity and physical fitness—to justify daytime TV programming aimed at self-improvement (cooking, exercise, and art programs, for example).

Content Analysis

Whereas the techniques just described measure cultural values consumers hold, content analysis measures these values as they are reflected in a culture's media and literature. Researchers employing content analysis review a culture's literature and mass communications to identify repetitive themes. In his famous study, McClellan identified the degree to which cultures were motivated by achievement by conducting a content analysis of the themes in children's stories.[22]

Belk applied content analysis to investigate how materialistic values are portrayed in comic books. Wealthy characters were portrayed ambivalently. On the one hand, some were portrayed as selfless and honest, while others were portrayed as spendthrifts. Overall, Belk concluded that these portrayals had a positive socializing influence on children by holding the work ethic in high esteem.[23] Content analyses have also been performed to determine whether the portrayal of African Americans and females in advertising is an accurate reflection of their role in society.

CULTURAL VALUES AND CONSUMER BEHAVIOR

As we have seen, marketing strategies generally attempt to reflect core cultural values of American society.

Means-End Chain

The role of cultural values in influencing consumer behavior has been described by Gutman as a **means-end chain** in that the means (product attributes) are the vehicle for attaining cultural values (the ends) with consumption goals as an intermediary between them (see Figure 14.1).[24] As such, product attributes are a reflection of cultural values.

Gutman's conceptualization relies on two theories. The first is Rokeach's distinction between cultural (terminal) values and consumption (instrumental) goals as shown in Figure 14.1. Gutman makes Rokeach's conceptualization more ap-

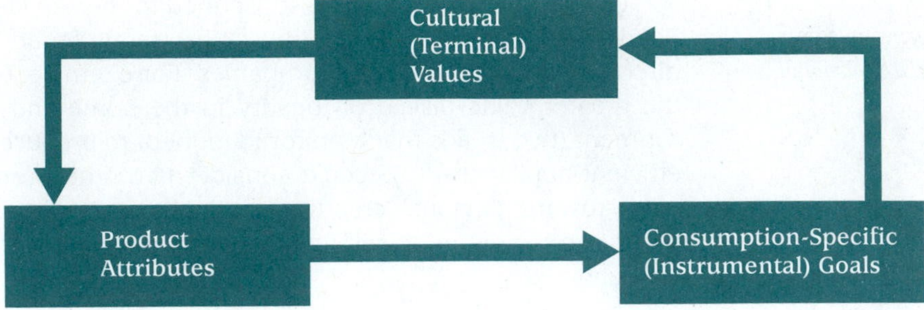

FIGURE 14.1 The Culture-Consumer Behavior Interface

plicable to marketing by adding another factor, product attributes, as a means of attaining consumption goals.

The second theory underlying the means–end chain in Figure 14.1 is Rosenberg's expectancy-value theory.[25] Rosenberg posits that consumers will evaluate products based on the degree to which they are instrumental in achieving cultural values. Consumers evaluate the projected consequences of their actions and will buy products that achieve the desired consequence. Thus, a consumer who values a world of beauty (a terminal value) will favor product attributes such as biodegradability because the consequence of buying a biodegradable product is to help preserve the environment. Applying Rosenberg's theory, the means–end chain leading to the purchase of the product is:

- Product attribute: Biodegradability.
- Consumption consequence: Helping to preserve the environment.
- Cultural (terminal) value: A world of beauty.

In short, the theories of Gutman, Rokeach, and Rosenberg all reflect the means–end chain in Figure 14.1, leading to the attainment of cultural (terminal) values through product attributes and consumption goals.

Laddering

Reynolds and Johnson applied the means–end chain to the development of marketing strategies through a process they called **laddering.**[26] (See the Strategic Applications box.) Laddering involves a series of consumer interviews to determine the links among product attributes, consumption goals, and cultural values. Consumers are "helped up the ladder" through a series of probes that start with concrete product attributes and then uncover more abstract consumption goals and even more abstract cultural values. As an example, a consumer might state a preference for a flavored potato chip with a strong taste. Probes show that she favors these attributes because they cause her to eat less which results in her losing weight and looking better (consumption goal). This results in greater self-esteem (a terminal value).

Marketers can then use the three components of the means–end chain in the ladder to develop marketing strategy as follows:[27]

1. *Message elements:* The specific product attributes to be communicated in advertising. In the preceding example, advertising would focus on flavor and taste as key elements.
2. *Consumer benefits:* The positive consumption consequences of using the product. The key requirement in the preceding example is to link the product attributes of flavor and taste to the benefit of weight control.
3. *Leverage point:* The way advertising attempts to associate the attributes and benefits to the terminal values and to activate them. The executional requirement in the advertising is to show that weight loss as a result of product consumption creates greater self-esteem. This can be done by portraying self-confident and attractive consumers in the advertising or by showing greater peer group acceptance as a result of product usage.

Once the marketer develops advertising, it is evaluated based on its ability to climb up the means–end ladder from message element to consumer benefit to leverage point.

STRATEGIC APPLICATIONS OF CONSUMER BEHAVIOR

▶ Federal Express Uses Laddering to Change Its Advertising

Laddering was applied to the development of advertising strategies for Federal Express by generating a detailed means–end map of the value secretaries placed on overnight delivery (see Figure 14.2). Specific attributes such as reliability and on-time delivery were associated with positive goals resulting from the use of overnight delivery services, such as to get promoted or to avoid looking bad. In turn, these goals led to terminal values such as peace of mind, control, and self-esteem.

The three means–end chains shown in Figure 14.2 represent three segments in the overnight delivery market emphasizing different attributes, consequences, or terminal values. One segment values peace of mind and being in control of the office. The other two emphasize self-esteem and accomplishment but through different consumption benefits and product attributes. The left-hand chain suggests that these terminal values can be attained through the intermediate consumption goals of doing more and saving time and through the availability of a drop box for convenience (product attributes). The middle chain shows that self-esteem and accomplishment are attainable through the consumption goals of making more money and getting promoted and through product attributes based on reliability and on-time delivery.

Before the study was performed, Federal Express used a humorous approach that demonstrated the problems with relying on competitive services. The attributes emphasized were reliability and on-time delivery, and the consumption benefits were less worry and avoiding looking bad to the boss. The message was targeted to the right-hand segment in Figure 14.2, but the message was not being translated into positive terminal values. Federal Express needed to differentiate itself from competitors by focusing on its strengths rather than on competitors' weaknesses. Further, management wanted to ensure that competition could not dominate any such point of differentiation.

Federal Express's unique point of differentiation was its satellite communications system to ensure reliability and on-time delivery. The company developed a new advertising campaign that kept the humorous execution while focusing on the satellite communication system. It emphasized the superiority of the tracking system (product attribute) in ensuring reliability and making work easier (consumption benefits). Most important, an evaluation of the campaign found that it did reach the top of **the ladder by translating consumption benefits into terminal values. Secretaries saw FedEx's services as a means of being in control and attaining peace of mind.

Federal Express reinforced this message of reliability when it offered NetShip in 1996, an Internet-based service that not only allowed customers to track shipments, but to arrange package pickup and print tracking numbers. The service was meant to satisfy the two key terminal values in Figure 14.2: accomplishment and control.

Sources: "Federal Express Delivers Shipping to the World Wide Web" *Fedex Internet Homepage,* July 16, 1996; Thomas J. Reynolds and Alyce Byrd Craddock, "The Application of the Meccas Model to the Development and Assessment of Advertising Strategy: A Case Study," *Journal of Advertising Research* 28 (April/May 1988), pp. 43–54.

In the next two sections, we consider the two main cultural interfaces in Figure 14.1: the impact of culture on the product and on consumption.

CULTURE AND PRODUCTS

The cultural meaning of products and services is often expressed in symbolic form. As we saw in Chapter 3, consumers frequently buy products for their symbolism rather than for their utility. Marketers try to establish symbols that equate the product with positive cultural values. McDonald's golden arches are meant to be a reflection of fun and family values; the Marlboro cowboy is a portrayal of rugged individualism and independence; the Mercedes emblem is meant to portray status and security.

▶FIGURE 14.2
A means–end ladder for overnight delivery services
Source: Thomas J. Reynolds and Alyce Byrd Craddock, "The Application of the Meccas Model to the Development and Assessment of Advertising Strategy," *Journal of Advertising Research* (April/May 1988), p. 45.

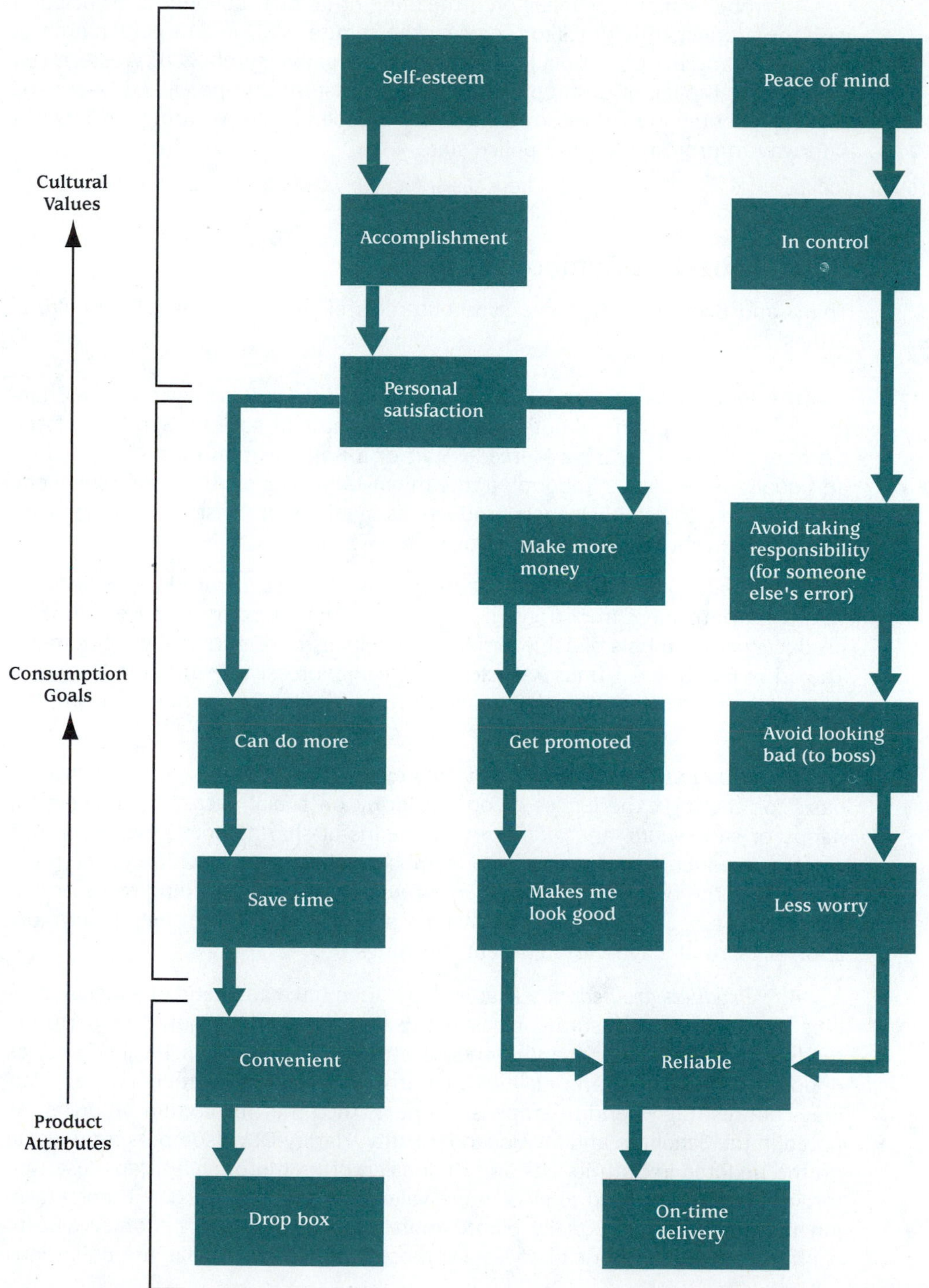

A symbol sometimes takes on a meaning of its own beyond its association with the product and comes to represent the culture. McDonald's golden arches, Levi jeans, and the Coca-Cola logo have become global symbols of Western culture. Before the fall of Communism, youths in Eastern Europe valued Levi jeans as a representation of Western culture and independence. Wearing Levis was a safe way to protest against a police state.

http://www.levi.com/

Role of Product Symbolism

Tharp and Scott identified five symbolic roles of products that reflect cultural values:[28]

1. *Products are a means of communicating social status.* As we saw in Chapter 11, products often connote a consumer's status in society. Symbols of status may be a Gucci scarf, a Mercedes car, or a Rolex watch. In the inner cities, an equally important symbol of status might be a pair of Air Jordan sneakers. Marketers try to establish their products as symbols of prestige, whether aiming at affluent business executives or inner-city kids.

2. *Products are a means of self-expression.* As such, products reflect the values that are most important to consumers. Marketers try to associate their products with symbols of achievement, individualism, or personal development. The ad in Exhibit 14.3 links XMI clothes to self-expressive generation Xers. The attempt is to associate the product with youth, freedom, and individualism, important values for this youth market.

3. *Products are a means of sharing experiences.* Products often provide a basis for sharing experiences. Food and drink on social occasions, flowers for happy or sad events, and gifts are all a means of sharing social events. In this respect, products have an important symbolic role since the nature of the product defines the occasion. Serving beer or wine at a party, sending roses or carnations for a special occasion, or giving a pen or a piece of jewelry as a graduation present all have very different meanings.

4. *Products are hedonic.* That is, they often have aesthetic or sensual qualities that give the consumer pleasure. Examples might be jewelry, perfume, foods, clothing, furniture, and works of art. The emphasis on the hedonic, as opposed to the utilitarian, qualities of a product reflect consumers' values. Various cultures might tend to emphasize one or the other for certain products. As noted in the Schouten and McAlexander study, Harley-Davidson puts more value on the hedonic in both its ads and the design of its motorcycles. Japanese motorcycle companies tend to place more value on the utilitarian. The French fashion industry has traditionally placed more emphasis on the hedonic value of clothing, whereas American styles are more likely to emphasize the utilitarian.

EXHIBIT 14.3
Appealing to the desire of generation Xers for self-expression

http://www.gm.com/

5. *Products are experiential.* That is, they remind consumers of past experiences. On a personal level, an engagement ring is experiential as is an old photo album or a record or CD that triggers memories of past events. Marketers sometimes attempt to project the experiential value of products. The ad for General Motors cars in Exhibit 14.4 effectively captures a teenager's experience in first getting a driver's license and the resulting feeling of power and freedom. GM is effectively associating its products with this positive experience.

Semiotics

http://www.unilever.com/

People often develop shared meanings from signs and symbols as a reflection of their cultural values. Consumer researchers have applied the field of *semiotics* to the study of product signs and symbols to better understand how people derive such meaning. (See Chapter 6 for a description of semiotics.) For example, when Lever introduced a new fabric softener with the symbol of a huggable teddy bear named Snuggle, it used semiotics to evaluate the symbolism of a bear. It found that the bear connotes aggression, but a teddy bear is seen as a

▶EXHIBIT 14.4
Projecting the experiential value of a product

softer and nurturing side of that aggression. The teddy bear is a logical symbol of tamed aggression and a good representation of a fabric softener that tames rough clothing.[29]

Such a semiotic analysis is based on three components: a sign (the symbol of a teddy bear), an object (Snuggle), and an interpretant (the consumer interpreting the symbol).[30] These three components represent the same interface between culture and consumer behavior as in Figure 14.1. Lever's analysis showed that the symbolism of the teddy bear was *instrumental* in attaining a *terminal* value (controlling nature) through a *consumption goal* (softening rough clothes) based on Snuggle's product attributes.

Because it demonstrates the different meanings various cultures place on the same signs and symbols, semiotics is an important tool in cross-cultural analysis. For example, in American society, animals are accepted as symbols of speed (jaguar) and freedom (eagle). However, in many Asian countries, animal symbolism is rejected since animals are seen as a lower life form.

Products as Myths and Fantasies

Marketers sometimes establish product symbols in the form of fantasies and myths to better link the product to cultural values. **Myths** are stories or character representations in fantasy form that attempt to portray cultural values. Advertising has a role in creating and maintaining such myths. McDonald's advertising has created a mythical world of food, fun, and fantasy. As one advertising executive said, "McDonald's advertising [portrays] a wondrous, magical place where everyone is welcome, safe, happy, loved, kind, sharing, caring and forever young at heart. The McDonald's that exists in the consumer's mind is a microcosm of everything America is supposed to be."[31] The golden arches are a universally recognized symbol of American culture, attracting foreign consumers as an American icon and providing a recognizable haven for American tourists.

Mythic images are also associated with imaginary characters: the Marlboro cowboy representing freedom and independence; Betty Crocker as the great mother image, representing the security of family and home-cooked meals; Mr. Goodwrench, the General Motors repairman, representing safety, security, and dependability.

Marketers also create mythologies around places. Pepperidge Farm's advertising takes us back to a time of farming communities and old-fashioned values. Similarly, advertising for Maxwell House 1892 coffee creates a mythology of a less-harried time when coffee tasted better.[32]

http://www.apple.com/
http://www.cocacola.com/

Marketers are also using the Internet to encourage consumers to communicate experiences and stories about their brands. Apple Computer and Coca-Cola encourage such storytelling on their Web sites. An annual digital storytelling festival on the Internet provides consumers with a venue for translating product experiences into myths and fantasies (see Exhibit 14.5).[33]

CULTURE AND CONSUMPTION

Culture not only influences the way products are portrayed, but it influences the way they are consumed. In particular, culture is important in defining the ritualistic role of consumption for many product categories.

Consumption Rituals

A **ritual** is a series of symbolic behaviors that occur in sequence and are repeated frequently.[34] *Grooming* is a ritual for most people since it involves a series of behaviors (showering, brushing teeth, using deodorants, brushing hair) that occur in sequence and are repeated frequently. Marketers will try to link their products to these rituals—for example, brush your teeth twice a day or shampoo frequently.

EXHIBIT 14.5 Using the Internet to create myths and fantasies

Gift giving is also a ritual that requires a sequence of events, namely, acquiring a gift, exchanging gifts, and then evaluating the receiver's reaction. The exchange of gifts, the types of gifts exchanged, and the occasions are all fairly well prescribed in our society. Some industries rely primarily on gift giving for sales. Gift giving at Christmas alone represents close to $40 billion in sales and is a substantial portion of yearly business for most retailers.

Holidays also involve ritual behavior in addition to gift giving. Christmas rituals prescribe the consumption of special foods and drinks. Holidays may also involve vacation rituals such as going to the same vacation spot and being involved in the same activities every year.

Each of these types of ritual behavior has three things in common. First, they involve **ritual artifacts,** often in the form of consumer products. Colored lights, mistletoe, wreaths, and Santa Claus representations are all artifacts associated with Christmas rituals. Second, rituals involve a **script** that prescribes how, when, and by whom products will be used. The use of the ring, cake, and photographs at weddings is fairly well scripted by society, for example. Third, rituals require that **performance roles** be prescribed for certain individuals.[35] The roles of the bride, groom, best man, and bridesmaids are all well-defined at weddings.

Marketers try to promote their products as artifacts in the process of ritual consumption. An ad for De Beers diamonds portrays a diamond ring as an artifact in a prewedding ritual, the engagement, with the tagline "What do you offer the woman of your dreams." Marketers can also portray the sequence of behaviors in rituals. An ad for Lubriderm lotion shows a brushing, cleaning, and moisturizing sequence in portraying a grooming ritual.

Rituals are likely to vary across cultures as a reflection of the predominant values of that culture. For example, gift-giving rituals in Japan emphasize the gift as a reflection of one's duty to others in one's social group. Gift giving is viewed as a shared moral imperative through which reciprocal obligations are fulfilled. In the United States, gift giving is of a more personal nature. Although there is often a sense of obligation in gift giving, it is more in the context of personal rather than group obligations.

Sacred and Secular Consumption

Culture also influences the way goods are consumed. An important distinction in this respect is between sacred and secular consumption.[36] **Sacred consumption** is the consumption of goods that promote beauty, the preservation of nature, and cooperation. Consumers who seek the sacred aspects of consumption are attracted to natural imagery or appeals to family ties. They favor food products with natural ingredients and fashions with simple styles.

Hirschman cites several campaigns that reflect such a sacred orientation to consumption:[37]

- *Gallo wines.* Accompanied by soft music, the opening visuals show the homecomings of family members for Christmas. Imagery includes snow on evergreens, wooden porches, red plaid flannel shirts, and down jackets. The gathered, multigenerational family sits at a wooden table bedecked with a turkey, yams, bread, and bottles of wine.
- *Tropicana orange juice.* A young woman, dressed in jeans and a cotton shirt, stands in an orange grove. She recalls eating oranges from her father's grove as a young girl. Her hands and face would get sticky from the sweet, delicious juice, and her mother would help her wash up when she returned home. [The announcer says] "Tropicana is natural and pure, just the way the rain and sun make it. . . . It comes fresh from nature, without any artificial additives."

These two ads emphasize natural food, natural settings, a rural environment, and family. Implicitly, nature is viewed as nurturing and life giving.

Another aspect of sacred consumption is the fondness and even reverence with which some consumers treat certain products. A piece of jewelry given on a special event or a suit or dress associated with business or social success will be worn in a more sacred fashion. The study of the Harley-Davidson subculture describes the reverence with which bikers treat their motorcycles. It is strictly taboo to touch another person's Harley without permission. The process of cleaning a Harley is an elaborate ritual involving careful cleaning and polishing. The garage or shed in which the motorcycle is kept is regarded almost as a shrine. The kinship with others (bikers call each other "bro") verges on a religious order. And when the Harley is ridden, it is in a sacred context in which the riding experience is "magical or otherworldly."[38]

Secular consumption is the consumption of goods that promote technology, the conquest of nature, and competition. Consumers who seek the secular aspects of consumption are attracted to products that improve control over one's life.

Hirschman also cites several campaigns that reflect such a secular orientation to consumption:[39]

http://www.alberto.com/

- *Static Guard.* A woman enters a restaurant in an elegant dress. When she removes her coat, static cling (an undesirable natural event) causes the dress to rumple unbecomingly. She is embarrassed. A technological product (Static Guard) is sprayed on the offending natural phenomenon and conquers it.
- *Oil of Olay.* An attractive woman states, "I don't intend to grow old gracefully. I intend to fight it every step of the way. I'm going to be 40 and wonderful." The announcer states, "Oil of Olay beauty fluid helps to replenish the fluids your skin loses with time."

These two ads emphasize control over nature through the use of manufactured products—in one case, to overcome an unwanted event; in another, to conquer aging. Here, nature is viewed as potentially harmful and the focus is on controlling it.

Depending on the values they wish to convey through the product or service, marketers will emphasize the sacred or the secular. Both Gallo and Tropicana use sacred imagery because they want to convey the natural aspects of their products. Static Guard and Oil of Olay use secular imagery because they want to portray their products as vehicles for controlling nature.

CHANGES IN CULTURAL VALUES IN THE 1990S

Several significant and interrelated changes occurred in the American consumer's value system from the 1980s to the 1990s. One, cited earlier, is a new reality about the limits of prosperity and the attainment of the American Dream. This change occurred largely as a result of the severe recession in the early 1990s and a decline in American economic and political leadership in the post-cold war world.

Three other changes started in the mid-1980s and have carried into the 1990s. They are:

1. A shift from valuing youth to valuing youthfulness.
2. Greater traditionalism, as reflected in a shift in focus from a "me" to a "we" orientation.
3. More emphasis on self-fulfillment.
4. Emergence of a new materialism.

New Reality

The **new reality** has had a profound effect on American consumers and their spending patterns. Many have come to realize that there are limits to growth in the American economy and that these limits translate into restricted future purchasing potential. As a result, consumers have become more price-conscious and value-oriented. As we have seen in previous chapters, consumers are less likely to be brand-loyal and more likely to buy lower-priced private brands and to comparison shop. A major change in buying motives is from prestige to value. Purchasing based on status is out; purchasing based on quality and performance is in.

The Monitor Service identified several dimensions of the new reality. One is a decline in commitment to organizational values and a greater willingness to explore other options. Despite the risks, starting one's own business or freelancing has gained new legitimacy as an alternate course to climbing the organizational ladder. As a result, the home is increasingly viewed as a work as well as a family center. Another dimension is a more constrained view of technology and the environment. People have shifted from a strong belief in technology and science as a means of conquering the environment to a belief in technology as a means of managing and preserving the environment. A manifestation of this shift is the greater emphasis consumers place on environmental protection.

This more sober consumer view is likely to continue until the turn of the century. Marketers have already adjusted by placing more focus on quality merchandise at lower prices. The acronym EDLP (everyday low prices) reflects a more common marketing strategy. These changes reflect not only an economic shift, but also a more basic shift in cultural values from achievement to security and from environmental control to environmental management.

Youthfulness versus Youth

As baby boomers have aged, there has been a significant change in the emphasis put on the traditional American value of youth. Increasingly, beauty and attractiveness are no longer the province of the young. Advertising is using models in their 40s and even 50s for beauty products, for example, Isabella Rosellini

http://www.lancome-usa.com/
http://www.revlon.com/

as a spokeswoman for Lancome and Lauren Hutton for Revlon. In fact, when a survey asked women to rank today's top 20 beauties, 16 were over 40.[40] As a result, the cultural emphasis seems to have shifted from youth to youthfulness, that is, retaining the feeling of youth as one gets older. As we saw in Chapter 11, advertisers are subscribing to this shift by portraying the mature market in more vibrant and youthful pursuits.

Greater Traditionalism

The shift to traditionalism represents a greater emphasis on family and patriotic values. Until the mid-1980s, a "me" orientation was fairly pervasive, especially among baby boomers and the youth segment. It reflected a need to live life "my way" and a fierce desire to live for today without concern for the more restrictive values that society or family might impose. The "me" orientation was a reaction to the self-sacrifice imposed on Americans by the Vietnam War, the disillusion brought on by Watergate, and subsequent economic dislocations. It started in the early 1970s, gained momentum through the early 1980s, and then began to wane by the end of the 1980s as many consumers began to deemphasize self-gratification.

The shift to a "we" orientation is reflected in a more traditional focus on family values, patriotism, and the work ethic. As evidence of this shift, a study of baby boomers found that 69 percent said they are more family-oriented than they thought they would be when they were younger.[39] Why this greater traditionalism? As we saw in Chapter 13, baby boomers have shifted away from the drive for affluence to a greater focus on personal development. An important component of personal development is the need to balance the competing demands of work, home, and recreational pursuits.

Two broad groups share a greater emphasis on traditionalism. The *new traditionalists* integrate family values with the new-age lifestyles reflected in the focus on personal development and self-actualization. *Old traditionalists* subscribe to traditional beliefs without acceptance of new lifestyles. Marketers have captured this old traditionalism by focusing on patriotic appeals such as Chevrolet's "Heartbeat of America," Miller's "Made the American Way," and Wal-Mart's "Buy American."

http://www.wal-mart.com/
http://www.chevrolet.com/

The two ads in Exhibit 14.6 reflect the new and the old traditionalism. The ad for the Ford Audio System emphasizes family togetherness, but in the context of a lifestyle that sees "life as more of an adventure than a routine." The ad for Haggar slacks epitomizes the "old" traditionalism, with a family portrayed in front of a church and the tagline "A feel for America."

Emphasis on Self-Fulfillment

A greater emphasis on self-fulfillment might seem to reflect more of an emphasis on "me" than "we," but the trend does not contradict the new traditionalism.

▶EXHIBIT 14.6
Ads that appeal to new traditionalists and old traditionalists

As we noted, during the 1980s many young people found that the self-indulgence of a "me" orientation was not sufficient. They sought a deeper satisfaction in their day-to-day lives. As a result, they redefined their priorities by reducing the importance of money and increasing the importance of personal self-enhancement and meaningful work. They sought several new dimensions in their lives:

- Physical fitness and well-being.
- Personal creativity as expressed through a wide variety of activities, hobbies, and other personal expressions of fulfillment.
- Cultural self-expression, that is, the wish to acquire more cultivation, knowledge, and appreciation of cultural topics.[41]

This focus on self does not mean that an individual cannot also obtain satisfaction from larger social units such as the family, community, or country. In fact, the new traditionalism suggests the desire to combine self-fulfillment with family values.

New Materialism

Greater emphasis on self-fulfillment might suggest a decrease in the traditional focus on materialism in American society, but this is not the case. The United States remains a materialistic, consumption-driven society. However, the nature of materialism has changed. In the past, affluence was desired as a means of enhancing one's social status through "conspicuous consumption." Today, the emphasis on wealth as a means of status is not as important. Wealth is seen as a means of expressing individualism rather than group conformity. As one writer noted, "[Consumers] are becoming more individualistic and are less defined by traditional social groupings. . . . For example, a consumer may drive a $40,000 luxury automobile and buy gasoline from a self-serve discounter. Another may buy designer suits from an exclusive retailer and $3 socks from a discount store."[42]

http://www.itthartford.com/

Affluence is seen not only as a means of expressing individualism, but also as a means of enhancing personal development. Booming expenditures on adult education, recreation, and travel reflect the focus on personal development. The ad for ITT Hartford in Exhibit 14.7 reflects the new materialism. The main theme is that the rewards for sound money management are fun and togetherness rather than higher social status.

SOCIETAL IMPLICATIONS OF CULTURAL VALUES

Cultural values can have both positive and negative effects on society. The increasing value placed on the preservation of the environment will have positive consequences in protecting the limited natural resources of this planet for future generations. The shift in values reflected in the new reality in the 1990s is also likely to be positive in the long run. In putting more emphasis on value, American consumers are becoming more efficient shoppers. Similarly, manufacturers are learning to do more with less by increasing their productivity and decreasing costs. This has enabled them to deliver the value that consumers seek.

There are also negative consequences to the impact of cultural values on society. Materialism may increase our standard of living. However, it also encourages the accumulation of wealth and creation of a greater gap between the haves and have-nots. The emphasis on youthfulness may promote an active and vibrant society, but it also encourages society to ignore the needs of the aged. This problem will become magnified with the aging of the American population into the next century. The emphasis on individualism may reflect America's pioneering spirit, but it has also created barriers to teamwork. Such barriers put

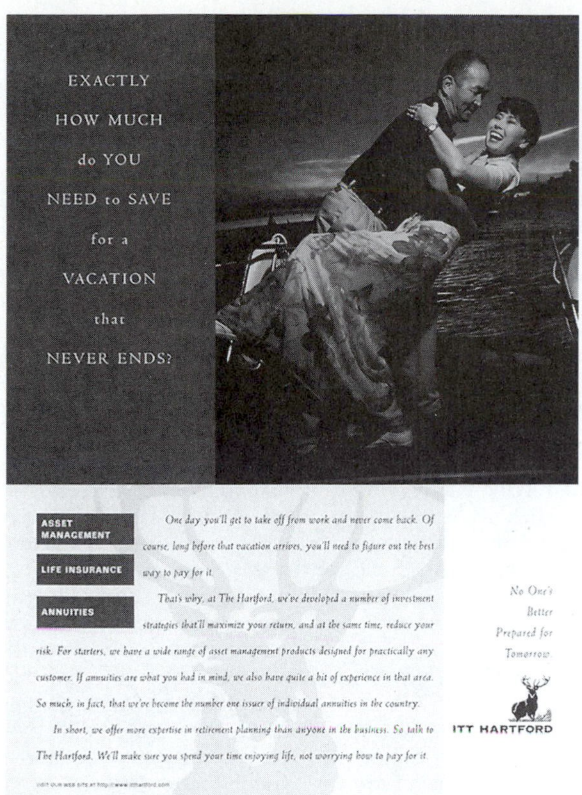

EXHIBIT 14.7
An example of the new materialism

many American companies at a disadvantage in competing with more group-oriented Japanese corporations.

Cultural values may also produce undesirable consumption consequences. Consider addictive consumption. While drug and alcohol consumption are the most serious abuses, addictions develop for many other products. The negative consequences of addiction to cigarettes is now widely recognized, even among lifelong smokers. Addictions can also develop for more mundane products such as chocolates, diet sodas, and snack foods. Compulsive purchasing behavior can be as socially undesirable as compulsive consumption. In the previous chapter, we saw that one result of addictive shopping is that consumers run up large debts that they often cannot repay.

Cultural values such as materialism may also encourage antisocial behavior such as theft, shoplifting, or insurance fraud. Loss of merchandise due to shoplifting has increased costs by an estimated $300 per year for a family of four.[43]

Overall, cultural values have a positive impact on consumers by directing their behavior in constructive ways. However, it is also important to recognize the negative consumption consequences of some cultural values.

SUMMARY

This chapter introduced the broadest environmental influence on consumer behavior: culture. Cultural influence is transmitted through societal values, which are learned from childhood through socialization and form permanent guides to understanding consumer behavior. Cultural values are terminal values or desirable end states to be attained. Another category of values, instrumental values, are the means of achieving these end states.

Cultural values have five key characteristics: they are learned, they are guides to behavior, they are permanent, they are dynamic, and they are widely held by members of society. Four such widely held values in American society are materialism, individualism, youthfulness, and a work ethic.

There are various means of identifying cultural values, including cultural inventories such as Rokeach's Value Survey, research services that conduct consumer surveys to determine changes in values such as the Monitor Service, field studies and observation, and content analysis of a society's mass media and literature.

In marketing terms, consumers seek to attain cultural values through a means–end chain in which (1) product attributes are a means for achieving (2) consumption goals that are instrumental in attaining (3) cultural values. The effect of culture on consumer behavior is reflected in its impact on the way products are portrayed and consumed. The means of portraying products in cultural terms is through symbols such as McDonald's golden arches. Marketers sometimes attempt to create myths and fantasies for products to strengthen their symbolism.

Culture is also important in defining a ritualistic role for many products. Consumers often purchase and consume products associated with grooming, gift giving, and holidays in a series of symbolic acts that reflect cultural values. One way to better understand the impact of culture on consumption is to view consumption as sacred or secular. Sacred consumption emphasizes beauty and the preservation of nature, whereas secular consumption emphasizes technology and the conquest of nature.

Several significant changes occurred in the American consumer's value system during the 1980s. The most important is a new reality that modifies the American Dream of unimpeded growth and recognizes future limits on purchasing power and spending. Other changes extending into the 1990s are (1) a shift in values from emphasizing youth to emphasizing youthfulness among older consumers; (2) a new traditionalism, reflected in a shift from a "me" to a "we" orientation; (3) a greater emphasis on self-fulfillment; and (4) the emergence of a new materialism that views wealth as a means of enhancing self-fulfillment rather than social status.

Cultural values can have both positive and negative effects on consumers and society. Some of the negative effects are addictive consumption, compulsive purchasing behavior, and antisocial behavior such as shoplifting or insurance fraud. Overall, cultural values have a positive impact on consumers by directing their behavior into constructive channels.

In the next chapter, we will focus on more specific components of culture: subcultural and cross-cultural influences.

QUESTIONS

1. Why is it rare for a marketing strategy to try to change cultural values?
2. What is meant by a *culture production system*? Cite some examples of such a system and how it might influence cultural values.
3. What is the distinction between terminal and instrumental values? What terminal and instrumental values might influence the purchase of a designer suit? A sports car?
4. What are the strategic implications of the changes in values between the 1980s and 1990s (labeled the *new reality*) for (a) advertising fax machines, (b) marketing disposable diapers, and (c) selling luxury goods?
5. What is the difference in the value placed on individualism in American and Japanese societies?
6. What changes have occurred in the work ethic in American society between the 1980s and 1990s? What are the strategic implications of these changes?
7. What are the theoretical underpinnings for Gutman's concept of a means–end chain as reflected in Figure 14.1?
8. What is the relationship between laddering and the means–end chain? How can marketers use laddering to develop advertising strategies?
9. What might be the role of product symbolism for the following products:

- A pair of designer jeans?
- A motorcycle?
- An engagement ring?

10. Why is semiotics useful in analyzing cultural influences on consumer behavior? Why is it particularly important to marketers in evaluating cross-cultural influences?
11. What do all consumption rituals have in common? How can marketers use these components in developing marketing strategy?
12. A manufacturer of plastic wrap is considering using the sacred dimensions of consumption to advertise the company's brand. A competitor decides to use the secular dimensions of consumption. How would each advertising campaign differ on this basis?
13. How have marketers reacted to changes in consumer values reflected in a "new reality"?
14. Assume a manufacturer of personal hair care appliances (hair dryers, rollers, and so on) wants to introduce two different lines: one directed to new traditionalists, the other to old traditionalists. What type of appeals could the manufacturer use to appeal to each segment?
15. What are the implications of the emphasis on self-fulfillment for positioning (a) a new line of perfumes directed to the working woman and (b) a line of exercise machines?
16. What do we mean by the *new materialism*? In what way does the ad in Exhibit 14.9 reflect the new materialism?

RESEARCH ASSIGNMENTS

1. Choose Web sites for four different products. How are the four widely held values of materialism, individualism, youthfulness, and the work ethic shown in these sites? Does each site showcase more than one of these values? Now analyze the site for Harley-Davidson (http://www.harley-davidson.com). Does it showcase any value other than individualism?
2. A study of automobile purchase preferences identified two segments based on cultural values: a self-enhancement segment and a social-recognition segment.[44] The two segments had very different need criteria for automobiles, different purchasing patterns, and different emphases on social issues. The self-enhancement group placed more emphasis on durability, environmental controls, and ease of repair. The social-recognition segment put more emphasis on luxury, prestige, and spaciousness. Regarding social attitudes, the self-enhancement group put more emphasis on equality, logic, and intellect; the social-recognition segment, on national security and law and order.
   - Use the attitudes toward the following five items to identify these two segments: (1) law and order, (2) national security, (3) religion, (4) individual freedom, and (5) logic. (The self-enhancement segment would place less emphasis on the first three items and more emphasis on the last two; the social-recognition segment would do the reverse.)
   - Select a sample of respondents and place them into one of the two segments based on their responses. (You may wish to form a third segment composed of those who do not clearly fit into one of the two segments.) Ask the respondents the criteria they emphasize in purchasing a particular durable good (a car, a stereo set, furniture, and so on). Determine particular brands or models owned.
   - What are the differences in (1) need criteria emphasized and (2) brand ownership between the self-enhancement and the social-recognition segments?

CROSS-CULTURAL AND SUBCULTURAL INFLUENCES

Chapter 15

LEVI STRAUSS THINKS GLOBALLY BUT ACTS LOCALLY

The previous chapter focused on the ways cultural values influence consumer purchasing behavior, primarily in the United States. There are two variations to the theme of cultural influences in a particular country. One is differences in values across countries, referred to as **cross-cultural influences.** The other is differences in values among groups within a country that distinguish them from society as a whole, referred to as **subcultural influences.**

In this chapter, we first consider cross-cultural influences and describe marketing strategies that adapt to local differences. A counterpoint to cross-cultural influences is **global influences,** that is, common needs and values across countries. We consider strategies that allow companies to market *world brands*—that is, brands such as Coca-Cola and McDonald's that are marketed similarly worldwide—based on global influences. We then turn to subcultures and define age, geographic, religious, nontraditional, and ethnic subcultures. We then focus on ethnic subcultures, namely African, Hispanic, and Asian Americans, because in many ways they represent distinct cultural values and purchasing patterns, account for one-fourth of the U.S. population, and represent close to $700 billion in purchasing power. On this basis alone, they are the ninth most powerful entity in the world, surpassing Canada or Sweden. Furthermore, these three groups are expected to account for nearly one-half of the U.S. population by the year 2050.[1]

http://www.levi.com/

http://www.mtv.com/

Levi Strauss closely follows both cross-cultural and subcultural trends. In its international operations it follows one basic principle: *think globally, but act locally.* The company recognizes that tastes in music, fashion, and technology are becoming more similar across the world because of greater facilities for travel and Internet communications and the global reach of media such as MTV. It has also recognized the increasing Americanization of consumption values abroad as more consumers crave American goods. Levi jeans are the only U.S. apparel label that can be called a world brand. The company has achieved world brand status by marketing Levi's as an enshrined piece of Americana. Teenagers wearing Levi jeans portray common values whether in Bangkok, Leningrad, Paris, or Rio.

The "act local" part of Levi's strategy is based on adapting its American roots to each country through the actions of local managers. In France it associates its jeans with the freedom of the global teenager (see Exhibit 15.1). In Indonesia, managers selected a TV commercial showing Levi-clad teenagers cruising around Dubuque, Iowa, in a 1960 convertible. In Japan, local managers use past movie stars such as Marilyn Monroe because of the obsession for American movie icons among Japanese youth.[2] The company is finding fertile ground in Eastern Europe and Russia since consumers in these countries hunger for any symbol of Americana, from McDonald's arches in Moscow to Coca-Cola cans in Warsaw.

EXHIBIT 15.1
Levi Strauss & Co.'s global perspective

http://www.dockers.com/

Levi Strauss is also extending its global reach through retail stores. In 1997, it introduced stores throughout Europe called Dockers & Co. to capitalize on the value that European consumers put on the name Dockers. The stores will make a full line of clothing available under the Dockers label.[3]

Many companies also target subcultures within their domestic markets. We saw in Chapter 1 that Levi effectively targets age segments—buttonfly jeans for teens, Dockers for baby boomers, Action Slacks for the mature segment. Each of these age groups could be considered a subculture in a broad sense because they have similar values and consumption needs—for example, the desire to look youthful yet the need for a looser fit among the mature segment.

Levi has also been effective in targeting the three basic ethnic subcultures and does so in much the same way as it targets markets cross-culturally: by using common themes but varying the message in selected media targeted to these groups. For example, when the company advertises its products to Hispanic Americans, it shows warm scenes in a family setting to appeal to this group's strong sense of family values.

CROSS-CULTURAL INFLUENCES

Marketing abroad has become an increasingly important part of American business. Today, three out of four manufacturing jobs are linked to products sold abroad, directly or indirectly. American companies such as Procter & Gamble, Colgate-Palmolive, Kellogg's, Coca-Cola, IBM, Gillette, and Johnson & Johnson earn more of their revenue abroad than in the United States. Many foreign-owned companies, such as Nestlé, Lever, and Shell Oil, which are often mistaken for American companies, earn a significant percentage of their revenues in the United States.

http://www.pg.com/

As foreign markets emerge and offer opportunities for growth, marketing abroad is likely to increase in importance. American firms are finding opportunities in Eastern Europe and Russia with the development of free-market systems. For example, Procter & Gamble has "spent millions of dollars researching the Russian consumer's mind and blitzing the airwaves with commercials that offer almost comic contrast to the dismal hardships of everyday life."[4] It is introducing Russian consumers to brands that offer unheard of benefits such as dandruff control and skin moisturizing. On gift-giving occasions, Russian consumers wrap bars of Camay soap and bottles of Pert Plus shampoo to give to loved ones. Before Camay was introduced (at a cost eight times that of Russian soaps), the only soaps available were coarse bars wrapped in brown paper.

China, the world's largest market, is becoming more consumption-oriented with the establishment of free trade zones in Southeast China. The turnover of Hong Kong to the Chinese government in 1997 is likely to spur the trend among Chinese consumers to become more brand-oriented. The regular appearance of

http://www.cocacola.com/

American brands such as Coca-Cola, Contac cold capsules, and Head and Shoulders shampoo on Chinese TV is further evidence of the development of a consumer society.[5] Coca-Cola figures that if the Chinese drink half as much Coke as Americans, the additional income would far exceed the company's total revenues.

The other side of the coin is the opportunity for foreign companies to market in the United States. Cross-cultural considerations apply equally in this case, as foreign companies have to become aware of the differing needs of American consumers and the nature of U.S. business customs. Japanese marketers have been particularly successful in challenging the leadership of American companies in autos, computers, and electronics. They have done so by adapting their products to the needs of American consumers—for example, by recognizing the need for compact, well-designed electronics products at reasonable prices.

http://www.mcdonalds.com/

Companies have generally been successful in marketing abroad by recognizing local differences in consumer needs and customs. To do so, such companies have had to acculturate themselves by learning local consumers' needs and values. Thus, despite McDonald's world brand status, it varies its offerings by selling beer in Germany, wine in France, mango milk shakes in Hong Kong, mutton pie in Australia, and McSpaghetti in the Philippines to compete with local noodle houses.[6] However, there is the danger that companies will assume that what works at home will work abroad. Such companies take an **ethnocentric** view of foreign consumers; that is, they assume foreign consumers have the same norms and values as domestic consumers.

Such an ethnocentric view is bound to fail. For example, P&G assumed that a 1990 campaign for Camay soap in Europe would also be successful in Japan. The campaign depicted a Japanese husband who walked in on his wife as she sat in a bathtub and complimented her on her complexion. Although the basic premise of the campaign—that women want to be attractive to men—is universally correct, the campaign flopped. Unlike most Europeans who considered the campaign sexy, the Japanese regarded it as bad manners to intrude on a woman's privacy.[7]

Cultural Variations Influencing Consumer Behavior

International marketers subscribing to an acculturated view of foreign markets have been affected by two cross-currents. First, they recognize differences in customs and values between countries and a need to adapt marketing strategies to these differences. Second, they also recognize a greater commonality between countries in cultural values as the result of global communications through TV and more frequent travel.

Cross-cultural differences require companies to develop localized strategies on a country-by-country basis, whereas global influences provide them an opportunity to standardize strategies. In this section, we consider cross-cultural variations that influence consumer behavior. In the next section, we consider global influences.

There are at least four cross-cultural factors that influence marketing strategies abroad: differences between countries in (1) consumer customs and values, (2) language, (3) symbols, and (4) the economic environment.

Consumer Customs and Values

American business people often take an ethnocentric view by assuming the values of American consumers are universal. However, the traditional American values of achievement, materialism, individualism, and youthfulness are not nearly as strong in other parts of the world. In many Asian countries, acceptance of one's place in society is more important than individual initiative in influencing behavior. Differences in the perspective of time also exist. Americans structure their day into times for work and pleasure based on business, family, and individual needs. In many South American and European countries, however, people are more likely to mix business with pleasure and being late for an appointment may be the norm.

Such differences in cultural values affect consumers' purchasing behavior. A failure to account for these differences is likely to spell trouble for the foreign marketer. For example, P&G failed in Russia when it introduced Wash & Go, a combination shampoo and conditioner. Shampoo was a relatively new concept to Russians who still washed their hair with soap, and a hair conditioner was completely foreign. In fact, many Russian consumers mistook the claim as "air conditioner." Wash & Go was quickly popularized into a euphemism for washing down a vodka before heading out.[8]

http://www.ford.com/

When American companies have accounted for foreign consumers' norms and values, they have been effective. Ford recognized a growing independence among Japanese women. In a traditionally male-dominated society, many more women were working full time. In 1990, Ford began targeting its Festiva car to single, young Japanese working women (see Exhibit 15.2). In the past, Japanese carmakers had assumed Japanese women would have deferred to fathers, husbands, or brothers in the purchase decision for a car.

Differences in cultural values among countries are likely to result in differences in product preferences and product usage.

Product Preferences. Product preferences are likely to differ sharply across countries. For example, the five brands with the strongest image in the United States are Coca-Cola, Campbell's, Disney, Pepsi, and Kodak. Yet none of these brands make it among the top 10 in Japan. Conversely, the strongest brands in Japan—Sony, National, Mercedes-Benz, Toyota, and Takashimaya—are not among the top 10 in the United States.

http://www.cambellsoup.com/

A lack of awareness that product preferences are culturally based can lead a company into trouble. Campbell was forced to call it quits in Brazil despite a $2 million award-winning advertising campaign because it failed to recognize

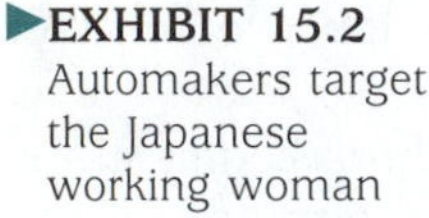

EXHIBIT 15.2
Automakers target the Japanese working woman

that many Brazilian women felt inadequate if they did not make soup from scratch for their families.[9] The company also failed to account for cultural values when it introduced its line of condensed soups in Britain. It was not sensitive to the fact that English consumers preferred ready-to-eat soups and were unaware of the condensed soup concept. Campbell's cans were at a disadvantage in the store because English consumers considered them small. In addition, the variety of flavors was not tailored to English tastes. It took several years of low sales to make the company aware of the difficulties and the required adjustments.

Product Usage. When operating abroad, American executives must consider differences in product usage. Consider the following:

http://www.colgate.com/

- Venezuelan women wash their laundry by using slivers of bar soap they knead together to form a paste. After Colgate researchers observed this process, they decided to put the paste in a plastic bowl and market it. The result was Axion soap paste, the leading laundry cleaner in Latin America.[10]

http://www.singer_nv.com/

- The Singer Company found that its predominant form of promotion—demonstration classes for women—had to be altered in Moslem countries.[11] Women were not allowed to leave the home to attend sewing lessons at Singer centers. One Singer representative in the Sudan was jailed for attempting to encourage women to attend classes. Once the men in those countries began to attend classes, however, they were convinced that sewing lessons would be of value to their wives, whom they then ordered to take lessons.
- Pepsodent tried to sell its toothpaste in Southeast Asia by using the same basic appeal as it did in the United States—getting teeth whiter. However, the campaign was ineffective in some regions because of the custom of chewing betel nuts to achieve the social prestige of darkly stained teeth.[12]
- People in Peru and Bolivia used powdered milk donated by the United States to whitewash houses. Why? They cannot drink milk because they do not retain an enzyme enabling them to digest it.[13]

Language

Language provides the means of communicating the customs and beliefs of a culture. Marketers must be aware of the meaning and subtleties of languages and dialects when selling in foreign markets. Many marketing blunders have resulted because of a lack of awareness of language. For example:

- When Coca-Cola was introduced in China, shopkeepers made their own signs in calligraphy with the words *ke kou ke la,* which translated into "bite the wax tadpole," an association that is not likely to encourage sales. When the company discovered this, it researched 40,000 Chinese characters and came up with *ko kou ko le,* which not only sounds more like the real thing, but also means "may the mouth rejoice."[14]

http://www.pepsi.com/

- PepsiCo had to change its slogan "Come alive with Pepsi" in certain Asian countries because the theme translated into "Bring your ancestors back from the dead."[15]

http://www.gm.com/

- General Motors discovered it could not use the name Nova on its models worldwide because in Spanish-speaking markets the name translated into "won't go" (*No va*).[16]
- Gillette had to change the name of its Trac II razor in many foreign markets when research showed that trac in some Romance languages means "fragile."[17]

Symbols

Symbols in a culture also influence purchasing behavior. Companies must be particularly sensitive to the use of color in advertising. Pink is associated with femininity in the United States, but yellow is considered the most feminine color in much of the rest of the world.[18] People in many Latin American countries disapprove of purple because it is associated with death. In contrast, purple connotes quality in China.[19] The Marlboro cowboy is shown in a lighter colored hat in Hong Kong and China compared to the rest of the world because of the positive cultural significance of the color white in China.

Symbols other than color also influence behavior. Two elephants are a symbol of bad luck in many parts of Africa. This forced Carlsberg to add a third elephant to its label for Elephant Beer. A moon appears frequently in Chinese ads because it is a traditional symbol of good luck in that country. The word for the number four in Japanese also means death, so Tiffany sells glassware and china in sets of five in that country.

Economic Environment

A country's economic environment influences consumer behavior. Three factors are particularly important: a country's standard of living, its economic infrastructure, and its economic policies.

As one of the most advanced industrial nations in the world, the United States' high standard of living allows for widespread ownership of electronics, appliances, and automobiles. Underdeveloped countries do not approach the level of ownership of TVs and telephones in the United States (over 95 percent). When Kellogg introduced its cereals into Southeast Asia, it knew it would have to try to change breakfast eating habits to influence Asian consumers to accept cereals. It also knew that a TV campaign would not be an effective way to do so because of limited TV ownership. Similarly, marketing researchers investigating consumer attitudes and behavior abroad cannot rely on collecting information by telephone in many countries because only upscale households have phones.

http://www.kelloggs.com/

The facilities a country uses to conduct business—media, telecommunications, transportation, and power—are known as the country's *economic infrastructure*. Media, telecommunications, and distribution facilities in many underdeveloped countries are primitive. For example, although consumers in Russia and Eastern Europe crave American goods, difficulties abound in marketing them because of archaic distribution networks and limited facilities for advertising. Marketers cannot take for granted basic requirements such as good road networks and warehousing facilities. Companies targeting less-developed countries face similar limitations in implementing marketing strategies.

A country's economic policies also influence consumer behavior. Many countries have instituted tariff barriers against imports to protect domestic industries, thus limiting their consumers' access to foreign goods. While tariffs have been reduced substantially in the post-World War II period, they still remain as barriers to consumer choice in many countries.

GLOBAL INFLUENCES ON CONSUMER BEHAVIOR

Supporters of global strategies in international marketing cite increased similarity in tastes and values across countries. Improvements in transportation and communication have resulted in distribution of products and transmission of advertising messages on a worldwide basis. The increasing availability of the World Wide Web will provide a further spur to global communications. As a result of these trends, brands such as Coca-Cola and Levi Strauss and fast-food outlets such as McDonald's and Pizza Hut can be regarded as world brands.

http://www.polaroid.com/

Certain values such as materialism, desire for beauty, nurturing of children, and security exist in most countries. If consumers can associate these values with a product category, a standardized marketing strategy across countries may be possible. For example, Polaroid developed a single global campaign based on the theme of pictures as a universal language. The campaign was successful because a theme of communicating through pictures was relevant to most cultures.[20]

Several factors have increased global influences on consumer behavior, including the availability of common TV programs from global cable networks, common values among teenagers worldwide, a general decrease in trade barriers, and the Americanization of values on a global basis.

Worldwide Communications

http://www.cnn.com/

Because of the advent of worldwide cable networks, television has become a global medium. Propelling this phenomenon is the global influence of MTV, the rock video channel, and CNN, the worldwide news channel. MTV estimates its audience at 210 million in 78 countries and expects to come close to tripling its audience by the turn of the century. CNN reaches 78 million households in more than 100 countries.[21] Because of such global media facilities, marketers can more easily create world brands by advertising them across many countries with a single theme. In Europe, MTV's 200 advertisers almost all run unified, English-language campaigns across its 78-nation broadcast area.[22]

One communications theory proposes that individuals tend to see the world around them largely based on information from the mass media. Therefore, heavy viewers of TV will develop similar perceptions of reality because they are exposed to similar stimuli. This effect, known as **mainstreaming,**[23] means that global TV networks such as MTV and CNN are promoting similar norms and values on a global basis.

The Global Teenager

Mainstreaming has encouraged the development of a global teenager, that is, teens with similar values across countries. MTV aired its first global show in 1989 because it "bet that teen tastes and attitudes are now sufficiently similar to warrant a global assault."[24]

MTV is not the only factor that has encouraged the development of the global teenager. Greater travel and better global communication have also spurred the development of common norms and values among teens worldwide. As the director of MTV in Europe said, "Eighteen-year-olds in Paris have more in common with 18-year-olds in New York than with their own parents. They buy the same products, go to the same movies, listen to the same music, sip the same colas."[25] As a result, a Russian rock band could be mistaken for an American group. Thai, French, and Brazilian teenagers are wearing the same brand of jeans, and teenagers in Asia, Western Europe, and Latin America are using the Sony Walkman.

http://www.swatch.com/

A growing number of marketers have begun targeting the global teenager. Swatch has a worldwide campaign for the simple reason that it sells 60 percent of its watches to teenagers. The company advertises the same image around the world, but varies the copy in its print ads to adapt to different languages. Exhibit 15.3 is an American print ad targeted to global teenagers.

Universal Demographic Trends

In Chapter 11, we described key demographic trends in the United States such as the increasing proportion of working women, the greater proportion of single-member households, increasing divorce rates, later marriages, and fewer chil-

▶EXHIBIT 15.3
Targeting the global teenager

dren per household. These trends are not restricted to the United States; they apply to most of the developed countries of the world, from France to Taiwan.

These common trends encourage global marketing strategies. For example, the increasing divorce rate in France, Japan, Sweden, Russia, and the United States was one factor behind the global success of Toys R Us. The company realized that parents who separate are more likely to give toys to their children.[26] Similarly, the increasing proportion of working women in Thailand, Malaysia, and Hong Kong led Jusco, a Japanese supermarket chain, to open stores in these countries. Although most women in these countries shop in open-air markets and small grocery stores, Jusco recognized that working women no longer have the time to shop in traditional ways and would want the time-saving convenience of supermarkets.[27]

http://www.toysrus.com/

Decrease in Trade Barriers

Trade barriers are decreasing worldwide, facilitating the flow of goods among nations and the consequent emergence of common tastes and values. The North American Free Trade Agreement (NAFTA) will facilitate the flow of goods between the United States, Canada, and Mexico, and the demise of Communism has opened markets previously closed to many Western goods.

The elimination of trade barriers in 1992 among the 12 nations of the European Community is likely to lead to a **Euroconsumer,** one who has many shared values with consumers in neighboring countries. As one European manager for Lever said, "Europeans share yearnings for odor-free underarms; fresh-smelling breath; and soft, easy-to-wash clothing."[28] As a result, companies are trying to sell products the same way across Europe, leading to the development of a **Eurobrand,** that is, a brand with several languages on the same package under the same brand name. Sara Lee has selected the Diam name as its Eurobrand for socks, underwear, and lingerie. Using a common strategy, Sara Lee can sell these items to all European Community countries (see Exhibit 15.4).

http://www.unilever.com/

Americanization of Consumption Values

The globalization of communications, decreasing trade barriers, and the demise of Communism have spurred the acceptance of American consumption values across the globe. Consumers in all parts of the world crave American goods as status symbols. In so doing, they adapt American consumption values to be consistent with local language, meaning, and beliefs, a process known as **cooptation.**[29] One author has coined the term "McWorld" to describe the cooptation of American consumption values.[30] Consider the following examples:

- In Russia, youthful consumers have turned to Western goods to maintain their traditionally disheveled look. They wear Chicago Bears and L.A. Lakers T-shirts, knock-off high-top basketball sneakers, and baseball caps.

http://www.nfl.com/bears
http://www.nba.com/lakers

EXHIBIT 15.4
An example of a Eurobrand

The taste for fast foods has caught on like wildfire, with an *Amerikanski gamburgeri* and a Budweiser being on the top of the list for chic.[31]

- In Japan, the Americanization of consumption values goes beyond a craving for American movie icons in commercials. Japanese consumers are equally in the throes of the fast-food craze with a fierce loyalty to *Bi-gu Ma-kus*. Japan now accounts for close to 10 percent of McDonald's sales worldwide. Japanese consumers also insist on American labels. For example, the L. L. Bean label is associated with a ruggedly functional American look that is now regarded as a status symbol, if not an icon, in Japan.[32]
- In Brazil, one executive attributed the failure of the Jack-in-the-Box chain to the fact that "there was nothing in them, like in McDonald's, to evoke for Brazilians 'the American way of life.'"[33]
- In Holland, an Amsterdam taxi driver points out a pedestrian dressed in a New York Yankee jersey, bluejeans, and green-striped Air Jordans. "I can smell an American anywhere," he says, "but that's a Dutchman." ("Why?" asks his passenger.) "Because he looks too much like an American."[34]

http://www.llbean.com/

http://www.jackinthebox.com/

American companies are taking advantage of this trend by using American themes, American celebrities, and English slogans in their advertising. However, this does not mean that American companies are being ethnocentric. These companies are actually following the desires of foreign consumers rather than assuming that American values can be imposed on them. Further, companies do adjust American-oriented ads to local needs and tastes. When Reebok advertised in France, it deleted a boxing theme from Planet Reebok commercials because of French consumers' aversion to any depiction of violence.[34]

http://www.reebok.com/

APPLICATIONS OF CROSS-CULTURAL AND GLOBAL INFLUENCES

Whether to sell on a localized basis, a global basis, or somewhere in between is perhaps the most important decision a marketer selling abroad must make. Such a decision must be based on the extent of cultural differences across countries and on the degree to which common norms, tastes, and values justify a more global approach. At one extreme, a company could follow a completely localized strategy by adapting product characteristics, advertising, and distribution requirements to the particular needs of each country it serves. Such a strategy may be unfeasible because of the costs of running a separate campaign in every country.

At the other extreme, a company could follow a completely global campaign. Coca-Cola has achieved world brand status through its objective of "one look, one sight, one sound," meaning that its advertising message is being constantly reinforced, whether consumers see it at home or abroad. Although such an approach may achieve a universal image and important economies of scale, some adjustment to local conditions is almost always necessary.

As a result, companies rarely follow a completely global strategy. Some degree of adaptation to local consumer needs is required. Such an approach reflects the "think globally, but act locally" strategy employed by Levi Strauss. We will refer to this strategy as **flexible globalization,** that is, an attempt to standardize marketing strategies across countries but to be flexible enough to adapt components of the strategy to local conditions. Such strategies are becoming the norm due to the shortcomings of a strictly local or global approach.

Since some companies follow a more localized approach and others more global strategies, we will consider these two approaches first. We then will describe the increasingly common strategy of flexible globalization designed to achieve the advantages of both local and global strategies.

Localized Strategies

Because of substantial differences between countries in tastes, customs, and product usage, many companies opt to localize their marketing strategies abroad. For example:

EXHIBIT 15.5
An American product reformulated to satisfy cultural norms

http://www.dominos.com/

- Heinz alters its ketchup to reflect local tastes. Americans like a relatively sweet ketchup, whereas Europeans prefer a spicier variety. In central Europe and Sweden, Heinz is selling a Mexican variety and a curry-flavored ketchup. In contrast to many companies that emphasize their American roots, Heinz plays down the fact that ketchup is a typically American product, preferring to let consumers think it is of more local origins.[35]
- Kellogg managed to attract Indians to its cereals, despite the fact that barely 3 percent of the country reported eating cereal in surveys, by advertising the benefits of a lighter and more nutritious morning meal. One tactic it used was to introduce rice flakes made of *basmati,* a premium aromatic rice (see Exhibit 15.5).
- Domino's Pizza also follows a localized strategy by varying its pizzas with what it calls "cultural toppings." For example, pizzas are topped with sweet corn in the United Kingdom, salami in Germany, and prawns in Australia. In Japan, Domino's offers a chicken teriyaki gourmet pizza for $15.[36]

Many companies also take a localized approach to advertising because of differences in needs or customs between countries. Renault advertised its Clio differently to various European countries because of differences in the features consumers consider most important in a car. The company emphasized road performance and features in Portugal, security and safety in France, self-image in Spain, style in Italy, and "new" in Belgium (see Exhibit 15.6).

▶EXHIBIT 15.6
Examples of localized strategies for one product

Italy

France

Belgium

Portugal

PASION
Clio
RENAULT
Clio

Spain

The Limits of Localized Strategies

The limitation of a localized international strategy is the inability of management to recognize the need to adapt to local tastes and customs (see Exhibit 15.7). Marketers have often attempted to export domestic strategies abroad and have gotten into trouble as a result.

http://www.snapple.com/

For example, when Snapple was first sold in Japan, ads declared that "The Snapple Phenomenon Has Landed," and Japanese consumers grabbed it up as part of their obsession for American products. But sales quickly dried up because consumers did not buy again. Why? Japanese consumers like a clear, unsweetened tea. Snapple had a cloudy appearance, a sweet fruit-juice flavor, and fruit sediment in the bottle.

http://www.QuakerOats.com/

Despite the evidence, Quaker (owners of Snapple) would not change the drink to suit local tastes. As one Japanese marketer said, "For all the talk about the Americanization of lifestyles here, Japanese taste buds remain traditional."[37]

Global Strategies

The cross-cultural differences just cited suggest that companies should vary their strategy for a product from country to country. However, in some cases, a company can use the same promotional campaign and positioning in each country if the product has a more global appeal. There may be compelling reasons for following a more global strategy. The resulting standardization in marketing strategies across countries results in important economies of scale. Coca-Cola saves about $8 million a year by producing similar ads across countries.[38]

Companies such as PepsiCo, Coca-Cola, Black & Decker, Singer, Levi Strauss & Co., and Goodyear have followed a global approach because they believe their products have universal appeal. By reinforcing the same theme in their advertising, companies can build a world image and a competitive advantage in their product category. Pepsi, whose strength has always been teenagers, uses this tag line in its Russian commercials, "The new generation chooses Pepsi," which is a variation on its universal theme of "The choice of a new generation."[39] Its

▶EXHIBIT 15.7
The limits of localized strategies: An American view of the world

red, white, and blue can is a universal symbol, regardless of language (see Exhibit 15.8).

Mars also sells its brands using a global strategy. In fact, the company actually killed off several highly successful brand names in Europe so that it could standardize the names under which its candies are sold worldwide. As a result, its best-selling Marathon bar in Britain was renamed Snickers, and its Raider chocolate biscuit, Europe's most successful, became Twix—brand names that are used on a worldwide basis.[40]

Limits of Global Influences

The focus on global influences might suggest that a company can market one standardized product with a uniform, worldwide advertising campaign. This is rarely the case. No matter how universal the product is, some adaptation to local customs and language is necessary. Even the most universal of brands, Coca-Cola, does not follow a strictly global approach. It makes variations in the brand's formula in certain countries; and while Coca-Cola uses a global theme, it creates

EXHIBIT 15.8
Pepsi's global strategy

variations in its advertising for each country. When the company launched its General Assembly campaign in 1987, showing children of the world singing the Coke jingle in one big assembly, each country's ads focused on a closeup of a local youngster. Thus, a unifying theme was adapted to different countries.

There are also limits to global communications. For example, despite the increasingly global reach of MTV, in Australia all commercials have to be reshot with Australian film crews.[41]

When a company follows a strictly global approach with little adaptation to local needs, it runs into trouble. Parker Pen tried to standardize every component of its marketing strategy in 154 countries but failed because of inadequate attention to local differences. Its global advertising campaign overlooked the fact that Scandinavia is a ballpoint pen market, whereas consumers in France and Italy want fancier pens.[42]

Another limitation to global strategies is the development of a backlash to the Americanization of consumption values. As a result of the recent recession, Japanese consumers seem to be shifting from their obsession with American products to a return to more traditional products. In some ways, this trend mirrors the "new reality" in American culture described in the previous chapter since both trends reflect greater restraint in spending due to economic uncertainty. The reaction to the Euro Disney theme park outside Paris also reflects a backlash against American values. Many French consumers viewed the park as a threat to traditional French culture and values. One author described this backlash as a reaction to "the numbingly homogenizing thrust of McWorld, which brings its blue jeans and MTV to Hindus and Muslims, Serbs and Croats alike."[43]

Flexible Globalization

The trend in international marketing has been to move toward a compromise between global and local strategies, which we have referred to as *flexible globalization.* This compromise requires the company to establish an overall marketing strategy but to leave implementation to local executives who are aware of national traits and customs.

http://www.harley-davidson.com/

For example, until 1992, Harley-Davidson insisted that local markets use its U.S. print advertising campaign. It then decided to customize its domestic strategy to account for different cultures. In Japan, Harley's local manager recognized that the American campaign featuring desolate scenes and the tagline "One steady constant in an increasingly screwed-up world" would not win over Japanese riders. So, he got permission to run a separate campaign juxtaposing American and Japanese images: American riders passing a geisha in a rickshaw or Japanese ponies nibbling at a Harley motorcycle.[44]

Similarly, Philip Morris uses the Marlboro cowboy ads on a universal basis but creates significant local differences in implementation. In Hong Kong, urban residents do not identify with horseback riding in the country, so the Marlboro cowboy is better dressed and shown in a pickup truck.[45] In Brazil, the cowboy becomes a rancher. In many countries, the cowboy cannot be shown at all, so the company uses western accoutrements such as a saddle horn, spurs, and cowboy boots to evoke the Marlboro image.

SUBCULTURAL INFLUENCES

In a society, individuals do not all have the same cultural values. Certain segments may be identified as subcultures because they have homogeneous values and customs that distinguish them from the society as a whole. The individual who identifies closely with a certain religious, ethnic, or national subculture will accept the norms and values of that group. As a result, members of a subculture frequently buy the same brands and products, read the same magazines and newspapers, and shop in the same types of stores.

Subcultures can be defined not only by race and religion, but by demographics and lifestyles as well. Common values among teenagers often set them apart from an adult-dominant society, thus defining a teen subculture. We saw in the last chapter that Harley-Davidson owners' lifestyles set them apart from society in many ways, constituting another subculture.

The religious, ethnic, national, and lifestyle diversity in American culture makes it distinct from most other societies which are much more homogeneous. The vast majority of people in most European countries are of the same race and religion. In Japan, most people consider themselves of common ancestry. It is rare to find a country where ethnic minorities represent over one-fourth of the population and no one religion dominates. Because of this diversity in American society, subcultural analysis is more important both from the standpoint of understanding consumer behavior and attempting to influence it.

Characteristics of Subcultures

The influence of a subculture on consumer behavior depends on several factors:

- *Subcultural distinctiveness.* The more a subculture seeks to maintain a separate identity, the greater is its potential influence. The Hispanic-American subculture is distinctive because many of its members have maintained their language as a means of cultural identification.
- *Subcultural homogeneity.* A subculture with homogeneous values is more likely to exert influence on its members. Hispanic Americans appear to be a diverse subculture composed of Mexicans, Cubans, Puerto Ricans, and individuals from South American countries. Some might consider each of these groups separate subcultures. However, in general, it is appropriate to talk of a Hispanic-American subculture because of common threads among all of these groups, namely, strong family and religious ties, conservatism, male dominance, and a common language.

- *Subcultural exclusion.* At times, subcultures have sought exclusion from or have been excluded by society. The Amish communities in Pennsylvania, Ohio, and Indiana have purposefully sought exclusion to maintain and protect their beliefs. African Americans have at times been excluded from a white-dominant society through the denial of educational and occupational opportunities. Exclusion tends to strengthen the influence of subcultures by isolating them from society and, thus, encourages the maintenance of subcultural norms and values.

United States: Melting Pot or Salad Bowl?

Distinctiveness, homogeneity, and exclusion interact to maintain subcultural identity separate from the general culture. In many subcultures, an individual is torn between maintaining a distinctive subcultural identity and integrating into the general society. The traditional path of immigrants in this country has been integration into the American "melting pot."

More recently, pressures to acculturate by accepting traditional, American middle-class values have lessened. For example, many Hispanic and Asian immigrants have a strong desire to maintain their language and heritage. This desire to maintain subcultural values has led one writer to refer to America in the 1990s not as a melting pot, but as a salad bowl "brimming with a polyglot, multihued potpourri of people who mix but don't blend. These immigrant groups have a need to maintain their separate identities rather than to meld into a cultural mainstream."[46] The challenge for marketers is to appeal to the separate identities of these subcultural groups while also appealing to the broader market.

TYPES OF SUBCULTURES

In the rest of this chapter, we consider subcultures in the United States by age, geography, religion, lifestyles, and ethnic identification. A key question is whether marketers should appeal to these groups with the same strategy they use for the general market or whether they should design specific campaigns targeted to particular subcultures.

http://www.metlife.com/

For example, Metropolitan Life's strategy has been to target particular ethnic groups with specific campaigns geared to their language and their customs. In appealing to Hispanic Americans, the company dispensed with Snoopy, the cartoon character, in its English-language ads and developed themes geared specifically to this segment for the Spanish-language media. Metropolitan has also developed specific ads targeted to Asian Americans. In each case, the company recognized that themes directed to the broad American market had to be adapted to the differing values and tastes of particular subcultures. Metropolitan is a trailblazer in this respect because many companies consider the 6 million Asian Americans too small a target.[47]

Age Subcultures

While some may debate whether age groups have sufficiently homogeneous and distinctive values to constitute a subculture, marketers have tended to identify the age groups cited in Chapter 12 as subcultures: teens, generation Xers, baby boomers, and the mature market. However, these age groups may be too broad to be defined as subcultures. More specific designations, such as younger versus older baby boomers or the "young" old versus the very old, do a better job of defining age groups with homogeneous norms and values.

Here we will cite the values that are sufficiently common to some of these age groups to qualify them as subcultures.

Teens

As adolescents, teens have in common a self-consciousness and search for identity that affects their purchasing behavior. Adopting a "funky" look, skate-boarding, and hip-hop music are manifestations of a search for identity. Part of this search for identity in the teen culture is a key conflict between the need to rebel and be independent from family and society and the need to be accepted for support and nurturing.

Generation Xers

Generation Xers have been described as being more cynical and alienated than other age groups, with income levels well below their expectations. They are the group that is best described by the "new reality" discussed in the previous chapter; they realize that they may not achieve the income potential of their parents and harbor some resentment for having to pay the future bill for an unbalanced budget and greater pollution control. There is also resentment toward their older baby boomer sisters and brothers for capturing better jobs and, in many cases, blocking their path to achievement.

Although this paints a somewhat depressing picture, a survey of women in their 20s found that this description of cynicism and alienation fits about 40 percent of generation Xers in one way or another.[48] This points to one of the basic problems of using age as a subcultural definition: common values often describe a minority of an age group. Other Xer subgroups were described as those who found fulfillment in their careers and those who were more traditional and family-oriented. As a result, it would probably be more appropriate to talk about three generation X subcultures than one.

Baby Boomers

Baby boomers should also be divided into at least two subcultures: younger and older. Many of the older baby boomers went through a transition from the rebellious 1960s and early 1970s of Vietnam and Watergate to a more materialistic lifestyle in the 1980s to a more inward and less materialistic outlook in the 1990s. They are best described by the trend toward self-fulfillment described in the previous chapter; the importance of money has become secondary to the importance of personal self-enhancement and meaningful work.

Not having gone through the societal upheavals of their older siblings, younger baby boomers are somewhat more conservative and materialistic. They can best be described by another trend described in the previous chapter: greater traditionalism, that is, a greater focus on family values, patriotism, and the work ethic.

The Mature Market

Those over 50 certainly cannot be described as a single subculture, although they do have certain values in common. Mature consumers want to lead active lives, to be self-sufficient, to look and act youthful, to reap the benefits of their past savings by enjoying new experiences, and to give something back to society, perhaps in the form of volunteer work or monetary contributions.

But the emphasis on these values will change over time, depending on which of the four age groups an individual is in, ranging from the younger mature group to the very old. For example, self-sufficiency becomes a much more important value than enjoying new experiences as one ages.

Geographic Subcultures

Geographic groups could also be identified as subcultures, but as with age groups, geographic designations may be too diverse to be labeled subcultures unless marketers can identify specific areas with homogeneous needs and values. Differences in tastes, lifestyles, and values are often distinct enough to define broader regional subcultures. For example, Easterners prefer to watch TV, read, and go to the movies, while consumers in the West prefer eating out, dancing, and visiting with friends. Consumers in the South prefer to stay at home, work around the house, and avoid organized entertainment.[49]

Subcultures can also be defined by regional clusters across the United States. This is the purpose of *geodemographic analysis,* as discussed in Chapter 11. For example, residents of retirement communities, whether in Florida, Arizona, or New Jersey, might be identified as a subculture because of common values regarding housing, medical care, and retirement benefits. Another regional grouping might be residents of college communities, from Chapel Hill, North Carolina, to Madison, Wisconsin, based on the similarities in tastes and expenditure patterns of two subcultures, college students and faculty.

Marketers' regional strategies reflect an international approach in thinking globally (that is, thinking in terms of the total U.S. market), but acting locally (targeting specific regions). For example, Campbell's follows a national strategy by advertising in the mass media and by capturing shelf space for its uniform red and white cans. But it targets its soups to regional tastes with a heavier dose of advertising and distribution of chicken noodle and tomato soups to northeasterners, cream of mushroom soup to Californians, and nacho cheese soup to southwesterners.

Religious Subcultures

Religious groups can also be regarded as subcultures as a result of traditions and customs tied to their beliefs and passed on from one generation to the next. As an example of differences in values, Catholics tend to be more traditional, with an emphasis on strong family ties; Protestants tend to value the work ethic as the avenue for success; Jews tend to emphasize individual responsibility for their actions and self-education; [50] and Muslims tend to be more conservative, with an emphasis on adherence to family norms.

Traditions and customs are reflected in purchasing behavior. Jews are less likely to eat pork and shellfish, Mormons are less likely to smoke tobacco and drink liquor, and Catholics are more likely to eat fish on Friday. The nonmaterialistic values of born-again Christians make them poor targets for credit cards but good targets for fast foods and do-it-yourself products.[51]

Religious affiliation can also influence the way consumers evaluate brands. For example, Hirschman found that Jewish consumers are more likely to seek information in the process of brand evaluation and to transfer that information on consumption experiences to others, possibly as a reflection of their emphasis on self-education.[52]

Nontraditional Subcultures: The Gay Community

Subcultures can also be grouped around nontraditional lifestyle choices—for example, the gay community. As this subculture grew more politically and economically visible through the 1980s, advertisers began actively courting it, mindful that gay couples tend to have more discretionary income than the average American, high-end tastes, and fierce brand loyalty. It is estimated that approximately 4 to 6 percent of the adult population is gay.[53]

Cigarette companies, clothing manufacturers, and carmakers are beginning to target their products to gay consumers. AT&T ran a direct-mail campaign targeted to gays by obtaining lists of subscribers to gay magazines.[54] The mailer came in a lavender envelope with a rainbow-colored cord and the tagline, "A Call for Change" (see Exhibit 15.9). Magazines are also being targeted to gays, with *The Advocate* being the leading gay magazine. Gays also have an active communications network with 200 Web sites to communicate about issues and to spread the word about companies that have the courage to target them.

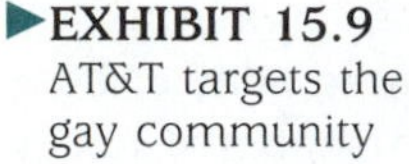

EXHIBIT 15.9
AT&T targets the gay community

Ethnic Subcultures

The most important subcultural entities in the United States are defined by ethnic origin, particularly by race and/or national origin. Consumers in a particular racial or national group are considered part of a subculture when they have a common heritage or environment that influences values and purchasing behavior.

As noted, we consider the three key ethnic groups—African, Hispanic, and Asian Americans—because they represent 25 percent of the U.S. population. But this figure understates their importance because, by the year 2050, they are projected to comprise nearly 50 percent of the U.S. population due to a combined population growth rate of 64 percent, nearly double the growth rate of 33 percent for the general population (see Figure 15.1).

As with age, geographic, or religious groups, we might consider these three ethnic groups to be too diverse to constitute subcultures. For example, the diversity that exists among lower-, middle-, and higher-income African Americans is probably as great as that for white consumers. However, as one writer noted, "Regardless of income brackets, African-Americans have a unique culture, and the African-American community has a distinct personality."[55] We will devote

FIGURE 15.1
Population projections for key minority groups: 1995–2050

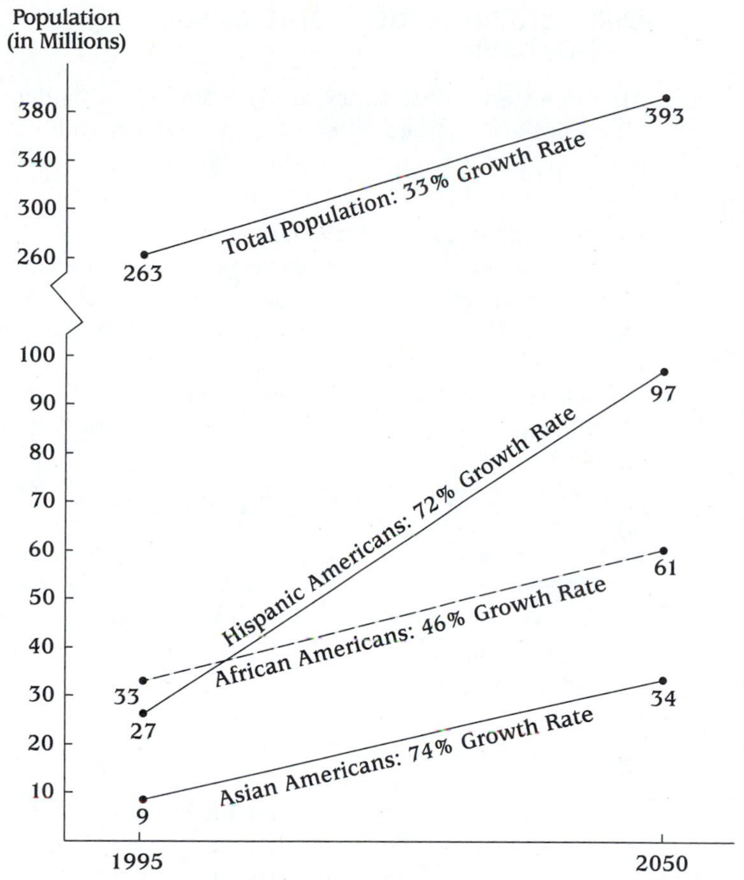

the remainder of this chapter to the three key ethnic subcultures: African Americans, Hispanic Americans, and Asian Americans.

AFRICAN-AMERICAN SUBCULTURE

More African Americans tend to identify with their ethnic group than whites do with theirs. About twice as many African Americans say that ethnic identity is more important than national identity.[56] This ethnic identity, plus the fact that African Americans differ in many ways from whites in their tastes and purchases, justifies characterizing them as a subculture. In this section, we first review differences in characteristics and purchasing behavior and then consider how companies direct marketing strategies to the African-American market.

Distinctiveness of Characteristics and Behavior

African-American consumers differ from whites by demographic characteristics. There are also marked differences in products and brands purchased, shopping behavior, prices paid, and media selected.

Demographic Characteristics

The 33 million African Americans made up 12 percent of the total U.S. population and accounted for $427 billion in purchasing power in 1996.[57] The median income of African-American households is less than two-thirds that of whites. Disparities in educational level parallel those in income. Only 13 percent of African-American adults had college degrees in 1995, compared to 24 percent of whites; and 74 percent had high school degrees, compared to 83 percent for whites.[58]

Lower income and educational levels among African Americans are the result of decades of discrimination. As barriers to equality have decreased, income and educational levels of African Americans have improved, resulting in a growing middle class. In the past 20 years, the rate of growth in annual income for African Americans has been about the same as for whites, and over 17 percent of African-American families have an annual income that exceeds $50,000.[59]

Educational levels have improved as well. Since 1960, the proportion of whites finishing high school increased by 47 percent, while that of African Americans increased by 73 percent, making them the fastest growing group to earn high school diplomas in the country.[60] Still, despite these positive trends, this country has a long way to go to achieve income and educational equality.

Another demographic factor that indicates increasing purchasing potential for African Americans is age. The average African-American consumer is six years younger than the average white consumer,[61] which means that a larger proportion of African Americans have entered their prime spending years in the 1990s, as compared to whites.

Some people might conclude that as the African-American middle class grows, it will lose its cultural identity. This is not the case. One study found that the greatest cultural affiliation occurs among affluent African Americans rather than among the underprivileged.[62]

Purchasing Patterns

Differences exist in purchasing patterns between African Americans and whites. African Americans spend proportionately more than whites for cosmetics, toiletries, and children's clothing; and whites spend more on medical care, entertainment, and insurance. These differences are largely the result of lower-income levels among African Americans, since lower-income households spend proportionately more of their dollars on necessities.

Since African Americans spend a greater proportion of their income on necessities, marketers might believe that they spend substantially less on luxuries. This assumption ignores the growing African-American middle class. One survey found that a greater proportion of African Americans owns CDs, pagers, and telephone answering machines than do whites. As for purchase intentions, the survey found that, in the next year, African Americans are more likely to purchase cars, furniture, home appliances, jewelry, and computers than are whites.[63]

These findings put to rest the misconception that the African-American market is a poor economic target. As a result, companies producing major appliances and electronics are increasingly targeting African-American consumers.

Marketing to African-American Consumers

Viewing African-American consumers as a homogeneous subculture can lead to oversimplified marketing strategies. Marketers can use most of the same demographic, lifestyle, and value criteria to segment the African-American market as they use to segment the white market. As a result, specific advertising, media, and product development strategies are required when selling to the African-American market.

Advertising

There has been a significant change in marketers' view of the African-American market. In the past, the market was regarded as homogeneous. Advertising not targeted to African Americans generally depicted whites. With the growth of the African-American and Hispanic-American markets, general advertising can no longer ignore these minorities. As one advertiser said, "In the old days, general was a code word for white. For any general program to be effective [today], you have to be aware of the sensitivities [of minorities.]"[64] This means that marketers are more likely to develop all-inclusive campaigns that depict minorities rather than targeting them separately. As a result, African Americans account for about 25 percent of the people in ads.[65] Further, African Americans are more likely to be depicted in more realistic rather than stereotypical roles.

An example of this approach is an ad for Kraft's Thick 'n Creamy Macaroni & Cheese, targeted to the general market, showing an African-American girl belting out the "Blue Box Blues" to encourage her father to make her Kraft for dinner.

Companies will still target African Americans for products designed to foster ethnic identification. For example, Exhibit 15.10 shows an ad for Creme of Nature that takes an ethnically aware approach by emphasizing the distinctive hairstyles of African-Americans and fostering African-American identity.

http://www.essence.com/

http://www.greyhound.com/

Despite these changes, marketers still occasionally make gaffes by failing to sufficiently research the African-American market. Greyhound discovered this when it bought time on African-American radio stations and aired a commercial with a country music soundtrack that few of the hoped-for customers could

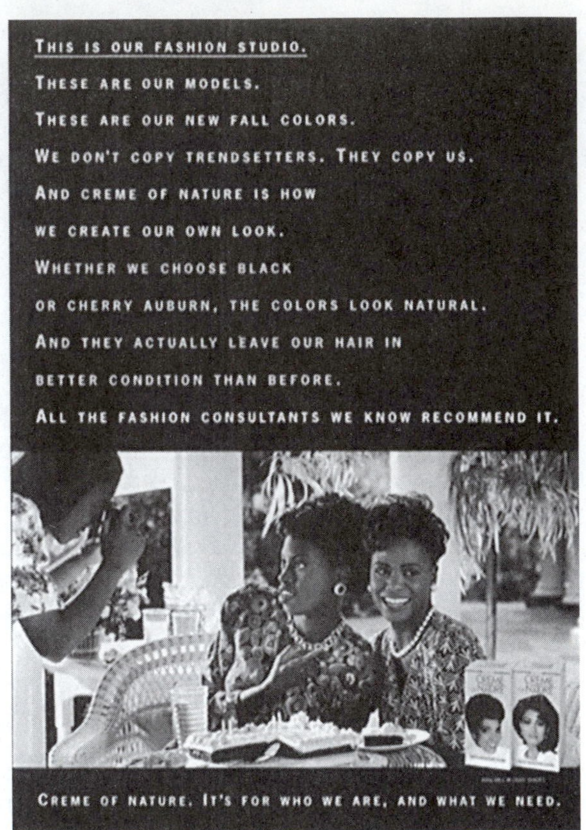

EXHIBIT 15.10
Appealing to African-American identity

relate to.[66] To prevent such gaffes, Fortune 500 companies are using African-American ad agencies to get it right. Chrysler used one such agency, Don Coleman & Associates, to advertise its Neon in an attempt to reverse a long-term loss in market share to imports in the African-American market. The print ads combined a view of the car with "jazzy visuals" designed to appeal to African Americans.

Media

Advertisers have an expanding range of broadcast and print media for reaching African Americans. There are hundreds of radio stations directed to African Americans across the country, over 200 African-American newspapers, and 22 national magazines.[67] Radio is particularly effective because African Americans listen to radio 20 percent more than the general public.[68] The one weak spot is television. There are few African-American TV stations in the United States, despite the fact that African-Americans spend 44 percent more time than whites watching TV. An exception is the Black Entertainment Network which reaches 53 percent of African-American households.[69]

Product Development

Cultural factors also play a large part in the design of new products. As African-American women emerged as a force in the workplace, they looked for cosmetics that suited their skin tones. A handful of African-American-run companies, such as Fashion Fair, filled the void until the major cosmetics companies estimated that the ethnic cosmetics market was worth at least $100 million in sales. As a result, Maybelline developed a line called Shades of You; Revlon, a line called Color Style.[70]

Product development is also required to meet the needs of the African-American community at large. JCPenney met this need in 1992 by opening boutiques in 20 markets that carry African-style clothing, housewares, and art.[71]

HISPANIC-AMERICAN SUBCULTURE

Because they have largely resisted assimilation of their language and customs into American society, Hispanic Americans (also called Latinos) are a distinct subculture. A 1990 survey found that almost 90 percent of Hispanics say that the Spanish language is the most important aspect of their culture. More than two-thirds of Hispanic Americans prefer to speak Spanish at home, and one-fifth do not speak any English.[72]

In this section, we will see the challenges and opportunities posed by the strong cultural identity of this fast-growing subculture.

Demographic Characteristics

Hispanic Americans make up the second largest minority group in the United States. In 1995, there were 26 million Hispanics in the United States, representing 10 percent of the population and close to $200 billion in purchasing power.[73] As shown in Figure 15.1, the Hispanic population should almost quadruple by 2050.

Among Hispanics, Mexicans represent more than 60 percent of the total, with most of the remainder being people of Puerto Rican and Cuban origin. Many are immigrants (one-third have come to the United States since 1981), and all are united by a common language and family bonds that make them nurture their heritage.

Hispanics tend to be younger, with a median age of 26, as compared to 34 for the rest of the population.[74] Their median income is about two-thirds that of the average American and their educational levels are well below average. However, both income and education levels are rising rapidly. Hispanic family size is also larger, with about 3.5 persons per household, as compared to 2.6 for the general population.[75] Hispanics are also more likely than whites or African Americans to live in metropolitan areas. Over 60 percent live in the top 10 urban areas in the United States.[76]

Hispanics have traditional and conservative values, which are shown in the respect they give their elders and their strong commitment to family. These values are reflected in the fact that, as one writer said, "Machismo is still strong and women's lib has a long way to go in Hispanic communities."[77] As a result of these values, one Hispanic marketer concluded, "The Spanish market will cling to its language, customs, and cultural background and will not, like other ethnic groups, be absorbed into the melting pot tradition of the U.S."[78]

These differences in values and customs justify defining the Hispanic market as a separate subculture, despite differences among Mexicans, Cubans, and Puerto Ricans.

Purchasing Patterns

Hispanic Americans are a highly brand-loyal segment of the market. One survey found that 62 percent of Hispanics buy the same food, beverage, and household items on a regular basis.[79] Hispanics are "significantly more likely to believe that advertising represents an honest and helpful portrayal of products."[80] They demonstrate faith in the quality of well-advertised national brands and are less likely to buy private brands and generic products. This is at least partly the result of their behavior in their native countries and explains why Colgate, which has a strong South American presence, holds a 70 percent market share among recent immigrants.[81]

http://www.colgate.com/

Because of their large family sizes, Hispanics also spend twice as much money per week as non-Hispanics on soft drinks, coffee, canned goods, household cleaners, and beauty aids. The brands they are loyal to also differ. For example, market share of the following brands among Hispanics is at least 20 percent higher than that for whites:

- Dove and Zest bar soaps.
- Coors and Budweiser beers.
- Avon and English Leather colognes.
- Alberto and Head & Shoulders shampoos.[82]

Marketing to Hispanic-American Consumers

The commitment of consumer goods companies to target the Hispanic-American market in the form of advertising and new products is increasing. In 1994, marketers spent $953 million in Hispanic advertising, compared to $633 million in 1989.[83] Although the Hispanic market is made up of various nationalities, marketers have generally avoided segmenting it because the small budgets allocated to Hispanics preclude preparation of separate campaigns for individual segments. Frito Lay treats Hispanic Americans as a single market because, in the words of one executive, the company tries to project a "consistent national image."[84]

http://www.fritolay.com/

However, differences in customs and language among various Hispanic groups warrant separate strategies for Mexicans, Cubans, and Puerto Ricans. Donnelley Marketing Information Services recently introduced a model that splits the market into 18 components. The model is so finely tuned that it describes a segment as "higher income, younger Puerto Ricans living in single family homes."[85]

One company that recognizes such differences is Anheuser-Busch. It follows a segmentation approach for Budweiser, the leading beer among Hispanics, by using different advertising for Mexican, Cuban, and Puerto Rican consumers. The purpose is to ensure that "each campaign should pick up on the regional nuances of [these] groups."[86] Thus, the Puerto Rican commercial is set in a disco and features salsa rhythms; the Mexican commercial is set in a rodeo to mariachi music; and the Cuban commercial takes place on a private boat because Cubans are the most affluent Hispanic group.

As a result of such targeted efforts, companies are directing advertising, product, and distribution strategies to Hispanic segments.

Advertising

Marketers must be aware of the norms, values, and language nuances of the Hispanic market. In failing to recognize these factors, some companies have made classic blunders. For example, Coors was left red-faced when its slogan, "Get loose with Coors," translated into Spanish as "Get the runs with Coors."[86]

Companies use two basic approaches to advertise to Hispanics. One uses the same ads as those in English; the other adapts the campaign to the specific values of the Hispanic market. Exhibit 15.11 shows both sides. The ad for Perry Ellis fragrances has appeared in Hispanic magazines such as *Vanidades* and in general circulation magazines. The danger with such an approach is that it may not reflect Hispanics' specific needs and values. Given the strong cultural identity of Hispanic Americans, they may not identify with a fragrance called America and an ad that pictures the vastness of the United States. Advertising approaches to the Hispanic market should reflect its conservative values and emphasis on family and children. This is better illustrated in Exhibit 15.11 by the ad for AT&T. The ad uses the experiential quality of a long-distance call to appeal to the desire of Hispanic Americans to communicate important experiences and events to relatives abroad. It appeals to basic family values with which Hispanic Americans can easily identify. One Hispanic marketer notes that using such values in ads "appeals to everything that unites us—heritage, tradition, family—without being heavy handed or a tear jerker."[87]

http://www.perryellisamerica.com/

http://www.att.com/

Media

Because a network of Spanish-speaking television stations exists, the Hispanic-American market is easier to target than the African-American market. There are 112 local Spanish TV stations plus two national Spanish networks, Univision and Telemundo. Radio is almost as effective as TV in reaching Hispanics, with about 125 Spanish-language stations nationwide.

EXHIBIT 15.11
Taking a general approach versus targeting Hispanic identity

Television and radio are effective in this market because Hispanics are more likely to tune into these media, and half of the time they tune into Spanish-speaking stations. While Hispanics are less likely to read magazines and newspapers than the average consumer, Spanish-language magazines and newspapers are becoming more important. *Vista,* a Sunday magazine newspaper supplement, reaches 1.2 million Hispanic households.[88] *Vanidades* magazine is aimed at Hispanic women in their late teens and early 20s, while *Cosmopolitan en Espanol* is targeted to the younger, more modern Hispanic woman. *Miami Mensual* is designed to reach affluent Hispanic audiences.

Product Development

In the product development area, there are parallels between Hispanics and African Americans. Estée Lauder designs makeup shades for Hispanic Americans as well as African Americans. Fabergé has also developed shampoos and conditioners specifically designed for the Hispanic woman's typically long and thick hair.[89]

http://www.gerber.com/

In foods, Frito-Lay introduced *Plantanitos* in the East because plantain chips are popular with Puerto Ricans and Cubans. Gerber Products Co. has added a 16-item tropical fruit line to appeal to Hispanics, while rice maker Riviana is testing new products for the Latino market in Los Angeles.[90]

Distribution

http://www.goya.com/

Hispanics tend to favor large supermarkets and department stores.[91] Many also shop in *bodegas,* small grocery stores that specialize in Hispanic foods and serve as a place for socializing. Hispanics value the personal interaction with friends and shopowners in the bodegas. One reason Goya Foods has been a successful marketer of Hispanic products is that it has cultivated strong relationships with bodega owners, who account for 45 percent of Goya's sales.[92] Similarly, by establishing strong distribution through bodegas, P&G has been successful as the largest marketer of Hispanic products. The company has a bilingual sales and distribution force that caters to bodegas in key metropolitan areas such as New York and Miami. To reinforce this presence, P&G reserves over $20 million a year for Hispanic media.

ASIAN-AMERICAN SUBCULTURE

Asian Americans are the third largest minority group, with 10 million people representing about 3.5 percent of the U.S. population and accounting for $120 billion in yearly purchasing power.[93] The reason for identifying Asian Americans as a subculture is the same as that for African Americans and Hispanic Americans: strong ethnic identity. Most are recent immigrants; 70 percent arrived in this country during the past 20 years.[94] Furthermore, 68 percent speak their native language at home.[95]

Asian Americans are more varied than Hispanic and African Americans, accounting for 29 distinct ethnic groups.[96] Chinese represent the largest group, followed closely by Filipinos and then by Japanese, Vietnamese, and Koreans. Despite this diversity, Asian Americans hold some values in common. They value close-knit family ties, put a high premium on education, and emphasize a strong work ethic.

They tend to be brand-loyal and like to buy status-oriented products. But because many are recent immigrants, they are not always familiar with brand names. For example, one survey found that 32 percent of Chinese residents in Los Angeles did not know what brand of laundry detergent they use, and 35 percent did not know what brand of soft drink they last purchased.[97]

Demographic Characteristics

Asian-Americans are the most highly educated and affluent minority group. About 40 percent have college degrees, compared to 22 percent for the general population, and their median income is 23 percent higher than that of other

Americans. The average age of this group is five years younger than that of the general population.[98] As Figure 15.1 shows, the Asian-American segment is projected to increase fourfold over the next half century, primarily because of a high rate of immigration. About 93 percent live in highly urbanized areas, and most of those areas are in the West with 39 percent living in California.[99]

Given the importance of the Asian-American market, it is surprising that more key demographic information on this market is not available. The U.S. Bureau of the Census separates basic income and educational information by whites, African Americans, and Hispanics. However, it does not group Asian-Americans as a separate category.

STRATEGIC APPLICATIONS OF CONSUMER BEHAVIOR

▶ California: On the Cutting Edge of Catering to Ethnic Identity

By the year 2000, California will become the first state in the United States where African, Hispanic, and Asian Americans constitute a majority of the population. In anticipation of that benchmark, marketers are pulling out all the stops to woo ethnic customers whom they largely ignored just a decade ago. In the process, they are learning that selling to ethnic shoppers requires considerably more effort than putting an Asian or a Latino actor in an English commercial.

These efforts are being felt most in the Hispanic community, which grew 70 percent between 1980 and 1990 and now accounts for a quarter of the state's population, and the Asian community, which doubled in the 1980s to become 10 percent of the state's total. Banks, phone companies, TV stations, and supermarket chains are all quickly learning about the diversity, nuances, and perceptions of these communities so they can apply a strategy that one consultant calls "international marketing within your own borders." This means that just as American strategies may not work abroad, marketers cannot assume that strategies designed for a homogeneous U.S. market will work in ethnic enclaves. New immigrants are often mystified by American norms, and those who have assimilated frequently retain their cultural identity.

In contrast, Bank of America showed more ethnic sensitivity in dealing with the fact that most of the new Latino residents from Mexico and Central America had never set foot in a bank. It embarked on a massive education campaign, including a slick soap opera video that followed a Latino couple through marriage, having children, and buying their first home—with explanations at each juncture about how a bank can help. The bank gives these videos to various outreach groups that socialize new Americans.

Some of the worst blunders have occurred because California marketers have not been sensitive to ethnic cultures. For instance, Met Life once tried appealing to Korean customers by running an ad picturing a family in traditional dress; the only problem was it was Chinese dress. Similarly, Coors was roundly criticized for sexual stereotyping during the 1988 Chinese New Year when it erotically portrayed a Chinese woman in the folds of a silk dragon. Marketers must also be sensitive to the nuances of a subculture's language. When Pepsi tried aiming its "Choice of a New Generation" campaign at Chinese Americans, it suffered a major embarrassment when the slogan was unintentionally translated into "Come and wake up your dead ancestors."

Asians pose more difficulties than Hispanics for California marketers because of the variety of languages they speak: Vietnamese, Cantonese, Mandarin, Korean, Tagalog (spoken by Filipinos), or Cambodian. One strategy for bridging the gap is to rely less on mass-market tools such as television and use the growing list of ethnic newspapers. Companies such as the Bank of America follow this strategy. Another strategy is to use members of a targeted ethnic group to help market products or services. In 1996, many HMOs in California (Oxford, Kaiser, and others) had recruited Cantonese and Spanish-speaking doctors to better target Chinese and Hispanic consumers.

It is often said that California leads the rest of the United States. As minorities become the majority in state after state, California's ethnic marketers will surely have much to teach the rest of the nation.

Sources: "Health: HMOs Say 'Hola' to Potential Customers," *The Wall Street Journal* (November 30, 1995), p. B1; "Catering to Consumers' Ethnic Needs," *The New York Times* (January 23, 1992), pp. D1, D8; "Solutions: Making a Connection," *Adweek* (October 7, 1991), p. 46; "California's Asian Market," *American Demographics* (October 1990), pp. 34–37.

Marketing to Asian-American Consumers

Because the Asian-American market is small, few marketers direct advertising strategies to it. Their philosophy is that Asian Americans need no special marketing effort and that general advertising campaigns will also attract this segment. These marketers also find targeted marketing difficult because of the community's diversity and range of native tongues. A recent survey discovered that most Asian Americans speak their native language at home, particularly Koreans (94 percent) and Chinese (90 percent.)[100]

As a result, Asian Americans are poor consumers of American media. On average, they watch only about 12 hours of English-language television a week and listen to only 80 hours of American radio, well below the national average. One survey found that about half of those polled did not read English-language magazines.[101] In addition, there is no national Asian cable TV network.

http://www.sears.com/

However, some companies are beginning to target Asian Americans because their youth and greater affluence make them an attractive market. Sears was the first major retailer to target Asian Americans in 1994 when it hired an ad agency to develop an ad campaign targeted to this segment. Nordstrom and The Gap use outdoor and point-of-purchase ads to attract Asian Americans in California.[102] Metropolitan Life focuses on the emphasis that Asian Americans place

EXHIBIT 15.12
Targeting Asian-American consumers

on education and stresses the role of saving for their future (see Exhibit 15.12). These attempts to target the broad Asian-American market are the exception, however. For most companies, it is difficult to implement such campaigns due to the diversity of the Asian-American market.

http://www.BankAmerica.com/

Specific Asian nationalities can be targeted because they tend to live in the same areas. For example, the heavy concentration of Chinese Americans in California made it possible for Bank of America to target this market selectively. The bank took English-language spots, dubbed them or added subtitles in Cantonese, and ran them on local Chinese-language cable TV stations. The bank also targeted immigrants in the central valley of California who were primarily from Southeast Asia by advertising in newspapers in Vietnamese, Cambodian, and Laotian. The ads urged readers to "come see us," as these recent immigrants mistrusted banks.[103] Bank of America's campaign is one of the few examples of marketing to specific segments of Asian Americans. Given the diversity of this market, such a segmented approach is essential.

SOCIETAL IMPLICATIONS OF CROSS-CULTURAL AND SUBCULTURAL INFLUENCES

The nature of cross-cultural and subcultural influences creates a number of societal issues that bear on consumer rights in the marketplace.

Cross-Cultural Issues

Consumers in foreign markets should have the same rights as those outlined in Chapter 2: the right to safe products, to full information, to adequate choice, and to redress of grievances. This should be true whether consumers live in developed or in Third World countries. One of the most contentious issues in international marketing is that consumers in Third World countries do not have adequate protection when it comes to product safety and full disclosure of product contents and performance. Some companies have even been charged with selling products that have misled and harmed consumers in underdeveloped countries.

http://www.nestle.com/

The most widely publicized case in this regard was Nestlé's infant formula products. Many infants died in Third World countries because the formula was often mixed with contaminated water from local sources. A worldwide boycott of Nestlé products ensued in the late 1970s. The company attempted to resolve the issue by following guidelines the United Nations set for promotion and distribution of infant formula. As a result, the boycott was lifted. The issue arose again in 1989 when Nestlé was charged with distribution of infant formula that did not conform to the spirit of the UN guidelines.[104] The issue has still not been fully resolved.

http://www.who.org/

Another issue drawing increasing attention is American cigarette companies targeting brands to consumers in less developed countries. Consumer advocates believe that it is unethical to encourage smoking in countries where famine and disease are prevalent. A World Health Organization study found that marketing campaigns by U.S. cigarette companies have "caused immediate jumps in consumption among women and teens, traditionally non-smoking groups in less developed economies."[105]

Consumer activists in Asian countries are accusing American companies of manipulating Asian youth. They charge that American companies are taking advantage of the globalization of American consumption values by linking cigarettes to such themes as the Marlboro cowboy or Joe Camel. One activist states that youth in underdeveloped countries are "smoking the American dream."[106] In Taiwan, one consumer group was successful in stopping a rock concert sponsored by R. J. Reynolds. Admission was by empty Winston packs.

Subcultural Issues

Many of these same issues arise regarding consumer rights of minority groups. We noted in Chapter 2 that minority consumers should have the same rights as others without being at a disadvantage. However, this is not always the case. Minority consumers in lower socioeconomic groups are often at a disadvantage when it comes to adequate brand alternatives, fair prices, and the assurance of product safety.

Another issue was the attempt by R. J. Reynolds to target Uptown cigarettes specifically to African Americans. Before Uptown came along, cigarette companies had devoted part of their advertising budget for their existing brands to African Americans and Hispanics, but none had ever developed a product with the intent of targeting it to a minority segment. Reynolds' plans provoked an outcry that was successful in getting the company to withdraw the product. However, apparently the lesson did not fully sink in. Shortly after it withdrew Uptown, Reynolds considered marketing a cigarette called Dakota to blue-collar women under 21.[107] Although there was no evidence Reynolds planned to introduce Dakota, the issue—attempting to target underprivileged consumers with potentially unsafe products—remains.

SUMMARY

Differing cultural norms and values result in different patterns of purchasing behavior in various countries. These cross-cultural influences require companies to adapt their marketing strategies to the local conditions of various countries. Four important cross-cultural factors influence marketing strategy: consumer customs and values, language, symbols, and the economic environment.

These cross-cultural factors encourage companies to adapt to local conditions. However, several factors are creating common tastes and purchasing preferences on a global basis. These include (1) global communications, (2) demographic trends across countries such as the greater proportion of working women, (3) a reduction in trade barriers worldwide, and (4) the Americanization of consumption values, particularly in Europe and Russia.

Based on these influences, three types of international marketing strategies were discussed. A localized strategy is important in adjusting to differences in norms and customs in various countries. A globalized strategy achieves economies of scale and a universal image but may fail to adapt to differences in needs and purchasing habits across countries. A company following flexible globalization thinks globally but acts locally by establishing a standard strategy but allowing countries to vary details to meet local needs and customs.

Subcultures are important to marketers because they represent groups with distinct values, customs, and purchasing habits. The more distinctive and homogeneous a subculture, the greater will be its influence on consumer purchases.

Subcultures in the United States can be identified on the basis of five things: age, geography, race, religion, or national origin. The three most important subcultures for marketers are African Americans, Hispanic Americans, and Asian Americans, who together represent close to one-fourth of the U.S. population. These subcultures also represent significant purchasing power—over $400 billion a year—and are profitable markets because they tend to be more brand-loyal.

Marketers have increasingly directed strategies to these groups. The African-American consumer market has seen more cosmetic and toiletry products directed to its specific needs. In addition, marketers have directed ads to African Americans through African-American magazines and radio; and ad campaigns have frequently attempted to foster African-American identity. Targeting marketing strategies to Hispanics is facilitated by some homogeneity in values. Companies such as Anheuser-Busch and Polaroid have developed Spanish-speaking ad campaigns for their national brands. However, companies find targeting ad campaigns to Asian Americans difficult because of the diversity of nationalities and languages within this broad segment. Overall, marketers have a long way to go in recognizing the potential of the African-, Hispanic-, and Asian-American markets and adequately targeting marketing efforts to these groups.

The chapter concluded by considering some societal implications of cross-cultural and subcultural influences, namely, the need to protect consumer rights abroad, particularly in Third World countries, and the need to protect the rights of underprivileged consumers at home.

In the next chapter, we consider another environmental factor: the influence of reference groups on consumer behavior.

QUESTIONS

1. What are the dangers of an ethnocentric view in marketing abroad? Provide some examples of these dangers.
2. What is meant by *mainstreaming*? How has mainstreaming contributed to the development of a global teenager? How does it facilitate the establishment of world brands?
3. What is the evidence that there is a global teenage market? How might a producer of designer jeans target the global teenager?
4. The chapter noted that many demographic trends that have occurred in the United States—an increasing proportion of working women, higher divorce rates, smaller families, and later marriages—have also occurred in most of the developed nations of the world. What are the strategic implications of these trends for a:
   - Car manufacturer in Japan considering a marketing campaign directed to women?
   - Large toy manufacturer in the United States considering exporting its products?
   - Manufacturer of household cleaning products considering a worldwide advertising campaign for its line?
5. What are the advantages and disadvantages of a globalized marketing strategy? What are the limits of implementing a truly standardized marketing strategy worldwide? When are such strategies most likely to work?
6. Localization of marketing strategies was suggested as a way to adjust to conditions in specific countries. What are the pros and cons of using a localized strategy?
7. What is meant by *flexible globalization*? Why is it becoming a more common strategy in international markets? Cite examples of (a) product strategies and (b) advertising strategies that have followed this approach.
8. What are the characteristics that identify a subculture? Would you identify residents of retirement communities as a subculture? Why or why not?
9. What are the marketing implications if America becomes more of a "salad bowl" than a melting pot in the 1990s?
10. On what basis could you support identification of the African-American consumer market as a subculture? On what basis could you argue against such an identification? What are the marketing implications of each position?
11. A company is considering three alternative strategies in marketing a hair care line to African-American consumers:
    a. Introduce two lines: one positioned to those who seek African-American identity; the other, to those who identify with white middle-class values.
    b. Introduce one line to appeal to both segments.
    c. Introduce one line to appeal only to those seeking African-American identity.

    What are the pros and cons of each strategy? Which would you select? Why?
12. Hispanic Americans have been described as a more homogeneous ethnic subculture than African Americans. Why? What are the marketing implications of a greater level of homogeneity?
13. An ad for a household cleanser targeted to Hispanic women uses an appeal showing the husband's approval when entering a sparkling clean home. Do you think such an appeal would be successful among Hispanic women? Among the general population? Why or why not?
14. What are the pros and cons of targeting Asian-American consumers?
15. What ethical issues might arise in marketing to foreign consumers, especially in less developed countries? To subcultures in a domestic market, especially to underprivileged consumers?

RESEARCH ASSIGNMENTS

1. How do IBM, Levi Strauss, and Pepsi adapt their Web sites to different cultures or countries? Do you feel these companies have created localized or globalized marketing strategies based on their Web sites? Do these companies target any subcultures within the United States? How is that shown in their Web sites? Do any of these companies target national subcultures outside of the United States?
2. A lively debate has ensued in the marketing community regarding the viability of a global strategy. As the chapter suggests, some marketers believe in the convergence of tastes and values and see globalization increasing in the future as a result of more travel and more universal communication facilities. Others believe that local differences between countries will dominate marketing strategies, regardless of the so-called trend to universal values. To familiarize yourself with this issue, read the following:
   - Theodore Levitt, "The Globalization of Markets," *Harvard Business Review* (May-June 1983), pp. 92–102. (This article supports the notion that markets are becoming more global and that the trend should be toward more standardized strategies.)
   - "Marketers Turn Sour on Global Sales Pitch Harvard Guru Makes," *The Wall Street Journal* (May 12, 1988), p. 1. (The article debates Levitt's position.)
   - Teresa Domzal and Lynette Unger, "Emerging Positioning Strategies in Global Markets," *Journal of Consumer Marketing* 4 (Fall 1987).
   - "Goodbye Global Ads," *Advertising Age* (November 16, 1987), pp. 22–24. (This article argues against globalized strategies.)

   Interview at least 10 marketing executives in multinational companies. The companies can be large or small, manufacturers or distributors, product or service companies. The important objective is to talk to managers with experience in marketing abroad. Ask these managers to comment on the following:
   - Do they think tastes and values are becoming more similar worldwide? If so, is this trend likely to facilitate globalized marketing strategies in the future?
   - Will decreasing trade barriers affect the company's operations? If so, in what ways? If not, what general opportunities do they think these events will create for American businesses?
   - Under what circumstances do they believe globalized strategies are more effective? When are localized strategies more effective? For what types of product categories or services?
   - What products or services have they been involved with abroad? What types of strategies did they use?
   - Did they adapt strategies to the customs and values of specific countries? How?

   Once you have collected this information, summarize the views of the executives you have interviewed. Consider the following:

   a. What differences in views emerged regarding the issues you investigated?
   b. Were there differences in views by type of company (for example, product versus service companies, producers of packaged goods versus durable goods)? If so, why do you believe these differences in views emerged?
3. Identify an ethnic group that can be regarded as a subculture (whether by race, religion, or national origin). Interview 30 people in this group and 30 people in the general population.
   a. Ask respondents to:
      - Rate their agreement with lifestyle items such as those in Table 11.1.
      - Indicate how frequently they purchase products such as cosmetics, household cleaners, and soft drinks.

   b. Do your findings justify identifying the group you selected as a subculture? Specifically:
      - What are the differences in values, lifestyles, and purchases between the subcultural group and the general group?
      - Is the subcultural group more homogeneous in lifestyles and values than the general group?

   c. What are the implications of your findings for developing (a) products and (b) advertising strategies for the subcultural group?

PART VI

GROUP INFLUENCES

In this last section of the book, we consider group influences on consumers. We describe the influence of face-to-face groups with particular emphasis on reference groups in Chapter 16 and households in Chapter 17.

Reference groups are important because they are made up of friends and family to whom consumers constantly refer for information and opinions. The household unit is the most important reference group and deserves special attention. The influences of spouses on each other and on their children are essential in understanding consumer decisions. Often, key decisions are made by nontraditional households, for example, single-parent families and unmarried couples.

In the last chapter, we describe group communications. Group communications occur within groups through a process of word-of-mouth influence. Such communications are considered the most credible since they come from friends, family, and neighbors. Communications also occur across groups through a process of diffusion of information and influence. Such a process is likely to occur for new products as information on and adoption of new products spreads across groups.

REFERENCE GROUP INFLUENCES

Chapter 16

MARKETERS CAN INFLUENCE GROUPS, AND GROUPS CAN INFLUENCE MARKETERS

One of the most important environmental influences on consumer behavior is the face-to-face group. A consideration of the influence of groups is based on the **reference group,** that is, a group that serves as a reference point for the individual in forming his or her beliefs, attitudes, and behavior. In this chapter, we:

- Describe various types of reference groups.
- Evaluate the roles they play.
- Explore the ways they influence the individual consumer.
- Consider the marketing strategy implications of reference group influences.

Marketers frequently advertise their products in a group setting—the family eating breakfast cereals, friends having a soft drink after a game of touch football, a neighbor admiring a new car. The purpose is to mirror the influence that friends and relatives have on consumers. The Macintosh ad in Exhibit 16.1 is an example. It associates the product with a group of school friends. The implication is that the product is accepted by schoolmates because it will enhance learning.

▶EXHIBIT 16.1
Depicting a reference group in advertising

Another strategy is for marketers to use "typical consumers" in testimonials for the product. The typical consumer reflects the purchaser's norms and values and acts as a representative of the consumer's reference group. For example, in a print ad campaign for Dove soap, six women cite the benefits of the product under the tagline, "Women from Scranton to Sacramento will tell you Dove is better."

http://www.nike.com/

Marketers also use celebrities as spokespersons to try to mirror group influence. In this case, the celebrity represents a member of a group the consumer admires at a distance rather than an actual member of the consumer's reference group. The assumption is that consumers are likely to be influenced by these individuals because they want to identify with the celebrity. Nike, for example, has used sports stars such as Michael Jordan, Carl Ripken, Jr., and Andre Agassi in its advertising to attract purchasers who identify with these stars. It even uses Dennis Rodman, the counterculture basketball star, to represent the cynical and authority-hating values that appeal to many generation Xers.

http://www.harley-davidson.com/

These examples illustrate marketers trying to influence the reference group. But if the group is sufficiently visible and cohesive, it can influence marketing strategy. An example is Harley-Davidson owners. Many owners have adopted jeans, black boots, T-shirts, and black leather jackets as the "Harley-Davidson uniform." The company did not initiate this association, but once it was established, Harley-Davidson cultivated it by coming out with a full line of clothing and accessories with the Harley-Davidson logo.[1]

In other such examples, hot rod groups influenced car designs during Detroit's "muscle car" era in the 1950s and 1960s, and equipment and clothing for skydivers and surfers have largely been determined by the norms and behavior of these groups.

WHEN DO REFERENCE GROUPS EXERT INFLUENCE?

Reference groups provide us with roles and standards of conduct that directly influence our needs and purchasing behavior. The family influences what the child eats for breakfast; the peer group, what the teenager listens to on the radio and watches on TV; and the organizational group, what the adult wears to work. In each case, the group provides the individual with information on how to act and often pressures the individual to conform to group norms.

In adapting to group norms, we not only subscribe to the values established by the family, peer group, or organization, but we also use them to define ourselves.[2] In fact, one essential element of self-concept is how we think others see us. This influence, referred to as the *looking glass self,* means that reference groups provide the points of comparison by which we evaluate our own attitudes and behavior.

The influence a group exerts on an individual's purchasing behavior depends on three factors: (1) the individual's attitude toward the group, (2) the nature of the group, and (3) the nature of the product.

Attitude Toward the Group

A study by Bearden and Rose found wide variations in an individual's susceptibility to group influence.[3] An individual's purchasing behavior is more likely to be influenced by the group if he or she:

- *Views the group as a credible source of information* about the product or service.[4]
- *Values the views and reactions of group members* regarding purchasing decisions.[5]
- *Accepts the rewards and sanctions meted out by the group* for appropriate or inappropriate behavior.[6]

Consider a member of a Harley-Davidson bikers group. He (most members are males) relies on other members for information and advice regarding servicing, maintenance, and product performance. The newer the member, the more likely he will look to others for such advice. Further, there is a hierarchy of expertise in the group, since certain members are relied on more than others for information.

Further, group members accept the rewards and sanctions of the group. In their ethnographic study of Harley-Davidson groups, Schouten and McAlexander report that as an individual gains more respect and authority in the group, he moves up further in the riding pack, with the group leader also leading the pack on the road.[7] New members ride further back in the pack. If they do not conform to the values and behavior of the group, they may be shunned and ridiculed as "weekend warriors."

Nature of the Group

As for the nature of the group, reference groups are more likely to influence a member's behavior[8] if they are:

- *Cohesive,* in that members have similar norms and values.
- *Frequently interacting,* thus creating more opportunities to influence members.
- *Distinctive and exclusive,* in that membership in the group is highly valued.

Harley-Davidson biker groups have each of these characteristics. The group is closely knit, with an increasing level of commitment by bikers over time. For many members, biking becomes an obsession, almost a full-time hobby. As a result, opportunities for interaction and influence increase. Further, membership becomes exclusive with members referring to each other as "brothers" and outsiders as "citizens."

Nature of the Product

The third factor that determines the degree of influence a group has on an individual is the nature of the product. Groups are more likely to be influential for (1) visible products such as clothing, cosmetics, and furniture and for (2) exclusive products that might connote status.[9]

Motorcycles are visible and the Harley-Davidson is the necessary mark of status for group membership. Of more interest are the visible indicators associated with the product. Each Harley group has its own distinct signs of membership such as tattoos, sew-on patches, pins proclaiming various accomplishments at rallies, and, most importantly, varying styles in customizing the bike.[10]

Before we consider the nature of these group influences in more detail, we will discuss the types of reference groups consumers can belong to.

TYPES OF REFERENCE GROUPS

Reference groups provide points of comparison by which to evaluate attitudes and behavior. A consumer can either be a member of a reference group, such as the family, or aspire to belong to a group (for example a tennis buff might aspire to associate with tennis pros). In the first case, the individual is part of a **membership group;** in the second, the individual is part of an **aspiration group.**

Reference groups can also be viewed negatively. For example, an individual may belong to or join a group and then reject the group's values. This type of group would be a **disclaimant group** for the individual.[11] Moreover, an individual may regard membership in a particular group as something to be avoided. Such a group is a **dissociative group.**

These four types of reference groups are shown at the top of Figure 16.1. Advertisers rarely appeal to the desire to avoid or disclaim a group, but they do appeal to the desire to be part of a group. Even appeals to nonconformity are made on the positive note of being different from everyone else, not on the negative note of dissociating oneself from certain groups. Marketers, therefore, tend to focus on positive reference groups, namely membership and aspiration groups.

Membership Groups

Because positive reference groups are important, Figure 16.1 further breaks down membership and aspiration groups. In the middle of Figure 16.1, positive membership groups are classified as primary or secondary and informal or formal. If a person has regular contact with certain individuals, such as family, friends, and business associates, those individuals are a *primary group.* Shopping groups, political clubs, and fellow skiers or joggers constitute a person's *secondary groups* because he or she has less frequent contact with them. Primary groups are more important to the consumer in developing product beliefs, tastes, and preferences and have a more direct influence on purchasing behavior. Reingen and his colleagues found that members of groups with the greatest contact in a variety of situations (that is, primary groups) were more likely to buy the same brands.[12] Because of their influence, these groups are more interesting to the marketer.

Groups also can be divided by whether they have a *formal* structure (a president, secretary, and treasurer) with specific roles (fund-raising, teaching, transmitting information) or an *informal* structure. The structures and roles of informal groups are implicit. This classification produces four types of membership groups as shown in Figure 16.1.

Primary Informal Groups

The family and peer groups represent **primary informal groups,** which are by far the most important groupings because of the frequency of contact and the closeness between the individual and group members. As a result, advertisers frequently portray consumption among friends and family. For example, by

FIGURE 16.1
Types of reference groups

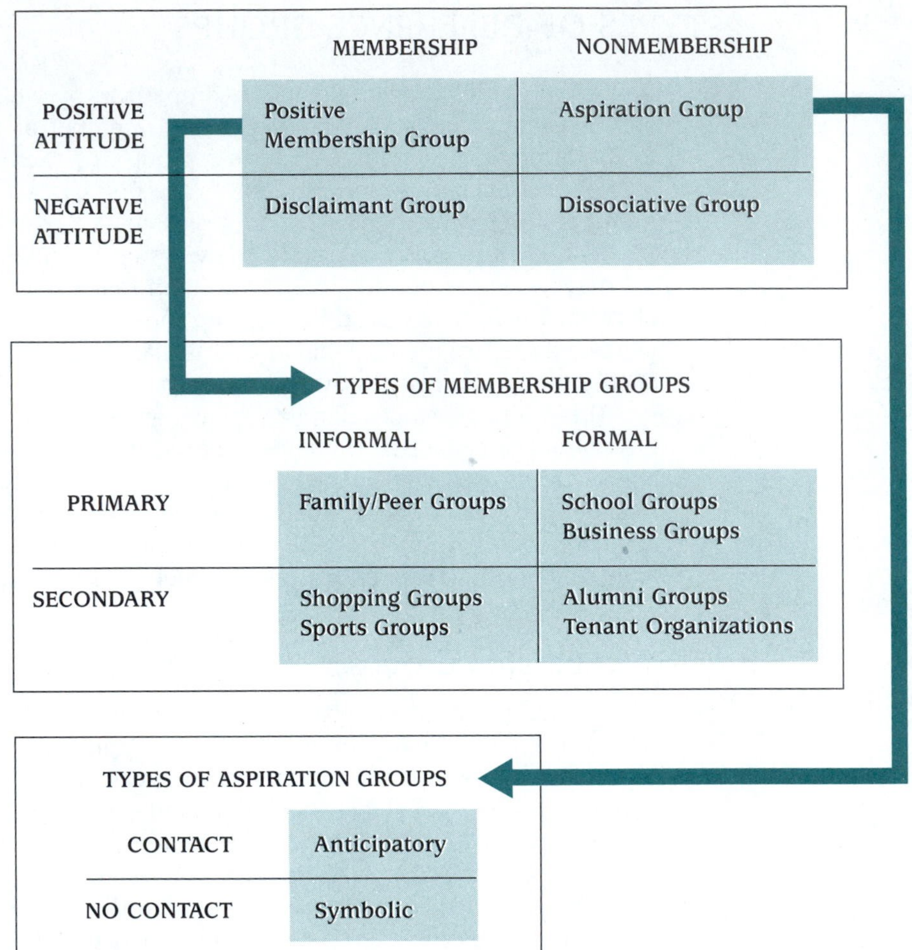

showing the Aussie family, the ad in Exhibit 16.2 tries to associate the company's hair care products with family usage.

Most Harley-Davidson rider groups are primary informal groups because of the importance of the group. Members come into frequent contact with each other, and the group is of paramount importance to members. Further, the structure and hierarchy in the group are implicit rather than formalized, with members achieving a leadership role based on a process of informal consensus.

Although each Harley group is cohesive and close-knit, these groups vary widely in their purpose, orientation, and membership. Some are regarded as "outlaw" groups in being countercultural and flouting authority, with names like Hell's Angels, Satan's Slaves, and Pagans. These are the traditional black leather set. Others are composed of semiretired or retired couples, known as "Mom and Pop bikers," with a preference for touring bikes with amenities like saddle bags, stereos,

▶EXHIBIT 16.2
Ads portraying primary and secondary group influences

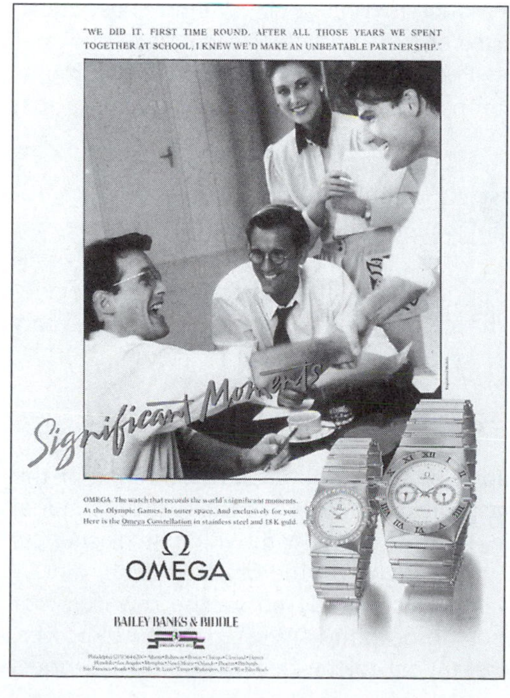

and heated handle bars. There are also born-again Christian clubs with names such as Trinity Road Riders that conduct devotional services featuring guest evangelists and a support group of bikers for recovering addicts and alcoholics.

The group resented most by the outlaw bikers is the RUBs (rich urban bikers), with more expensive clothing and highly stylized bikes, "riding . . . Harleys down the backroads of midlife crises."[13] Each of these are primary informal peer groups that differ in their norms and values and are highly important to group members.

Primary Formal Groups

Primary formal groups have a more formal structure than do family, friends, and peer groups. These are groups with which the consumer comes into regular contact but not as frequently as primary informal groups. Examples are school class groups assigned to a project or business groups working together on a daily basis. Advertisers portray membership in such groups as a means of winning product approval. For example, Omega associates its watch with positive moments for a business group. The indirect message is that Omega is associated with a successful group effort (see Exhibit 16.2).

Secondary Informal Groups

Secondary informal groups have no formal structure and meet infrequently. Examples are shopping groups or sports groups that get together once in a while. Such groups may directly influence purchases. In his study of shopping groups, Granbois examined the influence of secondary informal groups.[14] He found that when an individual shops in a group of three or more persons, compared to a smaller group, there is twice as much chance that he or she will purchase more than originally planned. Exhibit 16.2 also shows the use of secondary informal groups in advertising. The ad for Oliver Peoples eyeglass frames shows a member of a bowling group wearing the company's product.

Secondary Formal Groups

Secondary formal groups are the least important to the consumer and, therefore, to the marketer, as they meet infrequently, are structured, and are not closely knit. Examples include alumni groups, business clubs, and tenant organizations. While marketers of specialized products (such as travel agents or developers of executive programs) may have some interest in these groups, marketers of national brands generally do not portray or appeal to them.

Aspiration Groups

Two types of aspiration groups, anticipatory and symbolic, are classified at the bottom of Figure 16.1. **Anticipatory aspiration groups** are those an individual anticipates joining at a future time and, in most cases, with which he or she has direct contact. The best example is a group higher in the organizational hierarchy that an individual wishes to join. This desire is based on the rewards that have been generally accepted to be most important in Western culture: power, status, prestige, and money. Marketers appeal to the desire to enhance one's position by climbing to a higher aspiration group. Clothing and cosmetics are frequently advertised within the context of business success and prestige.

Manufacturers of men's clothing and fragrances traditionally have used such themes, and women's products increasingly rely on appeals to organizational aspirations because of the growing number of women in the work force. A good example of a direct appeal to aspiration group norms within the organization is the ad for Johnnie Walker Black Label (see Exhibit 16.7). The ad appeals to the anticipation of eventually arriving at the top in the business organization. The purchase of the product represents an acceptance of aspirational group norms.

Symbolic aspiration groups are those the individual admires but to which he or she is not likely to belong, despite acceptance of the group's beliefs and attitudes. Fisher and Price found that purchasing a product linked to the aspiration group is a means of establishing a vicarious connection with this group[15]—for example, a football fan buying a sports jacket or a jersey with the team's logo prominently displayed. An important condition for such influence is that the product is visually obvious, such as team-sponsored clothing.

http://www.sharp-usa.com/

Marketers appeal to symbolic aspirations by using celebrities to advertise certain products. The ad for the Sharp Camcorder showing Wayne Gretzky and his daughter (see Exhibit 16.3) is an example. Gretzky's appearance in the ad

►EXHIBIT 16.3 Appealing to a symbolic aspiration group

is based on his fame as a hockey star, not on his expertise in the product category. Anyone who vicariously associates with sports stars like Gretzky might be influenced to buy a Sharp Camcorder.

NATURE OF REFERENCE GROUPS

Reference groups have certain characteristics that affect their influence on consumers. They establish norms, roles, status, socialization, and power. We have seen each of these characteristics operating in the Harley-Davidson biker groups and will enumerate them below.

Norms

Norms are the (generally undefined) rules and standards of conduct the group establishes. Group members are expected to conform to these norms, which may relate to the appropriateness of clothes, eating habits, makes of cars, or brands of cosmetics.

Norms in Harley groups are fairly well defined regarding dress, maintenance requirements, assistance given to bikers within the group, and forms of addressing bikers outside the group. These norms are not documented but they are clearly understood.

Values

Values are shared beliefs among group members as to what behaviors are desirable and undesirable. As we saw in Chapters 14 and 15, values are largely defined by cultures and subcultures but they do vary substantially by family and peer group. One family may place more value on social status and another on personal enhancement independent of status.

The typical Harley rider's values include a strong dose of personal freedom and the bike as the means to achieve it. This emphasis on freedom and liberation from the constraints of society is as true for Mom and Pop bikers as for Hell's Angels. In addition, most biker groups demonstrate patriotic values, particularly since Harley-Davidson was the sole survivor of the American motorcycle industry. They regard owning a Japanese bike as unpatriotic. American flags abound at rallies and many bikes and clothing carry pro-USA messages.[16]

Roles

Roles are functions that the individual assumes or that the group assigns to the individual to attain group objectives. In group purchasing behavior, marketers can identify specific roles in an attempt to offer the best available brand or product category. The following roles have been identified in family decision making: the influencer, the gatekeeper (the individual who has the most control over the flow of information into the group), the decision maker, the purchasing agent, and the consumer.

Status

Status refers to the position the individual occupies within the group. High status implies greater power and influence. A chairperson of the board has the highest status within an organization but may be the weakest member of a weekly bridge club. Symbols of dress or ownership are frequently associated with both high and low status. For example, the chairperson's oak-paneled office symbolizes status but so does the janitor's uniform.

Status in Harley rider groups is "conferred on members according to their seniority, participation and leadership in group activities, riding expertise and experience, [and] Harley-specific knowledge."[17] Such status is represented by an informal hierarchy based on these factors.

Consumers sometimes purchase products to demonstrate status in a broader societal sense so that the message is one of wealth and implied superiority. The elegant dress and expensive car may be status symbols, but in some groups, symbolism operates in exact reversal to one's wealth and position. Jeans and small cars may be the norm among wealthy suburbanites, and large cars and more expensive clothes may be status symbols among lower socioeconomic groups.

Socialization

The process by which an individual learns the group's norms and role expectations is called **socialization.** The individual moving from one job to another must learn the informal rules and expectations from primary work groups along with the organization's formal rules and expectations.

Consumer socialization is the process by which consumers acquire the knowledge and skills necessary to operate in the marketplace. The two most important types are the socialization of children and the socialization of new residents in a community. (We will consider the socialization of children in more detail in Chapter 17 on household decision making.)

Based on their own experiences with a Harley riders group, Schouten and McAlexander describe their own process of consumer socialization as learning "models for appropriate consumption behavior from a variety of sources including other bikers and the media."[18] Because of the arms-length attitude of veteran riders, newcomers tend to rely on Harley-Davidson's promotional literature, catalogs, and corporate magazine for initial instruction regarding the appropriate "look." These commercial sources of information are reinforced by the new rider's attempts to emulate role models within the group and by pressures for conformity from the group.

Power

The influence that a group has on an individual is closely related to the group's power. Various sources of group influence have been identified[19] but three are particularly relevant for marketing strategy: expert power, referent power, and reward power.

Expert Power

To have **expert power,** an individual or group must have experience and knowledge. A consumer may accept a friend's purchase recommendation if the friend is regarded as more knowledgeable or experienced with the product. A sales representative also may be regarded as an expert source as long as he or she has established credibility with the consumer.

Referent Power

The basis for **referent power** is the individual's identification with members of the group. The greater the similarity between the individual's beliefs and attitudes and those of group members, the greater the referent power of the group. The individual either is a member of a group or may aspire to belong to a group because of common norms and values.

Reward Power

Reward power is based on the group's ability to reward the individual. The business organization can reward an employee with money and status. The family can reward the child with praise and approval. Social groups can also provide rewards in purchasing behavior. Compliments on clothes or looks provided by a relevant group member reinforce the consumer's choice.

Groups that have reward power may also have coercive power over the individual. That is, the group "giveth and taketh away." The greater the importance of the group, the greater is its power to express disapproval and even punishment. The organization has the power to fire an individual, parents to punish a child, and social groups to exclude individuals for deviant behavior.

These three sources of group influence are not mutually exclusive. Harley rider groups exert all three forms of influence on members. Veteran riders exert expert power over new members in the process of consumer socialization by demonstrating the right look, riding techniques, maintenance procedures, and language. The group exerts referent power through imitation by new members of veteran riders. And the group exerts reward power through demands for conformity and rewards members with greater status within the group for such conformity.

REFERENCE GROUP INFLUENCES ON CONSUMERS

The three types of group power suggest the ways reference groups influence consumer choice.[20] First, expert power suggests **informational influence.** The testimonial of an expert in an advertisement or the experiences of a knowledgeable friend are informative communications. Second, referent power suggests that groups have **comparative influence** in permitting a comparison of the individual's beliefs, attitudes, and behavior to those of the group. As referents, groups provide the consumer with the basis for evaluating his or her self-image. Third, reward power suggests that reference groups have **normative influence** by directly influencing attitudes and behavior based on group norms and encouraging compliance with these norms.

Table 16.1 shows each type of influence within the context of consumer behavior by citing the type of influence exerted on the consumer, the objectives for the consumer, the basis for group influence, and the effects on behavior.[21]

Informational Influence

A consumer will accept information from a group if he or she considers the group a credible source of information and expertise and if he or she believes the information will enhance knowledge about product choices.[22] As we saw in the Harley rider's socialization process, information can be obtained directly from group members the consumer regards as knowledgeable or by observing the behavior of group members.

Consumers are more likely to seek expert advice from personal sources such as friends and neighbors than from commercial sources such as advertising because they regard personal sources as more trustworthy. Consumers may regard a manufacturer's advertising claim with suspicion because of the company's vested interest in promoting the product.

Table 16.1 illustrates the nature of informational influence by describing the consumer's objectives as obtaining knowledge, the condition for accepting in-

TABLE 16.1
Types of influence exerted by reference groups

Nature of Influence	Objectives	Perceived Characteristics of Source	Type of Power	Behavior
Informational	Knowledge	Credibility	Expert	Acceptance
Comparative	Self-maintenance and enrichment	Similarity	Referent	Identification
Normative	Reward	Power	Reward or coercion	Conformity

Source: Based on Robert E. Burnkrant and Alain Cousineau, "Informational and Normative Social Influence in Buyer Behavior," *Journal of Consumer Research* 2 (December 1975), p. 207. Reprinted with permission from The University of Chicago Press.

formation as credibility, the source of power as expertise, and the final behavior as acceptance of influence. Table 16.2 lists various types of statements that illustrate informational, comparative, and normative influences. Park and Lessig used the statements in a study to determine the relative importance of these three influences in the selection of 20 products.[23] Statements 1 and 2 reflect the objective of seeking information from expert sources or friends and neighbors with reliable information. In addition, observation (Statement 3) is regarded as an important source of information.

There are two conditions under which informational influence is likely to be most important. First is when there is social, financial, or performance risk in buying the product.[24] A consumer buying a car will seek information from knowledgeable friends, relatives, or salespeople because of the social visibility of a car, the costs of buying, and possible mechanical failures. In this case, the advice of

TABLE 16.2
Conditions reflecting informational, comparative, and normative influences

Informational Influence

1. The individual seeks information about various brands of the product from an independent group of experts, or from those who work with the product as a profession.
2. The individual seeks brand-related knowledge and experience (such as how Brand A's perfume compares to Brand B's) from those friends, neighbors, relatives, or work associates who have reliable information about the brands.
3. The individual's observation of what experts do influences his or her choice of a brand (such as observing the type of car that police drive or the brand of TV that repair people buy).

Comparative Influence

4. The individual feels that the purchase or use of a particular brand will enhance the image that others have of him or her.
5. The individual feels that the purchase of a particular brand helps show others what he or she is or would like to be (such as an athlete, successful business person, etc).
6. The individual feels that those who purchase or use a particular brand possess the characteristics that he or she would like to have.
7. The individual sometimes feels that it would be nice to be like the type of person advertisements show using a particular brand.

Normative Influence

8. The individual's decision to purchase a particular brand is influenced by the preferences of people with whom he or she has social interaction.
9. The individual's decision to purchase a particular brand is influenced by the preferences of family members.
10. The desire to satisfy the expectations that others have of him or her has an impact on the individual's brand choice.

Source: Adapted from C. Whan Park and V. Parker Lessig, "Students and Housewives: Differences in Susceptibility to Reference Group Influence," *Journal of Consumer Research* 4 (September 1977), p. 105. Reprinted with permission from The University of Chicago Press.

an expert is probably more important than that of a referent. Second, if the individual has limited knowledge or experience regarding the product, informational influence is likely to be most important. A consumer with little knowledge of technical products such as computers, cellular phones, or fax machines is likely to seek expert advice.

Marketing studies provide evidence of the importance of personal sources of information. A study by Robertson found that personal sources were more important than commercial sources for purchases of small appliances and were somewhat more important for food items.[25] This study shows that expert power may be based on the usage and experience of friends and neighbors as well as on professional expertise.

Comparative Influence

Consumers constantly compare their attitudes to those of members of important groups. In so doing, they seek to support their own attitudes and behavior by associating themselves with groups with which they agree and by dissociating themselves from groups with which they disagree. As a result, the basis for comparative influence is in the process of comparing oneself to other members of the group and of judging whether the group would be supportive.

For example, if a family moves into a new home and meets new neighbors, the parents might compare the neighbors' attitudes toward political issues, education, and child rearing with their own. The parents also identify brands and products the neighbors purchase. New residents naturally will be attracted to neighbors who are similar to themselves because those neighbors reinforce existing attitudes and behavior. This is the main reason why neighborhoods are made up of people with similar social and economic characteristics.

Table 16.1 shows that comparative influence is a process of self-maintenance and enrichment. The individual's objective is to enhance his or her self-concept by associating with groups that will provide reinforcement and ego gratification. The source of power is referent power, and the individual's behavior toward the group is one of identification. Table 16.2 shows that the conditions relating to comparative influence deal with the enhancement of an individual's self-image through membership in a group (Statements 4 and 5) or identification with other people who are liked and admired as members of an aspiration group (Statements 6 and 7).

Comparative influence implies that those being influenced should have characteristics similar to those doing the influencing. A study by Moschis found that consumers are likely to seek information from friends viewed as similar to themselves and to regard such sources as credible.[26] The study concluded that advertisers should try to use spokespersons whom consumers perceive as being similar to themselves (that is, "typical consumers"). The notion of similarity between influencer and influencee also extends to customer-salesperson interactions. Several studies have found that when a customer sees the salesperson as similar in terms of tastes, attitudes, and even religion, the salesperson is likely to be effective.[27]

Comparative influence may also be due to proximity. Several studies have shown that influencers and influencees tend to live close to each other.[28] One study of elderly residents of a retirement community found that 81 percent of the exchange of information and advice about a new product occurred between persons who live on the same floor.[29]

Normative Influence

Normative influence refers to the influence a group exerts on its members to conform to its norms and expectations.

Conditions for Conformity

A consumer is motivated to conform to the norms and behavior of the group if:

- *The individual is committed to the group and values membership in it.*[30] In general, Harley owners are highly committed to their biker groups. The less committed the individual, the less the pressure to comply. Groups identified with disdain by regular bikers such as the RUBs (rich urban bikers) and SEWERS (suburban weekend riders) are less likely to have the close-knit structure of some outlaw groups and committed Mom and Pop bikers. As a result, there is less pressure to comply to modes of dress or to accept the status hierarchy of the group.
- *The group provides significant rewards for compliance and punishment for lack of compliance.* The primary reward for compliance with group norms is acceptance. One study found that consumers used friends and relatives as sources of information for products because they provided positive social interaction.[31] The greater the commitment to the group, the greater the importance of rewards and punishment. To the highly committed biker, moving up in the pack is going to be much more important than it is to the RUB or SEWER. Similarly, being ignored by the group for wearing what is regarded as nerdy clothes or making ingratiating remarks is going to be less devastating to the RUBs and SEWERs than to the outlaws.
- *The individual's behavior in conforming is visible to members of the group.*[32] Such rewards are more likely if the behavior is visible. A group can exert normative influence in the purchase of clothes, furniture, and appliances because these items are visible. An important factor in Harley-Davidson's decision to leverage its name and logo into clothing and accessory products was the visibility of these items in Harley groups and the fact that wearing them was a form of free advertising for the company. Whyte demonstrated the importance of visibility in his study of a Philadelphia suburb's purchase of air conditioners.[33] Re-

> search indicated the direct influence of friends and neighbors in purchasing the product, but the most apparent influence was seeing an air conditioner in a neighbor's window. Normative influence may also occur for items such as mouthwash and denture adhesive, even though the items themselves are not visible, because of fear that lack of use may be visible (bad breath, loose dentures).

Visibility is less important in exerting informational and comparative influence because, in these cases, the objective is not conformity but knowledge and self-enhancement. The consumer could obtain information from the group and gain satisfaction in identifying with the group without any overt action.

According to Table 16.1, normative influence is based on the individual's desire to receive the rewards of the group. The basis for power is reward or coercion; the resulting behavior toward the group is conformity and compliance. Table 16.2 indicates that conditions reflecting normative influence deal with a desire to conform to group preferences (Statements 8 and 9) and to satisfy the expectations of group members (Statement 10).

Conformity in Consumer Behavior

Conformity to group norms is the ultimate goal of normative influence, as it means that consumers will buy the brands and product categories the group approves. Marketers are interested in such imitative behavior because it implies a snowball effect once the most influential members of a group accept products. The idea of "keeping up with the Joneses" reflects imitative behavior.

Various studies have confirmed that individuals do imitate group behavior. These studies have been largely experimental and were inspired by social psychology studies demonstrating individual conformity to group norms. One of the most famous of these experiments brought groups of seven to nine college students together to judge the length of lines drawn on a card.[34] All group members but one were instructed to give the same incorrect response. The subject, who was not aware of the experiment, was confronted with the obviously incorrect choice of a unanimous group. In 37 percent of the cases, the subject went along with the group, even though the choice appeared to contradict his or her senses.

In an experiment by Venkatesan, three identical men's suits labeled "A," "B," and "C" were described to respondents as being of different quality and manufacture.[35] Three of four students in each group were told to pick Suit B. In the majority of cases, the fourth student also picked Suit B.

Social Multiplier Effect

The desire to emulate the behavior of a group often leads an individual to buy the same brand or product. Such imitative behavior reflects a **demonstration principle.** First formulated by economist James Duesenberry,[36] the demonstration principle states that with the American consumer's increased mobility and purchasing power, consumers increasingly will come into contact with new products and will have the purchasing power to buy them. For example, when compact disc players were first marketed, once one family bought one, friends and neighbors came into contact with the product. Since these people were likely to have the same level of purchasing power, they also bought CD players. In turn, other individuals came into contact with the recently acquired product, and the pattern of ownership spread within the group and to other groups. The demonstration principle is similar to the idea of "keeping up with the Joneses" because of the element of social pressure to own new products. We will refer to it as the **social multiplier effect** because ownership increases in multiples as a function of group influence and product visibility.

One of the best examples of the social multiplier effect is a 1928 ad for Victrola (Exhibit 16.4). The headline "Keeping Up With the Joneses" was the main appeal for buying the new phonograph player. The copy illustrates the social multiplier in action: "The day it came, we celebrated by having the neighbors come over."

The social multiplier effect illustrates the volatility of group influence in the American economy. Certain brands or product categories may be highly visible today and representative of group norms, but 5 or 10 years from now such influence may become minimal. Because of the social multiplier effect, products

▶EXHIBIT 16.4
A 1928 example of the social multiplier effect

that once were considered a luxury (refrigerators, automobiles, air conditioners) are now considered a necessity. Others such as portable radios and record players have become obsolete due to technological advances. To a large degree, the social multiplier effect has powered the American economy to higher standards of living.

Rejection of Conformity

Many individuals will react to group pressures for conformity by rejecting them. As we will see, rejection of group pressures to conform has major societal implications, particularly for teenagers. If society could increase the teenager's willingness to reject peer pressures to smoke, drink, and take drugs it could save millions of lives and billions of dollars in medical expenses.

The likelihood of rejecting pressures to conform depends on:

- *The strength of the individual's value system.* If the group sanctions behavior that contradicts deep-seated norms and values, group pressures are likely to be rejected. The teenager that believes that cigarettes are life-threatening and has seen a parent die of lung cancer is unlikely to accept peer pressures to start smoking.
- *The intensity of group pressures to conform.* When group pressures become too intense, consumers may reject group norms and demonstrate independence. In the experiment where all but one respondent purposefully misjudged the length of a line, when pressure was put on the individual to go along with the other three, the chances of conforming actually went down. Students reacted negatively to such pressure. This situation, known as **reactance,** suggests that consumers will conform to group pressures only to a certain point.[37]
- *The commitment of the individual to the group.* As we saw, the greater the individual's commitment to the group, the greater the likelihood he or she will conform to group norms. But conflict arises if the group is highly important to the individual yet contradicts the individual's value system. According to *balance theory,* to resolve this conflict, the individual will either reduce commitment to the group and maintain his or her values, maintain commitment to the group and modify values so as to conform, or some combination of the two. The teenager cited above is unlikely to yield to pressures to smoke and will probably reduce commitment to the group.
- *The value placed on individuality.* Many people place a high value on individuality and lack of conformity. They like to stand apart from the crowd yet may not be totally divorced from group membership. Schouten and McAlexander encountered a member of the Hell's Angels in Amsterdam who clearly desired to stand apart from the traditional mode of dress and behavior of the group. This individual unabashedly rode his chopper in full colors (i.e., wearing his official club insignias)

> over a white T-shirt, flowered bermuda shorts, and red converse sneakers instead of the uniform black T-shirt, greasy blue jeans, and black boots of the outlaw biker.[38] Most Hells Angels wouldn't be caught dead in this outfit. This biker was obviously unwilling to compromise his independence in the interest of conformity.

Some advertisers seek to identify their products with such independence and lack of conformity.

Information, Comparison, or Conformity?

Is group influence on consumer purchasing behavior due primarily to the information supplied by groups, the identification with groups, or the pressure that groups bring to bear on individuals? The obvious answer is that all three components influence consumers. The type of influence that is most important, however, may be a function of the type of product being evaluated.

Type of Influence by Product

Park and Lessig measured the relative effects of informational, comparative, and normative influence in the purchase of 20 products.[39] They asked a sample of college students to rate the 20 products by the statements listed in Table 16.2. The types of products most likely to be subject to informational influences are those that are technologically complex (autos, color TVs, air conditioners) or require objective informational criteria for selection (insurance, physicians, headache remedies). The products most subject to comparative influence are those that serve as a means of self-expression and identity (autos, clothing, furniture). Automobiles and clothing are also subject to normative influence because they are visible and are, therefore, a means of conforming to group norms.

Schouten and McAlexander found that motorcycles and related clothing were subject to all three influences: informational because of the technical complexity of motorcycles, comparative because of self-identity with the product, and normative because of the visibility of motorcycles and clothing as a means of identifying conformity.[40]

Influence by Product Category versus Brand

After examining various studies of group influence, Bourne found that groups could exert influence on the ownership of a product, the decision on what brand to buy, or both.[41] By focusing on two product characteristics—product exclusivity and visibility—Bourne was considering normative rather than comparative or informational influence. Bourne determined that groups would be more likely to influence the *product decision* for exclusive products such as yachts or sports cars because owning such products would in itself make a statement. If the product were visible but not exclusive (owning a watch), groups would be more likely to influence the *brand decision* such as buying a Rolex watch. In this case, it is the visibility of the brand rather than the product that makes it subject to group influence.

If the product is not exclusive or visible, consumers will make purchase decisions based on product attributes alone. Energy efficiency or size is more likely to influence the choice of a refrigerator rather than a neighbor's comments.

What Is the Most Important Component of Group Influence?

Evidence regarding the relative importance of information, comparison, and conformity is mixed. The studies of comparative and normative influence suggest that consumers use groups as a means of identification and reward, but they may well be using groups more for the information supplied.

Hansen believed that many of the studies purporting to find conformity to group norms actually may represent the processing of information supplied by groups.[42] A consumer's tendency to buy the products and brands the group purchases can be interpreted in two ways: (1) conformity to group norms or (2) an assertion of quality (the uniformity of purchasing behavior within the group shows that the brand is in fact highest in quality). The latter case does not represent conformity; it represents action based on credible information.

Burnkrant and Cousineau supported the notion that groups are more important in supplying information than in influencing compliance to group norms.[43] They found that the consumer's belief in the credibility of information provided by peers influenced the ratings of brands of coffee more than any pressure to conform to group norms. Similarly, Park and Lessig found that informational influence was more important to college students than comparative or normative influence for most of the products studied.[44] Ward and Reingen also supported the importance of groups as sources of information rather than of conformity. They found that group members moved toward the group's position not because of pressures to conform to group norms, but because of discussions and "shared knowledge that leads to a change in beliefs."[45] Summarizing these studies, Kaplan and Miller conclude that "in general, informational influence produces more frequent and stronger shifts (in beliefs) than does normative influence."[46]

These findings suggest that marketers should place more emphasis on the group as a source of information than as a source of compliance. Ads should picture typical consumers citing their experiences and providing information on relevant product attributes. Rather than picturing friends and neighbors marveling at a sparkling floor (compliance to group norms of cleanliness), ads might be more relevant if they show group members transmitting information on the product to the prospective buyer. Such an approach shifts the emphasis from conformity to information. An ad for Mannington floors shows attendees at a wedding reception admiring the floor in the couple's new home. The studies cited suggest that this may be the wrong approach. A "typical consumer" approach may be more effective by supplying information. Consumers are more likely to identify with typical consumers than with models used to simulate group influence. Using typical consumers tends to lessen the skepticism many consumers have regarding advertising claims.

Group Influence versus Product Evaluation

If group influence is such an important source of information, does it supplant objective product evaluation? That is, do many consumers say, "Since most of my friends recommend it, I may as well use it because it must be good," and as a result forego a process of brand evaluation? In many cases, yes; *reference group influence can be a substitute for brand evaluation.*

Rosen and Olshavsky's study supports the likelihood that group recommendations often supplant brand evaluation.[47] They studied brand selection for two disparate product categories, pizza and stereos. They considered three possibilities: that consumers will (1) go along with the group's recommendations without evaluating brand alternatives, (2) evaluate alternative brands, or (3) rely on group recommendations to narrow the choice to a few brands and then evaluate these brands.

They found that group recommendations outweighed brand attribute evaluations for both product categories. That is, in most cases, consumers either totally relied on the group's recommendations or used these recommendations to narrow the choice to a few brand alternatives. Surprisingly, this was as true for a high-risk product such as a stereo as for a low-risk product such as pizza. Based on such evidence, Moschis concluded that as a result of relying on peers for information, "consumers often choose products without evaluating them on the basis of objective attributes."[48]

STRATEGIC APPLICATIONS OF REFERENCE GROUP INFLUENCES

Marketers have used the three types of group influence—informational, comparative, and normative—to develop both advertising and personal selling strategies.

Advertising Strategies

Advertising strategies have portrayed informational influence using expert spokespersons, comparative influence by portraying typical consumers, and normative influence by showing the rewards of using a product or the risks of not using it.

Portraying Informational Influence

Marketers have tried to convey informational influence through advertising as a counterweight to the dominant influence of friends and relatives. They have attempted to exert informational influence by using expert spokespersons to communicate product features and performance.

Marketers have used two approaches to portraying expert spokespersons. One is to portray the role the expert plays—a doctor for a medical product or an engineer for a technical product. A second approach is to show a celebrity http://www.warner-lambert.com/

who has expertise in the product area—a tennis star's testimonial for a tennis racket, for example. Exhibit 16.5 shows both approaches. The ad for Benadryl is a tongue-in-cheek portrayal of expert medical roles. Even though children are portrayed, the message is clear: the medical profession stands behind Benadryl as a safe and effective allergy medication for children.

The second approach uses celebrities to provide product testimonials. Such testimonials are accepted only to the degree that consumers view the spokesperson as being an expert on the product. Exhibit 16.6 shows Andre Agassi in an ad for Nike tennis apparel. Consumers are likely to view a testimonial from Agassi for the product category as credible.

http://www.gm.com/
http://www.generalmills.com/

Advertisers also create their own experts. General Motors has established Mr. Goodwrench as an expert in car maintenance. General Mills created Betty Crocker in 1921, and she has become "a sort of 'First Lady of Food,' the most highly esteemed home service authority in the nation."[49] Also, Reuben H. Donnelley, the leading source of direct-mail coupons, has established Carol Wright as the expert spokesperson on how to achieve value through coupon redemptions.

EXHIBIT 16.5
Conveying informational influence

Portraying an expert role

Using an expert spokesperson

Portraying Comparative Influence

http://www.ford.com/

Advertisers can portray comparative influence by using two types of referents. One is an *actual referent* in the form of a "typical consumer" who persuades consumers that people like themselves have chosen the advertised product. The typical consumer is a referent because, by citing common needs and problems, he or she is portrayed as similar to the prospective purchaser. The Ford ad in Exhibit 16.6 is an example. The individuals pictured are typical consumers whom Ford asked to brainstorm regarding what they want in a car. A consumer in the market for a car could easily identify with these individuals.

A second approach is to use a *symbolic referent,* that is, a celebrity the consumer empathizes and identifies with because he or she is likeable or attractive. The ad for the Sharp Camcorder showing Wayne Gretzky and his daughter (see Exhibit 16.3, page 541) is an example. Gretzky's appearance in the ad is based on his fame as a hockey star, not his expertise in the product category. Anyone who identifies with sports stars like Gretzky might be influenced to buy a Sharp Camcorder.

Whereas the Ford ad depicts referents as part of a consumer's membership group, the Sharp ad shows a referent as part of the consumer's aspiration group. In the case of Ford, consumers consider themselves similar to the referent; in the case of Wayne Gretzky, consumers would like to identify with the referent.

▶EXHIBIT 16.6
Using actual versus symbolic referents in advertising

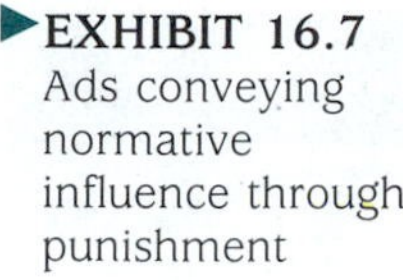

EXHIBIT 16.7
Ads conveying normative influence through punishment

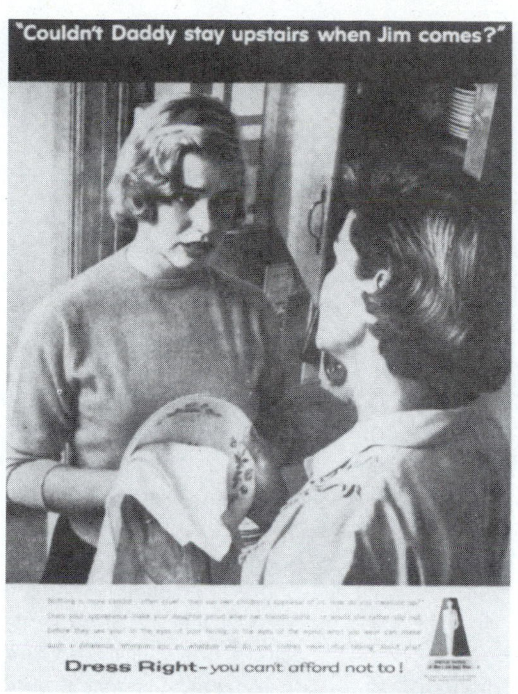

Since most consumers realize they will never meet Wayne Gretzky, he is portrayed as a symbolic referent.

Portraying Normative Influence

Marketers have tried to portray normative influence by showing group approval in advertising. Praise for a good cup of coffee, a shiny floor, glorious hair, good sherry, and a quiet and comfortable ride are all examples of advertising's simulation of social approval. In each case, an individual who is important to the consumer (spouse, neighbor, friend, business associate) has expressed approval of the consumer's choice.

Marketers have also used normative influence to show the potential results of not using the product. Poligrip uses the fear of social disapproval due to loose dentures, and Dial demonstrates the fear of group ostracism due to body odor. In each case, use of the product changes disapproval to approval, which demonstrates the fact that coercive power and reward power are linked. Such appeals use the fear of a group's coercive power to gain compliance to group norms. An ad campaign for the Men's & Boy's Wear Institute that ran in the early 1950s is a classic example of an appeal to the fear of group rejection if the product is not used. It shows a daughter who does not want her father to meet her boyfriend because she is ashamed of the way he dresses. The tagline, "Dress right, you can't afford not to," implies that poor clothes can lead to failure. Although dated, the ad is a clear use of normative influence through punishment.

STRATEGIC APPLICATIONS OF CONSUMER BEHAVIOR

▶ When Should Advertisers Use Celebrities as Experts or Referents?

Around 20 percent of all commercials use some sort of celebrity endorser, with these celebrities making about 5 percent of their income from endorsements. Celebrities are best used as experts when consumers see them as being knowledgeable about the product category and conveying legitimacy in their message. Phil Mahre, the Olympic ski champion, is an effective spokesperson for K2 skis; Mark Messier for Louisville hockey products, Charles Barkley for Nike basketball sneakers, and Monica Seles for Yonex tennis rackets. Expert spokespersons do not necessarily have to represent products associated with their professions. Consumers see Jimmy Connors and Nolan Ryan as expert spokespersons for analgesics because consumers believe these aging sports stars must know what they are talking about when it comes to relieving aches and pains.

Celebrities have been used as referents when they come across as likeable and attractive; that is, they are someone with whom many consumers would like to identify. The product has to be one that lends itself to identification with the celebrity as a referent, however. Bill Cosby was an effective referent for Jell-O pudding pops because the ads were directed to fans of his TV show who saw him as a likeable family role model. Elizabeth Taylor is an effective referent for her perfume line because of the strong emotional bond with her fans.

When advertisers stray from the principles that experts must communicate knowledge and legitimacy and that referents must communicate likeability and attractiveness, they get into trouble. Bill Cosby bombed as a referent for E. F. Hutton, the brokerage house, because his good guy image did not convey any special expertise or credibility for financial services. When Cosby intoned the tagline "When E. F. Hutton talks everybody listens," one observer said "When Cosby talked, nobody listened," meaning that celebrities can serve to reflect group influence only when they are relevant role models for the product.

Of even more concern, the use of referent spokespersons could backfire if they lose their appeal. O. J. Simpson's value as a referent spokesperson for Hertz was lost overnight with the allegation that he murdered his wife. Similarly, Marky Mark's value as a spokesperson for Calvin Klein apparel dissipated when it was discovered that he had made a series of racial slurs in his younger days. These risks have led companies like Diet Coke, Hershey, and Levi Strauss to use deceased celebrities such as Humphrey Bogart, Marilyn Monroe, and James Dean as referent spokespersons. They are sure to remain likeable and to stay out of trouble.

Sources: "Marketers Are Always Looking for Good Pitchers," *Brandweek* (February 26, 1996), p. 27; "New Tactics on Celebrity Endorsement," *The New York Times* (April 3, 1992), p. D5.

Personal Selling Strategies

Marketers also use the three types of reference group influences to develop sales strategies to influence customers. Informational influence is used when the salesperson is considered to be knowledgeable about the product category and a legitimate source of information. Such influence reflects expert power. Comparative influence applies when a consumer perceives the salesperson as someone with similar needs and characteristics. Under such circumstances, the salesperson is likely to exert influence through referent power. Normative influence applies to the relative bargaining power of the buyer and seller to achieve favorable terms of sale. Such influence reflects reward or coercive power.

Sales Strategy Implications of Informational and Comparative Influence

Applications of informational and comparative influence suggest two general approaches to customer-salesperson interactions:

1. The salesperson can be an objective source of information (expert influence).
2. The salesperson can attempt to reinforce the customer's ego and social needs by demonstrating similar needs, concerns, and predispositions (referent influence).

Weitz has attempted to determine the conditions in which salespersons should establish expertise rather than similarity.[51] Expertise should be established if (1) the salesperson has the knowledge and credentials to be seen as an expert, (2) the customer is engaged in a high-risk, complex buying task requiring expertise, and (3) the salesperson does not regularly sell to the buyer, which creates a need to impress the buyer. Conversely, similarity is best established when the salesperson is in fact similar, the buying task is simple and low risk, and the salesperson regularly sells to the buyer.

Based on findings such as these, expertise appears to be more important in a problem-solving approach, particularly for complex goods such a personal computers or music systems due to their greater complexity and variety. In addition, many consumer services fall into this category. For example, the variety of financial offerings available to consumers requires more expertise on the part of insurance agents, stockbrokers, and financial advisers. Whether the emphasis is on expertise or similarity, the burden falls on the salesperson to develop a proper impression of the customer and to formulate a sales strategy accordingly.

Sales Strategy Implications of Bargaining Power

Normative sales influence rests on **bargaining power,** that is, the degree of influence the buyer and seller have on each other to achieve favorable terms of sale. Bargaining is most likely to occur when there is a need to negotiate price, delivery, and product specifications. On this basis, bargaining is likely for products such as cars, appliances, furniture, real estate, and second-hand items. In such cases, the consumer's willingness and ability to bargain may directly influence the sales outcome. One study found that the major reason certain customers can obtain items for lower prices is because of their bargaining strength and knowledge.[52]

Not only does the process of bargaining heighten the complexity of the customer-salesperson interaction, but it also gives rise to conflicts over economic goals. Research has focused on the types of bargaining strategies buyers and sellers develop to resolve conflicts and reach agreement over terms of sale. Two broad strategies are competitive and coordinative bargaining behavior. In **competitive bargaining behavior,** the party with stronger bargaining power exerts that power to force concessions from the weaker party. In **coordinative bargaining behavior,** the parties approach bargaining in a problem-solving manner to achieve these goals. Bargaining power is less likely to be exerted in an arbitrary manner.[53]

Several studies have confirmed that satisfactory sales agreements are most likely to occur when coordinative strategies are used. Competitive bargaining power results in sales agreements under some conditions. According to Schurr and Ozanne, the factor most likely to lead to agreement in competitive bargaining is trust in the seller. Even though a buyer expects tough bargaining, if the buyer trusts the seller, agreement on the terms of sale is likely.[54]

SOCIETAL IMPLICATIONS OF REFERENCE GROUP INFLUENCES

The portrayals of reference group influences in this chapter have been generally positive: as sources of information, as means of self-identification, and as sources for rewards for conformity. But as we saw, at times group pressures may conflict with an individual's value system or pressures to conform may be intense.

These issues become most important when it comes to the consumption of potentially harmful products—drugs, cigarettes, and alcohol. Two issues arise in this respect: (1) trying to discourage peer group pressures to use these products and (2) marketers' responsibilities in portraying peer group influence.

Discouraging Conformity

Teenagers are particularly susceptible to peer group pressures to conform because of typical stages of adolescent rebellion from parental authority and a search for self-identity. Peer groups are particularly important to teenagers, and fears of disapproval and rejection for not conforming to the group are common. If the use of drugs, cigarettes, or alcohol is compatible with group values, pressures to conform by using these products may be severe.

Rose, Bearden, and Teel examined how pressures to conform influence illicit drug and alcohol consumption among high school and college students.[55] To demonstrate the strength of peer pressures, even for harmful products, more than two-thirds of the students in the study were concerned with the implications of accepting or rejecting drugs and alcohol in the eyes of their peers. The researchers felt that if they could find ways to encourage young people to seek explanations for a peer group sanctioning illicit drug and alcohol use, then the pressure to conform might be reduced. That is, if group members could explain why their peer group sanctions such illicit use, then they might find it easier to reject group pressure.

Rose and his colleagues used *attribution theory* to examine students' explanations for the acceptance by their group of illicit drug and alcohol usage.[56] As we saw in Chapter 10, attribution theory says that consumers seek to attribute causes to events (that is, why the group encourages drug usage). When an individual could attribute reasons for a group's use of drugs and alcohol by saying "they just want to get high" or "they don't think they will get caught," such attributions encouraged the individual to dissent from the group's actions. Such attributions provide a rationale for the potential dissenter to refuse to go along with the group.

The implication is that if plausible reasons for the group's deviant behavior are provided, that makes it easier to dissent. Current public service campaigns based on the slogan "Just Say No" or Bob Dole's theme to discourage drug use in the 1996 presidential election—"Just Don't Do It"—may stress assertiveness, but do not really provide an attribution for rejecting group pressures. Rose, Bearden and Teel's research suggests that campaigns should emphasize themes like "If your friends want to get high, that doesn't mean you have to," or "Fitting in with your friends is no reason to drink." In each case, the reason for the group's actions is directly addressed.

Marketers' Portrayal of Peer Group Influence

Marketers frequently portray peer groups in social situations in print ads for cigarettes and alcohol, implying that the product is "in" with the group. In most cases, the groups portrayed are young adults. A key issue is whether such advertising is socially responsible. In fostering group identity with their brands, marketers are encouraging liquor and cigarette consumption among young adults. The decision by some liquor companies to lift the self-imposed prohibition against TV advertising is likely to magnify concerns about portraying peer groups in commercials.

On the other side of the coin, it could be argued that young adults are subject to group influence for a wide variety of products and should be free to choose the brands and products they want to consume. But liquor and cigarette commercials will be seen by teenagers and young children, and are likely to make an impression.

Overall, marketers of cigarettes, liquor, and beer must be sensitive to portraying group acceptance of their products, especially among younger consumers.

SUMMARY

This chapter focused on reference group influences on consumer behavior. Reference groups can be classified into membership groups and aspiration groups. Membership groups can be classified further into formal and informal groups and primary and secondary groups. By far the most influential groups are informal primary groups, represented by family and peer groups. Aspiration groups can also be divided into groups in which the consumer anticipates membership (anticipatory groups) and groups that the consumer admires at a distance (symbolic groups).

These group designations are important, as advertisers frequently portray group influences directly (for example, one friend advising the other) or employ spokespersons to influence consumer aspirations.

Reference groups serve a number of important functions. They provide norms of conduct, assign roles within the group to individuals, designate status positions within the group, and are a vehicle for consumer socialization. They also influence individuals by exerting three types of power: expert, referent, and reward.

These three types of power correspond to the three types of influence. Groups exert informational (expert) influence, comparative (referent) influence, and normative (reward) influence. Informational influence depends on the credibility of the source of information, comparative influence on the degree of similarity between the consumer and influencer, and normative influence on the levels of reward or punishment meted out by the group.

Marketers have emphasized normative influence most, since it results in conformity to group norms. Conformity is most likely when products are visible and related to group norms. Such conformity may produce a social multiplier effect: one consumer buys a product, and others come into contact with the consumer and are influenced to buy. Their purchase in turn results in a spread of ownership throughout the group and, eventually, to other groups.

Marketers have used informational, comparative, and normative influence in establishing advertising and personal selling strategies. In advertising, informational influence is portrayed through expert spokespersons, comparative influence through typical consumers, and normative influence by showing the rewards of using a product or the risks of not using it. In personal selling, informational influence is established by the expertise of the salesperson, comparative influence by the similarity of the salesperson to the customer, and normative influence by the relative bargaining power of the salesperson and the customer.

Reference group influences raise certain issues regarding the potential negative effects of groups in influencing individuals to consume potentially harmful products such as cigarettes, drugs, and alcohol. Public service advertising should develop campaigns that encourage rejection of peer group norms that sanction use of harmful products. Cigarette and liquor advertisers should also avoid ads that portray acceptance of these products in a group context.

In the next chapter, we will consider one of the key sources of group influence: the family.

QUESTIONS

1. When are reference groups most likely to exert influence?
2. What is meant by the "looking glass self"? How does this concept affect consumer behavior?
3. What is the distinction between aspiration groups and membership groups? Are both types of groups relevant for marketers? In what ways?
4. What is the distinction between symbolic and anticipatory aspiration groups? How do the Wayne Gretzky ad in Exhibit 16.3 and the Ford ad in Exhibit 16.6 depict one or the other of these group influences?
5. How do Harley rider groups reflect the key characteristics of reference groups in regard to norms, values, roles, status, and socialization?

6. How are expert, referent, and reward power translated into informational, comparative, and normative influences?
7. What do we mean by "reactance"? Cite some examples. Is a marketer likely to illustrate reactance in advertising? Why or why not?
8. What do we mean by the "social multiplier effect"? What conditions are required for the social multiplier to take effect? Cite some examples of the workings of the social multiplier.
9. What types of products are most likely to be subject to informational influence, comparative influence, and normative influence? Why?
10. Under what conditions should an advertiser use a spokesperson as a referent? As an expert? What are the risks of each strategy?
11. Under what conditions are a salesperson's (a) referent power or (b) expert power likely to be more important in influencing the customer?
12. What are the implications of the research by Rose, Bearden and Teel cited on p. 561 for attempting to discourage conformity to negative group influences such as drug, alcohol, and cigarette consumption?

RESEARCH ASSIGNMENTS

1. How are spokespersons used on the Internet? Do you believe they are effective in this medium?
2. Give examples of how the Internet is used to influence consumers in informational, comparative, or normative ways.
3. Ask a group of students to evaluate four identical unlabeled cans of soda. Four students should do the evaluation at the same time. Have three students act as "ringers" and ask them to state a preference for the same can of soda. The fourth student will be an actual respondent. Conduct about 20 such tests so that there are 20 actual respondents. In one-half of the cases, the ringers should express a preference in a low-keyed manner. In the other half, they should be adamant about their preference (for example, "Wow, this soda is much better!"). One would expect that on a random basis, the fourth student would agree with the other three 25 percent of the time.
   - Is the proportion who conform significantly greater than the 25 percent chance expectation?
   - Is there a difference in acceptance between those who were subjected to a low-keyed preference and those who were subjected to a more definite preference?

   Once the taste test is completed, ask the actual respondents to rate themselves on (a) self-confidence and (b) predisposition to take risk (for example, "I like to try new and different things"). Do those who conformed differ from those who did not on these two characteristics?
4. Identify a salesperson who is willing to cooperate in an experiment. The salesperson could be a local merchant or a student with a job in sales. Develop a scenario in which the salesperson attempts to influence customers by (a) expressing similar interests and opinions (referent appeals), (b) acting knowledgeable (expert appeals), and (c) a combination of both. Determine the influence on the customers, using sales results or likelihood of a purchase. Which appeals were most successful? Why?

   If possible, replicate the experiment in another type of store.
   - Were the same results obtained?
   - If not, why were there differences between the two types of stores? To what extent did differences in the product categories influence the results of the experiment?

HOUSEHOLD DECISION MAKING

Chapter 17

TYSON FOODS RECOGNIZES CHILDREN'S PURCHASE INFLUENCE

The last chapter focused on the importance of reference groups in influencing a consumer's purchasing behavior. By far the most important reference group is the household, the majority of which are family units. Not only do members of a household influence one another's purchasing decisions, they are also frequently involved in making joint decisions. The frequency of joint purchasing decisions for items such as cars, furniture, appliances, and other durable and electronic products suggests the importance of studying the nature of household decision making.

This chapter focuses on both joint and individual decision making within the family. We consider:

- Traditional and nontraditional households.
- A model of household decision making.
- The relative influence of the husband and wife in household decision making.
- The parent-child interaction in the purchasing process.

http://www.tyson.com/

- The strategic implications of household influences.
- The broader societal issues involved in the consumer socialization of children.

The strategic importance of joint decisions is apparent when auto manufacturers advertise features and performance as well as style in women's magazines in recognition of their increasing influence over a traditionally male-dominant purchasing decision, or when marketers of food and household products advertise to men because of their greater involvement in shopping tasks.

Marketers have also been paying more attention to the influence of children on household decisions. With the great majority of mothers in the work force, three out of four American children now have no full-time parent at home. The greater proportion of single-parent households and dual-earning households means that adults are coming to rely more on children for shopping and meal preparation. The term *latchkey kids,* that is, children with no parent at home after school, reflects the increasing independence and more rapid consumer socialization of children. As a result, children are the prime purchase influencers for a wide array of products, even though parents are the ultimate decision makers. Their role in the household is reflected in one estimate that they exert direct or indirect purchase influence over $130 billion in household expenditures.[1]

Tyson Foods is keenly interested in childrens' influence on household decisions. It targets its Looney Tunes microwaveable meals to latchkey kids because these meals are easy to prepare, and over 80 percent of 6- to 14-year-olds use microwave ovens. Tyson realizes that children under 14 are unlikely to be the decision makers for packaged foods, but they can certainly exert influence on their parents. So, its strategy is to try to encourage children to ask their parents to buy the products. In licensing Warner Brothers' Looney Tunes characters for use on its packages, Tyson featured the characters trying to upstage each other in TV commercials to kids. Tyson advertised to parents as well to try to gain their approval when kids request Looney Tunes products. Print ads emphasize the nutritional value of the meals through the same Looney Tunes characters but are placed in adult media.

Tyson's strategy recognizes the dynamics of parent-child influences in its advertising to children. Parents are more likely to be influenced by children for a wide range of products; and even if they are not the prime decision makers, children are increasingly targeted for these products. The unresolved issues are whether such advertising to children is responsible and whether children should be encouraged to use products such as microwaveable meals.

TYPES OF HOUSEHOLDS

Our focus in this chapter is on household purchasing influences. A **household** is composed of individuals living singly or together with others in a residential unit. Since we are concerned with group influences, we will focus only on multi-person households in this chapter. The majority of households, 63 percent, are in family units. A **family** is two or more people living together who are related by blood or marriage. A family is, therefore, a category of a household.

The 99 million households in the United States in 1995 were composed of the following categories:[2]

1. Married couples with children under 18: about 25 percent of all households.
2. Married couples with children 18 and over: about 14 percent of households.
3. Married couples without children: 15 percent.
4. Single parents living with children under 18: 9 percent.
5. Unmarried couples (both heterosexual and gay) and other households (roommates, college students): 6 percent.
6. Individuals living with others (either relatives such as single parents living with children over 18 or individuals living with siblings, or nonrelatives such as roommates or college students): 6 percent.
7. People living alone: 25 percent.

Traditional Households

Households can be divided into traditional and nontraditional. Traditional households are represented by the first two categories, married couples with children, representing 39 percent of all households. A substantial number of households are in the nontraditional category, 36 percent, representing married couples without children, single-parent households, unmarried couples, and individuals living with others.

The proportion of traditional households has been decreasing steadily, from 70 percent of all households in 1950 to the current 39 percent.[3] A number of factors cited in Chapter 12 explain this decrease: higher divorce rates, later marriages, and a decreasing birthrate.

Traditional families can further be categorized as nuclear or extended. **Nuclear families** are married couples with one or more children under 18, and **extended families** are nuclear families with at least one grandparent living at home. At the turn of the century, this three-generational unit (often including aunts and uncles) was the norm. A government study found that in 1900, half of all households in Boston were extended families. Today, mobility, geographic dispersion, changing patterns of immigration, and a decrease in transgenerational ties have made the extended family almost extinct. By 1976, only 4 percent of households were extended families.[4] Today, the figure is probably lower. The virtual extinction of the extended family means that nuclear and traditional families are synonymous.

More recently, developing countries such as the Philippines and Malaysia have seen a decrease in the extended family as newly wealthy couples are moving out of extended families and forming Western-style nuclear ones.

In the United States, the nuclear family is decreasing. In the 1950s, the nuclear family was the norm as portrayed in TV programs like "Leave It to Beaver" or "Ozzie and Harriet." The husband was the breadwinner, the wife took care of the home, and the children (two or more) were in grade school. Whereas close to 50 percent of households could be classified as nuclear in 1950, today about half that number fit the traditional mold.

A countertrend is the greater number of older children living with their parents. Some generation Xers are choosing to save money by living at home in the face of a tight job market. Others are moving back in with their parents. As a result, the Census Bureau is projecting that the second traditional category listed, married couples with children over 18, will grow slightly in the next 15 years.[5]

Nontraditional Households

Nontraditional households (categories 3 to 6 in the list) have increased proportionately as traditional households have declined. Let us consider each of the nontraditional household categories.

- *Married couples without children.* Many members of the baby boom generation decided to marry later. This trend was a function of the "me" orientation that began to develop in the midst of the Vietnam War and Watergate. Over time, it became the norm as more baby boomers focused on self and professional interests and delayed family formation. The later they got married, the more likely it was that they would be childless, for both biological and lifestyle reasons.

  Married couples without children have more discretionary income and a different set of purchasing priorities than the nuclear family. They are good targets for travel, entertainment, and higher priced durable goods and electronic items.
- *Single parents with children under 18.* With one of every two marriages ending in divorce and over one million divorces a year, single-parent households are likely to continue to increase. Today, 28 percent of all children live in single-parent households.[6]

  Over three-fourths of single-parent households are headed by a female. As we saw in Chapter 12, many live in poverty. Adding to the financial burden is the limited time a working parent has to spend with his or her child. Single parents are likely to spend more on their children, partly out of guilt. And, children in single-parent households are likely to have more influence over a wide range of purchases and more purchasing power.
- *Individuals living with others.* This catch-all group is also likely to grow as the number of individuals who decide not to marry or remarry increases. The proportion of married couples decreased from 75 percent

of all households in 1960 to 54 percent today.[7] One alternate to living alone is to live with another relative, with a sibling, or with a friend. In addition, single parents as well as married couples are finding that children are living with them longer to save money on housing and other necessities.

- *Unmarried couples.* This group, divided between heterosexual and homosexual couples, represents what is often referred to as an alternative lifestyle. Unmarried couples are also likely to increase in numbers. Many heterosexual couples are choosing not to follow convention and to remain unmarried. Homosexual couples have probably been undercounted by the Census Bureau in the past due to the stigma of homosexuality. As this group becomes increasingly accepted, it is also likely to increase in numbers.

  Unmarried couples tend to have higher disposable income because they are dual-earning households with higher than average income levels. As we saw in Chapter 15, gay couples are an affluent group and a good target for luxury goods. In general, unmarried couples would be good targets for discretionary expenditures on travel, entertainment, and high-priced durable goods.

http://www.census.gov/

Overall, nontraditional households are likely to continue to increase in importance relative to traditional households. One indication of this trend is the Census Bureau's projection that the nuclear family will decrease from 25 percent of all households in 1995 to 20 percent by 2010.[8]

Purchasing Patterns by Household Life Cycles

Spending patterns will vary by type of household depending on the age of household members, their marital status, and whether there are children in the household. Spending patterns will also change as a household moves from one category to another, for example, going from a young married couple without children to one with young children, teenagers, and children no longer living at home (*empty nesters*), or from a married couple with children to a divorced couple with the children rotating between two single-parent households.

These changes are not captured by the household types just described. An important dimension in understanding these *changes* in spending patterns is the **family life cycle,** that is, the progression of a household through various stages as its members get older. As noted, this progression is not only a function of age, but it also reflects income and changes in family situation that affect every facet of purchasing behavior.

The Family Life Cycle

In the mid-1960s, two researchers, William Wells and George Gubar, proposed eight stages to describe the family life cycle.[9] The stages described in Table 17.1

TABLE 17.1
The traditional family life cycle

1. ***Young Singles*** Single people under the age of 35. Incomes are low since they are starting a career, but they have few financial burdens and a high level of discretionary income.
2. ***Newly Married*** Newly married couples without children. High level of discretionary income because the wife is usually working.
3. ***Full Nest I*** Married couples with the youngest child under 6. Greater squeeze on income because of increased expenses for child care.
4. ***Full Nest II*** Married couples with children from 6 to 12. Better financial position since parents' income is rising. Most children are "latchkey kids" because both parents are working.
5. ***Full Nest III*** Married couples with teenage children living at home. Family's financial position continues to improve. Some children work part-time. Increasing educational costs.
6. ***Empty Nest I*** Children have left home and are not dependent on parental support. Parents are still working. Reduced expenses result in greatest level of savings and highest discretionary income.
7. ***Empt Nest II*** Household head has retired, so couple experiences sharp drop in income. Couple relies on fixed income from retirement plans.
8. ***Solitary Survivor*** Widow or widower with lower income and increasing medical needs.

Source: William D. Wells and George Gubar, "Life Cycle Concept in Marketing Research," *Journal of Marketing Research* 3 (November 1966), pp. 355–363.

reflect the progression of a traditional family from marriage to retirement. The categories in Table 17.1 affect both what is bought and the decision process by which it is purchased. This scheme was based on an analysis of demographic and spending data from the 1960 Census. Given its traditional focus, the concept was referred to as a *family* rather than a *household* life cycle. Until recently, it was a very useful framework for classifying families.

The Household Life Cycle

Demographic changes since 1980 resulted in the growth of nonfamily households, meaning that the relevant concept today is a **household life cycle.** As a result, researchers have suggested more modernized family life-cycle categories. For example, Murphy and Staples suggest new categories such as younger or middle-aged divorced couples and older married couples without children.[10]

Table 17.1 presents one life-cycle sequence, the traditional family life cycle. But there are hundreds of different sequences when one accounts for nontraditional categories. Table 17.2 lists several examples of nontraditional categories.

TABLE 17.2
Nontraditional household life cycles

Sequence 1
• Young married couple with children
• Young divorced parent
• Single parent with older children
• Older, unmarried
Sequence 2
• Young divorced couple without children
• Middle-aged married couple without children
• Older married couple without children
Sequence 3
• Young married couple with children
• Middle-aged divorced parent
• Middle-aged married parent with children and stepchildren
Sequence 4
• Young unmarried couple without children
• Middle-aged married couple without children
• Older married couple without children
• Widow

One is a young married couple with children that get divorced and one of the spouses never remarries (sequence 1). Another nontraditional sequence is a couple that divorces in middle age and one of the spouses remarries and establishes a family with children and stepchildren (sequence 3). Clearly, there will be different purchasing patterns if a divorced individual does or does not have children and remarries or stays single. The life cycles in both Tables 17.1 and 17.2 can be incorporated into a concept of a household life cycle. But given that one in two marriages today end in divorce,[11] the life-cycle sequences in Table 17.2 are probably more important than those in Table 17.1.

Nature of Purchases

Income constraints and family responsibilities define many of the purchase decisions of families along both the traditional and nontraditional life cycles. For example, both young singles and newly married couples have significant discretionary income, the latter because husband and wife are likely to be employed. Whereas young singles spend more on clothing, entertainment, vacations, and other leisure pursuits, newly marrieds spend more on the required trappings of a new household. One study found that they account for 41 percent of all stereo sales and 25 percent of sales of bedroom furniture.[12]

When children arrive (Full Nest I), the couple is likely to move into a new home, purchase baby-related products, and buy home appliances. Discretionary income declines. As the children grow older (Full Nest II and III), the family buys more food and household items. Parents are likely to allocate money to home improvements and to replacement of old cars and appliances. They also begin to spend more on children and teen-related items such as clothing, electronic toys, and recreational products. In the later stages of the full nest, educational costs increase.

In the empty nest stage, discretionary income increases, and parents can afford to spend more money on themselves. Spending for travel and luxury items increases. In the later stages of the empty nest and in the solitary survivor stage, parents generally retire from work. Their income begins to decrease, and they spend more on medical expenses.

The life-cycle sequences in Table 17.2 provide similar implications for purchasing patterns. Single parents are three times as likely to be females. As a result, many divorced women see a major decrease in financial resources, despite possible alimony payments. Given the limited amount of time a young single parent has to spend with his or her children, a disproportionate amount of money is likely to be spent on toys and day-care centers. As the household moves into the middle-aged single-parent category, children are likely to play an increasingly important role in shopping, meal preparation, and selection of food and household items.

There are also ramifications that arise from the change in living status. Going from a family to a single parent may mean different needs for appliances and household furnishings. If the single parent remarries, the likelihood of stepchildren increases family size and creates a whole different set of needs regarding appliance shopping expenditures. For example, larger families will mean bigger washloads and buying economy size packages in the supermarket.

Nature of Household Decision Process

The household life cycle operates in influencing the nature of decision making. Joint decision making is most likely early in the household's life cycle. As husband and wife or unmarried couples gain experience, they are willing to delegate responsibilities for decisions to each other. If a family has children, joint decisions are even less likely as time becomes more constrained and husband and wife assume specific roles.

Regarding patterns of family influence, the husband tends to be more influential in the early stages of the life cycle. Over time, the wife becomes more assertive in decision making, particularly if she is employed and has some financial leverage over decisions. The arrival of children affects family influences for the simple reason that an additional person often must be considered in the decision process. Children not only act as influencers over a wide range of decisions, but they also serve as occasional mediators in any disagreements between husband and wife. One study of vacation decisions found that children "may have the potential to influence family decisions by forming alliances with either husband or wife to produce a 'majority' position."[13]

A MODEL OF HOUSEHOLD DECISION MAKING

As we saw, households are likely to vary in the way they make their purchasing decisions depending on their stage in the life cycle. But there are certain common denominators in household decision making. Figure 17.1 presents a model of household decision making. As the model shows, household decision making is different from individual decision making because of three factors: (1) the likelihood of joint decisions, (2) different role specifications for family members in the process of decision making, and (3) the need to resolve conflicts among family members when making purchasing decisions. These three areas are highlighted in Figure 17.1.

Consider the following example of household decision making. Larry Philips, a recently divorced father, plans to take his two children, Laurie, 14, and Michael, 12, on a one-week summer vacation. Larry could make the decision on his own, but a joint decision is likely for three reasons. First, the decision is *important* to all of them. Second, the *perceived risks* of the decision (the expense, the fact that they

FIGURE 17.1

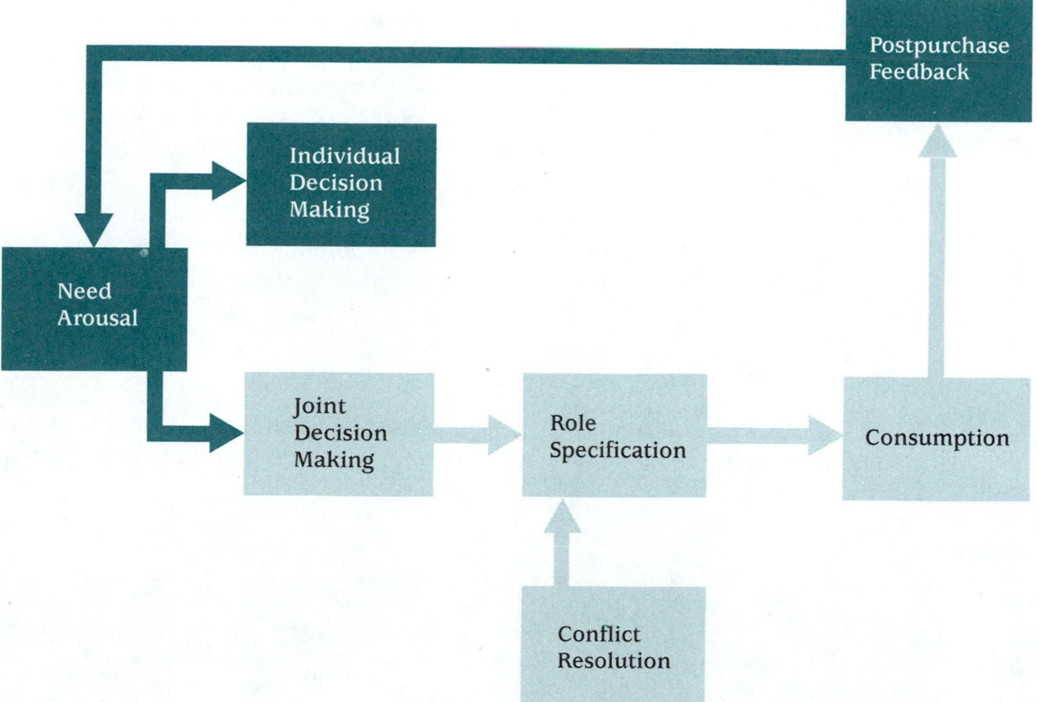

will be close together, and the importance of having a good time) are fairly high. Third, there is *no time pressure* as it is May and they plan an August vacation.

Once the need for a joint decision has been established, Figure 17.1 shows that decision roles will be specified for individuals in the household. Role specification may be explicitly assigned to an individual, or it may be assumed that an individual in the household will perform the role. If an individual makes a decision, all these roles would be fulfilled by one person.

Figure 17.2 shows five roles required in decision making. When Larry told his kids they would go on vacation, Laurie and Michael began collecting information on a motor trip through various regions of the United States. They were the initial *information gatherers* in the process of *information search* and made Larry aware of various options: a trip to national parks in Utah and Arizona, to the Columbia River basin in Oregon, and to Yosemite National Park, or the Lake Tahoe region in California.

The prime *influencers* are the children who specified the alternative vacations. The *decision maker* will be the father since he controls the logistics of the vacation and the budget. When Larry was married, the *purchasing agent* for any vacation was his wife since she worked in a travel agency and easily made the arrangements. Since they are still friends, Larry could rely on her to serve the same role and make the air, hotel, and car rental reservations.

In the process of collecting information and evaluating alternative vacation spots, a *conflict* arises between the two children. Michael would like to go to Oregon for white water rafting. Laurie would like to go to the Southwest because she is interested in Native American culture. Larry settles the conflict by deciding they will go to the Southwest this year and Oregon next year.

After their vacation, they decided they all thoroughly enjoyed it (*postpurchase evaluation*) and discuss going back to the Southwest if they can accommodate Michael and find a spot with white water rafting.

In this section, we will consider three components that distinguish family from individual decisions: joint decision making, role specification, and conflict resolution.

Joint Decision Making

Under what conditions are purchasing decisions likely to be made jointly by the family, and under what conditions are they likely to be made by an individual

FIGURE 17.2
Required roles in joint decisions

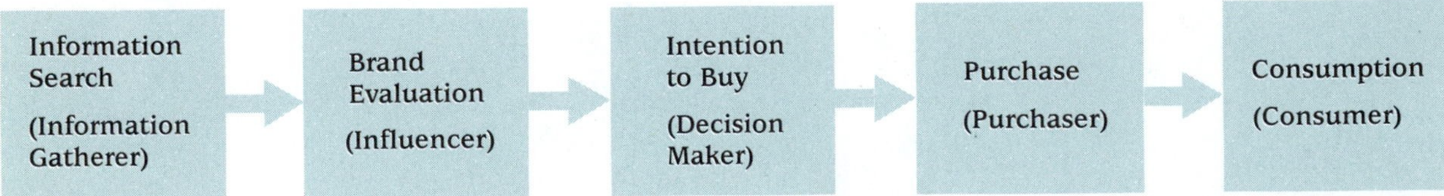

family member? Sheth found that joint decision making is more likely in the following situations:[14]

1. *When the level of perceived risk in buying is high.* Because a wrong decision will affect the whole family, a joint decision is likely to occur to reduce risk and uncertainty. A decision regarding the purchase of a new home is invariably a joint decision because of the financial risks, the social risks involved in neighborhood interaction, and the psychological risks.

Some evidence suggests that joint decision making may encourage the group to make riskier decisions because all members of the group can share the blame for a wrong decision. This so-called **risky shift phenomenon** would mean that a decision the husband and wife make may result in the purchase of a more expensive house than if either spouse made a decision alone. Woodside studied whether a risky shift occurs in consumer decisions and found that wives were more willing to make riskier decisions for a variety of products after group discussion.[15]

2. *When the purchasing decision is important to the household.* Importance is closely related to risk. However, in some cases, the decision may be important and the risk low—for example, deciding whether to return to the same vacation resort the family has gone to for the past five years. Decisions to buy major appliances and automobiles are generally joint decisions because of their importance. Decisions for low-involvement products are more likely to be made individually because it may not be worth the time and effort to engage in joint decisions for such products.

3. *When there are few time pressures.* Time pressures will encourage one member of the family to make the purchase decision. The greater number of dual-earning households has created greater time pressures, a situation that encourages individual decision making for many products that ordinarily might be purchased on a joint basis.

4. *For certain demographic groups.* Several demographic factors are likely to encourage joint decision making:

- Joint decision making is less likely among upper and lower socioeconomic groups. Lower-income households are more female-dominant; higher-income households are more male-dominant. The middle-income groups are most likely to engage in joint decision making.[16]
- Younger families show a higher frequency of joint decision making. One study found the greatest amount of shared decisions in the first year of marriage.[17] As the family gets older, joint decisions tend to decrease. Family members learn to make decisions that are acceptable to each other, and there is less need for shared decisions.[18]
- Joint decision making is more likely if there are no children in the family. As a family adds children, roles become more clearly defined, and

husband and wife are more willing to delegate authority to each other. Thus, the need for joint decision making is reduced.[19]

- Joint decision making is more likely if only one of the parents is working, as time pressures are less.

Role Specification

Household members can play one or more of the five roles shown in Figure 17.2:

1. The *information gatherer* (sometimes called the *gatekeeper*) influences the family's processing of information by controlling the level and type of stimuli the family is exposed to. The information gatherer has the greatest expertise in acquiring and evaluating information.
2. The *influencer* establishes the decision criteria by which brands are compared (cost, durability, and so on) and influences the other family members' evaluation of alternative brands.
3. The *decision maker* decides which brand to purchase, probably because he or she has budgetary power and, therefore, final approval.
4. The *purchasing agent* carries out the decision by purchasing the product for the family.
5. The *consumer* uses the product and evaluates it, giving some feedback to other family members regarding satisfaction with the chosen brand and desirability of purchasing the same brand again.

From the marketer's standpoint, one of the most important distinctions is that between the purchaser and consumer. Many strategic decisions are made without recognizing this important distinction. In many cases, the purchasing agent may have little importance since the consumer is making the postpurchase evaluation and will decide on future brand purchases. In other cases, the purchaser may decide the brand for others in the family, particularly if the decision is made in the store. A study by *McCall's* magazine found that almost one-third of beer consumers delegated the brand decision to the purchasing agent (in most cases the wife) and that the purchasing agent was aware of the consumer's beer preferences 90 percent of the time.[20]

Conflict Resolution

Whenever two or more people are involved in decision making, some conflict is likely in purchasing objectives, attitudes toward alternative brands, and the selection of the most desirable alternative. The family is no exception. Because households are small, closely interdependent groups, joint decisions are likely to lead to conflict. Research has shown that conflicts exist in the selection of housing,[21] automobiles,[22] and family planning.[23] In family planning, the differences were not whether to engage in family planning but the choice criteria.

Husbands emphasized the positive effects of small family size on living costs, whereas wives viewed small families as an advantage in giving them more time.

The marketer must be aware of such conflicts and adjust marketing strategies accordingly. For example, families frequently visit automobile showrooms together. The husband may emphasize roominess and style to impress business associates, and the wife may be concerned with gas economy and service costs—or the husband may emphasize cost; the wife, style. In any case, differences are likely to occur, and the sales representative must appeal to both parties.

Household Strategies to Resolve Conflict

Households use various strategies to try to resolve conflicts. Conflicts may arise over (1) which choice to select, or (2) the criteria used to evaluate alternative choices. Most conflicts in households are over product alternatives rather than goals and usually are resolved by *consensus*. This is because the household is a cooperative group, that is, one whose members' goals are usually compatible. Conflict over buying goals is more serious and leads to *politicking* among family members.

Davis studied various strategies to resolve conflicts by consensus and politicking.[24] To reach consensus, households usually engage in problem solving through discussion and compromise. The compromise reached in the vacation decision described earlier is an example. Consensus could also lead the household to opt for an individual rather than a joint decision as a means of avoiding conflict; thus, responsibility for the decision is delegated to one member of the family.

When family members disagree about goals, they use politicking. One way to politick is to form coalitions, as when children support one parent over another in a conflict. Coalitions may also be formed to bring dissenters into line. Everyone in the family wants to buy a stereo console except the teenage son, who wants to buy components. The weight of family opinion forces the teenage son to comply. Another form of politicking is through coercion. For example, the parent may threaten to reduce an allowance if the child uses most of it to purchase candy, or one spouse may threaten another ("Since you bought that suit, I have a right to buy the winter coat I saw").

Spiro studied these conflicts in the context of husband-wife relationships and found that traditional (husband-dominant) families were more likely to use politicking strategies. By contrast, more contemporary families (families with greater equality between husband and wife) tended to use problem-solving strategies, particularly reliance on a spouse's expertise.[25]

Several studies examined such husband-wife problem solving. Park examined husband-wife problem-solving strategies in buying a home and described them as a process of *muddling through*. Since there is little preplanning in the purchase of a home, the spouse who felt most strongly about a point won out (for example, "If you really want a two-car garage, it's OK with me").[26] Corfman and Lehmann also found that couples often resolve conflicts by choosing the alternative of the spouse with the strongest preference.[27] If neither spouse has a strong preference, the spouse who has had his or her way less often in the past makes the selection. In other words, if no one has a strong preference, couples "take turns" in getting their way.

When Are Conflicts Most Easily Resolved?

There are three situations in which family conflicts are most easily resolved. The first occurs when the family recognizes one person as the legitimate authority. Conflict is simply resolved by delegating decision making to this individual. The second occurs when one family member is more involved in the decision than the others. The family may agree that the highly involved individual will make the decision. The third situation is when one family member may be more empathetic to another's needs.

Burns and Granbois studied the influence of husbands and wives in automobile decisions to determine if these three factors—recognized legitimacy, involvement, and empathy—reduce conflict.[28] They found that each factor facilitated conflict resolution. Conflict was less likely if the husband and wife agreed that the decision should be made jointly or by one of them alone. Even if the couple failed to agree on authority, conflict was less likely if one of them was more involved in the purchase. Finally, conflict was less likely if one of the spouses was more empathetic. For autos, the husband was more involved and less empathetic to the wife's needs. Therefore, the wife was more likely to cede decision authority to the husband. Menasco and Curry's study of husband-wife choices of investment options supported these findings. Spouses gravitated to one or the other's preferences as a result of empathy.[29]

HUSBAND-WIFE INFLUENCES

Given the fact that 63 percent of households are family units, we will focus on husband-wife influences in this section and parent-child influences in the next. The relative influence of the husband and the wife is likely to vary according to four things: (1) type of product considered, (2) the nature of purchase influence, and (3) family characteristics.

Type of Product

Traditionally, husbands have been regarded as the dominant decision makers for products such as automobiles, financial services, and liquor. Wives have been viewed as the prime decision makers for foods, toiletries, and small appliances. However, as we saw in Chapter 13, many of these roles have merged and even been reversed due to the greater proportion of working wives and changes in family norms.

In 1974, Davis and Rigaux undertook one of the most detailed studies of husband-wife influences by product category.[30] They studied family decision making for 25 products and classified them into one of four categories:

1. Products for which the husband tends to be the dominant influence.
2. Products for which the wife tends to be the dominant influence.
3. Products for which decisions are made by either the husband or the wife, with either person equally likely to be dominant (autonomous decisions).
4. Products for which decisions are made jointly by husband and wife.

Putnam and Davidson's 1987 update of their study is shown in Figure 17.3.[31] The higher the product is on the vertical axis, the more likely it is that the wife will be the dominant influence. The farther to the right it is on the horizontal axis, the more likely the decision is to be a joint one. Therefore, products in the upper left are wife-dominant, products in the middle left are based on individual decisions by either husband or wife (autonomous), and products in the lower left are husband-dominant. Products to the right are joint decisions and involve both husband and wife as equal influences. Products to the left are individual decisions.

Some of the product classifications in Figure 17.3 confirm previous studies. Husbands are more dominant in decisions for lawnmowers, sports equipment,

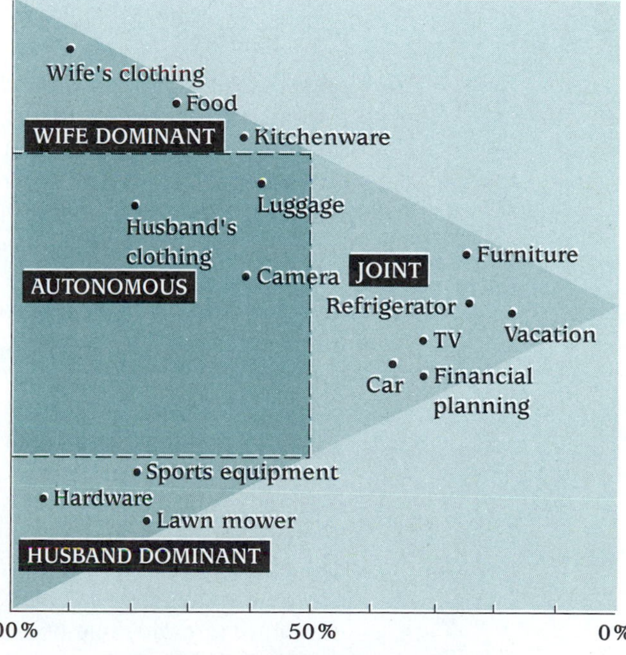

FIGURE 17.3
Husband-wife rules in family decisions by product category

Sources: Original study in Harry L. Davis and Benny P. Rigaux, "Perception of Marital Roles in Decision Processes," *Journal of Consumer Research,* 1 (June, 1974), p. 54. Figures based on Mandy Putnam and William R. Davidson, *Family Purchasing Behavior: II, Family Roles by Product Category* (Columbus, OH: Management Horizons, Inc., a division of Price Waterhouse, 1987).

and hardware items. Wives dominate decisions for food, clothing, and kitchenware. Either the husband or the wife will make decisions for cameras and for the husband's clothing on an individual basis. They will most likely make joint decisions for vacations, furniture, and refrigerators.

A number of items changed their position between the original study in 1974 and the 1987 study. Cars, TV sets, and financial planning moved from a husband-dominant position to joint decision making, reflecting the greater influence of working wives.

The classifications in Figure 17.3 have important implications for marketers. If a product is in the husband- or wife-dominant category, marketers must tailor messages to one spouse or the other and must select media that are male- or female-dominant. If the product is in the joint decision category, marketers must tailor the message for the couple and must select media that are likely to reach both spouses. If the product is in the autonomous category, either spouse could make the decision. In some cases, the husband is dominant; in others, the wife. Therefore, there are two audiences, and marketers may need two campaigns. An advertiser of men's clothing might recognize the wife's influence by introducing two campaigns, one directed to the wife and the other to the husband, using different appeals. Trying to develop one campaign to appeal to both spouses may not be as effective.

Nature of Purchase Influence

The nature of the purchase influence may specify husband-wife roles. The most important classification by purchase influence defines instrumental versus expressive roles in family purchasing.[32] **Instrumental roles** are related to performing tasks that help the group make the final purchasing decision. Decisions on budgets, timing, and product specifications would be task-oriented. **Expressive roles** facilitate expression of group norms and provide the group with social and emotional support. Decisions about color, style, and design are expressive since they reflect group norms.

Historically, the husband has been associated with the instrumental role and the wife with the expressive role.[33] However, we saw in Chapter 13 that as more wives enter the work force, husbands are more likely to assume household roles and wives budgetary and planning roles. As a result, instrumental and expressive roles are becoming more intermingled between husband and wife.

Several studies found that working wives are less likely to accept traditional homemaking tasks associated with expressive roles.[34] In their study, Ferber and Lee suggested that the wife may be just as likely as the husband to fulfill certain instrumental roles.[35] They identified the role of the *family financial officer* in the family, that is, the person who pays the bills, keeps track of expenditures and determines the use of leftover money. Clearly, this is an instrumental rather than an expressive role because it is budgetary. Yet, in most cases, by the second year of marriage, the wife was likely to be the financial officer.

Family Characteristics

Even though husbands tend to dominate decisions for certain product categories and wives for others, these roles may vary in the degree of dominance within each family. In some families, the husband may be more dominant, regardless of the product being considered (patriarchal families); in others, the wife may be more dominant (matriarchal families).

Various studies show that a husband will generally be more influential in the purchase decision than his wife when:

1. His level of education is higher.
2. His income and occupational status are higher.
3. His wife is not employed.
4. The couple is at an earlier stage in the family life cycle (young parents).
5. The couple has a greater than average number of children.[36]

The opposite is true for a wife-dominant family: the wife is employed, has a higher level of education than the husband, and so forth. One study by Skinner and Dubinsky confirmed this profile. Wives who were more involved than husbands in forming insurance decisions tended to be employed and better educated than their husbands.[37]

The profile of the husband-dominant family suggests a family with traditional values and attitudes toward marital roles. The husband's higher income provides him with financial power within the family. When there is a nonworking wife with a lower level of education, more traditional values usually prevail. A survey of 257 married women supported the more traditional orientation of the husband-dominant family.[38] Wives were classified as conservative, moderate, or liberal with regard to female roles. Women who had liberal views of their role were much more likely to make purchase decisions than were conservative women. They were also more than twice as likely to make decisions about family savings, vacation plans, and major appliances than were conservative women. Conversely, a study of husbands found that those with conservative perceptions of their marital role believed they had more influence on decisions for vacations, insurance, and savings than did husbands with more liberal views.[39]

Both studies indicate that traditional (conservative) views of marital roles encourage greater male influence and contemporary (liberal) views encourage greater female influence.

Changing Patterns of Husband-Wife Influence

As we saw in Chapter 13, changes in marital roles have led to the husband's greater influence in decisions the wife has traditionally assumed (see the Gerber ad in Exhibit 17.1) and the wife's greater influence in areas traditionally assumed to be the husband's domain (see the Whirlpool ad in Exhibit 17.1). Men bought 25 percent of the groceries in 1992, up from 17 percent in 1987. Further, they made more than half the household decisions for soaps, cereals, soft drinks, and snack foods.[40] One advertising agency suggested that changing mens' roles might result in household products being advertised more frequently in mens' magazines such as *Esquire* and *Playboy*.[41]

Other studies have cited women's increasing role in decisions about insurance, automobiles, and financial services as a result of the greater economic power of working wives.[42] As one researcher noted, an employed wife results in a more equal distribution of family power between husband and wife and will, therefore, lead to more joint decisions.[43] As we saw in Figure 17.3, wives are increasingly making joint decisions with husbands for cars and financial planning. Another study found wives more likely to make joint decisions for insurance as well.[44]

The implications for marketing are direct. Marketers for a wide range of products can no longer rely on traditional buying patterns. Producers of food products and household items should direct more effort toward husbands. Marketers of a wide range of "big-ticket" products and services should direct more effort toward wives.

EXHIBIT 17.1
Changes in husband's purchasing roles

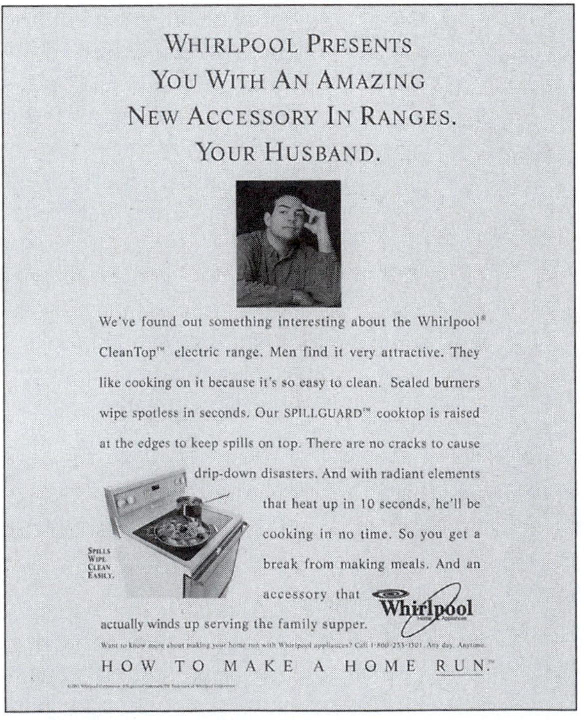

PARENT-CHILD INFLUENCES

Children are playing a more important part in family decisions in both traditional and nontraditional families. In almost 70 percent of traditional families, the husband and wife work. Dual-earning households foster greater self-reliance among children, often requiring them to shop and prepare meals. In nontraditional families, the rapid increase of single-parent households has also increased the number of children involved in shopping and meal preparation.

As a result, children are likely to influence decisions for products the whole family consumes. One study estimates that children influence $132 billion in family expenditures over 62 product categories. The bulk of this influence is in food and beverage products.[45]

Studies of parent-child influences in purchasing have been divided between research on children 12 or under and on adolescents 13 to 17 years old. Research on younger children has focused on how they learn about purchasing and consumption tasks (the child's socialization in the marketplace) and on the mother-child interaction in the purchasing process. Research on adolescents has been directed toward the relative influence of parents and peer groups in teenage purchasing decisions. This focus is due to the general belief that children rely more on parents for norms and values when they are younger and more on their peer group as they grow older. In the following sections, we first consider the consumer socialization of children, then the mother-child interaction, and finally the peer group-adolescent interaction.

Consumer Socialization of Children

Consumer socialization is the process by which "young people acquire skills, knowledge, and attitudes relevant to their functioning in the marketplace."[46] Children learn about purchasing and consumption primarily from their parents. While television may have a persuasive influence on what children see and how they react to certain brands, "the family is instrumental in teaching young people rational aspects of consumption, including basic consumer needs."[47] The role of parents in trying to teach their children to be more effective consumers is illustrated by the following findings:

- Parents teach price-quality relations to their children, including experiences with the use of money and ways to shop for quality products.[48]
- Parents teach their children how to be effective comparison shoppers[49] and how to buy products on sale.[50]
- Parents influence children's brand preferences.[51]
- Parents have influenced children's ability to distinguish fact from exaggeration in advertising.[52]

Methods of Socialization

How do children learn these various facets of purchase and consumption behavior from their parents? Children watch and imitate parental behavior because parents serve as role models. Children also co-shop with the parent. Grossbart, Carlson, and Walsh found that mothers who co-shop have more explicit consumer socialization goals for their children. They seek to expose children to the experiences associated with visiting stores and use these occasions to teach children consumer skills.[53]

Children are also socialized through direct experience. The increase in dual-earning and one-parent households has resulted in children often shopping on their own. As a result, the process of consumer socialization is occurring much earlier and much faster than it used to.

Television and the school environment are also important sources of socialization. Children learn to make associations from TV ads and programs. According to **cultivation theory,** children learn about a culture's norms and values from the media. The greater the children's exposure to TV, the greater the likelihood that they will accept the images and associations seen. Thus, young children may learn that using a deodorant is a must in social situations, and many begin to use the product even though body odor does not occur until adolescence.

http://www.scholastic.com/

http://www.discovercard.com/

Schools are becoming a more controversial source of consumer socialization. Whittle Communication's Channel One gives schools TV equipment for the right to broadcast 2 minutes of commercials and 10 minutes of programming a day. Similarly, Scholastic Inc. creates school magazines and posters for corporations to sponsor. These ventures have provoked charges of excessive commercialism in the schools. However, some of the efforts may be constructive. Sears Roebuck's Discover Card division supports Scholastic's *Extra Credit* magazine, which teaches kids about personal finances and economics.[54]

One additional source of socialization is other children. Younger children may emulate older children's behavior and, in so doing, develop consumption skills. The child's peer group can also affect consumer socialization by influencing brand preferences and purchases.

Stages in Consumer Socialization

Children go through various stages of consumer socialization. James U. McNeal studied the process of children's socialization over many years. He and his colleagues developed a five-stage process:[55]

1. *Observing* (average age—six months): In the first stage, children construct mental images of marketplace objects and symbols like Ronald McDonald. They begin to understand that stores are sources of good things.
2. *Making requests* (average age—two years): Children begin to make requests for desired objects at home, particularly as TV advertising becomes a meaningful stimulus. They make requests only when in the presence of store objects because they cannot carry representations in their mind. The reminder effect does not yet operate when they are in

a store. Almost half of children's first in-store requests are for ready-to-eat cereals. Another 30 percent are for snack items.

3. *Making selections* (average age—three and one-half years): Children begin to develop memory of store locations for certain products and locate and retrieve satisfying products by themselves. Many master self-service layouts.
4. *Making assisted purchases* (average age—five and one-half years): Children are asking and receiving permission to obtain objects in the store. The child now has the ability to spend his or her money.
5. *Making independent purchases* (average age—eight years): Children are now buying on their own without parental assistance. They gain a better understanding of money and become mature enough to convince parents they can make responsible purchases on their own.

The Swiss psychologist Jean Piaget viewed socialization in the context of three phases of a child's cognitive development.[56] Children from age three to seven are in a *preoperational stage* when cognitive structure is poorly organized and language skills are developing. In this stage, parents may permit some limited purchase choices on an assisted basis—for example, in the flavors of ice cream or beverages. This would be equivalent to McNeal's stages 3 and 4.

From 8 to 11 years of age, children are in a *concrete operational stage* in which they are developing more complex abilities to apply logical thought to concrete problems. In this second phase of socialization, children start developing persuasive techniques learned from their peers to influence their parents to buy them what they want (e.g., "Everyone's got one except me"). This would be equivalent to McNeal's stage 5.

In the third stage (12 to 15 years old), children enter a *formal operational stage* in which their ability to think abstractly and to associate concepts and ideas is more fully developed. In this third stage, children have greater financial resources and cognitive capabilities to make decisions on a wider range of products. Many of them will influence parental purchases for adult items such as cars, computers, and electronics. This phase goes beyond McNeal's five stages and represents a child's ability to influence others, especially parents, and to build purchasing power for major purchases such as a computer.

Role of Parents in Consumer Socialization

Carlson and Grossbart studied the role of parents in children's socialization as consumers.[57] They identified four types of families:

1. *Authoritarian parents* seek a high level of control over their children and expect unquestioned obedience. They try to shield children from outside influences and are more likely to engage in socially oriented communications.
2. *Neglecting parents* are distant from their children and do not exert much control over them. They do little to maintain or encourage their children's capabilities.

3. *Democratic parents* foster a balance between parents' and children's rights. They encourage children's self-expression and value autonomy. They are warm and supportive, but they also expect mature behavior from their children. If they regard children as "out of bounds," they use discipline. Democratic parents are more likely to engage in conceptually oriented communications.
4. *Permissive parents* seek to remove as many restraints from children as possible without endangering them. They believe children have adult rights but few responsibilities.

Although these categories are not all encompassing, Carlson and Grossbart used them to study parent-child interactions. They found that democratic and, to a lesser extent, permissive parents had the most active role in children's socialization as consumers. These parents shop with their children and are more likely to seek their advice compared to authoritarian and neglecting parents. Democratic parents also are more likely to view TV with their children, but they express more concern about advertising to their children and try to control their TV viewing. As expected, authoritarian households place the most restrictions on children's consumption behavior.

In another study, Moschis found that parents are the main source of consumer socialization when they encourage communication and independence. The peer group and television are stronger sources of socialization when parents encourage obedience and deference in their children (that is, authoritarian parents).[58]

One implication of these studies is that families most involved in children as consumers are also most concerned about the legitimacy of advertising to children. Marketers should try to increase the value of advertising in the eyes of these parents by providing more information on nutrition or product safety, for example. In so doing, they would allay some of the concerns of democratic parents by showing the positive role that advertising can play in the socialization process.

Intergenerational Influences

The process of consumer socialization is intergenerational; that is, influences are passed on from one generation to the next. Such influences are most apparent when researchers study brand preferences of parents and children. One study found that 93 percent of college freshmen patronize the same bank as do their parents.[59] State Farm Insurance's study found that about 40 percent of married couples held auto policies with the same company as the husband's parents.[60]

http://www.statefarm.com/

Such influences tend to decrease with consumers' age. The State Farm study found that 65 percent of husbands in their 20s had the same auto policy as their parents. However, by the time they were in their 50s, only 25 percent had a policy with the same company.[61]

Intergenerational influences are not one-directional. That is, they also pass from children to parents. The ad in Exhibit 17.2, for example, shows a daugh-

▶EXHIBIT 17.2
An example of intergenerational influence from child to parent

ter influencing her mother to get the right sources of nutrition. Adolescents are likely to influence parents' preferences for products involving new technologies. For example, a survey by a leading research firm found that 57 percent of teens influenced the choice of a personal computer.[62]

Intergenerational influences are likely to be stronger in many foreign countries that have a greater proportion of extended families. Childers and Rao compared family influences in Thai and U.S. families and found that the greater number of extended families in Thailand resulted in stronger intergenerational influences.[63] Because of a close-knit traditional family structure, brands that parents and grandparents purchase exert a stronger influence than they do in U.S. families.

Children's Influence in the Purchasing Process

Figure 17.4 shows the products that children 12 and under buy and influence their parents to buy. The extent of children's influence varies sharply by prod-

CONSUMER BEHAVIOR AND THE NEW TECHNOLOGIES

▶ Socializing Children on the Internet: Meet the Net Generation

The two-year-old is sitting on her father's lap, takes the mouse out of his hand, and manipulates it through a colorful CD-ROM program for kids. A seven-year-old turns on the family computer to Netscape, types in an Internet address for kids' games, and spends a few hours having fun. A 12-year-old also gets on the Internet to the site for Levi jeans to check out the latest styles and costs.

Welcome to the Net Generation, the children of younger baby boomers. They are defined by their lack of awe for the new technologies, have grown up with computers, and treat them like any other household appliance. One study found that it takes less than five minutes to teach a four-year-old how to use a mouse compared to several hours for adults. Two-thirds of kindergarten kids have used a computer. By the time they are 12, they are probably more adept than their parents at downloading software and accessing information on the Internet. By one estimate, more than 7 million children under 18 have their own Internet accounts.

The opportunity for socializing kids on the Internet is immense. Children are spending more and more time on the computer, and time on the computer is time taken away from television. Children watched an average of 17.6 hours of TV a week in 1995, one hour less than in 1990, and this trend is likely to continue as access to the Internet becomes even easier and less expensive.

As a result, the Internet may become almost as important a vehicle as TV for kids to get information on the latest fashions, new electronic products and games, and store availability. We can easily imagine a 12-year-old influencing her parents to buy a Volvo by downloading information on safety statistics from the Internet. Or how about a 10-year-old who is interested in cooking downloading recipes from a Pillsbury site?

Marketers are beginning to target specific sites to the Net Generation. The site for Levi jeans provides them with fashion information. Procter & Gamble's Internet site, which showcases all the company's products, has a site for Sunny Delight targeted to children. It features an on-line treasure hunt with college scholarships as prizes.

It looks like the process of socialization for the Net Generation is going to be a whole new ball game.

Sources: "The Rise of the Net-Generation," *Advertising Age* (October 14, 1996), pp. 31, 43; "P&G Steps Up Ad Cyber-Surfing," *The Wall Street Journal* (April 18, 1996), p. B14.

uct category. Children are most likely to buy product categories one would expect—candy, gum, toys, soft drinks, and snack foods. A significant proportion use their own money to buy presents, books, fast foods, and even clothing and sports equipment. In addition, a large proportion of children also influence their

FIGURE 17.4 Products purchased and influenced by children

Sources: Influence data reprinted with permission © *American Demographics*. February, 1992. For subscription information, please call (800) 828-1133. Purchase data from "Young Consumers, Perils and Power," *The New York Times* (February 11, 1990); based on a study by Yankelovich, Clancy, and Shulman (Copyright 1990 by The New York Times Co. Reprinted by permission.)

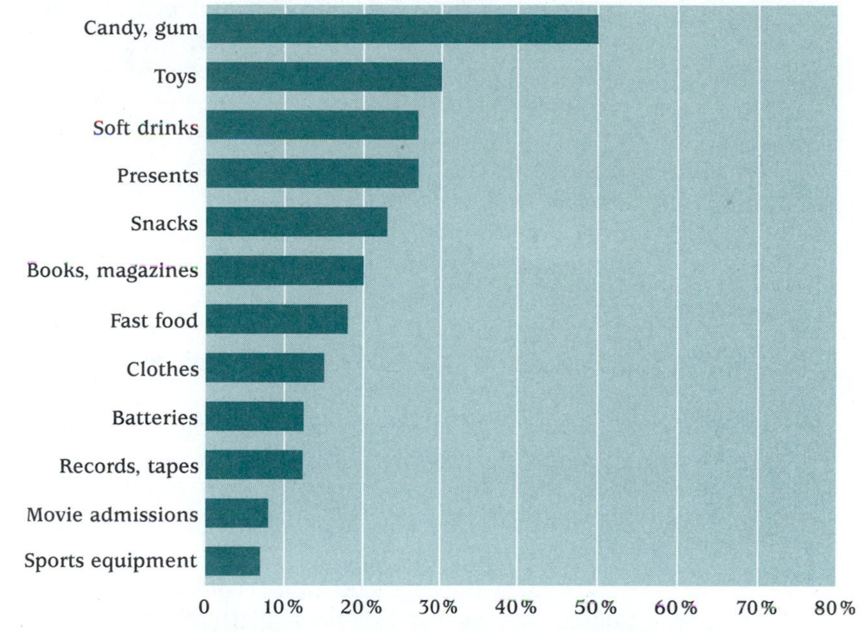

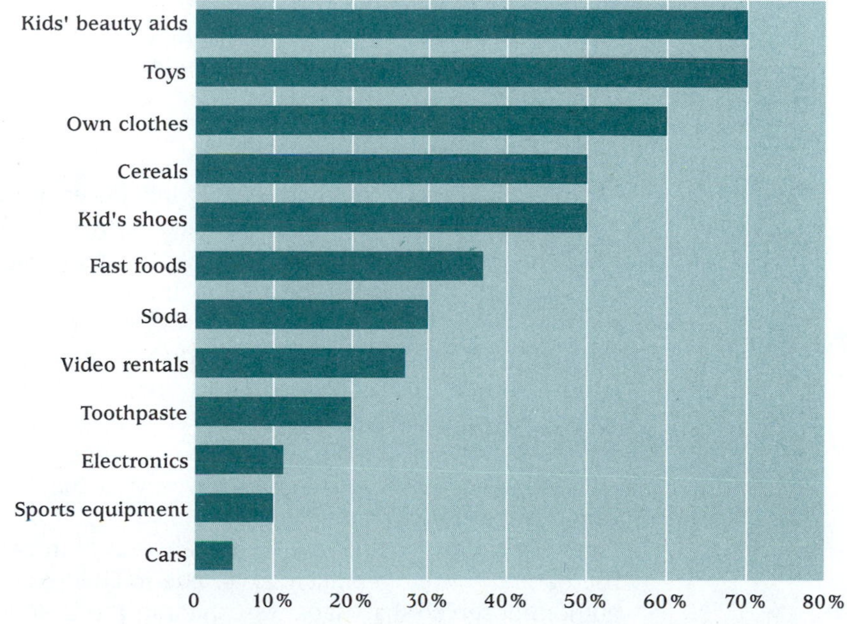

parents' purchases of these same items, particularly clothing. Figure 17.3 also shows that a significant number influence the purchase of such adult-oriented items as cars and electronic products.

Children's involvement may go beyond influencing parents. In some cases, parents and children make joint decisions, particularly when the child is highly involved in the decision. For example, many parents will decide jointly with the child on the choice of a summer camp, private school, or a family vacation. Hyatt hotels offers its guests the services of "Camp Hyatt," a facility that offers separate programs for kids such as sports lessons, movies, and video games, permitting parents to be alone. To demonstrate the influence of children in vacation decisions, Hyatt follows up by sending kids news of contests and certificates for resort attractions. One Hyatt executive says, "There is nothing like a seven-year-old asking 19 times, 'When are we going back to that hotel' to get parents to go back."[64]

http://www.hyatt.com/

Children's influence will vary by age.[65] Ward and Wackman found that only 21 percent of the mothers yielded to clothing requests from 5- to 7-year-old children, but 57 percent yielded to requests from 11- to 12-year-old children. Music tapes and CDs were another category in which children's influence increased markedly with their age.[66]

Greater affluence and earlier consumer socialization of children may be resulting in a greater likelihood that children will get their way. Another reason that children are more likely to get their way is that parents feel guilty for leaving children at home and are more permissive in letting them buy what they want. As a result, marketers have begun to treat children as influentials for adult-oriented products. The ad for the digital thermometer in Exhibit 17.3 is directed to adults, but it portrays the child's influence.

Parent-Child Interaction

The focus in research on parent-child influences in purchasing has been on the interaction between mother and child. Several researchers have considered mothers' responses to children's request to purchase various products.

Ward and Wackman found that the older children were, the more likely mothers were to yield to their request.[67] However, older children made fewer purchase requests because they could make more purchase decisions independently. They are more likely to look to the peer group and disregard parents as sources of information, and parents view them as more competent in making purchasing judgments.[68]

An interesting cross-cultural study of younger children's influence found that American children made the most requests (19 over a two-week period) and Japanese children made the fewest requests (9 in two weeks). However, Japanese parents were more likely to accede to children's requests when made. The authors observed that "Japanese children are encouraged to be respectful and harmonious in the family and purchase requests may be viewed as 'pushy'; how-

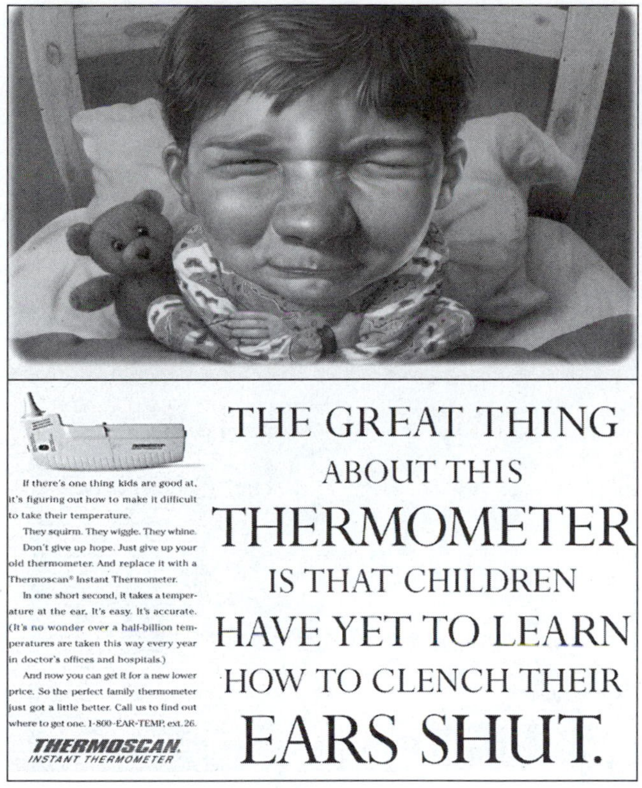

EXHIBIT 17.3
An ad depicting children's influence on the purchase of adult products

ever, since Japanese parents are highly indulgent of their children, they most often agree to buy requested items."[69] When it came to American parents, they were more likely to negotiate and discuss purchase requests with the child or to just say no. The ad in Exhibit 17.4 reflects the American mother's willingness to say no by associating the product with a rare yes on the mother's part.

Parent versus Peer-Group Influence Among Adolescents

The purchasing influence of teenagers has increased as working parents have shifted more responsibilities to them for shopping and other chores. One survey found that, on average, teenage girls spend over an hour a week shopping for the family and that over 80 percent do some cooking at home. One marketing expert concluded that teens' influence in food shopping is almost on a par with their mothers'. Another survey found that from 40 to 60 percent of teenagers have a say in family decisions for personal computers, cars, and TV sets, and about 70 percent influenced family vacation decisions.[70]

EXHIBIT 17.4
An example of a mother-child purchase interaction

When do adolescents exert the most influence on purchases? In a survey of 429 college freshmen's influence on family decisions for durable goods, Beatty and Talpade found that they saw themselves as exerting the most influence when they:[71]

- *Have more purchasing power.* The greater the teenager's purchasing power, the more likely the parent will respect his or her purchasing opinions.
- *Have more perceived knowledge of the product.* Teenagers often have more knowledge than parents for products such as computers, stereo equipment, camcorders, and cellular phones. In such cases, parents are more likely to accept the teenager's opinions.
- *Regard the product as important.* The more important the product to the teenager, the more likely it is that he or she will exert purchasing influence on the family decision.

Such teenage influence is often ascribed to the greater independence of adolescents. The traditional view is that as children enter adolescence, they shift their allegiance from parents to the peer group, and parental purchase influence declines. However, various studies suggest that children continue to rely on parents for information and influence into adolescence. One study found that high school students were just as concerned with parents' approval as were elementary school students.[72] Another found that 16- to 19-year-olds were more likely to be influenced by parents than by friends in the purchase of sports equipment and small appliances.[73] A study by Moschis and Moore found that the fact a parent liked the product was a more important criterion than the fact a friend liked the product.[74] This means that joint decision making is not a one-way street; adolescents and parents influence each other.

The importance of parents in purchasing decisions does not diminish the importance of the peer group. In the same study, Moschis and Moore found that as teenagers get older, they rely on more information sources, and peer groups become increasingly influential in purchase decisions.[75]

HOUSEHOLD DECISION MAKING AND MARKETING STRATEGIES

Household decision making influences every phase of marketing strategy: the advertising message, the media selected, product development, pricing strategies, and distribution. In this section, we consider the marketing implications of (1) children's socialization, (2) decision making in traditional households, and (3) decision making in nontraditional households.

Children's Socialization

Marketers have attempted to influence children's consumer socialization by getting kids to recognize company and brand names early even if these companies do not sell children's products. Yogurt, a decidedly adult, health-oriented category, is an example. Children generally tell their moms that they hate the taste. However, as baby boomer parents began to extend their nutritional orientation to their children, yogurt marketers saw an opening. In 1993, Dannon introduced Sprinkl'ins, with a thicker consistency that children like, and Yoplait introduced Trix, with fruit flavors layered into the cup. Advertising targets children with fun themes while targeting moms with nutritionally oriented benefits. The president of Yoplait explains the consumer socialization strategy for children in saying, "If you can get kids hooked on yogurt, you can develop a habit that hopefully will continue through their entire life."[76]

Another producer of adult products, Black & Decker, has engaged in a similar strategy. The company manufactures power tools and appliances. It licensed its name to a line of toys that are miniature versions of its small appliance line.

One company executive reasoned, "Youngsters don't buy Black & Decker drills. But they might someday if they start out on toy Dustbusters."[77]

Socialization strategies have also been educationally motivated. First National Bank of Tennessee introduced a savings club for children under 12 to teach them fiscal responsibility with a marketing campaign featuring Moola-Moola, a fuzzy monster who visits schools. One executive says, "If they have an account here when they're young, where are they going to keep it when they do get more money?"[78]

We also saw that marketers are beginning to use the Internet to influence the socialization of children (see the Consumer Behavior box earlier in the chapter). Advertising and information on Web sites will become increasingly influential.

Traditional Households

Implications for marketers from family decisions center on the husband-wife and parent-child relationships. The key question is, Who has the dominant influence?

Husband-Wife Influences

If the husband or wife are dominant in decision making, the marketer will direct the advertising message to the needs of the dominant party and select media to reach either the husband or the wife. A more difficult strategic issue arises when spouses make decisions jointly or autonomously. If the decision is joint, should marketers direct separate messages to husband and wife, or should they design one campaign to appeal to both? In car advertising, some manufacturers have used separate campaigns on the assumption that husband and wife emphasize different benefits. Chevrolet, for example, began targeting 30 percent of its ad budget to women, gearing its themes to fashion and style. However, one study found that 65 percent of women felt misrepresented by such advertising because it implied they were not very interested in performance.[79] Increasingly, automakers are targeting their campaigns to both husband and wife, with performance as the primary benefit and style as a secondary theme (see the Nissan ad in Exhibit 17.5).

http://www.chevrolet.com/

If the decision is autonomous—that is, the decision is made by husband or wife and either one is equally likely to make it—the marketer is faced with a difficult choice. Should the advertising budget be split equally between male- and female-oriented media, or should the marketer appeal to one or the other? Men's clothing is a good example. The marketer could advertise men's clothing in women's magazines, in men's magazines, or in both. If both are used, marketers need two separate campaigns. The danger of this approach is that the media budget may be spread too thin. A joint decision poses a different problem.

As patterns of husband-wife influence have changed, marketing strategies have adapted. For example, until recently, life insurance was designed primarily to the husband's specifications, but companies now are developing policies geared specifically to the working wife. Similarly, marketers can no longer assume that the coupon redeemer is necessarily the wife. Husbands' increas-

EXHIBIT 17.5
An auto campaign that targets both husband and wife

ing involvement in food shopping means they are more likely to redeem coupons.

Parent-Child Influences

A similar strategic issue is whether to target the child alone or to target both child and parent when both have influence on the purchase decision. Marketers generally reach the parent and child separately to emphasize different benefits. Banquet's Kid Cuisine follows a strategy similar to Tyson's in advertising to both parents and children. Banquet advertises its microwaveable product to children on the Nickelodeon cable channel and on TV shows such as "The Simpsons" and "Step by Step," while it targets nutritionally oriented print ads to mothers in magazines such as *Good Housekeeping* and *Parents*.

In contrast, Hawaiian Punch targets kids rather than parents with themes like "The only 'Punch' that won't get you sent to the principal's office," and "If you tried blending 7 Natural Fruits, you'd make a mess and Mom would have a cow."[80] The company may feel that kids often make the purchase decision without parental influence.

Marketers are also increasingly willing to change the characteristics of adult products to suit the needs of children. Procter & Gamble launched Pert Plus for Kids in a tear-free formulation.[81] The company also introduced a sparkle-filled version of Crest toothpaste to get children to brush.[82]

Nontraditional Households

A different set of strategic issues arise when dealing with nontraditional households. Nontraditional households represent diverse groupings that require specific targeting—for example, single-parent households, gay households, college roommates, friends living together, and so forth. The following strategic questions arise in targeting these groups:

http://www.ikea.com/

http://www.cambellsoup.com/

- *Is the nontraditional household grouping large enough to target?* A grouping such as single-parent households represented about 9 million households in 1995, certainly a grouping large enough to target for most products. But the key question is whether a separate effort is required to target such a group or whether a general campaign will be sufficient. If a company like Tyson wants to target parents of latchkey kids, advertising depicting single-parent households might be warranted. Similarly, marketers such as Ikea are targeting the gay market even though they represent only 3 percent of households, because they are an affluent group with significant purchasing potential.
- *Can appeals be geared to the particular needs of these groups?* Tyson could reasonably appeal to single-parent households because almost all single parents work and have latchkey kids. In contrast, Campbell's Soups would probably not advertise their condensed soups specifically to single parents because the same appeals would be used for all families with children. If the needs of the group do not differ from the general population, then a separate marketing campaign is not warranted.
- *Are media vehicles available to reach nontraditional households?* The absence of specific media vehicles would inhibit reaching nontraditional households. For example, to reach single parents through print media, magazines would have to be available that are targeted to this group and are widely read. The absence of such magazines means that prime-time TV would have to be used to reach the working single parent, an expensive alternative given the size of the segment.

MEASUREMENT OF HOUSEHOLD INFLUENCE

Most of the research studies cited concerned family decision making. But questions arise as to the validity of measures of husband-wife and parent-child influence.

Three approaches have been used in determining husband-wife influences: (1) interview both together, (2) interview each separately, (3) interview the wife to determine her influence and the husband's.

Most studies that interviewed husbands and wives separately found a moderate level of agreement between them as to their respective influence.[83] One study found that 68 percent of husbands and wives agree about their roles across

25 product categories.[84] Disagreement over influence is usually about who makes the decision. Another study found that 90 percent of husbands say they make the primary decision to buy auto accessories, whereas only 55 percent of wives say husbands control these purchases. Conversely, 44 percent of wives say they make the decision for major appliances, but only 25 percent of husbands agree that their wives make the decision.[85]

These studies suggest that interviewing one spouse to determine the influence of another may not be a reliable means of determining family influence. Interviewing both spouses together to obtain some consensus may be more effective.

Another issue is who should be interviewed in parent-child studies. In most cases, parents are interviewed to estimate the children's influence. Studies generally have relied on mothers' reports of children's purchase requests with little attempt to gauge the nature of children's purchase influence beyond determining their reaction to their mothers' purchase decision. Recently, children have begun to be studied to determine their perceptions of family decision making.[86] Such studies generally have been with adolescents rather than with younger children because adolescents are easier to interview. In one of the few studies to interview parents and children, Foxman and her colleagues evaluated the purchase influence of husbands, wives, and adolescent children.[87] They found that, compared to parents' ratings, children overestimated their influence.

Another issue is determining the nature of family influence. The measure of influence most typically used—husband decides, equal influence, or wife decides—does not indicate the nature of the influence. If the wife decided about a piece of furniture, was it because the husband was not interested, a decision was made to delegate authority to the wife for the purchase, or the husband and wife engaged in negotiations? Determining the nature of influence requires more complex measures and in-depth interviews involving both spouses.

SOCIETAL IMPLICATIONS OF FAMILY INFLUENCE

The primary societal issue in family decision making is the effect of advertising on children. We saw in Chapter 2 that the primary concern is the inability of children to process advertising information adequately because of undeveloped cognitive capacities.

Armstrong and Brucks cite two issues regarding the effects of children's advertising in the context of family influence.[88] First, does children's advertising increase parent-child conflict? Second, does such advertising create undesirable consumer socialization by teaching children poor consumption and social values?

Increased Parent-Child Conflict

http://www.ftc.gov/

Critics of children's advertising suggest that advertising may undermine parental control. Seeing ads makes children badger their parents for products they cannot afford or do not want to give to their children. As one Federal Trade Commission critique says, the effect is to turn the child unwittingly into an "assistant salesperson."[89]

Advertisers say that children's requests of parents are a natural part of the parent-child relationship. They also cite polls showing little support from parents for increased advertising regulation.

Undesirable Consumer Socialization

http://www.bausch.com/

Critics claim that children's advertising teaches materialism, impulsiveness, and immediate gratification. As a result, it creates poor consumption values. Further, in fostering impulsive choices, advertising encourages children to buy inappropriate products such as expensive or unneeded toys, sugared cereals, and junk food.[90] For example, status-conscious 15-year-olds in Southern California were buying Bausch & Lomb's Killer Loop sunglasses for up to $120 because they were "in." Advertising may also create favorable attitudes toward harmful products such as cigarettes. As we saw in Chapter 2, R. J. Reynold's Joe Camel campaign has been faulted on this score.

Consumers Union, which publishes a version of its *Consumer Reports* for kids, summarized the criticisms of marketers for negative influences in socializing children: "At a time when kids need to learn how to consume thoughtfully, numerous promotional messages are teaching the opposite."[91]

Defenders claim that advertising provides information that helps children make more informed decisions. They cite consumer socialization as a parental, rather than an advertising, responsibility. Further, they note that advertisers have been instrumental in promoting positive socialization by funding such high-quality children's programs as CBS Schoolbreak Specials and ABC Afterschool Specials.

Alternative Solutions

We saw in Chapter 2 that stricter regulations have limited the amount of commercial time on children's programs and required clearer division between programs and commercials. Further, an industry-sponsored organization, the Children's Advertising Review Unit, monitors TV ads on children's programs to determine their suitability and issues complaints against advertisers who violate their guidelines.

These efforts do not address how to prepare children to better process and evaluate advertising. Advertisers might try to develop commercials that children can process more easily, assuming such commercials are responsible. For example, Peracchio found that when ideas and events were repeated visually and were put in a relevant context, younger children were as effective as older children in processing information.[92] Advertisers using repetitive themes in a salient context might improve children's processing of the message, but the question remains whether the message is responsible and improves children's consumer socialization skills.

Ultimately, the primary role for improving children's skills in evaluating advertising rests with the parents. As Armstrong and Brucks note, "Parents can [best] monitor their children's television viewing, get children to think about advertising claims, evaluate children's purchase requests, and help children compare advertising claims against product performance."[93] However, such consumer socialization requires active and involved parents. In this respect, little can be done to protect children from undue advertising influence if parents simply do not care.

SUMMARY

This chapter focused on the most important reference group: the household. Both traditional households (married couples with children) and nontraditional households (single parents, unmarried couples, gay couples, friends living together) were described. The proportion of nontraditional households is increasing as a result of couples marrying later or not marrying at all and a higher divorce rate.

The chapter also considered the purchasing implications of changes in household composition over time. Originally, such changes were considered in the context of a family life cyle that described a progression from single to married to married with children to empty nesters. As a family moved from one stage to another, their discretionary income, need for household appliances, and expenditures on food, clothing, and education changed. Given the increase in nontraditional households, a more appropriate context is the household life cycle which incorporates changes such as married, divorced single parents, remarried with stepchildren. The focus on purchasing implications changes when one considers the needs of a single parent as opposed to a married couple and the formation of a family with stepchildren.

The chapter then considered a model of household decision making and identified three distinguishing characteristics of household decisions. First, decisions within households are likely to be made jointly. Joint decisions are more likely when perceived risk is high, the purchase decision is important to the family, and there are minimal time pressures.

Second, family members have prescribed roles in the decision process. Family members can perform the roles of information gatherer, influencer, decision maker, purchasing agent, and consumer. Third, joint decisions invariably produce some conflict in purchase objectives. As a result, families develop strategies to resolve purchase conflicts through persuasion, problem solving, or bargaining.

Husband-wife influences dominate the family purchasing process. Four types of decision processes were defined: (1) husband-dominant, (2) wife-dominant, (3) autonomous (either husband or wife is equally likely to make an individual decision), and (4) joint decision making. Traditionally, husbands dominate decisions for cars and insurance; wives, for food and toiletries. However, these traditional domains have become blurred as working wives have gained more influence in household decisions for automobiles and financial services.

Parent-child influences were also considered. Children exert more influence over family purchase decisions, especially in single-parent and dual-earning households. An important aspect of parent-child interaction is children's consumer socialization. Parents teach children how to be effective consumers and influence their brand preferences. Purchase influences and consumer learning are intergenerational in that they are passed from one generation to another.

The chapter also considered the strategic implications of household decision making. The strategic implications of the socialization of children and of husband-wife and parent-child influences were considered.

In the last section, we considered the societal implications of advertising to children in the context of household influences. Advertising may have two negative consequences in regard to the parent-child relationship. First, it may create parent-child conflict by encouraging children's purchase requests. Second, it may instill poor consumption values. Both government and industry have a role in regulating children's advertising. However, ultimately, it is the parents' responsibility to try to counter any negative effects of advertising by trying to improve their children's capacity to process and evaluate advertising messages.

In the next chapter, we consider another essential component in understanding groups: the nature of group communications.

QUESTIONS

1. Why is the number of nontraditional households increasing? What are the strategic implications of this trend?
2. Why is it more relevant to talk about a household life cycle than a family life cycle?
3. What are the differing purchase implications of a family and a household life cycle?
4. Are families likely to make the following product decisions on a joint basis or on an individual basis? Why?
   - Life insurance
   - Hair shampoo
   - Toothpaste
   - Compact disc players
5. What strategies could households use to resolve the following conflicts:
   - The wife wants a smaller house than the husband does because it is easier to maintain. The husband wants a larger house to impress friends and business associates.
   - The single parent wants his 14-year-old daughter to save her money to buy a computer. She wants to spend it on clothing.
   - The teenage son wants a car. The teenage daughter wants to go on a summer vacation with friends. Parents cannot afford both.
6. Advertising campaigns for products in which spouses make decisions on an autonomic basis are more difficult to formulate because either spouse could make an individual decision. The advertiser could try to develop (a) separate campaigns for each spouse, (b) a joint campaign for both, and (c) a campaign aimed at one or the other. Under what conditions will each of these strategies be most effective?
7. What may be the effect of a contemporary versus a traditional view of the woman's role in the family on (a) the purchase of convenience foods, (b) family shopping behavior, and (c) the criteria used in selecting food products?
8. Instrumental roles traditionally have been associated with the husband; expressive roles, with the wife. What changes have taken place in American society that have caused a blurring of these traditional roles?
9. There has been a greater shift toward joint decision making for many product categories that have been within the husband's traditional domain (autos, financial planning) and the wife's (appliances, furniture). What are the implications of this shift for (a) new product development, (b) product-line strategies, and (c) advertising?
10. Why has the influence of children in family purchase decisions increased substantially?
11. What are the implications for children's consumer socialization in each of Piaget's three phases of child development?
12. How have marketers attempted to influence children's socialization as consumers?
13. What do we mean by the "Net Generation"? What are the marketing implications of this group's facility with new technologies?
14. Research has found that mothers are more likely to yield to children's requests that are made in the store rather than in the home.[94] Why do you suppose this is true? What are the strategic implications of this finding for (a) advertising and (b) in-store promotional policy?
15. What are some of the problems in measuring family influence in purchase decisions?
16. What may be the potential negative effects of advertising on the consumer socialization of children? How can children's consumer socialization skills be improved?

RESEARCH ASSIGNMENTS

1. Compare the Web sites for Levi Strauss (http://www.levi.com) and Kraft Foods (http://www.kraftfoods.com). What type of household does each site target? In what ways do the targeted households derive value from each site? As Internet usage increases among women, children, and families, in what ways will the Webt sites evolve?
2. Trace a family decision for two families: (a) a couple with two or more children and (b) a single-parent household. Be sure the product or service involves joint decisions by parent(s) and children (for example, a family vacation, selection of a college, purchase of an automobile). Identify each family member's (a) specific roles, (b) perceptions and attitudes of the alternatives being considered, (c) conflicts in decision making, (d) modes of conflict resolution, and (e) postpurchase evaluation.
   - What are the differences in the decision processes between the two families?
   - What are the implications of decision making for (a) advertising, (b) product-line development, (c) product positioning, and (d) pricing?
3. Conduct separate interviews with third- or fourth-grade children and their mothers to determine perceptions of each child's influence. A good way to do this is to make contact with an elementary school class. Interviews with children should be conducted in class with the teacher's cooperation. Mothers can be interviewed at home.
   - Ask mothers about the influence of their children and ask children about their influence relative to their mothers' for products such as cereal, toothpaste, candy, and fast-food restaurants. Use a simple scale that children can understand, such as "I make the decision," "My mother makes the decision," and "We both make the decision." Ask both mothers and children what brand they last purchased and to rate the brand from excellent to poor.
   - Is there agreement between mother and child on (a) degree of influence, (b) brand purchased, and (c) brand ratings?
4. Replicate Assignment 2 for 12- to 13-year-old girls buying clothes. In this case, ask children and mothers to divide up 10 points based on purchase influence. Determine degree of agreement on (a) purchase influence, (b) evaluation of store in which purchased, and (c) evaluation of clothing purchased.

GROUP COMMUNICATIONS: WORD-OF-MOUTH AND DIFFUSION PROCESSES

Chapter 18

CORONA SUCCEEDS BASED ON WORD OF MOUTH AND DIFFUSION

Group communications are central to consumer decision making since groups are the primary source of information and influence. Group communications occur within and across groups. Communication within groups, in the form of *word-of-mouth* influence, is the most influential type of communication since it comes from family, friends, and neighbors—all highly credible sources of information. Communication across groups occurs through a process of *diffusion of information and influence.* Such a process of diffusion is likely to occur for new products, as information and adoption of new products spreads across groups. Marketers must trace such diffusion processes since new products are a primary source of profits to the firm.

In this chapter, we first consider word-of-mouth communication by describing:

- The process by which it occurs.
- The nature of *opinion leadership,* that is, the influence that individuals that are interested in the product exert over others.
- How marketers attempt to influence word-of-mouth communications.

We then consider the process of diffusion by describing how information and influence are communicated to other groups. Consumers are categorized by the time they take to adopt new products as innovators, early adopters, the majority, and laggards. Particular emphasis is given to those who are among the first to adopt, namely innovators and early adopters. The chapter concludes with a consideration of the strategic implications of the diffusion process.

http://www.corona.com.tw/corona/index.html

The importance of communications within and across groups is illustrated by Corona beer. Before the beer was imported to the United States, many residents of the Southwest would bring it back while on vacation in Mexico. This led Corona to import the beer, first to Austin, Texas, where it began to appear in bars, chili parlors, and Mexican restaurants. The beer's popularity quickly spread by *word of mouth*. The next market was San Diego, where surfers and beach people adopted the brand. From there word spread up and down the California coast. That is, communications traveled across groups illustrating a process of *diffusion*. The brand began moving east and won acceptance in Chicago, where it was most popular among yuppies. By 1984, sales had grown from 300,000 to 1.7 million cases on the strength of word of mouth alone. All of this growth occurred on the basis of on-premises sales in bars and restaurants.[1]

In 1987, as the brand began appearing in supermarkets, sales hit 13.7 million cases, making Corona the second largest selling imported beer after Heineken. Limited advertising in select magazines began, but Corona planned no television advertising. By that time, Corona was being distributed on the Eastern Seaboard, where it once again relied on word of mouth, rather than advertising for sales. Although sales of Corona dipped in the early 1990s due to more intense competition from foreign beers, the power of word-of-mouth communication suggests that Corona is probably here to stay.

Corona reaped the benefits of word-of-mouth and diffusion processes without any overt attempt to stimulate them. In many cases, marketers try to directly influence word-of-mouth communication by depicting it in advertising or by trying to get opinion leaders to use a product and talk about it. For example, Canada Dry set up an advisory board of socially prominent women in major markets across the country to "serve Canada Dry club soda at their elegant dinner parties, talk it up to their socially prominent friends, and maneuver it into such upscale—and much publicized—events as the Boston marathon."[2] The company was seeking ways to compete with Perrier's sparkling water and came up with the idea of getting Canada Dry in the hands of local opinion leaders "in the hope of sparking a word-of-mouth campaign that would spread to a broader market [through a process of diffusion]."[3]

WORD-OF-MOUTH COMMUNICATION

Word of mouth is interpersonal communication between two or more individuals such as members of a reference group or a customer and a salesperson.

All of these people exert purchase influence through such communication. The adage "a satisfied customer is your best salesperson" illustrates the importance of word of mouth to the marketer: satisfied customers influence friends and relatives to buy; dissatisfied customers inhibit sales.

Such personal influence is most powerful because consumers generally regard friends and relatives as more credible and trustworthy than commercial sources of information. Moreover, seeking information from reference and family groups is a means of reducing the risk in a purchase decision. Consumers who consider purchasing an expensive item such as a car or socially visible items such as clothing or furniture are likely to obtain the opinion of "relevant others." Such opinions not only provide information to reduce financial and performance risk, but they also serve as a means of group sanction to reduce social risk.

Katz and Lazarsfeld conducted one of the first studies establishing the importance of word-of-mouth communication in a small midwestern community shortly after World War II. They found that word-of-mouth communication was the most important form of influence in the purchase of food products and household goods. In influencing consumers to switch brands, word of mouth was twice as effective as radio advertising, four times as effective as personal selling, and seven times as effective as newspapers and magazines.[4] Engel, Blackwell, and Kegerreis found that 60 percent of consumers cited word of mouth as the most influential factor in their use of a new auto diagnostic center.[5] In a 1990 study of personal computers, Herr, Kardes, and Kim found that word-of-mouth communication had a much stronger impact on brand evaluations than detailed brand information from a neutral source, *Consumer Reports* magazine.[6]

The importance of word of mouth is related to cultural values. In cultures dominated by group cohesion and adherence to group norms, communications from group members will have more influence. In Chinese and Japanese cultures, adherence to group norms is ingrained from childhood. As a result, word of mouth is an even more important influence in these countries than it is in the United States.

Nature of Word of Mouth

If marketers are to encourage positive word-of-mouth communication about their products, they must understand the:

- Types of word-of-mouth communication that occur.
- Process by which word-of-mouth communication occurs.
- Conditions for word-of-mouth communication.

Types of Word-of-Mouth Communication

A study by Richins and Root-Shaffer of personal influence in buying autos identified three types of word-of-mouth communication: product news, advice giving, and personal experience.[7] Product news is information about the product such as features of car models, new advances in car technology, or performance attributes. Advice giving involves expressions of opinions about the car or advice about which model to buy. Personal experience relates to comments about the performance of the consumer's car or why the consumer bought it. Product news is fairly straightforward, but the advice and personal experience dimensions of word-of-mouth communication could be either positive or negative.

These categories suggest that word of mouth serves two functions: to inform and to influence. Product news informs consumers; advice and personal experience are likely to influence consumer decisions. As a result, each type of communication is probably most important at different stages in the purchasing decision. Product news is important as a means of creating awareness about product features or about a new product. Once awareness is established, hearing about product experiences from a friend or relative gives consumers the ability to judge the relative merits of one brand or another. Finally, advice is most important in making the final decision, as the opinion of a "relevant other" regarding a purchase is likely to be influential.

Process of Word-of-Mouth Communication

The process of word-of-mouth communication has been described as a communication flow between opinion leaders and followers. Of key importance in this flow is whether the information being communicated is positive or negative.

Two-Step Flow of Communication. Katz and Lazarsfeld were among the first to identify the process of word-of-mouth communication. They described it as a two-step flow from the mass media to opinion leaders and from opinion leaders to followers (see top of Figure 18.1).[8] They believed that opinion leaders are more exposed to the mass media than are those whom they influence. As a result, opinion leaders are viewed as intermediaries between the mass media and other consumers. The majority of consumers—the followers—are viewed as passive recipients of information.

The principal contribution of the two-step flow theory is that it rejected the longstanding notion that the mass media were the principal means of influencing consumers and the principal sources of information. While the importance of personal influence relative to commercial influence is evident today, it was not as clear after World War II. Advertising was considered the dominant force. It was in the 1950s and, paradoxically, after the advent of television that advertising began to be viewed as a weaker force that was unlikely to change group-influenced purchasing choices. Advertising could reinforce existing product preferences, but it could not change negative opinions, particularly when consumers held them strongly.[9] The two-step flow theory encouraged the view that personal influence, not advertising, was the principal means of communication and influence.

▶**FIGURE 18.1** Two models of word-of-mouth communication

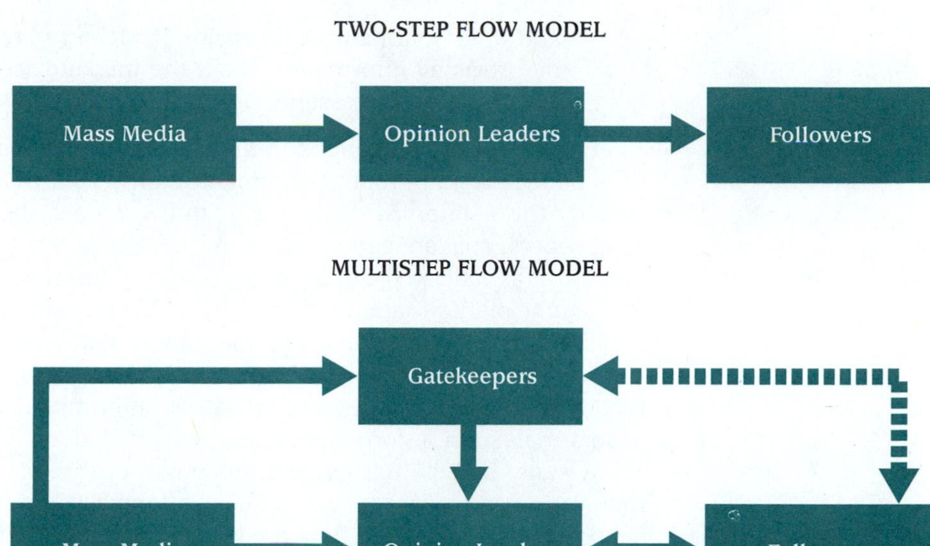

Multistep Flow of Communication. Although the two-step flow was important in understanding the process of personal influence, it was not an accurate representation of the flow of information and influence for three reasons:

1. Followers are not passive. They may initiate requests for information as well as listen to the unsolicited opinions of others.
2. Those who transmit information are also likely to receive it; that is, opinion leaders are also influenced by followers. Conversely, those who seek information are likely to give it. Word-of-mouth influence is frequently a two-directional flow between transmitters and receivers.
3. Opinion leaders are not the only ones to receive information from the mass media. Followers are also influenced by advertising. Moreover, opinion leaders may not control the flow of information from the mass media to the group. Katz and Lazarsfeld realized that there may be "gatekeepers" or "information gatherers" who serve this function.[10] **Gatekeepers** may be distinct from opinion leaders; they introduce ideas and information to the group but may not influence it.

   Researchers have also described *market mavens,* that is, individuals who are gatekeepers across many product categories because of their general expertise about places to shop, product characteristics, prices, and other marketing information.[11] Market mavens like helping others by providing information about the marketplace but, like gatekeepers, they may not necessarily be opinion leaders.

Because of the limitations in the concept of a two-step flow, a more realistic model of word-of-mouth communication would be a multistep flow, represented at the bottom of Figure 18.1. In this model, the mass media can reach gatekeepers, opinion leaders, or followers directly but are less likely to reach the followers (as indicated by the dashed line). Gatekeepers, although represented as a source of information to both opinion leaders and followers, are more likely to disseminate information to opinion leaders. Furthermore, word-of-mouth communication between opinion leaders and followers is represented as a two-directional flow: opinion leaders may seek information from followers, and followers may solicit information from opinion leaders.

A study by Still, Barnes, and Kooyman of the role of word-of-mouth communication and advertising in influencing moviegoers to see *Superman II* found support for the multistep flow model. The study found that followers cited both word of mouth and advertising as equally likely to influence them to see the movie. Thus, the pattern of influence can go from the mass media to followers without opinion leaders serving as intermediaries.[12] Moreover, the study found that the same individual could serve as both information provider and seeker, a pattern that supports the two-sided arrow between opinion leaders and followers in the multistep model in Figure 18.1.

Negative Word-of-Mouth Communication

Word-of-mouth communication can be negative as well as positive. Negative word of mouth is manifested in two ways: by communicating *direct experiences* such as poor product performance, lack of service, high prices, or rude sales personnel and by communicating *rumors* about a product or company.

Direct Experience. Negative word-of-mouth information tends to be more powerful than positive information. When consumers are dissatisfied, they complain to approximately three times as many friends and relatives as when they are satisfied. Richins' study of dissatisfied purchasers of clothing and appliances found that over half engaged in negative word-of-mouth communication about their experiences.[13] Such negative communication was most likely when:

- Consumers viewed the problem as serious.
- Consumers placed the blame for dissatisfaction directly on the manufacturer or retailer.
- Consumers believed that complaining directly to the source would not do any good.

In addition, Mizerski found that consumers are more likely to pay attention to negative than to positive information.[14] The power of negative word-of-mouth communication is illustrated by the fact that it killed the movie *Heaven's Gate* almost overnight, resulting in a $50 million loss for United Artists and the sale of the company by its conglomerate owner.[15]

As we saw in Chapter 2, most dissatisfied consumers do not complain about products to manufacturers or seek satisfaction by returning them. As a result, many companies conclude that their consumers are generally satisfied and that negative word of mouth is unlikely. This reaction effectively ignores the damaging effects of negative word-of-mouth communications. Other companies recognize that silence does not necessarily mean satisfaction. Companies such as Procter & Gamble, General Electric, and Whirlpool have encouraged consumers to provide product feedback through toll-free telephone numbers.

http://www.pg.com/

http://www.ge.com/

http://www.whirlpool.com/

Rumors. A type of negative word-of-mouth communication is false rumors about a company or product. Occasionally, false rumors have proved harmful to sales. One of the most pervasive was the rumor that Procter & Gamble was "in league with Satan," based on the company's 108-year-old logo—a man in the moon with 13 stars. The problem was that the man in the moon's curly hair looked like an inverted 666. That number has long been associated with Satan. The company withdrew the logo after a five-year effort, numerous court cases against rumor generators, and hundreds of thousands of dollars spent to dispel the rumor.[16] In the late 1980s, P&G brought the logo back on four products, only to have the rumors start afresh. By 1990, the company was reporting an average of 150 calls a day from consumers who wanted to know if the company had pledged its profits to the Devil.[17] In 1991, the company revised the logo by giving the man in the moon straighter hair. But that did not dispel the rumors. In 1995 P&G sued an independent Amway distributor for linking the company to a rumor that a large part of its profits go to support satanic churches.[18]

http://www.Amway.com/

Sometimes, advertisers try to combat rumors with advertising campaigns that attempt to set the record straight. Consumers may have misconceptions about a product or company, and marketers use advertising to combat this negative information. A good example is the ad in Exhibit 18.1. The misperception existed among consumers that Hunt-Wesson was owned by a rich Texas magnate called Hunt. The ad dispels the false rumor by identifying the true owner, the Norton Simon company, and the true company location, California.

There have been other rumors that have harmed companies. For example:

- Poprocks, a General Foods candy, was rumored to cause children to explode.[19]
- McDonald's was rumored to use red worms in its hamburgers and suffered a 30 percent decrease in sales in areas where the rumors circulated.[20]
- Entenmann's, the world's largest baker of fresh cake products, was rumored to be owned by the Reverend Sun Myung Moon's Unification Church.[21]
- Tropical Fantasy, a low-priced soft drink that competes with Coke and Pepsi in downscale inner-city areas, was rumored to have been manu-

http://www.mcdonalds.com/

▶EXHIBIT 18.1
Using word-of-mouth communication to set the record straight

factured by the Ku Klux Klan.[22] Its sales plunged 70 percent in a three-month period as a result.

In most of these cases, rumors eventually die. However, as we saw in the case of the P&G logo, they can be persistent. Entenmann's (actually owned by Warner-Lambert, the pharmaceutical conglomerate) fought the rumors of the association with Moon's Unification Church with advertising, press conferences, and letters of denial.[23] The Tropical Fantasy rumors prompted an investigation by a state district attorney's office to determine if competitors were behind the rumors.[24]

http://www.warner-lambert.com/

Conditions for Word-of-Mouth Communication

Word-of-mouth communication is not the dominant factor in every situation. For instance, Herr, Kardes, and Kim found that word of mouth is not as important in the evaluation of an automobile if (1) consumers already have a strong impression of the product, and/or (2) negative information regarding the product is available.[25] This means that word-of-mouth communication is unlikely to change the attitudes of consumers who have strong brand loyalties. A third condition in which word of mouth is unlikely to change attitudes is when consumers have doubts about a product because of credible negative information.

CONSUMER BEHAVIOR AND THE NEW TECHNOLOGIES

▶ The Internet: Taking Word of Mouth to a New Level

A whole new dimension in word-of-mouth communication is developing on the Internet. Until now, word of mouth has generally been viewed as communication between friends, relatives, and colleagues in small groups. But a new computer start-up, Firefly Network Inc., has expanded the dimensions of word of mouth. Through Firefly's Web site(http://www.firefly.com) an individual can get into contact with hundreds of others with similar tastes, judgments, and opinions, people that a consumer is likely to trust.

Firefly develops profiles of the people who use its site and groups them by similarity on a range of tastes, issues, and opinions. It then puts these individuals into contact with each other (if they choose). So far, the company is focusing on similarity in tastes for music and movies, but it plans to expand into mutual funds, restaurants, and books.

The site is also a potential advertising medium. Firefly plans to accept advertising banners on its site and place them in front of those consumers most likely to be interested in the company's products. In this manner, marketers can reach predefined involved consumers with customized pitches.

Of greatest interest is the chat lines on Firefly's site that provide the vehicle for expanding word of mouth beyond small groups. These sites lead to a sense of community as individuals get to know each other on line. And they lead to some surprising connections—for example, a 57-year-old inventor and ex-marine being put into contact with a 26-year-old immigrant from Poland because of common interests in Shakespeare and Baroque music.

With the likely diffusion of Internet usage, word of mouth is no longer what it used to be.

Source: "Why Firefly Had Mad Ave. Buzzing," *Business Week* (October 7, 1996), pp. 10–102.

Word of mouth is not dominant for every product category. It is most important when reference groups are likely to be sources of information and influence. This means that word of mouth is most important when:

- The product is visible and, therefore, purchase behavior is apparent.
- The product is distinctive and can more easily be identified with style, taste, and other personal norms.
- The product has just been introduced, and consumers have not formed impressions and attitudes about it.
- The product is important to the reference group's norms and belief system (for example, teenagers' reactions to a new rock CD or older consumers' reactions to a new salt-free breakfast product).
- Consumers are involved in the purchase decision and, as a result, are more likely to communicate about it and influence others.

- Consumers see the purchase of the product as risky and, thus, are more likely to initiate product-related conversations and to request information from friends and relatives.

Opinion Leadership

The influence of word-of-mouth communication in consumer behavior is tied closely to the concept of opinion leadership. As we saw earlier, individuals most likely to influence others through word of mouth are opinion leaders, and individuals most likely to be influenced are followers.

Nature of Opinion Leadership

The marketer must answer two questions before directing appeals to opinion leaders or attempting to stimulate positive word-of-mouth communication:

1. Is there a general opinion leader, or is opinion leadership specific to particular product categories?
2. Is opinion leadership really leadership?

Is There a General Opinion Leader? Most studies have found that there is no general opinion leader. Instead, *opinion leadership is product-specific*. That is, an opinion leader for one category is not likely to be influential across unrelated categories. Personal influence in one category carries over only to closely related categories. For example, opinion leaders for small appliances are likely to be opinion leaders for large appliances; or those who are influential for packaged foods are also likely to be influential for household cleansers and detergents.[26]

Although most studies suggest that a general opinion leader does not exist, three categories of consumers do suggest generalized influence across product categories: influentials, market mavins, and surrogate consumers.

Influentials. The Roper Organization, a well-known market research firm, has conducted yearly surveys since World War II to identify influentials.[27] Influentials are defined as those individuals who are active in community and public affairs. Specifically, influentials are identified as individuals who take part in three or more of the activities listed in Figure 18.2. On this basis, 10 to 12 percent of American adults are defined as influentials. Figure 18.2 shows the proportion of influentials who take part in each of the activities listed compared to the general population. For example, three-fourths have attended town meetings compared to less than 20 percent of the general population, one-half have attended a political rally, and one-third have made a speech compared to less than 10 percent of the general population.

Influentials tend to be upscale, and the majority are baby boomers. Well educated and well read, they are much more likely to be asked their opinions about products and services that depend on word-of-mouth recommendations such as restaurants, books, movies, and financial services. Influentials also tend to buy

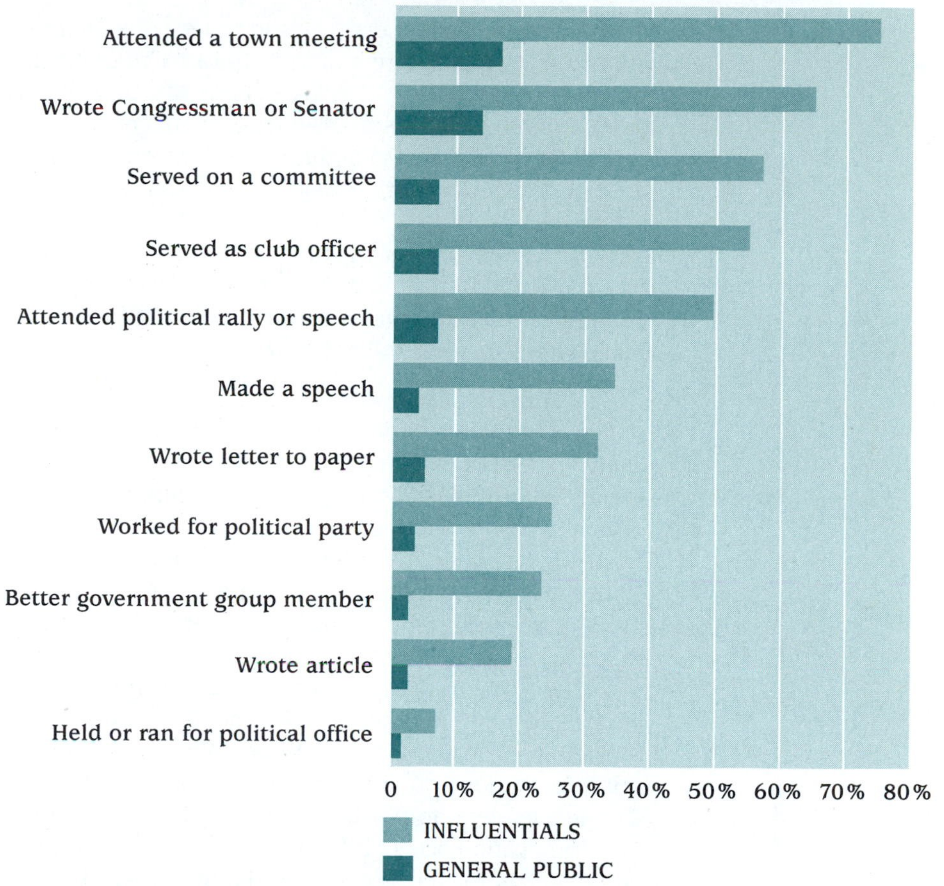

FIGURE 18.2 Defining the influentials

Source: "The Influentials," *American Demographics* (October, 1992), p. 32.

new products when they are first marketed. They were among the first to buy a VCR and health foods and among the first to have started jogging. They will probably be among the first to adopt electronic cars and Internet services. Overall, it is clear that influentials come close to being general opinion leaders. However, they are not influential in every product category.

Market Mavens. Market mavens come closer to being general gatekeepers than opinion leaders. Feick and Price found that a market maven has "information on many kinds of products, places to shop, and other facets of markets, and initiates discussions with consumers and responds to requests from consumers for market information."[28]

Although market mavens are not necessarily opinion leaders, they are more likely to influence as well as to inform. They are good targets for product information—messages about product changes, prices, and new products—because they are likely to pass on this information.

Surrogate Consumers. A surrogate consumer is "an agent retained by a consumer to guide, direct, and/or transact marketplace activities."[29] Surrogates can play a wide range of roles such as tax consultants, wine stewards, interior decorators, or financial managers. Their degree of influence varies, but in many cases, they are asked to assume the decision role for consumers. As such, they are not general opinion leaders but are clearly opinion leaders in their surrogate role.

Consumers use surrogates because they may not have the time, inclination, or expertise to go through information search and decision making. Also, consumers can use surrogates to narrow their choices, to collect information, or to make the actual purchase decision.

Is Opinion Leadership Really Leadership? A number of studies have consistently found that individuals who transmit information to others are also more likely to receive information from others. That is, a consumer who frequently expresses opinions about sports equipment will also be more likely to listen to others' opinions about such equipment. A study of the adopters of stainless steel razor blades when they were first introduced found that 75 percent of opinion leaders were also influenced by others.[30] A study of women's influence in four product categories found that 80 percent of the influencers also received information from others.[31]

These findings suggest that the key element in face-to-face influence is not leadership but social communication. Those who are most likely to do the influencing are also most likely to be influenced. Therefore, individuals who transmit information and influence about a product do not have to be group leaders. Opinion leaders do not dominate others or communicate in a one-sided way. Communication occurs both ways between transmitter and receiver. As a result, better terms for the two-way exchange in word-of-mouth communications are *opinion giver* and *receiver* rather than *opinion leader* and *follower.*

Characteristics of the Opinion Leader

Marketers are interested in identifying opinion leaders, since these consumers may be very influential *within a product category.* Identification of the demographic characteristics that distinguish opinion leaders from other purchasers in a product category would permit marketers to select media most likely to reach this influential group. In identifying the attitudes or lifestyles of opinion leaders, marketers can develop promotional themes to appeal to this group.

However, reaching opinion leaders with advertising is difficult because they tend to communicate with consumers similar to themselves. Studies have found little difference between the demographic and lifestyle characteristics of opinion leaders and followers.[32] As a result, media to reach opinion leaders have not been identified. In addition, developing a profile of the opinion leader is difficult because such a profile has to be product-specific. The characteristics of the fashion opinion leader may be totally different from those of the food opinion leader. Few generalizations can be made across product categories.

Despite the difficulties of identifying opinion leaders, some general traits have been identified. Opinion leaders are more likely to

- Be knowledgeable about the product category.
- Be involved in the product category.
- Be active in receiving communications about the product from personal sources.
- Be interested in new products.[33]
- Read magazines and other print media relevant to their area of product interest.[34]
- Be self-confident in their appraisal of the product category.[35]
- Be more socially active, as a reflection of their willingness to communicate with others.

Few demographic and lifestyle characteristics have been found to identify opinion leaders. As a result, a strategy of trying to pinpoint opinion leaders and reach them through specific media is likely to fail. These findings do not mean that the study of word-of-mouth communication provides the marketer with few strategic applications. Rather, they suggest that strategic applications are best directed to stimulating word-of-mouth communication through advertising or through some direct identification of opinion leaders.

Methods to Identify Opinion Leaders

Marketers have used three methods to identify opinion leaders: the sociometric technique, the key informant method, and the self-designating technique.

Sociometric Technique. In the **sociometric technique,** group members are asked to identify people with whom they communicate about a product or idea. Specific individuals are identified and can, in turn, be interviewed to trace the network of communication. In his study, Coleman traced word-of-mouth communication between doctors.[36] Figure 18.3 shows the pattern of communication among nine doctors in a community. This network is known as a **sociogram.** Obviously, Doctor 5 is an opinion leader since the eight other doctors seek his advice. Doctor 5 also adopted a new drug sooner than the other eight doctors. Doctor 6 appears to be the second most influential person in the network as indicated by the two-way flow of communication between him and Doctor 5 and the fact that two other doctors seek his advice.

Sociometric analysis is used only for studies of communications in small groups. Most marketing studies require information beyond a single social group. However, sociometric analysis could be useful in identifying the common characteristics of opinion leaders by studying several groups and constructing a number of sociograms.

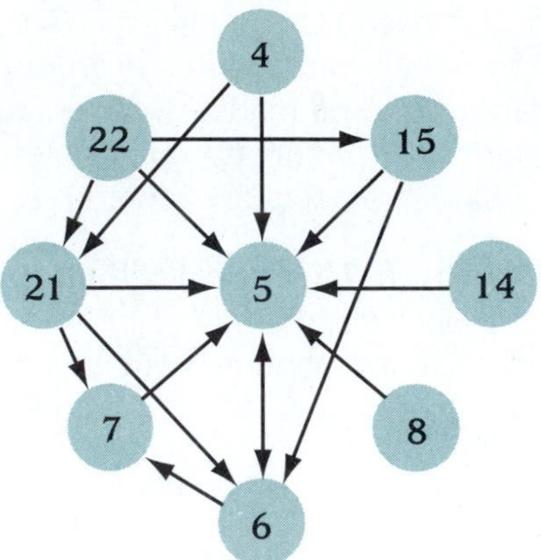

FIGURE 18.3 A sociogram of word-of-mouth communication among doctors

Source: James Coleman, "Social Processes in Physicians' Adoption of a New Drug," *Journal of Chronic Diseases*, 9 (1959), pp. 1–19. Reprinted with permission.

Key Informant Method. **Key informants** in a social group are asked to identify opinion leaders. Key informants are individuals who engage in frequent word-of-mouth communication within a group, but they are not necessarily opinion leaders. Using this technique, key informants would be asked to rate the prestige or leadership of members of their group. Like sociometric analysis, it is restricted to a particular social group.

Self-Designating Techniques. **Self-designating techniques** are often used by marketers because they identify opinion leaders beyond a single social group. As the name implies, this technique asks consumers a series of questions to determine the degree to which they perceive themselves as opinion leaders. The questions usually pertain to a particular product category and ask consumers to rate themselves on whether they are more or less likely to be asked advice about the product compared to their friends, and whether friends and neighbors regard them as a good source of advice about the product.[37]

Most of the marketing studies cited in this chapter have used the self-designating technique. These studies are surveys of brand and product influence that extend beyond a single social group; therefore, a self-designating method is necessary.

Strategic Applications of Word-of-Mouth Communication

Marketers try to influence word-of-mouth communication among consumers in various ways. They can try to:

1. Stimulate word of mouth through free product trials.
2. Stimulate word of mouth in advertising by suggesting that consumers tell friends about the product or service.

3. Simulate word of mouth through advertising showing typical consumers saying positive things about the product.
4. Portray communications from opinion leaders.

In this section, we consider each of these strategies.

Stimulating Word of Mouth Through Product Trial

Companies can try to stimulate word-of-mouth communication by offering products for trial. Such strategies are generally targeted to opinion leaders. If successful, product trial should stimulate a social multiplier effect since these individuals would disseminate information and exert a disproportionate amount of influence on friends and relatives.

http://www.chryslercars.com/

When Chrysler introduced its luxury LH models in 1992, Chrysler dealers in 25 areas of the country offered the cars for a test drive over a weekend to influential community leaders and business people. From October 1992 to January 1993, more than 6,000 individuals took Chrysler up on the offer. A subsequent survey found strong evidence of a social multiplier effect since Chrysler estimates approximately 32,000 people were involved in the test drive when one includes secondary drivers and passengers. The survey also found that 98 percent of respondents said they would recommend the car to a friend. The promotion was so successful that Chrysler then placed the cars at 19 luxury resorts for free use by guests.[38]

How can marketers identify such opinion leaders? Two approaches have frequently been used. First, because of the close relationship between opinion leadership and new product adoption, it is possible to identify consumers who are among the first to adopt a new appliance or other product with a purchase record and assume that these individuals are opinion leaders. A second approach is to identify influentials in a community based on the activities identified by the Roper Organization in Figure 18.2. Presumably, this is the method Chrysler used.

Stimulating Word of Mouth Through Advertising and Promotions

Advertisers can try to encourage consumers to talk about the product. One approach is to encourage consumers to "tell your friends" or to "ask your friends." The Acme Supermarket Chain advertises, "Tell a friend. Save at Acme." Commercials for Fabergé Organics shampoo urged users to tell two friends so they will tell two friends and so on as the faces on the screen multiply to show the spread of word of mouth.[39] For such strategies to work, the product must be in a strong position and word-of-mouth communication must be positive.

http://www.harley-davidson.com/

Another approach is to organize events to stimulate word of mouth. We saw in the last chapter that Harley-Davidson holds family-oriented events to get Harley owners together. Similarly, off-road vehicles like Jeep, Isuzu, and Land Rover hold jamborees to stimulate word of mouth. Jeep has been sponsoring these events for over 40 years. One Jeep executive says, "Our best endorsement is word-of-mouth. A jamboree makes for good cocktail talk. That just reinforces the Jeep name."[40]

http://www.jeepunpaved.com/

Simulating Word-of-Mouth Communication

By portraying recommendations from typical consumers, advertising can simulate word-of-mouth communication. In portraying personal influence, these ads seek to simulate direct contact by consumers with friends and relatives. The assumption is that the typical person in the ad is credible enough to convince consumers to believe the information this individual provides.

http://www.saturncars.com/

General Motors built its first advertising campaign for Saturn cars around word-of-mouth communication. When it introduced Saturn in 1991, GM received unsolicited letters from satisfied customers. These letters were then routed to the company's advertising agency and used in print ads. An example, showing one such customer, is in Exhibit 18.2. Saturn's president provided the rationale for simulating word of mouth as follows: "We want the actual owners to tell their stories. . . . The ads are just like listening to other people, like your neighbors, tell you about their new car."[41]

TV commercials have also attempted to simulate word of mouth. The most frequent approach is the "slice of life" in which a real-life situation is portrayed. For example, one consumer tells another about the virtues of a brand of coffee

▶EXHIBIT 18.2
Saturn simulates word-of-mouth by portraying actual consumers

▶EXHIBIT 18.3
Ads portraying accurate and inaccurate word-of-mouth communication

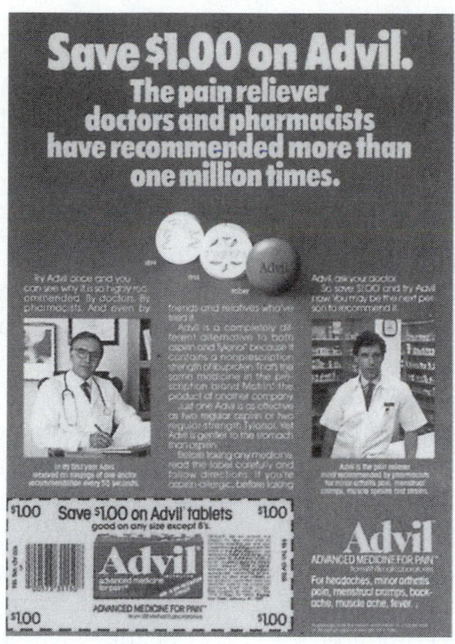

while making it. Another approach is the hidden camera showing people in TV commercials making unsolicited recommendations for the product.

Portraying Communications from Opinion Leaders

A strategy that is related to simulating word of mouth is to portray communications from opinion leaders that influence followers. The Advil ad in Exhibit 18.3 shows two opinion leaders for pharmaceuticals, a doctor and a pharmacist, expressing their approval for the product.

Companies will occasionally attempt to discourage and discredit certain types of word-of-mouth communication. Schering has used advertising to encourage consumers to rely on pharmacists rather than on friends or neighbors for information about medication. By depicting inaccurate sources of information, Schering's ad in Exhibit 18.3 attempts to discredit nonexpert medical advice.

http://www.sch-plough.com/

◆ THE DIFFUSION PROCESS

In this section, we consider communications across groups through the diffusion of information and influence over a wider segment of society. Research on word-of-mouth communication and opinion leadership view communications on a *micro* level since communications are among a small number of individuals. In contrast, research on the process of diffusion views communications on a *macro* level since communications and product ownership are traced across a large number of individuals over time.

Importance of New Products

http:///www.mmm.com/

http:/www.jnj.com/

From the marketer's standpoint, the most relevant area of study is the diffusion of new products, particularly those that can be classified as innovations. The adoption of new products is a critical question to marketers because new product success is linked to profitability. Companies such as 3M and Johnson & Johnson have a policy of ensuring that at least one-fourth of company sales should come from products introduced during the previous five years.[42] In areas with rapid technological change such as computers and consumer electronics, the majority of sales are likely to come from products introduced in the last two or three years.

The process of diffusion is exemplified by American consumers' acceptance of VCRs and their rejection of videodisc players. Videocassette recorders won quick acceptance because they provided an important benefit, recording capability. Furthermore, consumers could observe VCRs in use, and VCRs were compatible with frequent TV viewing. Diffusion theory would predict that innovations with these characteristics would be successful. Although videodisc players were observable and compatible with current TV usage, they did not produce any obvious benefit compared to VCRs because of their lack of recording capabilities. As a result, RCA lost hundreds of millions of dollars when its videodisc entry, SelectaVision, failed.

Diffusion Research and Marketing Strategy

Diffusion research traces the spread of product acceptance across its life cycle. Figure 18.4 shows the phases of the product life cycle from introduction to decline and the associated categories of product adopters by time of adoption. The diffusion process identifies innovators in the introductory period of the life cycle, early adopters during growth, the majority of adopters during the mature phase, and laggards (late adopters) during maturity and decline. These phases of adoption are important because they are linked to different marketing strategies during the product life cycle. In the introductory phase, the firm tries to establish distribution, build brand awareness, and encourage trial to begin the diffusion process. As the product takes hold, the firm can define its primary target, the early adopters. It is now trying to reinforce the toehold it has in the market by moving from an objective of creating awareness to one of broadening product appeals and product availability.

As the brand matures, competition intensifies and sales begin to level off. The firm starts to emphasize price appeals and sales promotions and begins to consider some product modifications to gain a competitive advantage. At this stage, the majority of adopters enter the market, based largely on the influence of the early adopters. Since others have already gone through an adoption process, the majority do not need to rely as much on the mass media for information. When the brand is in the decline phase, lower prices become more

FIGURE 18.4 Distribution of adopter categories

Source: Reprinted with the permission of The Free Press, a division of Macmillan, Inc. from *Diffusion of Innovations,* 3/e by Everett M. Rogers. Copyright © 1962, 1971, 1983 by The Free Press.

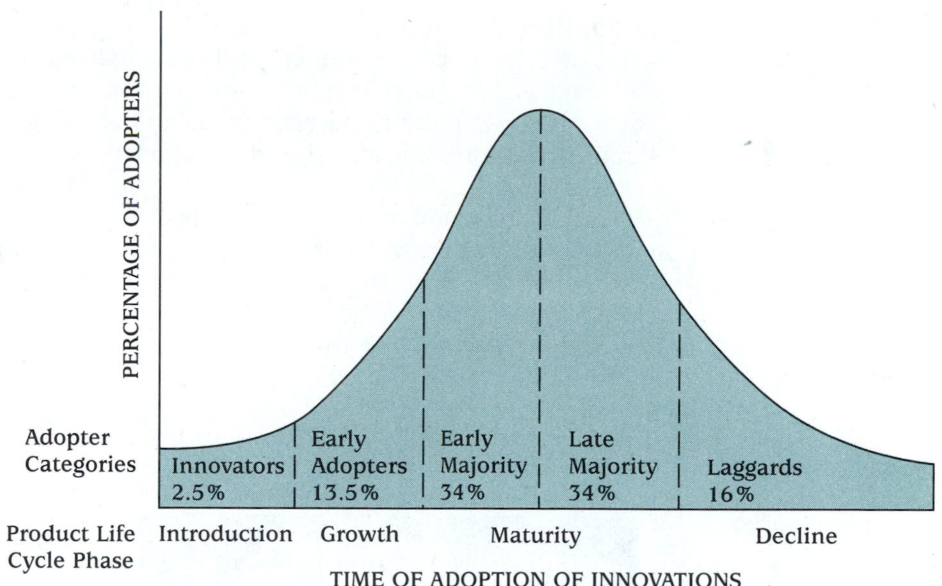

prevalent. The firm begins to consider either revitalizing the brand or deleting it. At this point, the latest adopters enter the market.

Because diffusion research traces the rate of acceptance of new products and identifies adopter categories by stages in the product's life cycle, it is directly tied to these strategic shifts.

Steps in the Diffusion Process

Diffusion is the process by which the *adoption* of an innovation spreads *over time* to other consumers through *communication.* Suppose a consumer buys a compact disc player soon after it is introduced. Through word of mouth, the consumer tells friends and relatives that the disc player provides finer sound and is easier to use than a record player. Others in the consumer's reference group buy. These individuals are regarded as early adopters. Over time, they begin to communicate positive experiences with disc players not only to members of their reference group, but also to other groups as well—casual acquaintances, sports clubs, and business associates with whom they have infrequent contact. At this point, diffusion begins to spread rapidly. The characteristics of these later adopters differ from those of earlier adopters, which means that the target for CD players in the earlier stages of adoption was different than it is now.

Based on this description, comprehending the diffusion process in marketing requires an understanding of (1) the nature of *adoption,* (2) the *time* of adoption (earlier or later), and (3) *communication* across groups. Most of the rest of this chapter is devoted to these three elements of diffusion.

Adoption Decision

The adoption of an innovation requires an individual or a group of consumers to make a decision regarding a new product. If adopters influence others to buy, both within their reference group and across groups, a diffusion process starts. Therefore, it is logical to think of adoption as the first step in the diffusion process.

The adoption of an innovation is likely to be an involving decision to those who are among the first to adopt. The steps of the adoption process are shown on the left in Figure 18.5 and reflect a high-involvement hierarchy of effects. These steps parallel those in the process of complex decision making shown on the right in Figure 18.5. The consumer:

FIGURE 18.5 Steps in the adoption process

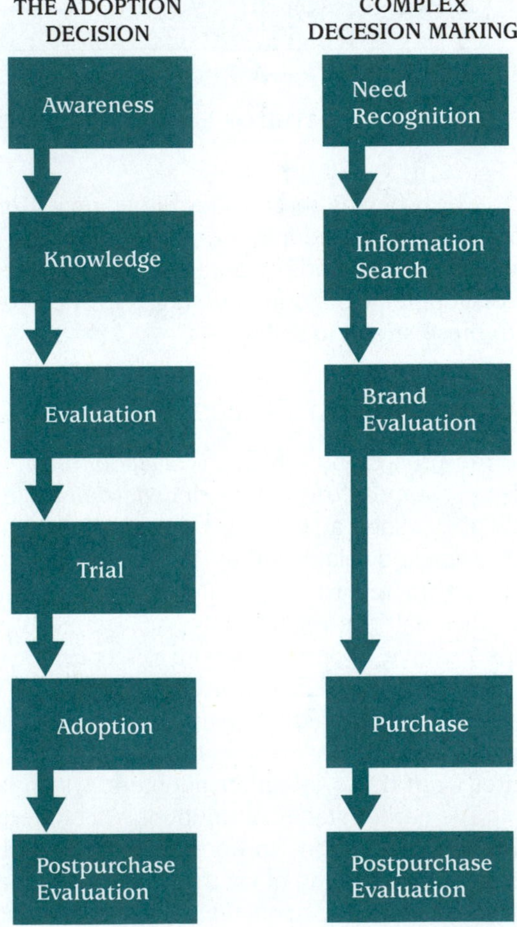

- Becomes *aware* of and recognizes a need for the product.
- Searches for information (*knowledge* acquisition).
- *Evaluates* the alternatives.
- Decides whether to try it before making a decision (*trial*).
- Makes a decision whether to *adopt* or not.
- *Evaluates* the product after the purchase.

Three components of this process should be emphasized in understanding diffusion. First, product trial is more important than in most other decisions because the product is new and risk is likely to be higher. For many, innovations such as electric cars are difficult to try on any sufficient basis to form a firm evaluation. Prospective adopters could take one out for a test drive or drive one if a friend has adopted. But trial is for a short period of time. Marketers will generally promote trial if they can. America Online offers 10 hours of free service in the first month of service to subscribers with the option to cancel at any time.

http://www.aol.com/

Second, postpurchase evaluation is likely to be more important because of the expense and complexity of many innovations and the rapid pace of technological change. Many personal computer owners already have discarded their original machines to obtain second- and third-generation technologies. If many of these adopters had discontinued the use of PCs because of dissatisfaction with their first purchase, the PC market would be shrinking instead of expanding.

Third, the outcome of the decision process can be rejection as well as adoption. A consumer evaluating a cellular telephone might have concluded that the unit is not worth the price just to gain the benefit of taking a phone anywhere. In this case, the consumer has rejected the innovation at the evaluation stage. If the consumer decides that the price may be worth the benefits, he or she will consider the product for trial. A high rate of rejection could mean failure, as was the case with consumer rejection of RCA's videodisc players because of their lack of recording capabilities. Or rejection could mean a slow rate of adoption, as is the case with the use of solar energy panels to heat homes.

The stages in adoption in Figure 18.5 are important to the marketer because they indicate the acceptance of the product and the effect of a promotional campaign based on answers to the following questions: To what degree is the public aware of the innovation? Is the public's information accurate? What are consumers' attitudes toward the innovation? What is the likelihood of trial and subsequent adoption? Are consumers satisfied after adopting the innovation?

Characteristics That Encourage Adoption. The likelihood of adoption and subsequent diffusion of a new product depend on the product's nature. If marketers can anticipate a product's likelihood of adoption, they can adjust strategies accordingly. For example, marketers can overcome resistance to adoption by offering free samples and lowering prices during an introductory period. Rogers and Shoemaker identified the following five characteristics that increase the rate of acceptance and diffusion of a new product.[43]

1. *Relative advantage* is the degree to which consumers perceive a new product as superior to existing substitutes—for example, the relative advantage of an electric car in saving money and reducing pollution or the relative advantage of cellular telephones in providing mobile communications.
2. *Compatibility* is the degree to which the product is consistent with consumers' needs, attitudes, and past experiences. If electric cars and cellular telephones are not markedly different from consumers' expectations regarding driving and phone usage, they are compatible. An aspirin product that could be taken without water when consumers are on the run failed in its test market because consumers were simply unaccustomed to taking pills without water. The product was not compatible with their past experiences and habits.
3. *Simplicity* is the ease in understanding and using a new product. Products such as electric toothbrushes, instant foods, and cook-in-the-bag vegetables are easy to understand and use. Computer companies such as Apple and IBM have tried to overcome the initial complexity of using personal computers by advertising their machines as user-friendly.

http://www.apple.com/

http://www.ibm.com/

4. *Observability* is the ease with which the product can be observed and communicated to potential consumers. Products that are highly visible are more easily diffused. Fashion items and cars are good examples.
5. *Trialability* is the degree to which a product can be tried before adoption. As noted, many innovations have little trialability. Limited trial is possible by demonstrations in showrooms or by using items such as fax machines or personal computers at work and determining if adoption for home use is desirable. One element that is related to trialability is *divisibility*. If consumers can purchase a product in small quantities, then trial is relatively easy. Shoemaker and Shoaf studied five packaged goods and found that almost two-thirds of consumers made trial purchases of new brands in smaller quantities than they usually purchased.[44]

Studies of these five factors generally agree that relative advantage and compatibility are most important in influencing adoption of an innovation. For example, LaBay and Kinnear found that adopters of solar energy systems rated these systems significantly higher than nonadopters on relative advantage and compatibility as well as simplicity.[45] Holak and Lehmann came up with similar findings for durable innovation categories.[46]

Characteristics That Encourage Rejection. Each of the five factors cited in the previous section could cause consumers to reject an innovation—namely, lack of relative advantage, incompatibility with previous habits and experiences, complexity, lack of observability, and inability to try the product. Ram and Sheth considered these factors in citing three major barriers to adopting an innovation: value barrier, usage barrier, and risk barrier.[47]

Value Barrier. The **value barrier** is a product's lack of relative advantage compared with substitute products. When first introduced, cellular telephones cost about $2,000 per unit. They were accepted in business markets because the advantage of mobile communications was worth the cost. However, the cost was too high for most consumers relative to the value they could get from regular telephones.

Manufacturers can overcome the value barrier in two ways. First, they can reduce the price through technological advances. Costs of cellular phones have decreased to bring the value of mobile communications into line with price for most consumers. The primary issue now is not the cost of the phone but the cost of monthly cellular service charges. Second, they can convey information to consumers through advertising to convince them of the product's value. Through the Charlie Chaplin campaign, IBM was able to convey the value of PCs to small business owners who doubted the worth of PCs relative to their cost.

Usage Barrier. A **usage barrier** occurs when an item is not compatible with consumers' existing practices or habits.[48] Systems that offer interactive in-home shopping and banking services by computer, for example, have encountered stiff resistance from consumers. The problem is that consumers like to interact with store personnel and to see the merchandise when they shop. Furthermore,

EXHIBIT 18.4
A product subject to a usage barrier

shopping is a social occasion for many consumers who shop with friends. For most consumers, computerized shopping is not compatible with their desire for the visual and social stimuli of shopping. Exhibit 18.4 shows a Gardenburger® Veggie patty ad aimed at overcoming a different usage barrier—the resistance some consumers feel toward healthful, low-fat foods.

Marketers have difficulty overcoming usage barriers because the innovation may be contrary to ingrained needs and usage habits. Advertising is unlikely to change consumers' needs and habits. One option that marketers have is to try to employ change agents to overcome usage resistance. **Change agents** are opinion leaders who have more influence and credibility than commercially sponsored means such as personal selling and advertising in convincing consumers to change their needs and habits. Companies producing farm seed and equipment use change agents by first targeting farm innovations to university agricultural extension people, the U.S. Department of Agriculture, and larger farmers who are receptive to modernization. Once these industry leaders adopt the innovation, it is more likely to be diffused to smaller farmers.

http://www.usda.gov/

Risk Barrier. A **risk barrier** represents consumers' physical, economic, performance, or social risk of adopting an innovation. When microwave ovens were first introduced, consumers expressed worries about physical risk from radiation. Technological improvements and consumer education overcame this perceived risk. Adopters of home computers had fears of economic and performance risks, which were largely overcome by decreasing prices and improved software. Dickeson and Gentry found that risk was further reduced because many consumers had experience with computer-related products such as programmable calculators.[49] Consumers' social risk of adopting designer jeans was also overcome when opinion leaders in consumers' peer groups accepted these products and when they were more generally accepted across groups.

One of the most effective ways to reduce consumer risk in adopting an innovation is through trial. Free samples are an effective tool for continuous innovations such as tartar control toothpaste. Car manufacturers offer a form of trial with test rides for new models. Some marketers can offer trial even for high-priced discontinuous innovations. For example, when Sony introduced its ProMavica electronic photography system, it distributed 150 prototypes of the product to its primary target, large newspaper publishers.[50] Distribution of the prototype permitted publishers to experience the product and encouraged diffusion from these opinion leaders to other newspaper and magazine publishers.

http://www.sony.com/

Time

Time is a key component of diffusion theory based on two measures: first, the time of adoption by consumers (whether consumers are earlier or later adopters of the innovation) and second, the rate of diffusion (the speed and extent with which adoption has taken place across groups).

Time of Adoption. Rogers developed a classification of adopters by *time of adoption*. Examining over 500 studies of diffusion, he concluded that there are five categories of adopters as shown in Figure 18.4: (1) innovators, (2) early adopters, (3) the early majority, (4) the late majority, and (5) laggards.[51] Using past research, Rogers determined that these categories follow a normal distribution. Rogers described each adopter category as follows:

1. *Innovators* represent on average the first 2.5 percent of all those who adopt. They are eager to try new ideas and products almost as an obsession. They have higher incomes, are better educated, are more cosmopolitan, and are more active outside of their community than non-innovators. In addition, they are less reliant on group norms, more self-confident, and more likely to obtain their information from scientific sources and experts.
2. *Early adopters* represent on average the next 13.5 percent to adopt the product. While they are not the very first, they adopt early in the product's life cycle. More reliant on group norms and values than innovators, they are also more oriented to the local community, in contrast to the innovators' cosmopolitan outlook. Early adopters are most likely to be opinion leaders because of their closer affiliation to groups. Since they are more likely to transmit word-of-mouth influence, early adopters are probably the most important group in determining whether the new product will be successful.
3. The *early majority* (next 34 percent to adopt) deliberate carefully before adopting a new product. They are likely to collect more information and evaluate more brands than early adopters do; therefore, the process of adoption takes longer. The early majority are an important link in the process of diffusing new ideas as they are positioned between earlier and later adopters.
4. The *late majority* (next 34 percent to adopt) are described by Rogers as skeptical. They adopt because most of their friends have already done so. Since they also rely on group norms, adoption is the result of pressure to conform. This group tends to be older and below average in income and education.
5. *Laggards* are the final 16 percent to adopt. They are similar to innovators in not relying on the group's norms. Independent because they are tradition bound, laggards make decisions in terms of the past. By the time laggards adopt an innovation, it has probably been superseded by something else. For example, they purchased their first television set when color television was already widely owned, and many still do not own a VCR. Laggards have the lowest socioeconomic status. They tend to be suspicious of new products and alienated from a technologically advancing society.[52]

Figure 18.6 shows product life cycles for record albums, cassettes, and compact discs from 1973 to 1989 that reflect time of adoption. Record albums are in the declining phase of the life cycle because of new technologies. By 1989,

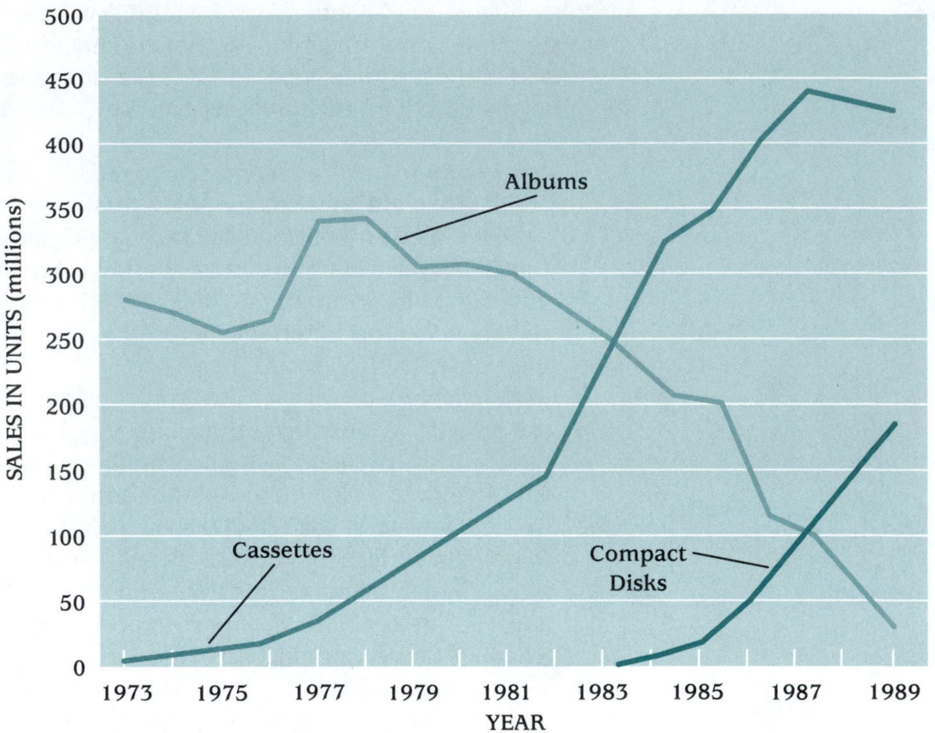

FIGURE 18.6 The life cycle for three product categories

Source: "Recording Enters a New Era, and You Can't Find It on LP," *The New York Times* (April 1, 1990), pp. 1, 24. Copyright © 1990 by The New York Times Company. Reprinted with permission.

about 35 million records were sold compared to 10 times that number in 1977. Cassettes have entered the mature phase of their life cycle, with sales leveling off for the first time in 1988. People first buying cassette recorders in 1990 were in the late majority category. In 1989, compact discs were still in the growth stage of the life cycle, with sales growing at an increasing rate. By 1989, most innovators and early adopters already purchased compact disc players, with majority starting to enter the market.

Adoption Curve. The difference between the product life cycle curve for records, cassettes, and CDs in Figure 18.6 and the adoption curve in Figure 18.4 is that the former depicts sales levels on the vertical axis and the latter depicts the percentage of adopters for a given time period. Both curves plot time on the horizontal axis. Both the product life cycle and adoption curves are generally shown as normal, bell-shaped curves. However, both may vary, depending on the type of product. Figure 18.7 illustrates some of the more common variations from the normal curve.

The first curve shows a product that has a long introduction stage because consumers adopt it slowly. This is typical of a major innovation. In this case, fewer individuals will adopt early but more will adopt in the late majority and laggard categories. The life cycle for record albums was gradual because their adoption was tied to ownership of a record player; it took at least 20 years for record players to achieve widespread adoption. Adoption of cassettes and compact discs is more rapid in a more technologically sophisticated and affluent society. The second curve is an innovation with a fast adoption rate and a short introductory stage. The rate of adoption for compact discs from 1983 to 1989 was fairly rapid, as shown in Figure 18.4.

The third curve in Figure 18.7 is a fad product with a rapid rise and a rapid decline. Movie spinoff products, such as Teenage Mutant Ninja Turtle dolls, follow such a curve. Sales for such a fad are likely to rise and fall sharply, so that the product life cycle looks more like a pinnacle than a bell. The adoption of Beanie Babies, bean bag creatures with names like Bones the Dog, caught on rapidly in 1996. The strategy for the frequently out-of-stock fad product was to create deliberate scarcity "which pumps up word-of-mouth demand to a frenzied level."[53] But the creators also know that demand is likely to be short-lived.

The fourth curve shows a product that has been frequently revitalized, going through periods of decline and subsequent growth. Such products go through phases of technological improvements, requiring adoption of new technology at each phase. Personal computers are an example. The curve shows adoption in three phases, the first PCs introduced, then the introduction of hard drives, and then laptops.

Adopters Versus Nonadopters. Rogers' classification deals with adopter categories; it does not account for nonadopters. However, not all families own compact disc players, electric toothbrushes, food processors, or VCRs. As we saw, many consumers reject innovations.

To account for such nonadopters, many marketing studies have used a simple three-part classification: early adopters, later adopters, and nonadopters.[54] The early adopter group includes Rogers' innovators. In most studies of the dif-

FIGURE 18.7
Variations from the normal adoption curve
Source: *Marketing: Principles & Strategy.* Second Edition by Henry Assael, copyright © 1993 by The Dryden Press,

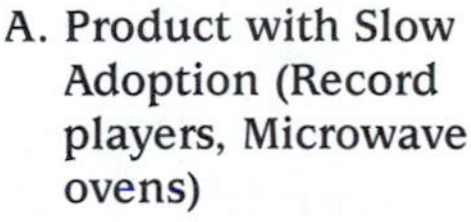

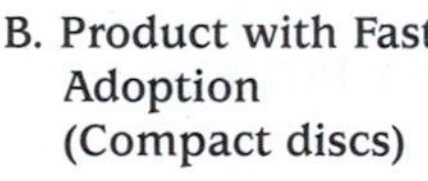

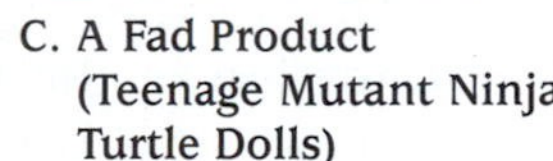

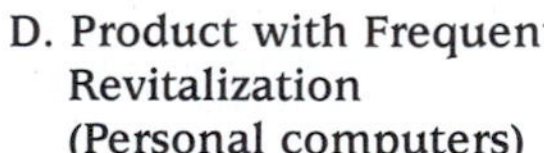

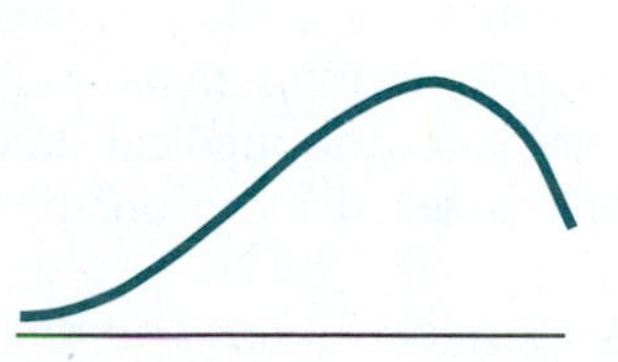

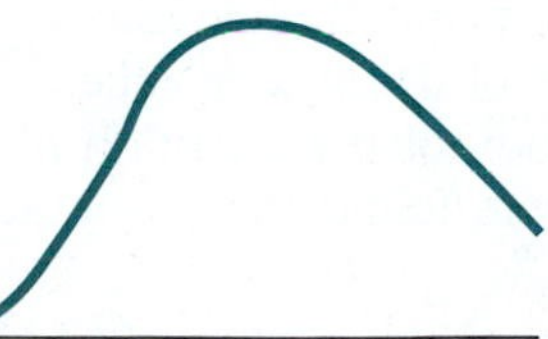

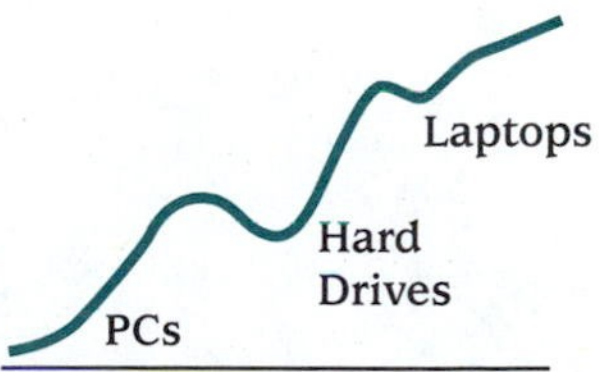

fusion of new products, such a classification is used because it simply is not feasible for management to direct marketing resources to the 2.5 percent of adopters represented by the true innovator. The later adopters combine the early and late majority and laggards. The nonadopter group provides for the possibility that a sizeable part of the market simply may decide not to buy the new product.

Rate of Diffusion. The rate of diffusion is the second key time-oriented measure. It is the *cumulative* level of adoption of a new product over time *across groups*. For example, it took only 10 years from introduction for 90 percent of U.S. households to own a TV set. Similarly, ownership of VCRs grew to 50 percent in just 6 years. Adoption for some other innovations is much slower. For example, by 1988 telephone answering machines had been on the market for 26 years, yet only 12 percent of American households owned one. The use of automatic teller machines grew to about 9 percent of consumers in 14 years.[55] In general, the speed of adoption of innovations seems to be increasing. In a study of 25 appliances, Olshavsky found that consumers are adopting new products more quickly than they used to.[56] Why are innovations being adopted more rapidly?

- Disposable income among U.S. households is increasing, making new products more affordable.
- Technological advances are more rapid, requiring quicker adoption cycles.
- Technology is becoming more standardized, reducing consumers' risk of adopting a new product.[57] When videocassette recorders were first introduced, consumers were reluctant to buy because two competing technologies were being marketed, Betamax and VHS. Eventually, the latter won out, creating a standardized product. Similarly, the rate of diffusion for PCs was fairly rapid because of acceptance of DOS as the industry-wide standard operating system.
- Information is being communicated quickly. The more rapidly people learn about a new product through the mass media and the Internet, the more rapid is communication within and across groups.

Communication in the Diffusion Process

Communication is the last key element in the definition of diffusion. When a product is first introduced, consumers tend to rely on the mass media for information. Advertising is designed to create awareness and convey information. A study of early users of a new automobile diagnostic center in a midwestern city found that early adopters of the service relied primarily on magazines and radio for information.[58] A study of the adoption of self-diagnostic medical devices among elderly consumers found that early adopters relied more on the mass media for information.[59]

Once awareness is created, early adopters will rely more on friends and relatives to help them evaluate new products. As Figure 18.8 shows, early adopters

FIGURE 18.8 Importance of mass media versus word of mouth in the adoption process

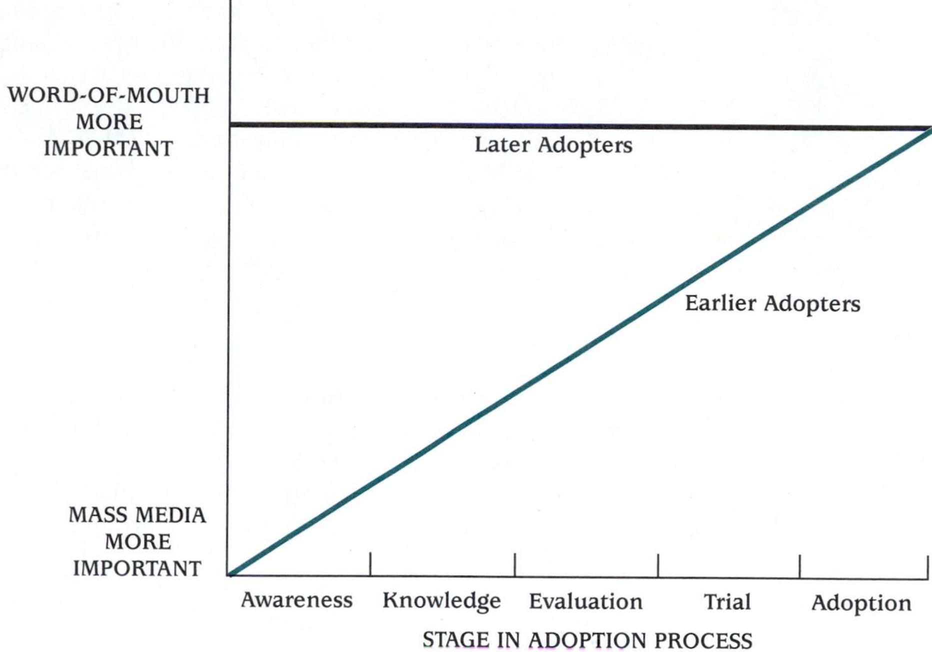

first rely on mass media for information. Word-of-mouth influence then increases in importance as early adopters move from awareness to evaluation, trial, and adoption. However, for later adopters, word of mouth is likely to be the dominant influence throughout the adoption process. Later adopters first learn of innovations from friends and neighbors rather than from the mass media. On this basis, advertisers can best encourage diffusion by using an informational campaign to create awareness among early adopters and by trying to stimulate favorable word-of-mouth communication among late adopters.

Word-of-Mouth Communication Across Groups. The studies cited show that if diffusion is to occur across groups, favorable word-of-mouth communication must first occur within groups. But favorable communications within groups is not sufficient for diffusion to take place. Diffusion requires the spread of information across different groups.[60] How is this process to occur if personal influence takes place primarily within a consumer's own peer group? It happens because consumers spread the word by interacting with individuals outside their personal networks.

Groups outside an individual's personal network are known as **heterophilous;** peer and family groups are **homophilous.**[61] Individuals within heterophilous groups are dissimilar, and ties holding them together are weak; individuals within homophilous groups tend to be similar and are bonded by stronger reference group ties. Associates at higher or lower levels in an organization or individuals with whom the consumer has occasional contact, such as tennis partners or carpool riders, are examples of members of heterophilous groups.

Consumers often spread the word about new products and ideas to passing acquaintances in heterophilous groups. This process has come to be known as *the strength of weak ties* because the weak ties of heterophilous groups are strong enough to fuel the process of diffusion.

The importance of communication to weaker groups is shown in a study by Brown and Reingen of the adoption of a personal service. They found that most word of mouth occurred among friends and relatives in homophilous groups. Word of mouth in heterophilous groups (weak ties) occurred in only 18 percent of communications among people.[62] However, when these weak ties did occur, they were very likely to be bridges across groups in communicating about the service.

Trickle Down and Trickle Up. One of the basic questions in analyzing communications across groups is how information and influence travel from one socioeconomic group to another.

In Chapter 12, we described the transmission of influence between socioeconomic groups as a trickle-down process from higher to lower groups (as with the diffusion of fashion items such as Izod alligator shirts) and a trickle-up process from lower to higher groups (as with the diffusion of jeans and rock music). Traditionally, the view has been that diffusion occurs from higher to lower social classes (trickle down). Two famous sociologists, Thorstein Veblen[63] and George Simmel,[64] stated this view. Both believed that the upper classes bought primarily for status and ostentation (*conspicuous consumption*) and that lower-quality duplicates of these products were then made for the lower classes (for example, knockoffs of Rolex watches or Gucci handbags and scarfs). Communication and influence moved from one class down to the next in the social hierarchy.

This view is reinforced by a description of innovators and early adopters as being in the highest and laggards as being in the lowest socioeconomic class. Thus, the transmission of influence from innovators and early adopters to laggards is a transmission from upper to lower socioeconomic classes.

However, as we saw in Chapter 12, the transmission of influence is occasionally from lower to upper socioeconomic groups. Innovators and early adopters of jeans and of bluegrass and rock music were those in lower socioeconomic classes who did not feel the need to conform to the norms of the dominant culture. They were free to innovate in clothing and music. Known as **grassroots innovators,** these individuals then disseminated their tastes to higher social classes. For example, African-American mule drivers working the coal mines of Appalachia created bluegrass music by fusing their instrumentation with white Appalachian music.[65] As the lower socioeconomic groups adopted bluegrass, it also began to be disseminated to a wider public through concerts, radio, and finally TV. The innovators and early adopters clearly were not the cosmopolitan, upscale consumers associated with early adopters. They were the lower-class African Americans and whites of Appalachia. We will be reporting studies in the next section that describe early adopters of many innovations as upscale. However, it is important to recognize that early adopters can be in any segment of society, depending on the innovation.

Trickle Across. The trickle-up process shows that early adoption of an innovation can go in either direction on the social scale. Another issue is whether social status is as relevant as it used to be in defining the transmission of influence, up or down. The views of Veblen and Simmel espousing a trickle-down effect were expressed at the turn of the century, a time when class distinctions were much sharper than today. The post-World War II period produced a leveling effect in socioeconomic status, making trickle-down and trickle-up effects less relevant. Moreover, the mass media rapidly communicate information on innovations to all classes. A more likely process of diffusion is one that occurs across groups, regardless of socioeconomic status, known as a **trickle-across effect.**

King's study of fashion adoption in the Boston area illustrates this leveling effect. King found that early buyers of new fashions were not the upper-crust elite. Almost two-thirds were middle class or lower. Moreover, there was no evidence that communications went from individuals of a higher social class to those of a lower class. Four-fifths of respondents were influenced by members of their own social class. Explaining these results, King stated, "The traditional upper-class fashion leader directing the lower levels is largely short-circuited in the communication process. Within hours after the exclusive Paris and American designers' showings, the season's styles have been passed to the mass audiences via newspaper and television."[66]

King's study tends to confirm a trickle-across, rather than a trickle-down, effect in the diffusion of fashion styles. King's ideas closely conform to the social multiplier effect. That is, individuals are more likely to come into contact with new products and ideas because of the leveling of social status in American society, and as a result, influence travels in a lateral fashion across markets. A trickle-down effect is much more marked in countries with sharp social class distinctions. In the United States, it is more likely that a trickle of information and influence across groups will result in the diffusion of new products.

Cultural Context of Diffusion

Cultural norms often determine the acceptance of new products and the rate of diffusion. Consumers reject many product innovations because they contradict cultural norms. This was the reason that prepared baby foods were rejected in Brazil and that condensed soups had a hard time winning acceptance in England. Brazilian mothers insisted on giving their babies homemade rather than prepared foods, and English consumers equated quality in canned soups with hefty soups in larger cans.

Two concepts that help us understand the diffusion of innovations in different cultures are **cultural context** and **cultural homogeneity.** Hall introduced the concept of cultural context by dividing cultures into two groups: those that rely primarily on verbal and written communication to transmit meaning (*low-context cultures*) and those that rely primarily on nonverbal communication (*high-context cultures*).[67] The concept of homophilous and heterophilous groups can also be extended to cultures by identifying uniform cultures with little difference in norms, values, and socioeconomic status among groups (homophilous) versus more disparate cultures with wider differences among groups (heterophilous).[68]

High-context cultures tend to be more homophilous. The emphasis on nonverbal communication means that such cultures will place more value on interpersonal contacts and associations. They put more value on the group than on the individual, and they emphasize subscribing to the norms and longstanding rituals of society. Low-context cultures place more value on individual initiative and rely more on the mass media for communication. Most Far Eastern countries would be described as high context/homophilous, whereas the United States and Western Europe would be described as low context/heterophilous.

The rate of diffusion would be expected to be faster in high-context/homophilous cultures because of their uniformity. The barrier in transmitting information from one dissimilar group to another is much lower. Further, the credibility of information on innovations is higher because the source is more likely to be friends and relatives rather than the mass media.

Takada and Jain compared the rate of adoption for three products—air conditioners, washing machines, and calculators—in high-context cultures (Japan, Taiwan, South Korea) versus a low-context culture (United States). In most cases, the rate of diffusion was more rapid in the three high-context cultures than it was in the United States for all three categories.[69]

Innovativeness and the Diffusion Process

By **innovativeness** we mean the predisposition of a consumer to adopt a product earlier than most others. We will look at the characteristics of those who adopt earlier and refer to them as innovators, recognizing that they represent Rogers' classification of both the true innovator group (the first 2.5 percent to adopt) and the early adopter group (the next 13.5 percent to adopt). The combination of innovators and early adopters into one group is necessary from a marketing standpoint, since the 2.5 percent of the market who are the first to adopt are too small a group to target. Therefore, the general designation of innovator refers to both true innovators and early adopters.

Nature of Innovativeness

Two key questions can be asked about innovators. First, can generalized innovators be identified, and if so, what are their characteristics? The answer will help marketers determine whether marketing strategy can be directed to a general group of innovators or whether specific target segments of early buyers have to be defined on a product-by-product basis. Second, is there a negative as well as a positive innovator? That is, can one trace a negative diffusion process leading to rejection of an innovation?

Characteristics of Innovators. It is likely that a general innovator exists for true (discontinuous) innovations. That is, the innovator who is among the first to consider buying an electric car will also be among the first to consider trying solar energy. One study found that early adopters of home computers were more likely to use automatic bill paying services, cable TV services, and automatic teller machines. They also were more likely to own programmable pocket calculators and video games.[70]

Various studies have shown that, across product categories, innovators tend to be:

- Opinion leaders.
- Risk takers.[71]
- Inner-directed, self-confident, and independent of group norms.[72]
- More likely to obtain information from mass media than through word of mouth.
- More likely to read newspapers and magazines and less likely to watch TV.[73]
- Open to new ideas and change.
- Relatively young and more mobile.

Also, most studies have identified innovators as cosmopolitan and in higher socioeconomic groups (although, as we noted, grassroots innovators are in lower socioeconomic groups and often from rural areas).

Most findings suggest that for less innovative products, a general innovator does not exist. That is, the individual who is one of the first to have adopted touch-tone telephone service will not necessarily be one of the first to have tried cook-in-the-bag vegetables. As with opinion leadership, innovativeness is likely to extend across related product categories, but an innovator in one category is not likely to be an innovator in an unrelated category. For most new products, marketers must define the target market on a product-by-product basis.

Some companies have sought to portray general innovators as users of their products or services. For example, the ad in Exhibit 18.5 refers to readers of Condé Nast magazines as those who are the first to adopt new ideas, new foods, and new services.

Are There Positive and Negative Innovators? We are assuming that the general innovator reacts positively to most discontinuous innovations. The same individual might reject an innovation, however. The consumer who was one of the first to accept VCRs, personal computers, and compact disc players might

EXHIBIT 18.5
Portraying a generalized innovator

have been one of the first to reject videodisc players. Midgley proposed three categories of adopters:[74]

1. *Active adopters* are those who have adopted the product and give favorable information about it.
2. *Active rejectors* are those who have tried the product, found it deficient, and give unfavorable information about it.
3. *Passives* are those who have adopted the product but do not give information or exert influence.

Leonard-Barton conducted one of the few marketing studies that distinguished between active adopters and rejectors. She found that rejectors frequently sought experts who evaluated the innovation negatively, possibly to justify discontinuing the use of the innovation.[75] In general, little documentation of a negative diffusion process is available. It may be that marketers are reluctant to provide evidence of failures, even though studies of negative diffusion could provide insights on ways to avoid future market failures.

Measuring Innovativeness

Innovativeness is a behavioral variable measured by the early adoption of new products. In contrast, opinion leadership is measured by consumers' perceptions regarding their interpersonal communications with others.

Innovativeness has been measured by three criteria. First, and most frequently, it has been measured by *adoption over time*. For example, Anderson and Ortinau identified personal computer innovators as those who purchased PCs prior to 1985.[76] Such a measure of innovativeness accounts for the time of adoption of the product.

A second criterion used to identify innovators is the *number of new products adopted*. Summers categorized consumers by number of new products adopted (from zero to six).[77] Such a criterion is useful in distinguishing between the product-specific and the general innovator. Any consumer who adopts innovations in all six product areas under study is likely to be a general innovator.

A third criterion used to measure innovativeness is how consumers view themselves. Such *self-designating measures* are used when the researcher wants to determine consumers' orientation to new products rather than measure specific adoption. Researchers could ask consumers whether they would be one of the first to buy a new product and whether they would buy immediately after it came out, within a week, a month, and so forth.

Strategic Applications of Diffusion Theory

Companies have attempted to influence both the likelihood of adoption and the rate of diffusion of innovations through marketing strategies.

Adoption

Companies have used various strategies to influence consumers to adopt innovations. They have tried to encourage trial through free samples and price promotions. If trial is not reasonable, companies have used advertising to create product awareness and to communicate product features. The ad for IBM's Web site in Exhibit 18.6 is an example. Companies also have tried to portray innovative behavior in advertising by showing astute buyers purchasing the most advanced products. The ads for Hewlett-Packard in Exhibit 18.7 portray innovative behavior by showing previous innovators of Hewlett-Packard products buying the company's personal computers.

http://www.hp.com/

In addition, marketers can attempt to overcome resistance to adoption by employing change agents. Pharmaceutical companies seek early adoption of medical innovations by respected hospitals, clinics, and physicians who have reputations as opinion leaders in the hope that these individuals and institutions will encourage others to adopt.

EXHIBIT 18.6
Creating awareness for a new product

Rate of Diffusion

Diffusion theory can provide marketers with guidelines for adjusting strategies according to the projected rate of diffusion. Marketers have two strategic options in influencing the rate of diffusion, as shown in Table 18.1. In a **skimming strategy,** marketers project a slow rate of diffusion. As a result, prices have to be set higher initially to sustain the costs of introduction. The strategy aims at "skimming the cream off the market" by aiming at the small, price-insensitive segment.

Such a segment is likely to be well defined by demographic and lifestyle characteristics. Advertising will probably be informationally oriented to create awareness and to supply necessary technical information. Distribution of the product will be selective. A skimming strategy is most likely for major innovations such as electric cars. There may be barriers to widespread acceptance because the product is not likely to be simple and may not be compatible with existing products or systems. Therefore, it is logical to establish a small and specific target for adoption.

The alternative to a skimming strategy is a **penetration strategy.** In this case, marketers encourage rapid and widespread diffusion by introducing the

▶EXHIBIT 18.7
Ads portraying adoption of an innovation

product at a low price. The intention is to try to sell to a general market through an intensive campaign that uses imagery and symbolism. Distribution is widespread. Because the market is so general, identifying the characteristics of early adopters may be difficult. A penetration strategy is likely for new products that are not major innovations such as diet soda or freeze-dried coffee since closely

TABLE 18.1
Strategic alternatives based on the diffusion curve

Rate of Diffusion	Slow	Fast
Marketing Strategy	***Skimming***	***Penetration***
Initial price	High	Low
Market segmentation	Target market is • Small • Well specified by demographics and lifestyle	Target market is • Larger • Harder to specify by demographics and lifestyle
Advertising	Informational approach	Use of symbols and imagery
Distribution	Selective	Intensive
Product characteristics	Discontinuous innovation	Continuous innovation

competitive product substitutes exist. Both diet soda and freeze-dried coffee were introduced at competitive prices on a widespread basis with intensive advertising campaigns using symbolism and imagery.

Once an initial strategy is established, diffusion theory can give marketers guidelines for changing marketing strategy, depending on where the product is on the diffusion curve. A product introduced by a skimming strategy eventually will move toward a penetration strategy. For example, personal computers were first introduced into the market at very high prices with little advertising and limited distribution. As technological improvements lowered prices, diffusion became more rapid. As adoption increased, distribution became more intense. Knowledge of the diffusion curve could have helped marketers of personal computers define the proper time to begin to shift from a skimming to a penetration strategy.

Similarly, marketers introducing a penetration strategy may find that a slow increase in prices is warranted when there is widespread acceptance of the product. Advertising and distribution will remain intensive, but the proper time for a change in pricing policy may be defined by the diffusion curve.

SUMMARY

Word-of-mouth communication among consumers is the most important source of information and influence in consumer behavior. Individuals who influence the purchasing behavior of other consumers are the opinion leaders; the consumers being influenced are the followers.

Several studies have documented the greater importance of word-of-mouth communication compared to commercial information sources. Word-of-mouth influence is more likely to be important when the product is visible, distinctive, and important to the group's belief system and when consumers are involved with the purchase decision and see it as risky.

The process of word-of-mouth communication can best be described as a transmission of information between opinion leaders and followers. The mass media often serve as the source of information, with gatekeepers (those most sensitive to product information) serving as intermediaries in the information flow. Marketers try to encourage positive word-of-mouth communication, but negative word of mouth may occur and it tends to be a more powerful influence on consumers than positive word of mouth.

The influence of word-of-mouth communication is tied closely to the concept of opinion leadership. Opinion leaders are likely to both transmit and receive information to and from others for specific product categories. The transmission of influence through word of mouth is most likely to occur in specific situational and social settings. Several methods used to identify opinion leaders were described, including the sociometric technique, key informant method, and self-designating technique.

Marketers have several strategic options in trying to encourage positive word-of-mouth communication about their product. They can (1) stimulate word of mouth through product trial, generally targeting opinion leaders; (2) stimulate word of mouth through advertising by encouraging consumers to transmit positive experiences with the product; (3) simulate word of mouth by portraying communications from typical consumers; and (4) portray communications from opinion leaders to followers.

The second major section in the chapter dealt with the diffusion of communications across groups. The diffusion process involves consumers' adoption of an innovation and communication to other groups over time. Adoption of a new product requires awareness, knowledge, evaluation, and trial. Consumers are more likely to adopt a product if it has a relative advantage, is compatible with their needs and past experiences, is visible, is simple to understand, and is easily tried. Consumers' rejection of an innovation can occur because of lack of perceived value, lack of compatibility with current habits and usage, and perceived risk in buying the innovation.

Time is a crucial part of the diffusion process because it determines the rate of diffusion. Time is also important in defining adoption. Adopter categories—innovators, early adopters, the majority, and laggards—are defined according to time of adoption. In communication among groups, information is likely to trickle up or down from one socioeconomic group to another or to trickle across similar groups, regardless of economic status. Because of the great mobility and lack of sharp socioeconomic distinctions in the United States, diffusion is likely to be based on a trickle-across effect.

Innovativeness was defined as a consumer's predisposition to buy a new product early. Innovators (that is, the true innovator group plus early adopters) may be generally predisposed to adopt innovations. General innovators tend to be better educated, more self-confident, more willing to take risks and accept change, and more socially active than other adopters. In addition, innovators are more likely to be opinion leaders.

Despite the fact that most findings are product-specific, diffusion research does provide important strategic implications. It helps marketers define those consumers who are first to adopt. Furthermore, it provides some basis for predicting the diffusion process and suggests guidelines for changes in strategy as marketers proceed on the diffusion curve.

QUESTIONS

1. What were the conditions that made it possible for Corona beer to be successful on word of mouth alone? What are the limitations of relying solely on word-of-mouth communications to market a product on a national basis?
2. It was stated that word-of-mouth communication is the most important influence on consumer behavior. Why? Under what circumstances are other types of communication (advertising, personal selling, information from government sources) likely to be more influential than word of mouth?
3. A major study documenting the importance of word-of-mouth communication—Katz and Lazarsfeld's study of influence in a Midwestern town—was conducted before the advent of television. Some have argued that TV provides a basis for simulating word-of-mouth communication and thereby reduces the importance of word-of-mouth influence.
   - Do you agree?
   - Is it possible that TV is a more important force than word-of-mouth influence for certain groups (for example, children)?
4. What are the likely roles of the three types of word-of-mouth communication—product news, product experiences, and advice—in the consumer's decision process?
5. What are the limitations of the two-step flow model of word-of-mouth communication? What evidence supports the multistep model of communications in Figure 18.1?

6. Why is negative word-of-mouth communication likely to be a more potent influence on consumer behavior than positive word of mouth?
7. What are the limitations of the concept of opinion leadership?
8. Marketing studies have not identified any distinctive characteristics of opinion leaders. Since it is so difficult to identify opinion leaders, can the concept of opinion leadership be used in developing marketing strategies? If so, in what ways?
9. What is the distinction between a marketing strategy of stimulating versus simulating word-of-mouth communication?
10. Cite an example of a value barrier, a usage barrier, and a risk barrier to adoption of an innovation. How can marketers overcome each barrier?
11. What do we mean by the "strength of weak ties"? Provide an example. Why is this concept important in the diffusion process?
12. The chapter cites two theories of communication between groups: a trickle-down and a trickle-across effect.
    - In what types of societies is a trickle-down flow of communication more likely?
    - Are there any groups or regions in the United States where a trickle-down flow is more likely to occur?
    - Is a trickle-up flow also possible? Cite examples.
13. What are the strategic implications of introducing a new product to a high-context/homophilous culture versus a low-context/heterophilous culture?
14. The chapter cites an important gap in diffusion research: the lack of any study of a negative diffusion process. The fact that marketing managers do not like to advertise failures may explain the lack of research on negative diffusion. Such studies, however, could provide insights on how to avoid product failures.
    - Cite an example of negative diffusion for a product.
    - What insights might a marketing manager gain from studying negative diffusion to better understand (a) word-of-mouth communication and (b) product positioning?

RESEARCH ASSIGNMENTS

1. In what ways can the Internet be used to foster word-of-mouth communication among consumers? How can a company influence on-line word-of-mouth communication? Try to find Web sites that show negative consumer opinions about a product or service (for example, nynexsucks.com). What recommendations do you have about managing this negative word-of-mouth communication?
2. Use a sociometric technique to trace conversations among a group of eight or nine teenagers or college students regarding opinions of rock CDs. Make sure the people you interview know each other. Try to develop a network to show who talks to whom. Ask these individuals to rate themselves on opinion leadership.
    - Do the sociometric and self-designating techniques agree regarding the identity of opinion leaders?
    - Ask the sample to rate themselves on their (a) interest in CDs, (b) self-confidence in buying and evaluating CDs, and (c) level of social activity compared to that of friends and acquaintances.
    - Opinion leaders would be expected to score high on these three criteria. Do your findings confirm this hypothesis?
3. Use the following questions to identify innovators for men's cosmetics. "How do you see yourself with regard to buying a new facial care preparation for men? As one of the first to buy? As one who purchases after a few others have tried it? As one who purchases after many people have bought it? As a nonpurchaser?" Identify the innovators as those who say they would be one of the first to buy. In addition to the innovativeness question, ask the sample of males: (a) lifestyle questions based on the statements listed in Table 11.1, (b) an opinion leadership question, (c) self-confidence questions in selecting cosmetics and toiletry items, and (d) questions about demographic characteristics.
    - What are the differences between the innovators and noninnovators on each of the items listed? (If your sample is large enough, split it into three groups—innovators, those tending to be innovators, and noninnovators—and determine differences among these groups.)
    - What are the implications of these differences for a marketing strategy for men's cosmetics in regard to (a) market segmentation, (b) advertising and product positioning, (c) pricing, (d) product development, and (e) distribution?

GLOSSARY

absolute threshold Level below which the consumer cannot detect a stimulus. Minimal stimulus values capable of being sensed.

acceptable price range A price range the consumer views as realistic. If the product is priced below this range, quality is suspect. If the product is priced above, the consumer refuses to buy.

acculturation The process of learning a culture different from the one in which a person was raised. Learning the values of another culture (e.g., a businessperson going abroad, immigrants moving to another country, foreign students).

activation One of the three factors required for retrieval of information from long-term memory. The linkages between nodes must be activated before retrieval can take place.

actual self The concept individuals have of themselves based on who they think they are.

adaptation level Point at which the consumer adjusts to a frequently repeated stimulus so that it is no longer noticed. Defined as the stimulus value (e.g., brightness, loudness) to which the consumer is indifferent and with respect to which stimuli above or below it are relatively judged.

advertising wearout Adaptation to a campaign over time that results in the consumer's boredom and fatigue; the consumer then "tunes out" the message.

affective (feeling) component of attitudes The favorable or unfavorable disposition toward an object. Consumers' evaluation of a brand on a positive to negative dimension represents the affective component of attitudes.

age cohort People of similar ages who have gone through similar experiences.

AIO inventories A list of consumer activities, interests, and opinions constructed to measure empirically lifestyle components.

anticipatory aspiration group Group that an individual aspires to belong to and anticipates joining at some future time.

archetypes Commonly shared memories.

aspiration group Group to which a consumer aspires to be associated with, but one of which he or she is not a member.

assimilation/contrast theories Combines the two views of assimilation and contrast theories in the belief that assimilation is more likely to occur if the disparity between experience and effect is likely. States that when consumers are only slightly disappointed, attitudes are likely to change in the direction of expectations and remain positive. When consumers are very disappointed, a negative change in attitude is likely to occur after the purchase and may be exaggerated.

assimilation effect Theory in social psychology that focuses on a desire to maintain balance between experiences and expectations by selectively accepting information consistent with expectations. The tendency in perception for the highly similar parts of a whole to look alike as much as possible; that is, to assimilate. Assimilation occurs when the stimulus differences among the parts are sufficiently small; if the differences are sufficiently large, the opposite phenomenon of contrast tends to occur.

attention The selective process of noticing a stimulus or certain portions of it. The momentary focusing of a consumer's cognitive capacity on a specific stimulus.

attitude-specific strategy Requires comparison of each brand alternative on specific attributes.

attitude toward the ad Consumers' predisposition to respond favorably or unfavorably to an ad.

attitudes Consumers' learned tendencies to evaluate brands in a consistently favorable or unfavorable way.

attribution theory States that people attribute a cause to their prior behavior.

baby boomers People born between 1946 and 1964, representing 76 million consumers.

baby busters The youths born between 1965 and 1976, representing 47 million consumers. Also known as generation Xers.

bait-and-switch pricing A form of deception in pricing practices that involves a low-price offer intended to lure customers into a store where a salesperson tries to influence them to buy higher-priced items.

balance theory A theory that asserts that unbalanced cognitive systems tend to shift toward a state of balance. Evaluation of an object is a function of consistently held beliefs about the object. When information about an object conflicts with consumers' beliefs, they will achieve balance by either changing their opinion about the object, about their source of information, or a combination of both. The result is a balance in beliefs about the information and the object.

bargaining power The extent of influence the buyer and seller have on each other to achieve favorable terms of sale.

behaviorist school Concerned with observing changes in an individual's responses as a result of exposure to stimuli. Developed two types of learning theories: classical conditioning and instrumental conditioning.

benefit segments Identification of a group of consumers based on similarity in needs. Often marketing opportunities are discovered by analysis of consumers' benefit preferences. Frequently, one or more segments are identified that are not being adequately served by existing alternatives.

blocking effect Using an image or stimulus to advertise a product that is already associated with another product.

brand equity The value of a brand in the consumer's mind.

brand leveraging A company will use a successful brand name on a product line extension, thus creating stimulus generalization.

brand loyalty Repeat buying because of commitment to a brand.

categorization Tendency of consumers to place marketing information into logical categories to process information quickly and efficiently and to classify new information.

category-based strategy Involves evaluation of a brand as a totality rather than a specific attribute.

cause-related marketing A firm sponsors a charity or sports event which is then linked to its name.

change agents Opinion leaders who have more influence and credibility than commercially sponsored means, such as personal selling and advertising, in getting consumers to change their needs and habits.

chunking/grouping information Organizing stimuli that summarize a wide range of information about a brand. A brand image is formed by information chunking, meaning the consumer is processing information by brand rather than by attribute.

classical conditioning An association is formed when a secondary stimulus is paired with a primary stimulus that already elicits a particular response.

closure A principle of perceptual integration describing a perceiver's tendency to fill in the missing elements when a stimulus is incomplete. Experience tends to be organized into whole, continuous figures. If the stimulus pattern is incomplete, the perceiver fills in missing elements.

cognitive (thinking) component of attitudes The tendency to act based on favorable or unfavorable predispositions toward the object; generally measured by an intention to buy scale. Beliefs link a brand to a set of characteristics and specify the extent to which the brand possesses each characteristic.

cognitive consistency A basic behavioral principle to which balance theory conforms. This principle states that consumers value harmony between their beliefs and evaluations. If one is inconsistent with the other, consumers will change their attitudes to create harmony in their cognitive structure.

cognitive economy The principle that consumers search for only as much information as they feel is necessary to adequately evaluate brands.

cognitive responses Thoughts consumers develop that support or counter claims made in marketing communication.

cognitive school Views learning as problem solving and focuses on changes in the consumer's psychological set.

Coleman-Rainwater Social Standing Hierarchy Often preferred to Warner's Index of Status Characteristics, this classification of social classes more directly reflects the power and prestige associated with each class and draws social class lines more sharply. The Social Standing Hierarchy also distinguishes between a middle class and a working class.

comparative influence The process of comparing oneself to other members of the group, providing a basis for comparing one's attitudes and behavior to those of the group.

compensatory method When a consumer uses a compensatory model, perceived strength of a given alternative on one or more evaluative criteria can compensate for weaknesses on other attributes. Generally requires consumers to evaluate a brand by a number of criteria.

competitive bargaining power The party with the stronger bargaining power exerts that power to force concessions from the weaker party.

complex decision making Making decisions through a process of active search for information. Based on this information, alternative brands are evaluated on specific criteria. The cognitive process of evaluation involves consumer perceptions of brand characteristics and development of favorable or unfavorable attitudes toward a brand. The assumption is that consumer perceptions and attitudes will precede and influence behavior.

conative (behavioral) component of attitudes The tendency to act based on favorable or unfavorable predispositions toward the object; generally measured by an intention to buy scale.

conditioned response A response that is the result of influence by primary and secondary stimuli.

conjunctive strategy A consumer accepts a brand only if it is acceptable on key attributes. The consumer would eliminate a brand seen as negative on one or two of the most important attributes, even if it is positive on all other attributes.

constant sum scale A scale in which values assigned to objects always add up to the same amount (e.g., assume you could select ten free bottles of soft drink in a store. How many bottles of the following brands would you select?).

consumer information processing The nature of the consumer's search for and reactions to marketing communications. The process by which consumers perceive information in four steps—exposure to information, attention, comprehension, and retention of information.

consumerism The set of activities of independent consumer organizations and consumer activists designed to protect the consumer. Concerned primarily with ensuring that the consumer's rights in the process of exchange are protected. A social movement seeking to augment the rights and power of buyers in relation to sellers.

consumer movement The activities that are generally encompassed under the heading of *consumerism* (see previous definition). Somewhat misleading term because there is no actual organization of consumers but, instead, a conglomeration of groups with separate concerns.

Consumer Product Safety Commission (CPSC) Agency established in the 1970s. It is empowered to set product safety standards to protect consumers from risk or injury.

consumer socialization The process by which consumers acquire the knowledge and skills necessary to operate in the marketplace. The two most important types of consumer socialization are the socialization of children and the socialization of new residents in a community.

context Setting.

continuity Principles of grouping that emerged from Gestalt psychology and that suggest that the basic flow of stimuli should be continuous and lead to a logical conclusion (e.g., the flow of a sales message).

contrast The opposite of adaptation. A change from the constant conditions a consumer is used to. Advertisers try to achieve contrast by using new, attention-getting stimuli.

contrast effect States that a disparity between expectations and experiences may lead the consumer to magnify the disparity. Implies that advertisers should moderate their claims so as not to increase consumer expectations to the point that dissatisfaction (e.g., a disparity between expectation and experience) is likely to result.

cooptation Adapting the consumption values of another country (i.e., America) to be consistent with local language, meaning, and beliefs.

coordinative bargaining power The parties approach bargaining in a problem-solving manner to achieve their goals. Bargaining power is less likely to be exerted in an arbitrary manner.

corrective advertising A means by which companies correct false claims publicly.

counterargument Thoughts consumers develop that are designed to counter existing information (e.g., a loyal RC Cola drinker develops thoughts to reject benefit claims Pepsi or Coca-Cola make).

cross-cultural influences Norms and values of consumers in foreign countries that influence strategies of multinational firms marketing abroad.

cultivation theory According to this theory, children learn about a culture's norms and values from the media. The greater children's exposure to TV, the greater the likelihood that they will accept the images and associations seen.

cultural context The concept of cultural context divides cultures into two groups: those that rely primarily on verbal and written communication to transmit meaning (low context cultures) and those that rely primarily on nonverbal communication (high context cultures).

cultural homogeneity Identifies uniform cultures with little difference in norms, values, and socioeconomic status among groups (homophilous) versus more disparate cultures with wider difference among groups (heterophilous).

cultural norms Those standards of behavior that govern proper social relations, means of ensuring safety, eating habits, and so forth. If behavior deviates from the cultural norm, society may place sanctions or restrictions on behavior.

cultural values an especially important class of beliefs shared by the members of a society as to what is desirable or undesirable. Beliefs that some general state of existence is personally and socially worth striving for. Cultural values in the United States include achievement, independence, and youthfulness.

culture The implicit beliefs, norms, values, and customs that underlie and govern conduct in a society. The norms, beliefs, and customs learned from society. Culture leads to common patterns of behavior.

culture production system The individuals and organizations responsible for creating and producing products designed to meet cultural goals.

database marketing Identifying individual consumers using databases of their characteristics and customizing product, service, or promotional offerings to meet their specific needs.

deceptive advertising Advertising that gives false information or that willfully misleads consumers about the brand's benefits.

decoding The sequence of steps in consumer information processing from exposure to attention to comprehension of a message. Consumers translate the message so it is understood and possibly retained in memory.

defense mechanism A strategy the ego uses to reduce tension. Conflicts that are not resolved in childhood influence later behavior in a manner of which the adult is unaware.

demographic characteristics Objective descriptors of individuals and households; include age, income, family size, and employment status.

demonstration principle Formulated by James Duesenberry, a Harvard economist, states that due to increased mobility and purchasing power in America, consumers will come into increasing contact with new products and will be more likely to buy them. Referred to as a social multiplier because ownership increases in multiples as a function of group influence and product visibility.

depth (focus group) interview An unstructured, personal interview in which the interviewer attempts to get subjects to talk freely and to express their true feelings. Can be conducted individually or in groups (focused group interiews). The latter have the advantage of eliciting more information because of group interaction.

deterministic models Demonstrate the linkages between variables that influence behavior and attempt to predict behavior based on these linkages.

diffusion The process by which the adoption of an innovation is spread over time by communication to members of a target market.

direct feedback Marketing communications that can be linked to sales results (e.g., retail advertising announcing a sale can be related to the number of shoppers coming into the store).

disclaimant group A group to which an individual belongs although rejecting its values.

disconfirmation of expectations Negative product evaluation resulting from consumption because expectations of product performance are not met. In such cases, consumers may develop more negative attitudes toward the product after the purchase.

dissociative group A group to which an individual may regard membership as something to be avoided.

ego Part of Freud's psychoanalytic theory—the individual's self-concept and the manifestation of objective reality as it develops in interaction with the external world.

elaboration likelihood model (ELM) An information processing model that postulates that the degree to which a consumer elaborates on a message depends on its relevance. The more relevant the message, the more elaborate the central processing that takes place. The less relevant the message, the more nonelaborate or peripheral processing takes place.

enculturation The process of learning the values of one's own culture from early childhood.

enduring involvement Continuous, more permanent involvement with a product; interest in product category on an ongoing basis.

Environmental Protection Agency (EPA) A government agency that sets controls on industry emissions, toxic wastes, and automobile pollution.

episodic memory Images in long-term memory that reflect our memory of past events.

equal interval scale A metric scale, meaning that a rating of "2" is equidistant from "1" and "3."

ethnocentric Assuming that foreign consumers have the same norms and values as domestic consumers.

ethnography The study of culture by observation. Anthropologists determine cultural values through field studies in which they live with a group or family and observe its customs and behavior.

Eurobrand A brand marketed in Europe with several languages on the same package under the same brand name.

Euroconsumer A person who has many shared values with consumers in neighboring countries.

evaluative strategies Processing strategies for brand evaluation that require the organization of information about alternative brands. Most likely to be used when involvement with a product is high.

expected price range The range of prices the consumer expects to find in the marketplace, which tends to be a wider range than the consumer's acceptable price range.

expert power Power based on the expertise of the individual or group derived from experience and knowledge (e.g., a salesperson has expert power if the consumer regards him or her as knowledgeable).

expert spokesperson Person who has a professional or technical relationship with a product or service.

exposure Occurs when consumer's senses (sight, hearing, touch, smell) are activated by a stimulus.

expressive roles Family purchase roles related to the need for social and emotional support (e.g., decisions regarding style, color, or design).

extended family A nuclear family with at least one grandparent living at home.

extended self Extends our concept of self to what we own, wear, and use. Incorporates some of our more important possessions into our self-concept.

extinction Elimination of the link between stimulus and expected reward. If a consumer is no longer satisfied with a product, a process of extinction takes place. Extinction leads to a rapid decrease in the probability that the consumer will repurchase the same brand.

factor analysis A mathematical procedure for determining the intercorrelation between items and reducing the items into independent components or factors to eliminate redundancy. Typically used to reduce a great amount of data into its more basic structure. An analytical technique that reduces purchasing motives to a smaller number of independent need criteria.

false advertising Involves a claim-fact discrepancy. A form of deceptive advertising.

family Two or more people living together who are related by blood or marriage.

family life cycle The progression of a family from formation to child rearing, middle age, and finally retirement. Also reflects changes in income and family situation.

Federal Communications Commission (FCC) A government agency that regulates communications media and practices. Among other things, it oversees advertising directed to children.

Federal Trade Commission (FTC) A government agency established in 1914 to curb the monopoly powers of big business and unfair trade practices. It is also a watchdog over deceptive advertising.

figure and ground Gestalt psychologists state that in organizing stimuli into wholes, individuals identify those stimuli that are prominent (the figure) and those stimuli that are less prominent (the ground or background). The figure appears well defined, at a definite location, solid, and in front of the ground. In contrast, the ground appears amorphous, indefinite, and continuous behind the figure. A principle of advertising is that the product should appear as the figure rather than as the ground.

flexible globablization An attempt to standardize marketing strategies across countries but to be flexible enough to adapt components of the strategy to local conditions.

focus group interview An unstructured, personal interview in which the interviewer attempts to get groups to talk freely and to express their true feelings. Has the advantage of eliciting more information because of group interaction.

Food and Drug Administration (FDA) A government agency created in 1906 to set product standards; it also requires disclosure of product contents.

forgetting Forgetting occurs when information stored in memory is lost or when new information interferes with retrieval of stored information. Occurs when the stimulus is no longer repeated or perceived. Lack of use of a product or elimination of an advertising campaign can cause forgetting.

framing Situation in which the usage puts the product in a relevant context for consumers.

fraudulent advertising A straightforward lie. A form of deceptive advertising.

frequency The number of times an individual consumer or household is exposed to a message marketers send.

functions of attitudes There are four functions served by attitudes: a utilitarian function, a knowledge function, a value-expressive function, and an ego-defensive function. Marketing strategies can attempt to influence attitudes serving each of these functions.

gatekeeper Information gatherer who controls the level and type of stimuli flowing from the mass media to the group. Has the greatest expertise in acquiring and evaluating information from various sources and is most aware of alternative sources of information but does not necessarily disseminate them.

geodemographic analysis Demographic data analyzed by geographic area, generally based on census data.

Gestalt psychology A German school of psychology that focuses on total configurations or whole patterns. Stimuli, such as advertising messages, are seen as an integrated whole. In short, the whole is greater than the sum of the parts.

global influences Common needs and values across countries.

grassroots innovator An innovator in a lower socioeconomic group (generally from a rural area) who disseminates tastes and influence to higher socioeconomic groups.

habit Repetitive behavior resulting in a limitation or absence of information seeking and evaluation of alternative choices.

hedonic need The need to achieve pleasure from a product; most likely associated with emotions or fantasies derived from consuming a product.

heterophilous groups Groups outside of an individual's primary social network or personal network. Secondary groups.

hierarchy of effects Stipulates the sequence of cognitive states the consumer goes through in reaching a tendency to act. Needs are formulated, beliefs are formed about the brand, attitudes develop toward the brand, and the consumer then forms an action predisposition.

high-involvement purchase Purchase that is important to the consumer; it is closely tied to his or her ego and self-image and involves some financial, social, or personal risk.

homophilous groups Groups that are part of an individual's personal network. Primary groups.

household Any individual living singly or together with others in a residential unit.

household life cycle A more modern version of the family life cycle that includes categories such as divorced couples, married couples without children, and remarried people with children and stepchildren.

ideal self The concept that individuals have of themselves based on who they think they would like to be.

id/libido Part of Freud's psychoanalytic theory. The component of personality that controls the individual's most basic needs such as hunger, sex, and self-preservation.

image A total perception of an object formed by processing information from various sources over time.

impulse buying A tendency to buy on whim with little preplanning.

Index of Status Characteristics (ISC) A multi-item index combining several socioeconomic variables into one index of social class. The ISC measures four variables: occupation, source of income, house type, and dwelling area.

indirect feedback When marketing communications cannot be directly related to sales results, marketers use indirect measures to evaluate the effectiveness of communications. Indirect criteria include exposure to and awareness, comprehension, and retention of the marketing communication

inertia A passive process of information processing, brand evaluation, and brand choice. The consumer frequently purchases the same brand by inertia to save time and energy.

inference Involves the development of an association between two stimuli; for instance, consumers may associate high price with quality.

informational influence The influence of experts or experienced friends or relatives on consumer brand evaluations.

information overload Consumers' ability to process information has been surpassed because of excessive information; as a result, decision making becomes less.

innovativeness The early adoption of a new product. Innovativeness is distinct from opinion leadership in that it is a behavioral variable (e.g., adoption). In contrast, opinion leadership is measured by the consumers' perception regarding their interpersonal influence on others.

inoculation theory A theory proposing that consumers can be "inoculated" against negative thoughts about a product when processing a marketing message with messages that anticipate these negative thoughts and refute them.

instrumental actions Actions necessary to complete the purchase of a brand (e.g., obtaining financing for a car).

instrumental conditioning Requires the development of a link between a stimulus and a response.

instrumental roles Family purchasing roles related to task-oriented functions meant to provide direction to the group. Decisions on budgets, timing, and product specifications are task-oriented.

instrumental values As defined by Rokeach, instrumental values are the means to attain cultural goals. As applied to consumers, instrumental values are consumption-specific guidelines.

integration The tendency to perceive stimuli as an integrated whole; for example, a brand image.

interference Occurs when a related information node blocks the recall of the relevant information. Competitive advertising often causes consumers to be unable to recall advertising for a related brand; or consumers may sometimes confuse one brand with another.

irresponsible advertising Advertising that depicts or encourages irresponsible behavior or portrays groups in an irresponsible manner.

just-noticeable difference (j.n.d.) The minimal difference that can be detected between stimuli. The consumer will not be able to detect any difference between stimuli below his or her differential threshold. The j.n.d. varies not only with (a) the sensitivity of the receptor and (b) the type of stimuli, but also with (c) the absolute intensity of the stimuli being compared.

Key informants Individuals who engage in frequent word-of-mouth communication within a group, but are not necessarily opinion leaders.

laddering As applied to the means-end chain, laddering involves a series of consumer interviews to determine the links among product attributes, consumption goals, and cultural values.

learning A change in behavior occurring as a result of past experience.

lexicographic strategy Requires consumers to rank product attributes from most important to least important. Consumers will choose the brand that dominates on the most important criterion. If two or more brands tie, then consumers will examine brands on the second attribute and so on until the tie is broken. A lexicographic rule follows a sequential approach.

lifestyle An individual's mode of living as identified by his or her activities, interests, and opinions. Lifestyle variables have been measured by identifying a consumer's day-to-day activities and interests.

limen The threshold level at which perceptions occur. Perceptions below the conscious level are subliminal. (*See also* subliminal perception.)

long-term memory The place where the consumer stores and retains information on a long-term basis.

low-involvement purchases Purchases that are less important to the consumer. Identity with the product is low. Because it may not be worth the consumer's time and effort to search for information about brands and to consider a wide range of alternatives, low-involvement purchases are associated with a more limited process of decision making.

mainstreaming The theory proposing that individuals tend to see the world around them largely based on information from the mass media. Therefore, heavy viewers of TV will develop similar perceptions of reality because they are exposed to similar stimuli.

marketing concept The philosophy that marketing strategies rely on a better knowledge of the consumer.

marketing stimuli Any component of a product's marketing plan (e.g., price, package, advertising, the store that sells the brand, and the brand itself). Most marketing stimuli are symbolic in nature; that is, representations of the product, not the product itself.

means-end chain Gutman describes the interface between culture and consumer-behavior as a means-end chain. That is, the means (product attributes) are the vehicle for attaining personal values (the ends) with the consumption goals as an intermediary between them.

membership group A group to which an individual belongs and in which he or she has face-to-face communication with other members. Groups to which a person is recognized by others as belonging.

memory Represents information that the consumer retains and stores and that the consumer can recall for future use.

micromarketing Reaching individual consumers based on their demographic characteristics. It is an extension of market segmentation in that it breaks the market down into more finite components.

misleading advertising A form of deceptive advertising that involves a claim-belief interaction. The advertisement interacts with a consumer's beliefs and results in a misleading claim.

moods Passing feelings that occur at a point in time (e.g., feeling happy, sad, silly, anxious, sexy, and so forth).

motivational research Research into consumer motives, particularly unconscious motives. These are determined through indirect assessment methods that include projective techniques and depth interviews. On this basis, hypotheses are developed regarding the motivations for consumer behavior.

motives General drives that direct a consumer's behavior toward attaining his or her needs.

multiattribute models Models that measure attitudes on a multidimensional basis by determining how consumers evaluate brands across product attributes. The sum of these ratings weighted by the value placed on each attribute represents consumers' attitude toward the brand.

myths Stories or character representations in fantasy form that attempt to portray cultural values.

new reality The realization that there are limitations to growth in the American economy and that these limits translate into restricted future purchasing potential.

node Each word or image in long-term memory. Each node is linked to other words or images (e.g., good food and fast service are nodes that a consumer may link to the McDonald's node).

noncompensatory method A model of attitude structure in which brands are evaluated on a few of the most important attributes. Weakness of a product or brand on one attribute cannot be compensated by its strength on another. As a result, the brand can be eliminated from consideration based on one or two attributes. Requires consumers to process information by attribute across brands.

nonevaluative strategies Strategies for brand evaluation that involve the use of a simple decision rule to avoid the necessity to evaluate brands (e.g., some consumers simply buy the cheapest brand).

normative influence The influence exerted on an individual to conform to group norms and expectations.

norms Rules of behavior in particular circumstances that specify actions that are proper and those that are improper. Beliefs held by a consensus of a group concerning the rules of behavior to which group members are expected to conform. Rules and standards of conduct (generally undefined) that the group establishes.

nuclear family Married couple who have one or more children.

overshadowing effect When a stimulus becomes as important as or more important than the unconditioned stimulus.

passive learning Occurs when consumers learn about brands with little involvement and purchase with little evaluation of alternative brands. Consumers are more likely to form attitudes after, rather than before, a purchase.

penetration strategy A strategic option establishing a competitive price for a new product entry. A mass marketing approach would be used. Most relevant for continuous innovation.

perceived risk Degree of risk consumers perceive in a purchase. Composed of two elements: (1) uncertainty about the decision and (2) potential consequences of the decision.

perception The process by which people select, organize, and interpret sensory stimuli into a meaningful and coherent picture. The way consumers view an object (e.g., their mental picture of a brand or the traits they attribute to a brand).

perceptual defense Consumers' distortion of information so that it conforms to their beliefs and attitudes. This function operates to protect the individual from threatening or contradictory stimuli.

perceptual equilibrium/disequilibrium Consumers seek to maintain equilibrium in their psychological set by screening out information that does not conform to their predispositions. When consumers choose information consistent with prior beliefs or interpret information to conform to these beliefs, they are processing information to ensure perceptual equilibrium. Acceptance of contradictory information means consumers are in a state of perceptual disequilibrium.

perceptual mapping A group of quantitative techniques that seeks to position various brands on a "map" based on the way consumers perceive them. The closer one brand is to another on the map, the more similar it is to the other brand. The basic assumption is that if consumers see two brands as being similar, they will behave similarly toward the two brands.

perceptual organization The organization of disparate information so that it can be comprehended and retained.

perceptual vigilance A form of selective perception whereby the consumers' needs determine the information perceived. The tendency of consumers to select the information that helps them in evaluating brands to meet their needs (e.g., words that connote important values are often perceived more readily. As a result, consumers will recognize preferred brand names more quickly than they will nonpreferred brand names.).

personality A person's consistent and enduring patterns of behavior. Represents a set of consumer characteristics used to describe target segments.

placement The second of three factors required for retrieval of information from long-term memory. Placement determines which other nodes consumers will connect the activated node to.

preteens Consumers who are between the ages of 8 to 12; together with teens, this market represents nearly 34 million consumers.

primary data Data collected for the specific purpose of answering research questions.

primary formal group Group the consumer frequently comes in contact with that has some formal structure (e.g., school or business groups).

primary informal group Group the consumer frequently comes in contact with that has no formal structure (e.g., the family and peer groups). These groups have the greatest influence on the consumer.

primary/intrinsic stimuli Unconditioned stimulus; that is, the initial stimulus (e.g., cowboy) that another stimulus is linked to (e.g., Marlboro cigarettes) to produce a conditioned response. In marketing, the product and its components (package, contents, physical properties) are primary stimuli.

primary (unconditioned) stimulus An object, character, or person that elicits a particular response.

product concept A bundle of product benefits that can be directed to the needs of a defined group of consumers through symbolism and imagery. The product concept represents the organization of marketing stimuli into a coordinated product position that can be more easily directed to consumers.

product positioning Communication of the set of benefits the product is designed to meet. Such benefits are communicated through advertising and other marketing strategies.

projective techniques Techniques used for detecting and measuring wants and attitudes not readily discernible through more direct methods. Consists of the presentation of ambiguous materials (e.g., ink blots, untitled pictured, etc.). In interpreting this material, the viewer "projects" tendencies of which he or she may be unaware or may wish to conceal. Diagnostic devices in which interpretation of ambiguous stimuli is taken to reveal something about the observer, based on previous experience and motivations, needs, and interests in play at the time.

proximity The tendency to group stimuli by proximity means that one object will be associated with another based on its closeness to that object.

psychoanalytic theory Theory developed by Sigmund Freud that emphasizes the conflict among id, ego, and superego in childhood and the resolution of these conflicts in adult behavior. The dynamic interaction of these elements results in unconscious motivations that are manifested in observed human behavior.

psychographic characteristics Consumer psychological characteristics that can be quantified. Represented by two classes of variables: lifestyle and personality.

psychological set The consumer's state of mind toward an object; that is, his or her needs, attitudes, and perceptions relative to various brands. The psychological set is represented at a given point in time prior to the decision process. It will change during the decision process when the consumer processes new information, resulting in changes in needs, attitudes, and perceptions.

qualitative research Designed to provide more information about consumers' underlying motives by asking them questions in an unstructured manner.

rank order of preference scale A nonmetric scale in which objects are ranked by order of preference. Values have ordinal meaning only.

ratio scale A scale that permits ratio comparisons.

reach The number of people exposed to the message that the marketer sends.

reference group Any group with which an individual identifies such that he or she tends to use the group as a standard for self-evaluation and as a source of personal values and goals. A group that serves as a reference point for the individual in the formation of beliefs, attitudes, and behavior. Such groups provide consumers with a means to compare and evaluate their own brand attitudes and purchasing behavior.

reference/standard price The price consumers expect to pay for a certain item that serves as a frame of reference by which consumers compare prices of alternative brands.

referent power Power based on the identification of the individual with members of the group. The greater the similarity of the individual's beliefs and attitudes with those of group members, the greater the referent power of the group. A salesperson has referent power if the consumer sees him or her as similar.

referent spokesperson A person to whom consumers can easily relate.

reinforcement Repeated satisfaction.

reinforcement strategies Used by marketers to reinforce positive attitudes rather than attempting to change them. Can be used to attract new users or appeal to existing users with new or existing products.

relationship marketing An area of marketing in which marketers must maintain a relationship with their customers after the purchase; service marketers attempt to establish a one-to-one relationship with consumers over time.

reservation price In the context of comparing prices of alternative brands, the higher end of the acceptable price range or the upper limit above which consumers would judge an article too expensive.

reward power Power based on the ability of the group to reward the individual.

risk barrier Represents the consumers' physical, economic, performance, or social risk of adopting an innovation.

risky shift phenomenon The hypothesis that joint decision making encourages the group to make riskier decisions because in this way, all members of the group can share the failure of a wrong decision.

ritual A series of symbolic behaviors that occurs in sequence and is repeated frequently—for example, those that occur in grooming and gift-giving and during holidays.

ritual artifacts In rituals, these are often in the form of consumer products. For example, colored lights, mistletoe, wreaths, and Santa Claus are artifacts of Christmas rituals.

roles Functions assumed by or assigned to individuals by the group in the attainment of group objectives.

sacred consumption Consumption of goods that promote beauty, the preservation of nature, and cooperation.

scanner data Data collected from scanners that link consumers' exposure to advertising and subsequent behavior.

schema A cluster of concepts or beliefs that represent an individual's perception of an object or situation.

secondary data Existing data from published sources or from company records.

secondary/extrinsic stimuli A stimulus that is repeatedly linked to a primary stimulus to produce a conditioned response. Communications designed to influence consumer behavior are secondary stimuli that represent the product or stimuli associated with the product (price, store in which purchased, effect of salesperson).

secondary formal group Group with some formal structure with which the consumer meets infrequently (e.g., alumni groups, business clubs, and tenant organizations). These groups are likely to have the least amount of influence on the consumer.

secondary informal group Group with no formal structure with which the consumer meets infrequently (e.g., shopping or sports groups).

secondary (conditional) stimulus A stimulus that is linked to a primary stimulus and evokes the same response.

secular consumption Consumption of goods that promote technology, the conquest of nature, and competition.

selection The first component of perception. Consumers pick and choose marketing stimuli based on their needs and attitudes (e.g., a car buyer will be more attentive to car ads).

selective perception Consumers perceive marketing stimuli selectively to reinforce their needs, attitudes, past experiences, and personal characteristics. Selective perception means that two consumers can perceive the identical ad, package, or product very differently.

self-concept/self-image theory A person's self-concept causes the individual to see herself or himself through the eyes of other persons. In doing so, an individual takes into account the other person's behavior, feelings, and attitudes. This evaluation is closely related to the perceptions of whether other persons in the reference group will approve or disapprove of the "self" presented to the reference group.

self-designating technique A set of techniques used to measure opinion leadership, innovativeness, perceived risk, or other marketing constructs. The method requires consumers to categorize themselves in a given topic area.

semantic differential A seven-point metric scale anchored by bipolar adjectives and used in marketing to measure beliefs about brands.

semantic memory Words and sentences stored in long-term memory that reflect facts and concepts that we remember.

semiotics A field of study established to study the interrelationship among three components: object (brand), the signs and symbols associated with the object, and the consumer who does the associating. To understand how people derive meaning from symbols, researchers must understand the shared meaning of various signs in a culture.

short-term memory The place where a consumer briefly evaluates perceived information to determine whether it is to be stored in long-term memory.

similarity A principle of grouping that suggests stimuli will be grouped together by similarity in their characteristics.

situational influences Temporary conditions or settings that occur in the environment at a specific time and place.

situational involvement Temporary involvement with a product only in specific situations, such as when a purchase decision is required.

skimming strategy A strategic option establishing a high price for a new product entry and "skimming the cream of the market" by aiming at the most price inelastic consumer. Advertising and sales promotion are limited to specific targets, and distribution is selective. The most relevant strategy for discontinuous innovations.

social class A division of society made up of persons possessing certain common social and economic characteristics that are taken to qualify them for equal-status relations with one another and that restrict their interaction with members of other social classes.

social judgment theory Sherif's theory that describes an individual's position on an issue based on his or her involvement with the issue. Sherif identified a latitude of acceptance, a latitude of rejection, and a latitude of noncommitment to operationalize this concept of involvement. The greater the involvement, the narrower the latitude of acceptance and the wider the latitude of rejection on various positions.

social mobility Movement of an individual or household from one social class to another.

social multiplier effect As a result of the demonstration principle, ownership increases in multiples as consumers come into contact with and acquire new products. The social multiplier effect illustrates the volatility of group influence in the American economy. (*See also* demonstration principle.)

social stratification The ranking of people in society by other members into higher or lower positions—such as upper, middle, and lower class—to create a hierarchy of respect or prestige.

socialization The process by which an individual learns the norms and values of the group and of society.

sociogram The diagram of a network of communications among individuals. A sociogram is developed by using a sociometric technique (see definition) to identify communications.

sociometric technique A method developed to describe the patterns of communication and influence among members of a group. Members of a group are asked from whom they get advice and to whom they go to seek advice or information in making a decision. Specific individuals are identified and can, in turn, be interviewed to trace the network of communication. Individuals with the most frequent communication links are identified as opinion leaders.

source bolstering When viewing ads in low-involvement situations, the tendency for consumers to react positively to the source of the message as opposed to the message itself.

source credibility The level of expertise and trustworthiness consumers attribute to the source of the marketing message.

source derogation When viewing ads in low-involvement situations, the tendency of consumers to react negatively to the source and, therefore, tend not to believe the message.

spurious loyalty When a brand achieves a minimum level of satisfaction, the consumer repurchases it on a routinized basis; the consumer appears to be brand loyal but is not.

status The rank of an individual in the prestige hierarchy of a group or community. The position the individual occupies within the group. High status implies greater power and influence within the group.

status symbol Possession that indicates a person's status in society—for example, a uniform or membership in an exclusive club.

stimuli Any physical, visual, or verbal communications that can influence an individual's response.

stimulus generalization Consumers' ability to perceive differences in stimuli. Allows consumers to judge brands selectively and to make evaluative judgments about preferences of one brand or another.

stochastic model Using probabilistic models of consumer learning to estimate the probability of consumers buying the same brand again.

subcultural influences Differences in norms and values among subcultures within a society.

subculture The part of the total culture of a society that is distinct from society in certain respects (e.g., an ethnic group, a social class group, a regional group). The ways of behaving that distinguish a particular group from a larger one.

subliminal embeds Tiny figures inserted into magazine ads by high-speed photography or by airbrushing.

subliminal perception Perception of a stimulus below the conscious level. If the stimulus is beneath the threshold of conscious awareness but above the absolute threshold of perception, it is known as subliminal perception. (The conscious level is referred to as the limen; thus, perception below the conscious level is subliminal or below the absolute threshold.)

subtyping Developing a subcategory of a broader category (e.g., Federal Express established the subcategory, overnight delivery, within the general category of package delivery).

superego Part of Freud's psychoanalytic theory. The component of personality that is the leash on the id and works against its impulses.

support arguments Thoughts evoked in response to advertising when viewed by consumers who support what is read or said.

symbolic aspiration group A group in which an individual does not expect to receive membership, despite the acceptance of the group's norms and beliefs.

symbolic interactionism The interaction between the individual and the symbols in his or her environment. Consumers purchase products for their symbolic value in enhancing their self-concepts.

teens Consumers who are between the ages of 13 and 17; together with preteens, this market represents nearly 34 million consumers.

terminal values As defined by Rokeach, terminal values are cultural goals to be attained. Applied to consumers, terminal values are their ultimate purchasing goals.

theory of reasoned action Proposes that to predict behavior more accurately, it is more important to determine the person's attitude to that behavior than to the object of behavior.

threshold level Level of sensory discrimination. Ability to discriminate stimuli.

trail theory A quantitative approach to the study of personality postulating that an individual's personality is composed of definite predispositional attributes called traits. The most empirical basis for measuring personality, it states that personality is composed of a set of traits that describe a general response predisposition.

transfer The third of three factors required for retrieval of information from long-term memory. Transfer determines the information consumers will retrieve from long-term to short-term memory. Generally, consumers will transfer information that is most important in making a decision.

transformational effect The effect that occurs when the attitude consumers have toward an ad carries over to the brand. Explains why consumers who cannot tell the difference between soft drinks in blind taste tests have strong brand preferences when they can choose labeled brands.

trickle-across effect The process of diffusion occurring across groups regardless of socioeconomic status. A horizontal pattern of diffusion.

trickle-down effect The process of information and influence traveling from higher to lower socioeconomic groups. A vertical pattern of diffusion.

trickle-up effect The phenomenon that occurs when lower-class groups influence the purchases of those farther up the ladder (e.g., jeans were originally designed for blue-collar workers and made their way up to designer jean status).

unconditioned response The response to primary (unconditioned) stimuli.

unplanned purchases A buying action undertaken without buying intention prior to entering the store. Four types of unplanned purchases are (1) pure impulse, (2) reminder effect, (3) suggestion effect, and (4) planned impulse purchases.

usage barrier Occurs when an item is not compatible with the existing practices or habits of consumers.

utilitarian needs Need to achieve some practical benefit from a product. Are associated with product attributes that define performance.

value barrier A lack of performance relative to price compared with substitute products.

value systems The relative importance cultures place on cultural values.

values Shared beliefs among group members as to what behaviors are desirable and undesirable.

vicarious (observational) learning When people imitate the behavior of others as a result of observing them.

vocabulary of product attributes and benefits A set of adjectives to describe a product's characteristics and benefits generally obtained from consumer depth interviews (e.g., a vocabulary for soft drink brands might include terms like mild, sweet, carbonated, thirst-quenching).

Weber's law A law of psychological relativity: Subject discriminations are not bound to absolute characteristics of stimuli but to relations between them. The size of the least detectable change or increment in intensity is a function of the initial intensity; the stronger the initial stimulus, the greater the difference needs to be (e.g., the higher the price of a product, the greater the price difference between two brands of that product must be for consumers to detect it).

word-of-mouth communication Interpersonal communication between two or more individuals such as members of a reference group or a customer and a salesperson. People exert purchase influence through such communication.

NOTES

Chapter 1

1. "Slow Fade," *Marketing & Media Decisions* (October, 1990), p. 64, and "Levi Strauss & Co.'s Dockers Weigh Into Casuals," *Adweek's Marketing Week* (September 24, 1990), p. 26.
2. *Marketing & Media Decisions* (October 1990), p. 64.
3. "Levi's Two New Campaigns Aim at Who Fits the Jeans," *The New York Times* (July 27, 1992).
4. "Levi's vs. the Dress Code," *Business Week* (April 1, 1996), pp. 57–58.
5. "For Levi's, a Flattering Fit Overseas," *Business Week* (November 5, 1990), pp. 76–77.
6. *Business Week* (April 1, 1996).
7. "Marketing: The New Priority," *Business Week* (November 21, 1983), p. 96.
8. "Sears' Turnaround Is for Real—For Now," *Business Week* (August 15, 1994), p. 102.
9. "Direct Selling Is Alive and Well," *Sales & Marketing Management* (August, 1988), p. 76; and "Fresher Face at Avon," *Management Today* (December, 1984), p. 60.
10. "Avon Answers Calling to Higher Scent Lines," *Advertising Age* (March 28, 1988), p. S-4.
11. "Consumer Schizophrenia: Extremism in the Marketplace," *Planning Review* (July/August 1992), pp. 18–22.
12. *John Naisbitt's Trendletter* (September 1995–February 1996), p. 5.
13. "P&G Steps Up Ad Cyber-Surfing; Tide Could Have a Major Effect," *The Wall Street Journal* (April 18, 1996), p. B14.
14. "Markets for Information," *American Demographics* (April 1995), pp. 47–54.
15. Don Peppers and Martha Rogers, *The One-to-One Future* (1993).
16. "Mass Customization Sparks Sea Change," *Business Marketing* (November 1993), p. 43.
17. *John Naisbitt's Trendletter* (September 1995–February 1996), p. 9.
18. "Digital Blue Jeans Pour Data and Legs into Customized Fit," *The New York Times* (April 8, 1994), p. A1.
19. "Matching Face with Image," *Business Marketing* (March 1989), p. 58.
20. David A. Aaker and George S. Day, *Marketing Research* (New York: John Wiley & Sons, 1980), p. 102.
21. Carrie Goerne, "Researchers Go Undercover to Learn About 'Laskerville,'" *Marketing News* (May 11, 1992), p. 11.

Chapter 2

1. "Friendly to Whom?" *The Economist* (April 7, 1990), p. 83.
2. "What Selling Will Be Like in the '90s," *Fortune* (January 15, 1992), pp. 63–64.
3. "Who's Doing What to Animals in Manhattan," *The New York Observer*, p. 1.
4. "Whales, Human Rights, Rain Forests—and the Heady Smell of Profits," *Business Week* (July 15, 1991), pp. 114–115.
5. "Can the Body Shop Shape Up," *Fortune* (April 15, 1996), pp. 119–120.
6. "Striving to Be Cosmetically Correct," *The New York Times* (May 27, 1993), pp. C1, C8.
7. "The Body Shop: Truth & Consequences," *DCI* (February 1995), pp. 54–62.
8. "The Body Shop Club: Frequency Marketing for Politically Correct Cosmetics," *Colloquy* (Spring 1993), p. 7.
9. George S. Day and David A. Baker, "A Guide to Consumerism," *Journal of Marketing* 34 (July 1970), p. 13.
10. See Robert O. Hermann, "Consumerism: Its Goals, Organizations and Future," *Journal of Marketing* 34 (October 1970), p. 56.
11. "Do Boycotts Work?" *Adweek's Marketing Week* (April 8, 1991), pp. 16–18; and "Facing a Boycott, Many Companies Bend," *The Wall Street Journal* (November 8, 1990), p. B1.
12. Ibid.
13. *New York Magazine* (February 11, 1991), p. 22.
14. "Suddenly, Green Marketers Are Seeing Red Flags," *Business Week* (February 25, 1991), p. 74.
15. "Cholesterol Crackdown," *Advertising Age* (May 20, 1991), pp. 1, 56; "P&G Gives In, Axes Its 'Fresh' Label," *Advertising Age* (April 29, 1991), p. 1; "U.S. Wants to Keep Menus Honest on Nutrition Claims," *The New York Times* (June 10, 1993), pp. A1, A23.
16. "Beware: Green Overkill," *Advertising Age* (January 29, 1991), p. 26; "Green Products Sprouting Again," *Advertising Age* (May 10, 1993), p. 12; "It's Green, It's Friendly, It's Wal-Mart 'Eco-store,'" *Advertising Age* (June 7, 1993), pp. 1, 4.
17. "How Green Is Your Market Basket?" *Across The Board* (January/February 1990), p. 50.
18. "The Green Revolution: Loblaws," *Advertising Age* (January 29, 1991), p. 38.

19. "How Green Is Your Market Basket?" *Across The Board* (January/February 1990), p. 50.
20. "Philip Morris Campaign Stirs Uproar in Europe," *The Wall Street Journal* (July 1, 1996), pp. B1, B5.
21. "Even Overseas, Tobacco Has Nowhere to Hide," *Adweek's Marketing Week* (April 1, 1991), p. 4.
22. Marie Anchrdoguy, "A Brief History of Japan's Keiretsu," *Harvard Business Review* 68 (July/August 1990), pp. 58–59.
23. "A History of Consumer Protest," *The New York Times* (September 16, 1985), p. 46.
24. "Earth Day '80 Dawns Tomorrow Amid Reflection and Plans for a New Decade," *The New York Times* (April 21, 1980), p. A16.
25. George A. Steiner, "New Patterns in Government Regulation of Business," *MSU Business Topics* 26 (Autumn 1978), pp. 53–61.
26. John S. Healey and Harold H. Kassarjian, "Advertising Substantiation and Advertiser Response: A Content Analysis of Magazine Advertisements," *Journal of Marketing* 47 (Winter 1983), pp. 107–117.
27. William L. Wilkie, Dennis L. McNeill, and Michael B. Mazis, "Marketing's 'Scarlet Letter': The Theory and Practice of Corrective Advertising," *Journal of Marketing* 48 (Spring 1984), p. 11.
28. "The Consumer Movement: Whatever Happened?" *The New York Times* (January 21, 1983), p. A16.
29. "Peterson Lists Alternatives to Defeated Consumer Bill," *Advertising Age* (February 13, 1978), p. 1.
30. "The Consumer Movement: Whatever Happened?" *The New York Times* (January 21, 1983), p. A16.
31. "Deregulation, Fast Start for the Reagan Strategy," *Business Week* (March 9, 1981), p. 62.
32. "It Sometimes Seems Like the Federal Tirade Commission," *The New York Times* (June 3, 1984), p. C5. See also, "Consumers Are Getting Mad, Mad, Mad, Mad at Mad Ave," *Business Week* (April 30, 1990), pp. 70–71; and "F.D.A. Is Preparing New Rules To Curb Food Label Claims," *The New York Times* (October 31, 1989), p. A1.
33. "U.S. Environmental Agency Making Deep Staffing Cuts," *The New York Times* (January 3, 1982), p. 20.
34. "The Consumer Movement: Whatever Happened?" *The New York Times* (January 21, 1983), p. A16.
35. "FTC Warns Agencies; Eyes Tobacco, Cable," *Advertising Age* (March 12, 1990), p. 6.
36. "Green Consumerism: The Trend Is Your Friend," *Directors & Boards* (Summer 1992), p. 47.
37. "Friend or Foe? Nature Groups Say Names Lie," *The New York Times* (March 25, 1996), pp. A1, A12; and "Green Concerns Influence Buying," *Advertising Age* (July 30, 1990), p. 19.
38. "Europe's Environmental Concerns Don't Make It to the Shopping Basket," *The Wall Street Journal* (August 18, 1995).
39. "Ecology Seals Vie for Approval," *Advertising Age* (January 29, 1991), p. 30.
40. *Business Week* (April 23, 1990), p. 99.
41. "Children's Health Is to Guide E.P.A.," *The New York Times* (September 12, 1996), p. A14.
42. *Business Week* (September 16, 1991), p. 86.
43. "Green Commitment: Fading Out?" *Progressive Grocer* (December 1992), p. 5.
44. "Government Dream Car," *The New York Times* (September 30, 1993), p. A1.
45. "An Alliance of 6 Big Consumers Vows to Use More Recycled Paper," *The New York Times* (August 19, 1993), p. A1.
46. "Tackling the Environment," *Progressive Grocer* (December 1992), p. 9.
47. John W. Hanley, "Monsanto's Early Warning System," *Harvard Business Review* 59 (November–December 1981), pp. 107–122.
48. "Labeling More Than a One-Word Answer: Church & Dwight Exec," *Advertising Age*, p. GR-11.
49. "FTC Green Guidelines May Spark Ad Efforts," *Advertising Age* (August 3, 1992), p. 1.
50. "Ad Claim Skeptics Still Bite," *Advertising Age* (May 7, 1990), p. S2.
51. "Alcohol Warnings Favored," *Advertising Age* (April 9, 1990), p. 1.
52. "Groups Put Heat on FTC," *The Wall Street Journal* (March 11, 1993).
53. *Advertising Age* (January 22, 1990), p. 1.
54. "Marketers Nervous Over Labeling Rules," *Advertising Age* (May 7, 1990), p. S8.
55. *Business Week* (September 25, 1989), pp. 42–44.
56. "Putting It Mildly, More Consumers Prefer Only Products That Are 'Pure,' 'Natural,'" *The Wall Street Journal* (May 11, 1993), p. B1.
57. "State Role in Labeling," *Advertising Age* (March 12, 1990), p. 73; and *The New York Times* (October 31, 1989), p. A1.
58. *The Wall Street Journal* (March 28, 1990), p. B1.
59. Ibid., p. B5.
60. "How Low Is Low? How Free Is Free?" *Advertising Age* (May 7, 1990), p. S10.
61. Ibid.
62. "Teen Smokers, Read This," *The New York Times* (August 23, 1996), p. A27.
63. "Poll Shows Camel Ads Are Effective with Kids," *Advertising Age* (April 27, 1992), p. 12.
64. Richard W. Pollay, S. Siddath, Michael Siegel, Anne Haddix, Robert K. Merritt, Gary A. Giovino, and Michael P. Eriksen, "The Last Straw? Cigarette Advertising and Realized Market Shares among Youths and Adults, 1979–1993," *Journal of Marketing* 60 (April 1996), pp. 1–16.

65. Rita Weisskoff, "Current Trends in Children's Advertising," *Journal of Advertising Research* 25 (February–March 1985), pp. RC12–14.

66. Ronald S. Rubin, "The Effects of Cognitive Development on Children's Responses to Television Advertising," *Journal of Business Research* 4 (1974), pp. 409–419.

67. Nancy Stephens and Mary Ann Stutts, "Preschoolers' Ability to Distinguish Between Television Programming and Commercials," *Journal of Advertising* 11 (April–May 1982), pp. 16–25.

68. Deborah L. Roedder, Brian Sternthal, and Bobby J. Calder, "Attitude-Behavior Consistency in Children's Responses to Television Advertising," *Journal of Marketing Research* 20 (November 1983), pp. 337–349.

69. Merrie Brucks, Gary M. Armstrong, and Marvin E. Goldberg, "Children's Use of Cognitive Defenses Against Television Advertising: A Cognitive Response Approach," *Journal of Consumer Research* 14 (March 1988), pp. 471–482.

70. See Kenneth D. Bahn, "How and When Do Brand Perceptions and Preferences First Form? A Cognitive Developmental Investigation," *Journal of Consumer Research* 13 (December 1986), pp. 382–393; Alan R. Wiman and Larry M. Newman, "Television Advertising Exposure and Children's Nutritional Awareness," *Journal of the Academy of Marketing Science* 17 (1989), pp. 179–188; and Deborah Roedder John and John C. Whitney, Jr., "The Development of Consumer Knowledge in Children: A Cognitive Structure Approach," *Journal of Consumer Research* 12 (March 1986), pp. 406–417.

71. "Kid's Kitchen May Face Safety Backlash," *Adweek's Marketing Week* (July 24, 1989), p. 25.

72. "A Little Booze for the Kiddies?" *Business Week* (September 23, 1996), p. 158.

73. "Issue: Secret Documents Reveal Industry Focus on Children, Addiction," *Action Alert,* Smoking Control Advocacy Resource Center (October 26, 1995), p. 2.

74. "FCC Adopts Limits on TV Ads Aimed at Children," *The New York Times* (April 10, 1991), p. D7; and "White House Gets Bill Reducing Ads on Children's TV Programs," *The New York Times* (October 2, 1990), p. A1.

75. "Ms. Kidvid Calls It Quits," *Time* (January 20, 1992), p. 52.

76. "Top Health Official Demands Abolition of 'Joe Camel' Ads," *The New York Times* (March 10, 1992), pp. A1, D1.

77. "Joe Camel Gets Reprieve, For Now," *Advertising Age* (June 6, 1994), p. 52.

78. "Tacky Toys with Crude Names," *Industry Week* (February 15, 1993), p. 26.

79. This section is based on the following references: "The Business of Privacy," *American Demographics* (October 1994); "Database Marketing Gone Amok," *Target Marketing* (December 1993); Ellen R. Foxman and Paula Kilcoyne, "Information Technology: Marketing Practice and Consumer Privacy," *Journal of Public Policy and Marketing*; "Invasion of Privacy: When Is Access to Consumer Information Foul—or Fair? *Marketing Information* (September/October 1993).

80. Executive Office of the President, Consumer Advisory Council, First Report (Washington, D.C.: U.S. Government Printing Office, 1963), pp. 5–8.

81. "For Want of a Wheel," *Regulation* 12 (1988), p. 7.

82. "Consumers in the Information Age," *The Futurist* (January–February 1993), p. 15.

83. David M. Gardner, "Deception in Advertising: A Conceptual Approach," *Journal of Marketing* 39 (January 1975), pp. 40–46. See also J. Edward Russo, Barbara L. Metcalf, and Debra Stephens, "Identifying Misleading Advertising," *Journal of Consumer Research* 8 (September 1981), pp. 119–131.

84. "Car-Rental Firms Leave Drivers Dazed by Rip-Offs, Options, Misleading Ads," *The Wall Street Journal* (June 1, 1990), p. B1.

85. "3 Diet Providers Settle with FTC," *New York Newsday* (October 1, 1993), p. 41.

86. William L. Wilkie, Dennis L. McNeil, and Michael V. Mazis, "Marketing's 'Scarlet Letter': The Theory and Practice of Corrective Advertising," *Journal of Marketing* 48 (Spring 1984), pp. 11–31.

87. "Critics Call Cuts in Package Size Deceptive Move," *The Wall Street Journal* (February 5, 1991), p. B1.

88. "Court Tells Craftmatic To Halt Deceptive Ads," *The New York Times* (February 12, 1992), p. D4.

89. Lawrence A. Crosby and Sanford L. Grossbart, "Voluntary Performance Information Disclosures: Economic Perspectives and an Experimental Test." In Andrew Mitchell, ed., *Advances in Consumer Research,* Vol. 9 (Ann Arbor, MI: Association for Consumer Research, 1982), pp. 321–326.

90. "Transition Unit Tells Plan for FTC," *Advertising Age* (February 2, 1981), p. 3.

91. "Antitrust, Consumer-Law Enforcement by FTC Has Been Reduced, Report Says," *The Wall Street Journal* (November 10, 1983), p. 7.

92. *Marketing News* (April 30, 1982), p. 1.

93. "Clinton U-Turn on Antitrust," *Investor's Business Daily* (September 8, 1993), p. 1.

94. "Antitrust Case Threatens the Image of Toys 'R' Us," *Advertising Age* (May 27, 1996), p. 6.

95. See Jagdip Singh, "Consumer Complaint Intentions and Behavior: Definitional and Taxonomical Issues," *Journal of Marketing* 52 (January 1988), pp. 93–107, for a model of consumer complaint behavior.

96. "More Firms Use '800' Numbers to Keep Consumers Satisfied," *The Wall Street Journal* (April 7, 1983), p. 31.

97. "Product Liability: Who Sues?" *American Demographics* (June 1995), pp. 48–55.
98. George S. Day, "The Mystery of the Dissatisfied Consumer," *Wharton Magazine* (Fall 1977), p. 47.
99. Ibid.
100. "Customer Satisfaction Research Can Improve Decision Making," *Marketing News* 4 (February 5, 1990), p. 13.
101. *The Wall Street Journal* (April 7, 1983), p. 31; see also Marsha L. Richins and Bronislaw J. Verhage, "Seeking Redress for Consumer Dissatisfaction: The Role of Attitudes and Situational Factors," *Journal of Consumer Policy* 8 (March 1985), pp. 29–44.
102. Eric Schnapper, "Consumer Legislation and the Poor," *Yale Law Journal* 76 (1967), pp. 745–768; and Louis G. Richards, "Consumer Practices of the Poor." In Sturdivant, *The Ghetto Marketplace,* pp. 42–60.
103. "After Uptown, Are Some Niches Out?" *The Wall Street Journal* (January 22, 1990), p. B1.
104. Ibid.
105. "Who Scores Best on the Environment," *Fortune* (July 26, 1993), p. 114
106. Robert L. Gildea, "Consumer Survey Confirms Corporate Social Action Affects Buying Decisions," *Public Relations Quarterly* (Winter 1994–95), pp. 20–21.
107. "Cause and Effects Marketing," *Brandweek* (April 22, 1996), pp. 38–40.
108. "Promoting with a Cause," *Promo* (February 1995), pp. 67–70.

Chapter 3

1. "Here Comes GM's Saturn," *Business Week* (April 9, 1990), pp. 56–62.
2. See "Volvo, Saturn Cultivate Their Cult Following," *Advertising Age* (March 24, 1994), p. S-12; and *Saturn: A Different Kind of Car Company* (Cambridge, Mass.: Harvard Business School Case, 1994).
3. *Advertising Age* (March 24, 1994) p. S-12.
4. *Saturn: A Different Kind of Car Company.*
5. M. Venkatesan, "Cognitive Consistency and Novelty Seeking." In Scott Ward and Thomas S. Robertson, eds., *Consumer Behavior: Theoretical Sources* (Engelwood Cliffs, N.J.: Prentice-Hall, 1973),pp. 354–384.
6. Thomas S. Robertson, "Low-Commitment Consumer Behavior," *Journal of Advertising Research* 16 (April 1976), p. 20.
7. Richard L. Celsi and Jerry C. Olson, "The Role of Involvement in Attention and Comprehension Processes," *Journal of Consumer Research* 15 (September 1988), pp. 210–224.
8. Dennis H. Gensch and Rajshekhar G. Javalgi, "The Influence of Involvement on Disaggregate Attribute Choice Models," *Journal of Consumer Research* 14 (June 1987), pp. 71–82.
9. See Giles Laurent and Jean-Noel Kapferer, "Measuring Consumer Involvement Profiles," *Journal of Marketing Research* 22 (February 1985), pp. 41–53.
10. Michael J. Houston and Michael L. Rothschild, "Conceptual and Methodological Perspectives on Involvement." In Subhash C. Jain, ed., *1978 Educators' Proceedings* (Chicago: American Marketing Association, 1978), pp. 184–187.
11. Celsi and Olson.
12. Jean-Noel Kapferer and Gilles Laurent, "Consumer Involvement Profiles: A New Practical Approach to Consumer Involvement," *Journal of Advertising Research* 25 (December 1985–January 1986), pp. 48–56.
13. Laurent and Kapferer, "Measuring Consumer Involvement Profiles."
14. Judith L. Zaichowsky and James H. Sood, "A Global Look at Consumer Involvement and Use of Products," *International Marketing Review* 6 (February 1988), pp. 20–34.
15. See Sharon E. Beatty and Scott M. Smith, "External Search Effort: An Investigation Across Several Product Categories," *Journal of Consumer Research* 14(June 1987), pp. 83–95.
16. Eric A. Greenleaf and Donald R. Lehmann, "Reasons for Substantial Delay in Consumer Decision Making," *Journal of Consumer Research* 22(September 1995), pp. 186–199.
17. See John Dewey, *How We Think* (New York: Heath, 1910), and Orville Brim et al., *Personality and Decision Processes* (Stanford, Calif.: Stanford University Press, 1962).
18. "Families Have Changed But Tupperware Keeps Holding Its Parties," *The Wall Street Journal* (July 21, 1992), pp. A1, A4.
19. Donald E. Vinson, Jerome E. Scott, and Lawrence M. Lamont, "The Role of Personal Values in Marketing and Consumer Behavior," *Journal of Marketing* 41 (April 1977), pp. 44–50.
20. Abraham H. Maslow, *Motivation and Personality* (New York: Harper & Row, 1954).
21. "Marketing to Mature Adults Requires a State of Being," *Marketing News* (December 9, 1991), p. 10.
22. Michael L. Ray, "Attitudes in Consumer Behavior." In Leon G. Schiffman and Leslie L. Kanuk, *Consumer Behavior* (Englewood Cliffs, N.J.: Prentice-Hall, 1978), pp. 150–154.
23. R. Lavidge and Gary A. Steiner, "A Model for Predictive Measurements of Advertising Effectiveness," *Journal of Marketing* 25 (October 1961), pp. 59–62; and Michael L. Ray, "Marketing Communication and the Hierarchy of Effects." In P. Clarke, ed., *New Models for Mass Communication Research* (Beverly Hills, Calif.: Sage Publications, 1973), pp. 147–175.
24. Jacob Jacoby et al., "Pre-Purchase Information Acquisition." In Beverlee B. Anderson, ed., *Advances in Consumer*

Research, Vol. 3 (Atlanta: Association for Consumer Research, 1975), pp. 306–314.

25. Joseph W. Newman and Richard Staelin, "Prepurchase Information Seeking for New Cars and Major Household Appliances," *Journal of Marketing Research* 9 (August 1972), pp. 249–257.
26. For a good review of compensatory and noncompensatory models, see William L. Wilkie and Edgar A. Pessemier, "Issues in Marketing's Use of Multi-Attribute Attitude Models," *Journal of Marketing Research* 10 (November 1973), pp. 435–438.
27. Greenleaf and Lehmann, p. 192.
28. For a review of the literature on postpurchase dissonance, see William H. Cummings and M. Venkatesan, "Cognitive Dissonance and Consumer Behavior: A Review of the Evidence." In Mary Jane Schlinger, ed., *Advances in Consumer Research,* Vol. 2 (Ann Arbor: Association for Consumer Research, 1975), pp. 21–31.
29. For a description of assimilation versus contrast theories, see Rolph E. Anderson, "Consumer Dissatisfaction: The Effect of Disconfirmed Expectancy on Perceived Product Performance," *Journal of Marketing Research* 10 (February 1973), pp. 38–44.
30. Elizabeth C. Hirschman and Morris B. Holbrook, "Hedonic Consumption: Emerging Concepts, Methods and Propositions," *Journal of Marketing* 46 (Summer 1982), pp. 92–101.
31. Sidney Levy, "Symbols for Sale," *Harvard Business Review* 37 (July–August), pp. 117–124; and Sidney Levy, "Symbolism and Lifestyle." In Steven Greyser, ed., *Toward Scientific Marketing,* Proceedings of the American Marketing Association Educators' Conference, 1964.
32. *A Case Study in Understanding Consumer Behavior* (Fountain Valley, Calif.: Coast Telecourses, 1988).
33. James H. Leigh and Terrance G. Gabel, "Symbolic Interactionism: Its Effects on Consumer Behavior and Implications for Marketing Strategy," *Journal of Consumer Marketing* 9 (Winter 1992), pp. 27–38; and Hirschman and Holbrook, "Hedonic Consumption."

Chapter 4

1. "The Brand's the Thing," *Fortune* (March 4, 1996), pp. 72–86.
2. Ibid.
3. For a good summary of these three learning theories, see Michael L. Ray and Peter H. Webb, "Three Learning Theory Traditions and Their Application in Marketing." In Ronald C. Curhan, ed., *Combined Proceedings of the American Marketing Association,* Series No. 36 (1974), pp. 100–103.
4. E. L. Thorndike, *The Psychology of Learning* (New York: Teacher's College, 1913); and J. B. Watson and R. Rayner, "Conditioned Emotional Reactions," *Journal of Experimental Psychology* 3 (1920), pp. 1–14.
5. Ivan Pavlov, *Conditioned Reflexes. An Investigation of the Physiological Activity of the Cerebral Cortex,* G. V. Anrep, ed. (London: Oxford University Press, 1927).
6. Chris Janiszewski and Luk Warlop, "The Influence of Classical Conditioning Procedures on Subsequent Attention to the Conditioned Brand," *Journal of Consumer Research* 20(September 1993), pp. 171–189.
7. Frances K. McSweeney and Calvin Bierley, "Recent Developments in Classical Conditioning," *Journal of Consumer Research* 11 (September 1984), pp. 619–631.
8. "Enduring Brands Hold Their Allure by Sticking Close to Their Roots," *The Wall Street Journal* (Centennial Edition, 1989), p. B4.
9. Terence A. Shimp, Elnora W. Stuart, and Randall W. Engle, "A Program of Classical Conditioning Experiments Testing Variations in the Conditioned Stimulus and Context," *Journal of Consumer Research* 18 (June 1991), pp. 1–12.
10. "Hostess, Wonder Bread Target Kids Again," *The Wall Street Journal* (November 17, 1995), p. B6.
11. B. F. Skinner, *The Behavior of Organisms: An Experimental Analysis* (New York: Appleton-Century-Crofts, 1938).
12. Peter D. Bennett and Robert M. Mandel, "Prepurchase Information Seeking Behavior of New Car Purchasers—The Learning Hypothesis," *Journal of Marketing Research* 6 (November 1969), pp. 430–433.
13. Eric Lapersonne, Gilles Laurent, and Jean-Jacques Le Goff, "Consideration Sets of Size One: An Empirical Investigation of Automobile Purchases," *International Journal of Research in Marketing* 12 (1995), pp. 55–66.
14. "Perrier Sets Slow Pace for U.S. Relaunch," *The Wall Street Journal* (March 7, 1990), pp. B1, B6; and "Perrier's Back," *Advertising Age* (April 23, 1990), pp. 1, 84.
15. *Advertising Age* (September 13, 1976), p. 124.
16. Michael L. Rothschild and William C. Gadis, "Behavioral Learning Theory: Its Relevance to Marketing and Promotions," *Journal of Marketing* 45 (Spring 1981), pp. 70–78.
17. Rom J. Markin, Jr., *Consumer Behavior: A Cognitive Orientation* (New York: Macmillan, 1974), p. 239.
18. Wolfgang Kohler, *The Mentality of Apes* (New York: Harcourt Brace & World, 1925).
19. Alan R. Andreasen and Peter G. Durkson, "Market Learning of New Residents," *Journal of Marketing Research* 5 (May 1968), pp. 166–176.
20. Chris T. Allen and Thomas J. Madden, "A Closer Look at Classical Conditioning," *Journal of Consumer Research* 12 (December 1985), pp. 301–315.
21. John A. Howard and Jagdish Sheth, *The Theory of Buyer Behavior* (New York: Wiley, 1969), pp. 27–28.
22. Joseph W. Newman and Richard A. Werbel, "Multivariate Analysis of Brand Loyalty for Major Household Appli-

ances," *Journal of Marketing Research* 10 (November 1973), pp. 404–409.

23. Donald R. Lehmann, William L. Moore, and Terry Elrod, "The Development of Distinct Choice Process Segments Over Time: A Stochastic Modeling Approach," *Journal of Marketing* 46 (Spring 1982), pp. 48–59.
24. Ted Roselius, "Consumer Rankings of Risk Reduction Methods," *Journal of Marketing* 35 (January 1971), pp. 56–61.
25. Klaus Peter Kass, "Consumer Habit Forming, Information Acquisition, and Buying Behavior," *Journal of Business Research* 10 (March 1982), pp. 3–15.
26. See Brian Wasnick and Cynthia Huffman, "Perceiving, Choosing, and Using: A Framework for Revitalizing Mature Brands," Working Paper, The Wharton School of Business, May, 1996.
27. W. T. Tucker, "The Development of Brand Loyalty," *Journal of Marketing Research* 1 (August 1964), p. 32.
28. Jacob Jacoby, "A Model of Multi-Brand Loyalty," *Journal of Advertising Research* 11 (June 1971), p. 26.
29. Jacob Jacoby and David B. Kyner, "Brand Loyalty vs. Repeat Purchasing Behavior," *Journal of Marketing Research* 10 (February 1973), p. 2.
30. "What Do People Want, Anyway?" *The New York Times* (November 8, 1987), p. F4.
31. "Brand Loyalty—Fact or Fiction?" *Advertising Age* (June 19, 1952), pp. 53–55; (June 30, 1952), pp. 45–47; (August 11, 1952), pp. 56–58; (September 1, 1952), pp. 80–82; (October 6, 1952), pp. 82–86; (December 1, 1952), pp. 76–79; (January 25, 1953), pp. 32–35.
32. Tucker, "The Development of Brand Loyalty."
33. Raymond J. Lawrence, "Patterns of Buyer Behavior: Time for a New Approach?" *Journal of Marketing Research* 6 (May 1969), pp. 137–144.
34. Robert C. Blattberg and Subrata K. Sen, "Market Segments and Stochastic Brand Choice Models," *Journal of Marketing Research* 13 (February 1976), pp. 34–45.
35. Lawrence, "Patterns of Buyer Behavior. . . ."
36. George S. Day, "A Two-Dimensional Concept of Brand Loyalty," *Journal of Advertising Research* 9 (September 1969), pp. 29–36.
37. Ibid.
38. See "Are There Consumer Types?" (New York: Advertising Research Foundation, 1964); and Ronald E. Frank, William F. Massy, and Thomas M. Lodahl, "Purchasing Behavior and Personal Attributes," *Journal of Advertising Research* 9 (December 1969), pp. 15–24.
39. Day, "A Two-Dimensional Concept. . . ."
40. James M. Carman, "Correlates of Brand Loyalty: Some Positive Results," *Journal of Marketing Research* 7 (February 1970), pp. 67–76.
41. Roselius, "Consumer Rankings. . ." and Jagdish Sheth and M. Venkatesan, "Risk-Reduction Processes in Repetitive Consumer Behavior," *Journal of Marketing Research* 3 (August 1968), pp. 307–311.
42. Carman, "Correlates of Brand Loyalty. . . ."
43. "Traditional Brand Loyalty," *Advertising Age* (May 18, 1981), p. S2; and "Hispanics: All for One?" *Advertising Age* (September 13, 1984), p. 3.
44. "Brand Loyalty Beats Price in Some Product Categories," *Marketing News* (November 28, 1980), p. 1.
45. Fred. D. Reynolds, William R. Darden, and Warren S. Martin, "Developing an Image of the Store-Loyal Customer," *Journal of Retailing* 50 (Winter 1974–1975), pp. 73–84.
46. Arieh Goldman, "The Shopping Style Explanation for Store Loyalty," *Journal of Retailing* 53 (Winter 1977–1978), pp. 33–46.
47. Ibid.
48. Robert D. Hisrich, Ronald J. Dornoff, and Jerome B. Kernan, "Perceived Risk in Store Selection," *Journal of Marketing Research* 9 (November 1972), pp. 435–439; and Joseph F. Dash, Leon G. Schiffman, and Conrad Berenson, "Risk and Personality Related Dimensions of Store Choice," *Journal of Marketing* 40 (January 1976), pp. 32–39.
49. *Supermarket Shoppers in a Period of Economic Uncertainty* (New York: Yankelovich, Skelly, and White, Inc. 1982), p. 16.
50. Goldman, "The Shopping Style Explanation for Store Loyalty."

Chapter 5

1. For a review of low-involvement consumer behavior, see Scott A. Hawkins and Stephen J. Hoch, "Low Involvement Learning: Memory Without Evaluation," *Journal of Consumer Research* 19 (September 1992), pp. 212–225; John C. Maloney and Bernard Silverman, eds., *Attitude Research Plays for High Stakes* (Chicago: American Marketing Association, 1979); and William L. Wilkie, ed., *Advances in Consumer Research,* Vol. 6 (Ann Arbor: Association for Consumer Research, 1979), pp. 174–199. See also the following sources: Ruth Lynne Zaichowsky, "Measuring the Involvement Construct," *Journal of Consumer Research* 12 (December 1985), pp. 341–352; Marsha L. Richins and Peter H. Bloch, "After the New Wears Off: The Temporal Context of Product Involvement," *Journal of Consumer Research* 13 (September 1986), pp. 280–285; Banwari Mittal and Myung-Soo Lee, "Separating Brand-Choice Involvement from Product Involvement via Consumer Involvement Profiles." In Michael J. Houston, ed., *Advances in Consumer Research,* Vol. 15 (Provo, UT: Association for Consumer Research, 1987), pp. 43–49; Sharon E. Beatty, Lynn R. Kahle, and Pamela Homer, "The Involvement-Commitment Model: Theory and Implications," *Journal of*

Business Research 16 (March 1988), pp. 149–168; Carolyn L. Costley, "Meta Analysis of Involvement Research," In Houston, *Advances in Consumer Research,* Vol. 15, pp. 554–562; Richard L. Celsi and Jerry C. Olson, "The Role of Involvement in Attention and Comprehension Processes," *Journal of Consumer Research* 15 (September 1988), pp. 210–224; Dennis H. Gensch and Rajshekhar G. Javalgi, "The Influence of Involvement on Disaggregate Attribute Choice Models," *Journal of Consumer Research* 14 (June 1987), pp. 71–82; and Jean-Noel Kapferer and Gilles Laurent, "Consumer Involvement Profiles: A New Practical Approach to Consumer Involvement," *Journal of Advertising Research* 25 (December 1985–January 1986), pp. 48–56.

2. "How King Kellogg Beat the Blahs," *Fortune* (August 29, 1988), pp. 55–64.
3. Harold H. Kassarjian and Waltraud M. Kassarjian, "Attitudes Under Low Commitment Conditions." In Maloney and Silverman, *Attitude Research Plays for High Stakes,* p. 8.
4. Nancy T. Hupfer and David M. Gardner, "Differential Involvement with Products and Issues: An Exploratory Study." In David M. Gardner, ed., *Proceedings of the 2nd Annual Conference of the Association for Consumer Research* (College Park, MD: Association for Consumer Research, 1971), pp. 262–269.
5. Tyzoon T. Tyebjee, "Refinement of the Involvement Concept: An Advertising Planning Point of View." In Maloney and Silverman, *Attitude Research Plays for High Stakes,* p. 106.
6. John L. Lastovicka, "Questioning the Concept of Involvement Defined Product Classes." In Wilkie, *Advances in Consumer Research,* Vol. 6, pp. 174–179.
7. See Michael L. Rothschild, "Advertising Strategies for High and Low Involvement Situations." In Maloney and Silverman, *Attitude Research Plays for High Stakes,* pp. 74–93. Recent research has suggested that attitudes are formed in low-involvement conditions on a noncognitive basis. Yet these attitudes are likely to be weaker than those formed on a cognitive basis in high-involvement conditions. See Chris Janiszewski, "Preconscious Processing Effects: The Independence of Attitude Formation and Conscious Thought," *Journal of Consumer Research* 15 (September 1988), pp. 199–209.
8. "Major Study Details Ads' Effects on Sales," *Advertising Age* (June 21, 1982), pp. 1, 80.
9. Sharon E. Beatty and Lynn R. Kahle, "Alternative Hierarchies of the Attitude-Behavior Relationship: The Impact of Brand Commitment and Habit," *Journal of the Academy of Marketing Science* 16 (Summer 1988), pp. 1–10.
10. Robert S. Wyer and Thoas K. Srull, "Human Cognition in Its Social Context," *Psychological Review* 93 (July 1986).
11. Beatty and Kahle, "Alternative Hierarchies. . . ."
12. Michael S. Mulvey, Jerry C. Olson, Richard L, Celsi, and Beth A. Walker, "Exploring the Relationships Between Means-End Knowledge and Involvement," *Advances in Consumer Research,* Vol. 21 (Provo, UT: Association for Consumer Research, 1994), pp. 51–57.
13. Jong-Won Park and Manoj Hastak, "Effects of Involvement on On-Line Brand Evaluations: A Stronger Test of the ELM," *Advances in Consumer Research,* Vol. 22 (Provo, UT: Association for Consumer Research, 1995), pp. 435–439.
14. Wayne D. Hoyer and Steven P. Brown, "Effects of Brand Awareness on Choice for a Common, Repeat-Purchase Product," *Journal of Consumer Research* 17 (September 1990), pp. 141–148.
15. John G. Lynch, Howard Marmorstein, and Michael F. Weigold, "Choices from Sets Including Remembered Brands: Use of Recalled Attributes and Prior Evaluations," *Journal of Consumer Research* 15 (September 1988), pp. 169–184.
16. For a similar four-part classification, see F. Steward DeBruicker, "An Appraisal of Low-Involvement Consumer Information Processing." In Maloney and Silverman, *Attitude Research Plays for High Stakes,* p. 124.
17. Rajeev Batra and Michael L. Ray, "Situational Effects of Advertising Repetition: The Moderating Influence of Motivation, Ability, and Opportunity to Respond," *Journal of Consumer Research* 12 (March 1986), pp. 432–445.
18. Hawkins and Hoch, "Low Involvement Learning. . . ."
19. Hoyer and Brown, "Effects of Brand Awareness. . . ."
20. "Former Customers Are Good Prospects," *The Wall Street Journal* (April 22, 1982), p. 31.
21. Dennis W. Rook, "The Buying Impulse," *Journal of Consumer Research* 14 (September 1987), pp. 189–199.
22. The first four types of unplanned purchasing behavior were proposed by Hawkins Stern, "The Significance of Impulse Buying Today," *Journal of Marketing* 26 (April 1962), pp. 59–62.
23. "Marketing Emphasis," *Product Marketing* (February 1978), pp. 61–64.
24. "Study Confirms Impulse Buying on Rise," *Promote* (October 12, 1987), pp. 6–8.
25. V. Kanti Prasad, "Unplanned Buying in Two Retail Settings," *Journal of Retailing* 51 (Fall 1975), pp. 3–12.
26. *Supermarket Shoppers in a Period of Economic Uncertainty* (New York: Yankelovich, Skelly, and White, Inc., 1982), p. 53.
27. Herbert E. Krugman, "The Impact of Television Advertising: Learning Without Involvement," *Public Opinion Quarterly* 29 (Fall 1965), pp. 349–356.
28. C. W. Sherif, M. Sherif, and R. W. Nebergall, *Attitude and Attitude Change* (Philadelphia: Saunders, 1965).
29. Richard E. Petty and John T. Cacioppo, *Attitudes and Persuasion: Classic and Contemporary Approaches* (Dubuque, IA: William C. Brown, 1981); and Richard E. Petty, John

T. Cacioppo, and David Schumann, "Central and Peripheral Routes to Advertising Effectiveness: The Moderating Role of Involvement," *Journal of Consumer Research* 10 (September 1983), pp. 135–146.

30. Herbert E. Krugman, "The Measurement of Advertising Involvement," *Public Opinion Quarterly* 30 (Winter 1966), pp. 584–585.
31. Robert C. Grass and Wallace H. Wallace, "Advertising Communication: Print vs. TV," *Journal of Advertising Research* 14 (October 1974), pp. 19–23.
32. Terry L. Childers and Michael J. Houston, "Conditions for a Picture-Superiority Effect on Consumer Memory," *Journal of Consumer Research* 11 (September 1984), p. 652.
33. Krugman, "The Impact of Television Advertising. . . ," p. 354.
34. Stephen W. Hollander and Jacob Jacoby, "Recall of Crazy, Mixed-Up TV Commercials," *Journal of Research* 13 (June 1973), pp. 399–42.
35. Celsi and Olson, "The Role of Involvement. . . ," and Gensch and Javagali, "The Influence of Involvement. . . ."
36. W. P. Dommermuth, "The Shopping Matrix and Marketing Strategy," *Journal of Marketing Research* 2 (May 1965), pp. 128–132; and Joseph W. Newman and Richard Staelin, "Prepurchase Information Seeking for New Cars and Major Household Appliances," *Journal of Marketing Research* 9 (August 1972), pp. 249–257.
37. R. A. Bauer, "The Obstinate Audience," *American Psychologist* 19 (May 1964), pp. 319–328.
38. Kassarjian and Kassarjian, "Attitudes Under Low Commitment Conditions. . . ," p. 10.
39. A. Benton Cocanougher and Grady Bruce, "Socially Distant Reference Groups and Consumer Aspirations," *Journal of Marketing Research* 8 (August 1971), pp. 378–381.
40. Sherif, Sherif, and Nebergall, *Attitude and Attitude Change*; and M. Sherif and C. E. Hovland, *Social Judgment* (New Haven, CT: Yale University Press, 1964).
41. Michael L. Rothschild and Michael J. Houston, "The Consumer Involvement Matrix: Some Preliminary Findings." In Barnett A. Greenberg and Danny N. Bellenger, *Proceedings of the American Marketing Association Educators' Conference*, Series. No. 41 (1977), pp. 95–98.
42. Ibid.
43. Gensch and Javagali, "The Influence of Involvement. . . ."
44. Petty, Cacioppo, and Schumann, "Central and Peripheral Routes to Advertising Effectiveness."
45. Richard E. Petty, John T. Cacioppo, and Rachel Goldman, "Personal Involvement as a Determinant of Argument-Based Persuasion," *Journal of Personality and Social Psychology* 41 (November 1981), pp. 847–855; and Petty, Cacioppo, and Schumann, "Central and Peripheral Routes to Advertising Effectiveness."
46. David W. Schumann, Richard E. Petty, and D. Scott Clemons, "Predicting the Effectiveness of Different Strategies of Advertising Variation: A Test of the Repetition-Variation Hypotheses," *Journal of Consumer Research* 17 (September 1990), pp. 192–203.
47. Meryl Gardner, Andrew Mitchell, and J. Edward Russo, *Strategy-Induced Low Involvement with Advertising*. Paper presented at the first Consumer Involvement Conference, New York University, June 1982.
48. Rothschild, "Advertising Strategies for High and Low Involvement Situations," p. 84.
49. Krugman, "The Measurement of Advertising Involvement."
50. Rothschild, "Advertising Strategies for High and Low Involvement Situations," p. 84.
51. Krugman, "The Measurement of Advertising Involvement."
52. Tyebjee, "Refinement of the Involvement Concept. . . ," p. 97.
53. Jerry B. Gotlieb, John L. Schlacter, and Robert D. St. Louis, "Consumer Decision Making: A Model of the Effects of Involvement, Source Credibility, and Location on the Size of the Price Difference Required to Induce Consumers to Change Suppliers," *Psychology & Marketing* 9 (May/June 1992), pp. 191–206.
54. John L. Lastovicka, *The Low Involvement Point-of-Purchase: A Case Study of Margarine Buyers*. Paper presented at the first Consumer Involvement Conference, New York University, June 1982.
55. Thomas S. Robertson, "Low-Commitment Consumer Behavior," *Journal of Advertising Research* 16 (April 1976), p. 23; and Henry Assael, "The Conceptualization of a Construct of Variety-Seeking Behavior," Working Paper Series #79-43, Stern School of Business, New York University, May 1979, p. 5.
56. Peter L. Wright, "The Choice of a Choice Strategy: Simplifying vs. Optimizing," Faculty Working Paper No. 163, University of Illinois, Department of Business Administration, 1974.
57. Rothschild and Houston, "The Consumer Involvement Matrix. . . ," pp. 95–98.
58. "Pepsi-Cola to Stamp Dates for Freshness on Soda Cans," *The New York Times* (March 31, 1994), pp. D1, D18.
59. Tyebjee, "Refinement of the Involvement Concept. . . ," p. 100.
60. Richard J. Lutz, "A Functional Theory Framework for Designing and Pretesting Advertising Themes." In Maloney and Silverman, *Attitude Research Plays for High Stakes*, p. 47.
61. Harper W. Boyd, Jr., Michael L. Ray, and Edward C. Strong, "An Attitudinal Framework for Advertising Strategy," *Journal of Marketing* 36 (April 1972), p. 31.
62. Frederick E. Webster, Jr., "Determining the Characteristics of the Socially Conscious Consumer," *Journal of Consumer Research* 2 (December 1975), pp. 188–196.

63. Lester W. Milbrath and M. L. Goel, *Political Participation,* 2nd ed. (New York: New York University Press, 1982).
64. Drew Hyman, "The Hierarchy of Consumer Participation: Knowledge and Proficiency in Telecommunications Decision Making," *The Journal of Consumer Affairs* 24 (Summer 1990), pp. 1–23.

Chapter 6

1. "Timex Data Link Watch Technology Integrated with Updated Microsoft Schedule+," *Timex Internet Site* (December 1996); and "Sweat Chic," *Forbes* (September 5, 1988), p. 96.
2. Flemming Hansen, *Consumer Choice Behavior* (New York: The Free Press, 1972).
3. William O. Bearden and Arch G. Woodside, "Consumption Occasion Influence on Consumer Brand Choice," *Decision Sciences* 9 (April 1978), pp. 273–284.
4. Kenneth C. Gehrt and Mary Beth Pinto, "The Impact of Situational Factors on Health Care Preferences: Exploring the Prospect of Situationally Based Segmentation," *Journal of Health Care Marketing* 11 (June 1991), pp. 41–52.
5. See, for example, C. Whan Park, Easwar S. Iyer, and Daniel C. Smith, "The Effects of Situational Factors on In-Store Grocery Shopping Behavior: The Role of Store Environment and Time Available for Shopping," *Journal of Consumer Research* 15 (March 1989), pp. 422–433.
6. "The Teen Market," *Product Marketing* (Spring 1982), p. S26.
7. "Sales Promotion: The Year in Review," *Marketing & Media Decisions* (July 1989), pp. 124–126; and "Ad Spending Outlook Brightens," *Advertising Age* (May 15, 1989).
8. Russell Belk, "Gift-Giving Behavior." In J. Sheth, ed., *Research in Marketing,* Vol. 2 (Greenwich, CT: JAI Press, 1979), pp. 95–126.
9. Keith Clarke and Russell Belk, "The Effects of Product Involvement and Task Definition on Anticipated Consumer Effort." In William Wilkie, ed., *Advances in Consumer Research,* Vol. 6 (Ann Arbor, MI: Association for Consumer Research, 1979), pp. 313–317.
10. A. Ryan, "Consumer Gift-Giving Behavior: An Exploratory Analysis." In D. Bellinger and B. Greenberg, eds., *Contemporary Marketing Thought* (Chicago: American Marketing Association, 1977), pp. 100–104.
11. John F. Sherry, Jr., "Gift Giving in Anthropological Perspective," *Journal of Consumer Research* 10 (September 1983), pp. 157–168.
12. John F. Sherry, Mary Ann McGrath, and Sidney J. Levy, "The Dark Side of the Gift," *Journal of Business Research* 28(1993):225–244.
13. Ibid, p. 237.
14. Joseph A. Cote, James McCullough, and Michael Reilly, "Effects of Unexpected Situations on Behavior-Intention Differences: A Garbology Analysis," *Journal of Consumer Research* 12 (September 1985), pp. 188–194.
15. William L. Wilkie and Peter R. Dickson, "Patterns of Consumer Information Search and Shopping Behavior for Household Durables." Working Paper Series (Cambridge, MA: Marketing Science Institute, 1985).
16. Marvin E. Goldberg and Gerald J. Gorn, "Happy and Sad TV Programs: How They Affect Reactions to Commercials," *Journal of Consumer Research* 14 (December 1987), pp. 387–403.
17. Margaret S. Clark, Sandra Milberg, and John Ross, "Arousal Cues Arousal-Related Material in Memory: Implications for Understanding Effects of Mood on Memory," *Journal of Verbal Learning and Verbal Behavior* 22 (1983), pp. 633–649.
18. Meryl P. Gardner, "The Consumer's Mood: An Important Situational Variable." In Thomas C. Kinnear, ed., *Advances in Consumer Research,* Vol. 11 (Ann Arbor, MI: Association for Consumer Research, 1984), pp. 525–529.
19. Russell W. Belk, "Situational Variables and Consumer Behavior," *Journal of Consumer Research* 2 (December 1975), p. 159.
20. S. Tamer Cavusgil and Catherine A. Cole, "An Empirical Investigation of Situational, Attitudinal and Personal Influences on Behavioral Intentions." In Kenneth Bernhardt et al., eds., *Proceedings of the American Marketing Association Educators' Conference,* Series No. 47 (1981), p. 161.
21. Russell W. Belk, "An Exploratory Assessment of Situational Effects in Buyer Behavior," *Journal of Marketing Research* 11 (May 1974), p. 160.
22. D. Bem, "Self-Perception Theory." In L. Berkowitz, ed., *Advances in Experimental Social Psychology* (New York: Academic Press, 1972), pp. 1–62.
23. Brian Sternthal and Gerald Zaltman, "The Broadened Concept: Toward a Taxonomy of Consumption Situation." In Gerald Zaltman and Brian Sternthal, eds., *Broadening the Concept of Consumer Behavior* (Ann Arbor, MI: Association for Consumer Research, 1975), p. 144.
24. Keith Clarke and Russell W. Belk, "The Effects of Product Involvement and Task Definition on Anticipated Consumer Effort." In William L. Wilkie, ed., *Advances in Consumer Research.*
25. William O. Bearden and Arch G. Woodside, "Interactions of Consumption Situations and Brand Attitudes," *Journal of Applied Psychology* 61 (1976), pp. 764–769.
26. Belk, "An Exploratory Assessment," p. 160; and Louis K. Sharpe and Kent L. Granzin, "Market Segmentation by Consumer Usage Context: An Exploratory Analysis," *Journal of Economics and Business* 26 (1974), pp. 225–228.
27. Bearden and Woodside, "Consumption Occasion Influence. . . ."

28. Belk, "An Exploratory Assessment. . . ."
29. Rajendra K. Srivastava, Allan D. Shocker, and George S. Day, "An Exploratory Study of the Influences of Usage Situation on Perceptions of Product Markets." In H. Keith Hunt, ed., *Advances in Consumer Research,* Vol. 5 (Ann Arbor, MI: Association for Consumer Research, 1978), pp. 32–38.
30. Russell W. Belk, "A Free Response Approach to Developing Product-Specific Consumption Situation Taxonomies." In Allan D. Shocker, ed., *Analytic Approaches to Product and Market Planning* (Cambridge, MA: Marketing Science Institute, 1979), p. 178.
31. Russell W. Belk, "Situational Variables and Consumer Behavior," *Journal of Consumer Research* 2 (December 1975), p. 160; Rajendra K. Srivastava, Mark I. Alpert and Allan D. Shocker, "A Customer-Oriented Approach for Determining Market Structures," *Journal of Marketing* 48 (Spring 1984), pp. 32–45; and Kenneth C. Gehrt and Mary Beth Pinto, "The Impact of Situational Factors on Health Care Preferences," *Journal of Health Care Marketing* 11 (June 1991), p. 47.
32. Sternthal and Zaltman, "The Broadened Concept. . . ," p. 146.
33. See Eric N. Berkowitz, James L. Ginter, and W. Wayne Talarzyk, "An Investigation of the Effects of Specific Usage Situations on the Prediction of Consumer Choice Behavior." In Barnett A. Greenberg and Danny N. Bellenger, eds., *Proceedings of the American Marketing Association Educators' Conference,* Series No. 41 (1977), pp. 90–94; and William O. Bearden and Arch G. Woodside, "Situational Influence on Consumer Purchase Intentions." In Arch G. Woodside, Jagdish N. Sheth, and Peter D. Bennett, eds., *Consumer and Industrial Buying Behavior* (New York: North-Holland, 1977), pp. 167–177.
34. James M. Daley and James H. Martin, "Situational Analysis of Bus Riders and Non-Riders for Different Transportation Methods," *Logistics and Transportation Review* 24 (June 1988), pp. 185–199.
35. Kenneth E. Miller and James L. Ginter, "An Investigation of Situational Variation in Brand Choice Behavior and Attitude," *Journal of Marketing Research* 16 (February 1979), pp. 111–123.
36. John L. Stanton and P. Greg Bonner, "An Investigation of the Differential Impact of Purchase Situation on Levels of Consumer Choice Behavior," *Advances in Consumer Research,* Vol. 8 (Ann Arbor, MI: Association for Consumer Research, 1980), pp. 639–643.
37. U. N. Umesh and Joseph A. Cote, "Influence of Situational Variables on Brand-Choice Models," *Journal of Business Research* 16 (1988), pp. 91–99.
38. Donald H. Granbois, "Improving the Study of Customer In-Store Behavior," *Journal of Marketing* 32 (October 1968), pp. 28–33.
39. Clarke and Belk, "The Effects of Product Involvement and Task Definition. . . ," p. 314.
40. Adrian B. Ryans, "Consumer Gift Buying Behavior: An Exploratory Analysis." In Barnett A. Greenberg and Danny N. Bellenger, eds., *Proceedings of the American Marketing Association Educators' Conference,* Series No. 41 (1977), pp. 99–104.
41. Ibid.
42. Bruce E. Mattson, "Situation Influences on Store Choice," *Journal of Retailing* 58 (Fall 1982), pp. 46–58.
43. Ibid.
44. Charles H. Ptacek and James Shanteau, "Situation Determinants of Consumer Decision Making," Working paper, 1980.
45. Brian Wansink and Michael L. Ray, "Advertising Strategies to Increase Usage Frequency," *Journal of Marketing* 60 (January 1996), pp. 31–46.
46. Peter R. Dickson, "Person-Situation: Segmentation's Missing Link," *Journal of Marketing* 46 (Fall 1982), pp. 56–64.
47. For an analytical method to position products by situations, see "CATALYST Measurement Mapping Method Identifies Competition, Defines Markets," *Marketing News* (May 14, 1982), Section 1, p. 3.
48. Ptacek and Shanteau, "Situation Determinants of Consumer Decision Making. . . ."
49. John Deighton, Caroline Henderson, and Scott Neslin, "Scanners and the Framing Effect," *Marketing & Media Decisions* (October 1989), p. 112.
50. "Perrier Rival Talks of Serendipity," *The New York Times,* p. 35.
51. Situational items taken from Russell W. Belk, "Effects of Gift-Giving Involvement on Gift Selection Strategies." In Andrew Mitchell, ed., *Advances in Consumer Research,* Vol. 9 (Ann Arbor, MI: Association for Consumer Research, 1982), pp. 408–412.

Chapter 7

1. "Arch Deluxe Life," *Brandweek* (May 27, 1996), pp. 22–31.
2. Ibid, p. 24.
3. "Red Symbols Tend to Lure Shoppers Like Capes Being Flourished at Bulls," *The Wall Street Journal* (September 18, 1995), p. A9B.
4. Ibid.
5. "Design Research: Beauty or Beast," *Advertising Age* (March 9, 1981), p. 43.
6. "Mary Kay Puts On a New Face," *Adweek's Marketing Week* (July 3, 1989), p. 4.
7. "P&G Discovers a New Look to an Old Product," *The New York Times* (January 28, 1993), p. D20.
8. "Crystal Pepsi, A Clear, Colorless Cola Is Being Launched in 3 Test Markets," *The Wall Street Journal* (April 13, 1992),

p. B7; and "Coke Hopes to Revive Tab as a Clear Cola," *The Wall Street Journal* (December 15, 1992), pp. B1, B8.

9. R. I. Allison and K. P. Uhl, "Influence of Beer Brand Identification on Taste Perception," *Journal of Marketing Research* 1 (August 1964), pp. 36–39.
10. William Copulsky and Katherine Marton, "Sensory Cues," *Product Marketing* (January 1977), pp. 31–34.
11. "Finding New Ways to Make Smell Sell," *The New York Times* (July 23, 1988).
12. Gerald J. Gorn, "The Effects of Music in Advertising on Choice Behavior: A Classical Conditioning Approach," *Journal of Marketing* 46 (Winter 1982), pp. 94–101.
13. R. Barton, *Advertising Media* (New York: McGraw-Hill, 1964), p. 109.
14. "Position in Newspaper Advertising: 2," *Media Scope* (March 1963), pp. 76–82.
15. "Betty Crocker Plans To Mix Ethnic Looks for Her New Face," *The Wall Street Journal* (September 11, 1995), pp. A1, A6.
16. John Revett, "FTC Threatens Big Fines for Undersized Cigarette Warnings," *Advertising Age* (March 17, 1975), p. 1.
17. For additional references on subliminal advertising, see Timothy E. Moore, "The Case Against Subliminal Manipulation," *Psychology and Marketing* 5 (1988), pp. 297–316; Anthony Pratkanis and Anthony Greenwald, "Recent Perspectives on Unconscious Processing: Still No Marketing Applications," *Psychology and Marketing* 5 (1988), pp. 337–354; Philip M. Marikle and Jim Chessman, "Current Status of Research on Subliminal Perception." In Melanie Wallendorf and Paul Anderson, eds., *Advances in Consumer Research,* Vol. 14 (Provo, UT: Association for Consumer Research, 1987), pp. 298–302.
18. See H. Brean, "What Hidden Sell Is All About," *Life* (March 31, 1958), pp. 104–114.
19. *New Yorker* (September 21, 1957), p. 33.
20. Timothy E. Moore, "Subliminal Advertising: What You See Is What You Get," *Journal of Marketing* 46 (Spring 1982), pp. 38–47.
21. M. L. DeFleur and R. M. Petranoff, "A Television Test of Subliminal Persuasion," *Public Opinion Quarterly* (Summer 1959), pp. 170–180.
22. "Subliminal Ad Okay If It Sells: FCC Peers into Subliminal Picture on TV," *Advertising Age* (1957).
23. Moore, "The Case Against Subliminal Manipulation," and Joel Saegert, "Why Marketing Should Quit Giving Subliminal Advertising the Benefit of the Doubt," *Psychology and Marketing* 4 (Summer 1987), pp. 107–120.
24. Chris Janiszewski, "Preconscious Processing Effects: The Independence of Attitude Formation and Conscious Thought," *Journal of Consumer Research* 15 (September 1988), pp. 199–209.
25. Wilson Bryan Key, *Media Sexploitation* (Englewood Cliffs, NJ: Prentice-Hall, 1976).
26. Dennis L. Rosen and Surendra N. Singh, "An Investigation of Subliminal Embed Effect on Multiple Measures of Advertising Effectiveness," *Psychology & Marketing* 9 (March/April 1992), pp. 157–172.
27. Brian Wansink, "Advertising's Impact on Category Substitution," *Journal of Marketing Research* 31 (November 1994), pp. 505–515.
28. Stuart Henderson Britt, Stephen C. Adams, and Alan S. Miller, "How Many Advertising Exposures Per Day?" *Journal of Advertising Research* 12 (December 1972), pp. 3–10.
29. "Packaging Research Probes Stopping Power, Label Reading, and Consumer Attitudes Among the Targeted Audience," *Marketing News* (July 22, 1983), p. 8.
30. "Tooth-Brushers Take a Shine to Baking Soda," *The Wall Street Journal* (March 2, 1992), pp. B1, B6.
31. Homer E. Spence and James F. Engel, "The Impact of Brand Preference on the Perception of Brand Names: A Laboratory Analysis." In David T. Kollat, Roger D. Blackwell, and James F. Engel, eds., *Research in Consumer Behavior* (New York: Holt, Rinehart & Winston, 1970), pp. 61–70.
32. M. Sherif and C. E. Hovland, *Social Judgment* (New Haven, CT: Yale University Press, 1964).
33. Ibid.
34. Fritz Heider, *The Psychology of Interpersonal Relations* (New York: John Wiley, 1958).
35. James T. Heimbach and Jacob Jacoby, "The Zerganik Effect in Advertising." In M. Venkatesan, ed., *Proceedings, 3rd Annual Conference* (Association for Consumer Research, 1972), pp. 746–758.
36. Douglas A. Fuchs, "Two Source Effects in Magazine Advertising," *Journal of Marketing Research* 1 (August 1964), pp. 59–62.
37. "What Have Snoopy and Gang Done for Met Life Lately?" *Adweek's Marketing Week* (November 13, 1989), pp. 2–3.
38. Kenneth E. Runyon, *Consumer Behavior and the Practice of Marketing* (Columbus, OH: Charles E. Merrill, 1977), pp. 302–303.
39. George S. Day, "Theories of Attitude Structure and Change." In Scott Ward and Thomas S. Robertson, eds., *Consumer Behavior: Theoretical Sources* (Englewood Cliffs, NJ: Prentice-Hall, 1973), p. 341.
40. Joseph W. Alba and J. Wesley Hutchinson, "Dimensions of Consumer Expertise," *Journal of Consumer Research* 13 (March 1987), pp. 411–454. For additional references on categorization, see Mita Sujan and Christine Dekleva, "Product Categorization and Inference Making: Some Implications for Comparative Advertising," *Journal of Consumer Research* 14 (December 1987), pp. 372–378; Joel B. Cohen and Kunal Basu, "Alternative Models of Categorization: Toward a Contingent Processing Framework," *Journal of Consumer Research* 13 (March 1987), pp. 455–472; Craig Thompson, "The Role of Context in Con-

sumers' Category Judgments." In Thomas K. Srull, ed., *Advances in Consumer Research,* Vol. 16 (Provo, UT: Association for Consumer Research, 1989), pp. 542–547; and Eloise Coupey and Kent Nakamoto, "Learning Context and the Development of Product Category Perceptions." In Michael J. Houston, ed., *Advances in Consumer Research,* Vol. 15 (Provo, UT: Association for Consumer Research, 1987), pp. 77–82.

41. Bobby J. Calder and Paul H. Schurr, "Attitudinal Processes in Organizations," *Research in Organizational Behavior* 3 (1981), pp. 283–302.
42. For additional references on schema, see Lawrence W. Barsalou and J. Wesley Hutchinson, "Schema Based Planning of Events in Consumer Contexts." In Wallendorf and Anderson, *Advances in Consumer Research,* Vol. 14, pp. 114–118; and Meera Venkatraman and Angelina Villarreal, "Schematic Processing of Information: An Exploratory Investigation." In Thomas C. Kinnear, ed., *Advances in Consumer Research,* Vol. 11 (Provo, UT: Association for Consumer Research, 1984), pp. 355–360.
43. Mita Sujan and James R. Bettman, "The Effect of Brand Positioning Strategies on Consumers' Brand and Category Perceptions: Some Insights from Schema Research," *Journal of Marketing Research* 26 (November 1989), pp. 454–467.
44. Douglas M. Stayman, Dana L. Alden, and Karen H. Smith, "Some Effects of Schematic Processing on Consumer Expectations and Disconfirmation Judgments," *Journal of Consumer Research* 19 (September 1992), pp. 240–255.
45. Joan Meyers-Levy and Alice M. Tybout, "Schema Congruity as a Basis for Product Evaluation," *Journal of Consumer Research* 16 (June 1989), pp. 39–54.
46. For additional references on perceptual inference, see Jeen-Su Lim, Richard W. Olshavsky, and John Kim, "The Impact of Inferences on Product Evaluations," *Journal of Marketing Research* 25 (August 1988), pp. 308–316; Valerie S. Folkes, Susan Koletsky, and John L. Graham, "A Field Study of Causal Inferences and Consumer Reaction," *Journal of Consumer Research* 13 (March 1987), pp. 534–539; Frank R. Kardes, "Spontaneous Inference Processes in Advertising," *Journal of Consumer Research* 15 (September 1988), pp. 225–233; and Gary T. Ford and Ruth Ann Smith, "Inferential Beliefs in Consumer Evaluation," *Journal of Consumer Research* 14 (December 1987), pp. 363–371.
47. See Arthur Asa Berger, *Signs in Contemporary Culture: An Introduction to Semiotics* (New York: Longman, 1984).
48. Teresa J. Domzal and Jerome B. Kernan, "Reading Advertising: The What and How of Product Meaning," *Journal of Consumer Marketing* 9 (Summer 1992), pp. 48–64.
49. See David Mick, "Consumer Research and Semiotics: Exploring the Morphology of Signs, Symbols, and Significance," *Journal of Consumer Research* 13 (September 1986), pp. 196–213.
50. "Firm's Eye-Catching Logos Often Leave Fuzzy Images in Minds of Consumers," *The Wall Street Journal* (December 5, 1991), pp. B1, B8.
51. Ben M. Enis and James E. Stafford, "Consumers' Perception of Product Quality as a Function of Various Informational Inputs." In Phillip R. McDonald, ed., *Marketing Involvement in Society and the Economy* (Proceedings of the American Marketing Association, Series No. 30, 1969), pp. 340–344.
52. "Penney Moves Upscale in Merchandise But Still Has to Convince Public," *The Wall Street Journal* (June 7, 1990), pp. A1, A8.
53. "A Corporate Campaign Tries Selling Toyota's U.S. Presence," *The New York Times* (July 21, 1993), p. D24.
54. "Penmanship with a Flourish," *Forbes* (April 3, 1989), p. 152.
55. See Robert Jacobson and Carl Obermiller, "The Formation of Expected Future Price: A Reference Price for Forward-Looking Consumers," *Journal of Consumer Research* 16 (March 1990), p. 420; and James E. Hegelson and Sharon E. Beatty, "Price Expectation and Price Recall Error: An Empirical Study," *Journal of Consumer Research* 14 (December 1987), p. 379.
56. Andre Gabor and C. W. J. Granger, "Price as an Indicator of Quality: Report on an Enquiry," *Economica* 46 (February 1966), pp. 43–70.
57. Akshay R. Rao and Wanda A. Sieben, "The Effect of Prior Knowledge on Price Acceptability and the Type of Information Examined," *Journal of Consumer Research* 19 (September 1992), pp. 256–270.
58. See Joel E. Urbany, William O. Bearden, and Dan C. Weilbaker, "The Effect of Plausible and Exaggerated Reference Prices on Consumer Perceptions and Price Search," *Journal of Consumer Research* 15 (June 1988), pp. 95–110.
59. E. Scott Maynes and Terje Assum, "Informationally Imperfect Consumer Markets: Empirical Findings and Policy Implications," *Journal of Consumer Affairs* 16 (Summer 1982), pp. 62–87.
60. Dhruv Grewal and Howard Marmostein, "Market Price Variation, Perceived Price Variation, and Consumers' Price Search Decisions for Durable Goods," *Journal of Consumer Research* 21 (December 1994), pp. 453–460.
61. Urbany, Beardan, and Weilbaker, "The Effects of Plausible and Exaggerated Reference Prices. . . ."
62. Donald R. Lichtenstein, Peter H. Bloch, and William C. Black, "Correlates of Price Acceptability," *Journal of Consumer Research* 15 (September 1988), pp. 243–252.
63. Akshay R. Rao and Kent B. Monroe, "The Moderating Effect of Prior Knowledge on Cue Utilization in Product Evaluations," *Journal of Consumer Research* 15 (September 1988), pp. 253–264.
64. Kent B. Monroe, "The Influence of Price Differences and Brand Familiarity on Brand Preferences," *Journal of Consumer Research* 3 (June 1976), pp. 42–49.

65. Jerry B. Gotlieb and Dan Sarel, "Effects of Price Advertisements on Perceived Quality and Purchase Intentions," *Journal of Business Research* 22 (1991), pp. 195–210.
66. Carl Obermiller, "When Do Consumers Infer Quality from Price?" *Channel of Communication* (Summer 1988), pp. 1–2.
67. Valerie A. Zeithaml, "Consumer Perceptions of Price, Quality, and Value: A Means-End Model and Synthesis of Evidence," *Journal of Marketing* 52 (July 1988), pp. 2–22.

Chapter 8

1. "Too Many Think the Bunny Is Duracell's, Not Eveready's," *The Wall Street Journal* (July 31, 1990), p. B1.
2. "Advertising Age Marketing 100," *Advertising Age* (July 5, 1993), p. SS-1.
3. Gabriel Biehal and Dipankar Chakravarti, "Information Accessibility as a Moderator of Consumer Choice," *Journal of Consumer Research* 10 (June 1983), pp. 1–14; see also Carolyn L. Costley and Merrie Brucks, "Selective Recall and Information Use in Consumer Preferences," *Journal of Consumer Research* 18 (March 1992), pp. 464–474.
4. Joseph W. Alba, Howard Marmorstein, and Amitava Chattopadhyay, "Transitions in Preference Over Time: The Effects of Memory on Message Persuasiveness," *Journal of Marketing Research* 29 (November 1992), pp. 406–416.
5. William B. Locander and Peter W. Hermann, "The Effect of Self-Confidence and Anxiety on Information Seeking in Consumer Risk Reduction," *Journal of Marketing Research* 16 (May 1979), pp. 268–274.
6. Keith B. Murray, "A Test of Services Marketing Theory: Consumer Information Acquisition Activities," *Journal of Marketing* 55 (January 1991), pp. 10–25.
7. Sharon E. Beatty and Scott M. Smith, "External Search Effort: An Investigation Across Several Product Categories," *Journal of Consumer Research* 14 (June 1987), pp. 83–95.
8. Narasimhan Srinivasan and Brian T. Ratchford, "An Empirical Test of a Model of External Search for Automobiles," *Journal of Consumer Research* 18 (September 1991), pp. 233–241.
9. Peter D. Bennett and Robert M. Mandell, "Prepurchase Information Seeking Behavior of New Car Purchasers: The Learning Hypothesis," *Journal of Marketing Research* 6 (November 1969), pp. 430–433.
10. Cynthia Huffman and Michael J. Houston, "Goal-Oriented Experiences and the Development of Knowledge," *Journal of Consumer Research* 20 (September 1993), pp. 190–207.
11. Beatty and Smith, "External Search Effort. . . ."
12. W. P. Dommermuth and E. W. Cundiff, "Shopping Goods, Shopping Centers, and Selling Strategies," *Journal of Marketing* 31 (October 1967), pp. 32–36; and Joseph W. Newman and Richard Staelin, "Prepurchase Information Seeking for New Cars and Major Household Appliances," *Journal of Marketing Research* 9 (August 1972), pp. 249–257.
13. John D. Claxton, Joseph N. Fry, and Bernard Portis, "A Taxonomy of Prepurchase Information Gathering Patterns," *Journal of Consumer Research* 1 (December 1974), pp. 35–42.
14. G. Stigler, "The Economics of Information," *Journal of Political Economy* 69 (1961), pp. 213–225; and Brian T. Ratchford, "Cost-Benefit Models for Explaining Consumer Choice and Information Seeking Behavior," *Management Science* 28 (February 1982), pp. 197–212.
15. Beatty and Smith, "External Search Effort. . . ."
16. Howard Beales, Michael B. Mazis, Steven C. Salop, and Richard Staelin, "Consumer Search and Public Policy," *Journal of Consumer Research* 8 (June 1981), pp. 11–22.
17. Jacob Jacoby et al., "Pre-Purchase Information Acquisition." In Beverlee B. Anderson, ed., *Advances in Consumer Research,* Vol. 3 (Atlanta: Association for Consumer Research, 1975), pp. 306–314.
18. Noel Capon and Marian Burke, "Individual, Product Class, and Task-Related Factors in Consumer Information Processing," *Journal of Consumer Research* 7 (December 1980), pp. 314–326.
19. Compiled from five studies by David L. Loudon and Albert J. Della Bitta, *Consumer Behavior* (New York: McGraw-Hill, 1979), p. 463.
20. W. P. Dommermuth, "The Shopping Matrix and Marketing Strategy," *Journal of Marketing Research* 2 (May 1965), pp. 128–132.
21. Newman and Staelin, "Prepurchase Information Seeking. . . ."
22. Girish Punj, "Presearch Decision Making in Consumer Durable Purchases," *Journal of Consumer Marketing* 4 (Winter 1987), pp. 71–82.
23. Jacob Jacoby, Donald E. Speller, and Carol A. Kohn, "Brand Choice Behavior as a Function of Information Load," *Journal of Marketing Research* 11 (February 1974), pp. 63–69.
24. J. Wesley Hutchinson and Joseph W. Alba, "Ignoring Irrelevant Information: Situational Determinants of Consumer Learning," *Journal of Consumer Research* 18 (December 1991), pp. 326–345.
25. Kevin Kerr, "Do Americans Have Too Many Brands?" *Adweek's Marketing Week* (December 9, 1991), p. 14.
26. "Free Choice: When Too Much Is Too Much," *The New York Times* (February 14, 1990), p. C1.
27. C. Whan Park and Henry Assael, "Has the Low Involvement View of Consumer Behavior Been Overstated?" Working Paper, University of Pittsburgh, 1983.
28. Herbert E. Krugman, "Memory Without Recall, Exposure with Perception," *Journal of Advertising Research* 17 (August 1977), pp. 7–12.

29. Jong-Won Park and Manoj Hastak, "Memory-Based Product Judgments: Effects of Involvement at Encoding and Retrieval," *Journal of Consumer Research* 21 (December 1994), pp. 534–547.

30. Richard E. Petty, John T. Cacioppo, and David Schumann, "Central and Peripheral Routes to Advertising Effectiveness: The Moderating Role of Involvement," *Journal of Consumer Research* 10 (September 1983), pp. 135–146; see also Scott B. Mackenzie and Richard A. Spreng, "How Does Motivation Moderate the Impact of Central and Peripheral Processing on Brand Attitudes and Intentions?" *Journal of Consumer Research* 18 (March 1992), pp. 519–529.

31. E. Tulving, "Episodic and Semantic Memory." In E. Tulving and W. Donaldson, eds., *Organization of Memory* (New York: Academic Press, 1972).

32. See Joan Meyers-Levy, "The Influence of a Brand Name's Association Set Size and Work Frequency on Brand Memory," *Journal of Consumer Research* 16 (September 1989), pp. 197–207.

33. Kevin Lane Keller, "Memory and Evaluation Effects in Competitive Advertising Environments," *Journal of Consumer Research* 17 (March 1991), pp. 463–476.

34. Kevin Lane Keller, "Memory Factors in Advertising Evaluations," *Journal of Consumer Research* 14 (December 1987), pp. 316–333.

35. Raymond R. Burke and Thomas K. Srull, "Competitive Interference and Consumer Memory for Advertising," *Journal of Consumer Research* 15 (June 1988), pp. 55–68.

36. Keller, "Memory and Evaluation Effects. . . ."

37. Meryl P. Gardner, Andrew A. Mitchell, and J. Edward Russo, "Strategy-Induced Low Involvement with Advertising," *Journal of Advertising Research*. See also Wayne D. Hoyer, "An Examination of Consumer Decision Making for a Common Repeat Purchase Product," *Journal of Consumer Research* 11 (December 1984), pp. 822–828.

38. For a similar distinction, see Mita Sujan, "Consumer Knowledge: Effects on Evaluation Strategies Mediating Consumer Judgments," *Journal of Consumer Research* 12 (June 1985), pp. 31–46; see also John G. Lynch, Jr., Howard Marmorstein, and Michael F. Weigold, "Choices from Sets Including Remembered Brands: Use of Recalled Attributes and Prior Overall Evaluations," *Journal of Consumer Research* 15 (September 1988), pp. 169–184.

39. Sujan, "Consumer Knowledge. . . ."

40. Douglas M. Stayman, Dana L. Alden, and Karen H. Smith, "Some Effects of Schematic Processing on Consumer Expectations and Disconfirmation Judgments," *Journal of Consumer Research* 19 (September 1992), pp. 240–255.

41. For example, Denis A. Lussier and Richard W. Olshavsky, "Task Complexity and Contingent Processing in Brand Choice," *Journal of Consumer Research* 6 (September 1979), pp. 154–165.

42. Naelm H. Abougomaah, John L. Schlacter, and William Gaidis, "Elimination and Choice Phases in Evoked Set Formation," *Journal of Consumer Marketing* 4 (Fall 1987), pp. 67–73.

43. Elizabeth C. Hirschman and Morris B. Holbrook, "Hedonic Consumption: Emerging Concepts, Methods and Propositions," *Journal of Marketing* 46 (Summer 1982), pp. 92–101.

44. James R. Bettman, "Perceived Risk and Its Components: A Model and Empirical Test," *Journal of Marketing Research* 10 (May 1973), pp. 184–190.

45. Ted Roselius, "Consumer Rankings of Risk Reduction Methods," *Journal of Marketing* 35 (January 1971), pp. 56–61.

46. Thomas S. Robertson, "The Touch-Tone Telephone: Diffusion of an Innovation." In Roger D. Blackwell, James F. Engel, and David T. Kollat, eds., *Cases in Consumer Behavior* (New York: Holt, Rinehart & Winston, 1969), pp. 274–297.

47. Michael L. Ray and Alan G. Sawyer, "Repetition in Media Models: A Laboratory Technique," *Journal of Marketing Research* 8 (February 1971), pp. 20–29.

48. John Deighton, "How to Solve Problems That Don't Matter: Some Heuristics for Uninvolved Thinking." In Thomas C. Kinnear, ed., *Advances in Consumer Research*, Vol. 11 (Provo, UT: Association for Consumer Research, 1984), pp. 314–319.

49. Terence A. Shimp and William O. Bearden, "Warranty and Other Extrinsic Cue Effects on Consumer's Risk Perceptions," *Journal of Consumer Research* 9 (June 1982), pp. 38–46.

50. Clive W. Granger and Andrew Billson, "Consumers' Attitudes Toward Package Size and Price," *Journal of Marketing Research* 9 (August 1972), pp. 239–248; and J. Edward Russo, Gene Dreiser, and Sally Miyashita, "An Effective Display of Unit Price Information," *Journal of Marketing* 39 (April 1975), pp. 11–19.

51. George S. Day, "Assessing the Effects of Information Disclosure Requirements," *Journal of Marketing* 40 (April 1976), pp. 42–52.

52. Hutchinson and Alba, "Ignoring Irrelevant Information. . . ."

53. Capon and Burke, "Individual, Product Class, and Task-Related Factors. . . ."

54. Jennifer Gregan-Paxton and Deborah Roedder John, "Are Young Children Adaptive Decision Makers? A Study of Age Differences in Information Search Behavior," *Journal of Consumer Research* 21 (March 1995), pp. 567–580.

55. Laura A. Peracchio, "How Do Young Children Learn to Be Consumers? A Script-Processing Approach," *Journal of Consumer Research* 18 (March 1992), pp. 425–440.

56. Irving Janis and Leon Mann, *Decision Making* (New York: Free Press, 1977); and Charles Schaninger and Donald Sciglimpaglia, "The Influence of Cognitive Personality

Traits and Demographics on Consumer Information Acquisition," *Journal of Consumer Research* 8 (September 1981), pp. 208–216.

57. Catherine A. Cole and Siva K. Balasubramanian, "Age Differences in Consumers' Search for Information: Public Policy Implications," *Journal of Consumer Research* 20 (June 1993), pp. 157–169.

58. Jacob Jacoby and Leon B. Kaplan, "The Components of Perceived Risk." In M. Venkatesan, ed., *Proceedings, Third Annual Conference* (Association for Consumer Research, 1972), pp. 382–393.

Chapter 9

1. Market share figures from "AT&T Discounts Signal a National Price War," *The Wall Street Journal* (May 30, 1996) p. B1. See also, "AT&T: Creating New Value in a 'Fast-Forward' Industry," *AT&T Internet HomePage,* Speech, June 11, 1996; and "Ma Bell Faces Up to Her Generation Gap," *Adweek's Marketing Week* (June 22, 1992), pp. 18–19.

2. Ibid.

3. Gordon W. Allport, "Attitudes." In C. A. Murchinson, ed., *A Handbook of Social Psychology* (Worcester, MA: Clark University Press, 1935), pp. 798–844. For a good review of attitudinal theories, see Richard J. Lutz, "The Role of Attitude Theory in Marketing." In Harold H. Kassarjian and Thomas S. Robertson, eds., *Perspectives in Consumer Behavior* (Glenview, IL: Scott, Foresman and Co., 1991).

4. Sharon E. Beatty and Lynn R. Kahle, "Alternative Hierarchies of the Attitude-Behavior Relationship: The Impact of Brand Commitment and Habit," *Journal of the Academy of Marketing Science* 16 (Summer 1988), pp. 1–10.

5. Scott B. Mackenzie and Richard A. Spreng, "How Does Motivation Moderate the Impact of Central and Peripheral Processing on Brand Attitudes and Intentions," *Journal of Consumer Research* 18 (March 1992), pp. 519–529.

6. See Michael Solomon, *Consumer Behavior* (Englewood Cliffs: Prentice Hall, 1966), pp. 162–163.

7. Peter D. Bennett and Harold H. Kassarjian, *Consumer Behavior* (Englewood Cliffs, NJ: Prentice-Hall, 1972), p. 81.

8. Elihu Katz and Paul F. Lazarsfeld, *Personal Influence* (New York: The Free Press, 1955).

9. James S. Coleman, Elihu Katz, and Herbert Menzel, *Medical Innovation: A Diffusion Study* (New York: Bobbs-Merrill, 1966).

10. Johan Arndt, "Role of Product-Related Conversations in the Diffusion of a New Product," *Journal of Marketing Research* 4 (August 1967), pp. 291–295.

11. Daniel Katz, "The Functional Approach to the Study of Attitudes," *Public Opinion Quarterly* 24 (Summer 1960), pp. 163–204.

12. Richard J. Lutz, "A Functional Theory Framework for Designing and Pretesting Advertising Themes," *Attitude Research Plays for High Stakes* (Chicago: American Marketing Association, 1979), pp. 37–49; and William B. Locander and W. Austin Spivey, "A Functional Approach to Attitude Measurement," *Journal of Marketing Research* 15 (November 1978), pp. 576–587.

13. For research on attitude formation and structure, see Mark P. Zanna, "Attitude-Behavior Consistency: Fulfilling the Need for Cognitive Structure." In Thomas K. Srull, ed., *Advances in Consumer Research,* Vol. 16 (Provo, UT: Association for Consumer Research, 1989), pp. 318–320; Michael D. Johnson, "On the Nature of Product Attributes and Attribute Relationships." In Srull, *Advances in Consumer Research,* Vol. 16, pp. 598–604; Morris B. Holbrook and William J. Havlena, "Assessing the Real-to-Artificial Generalizability of Multiattribute Attitude Models in Tests of New Product Designs," *Journal of Marketing Research* 24 (February 1988), pp. 25–35; Punam Anand, Morris B. Holbrook, and Debra Stephens, "The Formation of Affective Judgments: The Cognitive-Affective Model Versus the Independence Hypothesis," *Journal of Consumer Research* 15 (December 1988), pp. 386–391; Michael D. Johnson and Claes Fornell, "The Nature and Methodological Implications of the Cognitive Representation of Products," *Journal of Consumer Research* 14 (September 1987), pp. 214–228; and Robert E. Smith and William R. Swinyard, "Attitude-Behavior Consistencies: The Impact of Product Trial Versus Advertising," *Journal of Marketing Research* 20 (August 1983), pp. 257–267.

14. See Fritz Heider, *The Psychology of Interpersonal Relations* (New York: John Wiley, 1958).

15. Jagdish N. Sheth and W. Wayne Talarzyk, "Perceived Instrumentality and Value Importance as Determinants of Attitudes," *Journal of Marketing Research* 9 (February 1972), pp. 6–9.

16. See Richard J. Lutz, "An Experimental Investigation of Causal Relations Among Cognitions, Affect, and Behavioral Intentions," *Journal of Consumer Research* 3 (March 1977), pp. 197–208; Jagdish N. Sheth, "Brand Profiles from Beliefs and Importances," *Journal of Advertising Research* 13 (February 1973), pp. 37–42; Frank M. Bass and William L. Wilkie, "A Comparative Analysis of Attitudinal Predictions of Brand Preference," *Journal of Marketing Research* 10 (August 1973), pp. 262–269; and David E. Weddle and James R. Bettman, "Marketing Underground: An Investigation of Fishbein's Behavioral Intention Model." In Scott Ward and Peter Wright, eds., *Advances in Consumer Research,* Vol. 1 (Urbana, IL: Association for Consumer Research, 1973), pp. 310–318.

17. Martin Fishbein, "An Investigation of the Relationships Between Beliefs About an Object and the Attitude Toward That Object," *Human Relations* 16 (1963), pp. 233–240. For a good review of multiattribute models, see William L. Wilkie and Edgar A. Pessemier, "Issues in Marketing's Use of Multiattribute Models," *Journal of Marketing Research* 10 (November 1983), pp. 428–441.

18. Martin Fishbein, "Attitudes and the Prediction of Behavior." In Martin Fishbein, ed., *Readings in Attitude Theory and Measurement* (New York: John Wiley, 1967), pp. 477–492.
19. Martin Fishbein, "Some Comments on the Use of 'Models' in Advertising Research." In *Proceedings: Seminar on Translating Advanced Advertising Theories into Research Reality* (Amsterdam: European Society of Marketing Research, 1971), p. 301.
20. Michael J. Ryan and E. H. Bonfield, "The Fishbein Extended Model and Consumer Behavior," *Journal of Consumer Research* 2 (September 1975), pp. 118–136.
21. David T. Wilson, H. Lee Matthews, and James W. Harvey, "An Empirical Test of the Fishbein Behavioral Intention Model," *Journal of Consumer Research* 1 (March 1975), pp. 39–48.
22. S. Knox and L. de Chernatony, "The Application of Multiattribute Modeling Techniques to the Mineral Water Market," *Quarterly Review of Marketing* (Summer 1989), pp. 14–20.
23. Richard P. Bagozzi and Johann Baumgarten, "An Investigation into the Role of Intentions as Mediators of the Attitude-Behavior Relationship," *Journal of Economic Psychology* 10 (1989), pp. 35–62.
24. Edward F. McQuarrie, "An Alternative to Purchase Intentions: The Role of Prior Behavior in Consumer Expenditures on Computers," *Journal of the Marketing Research Society* 30 (October 1988), pp. 407–437.
25. Seymour Banks, "The Relationship Between Preference and Purchase of Brands," *Journal of Marketing* 15 (October 1950), pp. 145–157.
26. George Katona, *The Powerful Consumer* (New York: McGraw-Hill, 1960), pp. 80–83.
27. "Recession Coming? Ask the Consumer," *The New York Times* (April 4, 1990), p. D6.
28. Robert E. Knox and James A. Inkster, "Post-Decision Dissonance at Post Time," *Journal of Personality and Social Psychology* 8 (1968), pp. 319–323.
29. Herbert E. Krugman, "The Impact of Television Advertising: Learning Without Involvement," *Public Opinion Quarterly* 29 (Fall 1965), pp. 349–356.
30. James L. Ginter, "An Experimental Investigation of Attitude Change and Choice of a New Brand," *Journal of Marketing Research* 11 (February 1974), pp. 30–40.
31. Ida E. Berger and Andrew A. Mitchell, "The Effect of Advertising on Attitude Accessibility, Attitude Confidence, and the Attitude-Behavior Relationship," *Journal of Consumer Research* 16 (December 1989), pp. 269–279. See also Smith and Swinyard, "Attitude-Behavior Consistencies. . . ."
32. Russell H. Fazio, Martha C. Powell, and Carol J. Williams, "The Role of Attitude Accessibility in the Attitude-to-Behavior Process," *Journal of Consumer Research* 16 (December 1989), pp. 280–288.

Chapter 10

1. "Will Kmart Ever Be a Silk Purse," *Business Week* (January 22, 1990), p. 46.
2. "For Big or Small, Image Is Everything," *Adweek* (March 8, 1993), pp. 28–29.
3. "Loss Leader: How Wal-Mart Outdid a Once-Touted Kmart in Discount Store Race," *The Wall Street Journal* (March 24, 1995), p. A1.
4. James McCullough, Douglas MacLachlan, and Reza Moinpour, "Impact of Information on Preference and Perception." In Andrew Mitchell, ed., *Advances in Consumer Research,* Vol. 9 (Ann Arbor, MI: Association for Consumer Research, 1982), pp. 402–405.
5. S. P. Raj, "The Effects of Advertising on High and Low Loyalty Consumer Segments," *Journal of Consumer Research* 9 (June 1982), pp. 77–89.
6. Richard J. Lutz, "Changing Brand Attitudes Through Modification of Cognitive Structures," *Journal of Consumer Research* 1 (March 1975), pp. 49–59.
7. M. Sherif and C. E. Hovland, *Social Judgment* (New Haven: Yale University Press, 1964).
8. "Milk Mustaches Jump Off the Page," *The New York Times* (October 4, 1996), p. D5.
9. "How Lubriderm Shed Its Image as a Cream for Problem Skin," *Adweek's Marketing Week* (July 3, 1989), pp. 44–45.
10. Neil H. Borden and Martin V. Marshall, *Advertising Management: Text and Cases* (Homewood, IL: Richard D. Irwin, 1959), p. 126.
11. Benjamin Lipstein, "Anxiety, Risk and Uncertainty in Advertising Effectiveness Measurements." In Lee Adler and Irving Crespi, eds., *Attitude Research on the Rocks* (Chicago: American Marketing Association, 1968), pp. 11–27.
12. "Resorting to Blandishments to Fight Image of Blandness," *The New York Times* (August 10, 1992), p. D7.
13. Leon Festinger, *A Theory of Cognitive Dissonance* (New York: Harper & Row, 1957).
14. Daniel Katz, "The Functional Approach to the Study of Attitudes," *Public Opinion Quarterly* 24 (Summer 1960), pp. 163–204.
15. Sherif and Hovland, *Social Judgment.*
16. "The Pleasure Merchants of Club Med," *Marketing Communications* (April 1986), pp. 21–24.
17. John C. Maloney, "Is Advertising Believability Really Important?" *Journal of Marketing* 27 (October 1963), pp. 1–8.
18. Fritz Heider, *The Psychology of Interpersonal Relations* (New York: John Wiley, 1958).
19. Richard E. Petty and John T. Cacioppo, *Attitudes and Persuasion: Classic and Contemporary Approaches* (Dubuque, IA: William C. Brown Co., 1981).
20. See Peter Wright, "The Cognitive Processes Mediating Acceptance of Advertising," *Journal of Marketing Research,* 10 (February 1973), pp. 53–62.

21. Martin R. Lautman and Larry Percy, "Cognitive and Affective Responses in Attribute-Based versus End-Benefit Oriented Advertising." In Thomas C. Kinnear, ed., *Advances in Consumer Research,* Vol. 11 (Provo, UT: Association for Consumer Research, 1984), pp. 11–17.
22. George J. Szybillo and Richard Heslin, "Resistance to Persuasion: Inoculation Theory in a Marketing Context," *Journal of Marketing Research* 10 (November 1973), pp. 396–403.
23. See Robert B. Settle and Linda L. Golden, "Attribution Theory and Advertiser Credibility," *Journal of Marketing Research* 11 (May 1974), pp. 181–185.
24. Kenneth B. Runyon, *Consumer Behavior and the Practice of Marketing* (Columbus, OH: Charles E. Merrill, 1977), p. 287.
25. Shelby D. Hunt, "Post-Transaction Communications and Dissonance Reduction," *Journal of Marketing* 34 (July 1970), pp. 46–51.
26. D. Bem, "Attitudes as Self-Descriptions: Another Look at the Attitude-Behavior Link." In A. Greenwald, T. Brock, and T. Ostrom, eds., *Psychological Foundations of Attitudes* (New York: Academic Press, 1968). For applications of attribution theory to consumer behavior, see Bobby Calder, "When Attitudes Follow Behavior—A Self-Perception/Dissonance Interpretation of Low Involvement." In John C. Maloney and Bernard Silverman, eds., *Attitude Research Plays for High Stakes* (Chicago: American Marketing Association, 1979), pp. 25–36.
27. Herbert E. Krugman, "The Impact of Television Advertising Learning Without Involvement," *Public Opinion Quarterly* 29 (Fall 1965), pp. 349–356.
28. "Hail to the Chef," *Fortune* (February 11, 1991), pp. 52–54; and "M'm, M'm, Okay," *Adweek* (October 10, 1988), p. 22.
29. "Relationship Retailing: A Two-Way Street," *Direct Marketing* (February 1994), pp. 38, 41.
30. "Nestlé Banks on Databases," *Advertising Age* (October 15, 1993), pp. 16, S7, S10.
31. "Sensor Gets Big Edge in Women's Razors," *The Wall Street Journal* (December 17, 1992), p. B1.
32. *Media-Advertising Partnership for a Drug-Free America, What We've Learned About Advertising* (New York: American Association of Advertising Agencies, 1990).
33. *It Works* (New York: American Association of Advertising Agencies, 1991), pp. 31–37.

Chapter 11

1. "Meet Mike Quinlan, Big Mac's Attack CEO," *Business Week* (May 9, 1988), pp. 92–97.
2. "Big Mac Takes a New Break with a Familiar McD's Twist," *Advertising Age* (March 13, 1995), p. 3.
3. "Mickey, McD Hop Online," *Advertising Age* (August 28, 1995), p. 34.
4. "Burger King Hypes Herb Ads, but Many People Are Fed Up," *The Wall Street Journal* (January 23, 1986), p. 33.
5. "Conversations Overheard at a Table in Burger King," *Adweek* (August 21, 1995), p. 54.
6. "How the Bunny Charged Eveready," *Advertising Age* (April 9, 1991), p. 20; "Eveready Loses Power in Market," *Advertising Age* (July 11, 1988), p. 4; and "Too Many Think the Bunny Is Duracell's, Not Eveready's," *The Wall Street Journal* (July 31, 1991), p. B1.
7. *Advertising Age* (July 11, 1988).
8. *The Wall Street Journal* (January 23, 1986).
9. "What Happened to Advertising?" *Business Week* (September 23, 1991), p. 68.
10. Herbert E. Krugman, "Point of View: Limits of Attention to Advertising," *Journal of Advertising Research* 28 (October-November 1988), pp. 47–50.
11. Peter H. Webb, "Consumer Initial Processing in a Difficult Media Environment," *Journal of Consumer Research* 6 (December 1979), pp. 225–236.
12. Raymond R. Burke and Thomas K. Srull, "Competitive Interference and Consumer Memory for Advertising," *Journal of Consumer Research* 15 (June 1988), pp. 55–68.
13. Carl I. Hovland, Irving L. Janis, and Harold H. Kelley, *Communication and Persuasion* (New Haven, CT: Yale University Press, 1953). See also Grant McCracken, "Who Is the Celebrity Endorser? Cultural Foundations of the Endorsement Process," *Journal of Consumer Research* 16 (December 1989), pp. 310–321.
14. Henry Assael, Michael Etgar, and Michael Henry, "The Dimensions of Evaluating and Utilizing Alternative Information Sources." Working paper, New York University, March 1983.
15. See W. Watts and William McGuire, "Persistence of Induced Opinion Change and Retention of the Inducing Message Contents," *Journal of Abnormal and Social Psychology* 68 (1964), pp. 233–241; and G. Miller and J. Basehart, "Source Trustworthiness, Opinionated Statements and Response to Persuasive Communication," *Speech Monographs* 36 (1969), pp. 1–7.
16. C. Samuel Craig and John M. McCann, "Assessing Communication Effects on Energy Conservation," *Journal of Consumer Research* 5 (September 1978), pp. 82–88.
17. Ibid., p. 87.
18. Ruby Roy Dholakia and Brian Sternthal, "Highly Credible Sources: Persuasive Facilitators or Persuasive Liabilities?" *Journal of Consumer Research* 3 (March 1977), pp. 223–232.
19. A. Eagly and S. Chaiken, "An Attribution Analysis of the Effect of Communicator Characteristics on Opinion Change: The Case of Communicator Attractiveness," *Journal of Personality and Social Psychology* 32 (1975), pp. 136–144.

20. H. Sigall and R. Helmreigh, "Opinion Change as a Function of Stress and Communicator Credibility," *Journal of Experimental Social Psychology* 5(1969), pp. 70–78.
21. Michael A. Kamins and Henry Assael, "Two-Sided Versus One-Sided Appeals: A Cognitive Perspective on Argumentation, Source Derogation, and the Effect of Disconfirming Trial on Belief Change," Journal of *Marketing Research* 24 (February 1987), pp. 29–39; and Robert B. Settle and Linda L. Golden, "Attribution Theory and Advertiser Credibility," *Journal of Marketing Research* 11 (May 1974), pp. 181–185.
22. Roobina Ohanian, "The Impact of Celebrity Spokespersons' Perceived Image on Consumers' Intention to Purchase," *Journal of Advertising Research* 31 (February/March 1991), pp. 46–53.
23. William J. McGuire, "Attitudes and Attitude Change." In Gardner Lindzey and Elliot Aronson, eds., *Handbook of Social Psychology* (New York: Random House, 1985), pp. 233–346.
24. Timothy C. Brock, "Communication-Recipient Similarity and Decision Change," *Journal of Personality and Social Psychology* 1 (June 1965), pp. 650–654; and Arch J. Woodside and J. William Davenport, "The Effect of Salesman Similarity and Expertise on Consumer Purchasing Behavior," *Journal of Marketing Research* 11 (May 1974), pp. 198–202.
25. David Mazursky and Yaacov Schul, "Learning from the Ad or Relying on Related Attitudes: The Moderating Role of Involvement," *Journal of Business Research* 25 (1992), pp. 81–93.
26. Richard E. Petty, John T. Cacioppo, and David Schumann, "Central and Peripheral Routes to Advertising Effectiveness: The Moderating Role of Involvement," *Journal of Consumer Research* 10 (September 1983), pp. 135–146.
27. S. Ratneshwar and Shelly Chaiken, "Comprehension's Role in Persuasion: The Case of Its Moderating Effect on the Persuasive Impact of Source Cues," *Journal of Consumer Research* 18 (June 1991), pp. 52–62.
28. Paul W. Miniard, Deepak Sirdeshmukh, and Daniel E. Innis, "Peripheral Persuasion and Brand Choice," *Journal of Consumer Research* 19 (September 1992), pp. 226–239.
29. "Nonverbal Messages in Ads Gain New Importance," *Adweek* (January 4, 1988), p. 23.
30. R. E. Smith and S. Hunt, "Attribution Processes and Effects in Promotional Situations," *Journal of Consumer Research* 5 (December 1978), pp. 149–158; Daniel R. Toy, "Monitoring Communication Effects: A Cognitive Structure/Cognitive Response Approach," *Journal of Consumer Research* 9 (June 1982), pp. 66–76; and Lauren A. Swanson, "The Persuasive Effect of Volunteering Negative Information in Advertising," *International Journal of Advertising* 6 (1987), pp. 237–248.
31. For a survey of research on two-sided communications, see Ayn E. Crowley and Wayne D. Hoyer, "An Integrative Framework for Understanding Two-sided Persuasion," *Journal of Consumer Research* 20 (March 1994), pp. 561–574.
32. Kamins and Assael, "Two-Sided Versus One-Sided Appeals. . . ."
33. George J. Szybillo and Richard Heslin, "Resistance to Persuasion: Inoculation Theory in a Marketing Context," *Journal of Marketing Research* 10 (November 1973), pp. 396–403; and Kamins and Assael, "Two-Sided Versus One-Sided Appeals. . . ."
34. Smith and Hunt, "Attribution Processes and Effects. . ."; Toy, "Monitoring Communication Effects. . ."; and Swanson, "The Persuasive Effect of Volunteering Negative Information. . . ."
35. Mark I. Alpert and Linda L. Golden, "The Impact of Education on the Relative Effectiveness of One-Sided Communications." In Bruce J. Walker et al., *Proceedings of the American Marketing Association Educators' Conference,* Series No. 48 (1982), pp. 30–33.
36. Carl I. Hovland, Arthur A. Lumsdaine, and Fred D. Sheffield, *Experiences on Mass Communication* (New York: John Wiley, 1949), pp. 182–200; and W. E. Faison, "Effectiveness of One-Sided and Two-Sided Mass Communications in Advertising," *Public Opinion Quarterly* 25 (1961), pp. 468–469.
37. "Coors' Bud-Bashing Stays Regional," *Advertising Age* (March 23, 1992), p. 10; and "Coors Says Anheuser Pours Water on Reputation," *The New York Times* (August 14, 1992), pp. D1, D3.
38. William L. Wilkie and Paul W. Farris, "Comparative Advertising: Problems and Potential," *Journal of Marketing* 39 (October 1975), pp. 7–15; and "Comparative Ads," *Advertising Age* (September 22, 1980), p. 59.
39. William R. Swinyard, "The Interaction Between Comparative Advertising and Copy Claim Variation," *Journal of Marketing Research* 18 (May 1981), pp. 175–186.
40. "The Effects of Comparative Television Advertising that Names Competing Brands." Private report by Ogilvy and Mather Research, New York.
41. Jerry B. Gotlieb and Dan Sarel, "Comparative Advertising Effectiveness: The Role of Involvement and Source Credibility," *Journal of Advertising* 20 (1991), pp. 38–45; and Jerry B. Gotlieb and Dan Sarel, "The Influence of Type of Advertisement, Price, and Source Credibility on Perceived Quality," *Journal of the Academy of Marketing Science* 20 (1992), pp. 253–260.
42. Swinyard, "The Interaction Between Comparative Advertising and Copy Claim Variation."
43. Cornelia Pechmann and David W. Stewart, "The Effects of Comparative Advertising on Attention, Memory, and Purchase Intentions," *Journal of Consumer Research* 17

(September 1990), pp. 180–191. See also Cornelia Pechmann and S. Ratneshwar, "The Use of Comparative Advertising for Brand Positioning: Association Versus Differentiation," *Journal of Consumer Research* 18 (September 1991), pp. 145–160.

44. "Theories of Negativity," *Brandweek* (February 20, 1995), pp. 20–22.

45. Lynette S. Unger and James M. Stearns, "The Use of Fear and Guilt Messages in Television Advertising: Issues and Evidence." In Patrick E. Murphy et al., eds., *Proceedings of the American Marketing Association Educators' Conference,* Series No. 49 (1983), pp. 16–20.

46. "Study Finds Nonsmokers Living 2 Years More by Heeding Alerts," *The New York Times* (September 22, 1979), p. 6.

47. Mark A. deTuck, Gerald M. Goldhaber, Gary M. Richetto, and Melissa J. Young, "Effects of Fear-Arousing Warning Messages," *Journal of Products Liability* 14 (1992), pp. 217–223.

48. Punam Anand Keller and Lauren Goldberg Block, "Increasing the Persuasiveness of Fear Appeals: The Effect of Arousal and Elaboration," *Journal of Consumer Research* 22 (March 1996), pp. 448–460.

49. John F. Tanner, Jr., James B. Hunt, and David R. Eppright, "The Protection Motivation Model: A Normative Model of Fear Appeals," *Journal of Marketing* 55 (July 1991), pp. 36–45.

50. Marc G. Weinberger and Harlan E. Spotts, "Differences in British/American Television and Magazine Advertising: Myth or Reality." In Gary J. Bamossy and W. Fred van Raaij, eds., *Proceedings of the Association for Consumer Research,* European Summer Conference, 1992.

51. Calvin P. Duncan, James E. Nelson, and Nancy T. Frontczak, "The Effect of Humor on Advertising Comprehension." In Thomas C. Kinnear, ed., *Advances in Consumer Research,* Vol. 11 (Provo, UT: Association for Consumer Research, 1984), pp. 432–437; and Calvin P. Duncan and James E. Nelson, "Effects of Humor in a Radio Advertising Experiment," *Journal of Advertising* 14 (1985), pp. 33–40.

52. "After Serious 70s, Advertisers Are Going for Laughs Again," *The Wall Street Journal* (February 23, 1984), p. 31.

53. Brian Sternthal and C. Samuel Craig, "Humor in Advertising," *Journal of Marketing* 37 (October 1973), pp. 12–18.

54. Duncan, Nelson, and Frontczak, "The Effect of Humor. . . ."

55. Sternthal and Craig, "Humor in Advertising."

56. Cliff Scott, David M. Klein, and Jennings Bryant, "Consumer Response to Humor in Advertising: A Series of Field Studies Using Behavioral Observation," *Journal of Consumer Research* 16 (March 1990), pp. 498–501.

57. Marc G. Weinberger and Leland Campbell, "The Use and Impact of Humor in Radio Advertising," *Journal of Advertising Research* 31 (December/January 1991), pp. 44–52.

58. David M. Stewart and David H. Furse, *Effective Television Advertising* (Lexington, MA: D.C. Heath and Co., 1986).

59. Amitava Chattopadhyay and Kunal Basu, "Humor in Advertising: The Moderating Role of Prior Brand Evaluation," *Journal of Marketing Research* 27 (November 1990), pp. 466–476.

60. Dana L. Alden, Wayne D. Hoyer, and Chol Lee, "Identifying Global and Culture-Specific Dimensions of Humor in Advertising: A Multinational Analysis," *Journal of Marketing* 57 (April 1993), pp. 64–75.

61. Marshall McLuhan, *The Medium Is the Message* (New York: Random House, 1967).

62. David A. Aaker and Phillip K. Brown, "Evaluating Vehicle Source Effects," *Journal of Advertising Research* 12 (August 1972), pp. 11–16.

63. Herbert E. Krugman, "The Impact of Television Advertising: Learning Without Involvement," *Public Opinion Quarterly* 29 (Fall 1965), pp. 349–356; and Herbert E. Krugman, "The Measurement of Advertising Involvement," *Public Opinion Quarterly* 30 (Winter 1966–1967), pp. 583–596.

64. Peter L. Wright, "The Cognitive Processes Mediating Acceptance of Advertising," *Journal of Marketing Research* 10 (February 1973), pp. 53–62.

65. Martin R. Lautman and Larry Percy, "Cognitive and Affective Responses in Attribute-Based versus End-Benefit Oriented Advertising." In Thomas C. Kinnear, ed., *Advances in Consumer Research,* Vol. 11 (Provo, UT: Association for Consumer Research, 1984), pp. 11–17.

66. Scott B. MacKenzie and Richard J. Lutz, "An Empirical Examination of the Structural Antecedents of Attitude Toward the Ad in an Advertising Pretesting Context," *Journal of Marketing* 53 (April 1989), pp. 48–61.

67. Thomas J. Olney, Morris B. Holbrook, and Rajeev Batra, "Consumer Responses to Advertising: The Effects of Ad Content, Emotions, and Attitude Toward the Ad on Viewing Time," *Journal of Consumer Research* 17 (March 1991), pp. 440–453.

68. Ibid.; and Meryl Paula Gardner, "Does Attitude Toward the Ad Affect Brand Attitude Under a Brand Evaluation Set?" *Journal of Marketing Research* 22 (May 1985), pp. 192–198. See also Paul W. Miniard, Sunil Bhatla, and Randall L. Rose, "On the Formation and Relationship of Ad and Brand Attitudes: An Experimental and Causal Analysis," *Journal of Marketing Research* 27 (August 1990), pp. 290–303.

69. Andrew A. Mitchell and Jerry C. Olson, "Are Product Attribute Beliefs the Only Mediator of Advertising Effects on Brand Attitude?" *Journal of Marketing Research* 18 (August 1981), pp. 318–332.

70. Christopher P. Puto and William D. Wells, "Informational and Transformational Advertising: The Differential Effects of Time." In Thomas C. Kinnear, ed., *Advances in Con-*

sumer Research, Vol. 11 (Provo, UT: Association for Consumer Research, 1984), pp. 572–576. See also Julie A. Edell and Marian Chapman Burke, "The Power of Feelings in Understanding Advertising Effects," *Journal of Consumer Research* 14 (December 1987), pp. 421–433.

71. See Silk and Vavra, "The Influence of Advertising's Affective Qualities"; and Danny L. Moore and J. Wesley Hutchinson, "The Effects of Ad Affect on Advertising Effectiveness." In Richard P. Bagozzi and Alice M. Tybout, eds., *Advances in Consumer Research,* Vol. 10 (Ann Arbor, MI: Association for Consumer Research, 1983), pp. 526–531.
72. Silk and Vavra, "The Influence of Advertising's Affective Qualities."
73. "Naming the Competition in Advertising," *Listening Post* (New York: Ogilvy and Mather, 1984).
74. See Meryl Paula Gardner, "Mood States and Consumer Research: A Critical Review," *Journal of Consumer Research* 12 (December 1985), pp. 281–300.
75. Thomas R. Srull, "Memory, Mood, and Consumer Judgment." In Melanie Wallendorf and Paul Anderson, eds., *Advances in Consumer Research,* Vol. 14 (Provo, UT: Association for Consumer Research, 1987), pp. 404–407.
76. Marvin E. Goldberg and Gerald J. Gorn, "Happy and Sad TV Programs: How They Affect Reactions to Commercials," *Journal of Consumer Research* 14 (December 1987), pp. 387–403.
77. Morris B. Holbrook and Rajeev Batra, "Assessing the Role of Emotions as Mediators of Consumer Responses to Advertising," *Journal of Consumer Research* 14 (December 1987), pp. 404–420. See also Julie A. Edell and Marian Chapman Burke, "The Power of Feelings in Understanding Advertising Effects," *Journal of Consumer Research* 14 (December 1987), pp. 421–433.
78. Robert E. Burnkrant, H. Rao Unnava, and Kenneth R. Lord, "The Effects of Programming Induced Mood States on Memory for Commercial Information." Working Paper Series, The Ohio State University, October 1987.
79. J. R. Kennedy, "How Program Environment Affects TV Commercials," *Journal of Advertising Research* 11 (February 1971), pp. 33–38.
80. Gary F. Soldow and Victor Principe, "Response to Commercials as a Function of Program Context," *Journal of Advertising Research* 21 (April 1981), pp. 59–65.
81. "For Some Ads, Glum People Make the Best Sales Prospects," *The Wall Street Journal* (July 25, 1985), p. 23.
82. William J. McGuire, "An Information-Processing Model of Advertising Effectiveness." In H. L. David and A. J. Silk, eds., *Behavioral and Management Sciences in Marketing* (New York: Ronald/Wiley, 1978), pp. 156–180.
83. "Candid Camera: Volvo and the Art of Deception," *Adweek's Marketing Week* (November 12, 1990), pp. 4–5.
84. "Reebok: If the Shoe Fits," *Adweek* (January 7, 1991), p. 23.

Chapter 12

1. "Subaru, GMC Top Push to Win Over Women," *Advertising Age* (April 3, 1995), p. S-24; and "In the Fast Lane," *Brandweek* (July 5, 1993), p. 22.
2. Ibid.
3. "BMW Tailors for Women," *Brandweek,* (April 11, 1994).
4. "Ma Bell Faces Up to Her Generation Gap," *Adweek's Marketing Week* (June 22, 1992), p. 19.
5. "The Population Is Taking Off Again," *American Demographics* (December 7, 1992), p. 14.
6. U.S. Department of Commerce, Bureau of the Census, *Current Population Reports, 1991* (Washington, D.C.: U.S. Government Printing Office, 1991), Series P-25, No. 1045.
7. "Gerber Stumbles in a Shrinking Market," *The Wall Street Journal* (July 6, 1993), p. B1; and "Gerber: Concentrating on Babies Again for Slow, Steady Growth," *Business Week* (August 22, 1993), p. 52.
8. U.S. Bureau of the Census, *Statistical Abstracts of the United States, 1996* (Springfield, VA: National Technical Information Service, 1996), Table 118, p. 88 and Table 17, p. 17.
9. "Population Growth Outstrips Earlier U.S. Census Estimates," *The New York Times* (December 4, 1992), p. D18.
10. "Gerber Stumbles . . . ," *The Wall Street Journal* (July 6, 1993), p. B5.
11. "Selling by Evoking What Defines a Generation," *The Wall Street Journal* (August 13, 1996), pp. B1, B5.
12. "The Boomer Report," *Adweek's Marketing Week* (January 22, 1990), pp. 20–27; and Andrew P. Garvin, *The Boomer Report Newsletter.*
13. "The Baby Boomers Are Richer and Older," *Business Month* (October 1987), pp. 24–28.
14. "What the Baby Boomers Will Buy Next," *Fortune* (October 15, 1984), p. 31.
15. "Michelob Piles It On," *Advertising Age* (September 12, 1985), p. 32; and "The Going Gets Tough and Madison Avenue Dumps the Yuppies," *The Wall Street Journal* (December 9, 1987), p. 1.
16. "Boomers Come of Old Age," *Marketing News* (January 15, 1996), p. 1.
17. "Peace, Love and Tie-Dye Turn Off 'Anti-Boomers,'" *Adweek's Marketing Week* (April 9, 1990), p. 17.
18. "Low-Key Luxury," *Brandweek* (July 1, 1996), pp. 23–28.
19. "How to Talk to Young Adults," *American Demographics* (April 1993), p. 50.
20. "Move Over, Boomers," *Business Week* (December 14, 1992), p. 75.
21. "Soft Drink Makers Place Future in Youths' Hands," *Marketing News* (May 20, 1996), p. 18.

22. "Ugly Chic," *Forbes* (September 13, 1993), p. 200.

23. "Liz Claiborne Throws a Curve with New Brand for Gen Xers," *Marketing News* (July 1, 1996), pp. 1, 10.

24. "Big Blue's Hip Campaign Targets Cool Collegians," *Marketing News* (October 11, 1993), p. 6.

25. "Get Ready for Gen Y," *Brandweek* (May 15, 1995), pp. 36–37.

26. Ibid.

27. "The Next Baby Boom," *American Demographics* (October 1995), pp. 22–32.

28. "The Child Research, Custom, Consulting and Qualitative Divisions," *MSW Newsletter*.

29. "The Teen Dream," *Mediaweek* (July 22, 1991), p. 27.

30. "Their Generation: No More Kid Stuff," *Adweek* (June 15, 1992), p. 66.

31. "Japan's Prodigal Young Are Dippy About Imports," *Fortune* (May 11, 1987), p. 118.

32. "You Just Can't Talk to These Kids," *Business Week* (April 19, 1993), p. 104.

33. *Fortune* (May 8, 1989), p. 115; and "Targeting the 'Tween' Market," *Advertising Age* (November 23, 1987), p. 51.

34. "Single Parents," *American Demographics Desk Reference* (July, 1992), p. 12.

35. Ibid.

36. "They May Be Small, But They Spend Big," *Adweek* (February 10, 1992), p. 39.

37. "Yogurt Makers Sweet-Talk the Young Set," *The Wall Street Journal* (February 23, 1993), p. B1.

38. "P&G Heads Shampoo into Preteen Segment with Pert Line Extension," *Advertising Age* (April 20, 1992), p. 3.

39. "The Rise of the Next Generation," *Advertising Age* (October 14, 1996), pp. 31, 43.

40. "Getting Ready for the 'Click Here' Generation," *Adweek* (June 5, 1995), p. 17.

41. "New Polaroid Cool Cam Develops Kids' Interest," *Advertising Age* (September 19, 1988), p. 90.

42. "Children Come of Age as Consumers," *Marketing News* (December 4, 1987), p. 8.

43. *Fortune* (May 8, 1989), p. 115.

44. "Older Consumers Adopt Baby-Boomer Buying Behavior," *Marketing News* (February 15, 1988), p. 8.

45. "U.S. Companies Go for the Gray," *Business Week* (April 3, 1989), p. 67.

46. *Adweek* (July 22, 1991), p. 21.

47. "Ads for Elderly May Give Wrong Message," *The Wall Street Journal* (December 31, 1991), p. D4.

48. "Gray Hair Is Cool," *Forbes* (May 6, 1996), p. 116.

49. "U.S. Companies Go for the Gray," *Business Week* (April 3, 1989), p. 65.

50. "Lodging Chain to Give Older Guests a Choice," *The Wall Street Journal* (February 19, 1993), p. B1.

51. *Statistical Abstracts, 1996,* Table 82, p. 66.

52. "Single Parents," *American Demographics Desk Reference* (July, 1992), p. 12.

53. *Statistical Abstracts, 1996,* Table 66, p. 58.

54. "Rise in Never-Marrieds Affects Social Customs and Buying Patterns," *The Wall Street Journal* (May 28, 1986), p. 1.

55. "Home Alone—with $660 Billion," *Business Week* (July 29, 1991), p. 76.

56. "Feeding China's 'Little Emperors'," *Forbes* (August 6, 1990), pp. 84–85.

57. "Detroit Strives to Reclaim Lost Generation of Buyers," *The New York Times* (April 9, 1991), p. D4; and "To Detroit," *American Demographics* (January 1987), p. 29.

58. "Mapping Regional Marketing Differences," *Advertising Age* (June 16, 1986), p. S32.

59. *American Demographics* (January 1987), p. 24.

60. "Different Folks, Different Strokes," *Fortune* (September 16, 1985), p. 68.

61. Michael R. Solomon, *Consumer Behavior: Buying, Having and Being* (Boston: Allyn and Bacon, 1992), pp. 464–466.

62. *American Demographics* (March 1992), p. 31.

63. "Reaching the Real Europe," *American Demographics* (October 1990), pp. 38–43.

64. *Statistical Abstracts, 1996,* Table 721, p. 468.

65. "Imperfect Picture," *The Wall Street Journal* (April 24, 1995), p. R7.

66. "Put Down Your Rotary-Dial Phone," *The New York Times* (July 30, 1996).

67. "Selling to Women," *American Demographics* (April 1996), pp. 36–43.

68. "PC Makers, Palms Sweating, Try Talking to Women," *Business Week* (January 15, 1990), p. 48; and "Women Start Younger at Own Business," *The Wall Street Journal* (February 15, 1993), p. B1.

69. "Eating Habits Force Changes in Marketing," *Advertising Age* (October 30, 1978), p. 30.

70. Ibid.

71. *Statistical Abstracts, 1996,* Table 719, p. 467.

72. Ibid, Table 711, p. 462.

73. Ibid, Table 709, p. 461.

74. Ibid, Table 241, p. 159.

75. Ibid.

76. Reed Moyer and Michael D. Hutt, *Macromarketing* (New York: John Wiley, 1978), pp. 123–141; Clive W. Granger and Andrew Billson, "Consumers' Attitudes Toward Package Size and Price," *Journal of Marketing Research* 9 (August 1972), pp. 239–248; and J. Edward Russo, Gene Dreiser, and Sally Miyashita, "An Effective Display of Unit Price Information," *Journal of Marketing* 39 (April 1975), pp. 11–19.

77. "Kodak Will Advertise by the Numbers," *Adweek* (April 27, 1992), p. 2; and "Their Generation: No More Kid Stuff," *Adweek* (June 15, 1992), p. 66.
78. Del I. Hawkins, Roger J. Best, and Kenneth A. Coney, *Consumer Behavior* (Homewood, IL: Irwin, 1992), p. 33.
79. "Digital Blue Jeans Pour Data and Legs Into Customized Fit," *The New York Times* (November 8, 1994), p. A1.
80. "Chains Start to Tune in on Frequency," *Brandweek* (March 21, 1994), pp. 36–38.
81. Bernard Berelson and Gary A. Steiner, *Human Behavior: An Inventory of Scientific Findings* (New York: Harcourt, Brace & World, 1964), p. 453.
82. Robert W. Hodges, Paul M. Siegel, and Peter H. Rossi, "Occupational Prestige in the United States 1925–1963," *American Journal of Sociology* 70 (November 1964), pp. 290–292.
83. Thorstein Veblen, *The Theory of the Leisure Class* (New York: Macmillan, 1912).
84. Terence A. Shimp and J. Thomas Yokum, "Extensions of the Basic Social Class Model Employed in Consumer Research." In Kent B. Monroe, ed., *Advances in Consumer Research,* Vol. 8 (Ann Arbor, MI Association for Consumer Research, 1981), pp. 702–707.
85. W. Lloyd Warner, Marcia Meeker, and Kenneth Eells, *Social Class in America: Manual of Procedure for the Measurement of Social Status* (New York: Harper & Row, 1960).
86. W. Lloyd Warner and Paul S. Lunt, *The Social Life of a Modern Community,* Yankee City Series, Vol. 1 (New Haven: Yale University Press, 1941).
87. Richard P. Coleman, "The Continuing Significance of Social Class to Marketing," *Journal of Consumer Research* 10 (December 1983), p. 270.
88. "New Boundaries of Affluence," *Marketing Communications* (February 1986), p. 33.
89. Coleman, "The Continuing Significance of Social Class to Marketing," p. 272.
90. "The Emerging Middle Class," *Business Week, 21st Century Capitalism,* pp. 176–193.
91. "Women's On-the-Job Attitudes," *Research Alert* (February 5, 1988), p. 3.
92. "Reaching Downscale Markets," *American Demographics* (November, 1991), p. 40.
93. Andre Gabor and S. W. J. Granger, "Price Sensitivity of the Consumer," *Journal of Advertising Research* 4 (December 1964), pp. 40–44; David Caplovitz, *The Poor Pay More* (New York: The Free Press, 1963); and Frederick E. Webster, Jr., "The Deal-Prone Consumer," *Journal of Marketing Research* 1 (August 1964), pp. 32–35.
94. "The Middle Class Comes Undone," *Ad Forum* (June 1984), pp. 32–39.
95. "Class in America," *Fortune* (February 7, 1994), pp. 114–126.
96. Florence Skelly, "Prognosis 2000," Speech before New York Chapter of the American Marketing Association, December 15, 1977.
97. Sidney J. Levy, "Social Class and Consumer Behavior." In Joseph W. Newman, ed., *On Knowing the Consumer* (New York: John Wiley, 1966), pp. 146–160.
98. Ibid.
99. A. Marvin Roscoe, Jr., Arthur LeClaire, Jr., and Leon G. Schiffman, "Theory and Management Applications of Demographics in Buyer Behavior." In Arch G. Woodside, Jagdish N. Sheth, and Peter D. Bennett, eds., *Consumer and Industrial Buying Behavior* (New York: North-Holland, 1977), pp. 74–75.
100. "Nestlé Courts the LDC Middle Class," *The Wall Street Journal* (June 4, 1990), p. A13.
101. V. Kanti Prasad, "Socioeconomic Product Risk and Patronage Preferences of Retail Shoppers," *Journal of Marketing* 39 (July 1975), pp. 42–47.
102. Roscoe, LeClaire, and Schiffman, p. 74.
103. Doyle W. Bishop and Masaru Ikeda, "Status and Role Factors in the Leisure Behavior of Different Occupations," *Sociology and Social Research* 54 (January 1970), pp. 190–208.

Chapter 13

1. "How a Heart Attack Changed a Company," *The New York Times* (February 26, 1993), pp. C1, C6.
2. "One from the Heart," *Marketing & Media Decisions* (March 1990), p. 34; and "How a Heart Attack. . . ," *The New York Times* (February 26, 1993), p. C6.
3. "Healthy Choice Invades Bread Aisle," *Brandweek* (October 2, 1995), p. 6.
4. "Healthy Choice Sets Sights On Adventure; Bristol's 'Beauty Central,'" *Brandweek* (November 27, 1995), p. 14.
5. Joseph T. Plummer, "The Concept and Application of Life Style Segmentation," *Journal of Marketing* 38 (January 1974), pp. 33–37.
6. "The Brave New World of Men," *American Demographics* (January 1992), p. 40.
7. "Man: Forever the Forager," *Madison Avenue* (February 1986), pp. 88–90.
8. "For Many Fathers, Roles Are Shifting," *The New York Times* (June 20, 1993).
9. "Real Men Buy Paper Towels, Too," *Business Week* (November 1992), p. 75.
10. "Parents Magazines Make Room for Daddy," *Marketing News* (February 27, 1995), p. 1.
11. "Real Men Buy. . . ," *Business Week* (November 1992), p. 75.
12. "Do Real Men Shop?" *American Demographics* (May 1987), p. 13.

13. "Ads Awaken to Fathers' New Role in Family Life," *Advertising Age* (1994), p. S-8.
14. "In Ads, Men's Image Becomes Softer," *The New York Times* (March 26, 1990), p. D12.
15. "Working Women Now More Attractive—Y&R," *Advertising Age* (January 11, 1982), p. 76.
16. "Working Women Task Advertisers," *Advertising Forum* (July 1982), p. 35.
17. *Advertising Age* (July 26, 1982), p. M13.
18. *Advertising Age* (April 2, 1984), p. M10.
19. "Avon Products Is Abandoning Its Old-Fashioned Image in an Appeal to Contemporary Women," *The New York Times* (April 27, 1993), p. D21.
20. "The Message, Clever as It May Be, Is Lost in a Number of High-Profile Campaigns," *The Wall Street Journal* (July 27, 1993), p. B1.
21. "Shoppers Say 'Yes' to Less," *Progressive Grocer* (May 1984), p. 192; and "What Americans Eat Hasn't Changed Much Despite Healthy Image," *The Wall Street Journal* (September 12, 1985), p. 1.
22. "Wary Consumers Want More Health Ad Info," *Advertising Age* (December 4, 1989), p. 12.
23. "Low Fat Food: Feeding Frenzy for Marketers," *The New York Times* (September 27, 1995), p. D1.
24. *Fortune* (May 26, 1986), p. 62.
25. "Tempted by Taste, and Tiring of Tofu, Shoppers Are Bringing Home the Bacon," *The Wall Street Journal* (March 18, 1993), p. B1.
26. "'Eat, Drink and Be Merry' May Be the Next Trend," *The New York Times* (January 2, 1994), pp. 1, 14.
27. "How Reebok Fits Shoes," *American Demographics* (March 1993).
28. "Physical Fitness: It's All in the Balance," *Adweek* (August 17, 1992), pp. 36–37.
29. "Newest Corporate Refugees: Self-Employed but Low-Paid," *The New York Times* (November 15, 1993), pp. A1, D2; and "Do Homework Before Taking the Plunge," *New York Newsday* (November 21, 1993), p. 76.
30. "Americans Devote More of Their Shrinking Leisure Time to Arts," *Ad Forum* (February 1985), p. 10.
31. "The Great American Slowdown," *American Demographics* (June 1996), pp. 42–48.
32. Ibid.
33. "Notes to Myself: Cookies and Milk at 3 p.m.," *Forbes*, (April 22, 1996), p. 202.
34. "Little Wishes Form the Big Dream," *The Wall Street Journal* (September 19, 1989), p. B1.
35. "Nestlé Gives Carnation Breakfast Line a Makeover," *Adweek* (September 20, 1993), p. 13.
36. "Now, Food for the Otherwise Engaged," *The New York Times* (April 15, 1987).
37. "Little Wishes. . . ," *The Wall Street Journal* (September 19, 1989), p. B1.
38. "Many Food Companies Find the Prospects for Microwave Product Aren't That Hot," *The Wall Street Journal* (February 2, 1993), p. B1.
39. "Tomorrow's New Rich: Postwar Babies Are Grown Up," *Sales & Marketing Management* (October 6, 1981), p. 29.
40. *American Demographics* (January 1993).
41. "The QRCA Trends Project: How Qualitative Researchers See the Consumer of the 1990s," *Marketing Review*.
42. Ibid., p. 10.
43. "Marketers of Luxury Goods Are Turning from Self-Indulgence to Family Values," *The Wall Street Journal* (October 22, 1992), p. B1.
44. William D. Wells and Douglas J. Tigert, "Activities, Interests and Opinions," *Journal of Advertising Research* 11 (August, 1971), pp. 27–35.
45. See Arnold Mitchell, *Changing Values and Lifestyles* (Menlo Park, CA: SRI International, 1981).
46. "Timex and VALS Engineer a Psychographic Product Launch," *Ad Forum* (September 1984), p. 12.
47. Ibid., p. 14.
48. "VALS the Second Time," *American Demographics* (July 1991), p. 6.
49. Ira J. Dolich, "Congruence Relationships Between Self-Images and Product Brands," *Journal of Marketing Research* 6 (February 1969), pp. 80–85.
50. For example, Al E. Birdwell, "Influence of Image Congruence on Consumer Choice." In *Proceedings, Winter Conference, 1964* (Chicago: American Marketing Association, 1965), pp. 290–303; and Edward L. Grubb and Gregg Hupp, "Perception of Self-Generalized Stereotypes and Brand Selection," *Journal of Marketing Research* 5 (February 1968), pp. 58–63.
51. Robert E. Burnkrant and Thomas J. Page, Jr., "On the Management of Self-Images in Social Situations: The Role of Public Self-Consciousness." In Andrew Mitchell, ed., *Advances in Consumer Research*, Vol. 9 (Ann Arbor, MI: Association for Consumer Research, 1982), pp. 452–455.
52. Marsha L. Richins, "Social Comparison and the Idealized Images of Advertising," *Journal of Consumer Research* 18 (June 1991), pp. 71–83.
53. *American Demographics* (January 1993), p. 56.
54. See "Compulsive Buying: A Phenomenological Exploration," *Journal of Consumer Research* 16 (September 1989), pp. 147–157; and Alice Hanley and Mari S. Wilhelm, "Compulsive Buying: An Exploration into Self-Esteem and Money Attitudes," *Journal of Economic Psychology* 13 (1992), pp. 5–18.
55. Michael R. Solomon, "The Role of Products as Social Stimuli: A Symbolic Interactionism Perspective," *Journal of Consumer Research*, 10 (December, 1983), pp. 319–329.
56. Russell W. Belk, "Possessions and the Extended Self," *Journal of Consumer Research* 15 (September 1988), pp. 139–168, p. 146.

57. Ibid.
58. Michael R. Solomon and Henry Assael, "The Forest or the Trees? A Gestalt Approach to Symbolic Communication." In Jean Umiker-Sebeok and Sidney J. Levy, eds., *Marketing and Semiotics: New Directions in the Study of Signs for Sale* (Bloomington: Indiana University Press, 1988).
59. "In a Marryin' Mood," *Brandweek* (September 2, 1996), pp. 22–28.
60. Sidney J. Levy, "Interpreting Consumer Mythology: A Structural Approach to Consumer Behavior," *Journal of Marketing* 45 (Summer 1981), pp. 49–61.
61. Rena Bartos, "Ernest Dichter: Motive Interpreter," *Journal of Advertising Research* 26 (February-March, 1986), p. 20.
62. Ibid.; and "Work Motivates Psychoanalysis," *Advertising Age* (November 1, 1984), p. 45.
63. Dennis W. Rook, "The Ritual Dimension of Consumer Behavior," *Journal of Consumer Research* 12 (December 1985), pp. 251–264.
64. Mason Haire, "Projective Techniques in Marketing Research," *Journal of Marketing* 14 (April 1950), pp. 649–656.
65. "The Frontier of Psychographics," *American Demographics* (July 1996), pp. 38–43.
66. William D. Wells and Arthur D. Beard, "Personality Theories." In Scott Ward and Thomas S. Robertson, eds., *Consumer Behavior: Theoretical Sources* (Englewood Cliffs, NJ: Prentice-Hall, 1973), pp. 142–199.
67. *American Demographics* (July 1996), pp. 38–43.
68. Joel B. Cohen, "An Interpersonal Orientation to the Study of Consumer Behavior," *Journal of Marketing Research* 4 (August 1967), pp. 270–278.
69. Arthur Koponen, "Personality Characteristics of Purchasers," *Journal of Advertising Research* 1 (September 1960), pp. 6–12.
70. Morris J. Gottlieb, "Segmentation by Personality Types." In Lynn H. Stockman, ed., *Advancing Marketing Efficiency, Proceedings of the 1959 Conference* (Chicago: American Marketing Association, 1960), pp. 148–158.
71. Harold H. Kassarjian, "Personality and Consumer Behavior: A Review," *Journal of Marketing Research* 8 (November 1971), pp. 409–419.

Chapter 14

1. "Advertisers Put Consumers on the Couch," *The Wall Street Journal* (May 13, 1988), p. 21.
2. "Interactive Ad Campaigns," *Advertising Age* (Special Advertising Section, October 7, 1996), p. C12.
3. Richard A. Peterson, "The Production of Culture: A Prologomenon, in the Production of Culture." In Richard A. Peterson, ed., *Sage Contemporary Social Science Issues* (Beverly Hills: Sage, 1976), p. 722.
4. "Culture Shocks," *Advertising Age* (May 17, 1982), p. M9.
5. Milton J. Rokeach, "The Role of Values in Public Opinion Research," *Public Opinion Quarterly* 32 (Winter 1968), pp. 547–549; and Milton J. Rokeach, "A Theory of Organization and Change Within Value-Attitude Systems," *Journal of Social Issues* (January 1968), pp. 13–33.
6. Joseph F. Hair, Jr., and Rolph E. Anderson, "Culture, Acculturation and Consumer Behavior: An Empirical Study." In Boris W. Becker and Helmut Becker, eds., *Combined Proceedings of the American Marketing Association,* Series No. 34 (1972), pp. 423–428.
7. Bernard Berelson and Gary A. Steiner, *Human Behavior: An Inventory of Scientific Findings* (New York: Harcourt Brace & World, 1964), p. 652.
8. Lisa Penaloza, "*Atravesando Fronteras*/Border Crossings: A Critical Ethnographic Exploration of the Consumer Acculturation of Mexican Immigrants," *Journal of Consumer Research* 21 (June 1994), pp. 32–54.
9. Adapted from "Rewriting the Book on Buying and Selling—Angry and Anxious Americans Seek Out New Values," *Adweek* (November 30, 1992), pp. 20–23.
10. David M. Potter, *People of Plenty* (Chicago: University of Chicago Press, 1954).
11. Marsha L. Richins, "Special Possessions and the Expression of Material Values," *Journal of Consumer Research* 21 (December 1994), pp. 522–533.
12. "Japan to Get L. L. Bean's Outdoor Chic," *The New York Times* (March 5, 1992), p. D3.
13. "Smoothing Away Age Time," *Advertising Age International* (September 1996), p. 144.
14. John W. Schouten and James H. McAlexander, "Subcultures of Consumption: An Ethnography of the New Bikers," *Journal of Consumer Research* 22 (June 1995), pp. 43–61.
15. Ibid.
16. Russell W. Belk, John F. Sherry, Jr., and Melanie Wallendorf, "A Naturalistic Inquiry into Buyer and Seller Behavior at a Swap Meet," *Journal of Consumer Research* 14 (March 1988), pp. 449–470.
17. Ibid.
18. Lynn R. Kahle, Sharon Beatty, and Pamela Homer, "Alternative Measurement Approaches to Consumer Values: The List of Values (LOV) and Values and Life Style (VALS)," *Journal of Consumer Research* 13 (December 1986), pp. 405–409.
19. Pamela Homer and Lynn R. Kahle, "A Structural Equation Test of the Value-Attitude-Behavior Hierarchy," *Journal of Personality and Social Psychology* 54 (April 1988), pp. 638–646.
20. Daniel Yankelovich, *The Yankelovich Monitor* (New York: Daniel Yankelovich, 1974).
21. "Lifestyle's Monitor," *American Demographics* (May 1981), p. 22.
22. David C. McClellan, *The Achieving Society* (Princeton, NJ: Van Nostrand, 1961).

23. Russell W. Belk, "Material Values in the Comics," *Journal of Consumer Research* 14 (June 1987), pp. 26–42.
24. Jonathan Gutman, "A Means-End Chain Model Based on Consumer Categorization Processes," *Journal of Marketing* 46 (1982), pp. 60–72.
25. Milton J. Rosenberg, "Cognitive Structure and Attitudinal Affect," *Journal of Abnormal and Social Psychology* 53 (1956), pp. 367–372.
26. Thomas J. Reynolds and Jonathan Gutman, "Laddering Theory, Method, Analysis, and Interpretation," *Journal of Advertising Research* 28 (February/March 1988), pp. 11–31.
27. Thomas J. Reynolds and Alyce Byrd Craddock, "The Application of the Meccas Model to the Development and Assessment of Advertising Strategy: A Case Study," *Journal of Advertising Research* 28 (April/May 1988), pp. 43–59.
28. Mary Tharp and Linda M. Scott, "The Role of Marketing Processes in Creating Cultural Meaning," *Journal of Macromarketing* (Fall 1990), pp. 7–60.
29. "Agencies Scrutinize Their Ads for Psychological Symbolism," *The Wall Street Journal* (June 11, 1987), p. 25.
30. *Charles Sanders Pierce (Collected Papers),* Charles Hartshorne, Paul Weiss, and Arthur W. Burks, eds. (Cambridge MA: Harvard University Press, 1931–1958); and David Glen Mick, "Consumer Research and Semiotics: Exploring the Morphology of Signs, Symbols, and Significance," *Journal of Consumer Research* 15 (September 1986), pp. 196–213.
31. "Advertising as Myth-Maker: Brands as Gods and Heroes," *Advertising Age* (November 8, 1993), p. 32.
32. These examples are from "The Power of Mythology Helps Brands to Endure," *Marketing News* (September 28, 1992), p. 16.
33. "Sites Try a Little Tenderness to Maintain Traffic," *Advertising Age* (October 7, 1996), p. 44.
34. Dennis W. Rook, "The Ritual Dimensions of Consumer Behavior," *Journal of Consumer Research* 12 (December 1985), pp. 251–264.
35. Ibid., p. 253.
36. Elizabeth C. Hirschman, "The Ideology of Consumption: A Structural-Syntactical Analysis of 'Dallas' and 'Dynasty,'" *Journal of Consumer Research* 15 (December 1988), pp. 344–359; and Elizabeth C. Hirschman, "Point of View: Sacred, Secular, and Mediating Consumption Imagery in Television Commercials," *Journal of Advertising Research* 31 (December 1990/January 1991), pp. 38–43.
37. Ibid.
38. Schouten and McAlexander, "Subcultures of Consumption. . . ," pp. 50–51.
39. "Double Standards of Post-War Adults," *Research Alert* (June 24, 1988), p. 1.
40. Daniel Yankelovich, Florence Skelly, and Arthur White, "Social Trends Measured in Monitor No. 3," *The Yankelovich Monitor* (New York: Daniel Yankelovich, 1981).
41. "Door Ajar to Women of All Ages in Ads," *Advertising Age* (October 4, 1993), pp. S-2, S-4.
42. "Marketers Must Consider Component Life Styles," *Marketing News* (August 29, 1988), p. 9.
43. "Shoplifting: Bess Myerson's Arrest Highlights a Multibillion Dollar Problem That Many Stores Won't Talk About," *Life* (August 1988), p. 32.
44. Donald E. Vinson, Jerome E. Scott, and Lawrence M. Lamont, "The Role of Personal Values in Marketing and Consumer Behavior," *Journal of Marketing* 41 (April 1977), pp. 44–50.

Chapter 15

1. U.S. Bureau of the Census, *Statistical Abstract of the United States, 1996* (Springfield, VA: National Technical Information Service, 1996), Table 12, p. 14; "Minority Promotions Pick Up the Pace," *Advertising Age* (March 20, 1995), p. S-4; and "Reaching the New Immigrants," *Adweek's Marketing Week* (September 11, 1989), p. 24.
2. "For Levi's, a Flattering Fit Overseas," *Business Week* (November 5, 1990), pp. 76–77.
3. "Dockers Tailors Retail Agenda for European Growth," *Advertising Age* (September 16, 1996), p. 17.
4. "P&G Uses Skills It Has Honed at Home to Introduce Its Brands to the Russians," *The Wall Street Journal* (April 14, 1993), p. B1.
5. "The International Agenda," *Marketing* (July 1, 1995), p. 142; and "The Awakening Chinese Consumer," *The New York Times* (October 11, 1992), p. F1.
6. "Ad Fads: Global Sales Pitch by Harvard Guru Appears Much Easier in Theory, Marketers Find," *The Wall Street Journal* (May 12, 1988), p. 4.
7. "Global Ad Campaigns After Many Missteps, Finally Pay Dividends," *The Wall Street Journal* (August 27, 1992), pp. A1, A8.
8. "Arise Comrades, Cast Off Your Chains and Go Get a Coke," *Brandweek* (July 20, 1992), pp. 23–24.
9. "Pitfalls Lie Waiting for Unwary Marketers," *Advertising Age* (May 17, 1982), p. M-9.
10. "Seeing Is Believing," *Marketing & Media Decisions* (February 1988), p. 52.
11. J. Douglas McConnell, "The Economics of Behavioral Factors on the Multi-National Corporation." In Fred C. Allvine, ed., *Combined Proceedings of the American Marketing Association,* Series No. 33 (1971), p. 265.
12. David A. Ricks, *Big Business Blunders* (Homewood, IL: Dow Jones-Irwin, 1983), p. 65.
13. Albert Stridsberg, "U.S. Advertisers Win Some, Lose Some in Foreign Markets," *Advertising Age* (May 6, 1974), p. 42.

14. *Business Marketing* (July, 1984), p. 112.
15. Ricks, *Big Business Blunders,* p. 84.
16. "Maintaining a Balance of Planning," *Advertising Age* (May 17, 1982), p. M21.
17. "America's International Winners," *Fortune* (April 14, 1986), p. 44.
18. Ricks, *Big Business Blunders,* p. 33.
19. Charles Winick, "Anthropology's Contribution to Marketing," *Journal of Marketing* 25 (July 1961), p. 59.
20. Domzal and Unger, "Emerging Positioning Strategies in Global Markets," p. 29.
21. "Global Ad Campaigns. . . ," *The Wall Street Journal* (August 27, 1992).
22. Ibid.
23. Thomas C. O'Guinn, et al., "The Cultivation of Consumer Norms." In Thomas K. Srull, ed., *Advances in Consumer Research,* Vol. 16 (Provo, UT: Association for Consumer Research, 1989), pp. 779–785.
24. "The First Global Generation," *Adweek's Marketing Week* (February 6, 1989), p. 18.
25. "Global Ad Campaigns. . . ," *The Wall Street Journal* (August 27, 1992).
26. "A New Mass Market Emerges," *Fortune* (Fall 1990 Special Issue), p. 51.
27. Ibid., p. 56.
28. "In Pursuit of the Elusive Euroconsumer," *The New York Times* (April 23, 1992), p. B1.
29. Eric J. Arnould and Richard R. Wilk, "Why do the Natives Wear Adidas?" In Thomas C. Kinnear (ed.), *Advances in Consumer Research,* Vol. 11 (Provo, UT: Association for Consumer Research, 1984), pp. 748–752.
30. "Jihad vs. McWorld," *The New York Times Book Review* (August 20, 1995), p. 8.
31. "Arise Comrades. . . ," *Brandweek* (July 20, 1992), pp. 22–24; and "Pepsi Takes a Seat on Moscow Fast-Food Express," *The New York Times* (June 11, 1993), p. D1.
32. "Den Fujita, Japan's Mr. Joint-Venture," *The New York Times* (March 22, 1992), pp. F1, F6; and "Moose-Hunting in Japan?" *The New York Times* (February 28, 1993), Section 9, p. 4.
33. "Fast-Food Franchises Fight for Brazilian Aficionados," *Brandweek* (June 7, 1993), p. 20.
34. "Pushing U.S. Style, Nike and Reebok Sell Sneakers to Europe," *The Wall Street Journal* (July 22, 1993), pp. A1, A8.
35. "Heinz Aims to Export Taste for Ketchup," *The Wall Street Journal.*
36. "Pizza in Japan Is Adapted to Local Tastes," *The Wall Street Journal* (June 4, 1993), p. B1.
37. "Snapple in Japan: How a Splash Dried Up," *The Wall Street Journal* (April 15, 1996), pp. B1, B3.
38. Domzal and Unger, "Emerging Positioning Strategies in Global Markets," p. 26.
39. "Arise Comrades. . . ," *Brandweek* (July 20, 1992).
40. "In Pursuit of the Elusive Euroconsumer," *The Wall Street Journal* (April 23, 1992), p. B1.
41. "Global Ad Campaigns. . . ," *The Wall Street Journal* (August 27, 1992).
42. "Parker Pen," *Advertising Age* (June 2, 1986), p. 60.
43. *The New York Times Book Review* (August 20, 1995), p. 8.
44. "The Rumble Heard Round the World: Harleys," *Business Week* (May 24, 1993), pp. 58–60.
45. Ricks, *Big Business Blunders,* p. 52.
46. "Reaching the New Immigrants," *Adweek's Marketing Week* (September 11, 1989), p. 24.
47. "If You Want a Big, New Market," *Fortune* (November 21, 1989), p. 181; "Firms Translate Sales Pitches to Appeal to Asian-Americans," *The Wall Street Journal* (April 10, 1986), p. 35.
48. *The Mademoiselle Report: Redefining a Generation* (New York: Mademoiselle, 1994).
49. Michael Solomon, *Consumer Behavior* (Boston: Allyn and Bacon, 1992), pp. 464–465.
50. Elizabeth Hirschman, "American Jewish Ethnicity: Its Relationship to Some Selected Aspects of Consumer Behavior," *Journal of Marketing* 45 (Summer 1981), pp. 102–105.
51. "Bringing In the Sheaves," *American Demographics* (August, 1988), pp. 28–32.
52. Hirschman, "American Jewish Ethnicity. . . ."
53. "Out of the Closet," *Marketing Review* (March 1996), pp. 21–23.
54. "Playing to Gay Segments Opens Doors to Marketers," *Advertising Age* (May 30, 1994), p. S-6.
55. "Madison Avenue Blindly Ignores the Black Consumer," *Business and Society Review* (Winter 1987), p. 11.
56. "6 Myths About Black Consumers," *Adweek's Marketing Week* (May 6, 1991), p. 17.
57. "Study Says Blacks Spend More on Big-Ticket Items Than Whites," *Marketing News* (September 23, 1996), p. 27; and "Black, Hip and Primed (to Shop)," *American Demographics* (September 1996), pp. 53–58.
58. *Statistical Abstract, 1996,* Table 241, p. 159.
59. Ibid, Tables 710 and 711, pp. 461–462.
60. Ibid, Table 241, p. 159.
61. Ibid, Table 22, p. 23.l
62. "6 Myths. . . ," *Adweek's Marketing Week* (May 6, 1991).
63. "Motorola Gets Signal on Blacks' Pager Use," *The Wall Street Journal* (June 24, 1996), p. B6; and *Adweek's Marketing Week* (May 6, 1991), p. 18.
64. "Blending into the Mainstream," *Advertising Age* (July 17, 1995), p. S-2.
65. Rohit Deshpande, Wayne D. Hoyer, and Naveen Donthu, "The Intensity of Ethnic Affiliation: A Study of the Sociology of Hispanic Consumption," *Journal of Consumer Research* 13 (September 1986), pp. 214–220.

66. "The Difference in Black and White," *American Demographics* (January 1993), p. 49.
67. "Minority Marketing Looks to the 80s," *Advertising Age* (April 7, 1980), p. S19; and *Advertising Age* (October 19, 1981), p. S52.
68. "Arbitron Radio Survey," *The New York Times* (June 14, 1984), p. D21.
69. "Many Marketers Still Consider Blacks 'Dark Skinned Whites,'" *Marketing News* (January 18, 1993), p. 13.
70. "Mining the Non-White Markets," *Brandweek* (April 12, 1993), p. 29.
71. "Buying Black," *Time* (August 31, 1992), p. 52; and "J. C. Penney Finds Profit in Africa," *American Demographics* (November 1992), p. 12.
72. "Do All Hispanics Speak a Common Cultural Language?" *Ad Forum* (December 1984), p. 16.
73. *Advertising Age* (March 20, 1995), p. S-4.
74. *Statistical Abstract, 1996,* Table 22, p. 23.
75. Ibid, Table 68, p. 59.
76. "Marketing to Hispanics," *Advertising Age* (March 21, 1985), p. 13.
77. "Cultural Differences Offer Rewards," *Advertising Age* (April 7, 1980), p. S-20.
78. Ibid.
79. "Poll: Hispanics Stick to Brands," *Advertising Age* (February 16, 1993), p. 6.
80. *Listening Post* (June, 1984), p. 1.
81. "What Does Hispanic Mean?" *American Demographics* (June 1993), p. 50.
82. "The Effects of Hispanic Subcultural Identification on Information Search Behavior," *Journal of Advertising Research* (September/October 1992), p. 6; "Familiarity Breeds Success," *Adweek's Marketing Week Supplement* (September 25, 1989), p. 10; and "Competition Heats Up for Hispanic Consumer's Dollar," *Ad Forum* (July 1983), p. 29.
83. "Brand Loyalty Wavers; Private Label Gains," *Advertising Age* (January 23, 1995), p. 32.
84. "What Does Hispanic Mean?" *American Demographics* (June 1993), p. 50.
85. Ibid., p. 48.
86. "Minority Markets," *Credit Magazine* (January/February 1992), p. 9.
87. "Versatility, Values-And Hold the Cliches," *Adweek's Marketing Week* (July 9, 1990), p. 38.
88. *Business Week* (June 6, 1988), p. 64.
89. "Competition Heats Up. . . ," *Ad Forum* (July 1983), p. 30.
90. "Ethnics Gain Market Clout," *Advertising Age* (August 5, 1991), p. 12.
91. "The Effects of Hispanic. . . ," *Journal of Advertising Research* (September/October 1992), p. 56.
92. *Advertising Age* (February 13, 1989), p. S-12.
93. *Statistical Abstract, 1996,* Table 12, p. 14.
94. "The Asian-American Market for Personal Products," *DCI* (November 1992), p. 32.
95. "Asians in U.S. Get Attention of Marketers," *The New York Times* (January 11, 1990), p. D19.
96. " 'Hot' Asian-American Market Not Starting Much of a Fire Yet."
97. "Asian-Americans: The Three Biggest Myths," *Sales & Marketing Management* (September 1993), pp. 86–101.
98. *Statistical Abstract, 1996,* Table 22, p. 22, Table 241, p. 159, and Table 715, p. 464.
99. "A New Look at Asian Americans," *American Demographics* (October 1990), p. 30.
100. "Taking the Pulse of Asian-Americans," *Adweek's Marketing Week* (August 12, 1991), p. 32.
101. "Poll: Hispanics Stick . . . ," *Advertising Age* (February 16, 1993), p. 6.
102. "Sears Targets Asians," *Advertising Age* (October 10, 1994), p. 1.
103. "The Art of Reaching Asian Immigrants," *Adweek's Marketing Week* (January 1, 1990), p. 23.
104. Carol-Linnea Salmon, "Milking Deadly Dollars from the Third World," *Business & Society Review* (Winter 1989), pp. 43–48.
105. "Even Overseas, Tobacco Has Nowhere to Hide," *Adweek's Marketing Week* (April 1, 1991), p. 4.
106. Ibid., p. 5.
107. "New RJR Brand Under Fire," *Advertising Age* (February 19, 1990), pp. 1, 74.

Chapter 16

1. John W. Schouten and James H. McAlexander, "Subcultures of Consumption: An Ethnography of the New Bikers," *Journal of Consumer Research* 22 (June 1995), pp. 43–61.
2. William O. Bearden, Richard G. Netemeyer, and Jesse E. Teel, "Measurement of Consumer Susceptibility to Interpersonal Influence," *Journal of Consumer Research* 15 (March 1989), pp. 473–481.
3. William O. Bearden and Randall L. Rose, "Attention to Social Comparison Information: An Individual Difference Factor Affecting Consumer Conformity," *Journal of Consumer Research* 16 (March 1990), pp. 461–471.
4. Paul W. Miniard and Joel B. Cohen, "Modeling Personal and Normative Influences on Behavior," *Journal of Consumer Research* 10 (September 1983), pp. 169–180.
5. Bobby J. Calder and Robert E. Burnkrant, "Interpersonal Influences on Consumer Behavior: An Attribution Theory Approach," *Journal of Consumer Research* 4 (June 1977), pp. 29–38.
6. Vernon L. Allen, "Situational Factors in Conformity." In Leonard Berkowitz, ed., *Advances in Experimental Social*

Psychology, Vol. 2 (New York: Academic Press, 1965), pp. 133–175.

7. Schouten and McAlexander, "Subcultures of Consumption. . . ."
8. James H. Leigh and Terrance G. Gabel, "Symbolic Interactionism: Its Effects on Consumer Behavior and Implications for Marketing Strategy," *The Journal of Consumer Marketing* 9 (Winter 1992), p. 30.
9. Francis S. Bourne, "Group Influence in Marketing and Public Relations." In Rensis Likert and Samuel P. Hayes, Jr., eds., *Some Applications of Behavioral Research* (Paris: UNESCO, 1957).
10. Schouten and McAlexander, "Subcultures of Consumption . . . ," p. 49.
11. Leon G. Schiffman and Leslie L. Kanuk, *Consumer Behavior* (Englewood Cliffs, NJ: Prentice-Hall, 1978), p. 214.
12. Peter H. Reingen et al., "Brand Congruence in Interpersonal Relations: A Social Network Analysis," *Journal of Consumer Research* 11 (December 1984), pp. 771–783.
13. Schouten and McAlexander, "Subcultures of Consumption . . . ," p. 49.
14. Donald H. Granbois, "Improving the Study of Customer In-Store Behavior," *Journal of Marketing* 32 (October 1968), pp. 28–33.
15. Robert J. Fisher and Linda L. Price, "An Investigation into the Social Context of Early Adoption Behavior," *Journal of Consumer Research* 19 (December 1992), pp. 477–486.
16. Schouten and McAlexander, "Subcultures of Consumption . . . ," p. 53.
17. Ibid., p. 49.
18. Ibid., p. 56.
19. John R. French and Bertram Raven, "The Bases of Social Power." In D. Cartwright, ed., *Studies in Social Power* (Ann Arbor, MI: Institute for Social Research, 1959), pp. 150–167.
20. H. C. Kelman, "Processes of Opinion Change," *Public Opinion Quarterly* 25 (Spring 1961), pp. 57–78.
21. Robert E. Burnkrant and Alain Cousineau, "Informational and Normative Social Influence in Buyer Behavior," *Journal of Consumer Research* 2 (December 1975), pp. 206–215.
22. Ibid., p. 207.
23. C. Whan Park and V. Parker Lessig, "Students and Housewives: Differences in Susceptibility to Reference Group Influence," *Journal of Consumer Research* 4 (September 1977), pp. 102–110.
24. Margaret L. Friedman and Gilbert A. Churchill, Jr., "Using Consumer Perceptions and a Contingency Approach to Improve Health Care Delivery," *Journal of Consumer Research* 13 (March 1987), p. 503.
25. Thomas S. Robertson, *Innovative Behavior and Communications* (New York: Holt, Rinehart and Winston, 1971).
26. George P. Moschis, "Social Comparisons and Informal Group Influence," *Journal of Marketing Research* 13 (August 1976), pp. 237–244.
27. F. B. Evans, "Selling as a Dyadic Relationship—A New Approach," *American Behavioral Scientist* 6 (May 1963), pp. 76–79; and Timothy C. Brock, "Communicator-Recipient Similarity and Decision Change," *Journal of Personality and Social Psychology* 1 (June 1965), pp. 650–654.
28. See William H. Whyte, "The Web of Word of Mouth," *Fortune* (November 1954), pp. 140–143; and Sidney P. Feldman, "Some Dyadic Relationships Associated with Consumer Choice." In Raymond M. Haas, ed., *Proceedings of the American Marketing Association*, Series No. 24 (1966), pp. 758–775.
29. Leon G. Schiffman, "Social Interaction Patterns of the Elderly Consumer." In Boris W. Becker and Helmut Becker, eds., *Combined Proceedings of the American Marketing Association*, Series No. 34 (1972), p. 451.
30. Park and Lessig, "Students and Housewives. . . ."
31. Henry Assael, Michael Etgar, and Michael Henry, "The Dimensions of Evaluating and Utilizing Alternative Information Sources," Working paper, New York University, March 1983.
32. Park and Lessig, "Students and Housewives. . . ."
33. Whyte, "The Web of Word of Mouth. . . ."
34. S. E. Asch, "Effects of Group Pressure upon the Modification and Distortion of Judgments." In Harold Geutzkow, ed., *Groups, Leadership and Men* (Pittsburgh, PA: Carnegie Press, 1951).
35. M. Venkatesan, "Experimental Study of Consumer Behavior Conformity and Independence," *Journal of Marketing Research*, 3 (November 1966), pp. 384–387.
36. James Duesenberry, *Income, Savings and the Theory of Consumer Behavior* (Cambridge, MA: Harvard University Press, 1949).
37. Asch, "Effects of Group Pressure. . . ."
38. Schouten and McAlexander, "Subcultures of Consumption. . . ," p. 56.
39. Park and Lessig, "Students and Housewives. . . ."
40. Schouten and McAlexander, "Subcultures of Consumption. . . ."
41. Francis S. Bourne, "Group Influence in Marketing and Public Relations." In Rensis Likert and Samuel P. Hayes, eds., *Some Applications of Behavioral Research* (Paris: UNESCO, 1957).
42. Flemming Hansen, "Primary Group Influence and Consumer Conformity." In Philip R. McDonald, ed., *Proceedings of the American Marketing Association's Educators Conference*, Series No. 30 (1969), pp. 300–305.
43. Burnkrant and Cousineau, "Informational and Normative Social Influence. . . ."
44. Park and Lessig, "Students and Housewives. . . ."
45. James C. Ward and Peter H. Reingen, "Sociocognitive Analysis of Group Decision Making Among Consumers," *Journal of Consumer Research* 17 (December 1990), pp. 245–262.

46. Martin Kaplan and Charles Miller, "Group Decision Making and Normative Versus Informational Influence: Effects of Type of Issue and Assigned Decision Role," *Journal of Personality and Social Psychology* 53 (1987), pp. 306–313.
47. Dennis L. Rosen and Richard W. Olshavsky, "The Dual Role of Informational Social Influence: Implications for Marketing Management," *Journal of Business Research* 15 (1987), pp. 123–144.
48. Moschis, "Social Comparisons. . . ," p. 240.
49. Julian L. Watkins, *The 100 Greatest Advertisements* (New York: Dover Publications, 1959), p. 205.
50. "Doesn't Everyone Want to Smell Like . . . ," *The New York Times* (April 2, 1990), p. 144.
51. Barton A. Weitz, "Effectiveness in Sales Interactions: A Contingency Framework," *Journal of Marketing* 45 (Winter 1981), pp. 85–103.
52. G. David Hughes, Joseph B. Juhasz, and Bruno Contini, "The Influence of Personality on the Bargaining Process," *Journal of Business* 46 (October 1973), pp. 593–603.
53. Dean G. Pruitt, *Negotiation Behavior* (New York: Academic Press, 1981).
54. Paul H. Schurr and Julie L. Ozanne, "Influences on Exchange Processes: Buyer's Preconceptions of a Seller's Trustworthiness and Bargaining Toughness," *Journal of Consumer Research* 11 (March 1985), pp. 939–953.
55. Randall L. Rose, William O. Bearden, and Jesse E. Teel, "An Attributional Analysis of Resistance to Group Pressure Regarding Illicit Drug and Alcohol Consumption," *Journal of Consumer Research* 19 (June 1992), pp. 1–13.
56. Ibid.

Chapter 17

1. "Born to Shop," *American Demographics* (June 1993), pp. 34–39; and "'Parental Guidance' Lost on This Crop," *Advertising Age* (July 30, 1990), p. 26.
2. U.S. Bureau of the Census, *Statistical Abstract of the United States, 1996* (Springfield, VA: National Technical Information Service, 1996), Tables 66–68, pp. 58–59.
3. *Statistical Abstract, 1996,* Table 68, p. 59; and "Mass Marketing to Fragmented Markets," *Planning Review* (September 1984), p. 34.
4. Joseph A. Califano, Jr., *American Families: Trends, Pressures and Recommendations.* Preliminary report to Gov. Jimmy Carter, September 17, 1976 (mimeographed).
5. *Statistical Abstract, 1996,* Table 67, p. 58
6. Ibid, Table 82, p. 66.
7. Ibid, Table 66, p. 58
8. Ibid, Table 67, p. 58
9. William D. Wells and George Gubar, "Life Cycle Concept in Marketing Research," *Journal of Marketing Research* 3 (November 1966), pp. 355–363.
10. Patrick E. Murphy and William S. Staples, "A Modernized Family Life Cycle," *Journal of Consumer Research* 6 (June 1979), pp. 12–22.
11. *Statistical Abstract, 1996,* Table 90, p. 74.
12. Ben J. Wattenberg, "The Forming Families: The Spark in the Tinder," *Combined Proceedings of the American Marketing Association* (Chicago: American Marketing Association, 1975), p. 52.
13. Pierre Filiatrault and J. R. Brent Richie, "Joint Purchasing Decisions: A Comparison of Influence Structure in Family and Couple Decision-Making Units," *Journal of Consumer Research* 7 (September 1980), p. 139.
14. J. N. Sheth, "A Theory of Family Buying Decisions." In Jagdish N. Sheth, ed., *Models of Buyer Behavior* (New York: Harper & Row, 1974), pp. 17–33.
15. Arch G. Woodside, "Informal Group Influence on Risk Taking," *Journal of Marketing Research* 9 (May 1972), pp. 223–225.
16. Mira Komarovsky, "Class Differences in Family Decision-Making on Expenditures." In Nelson Foote, ed., *Household Decision-Making* (New York: New York University Press, 1961), pp. 225–265.
17. Robert Ferber and Lucy Chao Lee, "Husband-Wife Influence in Family Purchasing Behavior," *Journal of Consumer Research* 1 (June 1974), pp. 43–50.
18. Donald H. Granbois, "The Role of Communication in the Family Decision-Making Process." In Stephen A. Greyser, ed., *Proceedings of the American Marketing Association Educators' Conference* (1963), pp. 44–57.
19. William F. Kenkel, "Family Interaction in Decision-Making on Spending." In Foote, *Household Decision-Making.*
20. John S. Coulson, "Buying Decisions Within the Family and the Consumer-Brand Relationship." In Joseph W. Newman, ed., *On Knowing the Consumer* (New York: John Wiley, 1967), p. 60.
21. Raymond Loewy/William Snaith, Inc., *Project Home: The Motivations Towards Homes and Housing.* Report prepared for the Project Home Committee, 1967.
22. P. Doyle and P. Hutchinson, "Individual Differences in Family Decision Making," *Journal of the Market Research Society* 15 (October 1973), pp. 193–206.
23. T. Poffenberger, *Husband-Wife Communication and Motivational Aspects of Population Control in an Indian Village* (Green Park, New Delhi: Central Family Planning Institute, 1969).
24. Harry L. Davis, "Decision Making Within the Household," *Journal of Consumer Research* 2 (March 1976), p. 252.
25. Rosanne L. Spiro, "Persuasion in Family Decision Making," *Journal of Consumer Research* 9 (March 1983), pp. 393–402. See also William J. Qualls, "Household Decision Behavior: The Impact of Husbands' and Wives' Sex Role Orientation," *Journal of Consumer Research* 14 (September 1987), pp. 264–279.

26. C. Whan Park, "Joint Decisions in Home Purchasing: A Muddling Through Process," *Journal of Consumer Research* 9 (September 1982), pp. 151–162.
27. Kim P. Corfman and Donald R. Lehmann, "Models of Cooperative Group Decision-Making and Relative Influence: An Experimental Investigation of Family Purchase Decisions," *Journal of Consumer Research* 14 (June 1987), p. 2.
28. Alvin C. Burns and Donald H. Granbois, "Factors Moderating the Resolution of Preference Conflict in Family Automobile Purchasing," *Journal of Marketing Research* 14 (February 1977), pp. 77–86.
29. Michael B. Menasco and David J. Curry, "Utility and Choice: An Empirical Study of Wife/Husband Decision Making," *Journal of Consumer Research* 16 (June 1989), p. 95.
30. H. L. Davis and Benny P. Rigaux, "Perceptions of Marital Roles in Decision Processes," *Journal of Consumer Research* 1 (June 1974), pp. 51–62.
31. Mandy Putnam and William R. Davidson, *Family Purchasing Behavior: II, Family Roles by Product Category* (Columbus, OH: Management Horizons, Inc., a division of Price Waterhouse, 1987).
32. Bernard Berelson and Gary A. Steiner, *Human Behavior: An Inventory of Scientific Findings* (New York: Harcourt, Brace & World, 1964), p. 314.
33. William F. Kenkel, "Family Interaction in Decision-Making and Decisions Choices," *Journal of Social Psychology* 54 (1961), p. 260; and Davis and Rigaux, "Perceptions of Marital Roles. . . ."
34. Kenkel, "Family Interaction in Decision-Making. . . ," p. 152; and Mary Lou Roberts and Lawrence H. Wortzel, "Role Transferral in the Household." In Andrew Mitchell, ed., *Advances in Consumer Research,* Vol. 6 (Ann Arbor, MI: Association for Consumer Research, 1982), p. 264.
35. Ferber and Lee, "Husband-Wife Influence in Family Purchasing Behavior."
36. Benny Rigaux-Bricmont, "Explaining the Marital Influences in Family Economic Decision-Making." In Subhash C. Jain, ed., *Proceedings of the American Marketing Association Educators' Conference,* Series No. 43 (1978), pp. 126–129.
37. Steven J. Skinner and Alan J. Dubinsky, "Purchase Insurance: Predictors of Family Decision-Making Responsibility," *Journal of Risk and Insurance* 51 (September 1984), p. 521.
38. Robert T. Green and Isabella C. M. Cunningham, "Feminine Role Perception and Family Purchasing Decisions," *Journal of Marketing Research* 12 (August 1975), pp. 325–332.
39. William J. Qualls, "Changing Sex Roles: Its Impact Upon Family Decision Making." In Andrew Mitchell, ed., *Advances in Consumer Research,* Vol. 9 (Ann Arbor, MI: Association for Consumer Research, 1982), p. 269.
40. "Real Men Buy Paper Towels Too," *Business Week* (November 9, 1992), p. 75; and "Study Boosts Men's Buying Role," *Advertising Age* (December 4, 1989).
41. "Large Numbers of Husbands Buy Household Products, Do Housework," *Marketing News* (October 3, 1980), p. 3.
42. See "Working Women Now More Attractive—Y & R," *Advertising Age* (January 11, 1982), p. 76; and "A Long Drive for Recognition," *Advertising Age* (June 22, 1981), p. S24.
43. Harriet Holter, "Sex Roles and Social Change," *Acta Sociologica* 14 (Winter 1971), pp. 2–12.
44. Isabella C. M. Cunningham and Robert T. Green, "Purchasing Roles in the U.S. Family, 1955 and 1973," *Journal of Marketing* 38 (October 1974), p. 63; and Qualls, "Changing Sex Roles. . . ," pp. 267–270.
45. "The Littlest Shoppers," *American Demographics* (February 1992), pp. 48, 50.
46. Scott Ward, "Consumer Socialization." In Harold H. Kassarjian and Thomas S. Robertson, eds., *Perspectives in Consumer Behavior* (Glencoe, IL: Scott, Foresman, 1980).
47. George P. Moschis, "The Role of Family Communication in Consumer Socialization of Children and Adolescents," *Journal of Consumer Research* 11 (March 1985), pp. 898–913, at p. 902.
48. Scott Ward, Daniel B. Wackman, and Ellen Wartella, *How Children Learn to Buy: The Development of Consumer Information Processing Skills* (Beverly Hills, CA: Sage, 1977).
49. George P. Moschis, *Acquisition of the Consumer Role by Adolescents.* Ph.D. diss., Graduate School of Business, University of Wisconsin, Madison, 1977.
50. George P. Moschis and Roy L. Moore, "Purchasing Behavior of Adolescent Consumers." In Richard P. Bagozzi et al., eds., *Proceedings of the American Marketing Association Educators' Conference,* Series No. 45 (1980), pp. 89–92.
51. Joseph N. Fry et al., "Consumer Loyalty to Banks: A Longitudinal Study," *Journal of Business* 46 (October 1973), pp. 517–525.
52. George P. Moschis, "A Longitudinal Study of Consumer Socialization." In Michael Ryan, ed., *Proceedings of the American Marketing Association Theory Conference* (1984).
53. Sanford Grossbart, Les Carlson, and Ann Walsh, "Consumer Socialization and Frequency of Shopping with Children," *Journal of the Academy of Marketing Science* 19 (Summer 1991), pp. 155–162.
54. "Getting 'Em While They're Young," *Business Week* (September 9, 1991), p. 94.
55. B. J. Wadsworth, *Piaget's Theory of Cognitive Development* (New York: David McKay, 1971).
56. *American Demographics* (June 1993), pp. 34–39.
57. Les Carlson and Sanford Grossbart, "Parental Style and Consumer Socialization of Children," *Journal of Consumer Research* 15 (June 1988), pp. 77–94.

58. Moschis, "The Role of Family Communication," p. 899.
59. Fry et al., "Consumer Loyalty to Banks. . . ."
60. Larry G. Woodson, Terry L. Childers, and Paul R. Winn, "Intergenerational Influences in the Purchase of Auto Insurance," in W. Locander, ed., *Marketing Look Outward: 1976 Business Proceedings* (Chicago: American Marketing Association, 1976), pp. 43–49.
61. Ibid.
62. *Advertising Age* (July 30, 1990).
63. Terry L. Childers and Aksay R. Rao, "The Influence of Familial and Peer-Based Reference Groups on Consumer Decisions," *Journal of Consumer Research* 19 (September 1992), pp. 198–211.
64. "Getting 'Em While They're Young," *Business Week* (September 9, 1991), p. 94.
65. Leslie Isler, Edward T. Popper, and Scott Ward, "Children's Purchase Requests and Parental Responses: Results from a Diary Study," *Journal of Advertising Research* 27 (October–November 1987), p. 34.
66. Scott Ward and Daniel B. Wackman, "Children's Purchase Influence Attempts and Parental Yielding," *Journal of Marketing Research* 9 (August 1972), pp. 316–319.
67. Ibid.
68. Isler, Popper, and Ward, "Children's Purchase Requests. . . ."
69. "Children's Requests: When Do Parents Yield?" *Wharton Alumni Magazine* (Fall 1987), p. 19.
70. *Advertising Age* (July 30, 1990).
71. Sharon E. Beatty and Salil Talpade, "Adolescent Influence in Family Decision Making: A Replication with Extension," *Journal of Consumer Research* 21 (September 1994), pp. 332–340.
72. David C. Epperson, "Reassessment of Indices of Parental Influence in the American Society," *American Sociological Review* 29 (February 1964).
73. Paul Gilkison, "What Influences the Buying Decisions of Teenagers?" *Journal of Retailing* 41 (Fall 1965), pp. 36–41.
74. George P. Moschis and Roy L. Moore, "Decision Making Among the Young: A Socialization Perspective," *Journal of Consumer Research* 6 (September 1979), pp. 101–112. See also Ellen R. Foxman, Patriya S. Tansuhaj, and Karin M. Ekstrom, "Family Members' Perceptions of Adolescents' Influence in Family Decision Making," *Journal of Consumer Research* 15 (March 1989), pp. 482–491.
75. George P. Moschis and Roy L. Moore, "Purchasing Behavior of Adolescent Consumers." In Richard P. Bagozzi et al., eds., *Proceedings of the American Marketing Association Educators' Conference* Series No. 46 (1980), p. 93.
76. "Yogurts Sprinkle in Fun to Stir Kids," *Advertising Age* (February 8, 1993), p. S22.
77. "Growing Up in the Market," *American Demographics* (October 1992), pp. 47–48.
78. "As Kids Gain Power of Purse, Marketing Takes Aim at Them," *The Wall Street Journal* (January 19, 1988), p. 15.
79. "Auto Makers Set New Ad Strategy to Reach Women," *Advertising Age* (September 23, 1985), p. 80.
80. "Growing Up in the Market," *American Demographics* (October 1992), p. 49.
81. "Makers of Personal-Care Products Hope to Clean Up with Brands for Children," *The Wall Street Journal* (January 28, 1993), p. B1.
82. "The ABC's of Marketing to Kids," *Fortune* (May 8, 1980), p. 120.
83. C. Whan Park and Easwar Iyer, "An Examination of the Response Pattern in Family Decision Making." In Kenneth Bernhardt et al., *Proceedings of the American Marketing Association Educators' Conference,* Series No. 47 (1981), p. 148.
84. Davis and Rigaux, "Perception of Marital Roles. . . ."
85. "Who Buys the Pants in the Family?" *American Demographics* (January 1992), p. 12.
86. Michael A. Belch, George E. Belch, and Donald Sciglimpaglia, "Conflict in Family Decision Making: An Exploratory Investigation," in Jerry C. Olson, ed., *Advances in Consumer Research,* 7 (Ann Arbor, MI: Association for Consumer Research, 1980), p. 475.
87. Foxman, Tansuhaj, and Ekstrom, "Family Members' Perceptions of Adolescents' Influence in Family Decision Making."
88. Gary M. Armstrong and Merrie Brucks, "Dealing with Children's Advertising: Public Policy Issues and Alternatives," *Journal of Public Policy and Marketing* 7 (1988), pp. 93–113.
89. Ibid., p. 102.
90. Ibid., p. 101.
91. *Business Week* (September 9, 1991), p. 94.
92. Laura A. Peracchio, "How Do Young Children Learn to Be Consumers? A Script-Processing Approach," *Journal of Consumer Research* 18 (March 1992), pp. 425–440.
93. Armstrong and Brucks, "Dealing with Children's Advertising. . . ," p. 104.
94. Daniel B. Wackman, "Family Processes in Children's Consumption." In Neil Beckwith et al., eds., *Proceedings of the American Marketing Association Educators' Conference,* Series No. 11 (1979), pp. 645–652.

Chapter 18

1. "Olé," *Marketing & Media Decisions* (June 1987), pp. 95–98.
2. "Reaching Moneyed Markets," *The New York Times* (August 18, 1981), p. D19.
3. Ibid.; and "The Shifting Power of Influentials in Purchase Decisions," *Ad Forum* (July 1983), p. 55.

4. Elihu Katz and Paul F. Lazarsfeld, *Personal Influence* (Glencoe, IL: The Free Press, 1955).
5. James E. Engel, Roger D. Blackwell, and Robert J. Kegerreis, "How Information Is Used to Adopt an Innovation," *Journal of Advertising Research* 9 (December 1969), pp. 3–8.
6. Paul M. Herr, Frank R. Kardes, and John Kim, "Effects of Word-of-Mouth and Product-Attribute Information on Persuasion: An Accessibility-Diagnosticity Perspective," *Journal of Consumer Research* 17 (March 1991), pp. 454–62.
7. Marsha L. Richins and Teri Root-Shaffer, "The Role of Involvement and Opinion Leadership in Consumer Word-of-Mouth: An Implicit Model Made Explicit." In Michael J. Houston, ed., *Advances in Consumer Research,* Vol. 15 (Provo, UT: Association for Consumer Research, 1987), pp. 32–36.
8. Katz and Lazarsfeld, *Personal Influence*.
9. R. A. Bauer, "The Obstinate Audience," *American Psychologist* 19 (May 1964), pp. 319–328.
10. Katz and Lazarsfeld, *Personal Influence,* pp. 118–119.
11. Lawrence Feick and Linda Price, "The Market Maven: A Diffuser of Marketplace Information," *Journal of Marketing* 51 (January 1987), pp. 83–87.
12. Richard R. Still, James H. Barnes, Jr., and Mark E. Kooyman, "Word-of-Mouth Communication in Low-Risk Product Decisions," *International Journal of Advertising* 3 (1984), pp. 335–345.
13. Marsha L. Richins, "Negative Word-of-Mouth by Dissatisfied Consumers: A Pilot Study," *Journal of Marketing* 47 (Winter 1983), pp. 68–78.
14. Richard W. Mizerski, "An Attribution Explanation of the Disproportionate Influence of Unfavorable Information," *Journal of Consumer Research* 9 (December 1982), pp. 301–310.
15. "Status Shifts to Peer Influence," *Advertising Age* (May 17, 1984), p. M10.
16. "P&G Drops Logo; Cites Satan Rumors," *The New York Times* (April 25, 1985), p. D1.
17. "P&G Once Again Has Devil of a Time with Rumors About Moon, Stars Logo," *The Wall Street Journal* (March 26, 1990), p. B3.
18. "P&G Is Still Having a Devil of a Time," *Business Week* (September 11, 1995), p. 46.
19. Alice M. Tybout, Bobby J Calder, and Brian Sternthal, "Using Information Processing Theory to Design Marketing Strategies," *Journal of Marketing Research* 18 (February 1981), p. 74.
20. Ibid., pp. 73–74.
21. "A Puzzlement Over a Bakery Rumor," *The New York Times* (September 10, 1981), p. A16.
22. "Rumor Turns Fantasy into Bad Dream," *The Wall Street Journal* (May 19, 1991), pp. B1, B5.
23. "Entenmann's Fights Moonie Link," *Advertising Age* (November 23, 1981), p. 33.
24. "Rumor Turns Fantasy. . . ," *The Wall Street Journal* (May 19, 1991).
25. Herr, Kardes, and Kim, "Effects of Word-of-Mouth. . . ."
26. Charles W. King and John O. Summers, "Overlap of Opinion Leadership Across Consumer Product Categories," *Journal of Marketing Research* 7 (February 1970), pp. 43–50.
27. "The Influentials," *American Demographics* (October 1992), pp. 30–38.
28. Lawrence F. Feick and Linda L. Price, "The Market Maven. . . ."
29. Michael R. Solomon, "The Missing Link: Surrogate Consumers in the Marketing Chain," *Journal of Marketing* 50 (October 1986), pp. 208–218.
30. Jagdish N. Sheth, "Word-of-Mouth in Low-Risk Innovations," *Journal of Advertising Research* 11 (June 1971), pp. 15–18.
31. Summers and King, "New Product Interpersonal Communication. . . ."
32. Katz and Lazarsfeld, *Personal Communication;* and James H. Myers and Thomas S. Robertson, "Dimensions of Opinion Leadership," *Journal of Marketing Research* 9 (February 1972), pp. 41–46.
33. Proprietary study by a large appliance manufacturer.
34. "The Influentials," *Research Alert* (December 2, 1988), p. 1; and Rogin A. Higie, Lawrence F. Feick, and Linda L. Price, "Types and Amount of Word-of-Mouth Communications About Retailers," *Journal of Retailing* 63 (Fall 1987), pp. 260–277.
35. Fred D. Reynolds and William R. Darden, "Mutually Adaptive Effects of Interpersonal Communication," *Journal of Marketing Research* 8 (November 1971), pp. 449–454.
36. James Coleman, "Social Processes in Physicians' Adoption of a New Drug," *Journal of Chronic Diseases* 9 (1959), pp. 1–9.
37. Everett M. Rogers and F. Floyd Shoemaker, *Communication in Innovations* (New York: The Free Press, 1971).
38. "Put People Behind Wheel," *Advertising Age* (March 22, 1993), p. S28.
39. "The Shifting Power of Influentials. . . , *Ad Forum* (July 1983).
40. "Marketer of the Year: Donald Hudler," *Brandweek* (November 16, 1992), p. 21.
41. Ibid.
42. "Masters of Innovation," *Business Week* (April 10, 1989), p. 58; and "At Johnson & Johnson, a Mistake Can Be a Badge of Honor," *Business Week* (September 26, 1988), p. 126.
43. Everett M. Rogers and F. Floyd Shoemaker, *Communication of Innovations,* 2nd ed. (New York: The Free Press, 1971).

44. Robert W. Shoemaker and F. Robert Shoaf, "Behavioral Changes in the Trial of New Products," *Journal of Consumer Research* 2 (September 1975), pp. 104–109.

45. Duncan G. LaBay and Thomas C. Kinnear, "Exploring the Consumer Decision Process in the Adoption of Solar Energy Systems," *Journal of Consumer Research* 8 (December 1981), pp. 271–278.

46. Susan L. Holak and Donald R. Lehmann, "The Relationship Among Primary and Secondary Attributes of Innovative Consumer Durables." Working paper, University of Texas at Dallas, 1986.

47. S. Ram and Jagdish Sheth, "Consumer Resistance to Innovations: The Marketing Problem and Its Solutions," *Journal of Consumer Marketing* 6 (Spring 1989), pp. 5–14.

48. See also Hubert Gatignon and Thomas S. Robertson, "A Propositional Inventory for New Diffusion Research," *Journal of Consumer Research* 11 (March 1985), pp. 849–867.

49. Mary Dee Dickenson and James W. Gentry, "Characteristics of Adopters and Non-Adopters of Home Computers," *Journal of Consumer Research* 10 (September 1983), pp. 225–235.

50. "Sony: Sorting Out the Sales Suspects," *Business Marketing* (August 1988), pp. 44–48.

51. Everett M. Rogers, *Diffusion of Innovations* (New York: The Free Press, 1962).

52. Ibid., pp. 168–171.

53. "Mystique Marketing," *Forbes* (October 21, 1996), pp. 276–277.

54. Robert L. Anderson and David J. Ortinau, "Exploring Consumers' Postadoption Attitudes and Use Behaviors in Monitoring the Diffusion of a Technology-Based Discontinuous Innovation," *Journal of Business Research* 17 (1988), pp. 283–298.

55. Ibid.

56. Richard W. Olshavsky, "Time and the Rate of Adoption of Innovations," *Journal of Consumer Research* 6 (March 1980), pp. 425–428.

57. Gatignon and Robertson, "A Propositional Inventory. . ."; and Thomas S. Robertson and Hubert Gatignon, "Competitive Effects on Technology Diffusion," *Journal of Marketing* 50 (July 1986), pp. 1–12.

58. James F. Engel, Robert J. Kegerreis, and Roger D. Blackwell, "Word-of-Mouth Communication by the Innovator," *Journal of Marketing* 33 (July 1969), pp. 15–19.

59. H. David Strutton and James R. Lumpkin, "Information Sources Used by Elderly Health Care Product Adopters," *Journal of Advertising Research* 32 (July–August 1992), pp. 20–30.

60. Everett M. Rogers, "New Product Adoption and Diffusion," *Journal of Consumer Research* 2 (March 1976), pp. 290–301.

61. Gatignon and Robertson, "A Propositional Inventory. . . ," p. 857.

62. Jacqueline Johnson Brown and Peter H. Reingen, "Social Ties and Word-of-Mouth Referral Behavior," *Journal of Consumer Research* 14 (December 1987), pp. 350–362.

63. Thorstein Veblen, *The Theory of the Leisure Class* (New York: Macmillan, 1912).

64. George Simmel, "Fashion," *International Quarterly* 10 (October 1904), pp. 130–155.

65. "Grassroots Innovation," *Marketing Insights* (Summer 1991), pp. 44–50.

66. Charles W. King, "Fashion Adoption: A Rebuttal to the 'Trickle Down' Theory." In James U. McNeal, ed., *Dimensions of Consumer Behavior* (New York: Appleton-Century-Crofts, 1969), p. 172.

67. Edward T. Hall, *Hidden Differences* (New York: Doubleday, 1987).

68. Rogers, *Diffusion of Innovations.*

69. Hirokazu Takada and Dipak Jain, "Cross-National Analysis of Diffusion of Consumer Durable Goods in Pacific Rim Countries," *Journal of Marketing* 55 (April 1991), pp. 48–54.

70. Dickenson and Gentry, "Characteristics of Adopters and Non-Adopters."

71. Lambert, "Perceptual Patterns, Information Handling, and Innnovativeness."

72. David Riesman, N. Glazer, and R. Denney, *The Lonely Crowd* (New Haven, CT: Yale University Press, 1950); and Robert L. Brittingham, Brent G. Goff, and Robert C. Haring, "Refinancers and Non-Refinancers: A Comparative Analysis," *Journal of Retail Banking* 11 (Spring 1989), pp. 27–34.

73. John O. Summers, "Media Exposure Patterns of Consumer Innovators," *Journal of Marketing* 36 (January 1972), pp. 43–49.

74. David F. Midgley, "A Simple Mathematical Theory of Innovative Behavior," *Journal of Consumer Research* 3 (June 1976), pp. 31–41.

75. Dorothy Leonard-Barton, "Experts as Negative Opinion Leaders in the Diffusion of a Technological Innovation," *Journal of Consumer Research* 11 (March 1985), pp. 914–926.

76. Anderson and Ortinau, "Exploring Consumers' Postadoption Attitudes. . . ."

77. John O. Summers, "Generalized Change Agents and Innovativeness," *Journal of Marketing Research* 8 (August 1971), p. 314.

INDEX

A

B

D

E

G

H

I

J

K

L

M

N

O

P

Q

R

S

T

U

V

W

X

Y

EXHIBIT CREDITS

Chapter 1

Exhibit 1.1: Courtesy of Levi Strauss & Co. Exhibit 1.2: Courtesy of Levi Strauss & Co. Exhibit 1.3: Courtesy of Sears, Roebuck and Co. Exhibit 1.4: © 1996 Avon Products, Inc. Exhibit 1.5: Courtesy of Levi Strauss & Co. Exhibit 1.6: Used with permission of Panasonic Communication and Systems Co.

Chapter 2

Exhibit 2.1: Courtesy of The Body Shop. Exhibit 2.2: Courtesy of Health Education Board for Scotland and photographer Nick Price. Exhibit 2.3: Courtesy of Environmental Defense Fund. Exhibit 2.4: Used with permission of Reynolds Metals Company. Exhibit 2.5: Courtesy of Crane & Co. Inc. Exhibit 2.6: Used with permission of The Quaker Oats Company. Exhibit 2.7: Courtesy of Kirshenbaum & Bond. Art director: Jeff Curry. Copywriter: Tom Christman. Exhibit 2.8: Reprinted with permission, General Motors Corp. and the Nature Conservancy.

Chapter 3

Exhibit 3.1: © Saturn Corporation; used with permission. Exhibit 3.2a: Courtesy of Mullen Advertising and Fruit of the Loom, Inc. Exhibit 3.2b: Ad courtesy of Cartier, Inc. Exhibit 3.3: Godiva Chocolatier, 701 Fifth Avenue, New York City, © 1997. Godiva and the Gold Ballotin are registered trademarks. Exhibit 3.4: Courtesy of Schwinn Cycling & Fitness Inc. Exhibit 3.5: Reprinted with permission of Nike, Inc. Exhibit 3.6: Courtesy of Saab Cars USA.

Chapter 4

Exhibit 4.1: Courtesy of Intel Corporation. Exhibit 4.2a: Reprinted with permission of Nike, Inc. Exhibit 4.3b: Used by permission of General Mills Inc. Exhibit 4.3c: Courtesy of Bijan Fragrances Inc. Advertising agency—Bijan-in-house-creative director/Bijan art director Cynthia Miller. Exhibit 4.4: Used by permission of Campbell's Soup Company. Exhibit 4.5: Courtesy of Adbusters, The Media Foundation. Exhibit 4.6: Courtesy of Joseph Higgins. Exhibit 4.7a: Advertisement courtesy of Apple Computer, Inc. © Apple Computer, Inc. All rights reserved. Used with permission. Apple®, the Apple Logo, Macintosh®, Performa®, PowerBook®, and "The Power to Be Your Best®" are registered trademarks of Apple Computer, Inc. Exhibit 4.7b: © The Coca-Cola Company. "Coca-Cola," "Coke," and the contour bottle design are registered trademarks of The Coca-Cola Company.

Chapter 5

Exhibit 5.3: Courtesy of Bauer USA, Inc. Exhibit 5.3b: MIRACLE WHIP is a registered trademark of Kraft Foods, Inc. Ad used with permission. Exhibit 5.4a: Courtesy of Coustic. Exhibit 5.4b: Courtesy of The Selmer Company, Elkhart, IN. Exhibit 5.5a: Courtesy of Colgate-Palmolive Co. Exhibit 5.5b: Copyright Tom Arma. Reprinted by permission of Parmalat Brasil and Tom Arma. Exhibit 5.7: Ad courtesy of Anheuser-Busch, Inc.

Chapter 6

Exhibit 6.1: Courtesy of Timex Corporation. Exhibit 6.2b: Godiva Chocolatier, 701 Fifth Avenue, New York City, © 1997. Godiva and the Gold Ballotin are registered trademarks. Exhibit 6.3a: Courtesy of Baccarat, Inc. Exhibit 6.3b: © The Coca-Cola Company. Sprite and ECOUTE TA SOIF are registered trademarks of The Coca-Cola Company. Exhibit 6.4: Courtesy of Motorola Inc. Paging Products Group.

Chapter 7

Exhibit 7.1: Reproduced with permission of PepsiCo, Inc., 1997, Purchase, New York. Exhibit 7.2: Courtesy of Al-Dahlawi Co., Sole Agent-National/Panasonic/Technics, Jeddah, Saudi Arabia. Exhibit 7.3: Used by permission of General Mills Inc. Exhibit 7.4: U.S. Department of Health and Human Services/Public Health Service/Centers for Disease Control and Prevention. Exhibit 7.6: Courtesy of Barneys New York Advertising. Exhibit 7.7: © 1958 United Features Syndicate, Inc. Courtesy of United Media and Metropolitan Life Insurance Co. Exhibit 7.8: Reprinted with permission of Nike, Inc.

Chapter 8

Exhibit 8.1: © John Schakel/Unicorn Stock Photos. Exhibit 8.2a: Courtesy of Schwinn Cycling & Fitness Inc. Exhibit 8.2b: Courtesy of Bell Sports, Inc./Goodby Silverstein & Partners. Exhibit 8.3: Advertisement courtesy of Apple Computer, Inc. © Apple Computer, Inc. All rights reserved. Used with permission. Apple®, the Apple Logo, Macintosh®, Performa®, PowerBook®, and "The Power to Be Your Best®" are registered trademarks of Apple Computer, Inc. Exhibit 8.4: Used with permission of McDonald's Corporation. Exhibit 8.5: By Fallon McElligott/Rolling Stone. Used by permission. Exhibit 8.6: Courtesy of Johnson & Johnson.

Chapter 9

Exhibit 9.1a: Courtesy of Toyota Germany. Exhibit 9.1b: Courtesy of Toyota Motor Sales, U.S.A., Inc. Exhibit 9.2a: Reprinted with permission of Nike, Inc. Exhibit 9.2b: Courtesy of Reebok International Ltd. Exhibit 9.2c: Courtesy of Johnson & Johnson. Exhibit 9.2d: Courtesy of Pharmacia & Upjohn. Exhibit 9.3: Courtesy of Volvo Cars of North America and Messner Vetere Berger McNamee Schmetterer/Euro RSCG.

Chapter 10

Exhibit 10.1: Courtesy of Bozell Worldwide, Inc., Advertising. Exhibit 10.2: Courtesy of Warner-Lambert Company. Exhibit 10.3: Advertisement reproduced courtesy of The Quaker Oats Company. Exhibit 10.4: Courtesy, The Gillette Company. Exhibit 10.5: Courtesy of Cluett, Peabody & Co. Inc. Exhibit 10.6: Courtesy of Partnership for a Drug-Free America.

Chapter 11

Exhibit 11.2: Reprinted with permission of Nike, Inc. Exhibit 11.3: Courtesy of Bauer USA, Inc. Exhibit 11.4: Furnished by J. L. Jordan III, DDB Needham Worldwide. Exhibit 11.5: Advertisement courtesy of Apple Computer, Inc. © Apple Computer, Inc. All rights reserved. Used with permission. Apple®, the Apple Logo, Macintosh®, Performa®, PowerBook®, and "The Power to Be Your Best®" are registered trademarks of Apple Computer, Inc. Exhibit 11.6: Courtesy of Avis Rent A Car System, Inc. Exhibit 11.7a: Courtesy of Bell Sports, Inc./Goodby Silverstein & Partners. Exhibit 11.7b: Courtesy of the Ontario Brain Injury Association. Exhibit 11.8: Courtesy of Warner-Lambert Company. Exhibit 11.9: © Saturn Corporation; used with permission.

Chapter 12

Exhibit 12.1: Courtesy of Johnson & Johnson. Exhibit 12.2a: Special thanks to KinderCare Learning Centers, Inc., Portland, OR. Exhibit 12.2b: Courtesy of International Business Machines Corporation. Exhibit 12.3: Courtesy of Polaroid Corp. Exhibit 12.4a: Advertisement courtesy of Apple Computer, Inc. © Apple Computer, Inc. All rights reserved. Used with permission. Apple®, the Apple Logo, Macintosh®, Performa®, PowerBook®, and "The Power to Be Your Best®" are registered trademarks of Apple Computer, Inc. Exhibit 12.4b: Courtesy of Polaroid Corp. Exhibit 12.5a: Courtesy of Beiersdorf Inc. Exhibit 12.6: Courtesy of Toyota Motor Sales, U.S.A., Inc. Exhibit 12.7a: Courtesy of Regent International Hotels and Resorts. Exhibit 12.7b: U.S. Department of Housing and Urban Development. Exhibit 12.8a: Courtesy of Air France USA. Exhibit 12.8b: Reproduced with permission from Motorola, Inc. © 1996 Motorola, Inc.

Chapter 13

Exhibit 13.1: Copyright ConAgra Brands, Inc. Reprinted with permission. Exhibit 13.2: Courtesy of Simmons Company. Exhibit 13.3: Reprinted with permission of Nike, Inc. Exhibit 13.4: Courtesy of Bijan Fragrances Inc. Exhibit 13.5: Häagen-Dazs courtesy of Pillsbury Co. Exhibit 13.6: Courtesy of Great Brands of Europe, Inc. (Evian). Exhibit 13.7: Advertisement courtesy of Apple Computer, Inc. © Apple Computer, Inc. All rights reserved. Used with permission. Apple®, the Apple Logo, Mcintosh®, Performa®, PowerBook®, and "The Power to Be Your Best®" are registered trademarks of Apple Computer, Inc. Exhibit 13.8: Courtesy of Exxon Company, U.S.A

Chapter 14

Exhibit 14.1a: © 1997 Maytag Co. Exhibit 14.1b: Courtesy of Ford Motor Company. Exhibit 14.3: Courtesy of XMI Corporation. Exhibit 14.4: Reprinted with permission, General Motors Corp. Exhibit 14.5: Courtesy of Digital Storytelling Festival; graphic by Dana Atchley. Exhibit 14.6a: Courtesy of Ford Motor Company. Exhibit 14.6b: Courtesy of Haggar Apparel. Exhibit 14.7: Courtesy of ITT Hartford Group Inc.

Chapter 15

Exhibit 15.1: Courtesy of Levi Strauss & Co. Exhibit 15.2: Courtesy of Ford Motor Company. Exhibit 15.3: Courtesy of Swatch/SMH (US), Inc. Exhibit 15.4 Courtesy of DIM S.A. Exhibit 15.5 Courtesy of Kellogg Company. *Kellogg's®* and package design are registered trademarks of Kellogg Company. Exhibit 15.6: Courtesy of Renault. Exhibit 15.7: ON THE FASTRACK reprinted with special permission of King Features Syndicate, Inc. Exhibit 15.8: Reproduced with permission of PepsiCo, Inc., 1997, Purchase, New York. Exhibit 15.9: Courtesy of AT&T. AT&T direct marketing campaign for gay consumers created by agency Prime Access, New York. Exhibit 15.11a: Courtesy of Parlux Fragrances. Exhibit 15.11b: Courtesy of AT&T. Exhibit 15.12: Courtesy of Metropolitan Life Insurance Co.

Chapter 16

Exhibit 16.1: Advertisement courtesy of Apple Computer, Inc. © Apple Computer, Inc. All rights reserved. Used with permission. Apple®, the Apple Logo, Mcintosh®, Performa®, PowerBook®, and "The Power to Be Your Best®" are registered trademarks of Apple Computer, Inc. Exhibit 16.2a: © Redmond Products Inc. Exhibit 16.2b: Courtesy of Omega Watch Corp. Exhibit 16.2c: Courtesy of Oliver Peoples. Exhibit 16.3: Courtesy of Sharp Electronics Corporation. Exhibit 16.4: Reprinted by permission of RCA Corporation. Exhibit 16.5a: Courtesy of Warner-Lambert Company. Exhibit 16.5b: Reprinted with permission of Nike, Inc. Exhibit 16.6: Courtesy of Ford Motor Company. Exhibit 16.7: Courtesy of Men's and Boy's Wear Institute.

Chapter 17

Exhibit 17.1a: Courtesy of Gerber Products Company. Exhibit 17.1b: Advertisement reprinted by permission of Whirlpool Corporation. Exhibit 17.2: Courtesy of Ross Products Division, Abbott Laboratories. Exhibit 17.4: Used by permission of General Mills Inc. Exhibit 17.5: Copyright, Nissan (1997).

Chapter 18

Exhibit 18.1: Courtesy of Hunt-Wesson, Inc. Exhibit 18.2: © Saturn Corporation; used with permission. Exhibit 18.3a: © Whitehall-Robins; reprinted with permission. Exhibit 18.3b: Reproduced with permission of Schering Corporation. All rights reserved. Exhibit 18.4: Courtesy of Wholesome & Hearty Foods. Exhibit 18.5: Courtesy The Condé Nast Publications. Exhibit 18.6: Courtesy of International Business Machines Corporation. Exhibit 18.7: Courtesy of Hewlett-Packard.